Public Sculpture of Sussex

Public Monuments and Sculpture Association
National Recording Project

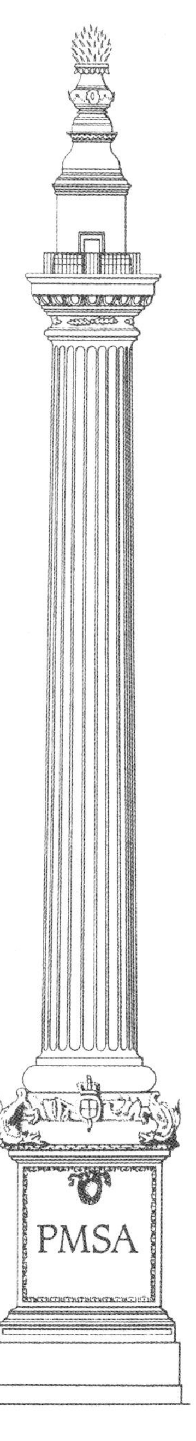

Public Sculpture of Britain Volume Seventeen

PUBLIC SCULPTURE OF SUSSEX

Jill Seddon, Peter Seddon and Anthony McIntosh

LIVERPOOL UNIVERSITY PRESS

First published 2014 by LIVERPOOL UNIVERSITY PRESS,
Liverpool, L69 7ZU

The National Recording Project is supported by the
National Lottery through the Heritage Lottery Fund

HERITAGE LOTTERY FUND

Copyright © 2014
Public Monuments and Sculpture Association

The right of Jill Seddon, Peter Seddon and Anthony McIntosh to
be identified as the authors of this work has been asserted by them
in accordance with the Copyright, Design and Patents Act 1988

British Library Cataloguing-in-Publication Data
A British Library CIP record is available

ISBN 978-1-78138-125-0 (cased)

Design and production, Grant Shipcott

Typeset in 9/11pt Stempel Garamond
by XL Publishing Services, Exmouth, Devon
Originated, printed and bound in Great Britain by
Henry Ling Ltd, Dorchester

The Henry Moore
Foundation

The Paul Mellon Centre
for Studies in British Art

This is the seventeenth volume in a series, the *Public Sculpture of Britain*, which will eventually cover the whole of the country. Public sculpture is defined very broadly to include not only commemorative and decorative monuments but also architectural sculpture and works inside public and semi-public buildings, excluding those in museums and art galleries.

Sussex is a mixture of the rural and the urban, from market town, rural village and country estate, to city, major seaside resort and new town development. All these different contexts are reflected in its public sculpture. Important sculptures from such contexts include works by Flaxman and others at Petworth House and the monument to William Powlett by Michael Rysbrack in the tiny rural church of Saint George, West Grinstead. There are also the imposing statue of Victoria to celebrate her Diamond Jubilee by Thomas Brock on Hove Seafront and the unusual monument to Edward VII, a figure representing Peace by Newbury Trent, on the border with Brighton. Brighton of course has a version of Chantrey's *George IV*, but also the monument to Mrs Fitzherbert by J.E. Carew at the Catholic Church of St John the Baptist at Kemptown. Significant contemporary examples in the county are Elisabeth Frink's *Desert Quartet* in Worthing, the first contemporary public sculpture to achieve Grade 2 listed status, and *Jet Stream* and *Slip Stream* by William Pye at Gatwick Airport. Public sculpture in Sussex celebrates monarchs, public worthies and historical events, and also exemplifies the particular nature of patronage in the nineteenth and twentieth centuries, with a specific concern for health and well-being in the county, especially in its hospitals. The range of contemporary and historic sculpture in the Royal Sussex County Hospital at Brighton is particularly impressive. Brighton's cemeteries contain the famous circus-horse memorial to the circus-owner J.F. Ginnett by the distinguished 'New Sculptor' Edwin Roscoe Mullins together with important and largely unknown monuments by William Wyon and others. At the same time, the county's emphasis on tourism and leisure activities has produced notable examples of important temporary sculptures and installations attached to festivals and other cultural events. The book demonstrates the various contributions to sculpture in the county from sculptors of major

historical significance to local craftspersons working within specific communities in the region.

The *Public Sculpture of Britain* is produced by the Public Monuments and Sculpture Association, which exists to encourage both the study and the conservation of public sculpture and monuments. The Association believes that the publication of detailed research into the commissioning, execution, installation and reception of public sculpture will both justify conservation policies and increase general awareness and appreciation of these important and very familiar works of art. The authors have been working on this volume for 10 years, mainly from Brighton University, and have produced a superb volume. Much information about a very wide range of public sculpture and monuments throughout Britain is also available on the Association's website, www.pmsa.org.uk.

For reasons of cost, the series of volumes only contains relatively small black and white illustrations, although nearly all the sculptures discussed are reproduced within them in some way. The Public Catalogue Foundation is well known for its excellent colour images of all publicly owned oil paintings in Britain, now available online in collaboration with the BBC at its website. The Association has formed a partnership with the Foundation intended to extend the Foundation's coverage to sculpture, including open air sculpture. So far as public sculpture is concerned, the Association will provide the expertise and thus the detailed research on public sculptures provided by the Association can eventually be studied alongside superb images which the Foundation will make available to all.

This series is very much a partnership between the Public Monuments and Sculpture Association and Liverpool University Press, where Anthony Cond, Alison Welsby, Patrick Brereton and Jenny Howard have collaborated to produce a splendid volume. It was designed by Grant Shipcott, who has worked on all the volumes in the series. The Paul Mellon Centre for Studies in British Art and the Henry Moore Foundation have continued their generous support for the series.

Edward Morris
Chairman of the Editorial Board

Contents

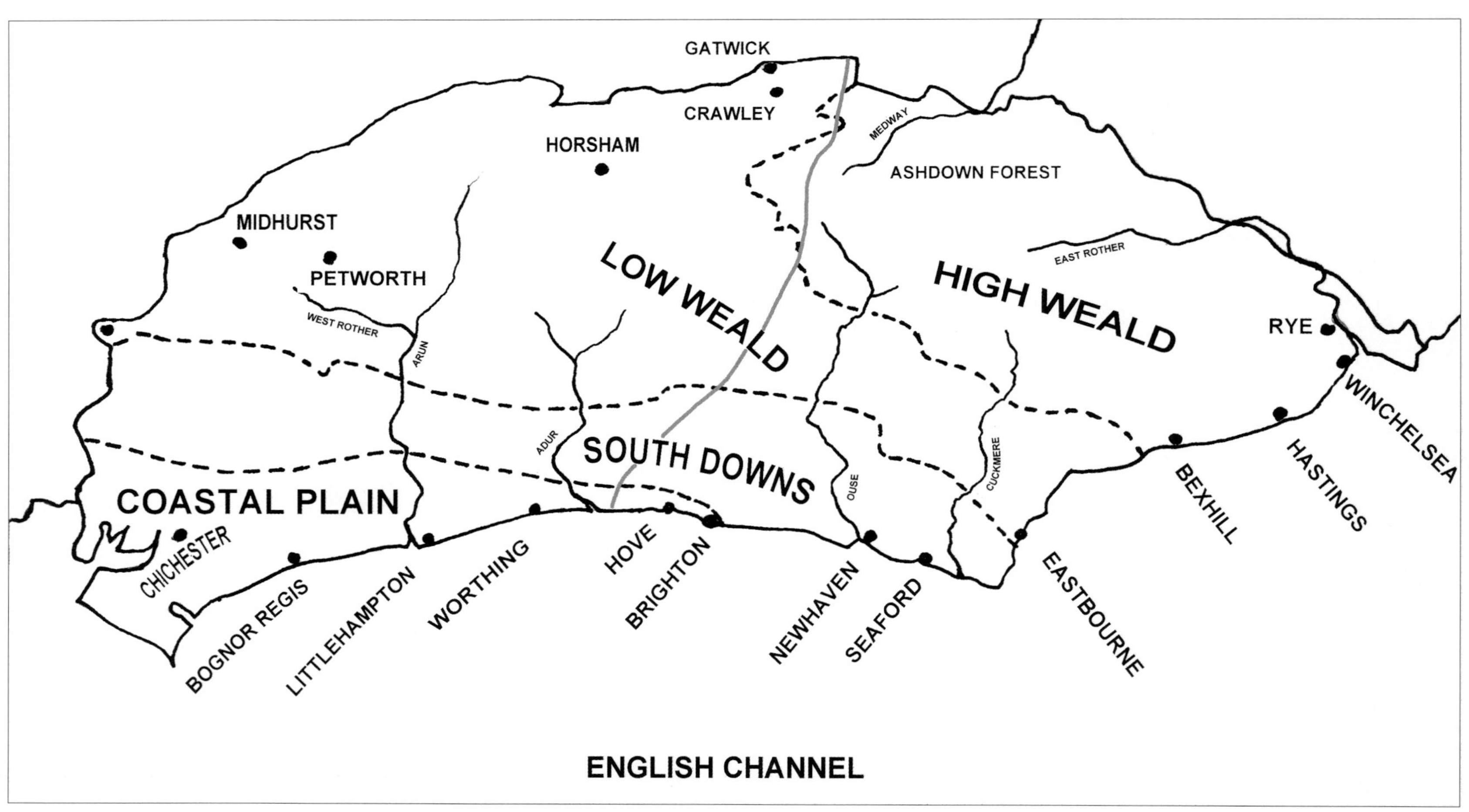

Map of Sussex showing geographical areas and rivers

Boundary between West and East Sussex

The physical geography of Sussex has four distinct areas running in horizontal, slightly tilting, bands from west/northwest to east/southeast (see map). Three of them run across most of the county in narrow strips; firstly, the small coastal alluvial plain from Chichester to Brighton; secondly, the chalk South Downs and their escarpments running from Petersfield to Eastbourne; and thirdly, the Low Weald or Sussex Vale, consisting largely of clay soils, beds of limestone and, most commonly, soft sandstone, running from Midhurst/Petworth in West Sussex to Pevensey Levels in the east. The fourth and final one in the east of the county is the High Weald, running from Ashdown forest in the north to Rye and Winchelsea on the eastern edge of the Sussex coast. These horizontal westerly to easterly directions are vertically intersected by four river systems rising in the north and flowing southwards into the English Channel. These are, together with their minor tributaries and streams, from west to east: the Rother/Arun, the Adur, the Ouse, and the Cuckmere. Lastly, in the High Weald, the rivers Medway and East Rother arise, flowing across to Kent and the Thames in one case and to the Channel coast at Rye in the other.

This geographical/geological structure accounts for differences in land ownership, farming practices and economic development in different areas of the county. It explains the spread of transport structures over time, the demographics of population and the locations of cities, towns and villages. Sussex is overwhelmingly a rural county, although industry, especially charcoal-burning iron forges, was significant between about 1550 and 1750. In terms of materials for large-scale public sculpture, and unlike some areas in Britain, Sussex in the nineteenth century lacked large-scale quarrying and, with some exceptions, large-scale foundries to support locally produced public sculpture.[1] Nevertheless, the county is also urban in certain places in a quite distinctive sense. This is best identified in its closeness to London, which operates like a 'dark star', its gravitational effect being a major influence on the county's economic, social and cultural development. Obviously, London provided a ready market for agricultural and market-garden produce, still a dominant factor in the county's economy. The relief statue of *Ceres* (1934) by James Woodford over the entrance to Brighton's Corn Exchange is a reflection of that very history. In relation to public sculpture and its development in the county, there are also other major factors fuelling urban development, such as the growth of seaside tourism, leisure industries and the question of health.

By the 1940s, 67% of the population of the county lived in towns, half of them in Brighton, Eastbourne and Hastings. In 1950, the total population of the county was over a million and 35% of that population lived in just four towns: Worthing, Brighton, Eastbourne and Hastings, that 35% living on 4% of the total land area of the county.[2] It is a reasonable assumption that in percentage terms, the figures from the early 1800s would not be much different. What this produced was an inverted T-shape centred on easy communication between London and the coastal towns and a lateral spread along the coast based on seaside resorts where most of the population and visitors to the county reside. Unsurprisingly, therefore, plotting on the map the spread and numbers of public sculptures and monuments in the county replicates almost exactly this pattern.

The development of the seaside resort from the 1750s onwards dramatically changed the shape and nature of the county. This was stimulated by three things: firstly, the appreciation of the health benefits associated with seawater drinking and bathing and the coastal climate of Sussex; secondly, the rapid development in road and rail transportation with falling journey times and cheaper connections to London; and thirdly, patterns of land ownership that facilitated the development of amenities such as baths, assembly rooms, libraries, high-density terraced housing development, and so on. Brighton, in particular, benefited from all three of these factors simultaneously, promoting its early development. Other resorts developed slightly later, particularly when railway connections improved.[3]

What such development also produced, and the coastal resorts of Sussex are a distinctive example of this, were public spaces in an urban environment where the social classes that make up the 'public sphere' could promenade, meet and mingle in circles of the 'polite', made up of aristocratic landowners and the increasingly wealthy, professional, commercial and industrial classes. Such public spaces were given over to the typical pursuits of a leisure resort, from theatres and assembly rooms to promenading and the 'constitutional' walk. Included in this was the pursuit and appreciation of the visual arts. Brighton, for example, had its drawing masters, galleries and print shops and some notable examples of public sculpture, such as Sir Francis Chantrey's statue of George IV erected in 1828.[4] That link between landed aristocrat and a widening bourgeois sphere, typical of Brighton, is well exemplified by a figure such as George O'Brien Wyndham, the 3rd Earl of Egremont. Instrumental in contributing to the subscription for Chantrey's statue of the king, he had a house in Brighton as well as being well-known for his patronage of key sculptors of the period, whose work he commissioned for display in the North Gallery of his country house at Petworth. A similar, later, example is furnished by the Dukes of Devonshire, the main landowners in Eastbourne, a town that developed rapidly once rail links to London were established. Monuments to the 7th and 8th Dukes of Devonshire were erected along the seafront at Eastbourne in 1901 and 1910, respectively.

The scale of a rapidly developing seaside resort service sector economy is not always fully appreciated. For example, between 1811 and 1821, Brighton was the fastest growing town anywhere in Britain, a fact confirmed by a glance at the table for population and employment figures in Brighton for this period provided in Sue Berry's book, *Georgian Brighton*.[5] Other towns such as Eastbourne, Worthing, Bognor Regis and Hastings followed Brighton's example from the 1840s onwards. This is Sussex's equivalent to rapid industrialisation elsewhere in Britain, but in this case based on a health and leisure economy. It is perhaps best exemplified in the development throughout the nineteenth century of that peculiar resort space, the seaside pier. The pleasures of walking, not just by, but over, the sea are explored by Fred Gray in *Designing the Seaside*.[6] Nevertheless, it should also be remembered that this economy had its losers in its unhealthy back streets behind the seafront façades. Hastings was after all the setting for Robert Tressell's famous novel *The Ragged Trousered Philanthropists* (1914). As David Solkin aptly puts it, 'the wealth of the "polite" depends on the poverty of the vulgar.'[7]

Apart from the commercial leisure activity of the seaside resort, there is from the early twentieth century onwards the discovery of the pleasures and health-giving benefits of the Sussex countryside, especially the Downs. Figures such as Edward Burne-Jones, who lived at Rottingdean, Rudyard Kipling who lived first at Rottingdean and then at Burwash, and Leonard and Virginia Woolf at Rodmell, are examples. In relation to the visual arts and that late nineteenth–early twentieth-century phenomenon of the rural art-based alternative group, Sussex has three key examples: the Guild of St Joseph and St Dominic at Ditchling, whose most famous figure is Eric Gill; the Bloomsbury Group based at Charleston farmhouse, near Firle; and the later example of Roland Penrose and Lee Miller's house, associated with Surrealism and Picasso, at Farley Farm. Each of these stands as an alternative to more dominant forces in society at large, either in terms of the religiosity of the late arts and crafts movement based at Ditchling, or the anti-establishment pacifism of Charleston, or the surrealist potential of the unconscious at Farley Farm. All three locations do contain items of sculpture by figures associated with these groups but it would be fair to say that such rural retreats are places where thoughts, ideas and alternative lifestyles were explored rather than being places where substantial sculptural pieces were produced. Eric Gill is a good instance of this. There are at least four examples of his work in the county, which display his skills as a letter and stone carver: the sundial in St Margaret of Antioch (1911) and the War Memorial (1919), both at Ditchling; the War Memorial (1921) at South Harting in West Sussex; and a plaque to Sir Harry Johnston in the nave of Poling church, West Sussex. This last piece is carved in the Perpetua typeface, which Gill designed in 1925. However, the major sculptural achievements of this highly significant and controversial figure are to be found elsewhere, particularly in London.

On a different but related note, the production and display of sculpture in a rural setting in recent years has been particularly associated with the phenomenon of the Sculpture Park. Sussex has one outstanding example in the Cass Sculpture Foundation at Goodwood near Chichester. The Foundation, set up in 1992 by Wilfred and Jeanette Cass, is sited in a stunning open-air 26-acre site in which sculpture is continually commissioned, displayed and then sold and circulated elsewhere. The presentation of much of the sculpture against the backdrop of woods and open fields is visually dramatic. However, the only permanently sited work is *Gate* by Wendy Ramshaw, at the entrance to the Foundation, installed in 2001.

A concern with health and well-being, a particular feature of Sussex and its history, has informed, and continues to inform, the public sculpture of the county. The Royal Sussex County Hospital (RSCH) was founded in 1828, called at that time the General Sea Bathing Infirmary. Designed by Charles Barry, its foundation stone was laid by the Earl of Egremont in 1826 and the hospital to this day displays a bust of him by Chantrey in Sussex House, currently one of the hospital's administration blocks. In the present day, private philanthropy such as Lord Egremont's has been replaced by the presence of public art programmes in a number of the county's hospitals and health organisations, particularly in Brighton, Worthing and Chichester. Much of this is the result of a successful coordination of a public arts policy aimed at using the visual arts to enhance the external and internal environment of such places to aid the healing process. The range of this work is varied and in the case of Brighton's RSCH includes interjections into the waiting rooms, corridors and lifts, which can be rather soulless spaces, inflicted on anxious and ill patients as they are moved about from ward to clinic or operating theatre. At Brighton Hospital there are over eight pieces of sculpture and environmental art installed, coordinated by Steve Geliot, a public artist liaising with other selected or commissioned artists, the Brighton and Sussex Universities Hospital Trust, supported by the Brighton and Hove Arts Commission, the Arts Council, and the Children and Young Peoples' Board of the Children's Hospital. This is part of a set of connections built as a consequence of the RSCH being a teaching hospital and the opportunities that provides for collaborative work and research across the arts and its application to medicine, health and well-being.

West Sussex has further significant examples of the use of artworks in the context of hospitals. In Chichester's Saint Richard's Hospital, a scheme was initiated in 1994 to provide artworks for its public areas, especially sculpture that made use of a cluster of themed courtyards, part of the design for a new main wing that opened in 1996. The scheme had a steering committee consisting of a hospital representative with a special interest in sculpture and an advisory group drawn from Chichester's local arts community. It is worth noting that from the total entries under Chichester in the database for Sussex sculpture and the catalogue of this book, 50% of them are attached to this particular hospital scheme, an indication of the level of activity in this area of public art since the 1990s. A similar interest in public art in a healing situation can be found just along the coast in Worthing Hospital. Recent development and new building there has included the use of public art, an early example being Peter Randall-Page's *Worthing Spiral* of 1997. More recent commissions have included *Penguins* (2002) by the one-time assistant to Antony Gormley, Ian Nutting. As in Chichester, just under 50% of the sculptures listed for Worthing in the Sussex public sculpture database are associated with this hospital scheme. Worthing also provides an interesting example of how such initiatives actually develop. In 1995 this particular hospital art project was registered as a charity by the hospital's chief anaesthetist, Roger Edwards. An accomplished amateur sculptor himself, he, together with arts administrator, Amanda Metcalfe, commenced the initiative through a mixture of private and public funding. Although this charity was dissolved in 1999, the basic idea persisted. The hospital has continued to commission work, especially in the context of new building development, a sign of their belief in the benefits of public art in this context.

All this activity in the region is part of a wider picture of increasing interest in this area of sculptural practice best evidenced by the *Prospectus for Arts and Health* produced jointly by the Department for Health and Arts Council England in 2007. Important also is the impact on areas of the county not necessarily rich in public sculpture. For example, on the database for Sussex, the percentage of entries for these institutions as part of the overall total for all public sculpture in Worthing and Chichester is just under 50%, whereas for Brighton, an area with a longer tradition of public art, it is just under 9%.[8] Another interesting feature of art patronage in such contexts is an even-handed spread between works by artists of significant national or international reputation and locally based sculptors and craftspersons. In this sense, it is an important source of work and commissions for artists based in the region. A key aspect of work in this context is the role of art in assuaging anxiety and in providing visual pleasure and distraction in what can be a stressful environment. Hence, the prominent use of forms derived from nature or the use of visual humour in the subject matter and approach taken. Although the values of memory and memorialising are not totally neglected, nevertheless the brooding histories associated with much

traditional public sculpture in our cities, towns and villages tend to be absent.

This is not just the case in hospitals, where the reason for such absence is clear. It can also be seen as part of a wider phenomenon in other recent public spheres. This is a context dominated by post-Second World War renewal and regeneration and a resurgent sense of utopian civic optimism from the 1960s onwards. This can be seen throughout the county, but particularly interesting examples can be found in the relatively recent demographic shift inland in Sussex during this period, with the growth of new town and suburban development in the Crawley/Horsham/Gatwick area. This is a location with an internationally important transport hub, an area until relatively recently of very low unemployment with commuter suburbs close to London. In such a region, 'new town' public art takes on particular flavours. One example is the genre of 'roundabout art' experienced from one's car as befits a new town like Crawley. The local council here has an art-on-roundabouts scheme inaugurated by Ray Smith's *Flying Spiral*. This large spiral, made of corten steel with an abstracted figure echoing the idea of flight at its top, was placed on a grassed area on the Hawth roundabout opposite Wealden Drive in Crawley in 2001. Further examples followed, such as the large football outside the Broadfield stadium and *Sixty Arrows* by Gary Breeze on the junction roundabout between Ifield Avenue and the High Street. There has been a considerable amount of this kind of public art/sculpture developed throughout the county in recent years, lending some credence to the concept of a 'public art mania' as an echo of the older late-nineteenth, early twentieth-century concept of 'statuemania'. Arising as a consequence of enlightened arts policy on the part of local councils, Arts Council England, notable individual arts administrators and arts organisations, a feature of such art is the linking of certain tropes of modernism to a civic context with its mix of local and universal themes. A good example from this area of Sussex is the fountain sculpture *Cosmic Cycle* in Horsham by Angela Conner. Unveiled in 1996, it consists of a large fountain bowl in which is placed a massive sphere made of polished steel partly cladded with concrete. This sphere rises up and disgorges water at appropriate moments in its cycle before descending to the bowl below. Set in a pedestrianised shopping precinct, it references Shelley (a poet associated with the town) and his poem on Mont Blanc. As befits its subject, the statement by the artist, inscribed on the monument, links ideas about cosmology, water and Shelley's concept of liberty to the monument's abstracted form and its 'watery performance'. In an echo of the unveiling ceremony of the much older Victoria Fountain in Brighton, the Horsham monument was unveiled to the sounds of Horsham Symphony Orchestra playing a new work by composer Martyn Harry, also inspired by Mont Blanc. This is not the only example of such 'fountain art' in this locality. There are also *Slipstream* and *Jetstream* at either end of the departure ramps in the North Terminal of Gatwick

Airport, designed by William Pye and installed in 1998. With dramatic fountains such as these, one is tempted, in the affectionate spirit of Osbert Lancaster, to label this kind of public art in the region, 'Gatwick Baroque!'[9]

The impact of enlightened patronage on public sculpture in the county has been frequently felt ever since the late eighteenth century, the 3rd Earl of Egremont being a prominent example. In more recent times, an example of significant patronage of the arts in general, and specifically the art of sculpture in the public realm, is to be found in the figure of Walter Hussey (1905–1985), Dean of Chichester Cathedral from 1955 to his retirement in 1977. The art historian Kenneth Clark called him 'the last great patron of art in the Church of England'.[10] The motivation behind both his personal collection and his public commissioning was, firstly, an enthusiasm for modernism, and secondly, the application of its devices and tropes to a traditional liturgical context. The artists involved with him read like a roll call of significant figures in modernism in the musical and visual arts including, among others, Britten, Moore, Auden, Sutherland, Piper, Walton, Feibusch, Tippet and Chagall. This legacy continues today through the Hussey Memorial Commission for Chichester Cathedral. One aspect of this continuing legacy is the selection of the best of contemporary talent and a far-sighted appreciation of what contemporary work can bring to an ancient medieval context, which inevitably can sometimes create controversy. The Spanish-born sculptor, Jaume Plensa, was selected in November 2010 to produce a new work for the cathedral. This artist, a previous winner of the PMSA Marsh Award for public sculpture, was selected from an impressive short list. His proposal ran into difficulties in gaining approval from the Cathedrals' Fabric Commission for England, which refused to approve it in February 2012, in spite of enthusiastic support from the current Dean, the Cathedral Chapter and Chichester Cathedral's own Fabric Advisory Committee. This proposal was particularly bold in its size and in the prominent suggested location within the nave space of the medieval Cathedral. In the view of the Fabric Commission, it would, 'have an adverse impact upon – and come to dominate – not only the nave space and principal views from the west end, but also the totality of visitors' and worshippers' experience of the Cathedral interior.'[11] Clearly, the Commission in this case felt that a line between respect for tradition and contemporary statement had been crossed.

Fundamental to initiatives behind Hussey's legacy is the belief that the old and the new can be brought into a confluence and given a context of respectful insertion where each could support and reinvigorate the other. It was Hussey, together with Bishop Bell, chair of the Bishop Otter College Council, who from the late fifties built up the college collection of artworks to enhance college buildings and surroundings. Founded in 1840, and now Chichester University, the original college was particularly noted for its commitment to art education. Of course, such activity, within the general expansion of higher education and the development of universities and colleges in the postwar period, is found elsewhere in Sussex. Sculpture using modernist forms in this context produced a genre that could be termed 'campus modernism'. Sussex examples from Brighton University's Falmer campus are *Brighton Lights* (1998) by Hamish Black and *Pollen Forms* (2004) by Steve Geliot.

The practice of public sculpture is a complex collaborative one, involving many different stakeholders both before and after the unveiling date of any particular example, its reception and meaning constantly changing. Sculpture in the public sphere and how a public responds to it and why is more complicated than it might at first appear. Sussex contains a number of intriguing examples that usefully highlight the broader significance of such interaction. Take, for example, *Desert Quartet* by Elisabeth Frink in Worthing. This work is a series of four bronze heads mounted within a loggia above the colonnade of the Montague Shopping Centre, Liverpool Gardens, Worthing. These four, instantly recognizable, Frink heads, according to Edward Lucie Smith, 'radiate authority'.[12]

Frink was awarded this commission in 1985 and worked closely with the architect of the Montague Centre on her proposal, which was a composition of horses and dogs designed specifically for this site. Unfortunately, the sculptor became too ill to complete the task so she offered these four heads (in fact, her penultimate work before her death in 1993) instead. They were based on a visit to the Tunisian Desert, hence the title *Desert Quartet*. Each head was an edition of 6, 24 in all, of near-perfect bronzes, cast from a plaster original and are, therefore, hardly unique to their site. However, whatever the compromises made, these works acquired a public context beyond being examples of work by a highly significant artist that happen to be placed in an outside architectural space. The controversy the pieces provoked when installed and unveiled on 13 June 1990 and also in 2007, when they were threatened with removal, provides an interesting example of Jurgen Habermas' theory of the public sphere as it might be applied to a work of art, demonstrating what he calls 'common concern' rather than individual economic market interests.[13]

The piece was commissioned by a local development company and at the time of its unveiling in June 1990, its director pronounced it, 'a major contribution to Britain's treasury of contemporary art [which] will give added distinction to a development which is already being acclaimed for its style'.[14] The reaction of the Worthing public was less favourable.[15] Fifteen years later, the developer, claiming ownership of the bronze heads, applied to the local council to have them removed while redeveloping the site, in order to replace them with something allegedly closer to Frink's original intentions. Given their original mixed reception, this did not seem an unreasonable suggestion. However, over the intervening period the sculptures had become an accepted part of the urban landscape and various groups challenged their removal, insisting that the developer no longer owned them because he had gifted them to the town. They further pointed out that a clause in the original planning permission for the commission had stipulated that they were to be permanently placed on this site. The campaign to oppose their removal and replacement included groups such as the PMSA, the Twentieth Century Society, the Worthing Society, with its specialist conservation group, and local Worthing citizens, including council members. As a result of this petition, the sculptures were Grade 2 listed, the first time such status was awarded to a cultural artifact less than 30 years old, signalling their special national importance. This Sussex example well represents that mediating confluence between the private concerns of individual citizens, civic societies, groups and associations, and the procedures of public authorities both local and national, in contrast to individual interests.

Sometimes there is a conflict of interest between local authorities who are often responsible for the ongoing repair of historic sculptures and public monuments and local citizens. Inevitably, spoilage, wear and tear, vandalism and graffiti take their toll on hard-pressed council budgets and arguments over inappropriate restoration sometimes erupt. An example is the case of the memorial in Brighton's Regency Square to the men of the Royal Sussex Regiment who fell in the Second Boer War of 1900–1902, known to Brighton residents more colloquially as 'The Bugler'. Erected in 1904, the monument's bronze figure, together with the associated plaques on its plinth, was given a thick coat of bronze metallic paint in 2008. From having a weathered dark patina, the Bugler was transformed into a vulgar, bright, garish figure standing against the sky and buildings of Regency Square. The Regency Square Area Society in its newsletter put the issue succinctly by quoting a letter to the local evening paper, *The Argus*. The letter indicated that the original patina was intended to enhance and preserve the monument and that 'for want of an expert restorer the Council has damaged the original surface'.[16] The Society put this issue to the Council, which defended its position via its property manager, who indicated that the monument had in fact been painted in the past. The restoration work had 'been done using a specialist paint treatment that is meant to weather down over time, whilst protecting the metal underneath.'[17] At the time of writing, the Council does indeed appear to have been correct about this. According to some reports, however, the monument's surface weathered back to its original dark patina in only a few weeks; it appears that possibly the paint literally fell off!

As with *Desert Heads*, what this illustrates is that in the public sphere, when a situation arises where people become nervous about proposed or actual adjustments to their familiar environment, they express that anxiety through whatever media are available to them. The monument dramatically depicts the vulnerable foot soldier in the form of a bugler calling his comrades to battle, a depiction in bronze of a poignant sound.

Monuments such as this one, seen by many people every day, are also part of a fading history and memory. Part of the purpose of a book such as this is not only to provide information for the specialist scholar of sculpture or of urban development, but also to rescue for the ordinary passerby the broader histories behind their familiar scenes. Memory and response to such objects depend, of course, on one's individual background. In relation to 'the Bugler', we were reminded of this when driving past it in 2012 with the South African sculptor, William Boschoff. His reaction, coming from an Afrikaans Boer community with its memories of those wars and of concentration camps set up by the British, was very different from our own, such camps being a particular feature of the Second Boer war of 1899–1902.[18]

Sussex, much as elsewhere, has its share of monuments that depict particular monarchs, public worthies, military heroes, social reformers, significant anniversaries, and so on. For example, in relation to the moment of Queen Victoria's Diamond Jubilee of 1897, there is a fine example by Thomas Brock at the end of Grand Avenue, Hove, facing the sea and promenade. Erected in 1901, this impressive statue with relief plaques on its pedestal representing Empire, Education, Commerce, Science and Art is a confident representation of the 'Pax Britannica' of Victorian Britain at the apex of its global spread and power. It is a precursor to Brock's larger, slightly later, ensemble outside Buckingham Palace, London. Today, with the hindsight of a bloody twentieth century, together with a more complex relationship to the figurative depiction of civic and public virtue, such works are divested of their original meanings, becoming to some extent mere markers in the city space, something we glance at when walking or driving past on the promenade.

Interjections into public spaces are now more likely to take the form of temporary installations, often attached to festivals or significant cultural or civic events, and here again Sussex has contributed notable and important examples to what are sometimes termed 'counter-monuments'. One such, during the Cultural Olympiad of 2012, was Richard Wilson's *'Hang on a minute lads, I've got a great idea'*. This consisted of a replica of the Harrington Legionnaire coach used in the 1969 film *The Italian Job*, perched on the edge of the roof of the De La Warr Pavilion in Bexhill. The final scene of this comic gangster caper showed exactly such a coach stacked up at its rear end with gold bullion, teetering over a cliff edge on one of those vertiginous roads for which North Italy is famous. The final line of the film, uttered by Michael Caine, provided the title of Wilson's piece. So here we have an object, an image from an iconic popular film, teetering off the roof of an iconic modernist Sussex building, the De La Warr Pavilion, a building conceived as a utopian popular resource for the south coast resort of Bexhill. A complicated system of hydraulics moved the replica bus up and down, recreating the amusing spectacle of the film's closing moments. There are many subtle references in the piece, such as the theme of gold coming to Britain during the London Olympics and also in its use of parapets, edges, Bexhill's sea and sky to reflect the imagery of the film's most famous moment. The installation was, as Wilson put it in an interview, 'a way of drawing a public to the grammar of art'.[19] What he meant by an 'art grammar' is perhaps an awareness of art history, of the traditions, meanings and iconography associated with the public monuments of the past that can no longer automatically be assumed to be a part of a wider culture.

This is by no means the only artwork in Sussex to signal the importance of cultural festivals for temporary monuments installed in public spaces. Of particular relevance is Brighton Festival, occurring each year for three weeks in May. In 2009 the sculptor Anish Kapoor, guest director of that year's festival, installed *C-Curve* on the South Downs above Brighton. This large, curved, polished mirror reflected, on its sides, downland landcape, sky and visitors. Significantly, it was positioned near the *Chattri Monument* set up on the Downs in memory of the open cremation of Sikh soldiers on that site in 1918. Perhaps the most interesting and most recent example of such temporary interjection into public space was by the Finnish artist, Kaarina Kaikkonen. Organised by the Brighton Gallery, Fabrica, with European and Arts Council funding, her piece called *Time Passing By* (2013) consisted of swathing the Clock Tower in central Brighton with items of clothing gathered from charity shops and local citizens. This was an unusual example of a work interfering with, and directly adjusting, a monument, investing it with different histories and meanings. The public response varied from cheerful amusement to more troubled associations, but at least in an ironic sense, the Brighton Clock Tower became for a time more visible and will hopefully remain so now that Kaikkonen's piece has been removed (see right).

There are some interesting examples in Sussex of the shifting nature of public response and reception. We can see this operating in the way monuments get 'affectionately' renamed. One such is Hamish Black's *Afloat*, installed on Brighton seafront near the Palace Pier in 1998. It is generally known in Brighton as 'the doughnut'. Black's sculpture has since become an icon of Brighton as a place, often appearing on publicity material and in one instance on the cover of the University of Brighton prospectus. One awaits with interest the outraged protests should there be any suggestion of removing it from its current location. Somehow the 'art grammar' of the piece, its scientific references to black holes, continental drift, morphology, its simple form, and so on, has not, as Richard Wilson might have put it, got in the way of the public appropriating its 'visual grammar', for their own purposes in response to its classic Sussex seaside setting near Brighton Pier.

Sussex, like other counties of Britain, is littered with memorials reminding us of the impact of political events, military campaigns and wars. It is, inevitably, the First World War that predominates, mention of subsequent wars being more usually added to those monuments with further inscriptions or relief plaques rather than being commemorated separately. As elsewhere in Britain, there is not a single city, town or village in the county of Sussex that lacks some kind of memorial to this event, even if it is only a simple village cross demonstrating the skills of the local stone mason rather than that of the sculptor. There are, of course, some spectacular sculptural examples of this category of monument in Sussex, often complex ensembles of the arts of statuary, architectural design and letter carving, employing the skills of sculptor,

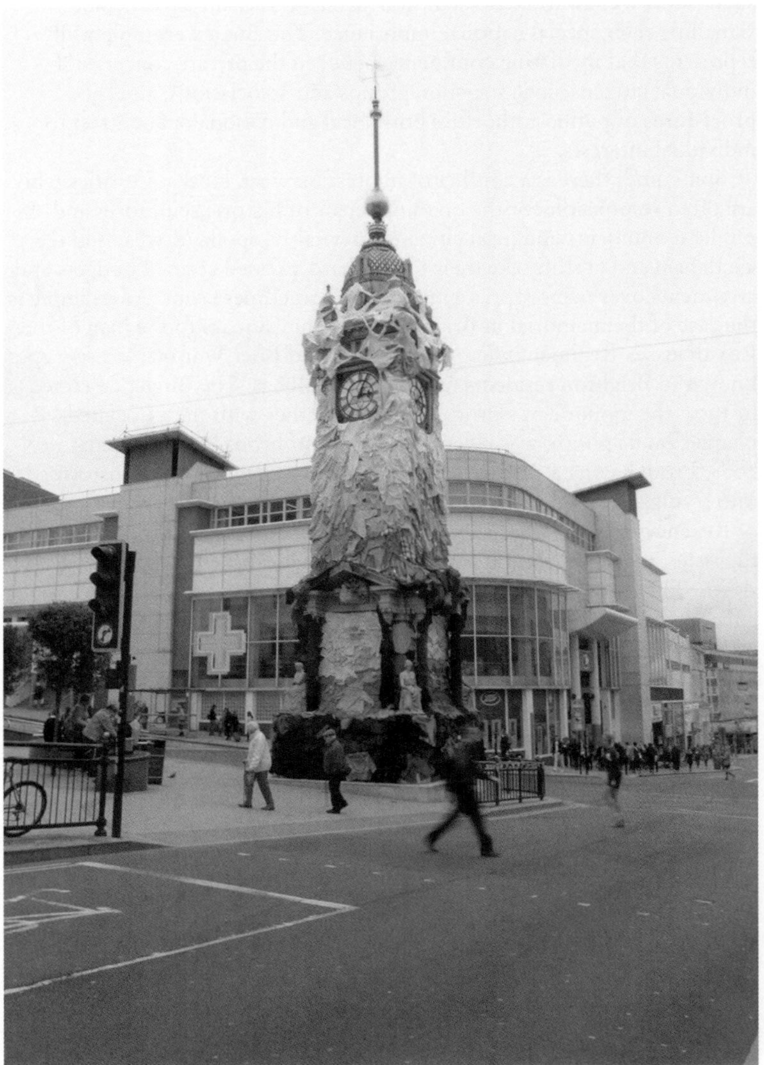

Kaarina Kaikkonen, *Time Passing By*

stone mason, bronze caster and foundry man, architect and builder, that must remind the viewer that public sculpture is a complex collaborative process requiring many varied skills and talents. Hastings, Brighton, Eastbourne and Lewes all have fine examples of First World War memorials, and it is worthy of note that the one in Alexandra Park, Hastings, erected in 1922, is a rare example of a war memorial by a female sculptor, Margaret Winser.

Sculptural practice has become increasingly expanded in recent years, to the point where artefacts once firmly outside its purview have now become 'sculpture' after the fact. Sussex contains one outstanding example of this in *The Long Man of Wilmington*. This work is supposedly a Neolithic earthwork made by exposing the chalk on a hillside of the South Downs above the village of Wilmington, so it might be better conceived as a drawing in chalk on the earth's surface rather than strictly as sculpture. Today it is not actually constructed from exposed chalk, but from concrete blocks laid in the turf in 1969 and painted white. It receives fresh coats of white paint from time to time with the assistance of local groups. It has now in a very real sense become sculpture since the impact of land art in the 1960s. Sculptors in Sussex have developed this idea of working directly with landscape and natural forms, such as in the piece in Hove Park by Chris Drury, entitled *Fingermaze*. Installed in 2006, it also consists of white stone blocks laid into the green turf, depicting a large fingerprint that can be walked along as a maze, leading, via its concentric whorls, towards its centre and back again.

Sussex is also rich in the vernacular tradition of folk and popular art with artifacts such as inn and village signs, wayside memorials, and so on. Such objects are often produced anonymously and are difficult to trace historically; to include all available examples in Sussex would distort this book beyond its focus and purpose, particularly as much of the material is of somewhat variable quality and interest. However, we have included a few examples where there is aesthetic impact and where this contributes significantly to the visual fabric around it. Good examples are the two carved, painted wooden figures of Henry VIII and Anne Boleyn over the entrance to the King and Queen pub in Brighton and the village sign in Mayfield, East Sussex. In a separate but related vein, a tradition of popular roadside temporary memorialising has grown in recent years, where, for example, flowers are tied to lampposts at scenes of traffic accidents or other forms of tragic death in public places.

A second area that expands the concept of public sculpture is the field of urban design, where street furniture, urban decoration, way-markers, public amenities such as benches and the provision of leisure areas, street lighting and so on blend with the idea of the public monument and public sculpture. This has been a particular feature of regeneration and redevelopment schemes in recent years. To include a comprehensive list of all such examples is again beyond the scope and focus of this book. However, in some cases, a talented artist or designer has been sought out

and commissioned. Work of real quality has been produced, examples being work from the riverside walk around the Ropetackle Development at Shoreham-by-Sea, the *Oyster Waymarkers* at Littlehampton, and work by Esther Rolinson at St Leonards-on-Sea and the County Library, Lewes. This emphasis on a considered relationship between space, site, context, object and audience, with a stress on social purpose and use, was the subject of *Mapping the Terrain: new genre public art*, edited by the American public artist and scholar, Suzanne Lacy, and published in 1995. An approach such as this has obvious appeal to local councils interested in regenerative and development schemes and in securing funding for such work in the interests of social cohesion. It also appeals to contemporary artists seeking alternative spaces for their work outside galleries and normal commissioning procedures. Nevertheless, it should not be forgotten that a somewhat older history lies behind it. A Brighton example of this is the opening of the Victoria Fountain in the Steine in 1846 when specially commissioned music, *The Fountain Quadrilles* by Charles Coote, was played by a concert band and local shops and businesses closed at 3 p.m. for a concert champêtre followed by fireworks.

Finally, a third and more contentious expansion of a definition of public sculpture in the post-Second World War period is the ubiquitous use of three-dimensional advertising and signage whose scale and impact on the urban public space can sometimes, when seen in a certain context, take on the condition of sculpture.

Apart from questions of sculptural quality and definition, what about quantitative measuring of sculptural activity over periods of time in the county? Although in Sussex a sculptural tradition has long existed, it should be acknowledged that much of it is centred on church monuments or architectural features, either free-standing or attached to buildings. However, the vast majority of items in this book run from 1750 to the present. If we simply count the numbers of sculptures installed over each of the individual decades making up this period of time and express those numbers as rough percentages, we can see the results in the diagram overleaf. The information it provides is not surprising; it very much confirms what one would expect to see, not only in Sussex but probably elsewhere as well. Starting in 1700 there is a small but steady amount of activity rising slowly in the Regency and early Victorian periods and then a pronounced spurt from around 1830 to the mid-1920s and early 1930s. The late nineteenth and very early twentieth centuries are the high point in the period christened by sculptural historians, 'statuemania', a cultural phenomenon referring to statues or monuments placed in city squares, piazzas, street junctions, avenues, boulevards and parks, meant to be seen and experienced fully in the round by a roving spectator.[20] The numbers of statues and monuments erected throughout Europe in this period are quite staggering. Of course, the actual number erected in Sussex is much smaller than in major metropolitan centres such as Paris, Munich, or

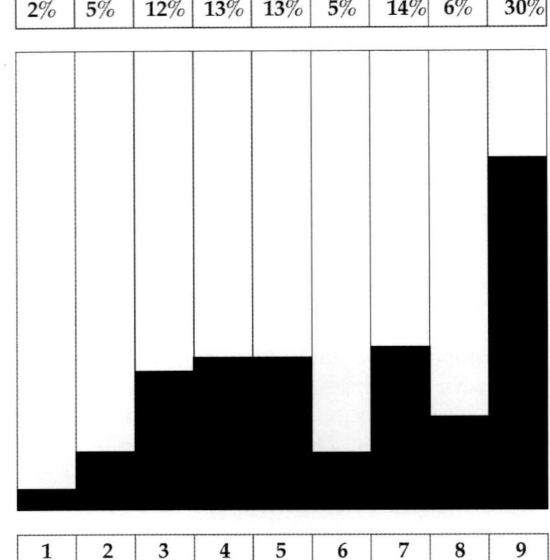

1	1700-1780
2	1780-1830
3	1830-1880
4	1880-1910
5	1910-1930
6	1930-1950
7	1950-1970
8	1970-1990
9	1990-2010

Percentage of monuments erected in Sussex 1700–2010

London, but nevertheless, particularly in its seaside littoral and along the leisure areas and promenades of places like Hastings, Eastbourne and Brighton, examples of 'statuemania' from this period can easily be found.

The diagram shows a significant drop in activity in the late 1930s and 1940s, particularly during and immediately after the Second World War. The next sharp rise upwards is during the 1950s and 1960s, the moment of postwar reconstruction and the welfare state. Compared to the rhetoric and tropes of earlier periods, the monuments and sculptures of this moment are often couched in the language of a modernism that expresses a notion of universal abstract form or, if it is figurative, that of utopian, universal values. Examples of the work of this period in Sussex include Richard Browne's *Family Group* on the wall of T.J. Hughes in Crawley (1959), Geoffrey Clarke's abstract work that echoes the crucifixion, above the door of the chapel at Bishop Otter Campus, University of Chichester (1962), John Skelton's *Symbol of Discovery* (1963) also in Chichester, and Uli Nimptsch's *Chris Ascendant*, St Winifred's Parish Church, Bognor Regis (1964). Perhaps the best exemplification of this particular moment is William Mitchell's *Spirit of Brighton* (1968), now unfortunately destroyed. There is then another dip in sculptural production in the mid-1970s, followed by a very steep rise from about 1990 to the present. This rise is often the result of public art projects, both permanent and temporary, suggesting that a good case could be made for the term 'public art mania'. This book contains many examples, from the highly successful

to those of more dubious quality and impact. The conflict between official taste and public rejection or alternatively between popular acclaim and elite anxiety, is played out in various ways. To take a Brighton example, one might compare the populist reception of Peter Webster's *Max Miller* statue (2005) commissioned by the Max Miller Appreciation Society with the attempt by *The Argus* newspaper to initiate protest against Charlie Hooker's *Twins* (1998) labeling them 'giant orbs'.

Regarding this book's organisation and use, the central catalogue section has been divided into East and West Sussex, much like the Sussex volume of *The Buildings of England*, by Ian Nairn and Nikolaus Pevsner. In our volume, towns and villages within each half of the county are listed alphabetically and the sculptures and monuments associated with each place are sorted according to location (in most cases street name). Ian Nairn, Pevsner's collaborator, was asked to complete the whole of Sussex but, as Pevsner comments, '… having completed West Sussex [he] found he could no longer bear to write the detailed descriptions which are essential for *The Buildings of England*. His decision filled me with sadness but I had of course to carry on … as things were, the volume called for two introductions.'[21] We are tempted to add that we know how he felt! Fortunately, although our catalogue is divided into two sections, in our case only one introduction was necessary. Therefore, the book is organised in such a way as to be of particular use to the resident or visitor curious enough to want to know more about familiar and not-so-familiar monuments. It is not completely comprehensive because, particularly with recent works of public art, it is often difficult to keep up. It is impossible to include and cover everything and to those artists, makers and others involved whose work we may have missed out we can only plead the necessity of choice. Nevertheless, we trust this volume is comprehensive enough to give a vivid snapshot of what is out there to see, enjoy and above all understand and is a basis for future work on the topic.

Notes

[1] All the foundries in the county tended to focus on the production and casting of ironwork. The Eagle Foundry in Gloucester Road, Brighton, in 1846 cast the iron dolphins and pool basin for the Victoria Fountain in Steine Gardens, Brighton. There were no local foundries specialising in the production of bronze sculpture using the lost wax process. There were in the sixteenth and seventeenth centuries over 100 foundries, mostly in the East Sussex Weald, producing ironwork. See aditnow.co.uk/ukminingregions.
[2] This statistical information can be found in Sutton, A. (ed.), *Sussex: Environment, Landscape and Society*, University of Sussex, 1983, pp. 221, 270–71.
[3] A useful discussion of the development and culture of the seaside resort and its peculiar public spaces is to be found in Farrant, S., 'The early growth of seaside towns, 1750–1840' in Sutton (1983), pp. 208–18.
[4] Seddon, J., 'The visual arts in Regency Brighton and Hove', *The Georgian Group Journal*, vol. XIII, 2003, pp. 273–80.

[5] Berry, S., *Georgian Brighton*, Chichester, 2005, p. 137.

[6] Gray, F., *Designing the Seaside: Architecture, Society and Nature*, London, 2006. See chapter 8, 'Walking on water', pp. 201–43.

[7] Solkin, D.H., *Painting for Money: the Visual Arts and the Public Sphere in Eighteenth Century England*, London and New Haven, 1992, p. 28.

[8] http://publicsculpturesofsussex.co.uk/

[9] Readers may be aware of the hilarious but revealing spoofs of art historical style terms in his books such as *Homes, Sweet Homes* (1949) and *A Cartoon History of Architecture* (1975).

[10] See Lubbock, T., 'Patrick Caulfield: serenely secular', *The Independent*, 14 April 2009.

[11] We are grateful to Ruth Poyner of Chichester Cathedral Visitors Centre for this information; visitors@chichestercathedral.org.uk.

[12] Lucie Smith, E., *Elisabeth Frink: Sculpture Since 1984 and Drawings*, London, 1994, p. 67.

[13] Habermas' book was first published in 1929, but for a full demonstration of its arguments in English, the reader should consult *The Structural Transformation of the Public Sphere; an Inquiry into a Category of Bourgeois Society* (trans. Thomas Burger and Lawrence Frederick), Cambridge, 1989.

[14] *Worthing Herald*, 1 June 1990, p. 5.

[15] Letters page, *Worthing Herald*, 22 June 1990, p. 10.

[16] Letters page, *Brighton Argus*, 23 May 2008, p. 11.

[17] *Regency Square Area Society Newsletter*, no. 223, June 2008.

[18] The South African sculptor, William Boschoff, visited Brighton and lectured to MA Fine Art students at Brighton University in May 2012.

[19] *The Guardian*, 4 July 2012.

[20] Hall, J., *The World as Sculpture: the Changing Status of Sculpture from the Renaissance to the Present Day*, London, 2000, p. 226.

[21] Nairn, I. and Pevsner, N. *The Buildings of England: Sussex*, Penguin, London, 1965, p. 11.

Acknowledgements

We are grateful for the support of the PMSA, the Heritage Lottery Fund, the Paul Mellon Centre for Studies in British Art, the Henry Moore Foundation, and the Faculty of Arts, University of Brighton. Many people, in a whole variety of ways, have assisted in the research and compilation of this volume and we are grateful to them all. We would particularly like to thank the following:

Prof. David Arnold
Josephine Barry (former curator) and staff at Petworth House
David Beevers (Keeper, Royal Pavilion, Brighton)
Anne Olivier Bell
Hamish Black
Chris Blade
Brighton Local History Centre staff
Michele Brooker (Lewes Public Library)
The late Jo Darke
Countess De La Warr
Douglas D'Enno
The Earl of March
Roger Edwards
Alice Fox
Nick Fox
Steve Geliot
Daniele Harwood (assistant to William Pye)
Prof. Charlie Hooker
Brian Lawe (chair) and Hastings Local History Group
Gina Lelliott
Charlotte Le Rossignol
Dr Paddy Maguire
Simon Martin and Sarah Norris (Pallant House)
Claire Mayoh (archivist, Henry Moore Institute)
Alison McCann (formerly Assistant County Archivist, West Sussex Record Office)
Geoff Metcalfe
William Mitchell
Prof. Catherine Moriarty
Dave Morris

Edward Morris
Diana Nason
Claire Nelson
Ruth Poyner (Chichester Cathedral)
Dr Brian Rigby and Bob Marshall, Otter Gallery, University of Chichester
Rocket Artists
Karina Rodriguez-Echavarria
The late Terry Sinnot
Wendy Walker (County Archivist, WSRO; formerly of East Sussex Record Office)
Peter Webster
Gaynor Williams

Photo Credits

Anthony McIntosh took most of the photographs in this book, with some photographs and diagrams provided by Peter and Jill Seddon. The authors would like to thank the following individuals and institutions for the provision of images and/or permission to reproduce them:

Time Passing By by Kaarina Kaikkonen (p. xiv), photo Ben Harding, courtesy of Fabrica Gallery, Brighton; *Terracotta Reliefs* by Alexander Fisher (p. 22), reproduced with the permission of Philippa Lyon, University of Brighton; *Captain Pechell Memorial Statue* (p. 37), courtesy of Brighton and Hove Museums; *Pomona the Lemon Gatherer* (p. 44) and *The Spink* (p. 45), by Quentin Bell, courtesy of Charleston Trust; *The Lazarus Panels* (p. 112), reproduced with the kind permission of Chichester Cathedral and permission to photograph other monuments in the cathedral; *Mother and Child* by Willi Soukop (p. 114) and *Murray Relief* by Peter Hodgkinson (p. 116), reproduced with the permission of the Otter Gallery, University of Chichester; *Slipstream* by William Pye (p.132), reproduced with the permission of the artist; *Memorial to Rob Needham* (p. 184) reproduced from the Robert Needham website; *Murmurations* by Chris Blade (p. 186), reproduced with permission of the artist.

ASHBURNHAM

Off A271 (Ashburnham Place)

The Ashburnham Family Chapel, Parish Church of St Peter (traditionally known as the Chapel of St James)

Monument to John Ashburnham

Sculptor: Thomas Burman (attrib.)

Installed: after 1671
Materials/dimensions: white and grey marble, 4.3 m high × 2.6 m wide × 1.7 m deep
Inscription (on plaque set into recessed arch):

HERE LYES IN THE VAULT / UNDERNEATH JOHN ASHBURNHAM / ESQ. OF THIS PLACE; SONN TO THE UNFORTUNATE / PERSON SR. IOHN ASHBVRNHAM WHOSE GOOD NATURE / AND FRANCK DISPOSITION TOWARDS HIS FRIENDS IN BEING / DEEPLY ENGAGED FOR THEM NECESSITATED HIM TO SELL THIS / PLACE (IN HIS FAMILY LONG BEFORE THE CONQUEST) AND ALL / THE ESTATE HE HAD ELSEWHERE NOT LEAVING TO HIS WIFE AND SIX / CHILDREN THE LEAST SUBSISTANCE WHICH IS NOT INCERTED TO / THE LEAST DISADVANTAGE OF HIS MEMORY (GOD FORBID IT SHOULD BE / UNDERSTOOD TO BE A CHARGE OF DISRESPECT UPPON HIM) BUT TO GIVE GOD THE PRAYSE, WHO SOE SUDDENLY / PROVIDED BOTH FOR HIS WIFE AND CHILDREN AS THAT WITHIN LESS THEN TWO YEARES AFTER THE DEATH OF / THE SAID SR. IOHN THERE WAS NOT ANY OF THEM BUT WAS IN CONDITION RATHER TO BE HELPFULL TO OTHERS THEN TO / WANT SUPPORTE THEMSELVES. MAY GOD BE PLEASED TO ADD THIS BLESSING TO HIS POSTERITY THAT THEY MAY NEVER / BE UNMINDFULL OF THE GREAT THINGS HE HATH DONN FOR THEM. THE WIFE OF THE SAID SR. JOHN ASHBUURNHAM WAS / DAUGHTER TO SR. THOMAS BEAMONT OF STAUGHTON IN THE COUNTY OF LECESTER. SHEE WAS VERY EMINENT / FOR HER GREAT TEMPER AND PRUDENCE. SHE DYED THE SEAVENTY FIFTH YEARE OF HER AGE AND BOTH THE / SAID SR. JOHN AND HIS WIFE LYE BURYED IN THE CHURCH OF ST. ANDREWS IN HOLBURNE LONDON / THE SAID MR. IOHN ASHBURNHAM MARRIED THE DAUGHTER AND HEIRE OF WILLIAM HOLLAND OF / WESTBURTON IN THIS COUNTY ESQ: WHO LYES ALSO HERE INTERRED AND BY WHOM HE HAD THESE EIGHT / CHILDREN. SHE MADE THE FIRST STEPP TOWARDS THE RECOVERY OF SOME PART OF THE INHERITANCE / WASTED BY THE SAID SR. JOHN FOR SHE SOULD HER WHOLE ESTATE TO LAY OUT THE MONY IN THIS PLACE / SHE LIVED IN GREATE REPUTATION FOR PYETY AND DISCRETION AND DYED IN THE SEAVEN AND THIRTITH / YEARE OF HER AGE. THE SECOND WIFE TO THE SAID MR. IOHN ASHBURNHAM WHO LYES ALSO HERE INTERRED / WAS THE WIDOW OF THE LORD POULETT OF HINTON SNT. GEORGE IN THE COUNTY OF SUMMERSETT. SHE / WAS DAUGHTER AND HEIRE TO CHRISTOPHER KENN OF KENT IN THAT COUNTY ESQ: WHO LEFT HER A GREATE / ESTATE IN LANDS NOW IN THE POSSESSION OF THE LORD POULETT. SHE WAS WORTHY IMITATION BY ALL / HER SEX FOR HER HONOURABLE AND RELIGIOUS CONVERSATION, SHE BROUGHT GREAT ADVANTAGES TO THE / FAMILY OF THIS PLACE. AND DYED AT THE AGE OF SEAVENTY YEARES AND FOUR MONTHES. AND HER MEMORY / IS PRECIOUS TO ALL CONSIDERING PERSONS THAT KNEW HER. THIS MR. IOHN ASHBURNHAM WAS OF THE / BEDCHAMBER TO THEIRE MATYES. CHARLES THE FIRST AND CHARLES THE SECOND WHO WHEN HE HAD / PERFORMED THE SERVICE TO GOD IN BUILDING THIS CHURCH AT HIS OWN CHARGE DYED IN THE / SIXTY EIGHT YEARE OF HIS AGE ON THE FIFETEENTH / DAY OF JUNE IN THE YEARE OF OUR LORD 1671

Status: not listed
Condition: fair (cracks to top of monument and left hand side column. Small shield broken off monument and resting on top of sarcophagus. Thumbs missing from furthest statue in recess. Crown on nearest statue to front chipped along upper edge. Evidence of previous repairs to sculptural relief particularly to the hands of the figures.
Owner/custodian: Ashburnham Thanksgiving Trust

Three recumbent figures, John Ashburnham (centre) and his two wives, surmount a sarcophagus extending into a recessed arch. His first wife, Frances Holland, is clothed in her shroud. A sculptural relief to the front of the sarcophagus represents his four sons and three daughters in kneeling position. A large plaque affixed to the wall inside the recessed arch bears the lengthy inscription and at the top of the monument is the Ashburnham coat of arms. The classical design of the tomb, and especially the recumbent figures, is rather old-fashioned for its date and contrasts with the much more adventurous baroque style of his brother William's tomb nearby, constructed only eight years later.

John Ashburnham was only 17 when his father died in 1620 in Fleet Prison, having had to sell his estate to the Relf family to clear his

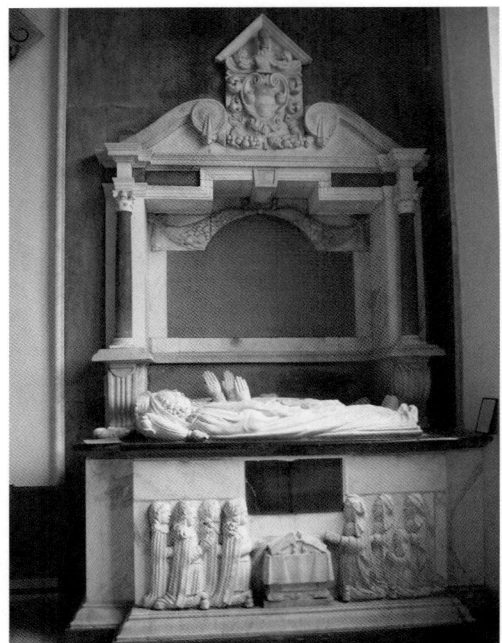

Thomas Burman (attrib.), *Monument to John Ashburnham*

Monument to William Ashburnham and Jane, Countess of Marlborough
Sculptor: John Bushnell

Installed: 1675
Materials/dimensions: white and grey marble,
 4.7 m high × 3.55 m wide × 1.5 m deep
Inscriptions (front of the sarcophagus): Under
 this Toombe (vizt: in the vault for this
 Family) / Lie the Bodies of JANE Countesse
 of Marlbrough, & William Ashburnham her
 husband, / Second sonne of Sr. John
 Ashburnham, She was Daughter to John
 Lord Butler of Hartfordshire, / She was
 married first to James Earle of Marlbrough
 Lord High Treasurer of England, / Who
 after seaven years died, and left her a young,
 beautiful and rich widow / When this
 William, comeing from beyond Sea; where
 he was bred a Souldier married her, and after
 / Lived almost five and forty yeares most
 happily with her, she was a very great lover
 and (through / Gods mercy) a great blessing
 to this Family, which is hoped will ever
 remember it with honouring her memory. /
 This William Ashburnham her husband lived
 after her to a great age, & gloried in nothing
 in this World / But this his Wife, and the
 almost unparallel'd love & intire friendship
 that for / Above fifty yeares was betweene
 his Deare Elder Brother John Ashburnham
 and himselfe / He was Cofferer to King
 Charles the 1st: & King Charles the second,
 he died without issue, / And by Gods
 blessing was a happy Preserver of his
 Brothers Posterity, / The praise and glory of
 it be to God alone
Status: not listed
Condition: fair (evidence of previous repairs to
 several places)
Commissioned by: William Ashburnham
Owner/custodian: Ashburnham Thanksgiving
 Trust

The large Baroque monument is set against a
dark grey marble back wall. Two cherubs pull

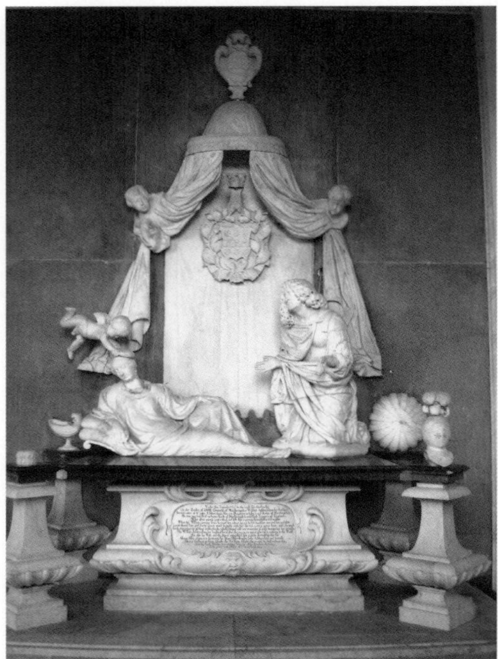

John Bushnell, *Monument to William Ashburnham and Jane, Countess of Marlborough*

debts. He finally managed to obtain a warrant
to reclaim the estate in 1639, using funds from
the sale of his wife's estate. Ashburnham began
a career at court and kept King Charles'
personal account book, travelling with him
during his evasion of Cromwell. When the King
was caught, Ashburnham was imprisoned in
Windsor Castle. After Charles' execution, the
estate was once again seized and he was
imprisoned and banished for some eight years.
After the Restoration, Ashburnham regained
his position of Groom of the Bedchamber and
was given an 80-year lease on Ampthill Park,
Bedfordshire. He was later elected MP for
Sussex. He rebuilt and refurnished the church
and together with his brother William rebuilt
Ashburnham Place, but John died before its
completion. The brothers are buried in the
crypt, containing 45 spaces, which John built.
The house and estate were gifted to the
Ashburnham Thanksgiving Trust in 1960.[1]

back a marble curtain above a sarcophagus on
which reclines the dying figure of Jane, the
Countess of Marlborough. Another cherub is
placing a wreath upon her head. The figure of
William Ashburnham, her husband, kneels on
the top step with a grief-stricken expression,
looking towards his wife. To either side of the
sarcophagus is a marble plinth; on the top of the
one to the right is a plumed helmet and on the
one to the left is a small crown. At the top of
the monument and also just underneath the
marble curtain are sculpted coats of arms.
Margaret Whinney states, '[t]his dramatic tomb,
with its intense expression of grief, and its
direct appeal to the spectator, was certainly a
novelty in England …'.[2]

William Ashburnham, who died in 1679,
fought in the Netherlands and in 1640 became
MP for Ludgershall in Wiltshire. He was later
Colonel of the King's 8th Regiment and in 1644

became Governor of Weymouth. In 1654 he was imprisoned in the Tower of London for being involved in a murder plot against the Protector, but was released for lack of proof. After the Restoration, he became Cofferer of the Household of Charles II. He was a close friend of Samuel Pepys, being mentioned several times in Pepys' diaries.

Notes
[1] The monuments are included by kind permission of the Ashburnham Thanksgiving Trust.
[2] Whinney, M., *Sculpture in Britain 1530–1830*, London, 1964, p.43.

Other sources
Ashburnham Christian Trust, *An Introduction to the History of Ashburnham Place*, Ashburnham, 2004.
Ashburnham family archive, East Sussex Record Office, Lewes (ASH/4501).
Llewellyn, N., *East Sussex Church Monuments 1530–1830*, Lewes, 2011, pp. 19–20.

BEXHILL-ON-SEA

Buckhurst Place

Set into the wall of Sainsbury's supermarket

Sculptural Relief
Sculptors: Joyce and Henry Collins

Installed: 1976
Materials/dimensions: small reliefs: polychrome *ciment fondu*, 65 cm high × 65 cm wide × 10 cm deep; arched panels (×3): polychrome *ciment fondu*, 2.45 m high × 4.2 m wide × 10 cm deep; large reliefs: polychrome *ciment fondu*, 1.2 m high × 1.2 m wide × 10 cm deep
Signatures (bottom right of third panel): HENRY & JOYCE COLLINS 1976
Status: not listed
Condition: good
Commissioned and owned by: J. Sainsbury plc

Three panels, on which are mounted individual rectangular and circular reliefs of varied sizes, are set in a row within shallow arched niches

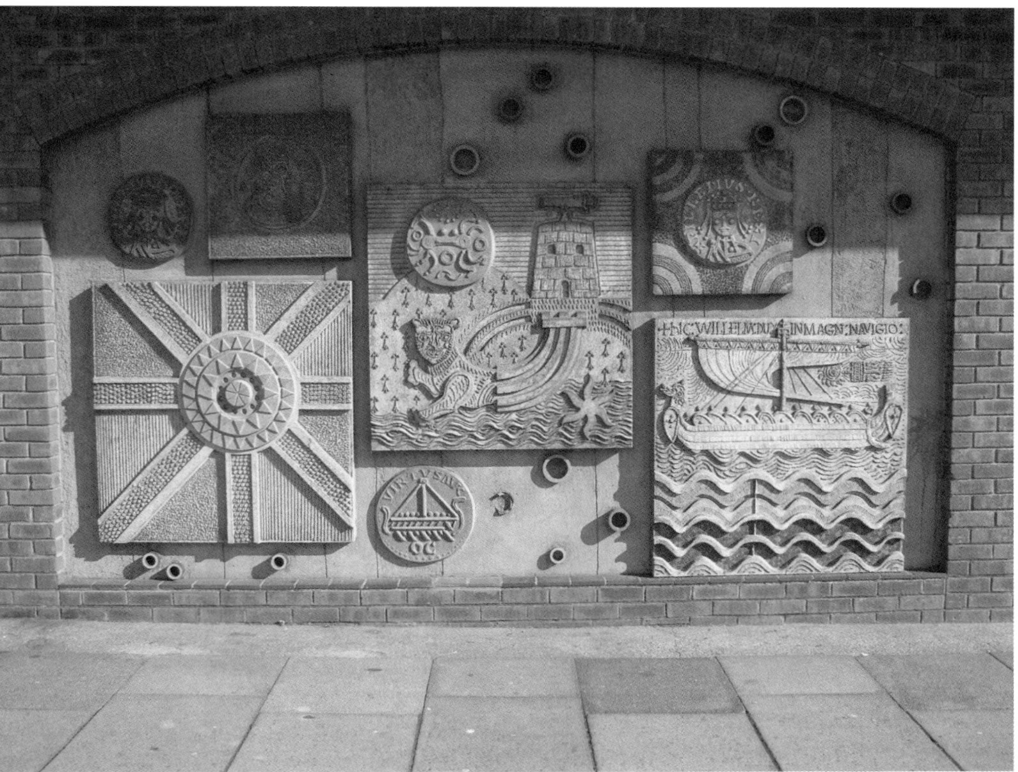

Joyce and Henry Collins, *Sculptural Relief* (detail)

along a brick wall on the exterior of the store. The stylised designs on the reliefs are all related to Bexhill and its environs, depicting marine life, historical events, including the Battle of Hastings, industry and local landmarks.

Joyce (née Pallot) and Henry Collins, whose work had achieved a public profile through their involvement in the Festival of Britain in 1951 and Expo 70 in Japan, were commissioned to provide reliefs for retail stores across the country, including Sainsbury's[1] and British Home Stores[2] as well as one in the foyer of the Post Office Tower, London.[3] Describing the meticulous research, with its emphasis on people and history, that he and his wife conducted for each project, Henry Collins wrote:

We do not aim for decoration for its own sake, or realism or fine art. We aim to put something together which adds dignity to a building and tells a story. We use formalized motifs which suit the concrete medium and respect the wall surface … [4]

Notes
[1] A Southampton branch has a relief dated 1978.
[2] BHS in Northumberland Road, Newcastle has a two-panel relief depicting the history of Newcastle. It is thought that it was originally commissioned by C&A, who owned the building. newcastle.gove.uk/core.nsf/a/pubartcitycentre (accessed 17 February 2011). [3] Commissioned in 1966. lightstraw.co.uk/ate/main/postofficetower (accessed 4 October 2010). [4] 'The scholarly murals of Henry and Joyce Collins, with a commentary by Henry Collins', *Concrete Quarterly*, 104, 1975, p. 15.

Other sources
'Obituary: Joyce Pallot', *Brightlingsea Gazette*, 29

June 2004. Pearson, L., 'Roughcast textures with cosmic overtones: a survey of British murals, 1945–80', *The Decorative Arts Society Journal*, vol. 31, 2007, pp. 116–137.
PMSA *Notes and Queries Archive*, 2009.
Usherwood, P., Beach, J. and Morris, C., *Public Sculpture of North-East England*, Liverpool, 2000, pp. 125–26.

De La Warr Parade

Opposite the Sackville Hotel and Middlesex Road

The Serpolet Sculpture

Designer: Peter Fairhurst

Metalworkers: Anvil Tubesmiths, Sedlescombe
Unveiled: 26 October 2002
Materials/dimensions: shot-blasted stainless steel, 1.6 m high × 1.33 m wide × 2.94 m deep
Inscriptions (metal plaque affixed to black granite at base of sculpture, south side): 1902 – BEXHILL ON SEA – 2002 / THE BIRTHPLACE OF BRITISH MOTOR RACING / THIS IMPRESSION OF M. SERPOLET'S / 'EASTER EGG' RECORD BREAKING CAR/ WAS UNVEILED, AS PART OF / BEXHILL'S CENTENARY CELEBRATIONS / BY / COUNCILLOR PETER FAIRHURST TOWN MAYOR / 26th OCTOBER 2002
Status: not listed
Condition: good (but overall weathering and possible knife marks to underside)
Commissioned and owned by: Rother District Council

This tubular steel structure represents in skeletal form the 'Easter Egg' car designed and made by the French manufacturer of steam cars, Leon Serpolet (also spelt Serpollet). The sculpture has elliptical wheels, suggesting the distortion characteristic of early photographs of speeding cars, and is embedded by steel poles into a tarmac base set on a grassed area. The piece cost £2500 and was designed by the mayor of Bexhill, Peter Fairhurst, who

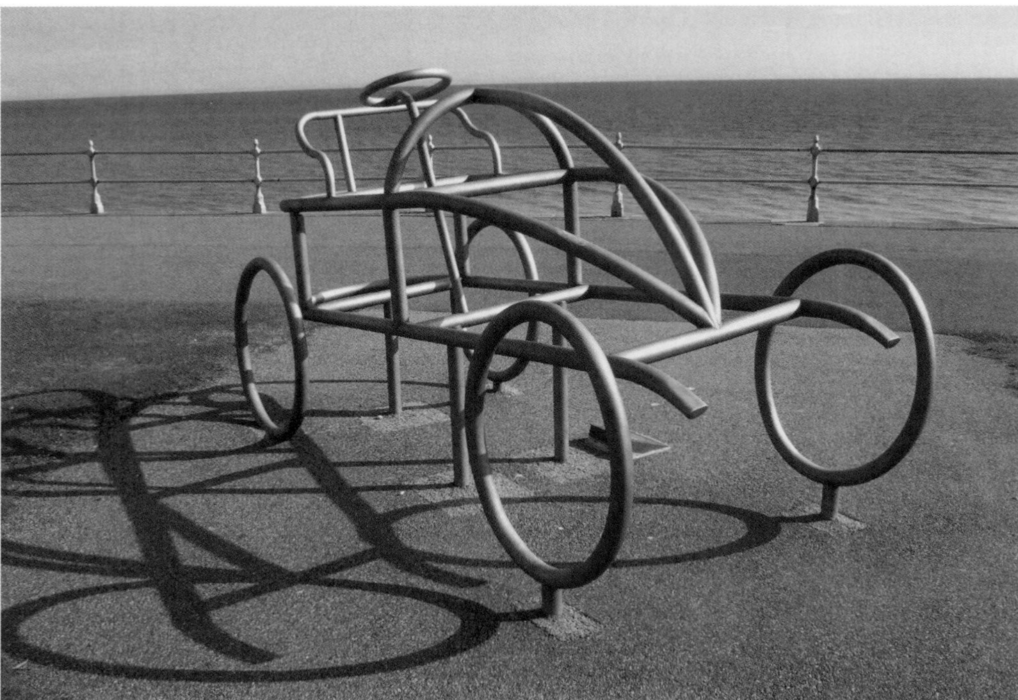

Peter Fairhurst, *The Serpolet Sculpture*

provided a drawing and a model to be made up by Anvil Tubesmiths. It depicts the car on the spot where M. Serpolet won the 1902 Bexhill Motor Trials, the first international motorsport meeting, with a speed of 54 mph. A reproduction of the original Serpolet car, known as the Easter Egg due to its rounded shape, can be found in the Bexhill Museum.

At the unveiling ceremony, a convoy of cars of the era, led by Old Town Preservation Society chairman Michael Kent on his 1899 Peugeot, motored the 1902 race route from Galley Hill to the Sackville Hotel with the mayor riding a reproduction Serpolet. The occasion was seen as marking the start of the landscaping and improvement of the seafront as part of the town's regeneration and the sculpture was the first of a planned series to adorn the parades.[1]

Note
[1] *Bexhill Observer*, 30 September 2002.

Other sources
Bexhill Observer, 22 July 2004.
bexhill100.co.uk/history/bexhillmotoringhistory (accessed 10 December 2010).
bonhams.com (accessed 10 December 2010).

London Road

In the centre of Town Hall Square

Henry Lane Memorial Drinking Fountain

Designers and builders: J.M. Whitehead and Sons Ltd, Rochester Row, London

Unveiled: 25 June 1898
Materials/dimensions: top section: red and grey granite, 1.8 m high × 40 cm wide × 40 cm deep; shaft/fountain: red and grey granite,

2.91 m high × 1.22 m wide × 1.22 m deep
Signature (north face to right of the fountain basin in inscribed letters): J.WHITEHEAD AND SONS LTD / WESTMINSTER
Inscriptions (above portrait relief in carved gilded letters): ERECTED 1898; (below relief): Lt COLONEL HENRY LANE / LATE 5th BENGAL LIGHT CAVALRY / BORN AT GHAZEEPORE INDIA/ 23RD OCT.R 1827 / DIED AT BROADOAK BEXHILL / 1ST APRIL 1895; (south face in carved letters): THIS MONUMENT / HAS BEEN ERECTED TO / THE MEMORY OF / LT COLONEL HENRY LANE / BY COLLEAGUES AND / FRIENDS OF THE DISTRICT OF / BEXHILL AND EAST SUSSEX / UNVEILED JUNE 25TH 1898 / BY MRS LANE, WIDOW / ASSISTED BY/ EARL DE LA WARR / AND LORD BRASSEY K.C.B.; (east face in carved letters): ARMY SERVICES / FOUGHT IN THE SUTLEJ CAMPAIGN 1845 / PRESENT AT MOODKEE, SOBRAON / ALLIWAL FEROZESHUHUR / PUNJAUB CAMPAIGN 1848 / PRESENT AT / COOJERAT AND CHILIANWALA / LUCKNOW / AND RELIEF OF LUCKNOW 1858; (west face in carved letters): LT COLONEL HENRY LANE / DC.JP.CA. / FIRST CHAIRMAN BEXHILL LOCAL BOARD / 1884 / FIRST CHAIRMAN / BEXHILL URBAN DISTRICT COUNCIL / 1894 / PRESIDENT / BEXHILL INSTITUTE / PRESIDENT BEXHILL LIBERAL ASSOCIATION / PRESIDENT / BEXHILL CENTRE ST JOHN AMBULANCE ASSOCIATION
Status: Grade II
Condition: fair (inscription on south face severely eroded; fountain not in working order)
Funded by: public subscription
Owner/custodian: Rother District Council

The memorial is a drinking fountain of square plan with the base built into the sloping ground. The pilasters on each face are of polished granite carved with decorative scrolls with a stone pediment above. Rising from the main cap is an ornamental shaft consisting of a moulded and carved base, developed from the square of the cap to an octagonal plan, then a cluster of polished granite columns with enriched stone capitals, finished with an ornamental terminal in stone. Immediately under the frieze on the north face is an alabaster portrait medallion of Colonel Lane, with laurel wreaths below it. There are fluted basins on two sides.

Colonel Lane, who had been born, and served in the army, in India, had subsequently been a local administrator and benefactor who, as the local newspaper described it, '[a]t a time when Bexhill was changing its condition from a little village to a flourishing health resort … did all in his power to smooth the way.'[1] There was strong local feeling that a memorial that also served a practical purpose to the local community was the best means of memorialising the colonel and the decision to erect a drinking fountain was universally approved. J.M. Whitehead and Sons won both first and second prizes in the competition for the design and the final selection was made by Colonel Lane's widow, who also unveiled the finished piece.

The cost of the memorial, £225, was raised principally in shilling public donations. The Earl De La Warr donated the land in front of the Town Hall to the Council in order for the memorial to be erected and the surrounding space was landscaped to provide an open space for the inhabitants to enjoy.

Note
[1] 'Bexhill and the late Colonel Lane', *Bexhill Observer*, 2 July 1898, p. 8.

Other sources
'Bexhill's tribute to the late Col. Henry Lane, J.P.', *Bexhill Chronicle*, 1 July 1898, p. 3.
'Memorial to the late Colonel Henry Lane, Bexhill', *Supplement to the Bexhill Chronicle*, 11 June, 1898.
Green, H. and Pinney, A., *Bexhill-on-Sea in Old Photographs*, Gloucester, 1989.

Marina
SEAFRONT
Bottom of Sea Road

War Memorial
Sculptor: Louis Frederick Roslyn

Unveiled: 12 December 1920
Materials/dimensions: sculpture: bronze, 2.2 m high × 70 cm wide × 40 cm deep; obelisk: Portland Stone, 8.5 m high × 1.5 m wide × 1.6 m deep
Signature (base of statue on left): L.F. ROSLYN
Inscriptions (south side at base): IN PROUD AND GRATEFUL MEMORY OF / THE MEN AND WOMEN OF BEXHILL WHO GAVE / THEIR LIVES IN THE FIGHT FOR FREEDOM / 1939–1945 / AT THE GOING DOWN OF THE SUN AND IN THE MORNING / WE WILL REMEMBER THEM[1]
Status: not listed

Louis Frederick Roslyn, *War Memorial*

Condition: fair (slight pitting and rusting on
  bronze surface, cracking along waistline of
  statue)
Owner/custodian: Rother District Council

The main element of the memorial is an obelisk,
with, affixed to the front, facing south, a female
winged figure representing 'Victory'. She holds
a wreath aloft in her left hand and a lowered
sword in her right. On the other three faces of
the obelisk are bronze panels inscribed with the
names of the fallen.

The memorial was unveiled by Brigadier
General H. O'Donnell after whom the British
Legion (Comrades) Club in London Road,
Bexhill is named. He became President of the
Bexhill Branch of the Legion on its formation
in 1921 and was the first local organiser of
Poppy Day.

Note
[1] The lines come from the fourth verse of *For The
Fallen*, by Laurence Binyon (1869–1943), first
published in *The Times* on 21 September 1914.

Other sources
Bartley, L.J., *The Story of Bexhill*, Bexhill, 1971.
Bexhill Chronicle, 18 December 1920.
Porter, J., *Images of England: Bexhill-on-Sea*, Stroud,
  1998.

St Augustine's Close, off Cooden Drive

*St Augustine's Church, on gable over main
entrance*

St Augustine

Sculptor: John Skelton

Architects: W.H. Randoll Blacking (1934); completed by H. Hubbard Ford (1960–1963)

Installed: c. 1963
Materials/dimensions: Clipsham stone; approx.
  4 m high × approx. 90 cm wide × approx.
  30 cm deep
Inscription (in lunette over main door): THE /

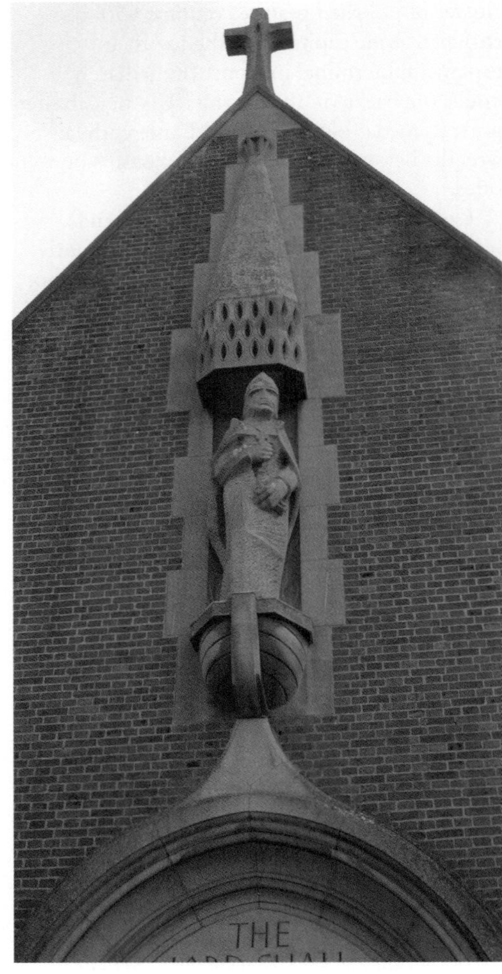

John Skelton, *St Augustine*

LORD SHALL / PRESERVE THY GOING / OUT &
THY COMING / IN: FROM THIS TIME / FORTH
FOR EVERMORE
Status: not listed
Condition: good
Owner/custodian: St Augustine's church

The large, rather severe, figure of Saint
Augustine of Canterbury stands on the prow of
a ship, holding a scroll in his left hand,
underneath a decorative canopy. The sculpture

and the lettering above the main door, also
executed by John Skelton, form the only
decoration on an otherwise plain brick exterior.
The sculptor has depicted the episode in the
saint's life when in 597 he landed on the Isle of
Thanet in Kent, having been sent by Pope
Gregory to convert the Anglo-Saxons to
Christianity. Augustine founded Britain's
second monastery in Canterbury and became
the first Archbishop of Canterbury. He is
regarded as a founder of the English church.

Sources
catholic.org/saints (accessed 20 June 2013).
Nairn and Pevsner (1965), p. 11.
Powers, A., 'John Skelton obituary', *The
  Independent*, 6 December 1999.

Brede Hill

*Lady Chapel in the Parish Church of St
George*

Our Lady of Brede

Sculptor: Clare Sheridan

Installed: 1941
Materials/dimensions: oak, 2.4 m high × 35 cm
  wide × 35 cm deep
Inscription (on base, to the front): THIS OAK
  TREE FROM BREDE PLACE WAS / CARVED BY
  CLARE SHERIDAN IN MEMORY / OF HER
  BELOVED SON / RICHARD BRINSLEY SHERIDAN
  / SEPTEMBER 20 1915–JANUARY 17 1937
Status: not listed
Condition: good (some splitting to base, due to
  ageing)
Owner/custodian: Parish Church of St George

The Madonna has her hands crossed either side
of her Child's head peeping from the folds of
her gown. This composition is a reference to the
angel's head above a pair of wings, emblem of
the soul in Renaissance paintings. The
proportions of the figure are tall and

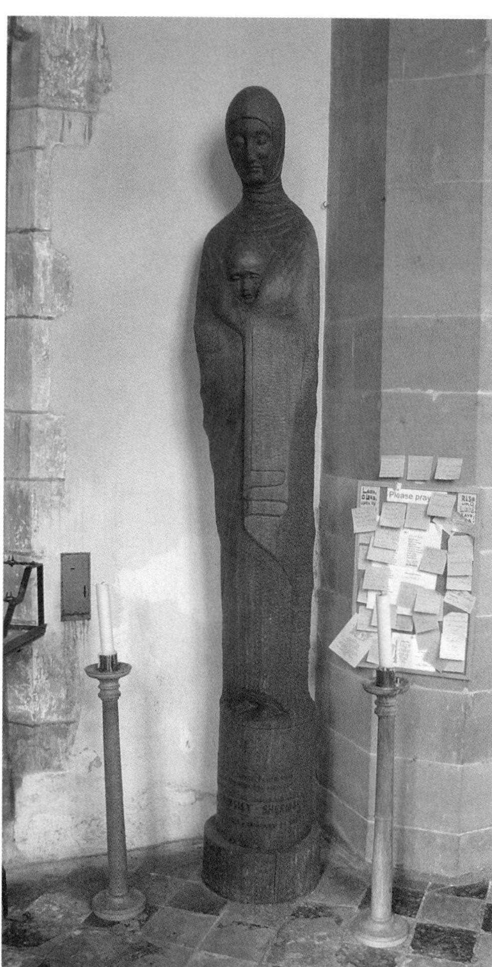

Clare Sheridan, *Our Lady of Brede*

cylindrical, based upon the classical Greek standard of a ratio of 1:8 between the measurements of the head and the rest of the body.

Sheridan wrote in detail about the conception and making of the statue in her autobiography.[1] She described it as having:

> … a Gothic feeling. At a distance the natural oak gives the illusion of stone. It has the same golden touch as the Caen stone which

is the background. The wood is carved as one carves stone. It is chiselled in the same way that stone is chiselled.[2]

She sculpted the piece from a tree trunk from the park at her family home, Brede Place, in memory of her 21-year-old son who had died suddenly, from peritonitis, in Constantinople, and was buried there. She declared that she 'would bring forth the Mother and Her little Son, the soul of Love translated into maternal form through my heart's sorrow …'.[3] Sheridan's husband, Wilfred, had died in action at Loos in 1915, five days before the birth of the son whose own early death affected her deeply for the rest of her life. When she later started working with stonemasons after moving to Galway in Ireland in 1947 she wrote, 'Dick is helping – giving me his transcendent strength'.[4]

Sheridan referred to the impossibility of obtaining materials such as bronze, marble or terracotta during the Second World War, deciding to use instead one of the dead trees close to hand.[5] Canadian soldiers, billeted in Sheridan's home, transported the heavy tree trunk to her studio and, on the completion of the statue, carried it to the church for the dedication, where it was fixed onto a concrete-embedded steel upright made by the local blacksmith, Jack Apps. Music at the dedication service included work by Shostakovich, a bust of whom Sheridan was then carving.

The fifteenth-century Lady Chapel was extended in the sixteenth century to form the Oxenbridge Chapel, named after the family who owned Ford (later Brede) Place, and are buried in the vault below it. The chapel remained in possession of the family as a private burial place until 1928, when it was restored to public use. The Frewen family, to which Sheridan belonged, has owned Brede place since 1708 and retained rights over the chapel. Sheridan explained that this, '[e]mpowered my father and my brother, each in their day, to refuse tentative offers of standardized Madonnas.'[6] She regarded her sculpture as,

'bringing back the holy symbol' to the church.[7] Clare Sheridan died in 1970 and is buried in the churchyard.

Notes
[1] Sheridan, C., *My Crowded Sanctuary*, London, 1945, chapter 22. [2] Ibid., p. 118. [3] Ibid., p. 115. [4] Letter to Jane Holder, 24 April 1948, papers of Clare Sheridan (1997.41, sh36 a–k), Henry Moore Institute archive, Leeds. [5] Sheridan (1945), p. 113. [6] Ibid., p. 114. [7] Ibid., p. 115.

Other sources
Crook, J., *St George's Church Brede*, Brede, revised edn 2004, np.
Leslie, A., *Cousin Clare: The Tempestuous Career of Clare Sheridan*, London, 1976, pp. 240–43.
Leslie, S., 'Clare Sheridan, sculptress', *New York Times*, 5 December 1920.
Swinfen, W. and Arscott, D., *Hidden Sussex*, Brighton, 1984, p. 35.

BRIGHTLING

The Street

Inside St Thomas à Becket Church on south interior wall of the nave

Memorial to John (Mad Jack) Fuller
Sculptor: Sir Francis Legatt Chantrey

Commissioned: monument 1819; bust 1820
Materials/dimensions: portrait bust: marble, 60 cm high × 55 cm wide × 30 cm deep; base: marble, 1.1 m high × 1.15 m wide × 20 cm deep
Signatures (underneath lower edge of bust): F CHANTREY R.A.; (on tablet) Henry Rouw
Inscription (on memorial plaque): JOHN FULLER ESQRE / OF ROSE HILL / BORN FEBRUARY THE XX MDCCLVII / DIED APRIL THE XI MDCCCXXXIV. / HE WAS ONE OF THE REPRESENTATIVES / FOR THIS COUNTY IN FOUR SUCCESSIVE / PARLIAMENTS / "UTILE NIHIL QUOD NON HONESTUM" / ERECTED AS A TRIBUTE OF ESTEEM AND AFFECTION BY HIS

Status: not listed
Condition: good
Owner/custodian: St Thomas à Becket Church

The memorial is set into the wall between two windows and is composed of a classical bust of Fuller in Roman dress within a shallow arched niche, below which is an inscribed rectangular tablet. It is surmounted by anthemion motifs at each corner, flanking Fuller's coat of arms and supported by leaf-shaped corbels.[1] As with his mausoleum (see below), Fuller planned this memorial long before his death. He ordered the portrait bust later than the tablet and the two were combined into a single monument. Ilene Lieberman suggests that this may have been the

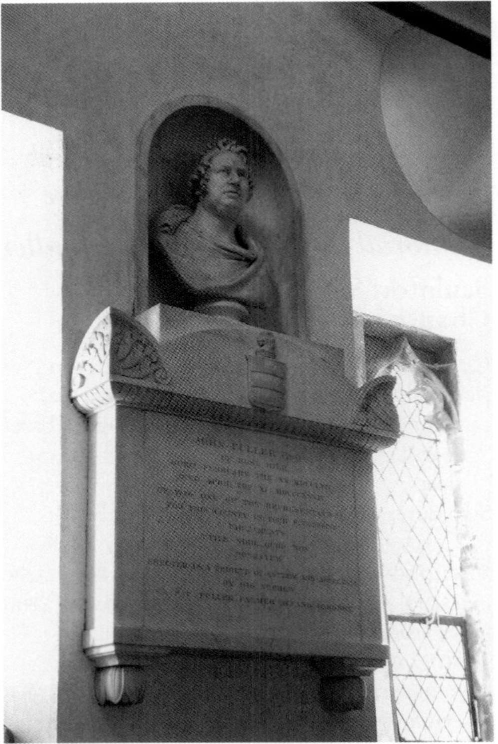

Sir Francis Legatt Chantrey, *Memorial to John (Mad Jack) Fuller*

responsibility of Henry Rouw, hence his signature on the tablet.[2] Chantrey executed a further bust by order of the Royal Institute, of which Fuller had been a sponsor, which was unveiled in 1835. Portrait drawings of Fuller by Chantrey are in the National Portrait Gallery.[3]

In addition to the epithet 'Mad', Fuller also earned the nickname 'Honest Jack', because he refused a peerage rather than forsake his party in the House of Commons. Delighted by this, he declared his intention of instructing his executors to place his bust in Brightling Church with the inscription: UTILE NIHIL QUOD NON HONESTUM (Nothing is useful which is not honest).

In the churchyard is 'Mad Jack's' mausoleum, a 25-foot high pyramid. He applied for permission to erect it in 1810 and planned and designed it with architect Sir Robert Smirke, regarded as the leading exponent of the Greek Revival. It is suggested that he based it on the Tomb of Cestius in Rome, as he had returned from an inspiring trip to Italy in 1805. John Fuller died at his London home on 11 April 1834 and his body was interred in his mausoleum on 18 April. As David Arscott has commented:

> There is sadly no truth in the rumour that he was buried sitting on an iron chair in full evening dress, with a bottle of port and a roast chicken on the table in front of him, awaiting the Resurrection.[4]

During 1987, cracks began to appear at the base of the pyramid and it was feared the structure could be slipping. A fund was set up, the foundations checked and the necessary repair work was successfully carried out.

The eccentric Fuller was a philanthropist and captain in the Sussex Yeoman Cavalry, who represented the County of Sussex in four successive Parliaments. The Fuller family were wealthy iron forgers, who also owned sugar plantations in Jamaica. The family motto was 'Carbone et Forcipibus' (by charcoal and tongs). During his years in public life, Fuller

made the acquaintance of many important figures in the arts, including Sir Walter Scott, the painter Henry Singleton and sculptors Joseph Nollekens and Peter Rouw, as well as his portraitist Chantrey. Among Fuller's close friends was J.M.W. Turner, whom he probably met through Lord Egremont of Petworth and who executed several paintings of Sussex whilst staying at Fuller's home, Rose Hill, in Brightling.[5] Fuller was also responsible for preserving Bodiam Castle and building the Belle Tout lighthouse, near Eastbourne, in 1832.

Notes
[1] The anthemion decorative motif, consisting of a number of radiating petals, was developed by the ancient Greeks from the Egyptian and Asiatic form known as the honeysuckle or lotus palmette. The corbel is a supporting bracket. [2] Yarrington A., Lieberman I., Potts A. and Baker, M. (eds.), 'The Chantrey Ledger', *Walpole Society*, vol. LVI, 1991/2, p. 121. [3] Ibid. [4] Arscott, D., *Curiosities of East Sussex: A County Guide to the Unusual*, Market Drayton, 1991, p. 42. [5] Hutchinson, G., *Fuller of Sussex: a Georgian Squire*, Brightling, reprinted 1997, pp. 81–86.

Other sources
Boyd, D., *Brightling Church Guide*, London, 1979, p. 21.
Gunnis, R., *Dictionary of British Sculptors 1660–1851*, London, 1953, p. 94.
Hutchinson, G., *Fuller: the Life and Times of John Fuller of Brightling 1757–1834*, Brightling, 1988.
Llewellyn (2011), p. 44.
Lower, M.A., *The Worthies of Sussex*, Lewes, 1865, pp. 96–98.
Nairn and Pevsner (1995), p. 425.

Brighton Square

THE LANES

In courtyard off Meeting House Square

The Dolphin Fountain

Sculptor: James Osbourne

Architect: Leo Panipucci, APP Partnership

Unveiled: 2 March 1992

Materials/dimensions: sculpture: patinated bronze, approx. 2 m high; plinth: ceramic mosaic tiles, approx. 1.88 m high × 1.5 m diam.

Inscription: (on small bronze plaque on side of plinth just underneath the sculpture): The Dolphin Fountain / dedicated to / The Royal Alexandra Hospital / for Sick Children / unveiled by / H.R.H. Princess Alexandra G.C.V.O. / 2nd March 1992 / Sculptor / James Osborne / 1940–1992; (on small bronze plaque on opposite side of plinth): THE COINS IN THE FOUNTAIN / will be donated to / The Royal Alexandra Hospital / for Sick Children

Status: not listed

Condition: good

Commissioned and owned by: South Bank Estates (Brighton Square) Ltd.

The fountain depicts two dolphins, leaping almost vertically, one above the other, with a child sat astride each animal. This is supported by a tiled circular plinth that sits within a large tiled fountain basin. The whole structure is sited in the centre of a circular brick paved area where tables and chairs are placed from the surrounding restaurants.

Osbourne used his own children as models and the original estimated cost was £5000. The fountain basin was designed to receive thrown coins, providing donations to Children in

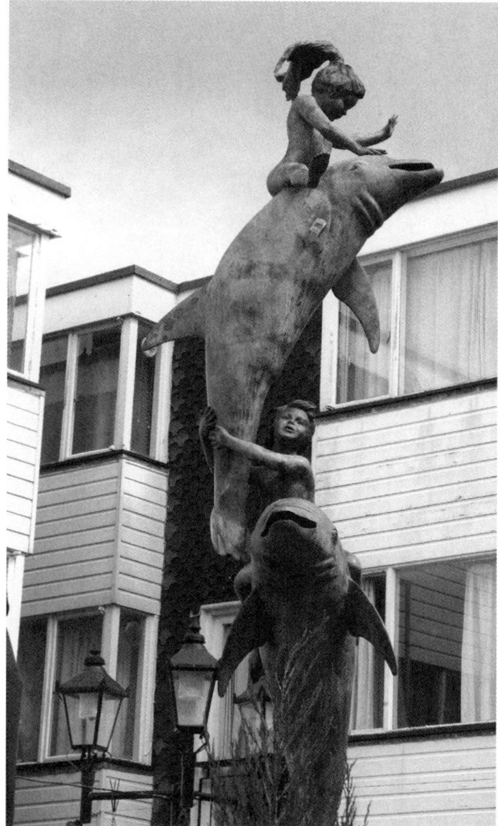

James Osbourne, *The Dolphin Fountain*

Need, later changed to the Royal Alexandra Hospital in Brighton. The sculptor was born in Brighton and raised large sums of money for various charities before his death in 1992.

Sources
Brighton History Centre Archive BHS SPB 123 13.
buses.co.uk/history/fleethist (accessed 21 June 2007).

KEMPTOWN

Bristol Road

St John the Baptist Church

The Church of St John the Baptist, known as the 'Mother Church of Brighton's Roman

Catholics'[1] was designed and built between 1832 and 1835 by William Hallett, with sculpture by John Edward Carew. The east end was extended by 60 feet in 1875 to designs by Gilbert Robert Blount, with further additions between 1887 and 1890. Wall decorations were carried out by Nathaniel Hubert Westlake from 1890 to 1921. The church is Grade II* listed.

The Irish sculptor J.E. Carew was employed almost exclusively by the 3rd Earl of Egremont from about 1820, mainly at Petworth House in West Sussex. From 1832–37 Carew lived near Petworth but also had a studio in Brighton, where the Earl owned property near St John's church and was a patron of the first Sussex County Hospital (see entry below) also in Kemptown.

The three sculptures listed below were executed by Carew over a period of 15 years. There is some debate as to the Earl's role in the commissioning of the pieces; Gunnis states that he published a disclaimer in the press that he had contributed money to the building or decoration of any Roman Catholic chapel.[2]

Above the font

St John the Baptist Baptising Christ

Installed: 1835

Materials/dimensions: white marble, 3.66 m high × 2.45 m wide

Condition: good (St John's finger and the dove's beak were damaged when moved for restoration in 1997. The relief was cleaned and re-gilded during the restoration. A join in the marble behind the figures has chips along its length)

The low-relief sculpture depicts St John, draped in animal skins and supporting a cross with his left arm, in the act of baptising the bowed figure of Christ, whose hands are placed together, facing downwards in supplication. Above their heads is depicted a dove, representing the Holy Spirit, emanating rays of light. It was originally the church's altarpiece, but currently stands

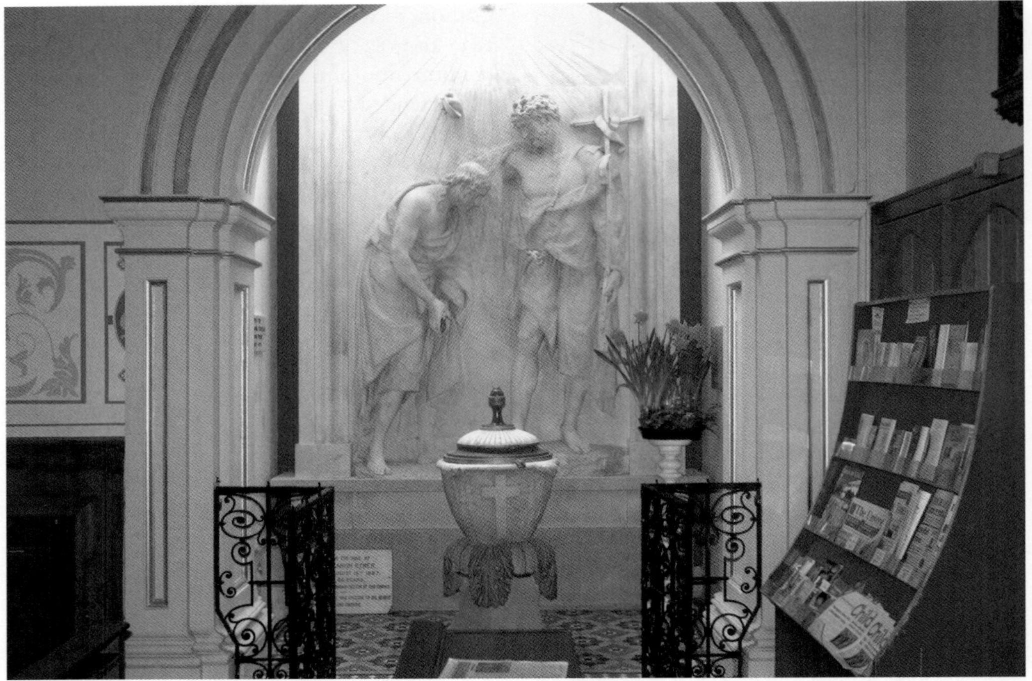

John Edward Carew, *St John the Baptist Baptising Christ*

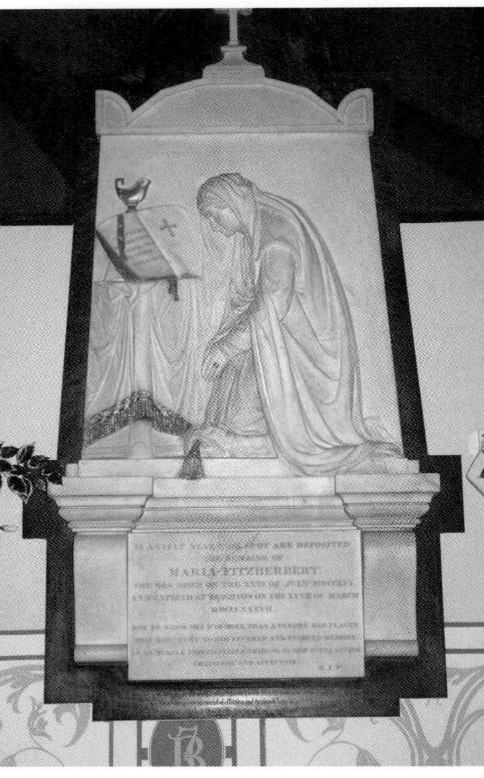

John Edward Carew, *Monument to Mrs Fitzherbert*

behind the baptismal font. The baptistery was finished in 1889 and the relief re-positioned there. Pevsner describes it as, '[r]emarkably good; in the Baroque tradition, not at all neo-classical.'[3]

Despite the Earl's wish to dissociate himself from the funding of the sculptures for the church, Carew, in the court case he brought against the executors following his patron's death, claimed that he was owed £3105 for this piece. Richard Westmacott, the sculptor, who appeared as a witness for the plaintiff, confirmed that, in his opinion, the sculpture was worth £3000.[4]

On east wall, next to baptistery
Monument to Mrs Fitzherbert

Installed: 1837

Materials/dimensions: relief sculpture: white marble with gilding, 2.74 m high × 1.22 m wide; grey marble surround, 3.05 m high × 1.35 m wide

Signature (bottom right-hand corner of relief): J.E. CAREW / SCULPTOR 1837

Inscriptions (on base of relief): IN A VAULT NEAR THIS SPOT ARE DEPOSITED / THE REMAINS OF / MARIA FITZHERBERT. / SHE WAS BORN ON THE XXVII OF JULY MDCCLVI. / AND EXPIRED AT BRIGHTON ON THE XXVII OF MARCH / MDCCCXXXVII. / ONE TO WHOM SHE WAS MORE THAN A PARENT HAS PLACED / THIS MONUMENT TO HER REVERED AND BELOVED MEMORY / AS AN HUMBLE THOUGH FEEBLE TRIBUTE OF HER EVERLASTING / GRATITUDE AND AFFECTION / R.I.P.; (on grey surround): In loving remembrance of our mother Mary Seymour, (Honble Mrs G.L.D. Darmer) the adopted child of Mrs Fitzherbert, / who placed this pious memorial of affection and gratitude here in 1837. She died in 1848. /

Her only surviving children, Blanche, Haygarth and Constance Leslie, place this record, 1910; (on book): 'IT IS A MORE / BLESSED THING / TO GIVE THAN / TO RECEIVE' ACTS. C.XX.V3

Condition: good (cleaned and regilded c. 1997 by specialist from the Victoria and Albert Museum)

Commissioned by: Mary Seymour (Mrs Fitzherbert's adopted daughter)

The memorial relief shows Maria Fitzherbert (née Smythe, 1756–1837) in profile, as a widow, wearing heavy classical drapery. She kneels before a table draped with a richly tasselled cloth upon which stand the broken gospels, symbolising either Fidelity or Religion, surmounted by the Lamp of Memory. She is wearing three wedding rings, as Catholic ecclesiastical law requires.

Mrs Fitzherbert, twice widowed and a devout Roman Catholic, was secretly married to George, Prince of Wales in 1785 in contravention of the Royal Marriage Act of 1772. She was disowned by the Prince in 1811, although she was granted a royal annuity and continued to live in Steine House (now the YMCA), in the centre of Brighton, that the Prince had built for her and where she died, aged 80. She was a friend of the Rev. Edward Cullin (1776–1850), who built the church, and patroness of the congregation.

On west wall, directly opposite Mrs Fitzherbert monument

Monument to the Reverend Edward Cullin

Installed: 1850
Materials/dimensions: stone with gilding, 2.45 m high × 1.35 m wide, with black painted stone surround
Signature (right-hand side, halfway down): JE CAREW SCULPTOR
Inscription (underneath portrait relief): PRAY FOR THE SOUL OF / THE REVEREND EDWARD CULLIN / UPWARDS OF THIRTY YEARS / PASTOR OF THIS CONGREGATION: / WHOSE INFLUENCE AND EXERTIONS PROCURED THE ERECTION OF / THIS CHAPEL: / WHOSE FRUGALITY AND SELF DENIAL / PROVIDED RESOURCES FOR / A SCHOOL FOR THE POOR: / WHOSE LIFE TRULY EXEMPLIFIED / THE LESSONS WHICH HE TAUGHT. / HE WAS BORN AT TRALEE IN IRELAND, JULY 8, 1776 / HE DIED AT BRIGHTON, MARCH 5, 1850, / IN THE 74TH YEAR OF HIS AGE. AND THE 40TH OF HIS PRIESTHOOD. / MAY HIS SOUL REST IN PEACE
Condition: good

A cherub's head and foliage are surmounted by a portrait profile in relief, topped by gilded chalice and cross set on a cushion with gilded tassels. Pevsner also remarks on the Baroque feel of this sculpture.[5]

Notes
[1] *The Church of St John the Baptist Brighton*, church leaflet nd. [2] Gunnis (1953), p. 79. [3] Nairn and Pevsner (1965), p. 432. [4] *Report of the Trial of the Cause, Carew Against Burrell Bart. And Another. Executors of the Late Lord Egremont at the Spring Assizes Held at Lewes on Wednesday March 18th 1840*, London, 1840, p. 9. [5] Nairn and Pevsner (1965), p. 432.

Other sources
Carder, T., *The Encyclopaedia of Brighton*, Lewes, 1990, entry 23.
Collis, R., *The New Encyclopaedia of Brighton*, Brighton, 2010, pp. 126–127.
Fr Foley, conversation, 31 March 2005.
Pugh, T., *The Church of Saint John the Baptist, Brighton 1835–1985*, Hove, 1985, pp. 11–36.
Rowell, C., *Petworth House*, Swindon, 1997, p. 89.

Church Street

Opposite north gate of the Royal Pavilion (previously in northern enclosure of Old Steine; moved for siting of war memorial 14 March 1922)

Statue of George IV

Sculptor: Sir Francis Legatt Chantrey

Commissioned: March 1822
Unveiled: 9 October 1828
Materials/dimensions: statue: bronze, 2.75 m high × 1.2 m wide × 1.2 m deep; pedestal: granite, 3.15 m high × 2.1 m (at widest) × 2.1 m deep (at deepest)
Signature (southern aspect of statue, bottom of robe): GEORGE IV / MDCCCXXVIII / CHANTREY.SC.
Status: Grade II
Condition: good
Funded by: public subscription
Owner/custodian: Brighton and Hove City Council

The king is depicted as a standing robed figure, with his head turned slightly to the right and his right hand outstretched. His left hand grasps the folds of his cloak of the Garter. Chantrey's

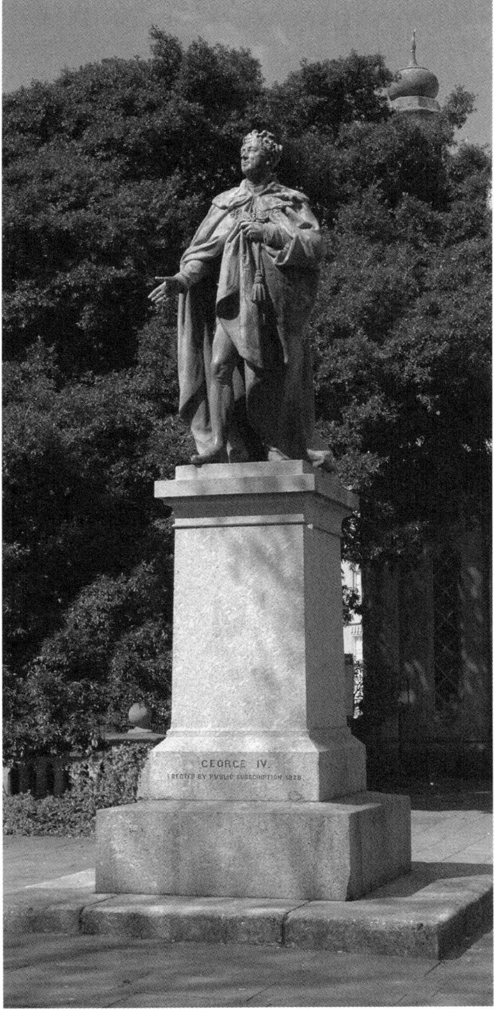

Sir Francis Legatt Chantrey, *Statue of George IV*

statue replaced an earlier one, of the then Price of Wales, made of Coade stone, executed by J.C.F. Rossi (sculptor to the Prince) and erected in 1802. It was considered an unflattering portrait, which weathered badly and was removed in 1819. The initiation of a public subscription for a new statue of the king was led by the 3rd Earl of Egremont, Lord Lieutenant of Sussex, who was an admirer of

Chantrey's work. It was his first successful bronze sculpture and replicated in Edinburgh (1831) and in marble at Windsor Castle (1829).[1]

The sculptor's fee was 3000 guineas and he was granted 4 tons of metal from the Ordnance Office to cast it.[2] Both Chantrey and Westmacott had become dissatisfied with the standards of casting attained by specialist firms and set up their own foundries, Chantrey's near his home in Pimlico, where the sculpture of the king was cast. Whinney points to this as, '… evidence of the changed position and wealth of the sculptors, who were, in fact, now *entrepreneurs* employing a variety of craftsmen, as well as artists.'[3]

Clifford Musgrave claims that the public subscription fell short of the estimated cost of the sculpture, even though the subscription lists remained open for eight years and Chantrey was thought to have made good the deficit.[4] This is contradicted by Chantrey's accounts and a letter from Lord Farnborough to Lord Egremont discussing plans for the deployment of the surplus of funds.[5]

A public dinner, with 120–130 guests, including the sculptor, took place in The Old Ship Hotel to celebrate the erection of the statue.[6] Originally sited in the Steine, the sculpture was re-erected in 1922 on a new base opposite the statue of Queen Victoria to make room for the building of the War Memorial. The moving of the statue and the question of its re-siting provoked much local debate.[7] It is, however, fitting that the king now stands closer to the Royal Pavilion, the Indo-Chinese architectural extravaganza that he commissioned from John Nash in 1813.

Notes
[1] Yarrington (1991), pp. 170–71. Yarrington points out that the marble version cost c. £830 more than the Brighton bronze and the cost of the Edinburgh statue was almost twice as much as the original (p. 236).
[2] Gunnis (1953), p. 93. [3] Whinney (1964), p. 279.
[4] Musgrave, C., *The Royal Pavilion: A Study in the Romantic*, Brighton, 1951, p. 71. [5] Yarrington (1991); Letter from Lord Farnborough to Lord Egremont, dated 30 October 1828. Petworth House

Archives, PHA Miscellaneous papers 1806–1837, West Sussex Record Office. Lord Farnborough was involved in several artistic causes, such as the establishment of the National Gallery and purchase of the Elgin marbles. He was frequently consulted by King George IV over the commissioning of architecture, sculpture and painting, including the reconstruction of Windsor Castle. [6] *Brighton Herald*, 18 October 1828. [7] *Brighton Gazette*, 18 January and 1 March 1922.

Other sources
A Pictorial and Descriptive Guide to Brighton and Hove, the South Downs, Shoreham, Bramber, Lewes, Newhaven, Seaford, etc. London, nd. c. 1937, p. 65.
Arscott, D., *Brighton and Hove: Events, People and Places over the Last 100 Years*, Stroud, 2000, p. 51.
Carder (1990), entry 161l.
Ford, J. and J., *Images of Brighton*, Richmond upon Thames, 1981, p. 36.
Open Air Statues and Memorials: Brighton History Centre: New Pamphlet Box 17 ref. JLR 6/5/87.

Ceres

Sculptor: James Woodford

Architect: Robert Atkinson

Installed: 1934
Materials/dimensions: complete sculpture: glazed terracotta, painted blue, yellow and brown, 2.3 m high × 4.8 m wide; figure of Ceres: terracotta, painted dark grey/blue with traces of gilding on torso, face and hands, 2.3 m high × 1.6 m wide
Status: Grade II
Condition: good (weathering to gold paint on figure)
Owner/custodian: Brighton and Hove City Council

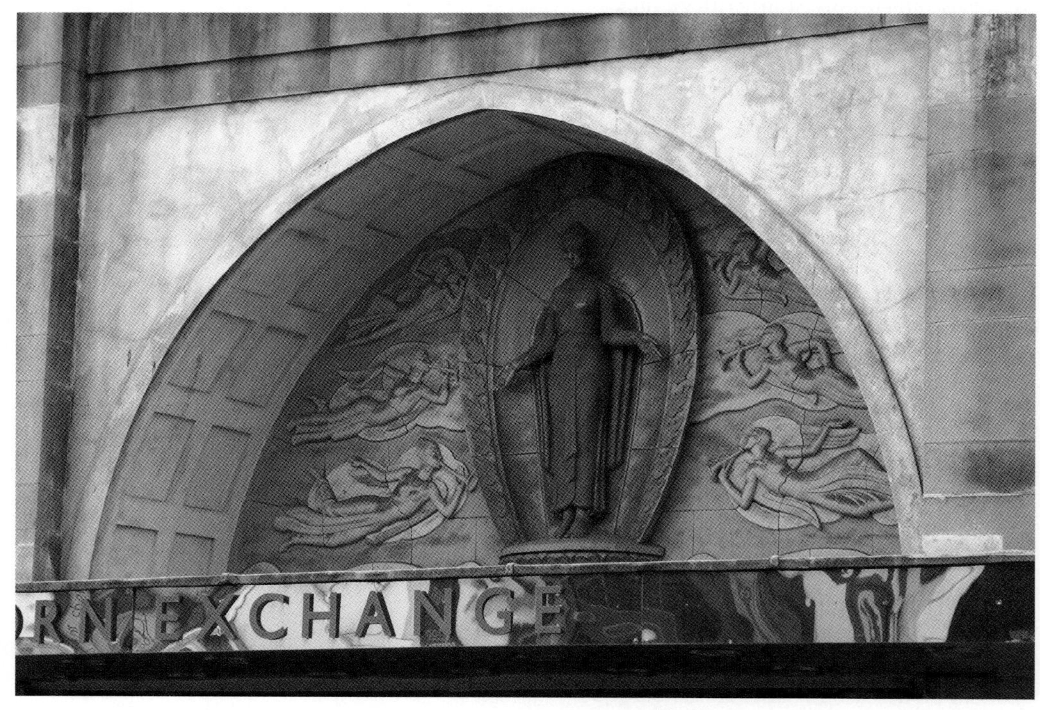

James Woodford, *Ceres*

The sculpture of Ceres, Roman goddess of agriculture and grain, is placed within a *vesica piscis*[1] on the tympanum directly over the building entrance. Her figure assumes an Asian posture and aspect, surrounded on both sides by flying and trumpeting angels on clouds against a blue sky.

The Corn Exchange was built in 1803–1808 by William Porden, originally as a riding school for the Prince of Wales, and forms the west wing of The Dome (originally the stables). It acquired its present name on 1 October 1868 when the Corn Market transferred there from the King and Queen Inn. It was a military hospital in the First World War and after the war became an exhibition and function venue. The new entrance was created, and other alterations carried out, by Robert Atkinson in 1934. Woodford was to further develop an agricultural theme in his carvings for the 1951–52 extension of the Ministry of Agriculture, Fisheries and Food in Whitehall, London, for which he provided a large coat of arms, flanked by sheaves of corn, over the central entrance, together with two allegorical figures and a series of decorative keystones depicting a variety of animal and sealife.[2]

Notes
[1] The shape formed by the intersection of two circles with the same radius, also known as a mandorla. It symbolises life and procreation.
[2] britishlistedbuildings.co.uk; artandarchitecture.org.uk (accessed 5 April 2013).

Other sources
Brighton Remembered: a Century of Pictures from the Archives of the Argus, Derby, 2002, p. 19.
'Canopy at the Corn Exchange, Brighton', *The Architect and Building News* (Supplement), 18 January 1935, p. 282.
Shapiro, M.S. and Hendricks, R.A., *A Dictionary of Mythologies*, St Albans, 1981, pp. 41–42.
The Architect and Building News, 11 January 1935, p. 66.

Church of St Nicholas of Myra

The church, dedicated to the patron saint of fishermen and sailors, children, pawnbrokers and Russia, was the parish church of Brighton until 1873. The original fourteenth-century flint building, due partly to a dispute over responsibility for its maintenance, had become severely dilapidated by the mid-nineteenth century and the vicar, Rev. H.M. Wagner, used the occasion of the Duke of Wellington's death in 1852, to argue for its rebuilding as his memorial due to the Duke's historical association with Brighton (see entry below). The vicar donated the first £1000 of the costs himself and nearly £5000 more was raised by public subscription. The architect was Richard Cromwell Carpenter, associated with the Cambridge Movement and Tractarianism. The interior of the church was extensively re-ordered in 2001; this involved returning the twelfth-century font, described by Pevsner as '[t]he best piece of Norman carving in Sussex', to its original position facing the west door.[1] Westmacott's memorial to his wife, Dorothy, a simple portrait bust (c. 1834), remains in a rather obscure position at the back of the nave wall.[2] In the eastern churchyard is the tall table-tomb, of Amon Wilds, designed by his son Amon Henry in 1833. The father and son, together with Charles A. Busby were responsible for some of the finest Regency architecture in Brighton and Hove.[3]

Beside font, previously in the Lady Chapel (moved 1900), then northwest corner of the nave (moved 2001)

Memorial to the Duke of Wellington

Sculptor: John Birnie Philip

Architect: Richard Cromwell Carpenter

Builder: Mr Bushby, Littlehampton
Unveiled: 8 April 1854

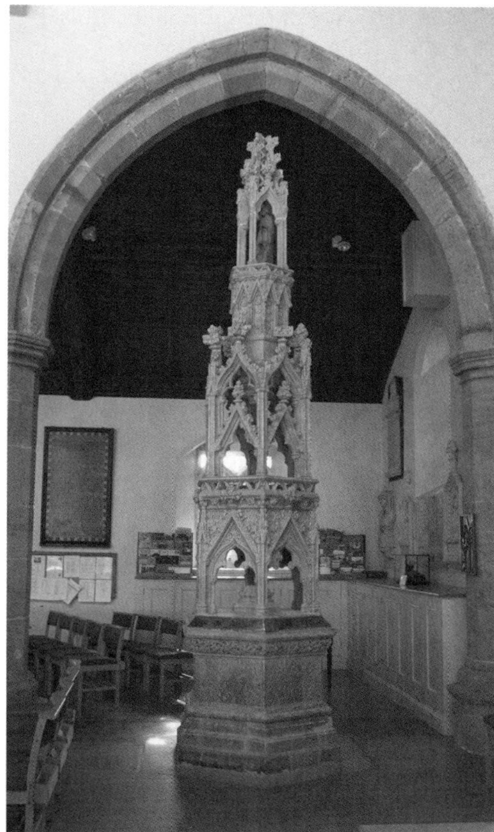

John Birnie Philip, *Memorial to the Duke of Wellington*

Materials/dimensions: stone and bronze, 5.63 m high × 1.45 cm diam.
Inscriptions (on 'ribbon' encircling bronze central column): Assaye - Torres Vedras - Vittoria - Waterloo; (on brass plates on each side of memorial): In memoriam / haec domus sacrosancta / Maximi Ducis Wellington / qua ipse adolescens / Deum colebat / reaedificatur (In memory of the great Duke of Wellington this sacred building in which, in his youth, he worshipped God, is restored)
Status: not listed
Condition: good (but some detailed carving

worn away; top of the spire on the cross is missing and may have been removed deliberately when the memorial was moved in order to accommodate its height)
Funded by: public subscription
Owner/custodian: Parish Church of St Nicholas of Myra

This Gothic Revival memorial is in the shape of an Eleanor Cross, with a hexagonal plan. The pedestal is covered with diaper work surmounted by a moulding, on the broad chamfer of which is an inscription, in old English characters in brass, each line being represented by an angle of the monument. From the pedestal rise two storeys, richly and elaborately decorated with open tracery work and crocketted pinnacles. These are separated by a pierced parapet; a similar one is on the third or upper storey, which is a solid stone drum, each face of which is also ornamented by sunken and carved panels. There follows a canopied niche with a pierced spire surmounted by a finial. The structure was described by John Wainwright, in 1916, as '… not a cross, but … something like a wedding cake …'.[4]

In the niche is an alabaster figure of St George, sheathing his sword over the dragon, which lies slain at his feet, symbolic of the career of the Duke. The drum and everything above it rests on a shaft of dark, polished marble which emerges from the pedestal and around which winds a scroll bearing the names of four of the achievements which mark different eras in Wellington's military career. Assaye represents the Duke's Indian Campaign; Torres Vedras, his successful defence of Portugal; Vittoria, the victory that delivered Spain; and Waterloo, the battle that defeated Napoleon's army.[5]

As a child in the 1780s, Wellington had studied for a time at an academy in Nile Street, Brighton (in what is now The Lanes in the city centre) and also attended St Nicholas Church. In 2001 the monument was moved from a corner by the tower to its present position

beside the font, thus addressing Pevsner's criticism that it was '… banished into a corner, but deserves better treatment'.[6]

North nave, to the side of the main altar
Mother and Child
Sculptor: Willi Soukop

Executed: c. 1950s
Materials/dimensions: statue, oak, 53 cm high × 13 cm wide × 11 cm deep; base, oak, 30 cm high × 25 cm wide × 13 cm deep
Status: not listed
Condition: good
Owner/custodian: Parish Church of St Nicholas of Myra

The small standing figure of the Virgin, in dark-stained oak holds the Christ child in front of her, '… reaching out to the world.'[7] They rest on a geometrical five-tiered bracket set into a stone pillar to the side of the altar.

Mother and child was a theme that the sculptor returned to continually throughout his career, even when his later work became more abstract. He produced examples, some composed with full-length figures, in wood and terracotta as well as stone. His work was frequently included in exhibitions of contemporary religious art and he received many commissions from churches and schools.[8]

Notes
[1] Nairn and Pevsner (1965), p. 427. [2] Busco, M., *Sir Richard Westmacott Sculptor*, Cambridge, 1994, pp. 151, 156. [3] Cooper, J., 'A.H. Wilds rediscovered!', *Regency Review: the Newsletter of the Regency Society*, November 2007, np. [4] Wainwright, J.B., *Notes and Queries*, London, 24 June 1916, p. 517. [5] *Brighton Herald Supplement*, 8 April 1854. [6] Nairn and Pevsner (1965), p. 428. [7] Day, F.A., *The Church of St. Nicholas of Myra: a History with Some Deviations*, Brighton, revised edn appendix. [8] A letter from Margaret Stack, 16 June 1953, refers to an exhibition on 'The Christian theme in contemporary arts' held in Park Lane House, London, 12 May–18 June and the interest of the Bishop of Coventry in Soukop's Mother and Child. Soukop papers correspondence 1/3.

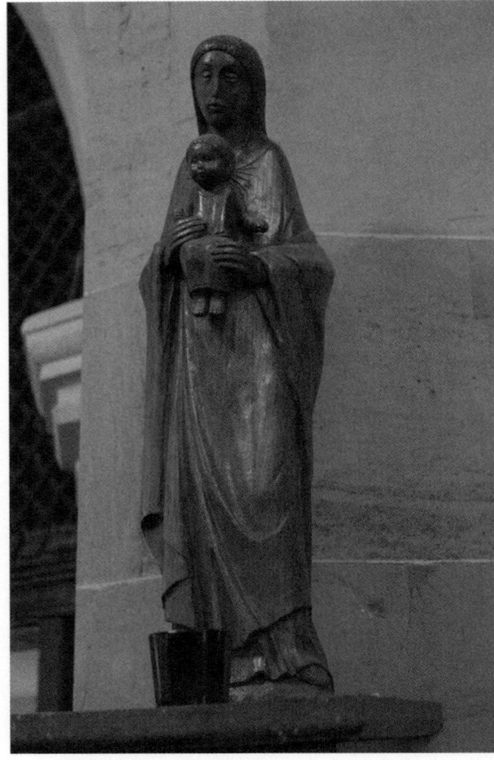

Willi Soukop, *Mother and Child*

Other sources
Arscott, D., *Dead and Buried in Sussex*, Seaford, 1997, p. 75.
Bianco, D., 'Amon Henry Wilds and the last enigma of Dr Gideon Mantell', *Friends of West Norwood Cemetery Newsletter*, no. 52, January 2005.
Cooper, J. and Jones, L., brightonsarchitecture.com/sacred.html#stnich (accessed 26 October 2010).
Dale, A., *Fashionable Brighton 1820–1860*, London, 1947.
Davey, H., 'Wellington at Brighton and Rottingdean', *Notes and Queries*, London, 24 June 1916, p. 517.
Kerney, M., 'Ammonites in architecture', *Country Life*, 27 January 1983, pp. 214–18.
Murray, J., *A Handbook for Travellers in Kent and Sussex*, London, 1858, p. 261
School of Architecture and Interior Design, Brighton Polytechnic, *A Guide to the Buildings of Brighton*, Macclesfield, 1987, pp. 12–19.
stnicholasbrighton.org.uk (accessed 14 December 2010).

Royal Sussex County Hospital

The Sussex County Hospital and General Sea-Bathing Infirmary was opened on 11 June 1828, in a building designed by Charles Barry. It has undergone almost continuous expansion, and several changes of title, ever since. The University hospitals now comprise a huge complex of buildings of different styles and dates, spreading out either side of the main Eastern Road. In 2007 the new Royal Alexander Children's Hospital (RACH) was incorporated into the site following its relocation from Dyke Road.

In the new building developments from the beginning of the twenty-first century there has been an increasing emphasis on the importance of the visual arts, not only in making patients' and visitors' surroundings more attractive, but also in aiding the healing process. This was first seen in the Millennium Wing, which not only incorporated the William Lasdun sculptures detailed below, but also decorative ceiling and lift panels in brushed stainless steel and printed Perspex by Christian Funnell, in the entrance to the Renal Unit, where they could be enjoyed by patients being wheeled about on trolleys.

The Audrey Emerton building, opened in 2005, displays in its entrance Homeostasis, a glass wall piece based on cell structures, by Michel and Jane Johansson of Float Glass Design, but it has been in the development of the new children's hospital that a coordinated arts policy has been most clearly demonstrated. Under the guidance of public artist Steve Geliot, Arts Coordinator at Brighton and Sussex University Hospital Trust and with active support from the Brighton and Hove Arts Commission, Arts Council England and the RACH Children's and Young People's Board, careful thought has been given to the creation and siting of artworks from the early stages of building development to provide a

welcoming, non-threatening and stimulating environment. The need for a quiet space for contemplation within a busy hospital, particularly for the families of sick children, was recognised through the creation of the Oasis room, with wooden screens pierced with abstract patterns created by Walter Bailey in 2007.

Abbey Road, Sussex House, mezzanine staircase landing

Bust of Lord Egremont

Sculptor: Sir Francis Chantrey

Commissioned: 1829
Installed: 1830
Materials/dimensions: white marble, 73 cm high × 60 cm wide × 33 cm deep
Inscriptions (on back of bust, under shoulders): BUST OF THE EARL OF EGREMONT, / EXECUTED AS A TOKEN OF RESPECT / FOR HIS MUNIFICENT DONATIONS / TO THE SUSSEX COUNTY HOSPITAL / CHANTREY. SC. 1830; (brass plaque on front of shallow wooden base): EARL OF EGREMONT / FIRST PRESIDENT OF THE HOSPITAL / Chantrey Sc / 1830
Status: not listed
Condition: fair (tip of nose has been repaired; large chip in base at back)
Owner/custodian: Brighton and Sussex University Hospital NHS Trust

Although this bust has the standard classical drapery around the shoulders, as a portrait it is far less classicising than four other busts commissioned by the Earl, on display at his former home, Petworth House. These are by George Garrard (1807), Joseph Nollekens (1815), William Behnes (1826) and J.E. Carew (1831–34). Chantrey's bust has a more contemporary feel, with a very direct gaze and alert manner; ironically, it appears to depict a younger man than the two earlier examples. His delineation of his sitter validates sculptor Derek Sellars's observation that '… Chantrey's subtle use of carefully judged inclinations of the heads

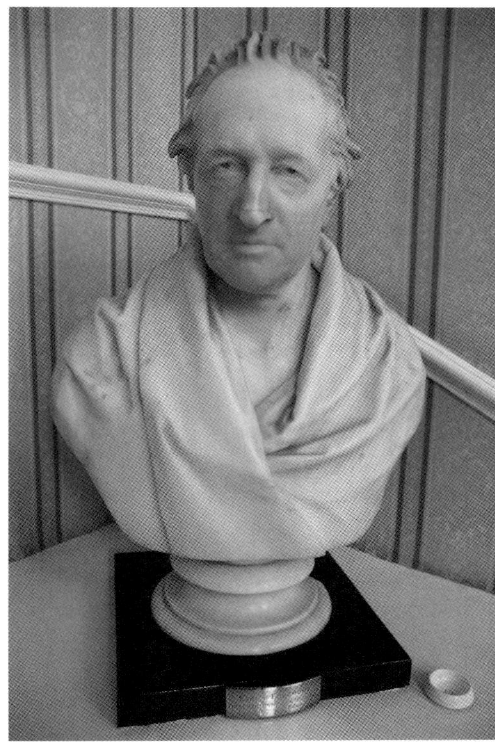

Sir Francis Chantrey, *Bust of Lord Egremont*

gives his best portraits vitality and a sense of personality. Therein lies their originality'.[1] The Earl had a longstanding friendship with Chantrey, whom he first visited in his studio in 1819 and tried to persuade to attempt an idealised classical subject, rather than the portraits for which he was well known. A proposed statue of the fall of Satan was abandoned.[2]

The 3rd Earl of Egremont was well known for his many acts of philanthropy, which were not limited to the area around his West Sussex estate. He laid the foundation stone of the first Sussex County Hospital building on 16 March 1826 and the bust commemorates his generosity to this cause. He also owned a house, East Lodge, sited between St James's Street and Upper Rock Gardens, from which he donated some land for the building of St Mary's church, also in Kemptown. Chantrey's ledgers show that the cost of the bust was £210, with subscriptions limited to 10 guineas; there was an oversubscription of £155 17s 6d.[3]

Level 6 courtyard, near Millennium Wing

Isis

Sculptor: William Lasdun

Constructed: 1998
Unveiled: 24 July 2000
Materials/dimensions: sculpture: marble resin, 2.5 m high × 60 cm wide; courtyard: coloured concrete paving slabs, 40 m × 13 m
Signature (bottom left-hand corner, back of plinth): SCULPTOR / W.LASDUN
Inscriptions (right-hand side of plinth): ISIS; (plaque on front of plinth): ISIS / by / WILLIAM LASDUN / 24TH July 2000; (inscribed in concrete surrounding bench at base): ISIS-ANCIENT EGYPTIAN GODDESS-HEALER OF THE SICK
Status: not listed
Condition: good (but considerable biological growth)
Commissioned by: Brighton Health Care through the Percent for Art scheme
Owner/custodian: Brighton and Sussex University Hospital NHS Trust

The sculpture depicts an abstracted figure of the ancient Egyptian goddess Isis, with a hooded head and stylised wings or drapery across her body. There is seating circling the base and the whole is set within a courtyard also designed by the sculptor.

The large enclosed courtyard was created as part of a major extension programme of new building at the hospital and a public art competition was held to provide a sculpture for this site. The commission was awarded to William Lasdun for his statue of Isis, who, according to myth, was a symbol of growth and nourishment, who used her wings to breathe new life into the old and sick. The goddess was

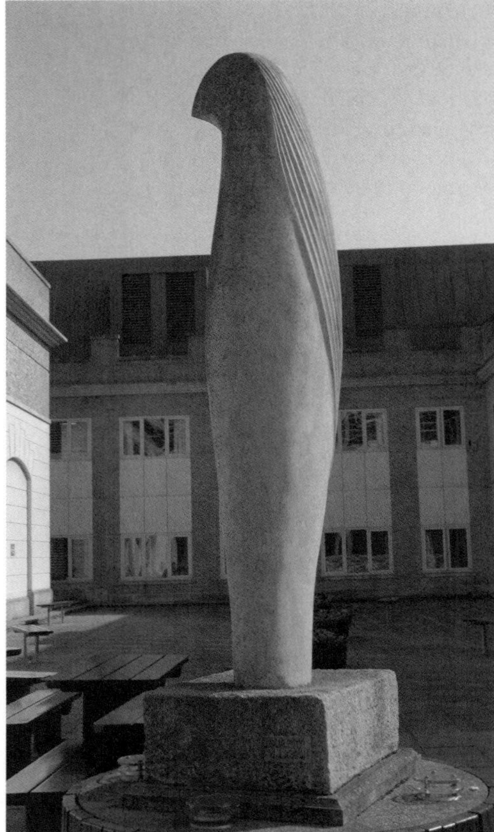

William Lasdun, *Isis*

often portrayed with a vulture's headdress that is alluded to in the half bird, half woman form of the sculpture.

The artist's brief for the design of the courtyard was to transform a rather bland space to provide a relaxing and calming area for the use of patients and staff. The layout of the paving echoes the wing form of the figure and forms a processional route to the statue of Isis, making reference to the river Nile, along which she travelled, and making a gesture towards the sea at Brighton.

On wall of Level 6 courtyard, near Millennium Wing

Peter Hiles Memorial

Sculptor: William Lasdun

Installed: 2002
Materials/dimensions: brushed stainless steel, 3 m diam.
Inscription (stainless steel lettering on wall immediately underneath sculpture); PETER HILES 1950–2001
Status: not listed
Condition: good
Owner/custodian: Brighton and Sussex University Hospital NHS Trust

The memorial is in the form of a pierced roundel in a shallow niche in the wall of the same courtyard in which the sculptor's *Isis* stands. It incorporates representations of a figure, a shire horse, cricket stumps and other objects, symbolising the interests of Peter Hiles. He was the leader of the commissioning team responsible for developing the Millennium Wing at the Royal Sussex County Hospital, who died of a brain tumour. A miniature version of the memorial was cast in silver and presented to his widow as a brooch.

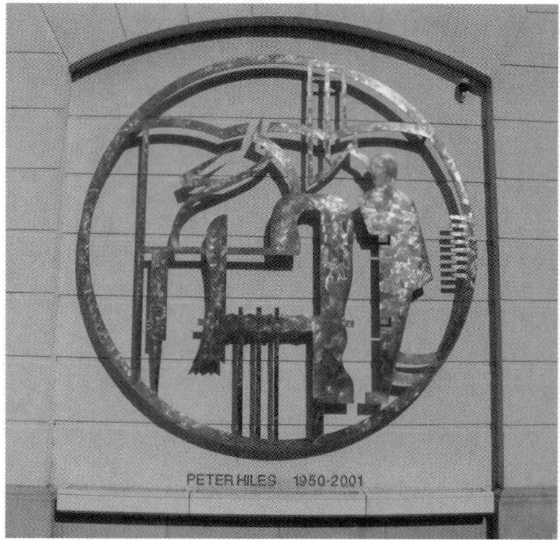

William Lasdun, *Peter Hiles Memorial*

Royal Alexandra Children's Hospital, first floor (level 6) outside Children's Assessment Unit

Life Begins

Sculptor: George Cutts

Installed: 2007
Materials/dimensions: polished stainless steel, 1 m high × 3 m wide
Status: not listed
Condition: good
Funded by: Southern FM Radio's 'Help a Local Child' Appeal
Owner/custodian: Brighton and Sussex University Hospital NHS Trust

This collection of interconnected highly polished spheres is placed on shock-absorbent matting and intended for children to play upon.

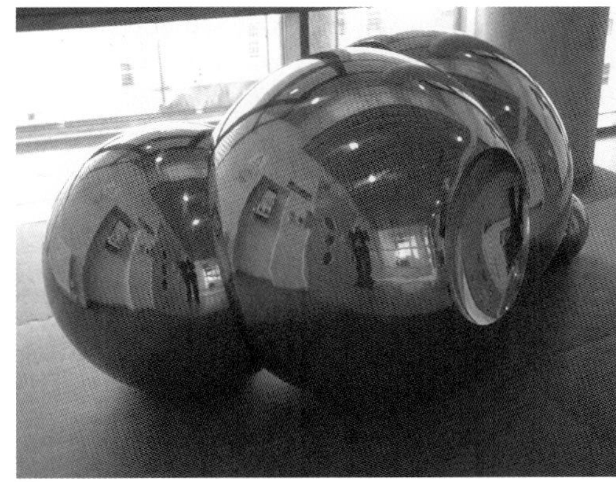

George Cutts, *Life Begins*

Outside north car park, opposite Royal Alexandra Children's Hospital

Boy and Girl

Sculptor: Jon Mills

Installed: 2007
Materials/dimensions: Boy: powder coated steel, part-painted blue and white, 4.2 m high × 80 cm wide × 20 cm deep; Girl: powder coated steel, part-painted pink and white,

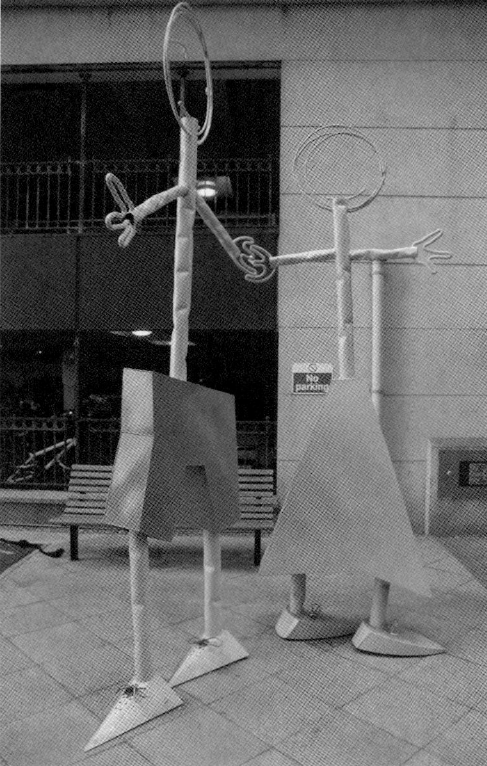

Jon Mills, *Boy and Girl*

approx. 3.75 m high × 92 cm wide × 24.5 cm deep
Status: not listed
Condition: good
Commissioned and funded by: Arts Council England and Brighton and Hove Arts Commission
Owner/custodian: Brighton and Sussex University Hospital NHS Trust

These tall but simple outline standing figures have been made using blacksmithing techniques of cutting, bending and welding metal. They are identifiable as male and female through the boy's blue shorts and girl's pink skirt. The couple are shown holding hands and gesturing towards the visitor and are intended as a welcome to the hospital.

Off Whitehawk Hill Road
Play area outside Royal Alexandra Children's Hospital

Buoys

Sculptor: Ally Wallace

Installed: 2009
Materials/dimensions: aluminium, each double cone-shaped element 1.45 m high × 50 cm wide
Status: not listed
Condition: good
Commissioned and funded by: Arts Council England and Brighton and Hove Arts Commission
Owner/custodian: Brighton and Sussex University Hospital NHS Trust

Ten columns, made up of between one and three double cone-shaped elements, painted in bold colours, are randomly grouped together on a grassed play area outside the entrance to the children's hospital, together with *Crumple Slide* by Walter Jack. They have been compared to toy blocks, but primarily reference the sea, which is considered to be, '… very appropriate standing in front of the new building, which has the feeling of a modern ark, from which the sea may be glimpsed.'[4]

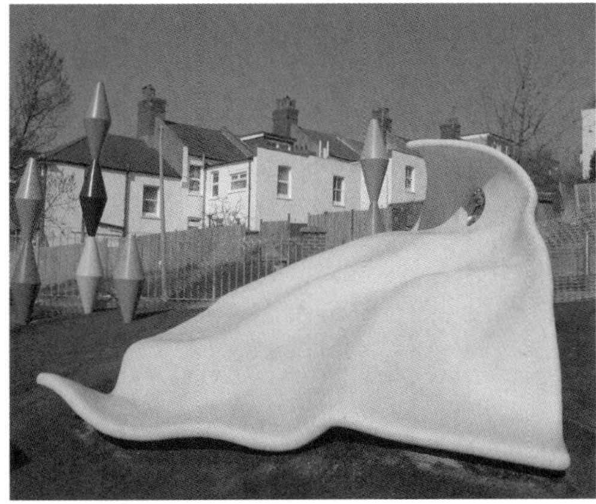

Ally Wallace, *Buoys*

Notes
[1] Sellars, D., 'Chantrey: the sculptor at work' in *Sir Francis Chantrey: Sculptor to an Age 1781–1841*, Sheffield, 1981, p. 49. [2] Kenworthy-Browne, J., 'The third Earl of Egremont and neo-classical sculpture', *The Sculpture Collection at Petworth House*, National Trust Swindon, nd, pp. 11–12. [3] Yarrington (1991), p. 251. [4] *The Royal Alexandra Children's Hospital Information Pack*, Brighton and Sussex University Hospitals NHS Trust, nd.

Other sources
Carder (1990), entries 162, 162a, 167c.
freenetpages.co.uk/hp/metaljon/html/sculpture_07 (accessed 25 November 2010).
lasdun.com/isis (accessed 24 November 2010).
Online Bulletin Brighton and Sussex University Hospitals NHS Trust, Southern Editorial Services, October 2002.
Rowell (1997).

Grand Junction Road

SEAFRONT

At roadside, next to entrance of Brighton Pier

The Fossil Tree (National Cycle Route Marker)

Sculptor: Jon Mills

Foundry: Taylors of Haverhill
Installed: 2000
Materials/dimensions: Cast iron, 1.75 m high × 85 cm wide × 6 cm deep
Inscriptions (on left branch): 2M HOVE; (on right branch): A / MILLENNIUM PROJECT / THE MILLENNIUM / COMMISSION / SUPPORTED BY FUNDS / FROM / THE NATIONAL LOTTERY / BRIGHTON MARINA 1 ½ M; (in central triangle at top): NATIONAL / CYCLE / NETWORK / 2; (on 'trunk'): The Royal Bank / of Scotland / This is one of / 1000 mileposts / funded by The / Royal Bank of / Scotland to / mark the / creation of / the / National Cycle Network; (bottom right of 'trunk'): CASTING BY TAYLORS FOUNDRY / HAVERHILL / FROM AN ORIGINAL BY JON MILLS

Status: not listed
Condition: good
Commissioned by: Sustrans (The National Cycle Network), sponsored by the Royal Bank of Scotland
Funded by: the Millennium Commission and National Lottery
Owner/custodian: Brighton and Hove City Council

The stylised tree with relief imagery of fossils depicts the passage of time from early primitive creatures to the ultimate demise of fossil fuel-driven technology. It indicates the distances from the pier eastwards to Hove and westwards to the Marina and was the first post to be

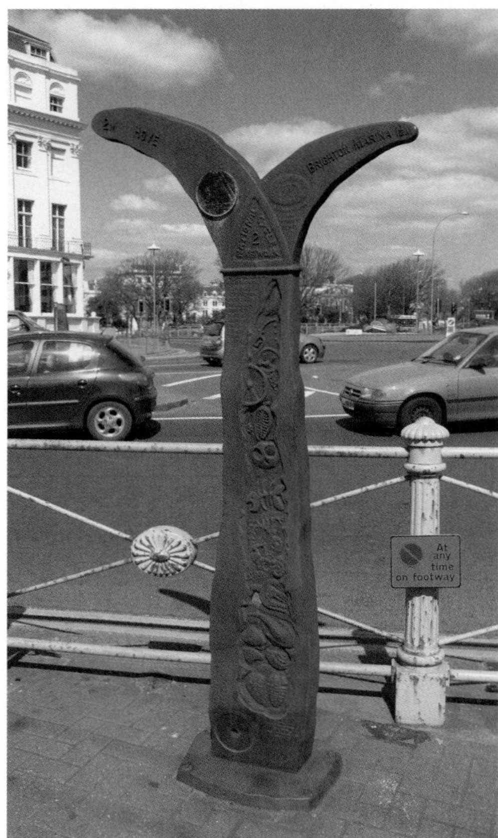

Jon Mills, *The Fossil Tree*

commissioned by Sustrans as part of the Millennium Time Trail, a four-dimensional voyage and puzzle around the National Cycle Network (established in 1977) developed to encourage increased use of this means of transport among children and adults. Throughout the UK there are almost one thousand cast iron mileposts on National Cycle Network routes, many of which carry embossed metal discs bearing a design that can be copied by making a pencil and paper rubbing to help record an individual journey. Over 60 different designs, divided into 5 sets, are repeated around the Network; there are 400 editions of this design. Each set joins up like a three-dimensional sculptural jigsaw to illustrate different aspects of Time. The five sets lead to a very rare sixth set – a final mystery to be solved and treasure to be discovered. There are at least two copies of most Time Trail Symbols in each region and the mileposts have been arranged so that the first two can often be collected during a single ride near a large town.[1]

Note
[1] *The Millennium Time Trail: Information*, Sustrans leaflet, nd.

Other sources
metaljon.com (accessed 13 December 2010).
sustrans.org.uk/what-we-do/national-cycle-network/mileposts (accessed 13 December 2010).

Promenade, at the top of East Street groyne

Kiss Wall

Sculptor: Bruce Williams

Unveiled: 22 September 1992
Materials/dimensions: aluminium magnesium alloy painted with dark blue car enamel, 4.2 m high × 1.55 m wide × 2 cm deep
Status: not listed
Condition: poor (paint surface on both sides of panel and flanking seats badly eroded; paint has been touched up in a different blue. Fly-posted stickers on lower halves of front and back of panel, graffiti on lower right-hand

side of back. There was originally a plaque with the artist's name and the sculpture's title. It was removed by vandals and never replaced by the council)
Commissioned by: Brighton Festival Trust
Funded by: British Gas and the Arts Council of England
Owner/custodian: Brighton and Hove City Council

The sculpture is a slightly curved aluminium panel on the surface of which photographs of six kissing couples, intended to reflect the diversity of Brighton's population, were transformed by computer into a dot screen drilled through the metal. Williams has

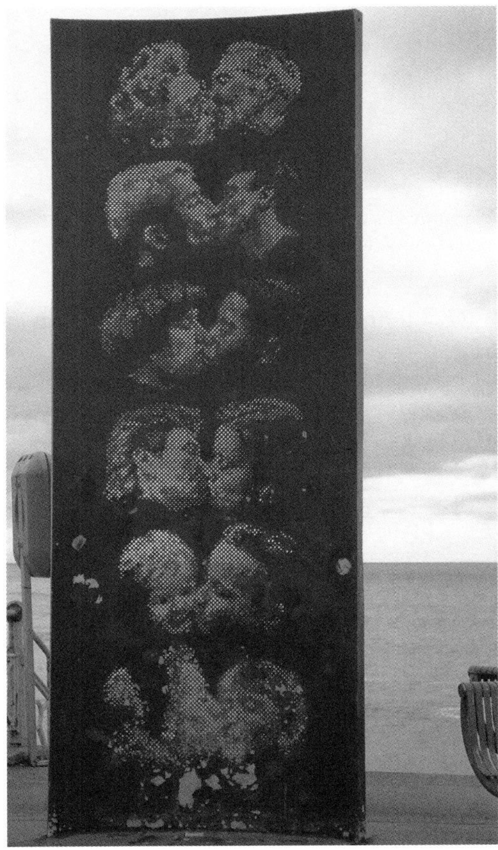

Bruce Williams, *Kiss Wall*

described his subject matter as:

> … a celebration … calling for equality, understanding and acceptance between all individuals … [it celebrates] a human contact not known to transmit the HIV virus. Indeed the sculpture affirms the kiss as a romantic and sexual or simply affectionate positive, untouched and even relieved by the dark background of Aids-consciousness.[1]

Williams won the commission in a national competition held in 1991.[2] He has been credited with pioneering the merging of digital printing and sculpture.[3] The clarity of the images is dependent upon the light conditions and the position of the viewer passing or standing in front of the piece. It can 'be read as projections of sunlight on the floor or as matrices of absence on the sheet itself.'[4] *Kiss Wall* was nominated for the 'Working for Cities' national public art award run by British Gas and the Arts Council of England.

Notes
[1] Berryman, L., 'Bruce Williams: a new public sculpture', *Arts Review*, 1992, p. 229. [2] Ibid.
[3] Rieser, M., 'Brave new world', *Printmaking Today*, vol. 9, Summer 2000, p.7. [4] Ibid.

Other sources
The Argus, 2 February 2006.
brighton.co.uk/arts/Public_Art (accessed 30 March 2011).
Graham, B., 'Long-term relationships: art in public', *Artists' Newsletter*, August 1993, pp. 30–31.
Graham, B., 'Long-term relationships: photography as permanent public art', *SF Camerawork Quarterly*, San Francisco, fall, 1993, stare.com/beryl/asunder/pubart (accessed 30 March 2011).

SEAFRONT

Opposite East Street, at the end of East Street Groyne, West of Brighton Pier

Afloat

Sculptor: Hamish Black

Foundry: Pangolin Editions

Installed: 1998
Materials/dimensions: patinated bronze, 2.5 m diam.
Signature (on base, facing the road): AFLOAT Hamish Black / 1998
Status: not listed
Condition: good (some graffiti)
Commissioned by: Brighton Borough Council
Funded by: National Lottery grant
Owner/custodian: Brighton and Hove City Council

The rounded shape of the sculpture, made of 2.2 tons of bronze, 5–6 mm thick, is derived from a toros (a speculative form for how black holes might look). Based on a globe, the points at the north and south poles are pushed together through the sphere, forming a central hole where they meet. The concentric radial indentations around its surface are the longitudinal lines. Major world continents exist as negative shapes cut out of the form in recesses deep enough to exclude light. The continents are not in realistic proportion to one another and they float, seemingly adrift, across the surface. The idea for the sculpture was initiated in 1995 as part of a series entitled 'One World'.

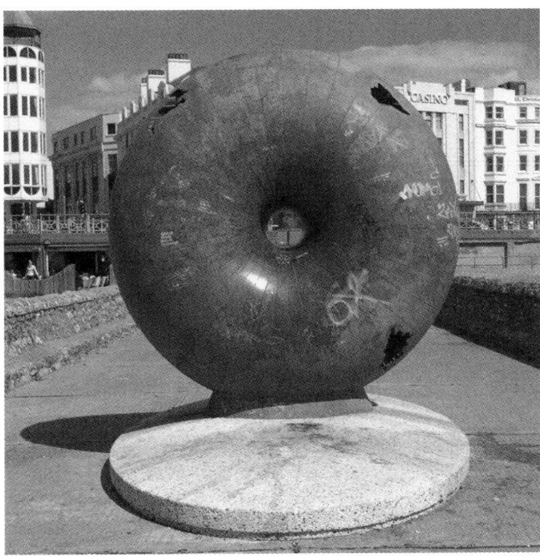

Hamish Black, *Afloat*

Afloat and Charles Hadcock's *Passacaglia* formed part of the Seafront Development Initiative in the late 1990s. Hamish Black was involved in the inception of the project and a maquette of his design, together with estimated costs and technical drawings, formed part of the grant application to the National Heritage Lottery fund.[1] The site for Black's piece, on the end of a small promontory, was selected to enable the viewer, when looking seawards, to see the horizon through the central hole in the sculpture. It appears as a line following through the lines of longitude. The blue/green patination forms a link to the ever-changing colour of the sky and the sea. Due to its shape, Black's sculpture is known locally as 'the doughnut'.

Note
[1] Mossop, S., *Brighton Seafront Sculpture Project: Teachers' Pack*, Brighton and Hove, 1998, p. 15.

Other sources
East Sussex Record Office, ACC 9753/20.
Moriarty, C., '"The sea goeth it all about": maritime themes in British public sculpture', *CRD Research Papers*, University of Brighton, 2001, pp. 7–8.

Grand Parade

Inside south entrance foyer of the University of Brighton (formerly on external wall of Brighton New School of Science and Art)

Terracotta Reliefs
Architect: J.G. Gibbins, Brighton
Designer: Alexander Fisher

Makers: Messrs Johnson, Ditchling Potteries
Unveiled: 3 February 1877
Materials/dimensions: terracotta, approx.
   1.10 m high × 2.6 m wide × 10 cm deep
Status: not listed
Condition: good
Funded by: public subscription
Owner/custodian: University of Brighton

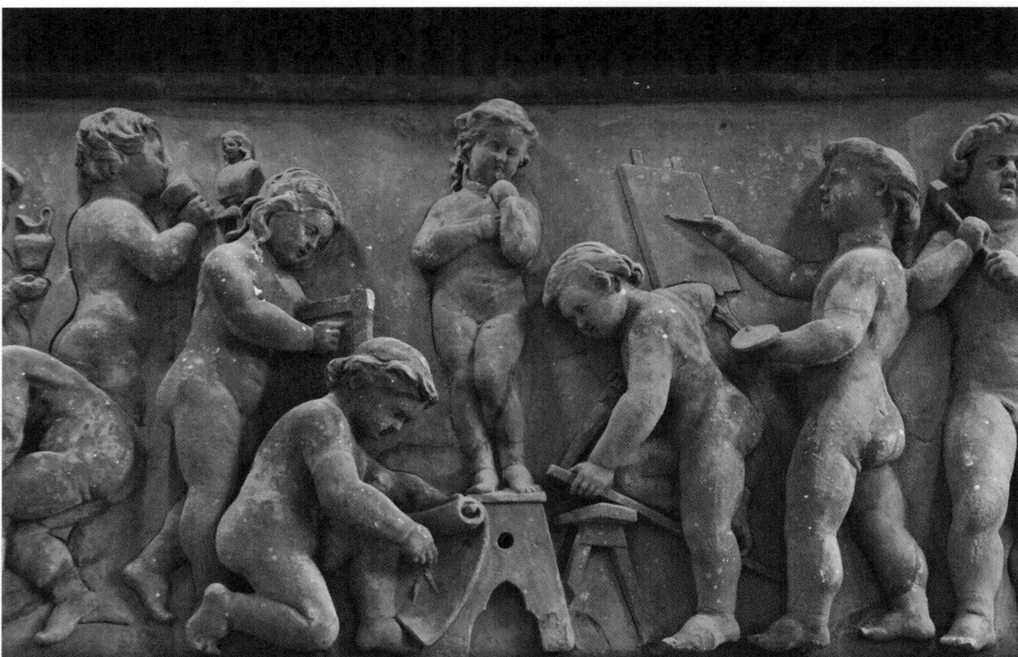

Alexander Fisher, *Terracotta Reliefs*

These terracotta panels were designed by the headmaster of the art school for the exterior of the new building. The one that was on the northern wing represents the arts with figures including:

> … Pottery … represented by a boy carrying an earthenware vessel; Architecture, by another constructing a toy house; Sculpture, by a sculptor at work on a bust; Geometry, by a fourth figure with compasses examining a scroll; Building Construction, by a youth with a saw and plank; Painting, by an artist at his easel.[1]

The panel that was on the southern wing represents the sciences, with the natural sciences symbolized by a boy examining a shell, a dinosaur skeleton and a boy chasing a butterfly with a net; the physical sciences are represented by boys with scientific instruments and test tubes, looking through a microscope and a telescope and standing in front of an electrical transformer; a boy holding a model of a railway train represents engineering. A clock for the front of the building, placed above the central panel, was presented by Mr. Boxell of Kings Road, Brighton.

Brighton had had a School of Art since 1858, originally housed in the Royal Pavilion. In the 1870s it was decided to combine the art school with a School of Science and a site was found at the bottom of Carlton Hill, in Grand Parade. Funds were raised by public subscription, with a Government contribution of £1000. The foundation stone was laid by Sir Henry Cole, K.C.B. in June 1876. The school was opened on 2 February 1877 by HRH Princess Louise, daughter of Queen Victoria. Large crowds turned out to greet her and her route from the station and the building itself were colourfully decorated.

The new building was designed in:

> … a modern Romanesque style, with the

façade in brick with Bath stone coping and
cornices. The columns flanking the entrance
were in polished red granite, those in the
windows in red Mansfield stone, with the
faced enriched by a series of terracotta panels
and lunettes.[2]

The two main panels and some of the lunettes
were preserved when the building was
demolished in the 1960s and installed in the
entrance to its successor.

Notes
[1] *Brighton Herald*, 3 February 1877. [2] Lyon, P.
and Woodham, J.M. (eds.), *Art and Design at
Brighton 1859–2009*, Brighton, 2009, p. 45.

Other source
Woodham, J.M. and Worden, S., *From Art School to
Polytechnic: Serving Industry and the Community
From Brighton 1859–1986*, Brighton, 1986, pp. 7–
13.

Kings Road

SEAFRONT

On beach opposite Kings Road arches

Passacaglia

Sculptor: Charles Hadcock

Foundry: James W. Shenton Ltd, Tipton, West
    Midlands
Installed: 1998
Materials/dimensions: recycled cast iron, 5 m
    high × 8 m wide × 1.5 m wide
Status: not listed
Condition: good (part removed 2006–07, not
    replaced)
Commissioned by: Brighton Borough Council
Funded by: National Lottery grant
Owner/custodian: Brighton and Hove City
    Council

The title of the sculpture is taken from an
Italian musical description for an instrumental
piece of old dance music in which a theme is
continually repeated. It takes the form of a tile
tessellation of 18 cast plates, inspired by the

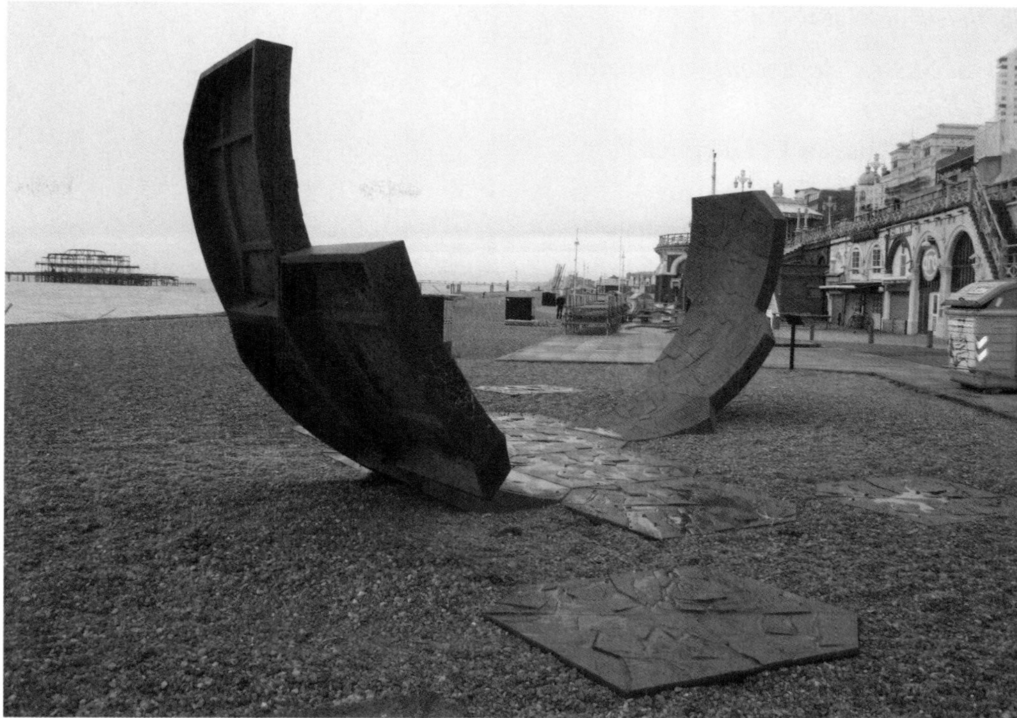

limestone terraces at Black Head, Co. Clare,
Ireland. Some tiles are flat, others curved and all
have textured surfaces that resemble York stone
paving. Their arrangement is based upon the
geometry and rules of proportion of the ancient
Roman architect Vitruvius. The reverse side of
each tile reveals the nuts and bolts of the
construction. In reaction to the flatness of the
beach landscape, Hadcock, whose design was
chosen in open competition, has introduced a
structure that rises up like a frozen wave or the
remains of a shipwrecked boat.

The sculpture weighs 20 tonnes and cost
£40,000. Its installation on the beach prompted
council leader Lord Bassam to exclaim, 'It's big,
it's brave and it's very Brighton. Like Brighton,
it will definitely have a strong reaction.'[1]

In 2004 structural cracks appeared in one of
the iron plates and the sculpture was removed
from the beach for investigation. When it was
returned in November 2007, the part that had

Charles Hadcock, *Passacaglia*

cracked was not replaced. This has changed the
appearance of the sculpture, but was done with
the agreement of the sculptor.

Note
[1] Windsor, J., 'Sculptor shapes up on the beach',
The Independent, 20 March 1998.

Other sources
'Brighton and Hove's public artwork guide', *The
    Argus*, 19 September 2008.
'Cast iron climbing frame is installed', *The Argus*,
    17 March 1998.
East Sussex Record Office, ACC 9753/20.
'Landmark back in Brighton', *The Argus*,
    5 November 2005.
Lewi-Turner, J. (Brighton Arts and Creative
    Industries Unit), email correspondence, 30 August
    2007.
Moriarty (2001), pp. 7–8.
Mossop (1998).
'Seafront sculpture in bad shape', *The Argus*,
    13 January 2004.

Royal Sussex Regiment Memorial (the Bugler)

Sculptor: Charles L. Hartwell

Architect: John W. Simpson

Builders: B&W Bennett, Lewes Road, Brighton
Metalworker: Walter Gilbert
Unveiled: 29 October 1904
Materials/dimensions: statue: bronze, 3.65 m
 high; obelisk: 5.48 m high
Signature (base of sculpture, east face):
 C. HARTWELL 1904
Inscriptions (on front of plinth): IN MEMORY /
 OF THE OFFICERS NON / COMMISSIONED
 OFFRS / AND MEN / OF THE ROYAL SUSSEX /
 REGIMENT WHO FELL / IN SOUTH AFRICA /
 1900–1902; (on front of base): LOUISBURG /
 QUEBEC 1759 / MAIDA / EGYPT 1882 / NILE
 1884–5 / ABU KLEA (with laurel wreath)
 1914–18 1939–45; (right-hand side of base):
 FIRST / BATTALION / ACTIVE SERVICE /
 VOLUNTEER COYS, followed by names of the
 dead; (on back of base): FIRST / BATTALION,
 followed by names of the dead; (on left of
 base): THIRD / BATTALION, followed by
 names of the dead
Status: Grade II
Condition: good (coated with metallic paint,
 subsequently removed and memorial
 restored 2009)
Funded by: public subscription and regimental
 funds
Owner/custodian: Brighton and Hove City
 Council

The statue is modelled on a sergeant from the
Royal Sussex regiment and makes reference to a
real incident that took place during the South
African campaign at Doornkop, with the bugler
sounding the charge. The Memorial cost £1400
(£803 from three Battalions of the Royal Sussex
Regiment) including artillery shells standing at
the four corners at a cost of 6s 7d each. It was
erected to commemorate the 152 soldiers of the

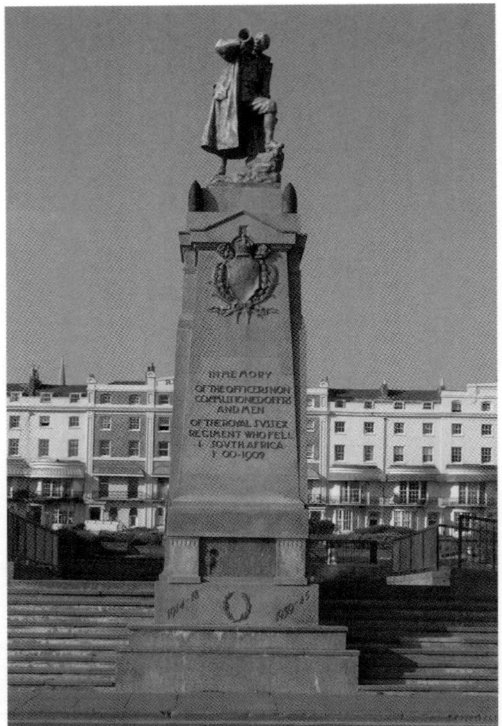

Charles L. Hartwell, *Royal Sussex Regiment
Memorial (the Bugler)*

Royal Sussex Regiment who died between 1900
and 1902 in the Boer War. The inscriptions
commemorate those lost in other conflicts; at
Quebec and Louisburg in 1759 and in Egypt in
the 1880s, as well as in the two World Wars. At
the time of its unveiling, by the Marquis of
Abergavenny, Lord Lieutenant of Sussex,
Regency Square was so filled with soldiers that
it was described as being 'under military
occupation'.[1]

Note
[1] *Brighton Herald*, 5 November 1904, p. 7.

Other sources
Moriarty, C., 'Remnants of patriotism: the
 commemorative representation of the greatcoat
 after the First World War', *Oxford Art Journal*,
 vol. 27, 2004, pp. 291–309.
Open Air Statues and Memorials, JLR 6/5/87.

*Between Brunswick Lawns and the
Esplanade opposite Brunswick Terrace*

Monument to Edward VII: The Peace Statue

Sculptor: Newbury Abbot Trent

Builder: William Kirkpatrick Ltd

Foundry: A.B. Burton
Unveiled: 12 October 1912
Materials/dimensions: winged figure: bronze,
 3.5 m high; pedestal: Stancliffe stone, with
 bronze plaques, 6.1 m high; stepped base:
 sandstone, 7.77 m square
Signature (on base of globe, right-hand side):
 N A TRENT SC LONDON; (on base of pedestal):
 NEWBURY A. TRENT. SC.
Inscriptions plaque on north face): EDWARD VII
 / 1901–1910; (west face, underneath coat of
 arms): FLOREAT HOVA; (plaque on south
 face): IN THE YEAR / 1912 / THE INHABITANTS
 / OF BRIGHTON AND HOVE / PROVIDED A
 HOME FOR / THE QUEEN'S NURSES AND
 ERECTED THIS MON- / UMENT IN MEMORY OF
 / KING EDWARD VII / AND AS A TESTIMONY OF
 / THEIR ENDURING LOYALTY; (plaque on east
 face): IN DEO FIDEMUS
Status: Grade II
Condition: fair (some guano damage and
 vandalism; some corrosion to base of
 pedestal; surrounding railings badly
 corroded)
Owner/custodian: Brighton and Hove City
 Council

The sculpture is of a draped, winged, female
figure, standing on a globe. The left hand holds
an orb; the right arm is raised holding an olive
branch. Although intended to symbolise peace,
iconographically the figure is part of a long
classical tradition of portraying the goddess

Nike as a winged victory, a 'sign of good omen', descending on the earth.[1] In this example, the globe is supported by dolphin-like figures (symbols of Brighton, alluding to the waters of the earth) with swags in their mouths. The statue stands atop a stone pedestal that carries bronze plaques on each side; that facing north bears a medallion portrait of the king; to the east and west, respectively, are the borough arms of Brighton and Hove. The memorial faces the promenade, with its back to the sea and has three steps surrounded by grass at its base.

It is a memorial to Edward VII 'The Peacemaker', who convalesced several times in Brighton, and marks the boundary with Hove. There was considerable public debate over the form that the memorial should take, with strong arguments in favour of 'practical charity' that would benefit 'the suffering poor'.[2] Public subscriptions raised by both Brighton and Hove councils in 1910 were spent on providing a home for the Queen's Nurses in Wellington Road, to which £1800 was contributed and which was considered the major part of the memorial, and on a monument to which £900 was allocated (it eventually cost £1000).[3]

Newbury Trent's design was chosen from 18 entrants in a public competition. He was not alone in employing a winged victory in a memorial to Edward VII. In 1912, the same year as the Brighton/Hove statue was unveiled, 'the Victory driving a four horse chariot on top of the Wellington Arch at Hyde Park Corner' was presented to the City of London in memory of the king.[4] For a year before the erection of the seafront statue, a wooden model of it stood in its place. The statue was unveiled by the Duke of Norfolk, Lord Lieutenant of Sussex, who stressed the importance of a monument to peace at a time when there was considerable anxiety about the outbreak of war on the continent.[5] The local newspaper reported that, '… it was felt that the figure is an artistic addition to towns that are not rich in beautiful statuary.'[6]

Known locally as the peace statue, and often mistaken for a war memorial, it was regarded as representative of a successful collaboration between two rival boroughs whose relations had not always been friendly. It resumed this symbolic role when Brighton and Hove became a unitary authority, following initial opposition, in 1995.[7]

Notes
[1] Warner, M., *Monuments and Maidens: the Allegory of the Female Form*, London, 1985, p. 133. We are grateful to Beverley Gowers, BA (Hons) History of Design for her discussion of this point. [2] *Brighton Gazette*, 16 October 1912. [3] Alexander, S., *Brighton Sculpture*, uncatalogued survey Brighton History Centre, nd, early 1980s. [4] Warner (1985), p. 143. [5] *Brighton Herald*, 19 October 1912. [6] Ibid. [7] *Sussex Today*, 13 April 1995.

Other sources
A Pictorial and Descriptive Guide to Brighton and Hove, p. 57.
Malcolm, J., *Bygone Brighton: Volume Two: Events*, Tunbridge Wells, 1980, p. 25.
Open Air Statues and Memorials, JLR 3/5/87.

Lewes Road

Cemeteries

The Extra-Mural Cemetery is the oldest of three cemeteries on the extensive site to the north of the town centre. It was built on arable land that once belonged to Scabe's Castle, a late eighteenth-century farm with buildings in Hartington Road. These were demolished in the 1900s when Hartington Place and Hartington Terrace were developed. The Brighton Extra-Mural Company laid out a private burial ground on 28 acres of land, 6 acres of which were donated by the Marquess of Bristol in 1850. The entrance was a castellated gateway with a round tower in Lewes Road and Amon Henry Wilds designed two mortuary chapels, of which only the Anglican one remains. The

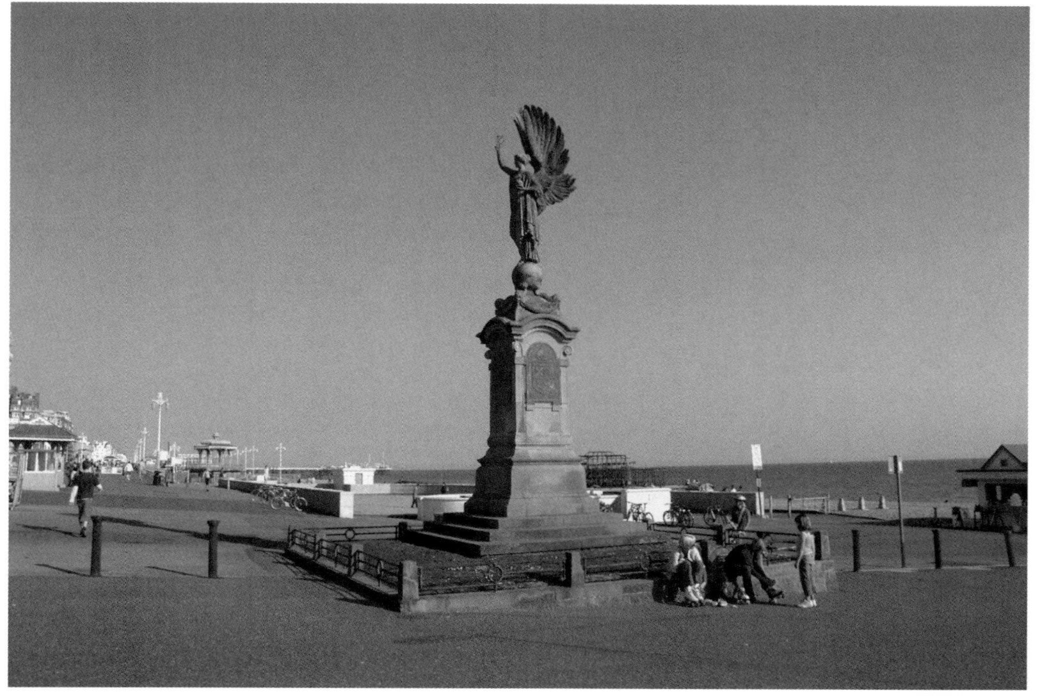

Newbury Abbot Trent, *Monument to Edward VII: The Peace Statue*

cemetery was consecrated on 14 November 1857 by the Bishop of Chichester, Dr A.T. Gilbert.

During the nineteenth century the cemetery was popular with visitors, for whom a guidebook was published. By 1956, however, it had become redundant, was purchased by the corporation and restored as an interesting and picturesque garden of remembrance, which contains many impressive Victorian tombs, including those of several important figures in Brighton's history.[1]

The adjoining Woodvale Cemetery was opened in 1857. The burial ground is Grade II listed and until 1902 was known as the Brighton Parochial cemetery.

Extra-Mural Cemetery, north side

Monument to Frederick William Robertson

Sculptor: William Wyon

Installed: c. 1855
Materials/dimensions: pylon: stone, 2.2 m high × 1.9 m wide × 1.17 m deep; inset rectangular relief: patinated bronze, 54 cm high × 85 cm wide × 25 cm deep
Inscriptions (bottom of rectangular plaque): WE THEN AS AMBASSADORS OF CHRIST; (bottom of bronze roundel): OTHER (?) MEN AND FELLOW TOWNSMEN; (east face): M.S. / THE REVEREND / FREDERICK WILLIAM ROBERTSON M.A. / PERPETUAL CURATE OF TRINITY CHAPEL BRIGHTON / BORN 3RD. OF FEBRUARY 1816 / DIED 15TH. OF AUGUST 1853 / HONORED AS A MINISTER / BELOVED AS A MAN / HE AWAKENED THE HOLIEST FEELINGS / IN POOR AND RICH IN IGNORANT AND LEARNED. / THEREFORE IS HE LAMENTED / AS THEIR GUIDE AND COMFORTER / BY MANY WHO IN THE BOND OF BROTHERHOOD / AND IN GRATEFUL REMEMBRANCE / HAVE ERECTED THIS MONUMENT. / GLORY TO THE SAVIOUR. WHO WAS HIS ALL; (west face): TO THE / REVD. F.W. ROBERTSON M.A. / IN GRATEFUL REMEMBRANCE OF HIS SYMPATHY / AND IN DEEP SORROW FOR THEIR LOSS / THE MEMBERS OF THE MECHANICS INSTITUTION / AND THE WORKING MEN OF BRIGHTON / HAVE PLACED THIS MEDALLION ON THEIR BENEFACTORS TOMB / A.D. 1855.
Status: Grade II
Condition: good (inscription on roundel damaged with letters missing from first word)
Commissioned and funded by: The Brighton Mechanics' Institute and Brighton Townspeople
Owner/custodian: Robertson family

The stone monument is in the form of a low Egyptian pylon facing east. A rectangular bronze plaque, donated by his congregation, on the east face, shows him preaching to them and a roundel on the west face, donated by the Mechanics' Institute, of which he was a founder, to working men. The stone frieze is carved with the symbol for Horus, Egyptian god of the sky, war and protection.

Robertson was a radical preacher at Holy Trinity Church, Ship Street, Brighton, which, during his ministry, became the most fashionable church in Brighton. His sermons attracted large congregations and were admired by Lord Shaftesbury, the Marquis of Lansdowne and Charles Dickens. He was a champion of the working classes and, '… particularly disliked the extreme degree of Sabbatarianism which opposed such things as the opening of the Great Exhibition of 1851 on Sundays.'[2] Robertson died at the age of 37 following a nervous breakdown and his funeral was a grand affair. Commemorative busts were erected in the Royal Pavilion (later moved to the Town Hall) and the Bodleian Library in Oxford.

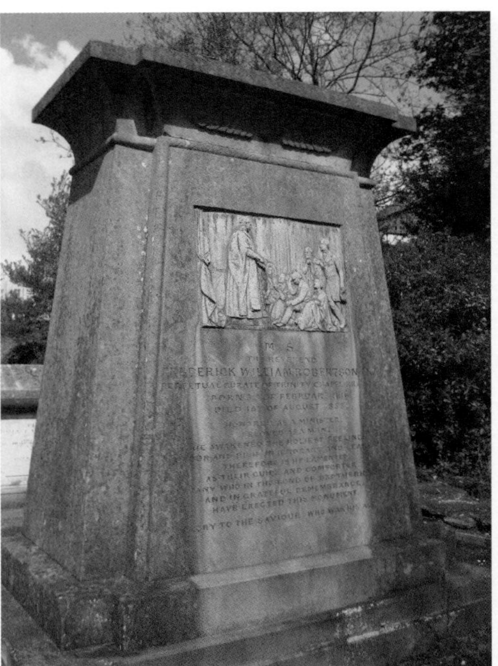

William Wyon, *Monument to Frederick William Robertson*

Extra-Mural Cemetery, north side, next to the Cemetery Chapel

Ray Family Mausoleum

Sculptor: unknown

Installed: c. 1850
Materials/dimensions: Mausoleum: knapped flint with granite dressings and asphalted roof; 6 m high × 7 m wide × 6.4 m deep; reliefs: stone; 1.75 m high × 1 m wide
Inscription (set into arch of the door frame): Keep innocency and take heed unto the thing that is right: for that shall bring a man peace at the last. (Psalm 37)
Status: Grade II
Condition: fair (cracks to pilasters either side of doorway; hands missing from classical figures above and at side of door; vegetation covering roof)
Commissioned and owned by: Ray family

The mausoleum is square in plan and partly set into the hillside. It has a pointed-arched entrance to the west set under a rectangular hood mould, the spandrels filled with quatrefoils, and over it a gabled niche

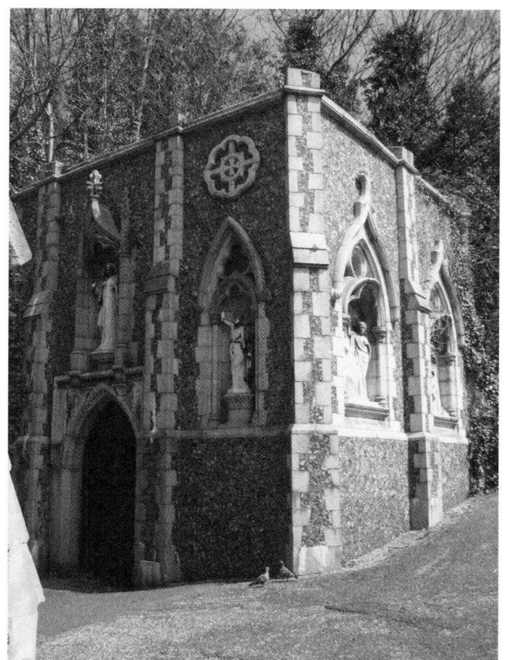

Unknown, *Ray Family Mausoleum*

Monument to John Frederick Ginnett

Sculptor: Edwin Roscoe Mullins

Installed: 1892
Materials/dimensions: statue: stone, 1.15 m × 1.4 m wide × 65 cm deep; plinth: Portland stone, 2.4 m × 2.6 m wide × 1 m wide
Signature: Illegible signature and date to back of integral base of pony.
Inscription (to front of monument): TO THE DEAR MEMORY OF / JOHN FREDERICK GINNETT / BORN IN 1819 AT LEA IN / ESSEX DIED AT BRIGHTON / JANUARY 12 1892:AND OF / HIS DEARLY LOVED WIFE / ANNIE MARIA: DAUGHTER / OF JOHN SNAPE OF LEAM-INGTON:IN HER 62ND YEAR. Other inscribed plaques at each corner and to the back of the monument record the names of other family members buried there
Status: Grade II
Condition: Good (but corrosion to the statue of the horse and some detail lost, signature illegible)
Commissioned and owned by: Ginnett family

The statue of a circus horse surmounts a stone plinth facing south-west onto one of the main cemetery roads. Described by Spielmann as '… one of the strangest subjects for treatment … that could be presented to a sculptor for solution', it commemorates John Frederick Ginnett, the eldest son of Jean Pierre Ginnett (d. 1861, buried in Kensal Green Cemetery) the founder of the Ginnett circus dynasty.[4] He was a celebrated horseman and performed for the King and Queen at Brighton in 1832. He took over his father's circus when he died and built several permanent circus buildings, including his hippodrome at Park Crescent Place, Brighton. John Frederick's sons, Claude, Frederick and Albert also worked in the circus business. The last of Ginnett's sons to be buried in the grave was Louis John, who died in 1947 and was a well-known portrait painter who taught at the Brighton College of Art in Grand Parade.[5] Descendents of Ginnett continue to work in the circus today.[6]

containing a classical female figure. The two principal fronts to west and south are divided by buttresses creating uneven bays on the west side, even bays on the south, and there is a high base with an offset through which the entrance breaks. The south bay to the west has a trefoiled niche under a pointed-arched hood mould with another Classical female figure in it and a cross in an octofoil above. On the south side there are two trefoiled panels under ogee hood moulds, with sculptural reliefs of Mary at the Sepulchre to the west, and to the east Gethsemane. The east face has a similar panel of Christ and St Peter.

It has been claimed that it was built for a barrister named Ray, but the oldest interment was that of Lucy Langford Ray in 1856. No male member of the Ray family was buried there until Robert Ray in 1871. The interior is fitted with shelves to take 42 coffins, but only 14 burials have taken place there.[3]

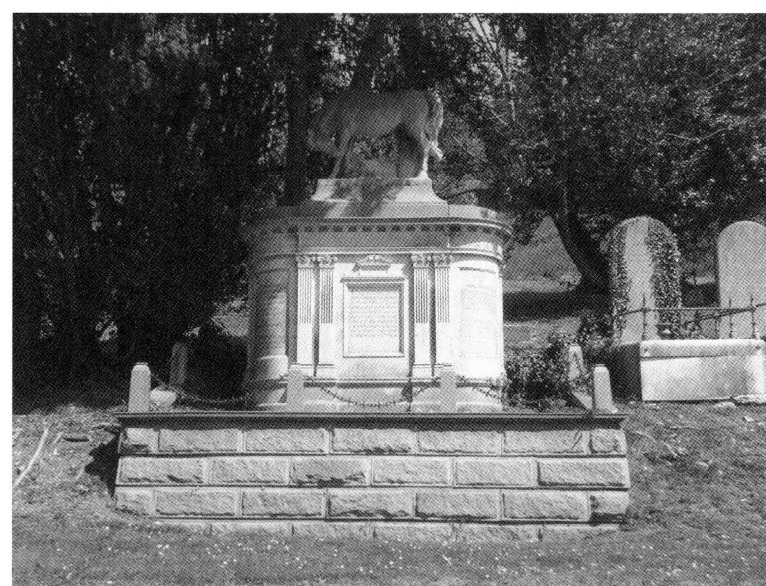

Edwin Roscoe Mullins,
Monument to John Frederick Ginnett

Notes
[1] Carder (1990), entry 33. [2] Dale, A., *Brighton Cemeteries*, Brighton, 1991 (1995 edn), p. 11. [3] Ibid. [4] Spielmann, M.H., *British Sculpture and Sculptors of Today*, London, 1901, p. 50. [5] Dale (1995). [6] circusginnett.com (accessed 27 October 2010).

Other sources
Beardsley, C., *Love: The Passionate Life and Preaching of F.W. Robertson*, Cambridge, 2009.
Collis (2010).
Robertson, F. W. and Brooke, S. A., *Life and Letters of Fred. W. Robertson, M.A.: Incumbent of Trinity Chapel, Brighton, 1847–53*, London, 1906.

London Road

A23 on northern boundary of Brighton

The Pylons

Architect: John Leopold Denman

Builder: Field and Cox Ltd.
Installed: 1928
Materials/dimensions: each pylon: Clipsham limestone, approx. 7 m high × 2.2 m wide × 3.3 m deep; each seat: Clipsham limestone, 1.4 m high × 11.2 m wide × 60 cm deep
Inscriptions (eastern pylon, south face, surmounted by the arms of the Duke and Duchess of York): THIS FOUNDATION STONE WAS LAID BY / HIS ROYAL HIGHNESS THE DUKE OF YORK / KG.RCKT.GCMG.GCVO. ON THE 30TH MAY 1928; (eastern pylon, north face, surmounted by a sculptural relief of a galleon): THESE PYLONS - ERECTED BY PUBLIC SUBSCRIPTION COMMEMORATE / THE EXTENSION OF THE COUNTY BOROUGH OF BRIGHTON ON / 1ST. APRIL 1928. / Alderman John L. Denman, F.R.I.B.A. / Charles Kingston J.P. Architect / Mayer, Field and Cox. Builder; (western pylon, south face, surmounted by the arms of the Duke and Duchess of York): THIS FOUNDATION STONE WAS LAID BY / HER ROYAL HIGHNESS THE DUCHESS OF YORK / G.B.E. ON THE 30TH. MAY / 1928; (western pylon, north face, surmounted by a sculptural relief of a female figure holding an ankh (key of life) and a torch: HAIL GUEST WE ASK NOT WHAT THOU ART. / IF FRIEND. WE GREET THEE. HAND & HEART: / IF STRANGER. SUCH NO LONGER BE: / IF FOE OUR LOVE SHALL CONQUER THEE.
Status: Grade II
Condition: good
Commissioned by: Sir Herbert Carden, Brighton Town Council
Funded by: public subscription
Owner/custodian: Brighton and Hove City Council

The pylons are wedge-shaped in plan, with the narrow end pointing inwards, towards the road; the two long sides, bearing inscriptions and emblems of Brighton and Sussex and the outer side, are very slightly concave in plan but with flat panels superimposed upon them, and concave-chamfered buttresses at the corners; the narrow end is treated as a tapering engaged column. The tops of the pylons are set back all round, and fluted. Low stone seats, segmental in plan and with stepped backs, curve around the bases of the pylons without touching them. They are finished with squat columns of stepped profile that once held bronze lamps.

The pylons, a Greek term for a monumental gateway to an Egyptian temple, function as large gate pillars, welcoming motorists to Greater Brighton. They were erected to mark the northern limit of the enlarged borough, which was created on 1 April 1928, although they stand 35 yards inside the boundary. Since the A23 was widened to become a dual carriageway, one stands at the eastern side of the road and one in the central reservation. The cost was born by a public subscription of £993 and a contribution from Herbert Carden, who had been responsible for much of the development of Greater Brighton, of £2555. Carden also chose the final wording of the inscriptions, suggestions for which had been submitted by readers of the local newspaper.[1]

Buried inside the pylons are coins and copies of the *Brighton and Hove Herald* and the

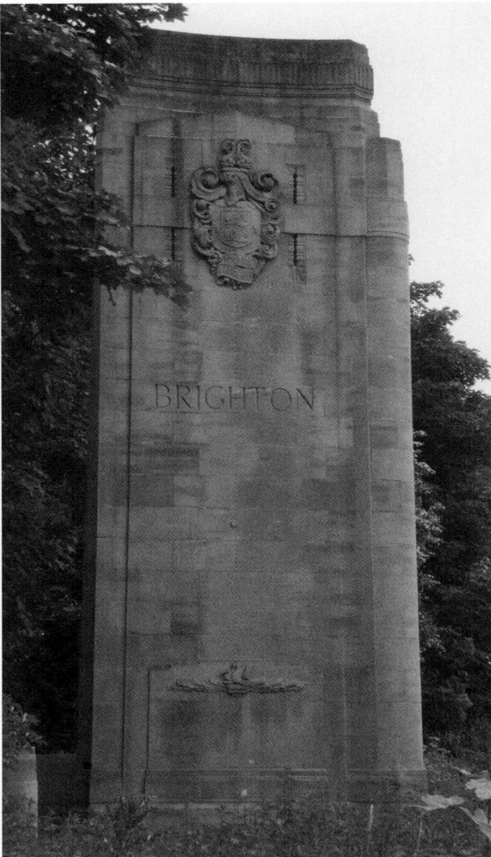

John Leopold Denman, *The Pylons*

Sussex Daily News in a teak box made by Messrs. T.B. Colman and Sons, Ltd, of Hove. Also buried is a bound book recording the laying of the foundation stones by the Duke and Duchess of York (later King George VI and Queen Elizabeth) given by Mr J.S. North. The book was illuminated by Mr W.H. Evans, A.R.C.A. (Lond.), Principal of the Brighton School of Art, and contains the borough coat of arms and an inscription describing the circumstances of the ceremony, followed by the names of the subscribers.[2]

Conservative councillor John Sheldon suggested a third pylon should be erected on the far western side of the road to mark the Millennium, but funding could not be raised. Denman also designed a stone seat at the top of Devil's Dyke on the South Downs Way to commemorate Councillor Carden's initiative to purchase 190 acres of downland in the area for public use.[3]

Notes
[1] 'Inscriptions on the pylons', *Brighton & Hove Herald*, 17 November 1928. [2] 'The Pylons: gateway to greater Brighton', *Brighton & Hove Herald*, 26 May 1928. [3] *Brighton and Hove Herald*, 2 June 1928; Carder (1990), entry 50.

Other sources
Collis (2010), p. 260.
Seldon, A., *Brave New City: Brighton and Hove Past Present Future*, Lewes, 2002, p. 73.

Madeira Drive

Facing Brighton Pier

Statue of Steve Ovett
Sculptor: Peter Webster

Unveiled: 24 July 2012
Materials/dimensions: statue: bronze, approx.
    1.5 m high × 59 cm wide × 59 cm deep;
    plinth: stone: 1.47 m high × 80 cm wide ×
    80 cm deep
Signature (on back of integral base): PETE
    WEBSTER
Inscriptions (front of integral base): STEVE
    OVETT: OLYMPIAN; (on front face of plinth)
    FREEMAN OF THE CITY / World Records
    /1500m / Koblenz 3min 31.36 sec / Reiti
    3min 30.77sec / Mile / Oslo 3min 48.80 sec /
    Two Mile / London 8 min13.50 sec
Status: not listed
Condition: good
Commissioned and funded by: private sponsors

The sculpture depicts Brighton-born Olympic athlete Steve Ovett (b. 1955) in the running position, with his right arm and left leg raised. It is a replica of an earlier statue, also by Peter Webster, commissioned by local tourism

official, Tony Hewison, in 1983. It was installed in Preston Park, where the athlete, who competed in three Olympic Games and held many world records, used to train. At the time, it was the most expensive public sculpture in Brighton, costing private sponsors £25,000 and it was also one of the few bronze sculptures to be installed in the city since the Victorian period.

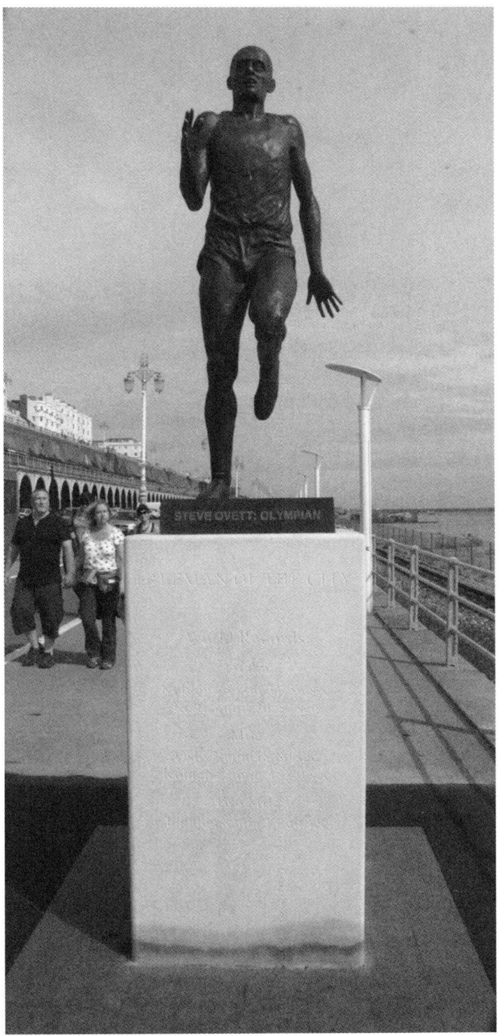

Peter Webster, *Statue of Steve Ovett*

The statue was vandalised and broken at the ankle six weeks after its unveiling in 1987, but was quickly restored. It was then stolen during the weekend of 2 and 3 September 2007. The figure was sawn off at the foot and broken up into pieces by the thieves in an attempt to melt it down for scrap.[1] Some parts were recovered by police, in a bonfire across the road from the park, at the site of a protest against the removal of trees by a developer, and a woman was arrested, but not charged. The right foot and signed base of the original statue remain in the flower bed at the perimeter of the park, but it was stated that it was impossible to reproduce the statue because the moulds no longer existed. A new version, however, was created, funded by local businessmen at a cost of £50,000. The new work occupies a much more prominent position on the seafront, near to the finishing line of the annual Brighton marathon. Ovett won a gold medal in the 800 metres at the Moscow Olympics in 1980 and the statue marks this distance from the pier and back. The athlete flew from his home in Australia to unveil the statue a few days before the start of the London 2012 Olympic games. He said at the ceremony, 'Brighton really did make me who I am. The chalk downland made my legs strong and the hills certainly made me fit.'[2]

Notes
[1] It would have required furnace facilities that could heat the bronze to about 1000 degrees to achieve this.
[2] Ridgeway, T., 'Steve Ovett statue unveiled on eve of 2012 games', *The Argus* 24 July 2012.

Other sources
The Argus, 4, 5, 6 and 7 September 2007; 21 January 2012; 29 May 2012.
Webster, P., 'The life and afterlife of a public sculpture', *Public Monuments and Sculpture in Sussex: Memory and Manifestation*, symposium, University of Brighton, 24 November 2007.
Peter Webster, telephone conversation, 28 January 2012.

14–16 Marlborough Place

Above entrance to King and Queen Inn

King and Queen

Architects: Clayton and Black

Builders: Heaton, Tabb and Company
Installed: 1931–32
Materials/dimensions: painted wood; approx.
 1.17 m high × 64 cm wide × 50 cm deep
Status: not listed
Condition: In 2013 a replica of the Queen
 figure was created and the King repaired
Owner/Custodian: King and Queen Inn

The two painted wooden statues stand on
platforms that extend outwards from a large
panelled window either side of the sign painted
with KING AND QUEEN, above the main
entrance. On the left is King Henry VIII in
typical dress; between his legs sits a bulldog.
On the right is Queen Anne Boleyn, with a cat
at her feet and her raised right hand holding an
orb.

There has been an inn on this site since 1779,
when a farmhouse sited on the western edge of
the Steine was granted a licence to serve alcohol
to the local agricultural community. The inn's
name originally referred to George III and
Queen Charlotte. In the early part of the
nineteenth century the Brighton Corn Market

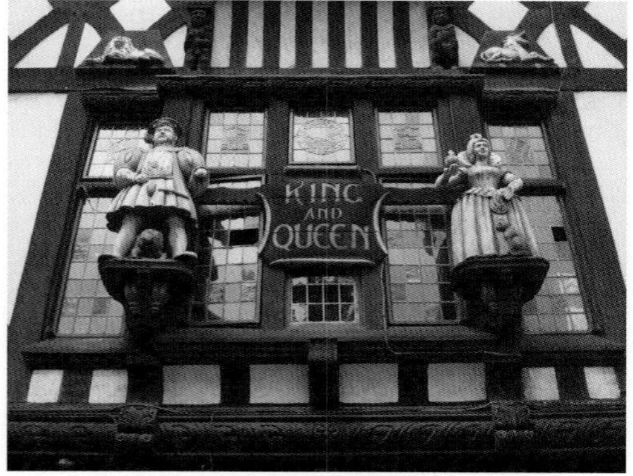

Clayton and Black, *King and Queen*

was held in the building before being moved in
1868 to the Royal Pavilion Riding House,
which became known as the Corn Exchange.

During the 1930s Clayton and Black rebuilt
the pub in an elaborate Tudoresque pastiche
including seemingly authentic details such as
tapestries and heraldic glass, carved oak timbers
and linen-fold panels. At the same time, the
figures of Henry VIII and Anne Boleyn,
regarded as more appropriate to the new style,
replaced the original Royal Couple.[1]

Note
[1] School of Architecture (1987), p. 47.

Other sources
Carder (1990), entry 189a.
Collis (2010), p. 195.

20–22 Marlborough Place

*Surrounding four windows of the Allied
Irish bank*

Allied Irish Bank Reliefs

Sculptor: Joseph Cribb

Architect: John Leopold Denman

Installed: 1933
Materials/dimensions: Portland stone, each arch
 3.5 m high × 2.6 m wide × 30 cm deep
Status: not listed
Condition: good
Owner/custodian: Allied Irish bank

Three windows at the front of the building are
set in concave-chamfered architraves of stone
decorated at the springing and above with small
carved panels illustrating the building trades,
including a portrait of Denman, the architect.
Denman and Cribb had collaborated in a
similar way the previous year (1932) on the
Brighton and Hove Herald building (now
Pavilion Buildings), for which the sculptor
carved a frieze and capitals including marine
motifs of tiny seahorses and shells.

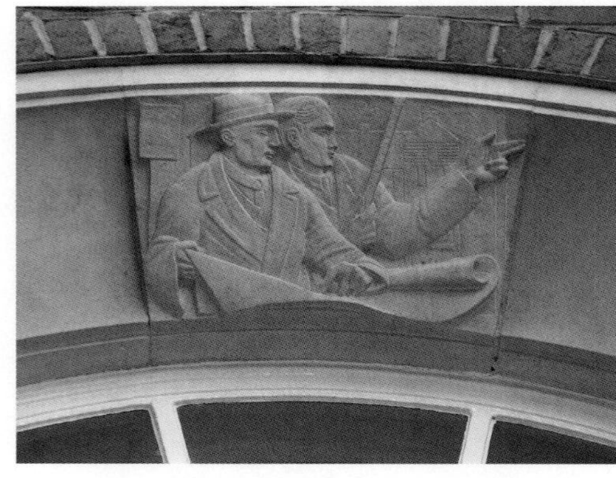

Joseph Cribb, *Allied Irish Bank Reliefs* (relief)

Sources
Collis (2010), p. 239.
Cribb, R. and Cribb, J., *Eric Gill and Ditchling: the
 Workshop Tradition*, Ditchling, 2007, p. 23.
James, N.P., *John Skelton: Axis Mundi*, London,
 2005, pp. 12–13.
regencysociety.org (accessed 26 October 2010).
School of Architecture (1987), p. 33.

Marlborough Place/Grand Parade

Church Street end of Victoria Gardens

Statue of Queen Victoria

Sculptor: Carlo Nicoli

Builders: The Sculptured Marble Company,
 London
Unveiled: 8 December 1897
Materials/dimensions: statue: Carrara marble,
 2.5 m high × 85 cm wide × 85 cm deep;
 pedestal: Carrara marble, 2.48 m high × 2 m
 wide (at widest) × 2 m deep (at deepest)
Signature (south aspect of statue, bottom of
 base): Nicoli
Inscriptions (in carved letters, front of lower
 plinth): Victoria Rg / 1897; (in lead letters
 inset into middle step of base): THE
 SCULPTURED MARBLE CO. / 11 QUEEN
 VICTORIA ST LONDON. EC
Status: Grade II
Condition: fair (weatherworn, with detail of

some carving lost; scroll damaged; copious
graffiti)
Commissioned by: Sir John George Blaker
Owner/custodian: Brighton and Hove City
  Council

The queen is depicted wearing the Garter sash
and a veil under her crown. She is in the act of
opening parliament, clutching an unfurled scroll
in her left hand. The original version of the
statue was sculpted by Nicoli in 1888 for
Amritsar in India and the scroll is likely to be
an 'allusion to the crown's assumption of direct
rule in India in 1858'.[1] Demand for public
statues of the Queen to commemorate her
Golden (1887) and Diamond (1897) Jubilees
was high throughout the Empire and the
Statuary and Granite Company (which
incorporated the Sculptured Marble Company)
issued an illustrated brochure with a choice of
three different figures of the Queen.[2] The
company 'stressed the importance of accurate
likeness, for which it relied on photographs,
rather than artistic effect.[3] Nicoli's sculpture
appears to be a realistic depiction of the ageing
Queen, which does not idealise her short, stout
figure. It was well received locally, but *The
Magazine of Art* was particularly scathing
about this work:

> This statue of Her Majesty the Queen
> impresses us neither as a portrait nor as an
> example of sculpture. But what can be
> expected when the commission was placed
> with a commercial sculptural company
> which undertakes to supply 'busts of
> statesmen and others executed from
> photographs', together with stairs, balusters,
> headstones and other marble works? We
> have received from them an eulogistic
> description of the Brighton statue
> accompanied by a biographical sketch of the
> 'eminent sculptor', which omits his name. Is
> the eminent sculptor – presumably an Italian
> – ashamed of his connection with
> commercial sculpture?[4]

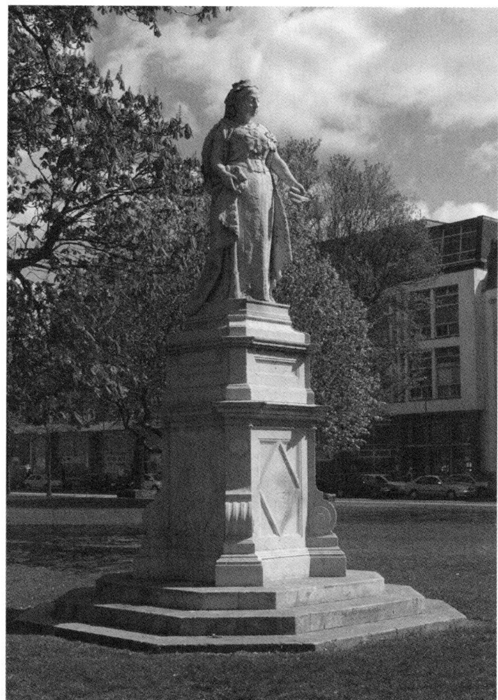

Carlo Nicoli, *Statue of Queen Victoria*

Sir John George Blaker, Mayor of Brighton
between 1895 and 1898, presented the statue to
the town at the opening of Victoria Gardens at
the time of the Queen's Diamond Jubilee on 22
June 1897. It was unveiled later that year by his
daughter, Miss Jessie Blaker. Given the statue's
association with India, it seems appropriate that
it stands facing the Indian-inspired fantasy that
is the Royal Pavilion, a building for which the
Queen, however, had an intense dislike.

Notes
[1] Darby, E.S., *Statues of Queen Victoria and of
Prince Albert: a Study in Commemorative and
Portrait Statuary 1837–1924*, unpublished PhD thesis,
Courtauld Institute of Art, London, 1983, p. 326.
[2] Ibid., p. 349. [3] Ibid., p. 326. [4] *The Magazine of
Art*, vol. 22, 1898, p. 168.

Other sources
Alexander (nd).
Brighton Almanack for 1898, Hove, 1898, p. 91.

Bob Speel (local historian), email correspondence 9
  December 2012.
Sussex Daily News, 22 and 23 June 1897.
Wales, T., *The Archive Photographs Series: Brighton
  and Hove*, Trowbridge, 1997, p. 24.
myweb.tiscali.co.uk/speel/place/brightn2 (accessed 22
  January 2008).

New Road

Edge of Pavilion Gardens

Statue of Max Miller

Sculptor: Peter Webster

Unveiled: 1 May 2005
Materials/dimensions: statue: bronze, 2.76 m
  high × 60 cm wide × 60 cm deep; pedestal:
  limestone facing over concrete, 1.2 m high ×
  78 cm wide × 60 cm deep
Signature (at top of base): Webster
Inscriptions (front of base): "The Cheeky
  Chappie"; (left of base): "There'll never be
  another"; (right of base): "Listen, listen";
  (back of base): "What if I am?"
Status: not listed
Condition: good
Commissioned and owned by: The Max Miller
  Appreciation Society

The life-sized bronze depicts Brighton-born
comedian Max Miller, known as 'the cheeky
chappie', on stage. Reference is made to his act
through his trademark stage clothing of flower-
patterned suit, plus fours, correspondent shoes
and a trilby hat and quotations from his stage
patter. The statue was modelled in clay and
plaster from photographic and video references
and cast using the lost wax method.

There was some debate over the positioning
of the statue opposite the Theatre Royal, as
Miller rarely appeared there, although he did
star regularly at the Dolphin Theatre
(demolished 1967). It was held in storage during
2007, while major works took place in the area,
resited a short distance from its original
position on 8 August 2007, and rededicated on
12 August 2007.

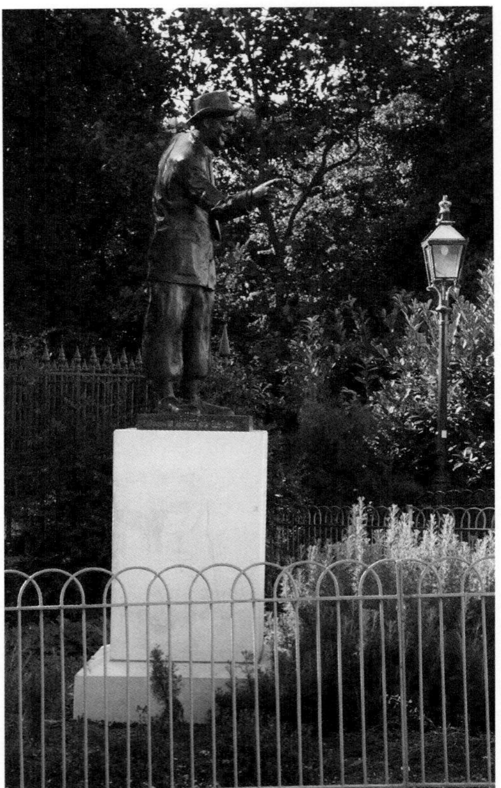

Peter Webster, *Statue of Max Miller*

Britain's top comedian from the 1930s to the 1950s, Max Miller starred in London's West End and in 14 feature films. He started his career as a song and dance man on Brighton seafront and his signature tune became 'Mary From The Dairy'. His act was risqué and filled with double entendres and regularly banned from the BBC airwaves.

Sources
J. Strutt (founder member Max Miller Appreciation Society), email correspondence, 30 September 2008.
Trimmingham, A., 'Those were the days', *Brighton and Hove Leader*, 23 August 2007, p. 4.
Walk of Fame: Official Guide, Brighton, 2003.

New England Road

On Circus Parade, outside Vantage Point

The Kissing Bridge
Sculptor: Nigel Boonham

Foundry: Burleighfield Arts Ltd
Unveiled: 9 September 1998
Materials/dimensions: concrete and bronze, 2.15 m high × 1.7 m wide × 40 cm deep
Signatures: base of male figure, facing west: Boonham/1982/2/3; bottom right: BURLEIFIELD [*sic*]
Status: not listed
Condition: good (some biological growth and graffiti)
Commissioned and funded by: Renison Investments Corporation (Vantage Point developers)
Owner/custodian: Vantage Point
Two stylised and elongated figures, male (west) and female (east), lean forward to form a dynamic arch, kissing at the point of the arch keystone. The sculpture is set in a gardened area, surrounded by shops and offices, including the Vantage Point office block. Nigel Boonham has written that:

> the idea for this sculpture originated after a conversation about being able to walk under

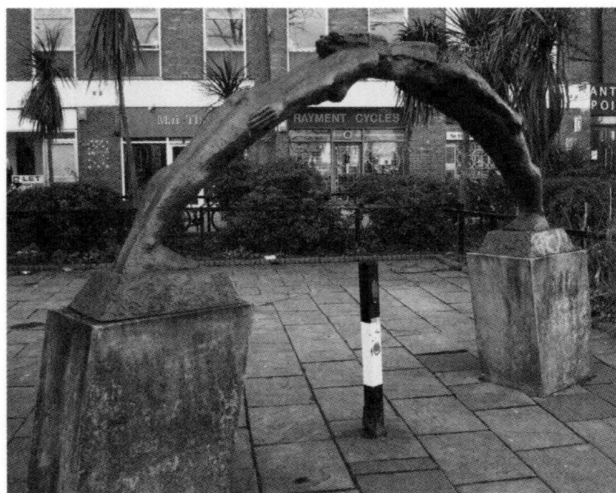

Nigel Boonham, *The Kissing Bridge*

a bronze. The concept was to bring the opposing poles together, man and woman, east and west, with the kiss being the keystone.[2]

It was not made to commission and was designed to be an intermediate study for a much larger sculpture and is the second cast of an edition of three; the first was bought in 1994 for a private house in East Ilsley, Berkshire and has since returned temporarily to the artist's studio on the sale of the house. It is occasionally temporarily exhibited elsewhere, for example in Chichester Cathedral. The Brighton sculpture was unveiled by the Duke of Gloucester.[3]

Notes
[1] boonham.com/s_kissingbridge (accessed 26 October 2010). [3] Nigel Boonham, email correspondence, 24 January 2008.

Other source
The Argus, 22 December 2003.

New Steine Gardens

Top of gardens, off St James's Street

Tay (Aids memorial)
Sculptor: Romany Mark Bruce

Foundry: Morris Singer, Braintree
Constructed: 2007–09
Unveiled: 9 October 2009
Materials/dimensions: sculpture: bronze, 3.35 m high × 72 cm wide × 23 cm deep; plinth: Portland stone, 1.2 m high × 1.2 m wide × 80 cm deep
Signatures (bottom, inner surface, right-hand column: ROMANY MARK BRUCE 2009; (bottom, inner surface, left-hand column): RMB 2009
Inscription (bronze plaque on front of plinth): Brighton and Hove Aids Memorial / 'TAY' / by Romany Mark Bruce / 2009
Status: not listed
Condition: good
Commissioned by: Councillor Paul Elgood

Funded by: public donations
Owner/custodian: Brighton and Hove City
    Council

The sculpture is formed of two abstracted male torsos, intertwined at the base, soaring upwards and away from each other, their heads tilted backwards. Their silhouette, especially when the piece is illuminated at night, resembles the red ribbon, symbol of HIV/Aids commemoration. The piece is named for Paul Tay, Bruce's best friend, who died in 1992. He described it as representing hope for the future.[1] The design was selected by a public online vote and the finished sculpture cost around £4200, with the sculptor donating his time free. A large section of the full-scale clay model had to be reconstructed in January 2009, prior to the moulds being made by the foundry, as extreme weather conditions had caused it to freeze, then melt and fall away from the metal armature.[2]

The sculpture was the result of three years campaigning for a permanent memorial to the hundreds of people in Brighton who have lost their lives to HIV/Aids in the past three decades, including the man whose name the piece bears. Considerable stress was placed upon the importance of having a physical structure to act as a focal point for acts of remembrance. It is only the second Aids memorial in the country, the first being in Manchester.

Tay was unveiled by David Furnish, board member of the Elton John AIDS Foundation, who said, 'This statue is for all those people [who died] and it's so important that come rain or sunshine we still remember them.'[3]

Following the ceremony there was an evening concert of remembrance at nearby St Mary's Church, from which a candlelit procession made its way to the statue where the names of the dead were read out.

Notes
[1] Ridgway, T., 'Past and future symbol', *The Argus*, 10 October 2009, pp. 20–21. [2] thelatest.co.uk/7/romany-mark-bruce (accessed 9 April 2013). [3] Ridgway (2009).

Other sources
Bauldry, J., 'Aids memorial ideas unveiled', *The Argus*, 7 September 2007, p. 9.
Romany Mark Bruce, Jubilee Library exhibition, Brighton, 3–31 May 2008.
romanymarkbruce.com (accessed 12 October 2009).

North Road

Set into the wall of the Brighthelm Church and Community Centre

Loaves and Fishes

Sculptor: John Skelton with Helen Mary Skelton

Architects: Wells-Thorpe and Suppel Ltd.

Unveiled: 10 October 1987

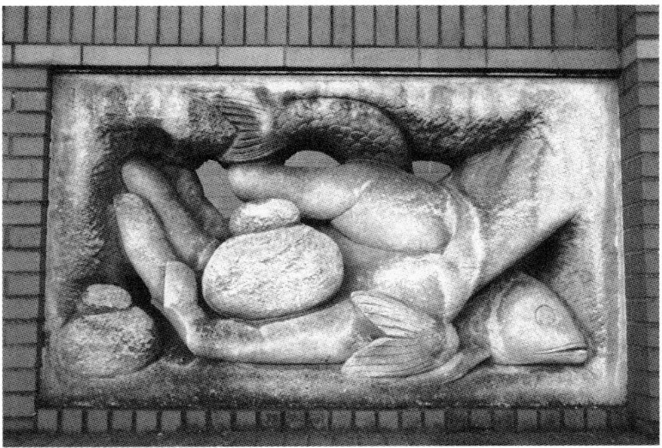

John Skelton with Helen Mary Skelton, *Loaves and Fishes*

Materials/dimensions: stone, 1.1 m high × 1.9 m wide × 40 cm deep
Signature: top left-hand corner: John Skelton (a further line illegible, possibly his daughter Helen Mary's name and a date)
Status: not listed
Condition: good (cleaned 2012)
Commissioned and owned by: Brighthelm Church and Community Centre

The sculpture is set into an open rectangle in the brick wall on the façade of the building. It depicts a hand holding a loaf of bread with intertwining fish above and below, referring to the biblical story of Christ feeding the five thousand with five loaves and two fishes. The sculpture was previously wrongly attributed to Eric Gill, Skelton's uncle, with whom he trained. Helen Skelton worked with her father and took over the workshop on his death.

Sources
Bailey, C., 'Obituary', *The Guardian*, 3 December 1999.
johnskelton.org.uk (accessed 26 October 2010).
Powers, A, 'John Skelton: obituary', *The Independent*, 6 December 1999.

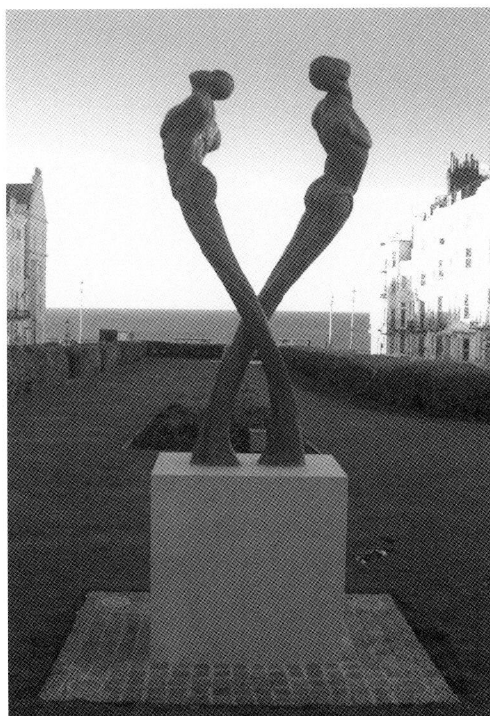

Romany Mark Bruce, *Tay (Aids memorial)*

South entrance to Royal Pavilion Gardens

Indian Memorial Gate
Designer: Thomas Tyrwhitt

Builders: Trollope and Colls
Unveiled: 26 October 1921
Materials/dimensions: Bath stone, 11.28 m high × 6.4 m wide × 5.6 m deep
Inscriptions (carved into wall to left of gate): THIS GATEWAY IS THE GIFT OF INDIA / IN COMMEMORATION OF HER SONS WHO / STRICKEN IN THE GREAT WAR WERE / TENDED IN THE PAVILION IN 1914 AND 1915; (carved into wall to right of gate): DEDICATED TO THE USE OF / THE INHABITANTS OF BRIGHTON BY / H.H. THE MAHARAJA OF PATIALA ON OCTOBER 26TH 1921 / B.N. SOUTHALL / MAYOR

Status: Grade II
Condition: good
Commissioned by: the Government of India
Owner/custodian: Brighton and Hove City Council

The gateway is designed in the sixteenth-century Gujerati style, square in plan and with a domed roof. Side walls and wooden gates close off the road.

The gift of the gateway to the people of Brighton commemorates the period during the First World War when the Royal Pavilion was temporarily transformed into a 724-bed hospital for the treatment of injured Indian troops. In total, 4306 patients passed through the hospital; 53 Hindu and Sikh soldiers who did not survive were cremated at the Chattri,

Thomas Tyrwhitt, *Indian Memorial Gate*

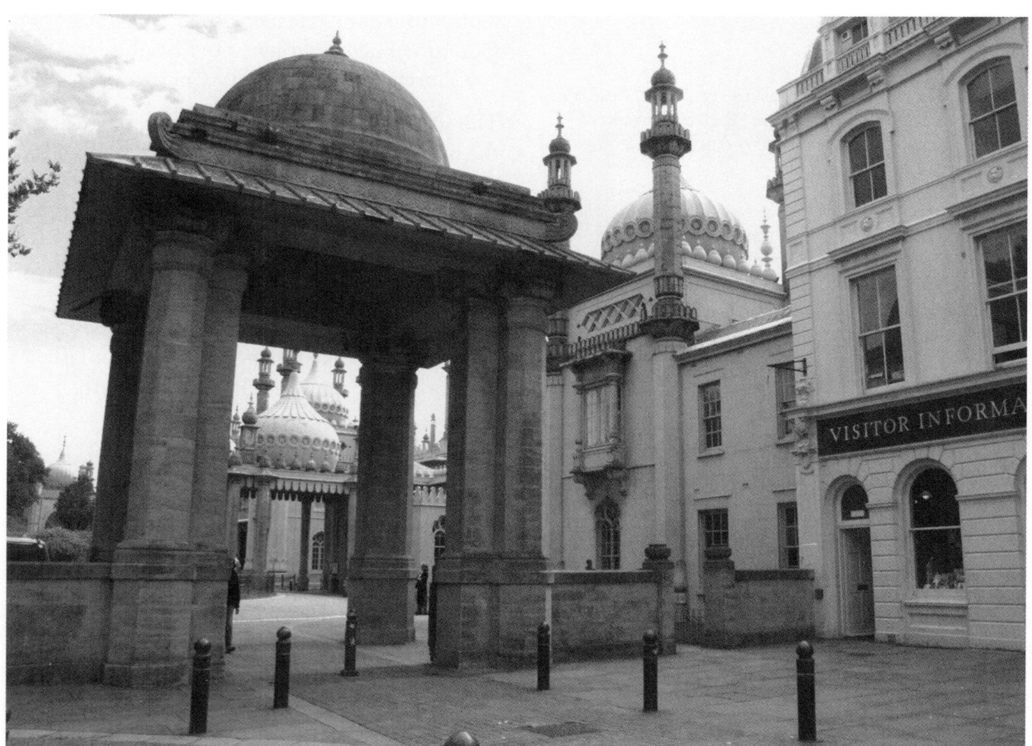

nearby on the downs at Patcham.

The guest of honour at the unveiling ceremony was Sir Bhupendra Singh, Maharajah of Patiala. After removing the Royal Standard, Union Jack and Star of India flags that had covered the gateway, he commented that:

> … the memories which Indian soldiers carried back to India of their treatment in the Royal Pavilion and of the visits of the King Emperor were a great imperial asset in these days of restlessness.[1]

Note
[1] 'Indian memorial gateway: the unveiling ceremony at Brighton', *The Argus*, 26 October 1921.

Other sources
black-history.org.uk/gateway (accessed 31 March 2011).
Brighton Gazette, 7 September 1921; 8 October 1921; 26 October 1921.
Carder (1990), entry 161.
Collins, J., *Dr Brighton's Indian Patients December 1914–January 1916*, Brighton, 1997, p. 30.
John, M., *Bygone Brighton: Volume Two, Events*, Tunbridge Wells, 1980, p. 26.
'Memorial gateway: Indian gratitude to people of Brighton', *The Argus*, 19 October 1921.
Open Air Statues and Memorials JLR6/5/87.
United Kingdom National Inventory of War Memorials (UKNIWM) ref. 16850.

Preston Road

In the rose garden in Preston Park (previously the Aquarium Clock Tower on the sea front)

Spring and Summer
Sculptor: unknown

Executed: 1874
Installed: 1928
Materials/dimensions: cast iron, 1.57 m high × 50 cm wide × 30 cm deep
Status: not listed
Condition: poor (the statues have been subjected to vandalism on several occasions and in October 2007 one was removed for repair. At some point they have been painted

in black and gold, out of keeping with their style and origins)
Owner/custodian: Brighton and Hove City Council

The two young male figures are dressed in short classical tunics, holding fruit and flowers appropriate to the season they represent. Local historian Simon Alexander has noted, 'The sculpture technique is detailed and realistic, with all the proportions accurately observed'.[1]

Originally there were four allegorical statues, two male and two female, which adorned the clock tower of the old Aquarium (opened in 1872), designed in a flamboyant Italianate Gothic style. It had a roofed entrance arch, supported at each corner by twinned columns surmounted by the bronze statues and a central shaft bearing the clock, ending in a small ovoid dome and steeple. It had octagonal tollhouses attached to each side. The clock tower, gateway and tollhouses were added to the aquarium in October 1874. They were demolished in November 1928 during modernisation by the Borough Engineer. The statues of the four seasons were moved Preston Park, but by 1979 there were only two remaining and nothing is known about the whereabouts of 'Autumn' and 'Winter'.

Note
[1] Alexander (nd).

Other sources
Beevers, D. and Roles, J., *A Pictorial History of Brighton*, Derby, 1993, pp. 19 and 23.
Carder (1990), entry 3.
David Cooper (Administrator City Parks), email correspondence, 22 October 2007.
Livingston, H., *Brighton and Hove Pictorial Memories*, Salisbury, 1999, p. 34.
mybrightonandhove.org.uk (accessed 18 September 2007).

Queens Road/West Street

Crossroads of Queens and Dyke Roads with West and North Streets

Jubilee Clock Tower
Architect: John Johnson

Builders: J. and T. Chappell, London and Brighton
Clockmakers: Gillett and Johnston, Croydon
Stonemasons: J.M. Whitehead and Sons Ltd.
Unveiled: 26 June 1888
Materials/dimensions: granite and Portland stone with enamel portraits and gilt copper sphere, 23.16 m high × 2.8 m wide × 2.8 m deep; each statue: 1.4 m high × 50 cm wide × 60 cm deep; each pedestal: 1.6 m high × 50 cm wide × 60 cm deep
Inscription (on plaque underneath portrait of Queen Victoria): THIS CLOCK TOWER / WAS PRESENTED TO THE PEOPLE OF BRIGHTON / IN COMMEMORATION OF THE / JUBILEE YEAR OF THE REIGN OF / HER MAJESTY QUEEN VICTORIA / BY / JAMES WILLING ESQRE. / THE MEMORIAL STONE WAS LAID BY / THE RIGHT HON. SIR ARTHUR OTWAY BART. / ON THE 20TH DAY OF JANUARY 1888 / EDWARD MARTIN MAYOR. / FRANCIS J. TILLSTONE. TOWN CLERK / JOHN JOHNSON ARCHITECT J.T. CHAPPELL BUILDER
Status: Grade II
Condition: good (restored 2002)
Commissioned and funded by: James Willing, local advertising contractor
Owner/custodian: Brighton and Hove City Council

The clock tower is built in a baroque revival style and has a life-sized allegorical statue representing one of the four seasons on each of the four faces of the base. Columns of polished red granite have carved capitals, supporting cornices and pediments with sculpted pairs of dolphins, representing Brighton's coat of arms. Each pair flanks the projecting prow of a boat, on the sides of which are inscribed directions to the sea, Kemptown, Hove and the station. Between the columns above the base are medallions with enamelled portraits of Queen Victoria, facing to the north, her late husband, Prince Albert, facing to the south, her son, Edward Prince of Wales, facing east and his wife, Princess Alexandra, facing west. The upper part of the tower has small coloured panels of enamelled iron with a carved cornice. The four clock faces are made of opal glass and are five feet in diameter; they were originally illuminated by gaslight. Above the clock is a copper cupola, then a 16-foot mast at the base of which is a gilt-copper sphere and weather vane.

The sphere is a time-ball, designed by Magnus Volk and controlled by landline from Greenwich Observatory. The ball rose hydraulically up the mast and fell on the hour. This was intended for the use of captains and

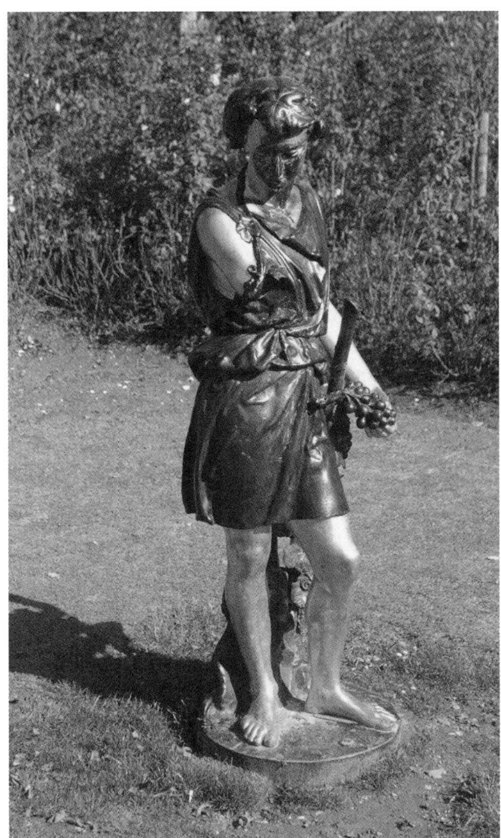

Unknown, *Spring and Summer*

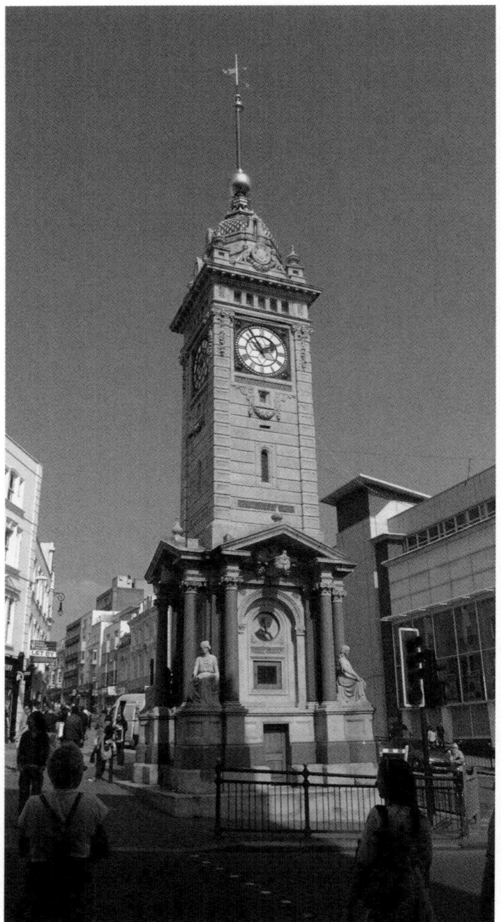

John Johnson, *Jubilee Clock Tower*

seafarers, so that they could synchronise their chronometers with the Greenwich Observatory Clock's one o'clock 'gun'. It functioned only for a few years and was stopped following complaints about the noise. Following restoration in 2002 the mechanism to the top of the tower was re-designed; Frost Brothers of Worthing currently hold the contract for maintaining the clock, but the falling ball mechanism has not recently been in operation.[1]

The clock tower cost £2000 and was gifted to the town by James Willing. It was

commissioned to commemorate Queen Victoria's Golden Jubilee and the foundation stone was laid by Sir Arthur Otway Bart, director of Brighton Railway and of Newhaven Harbour, on 20 January 1888, Willing's seventieth birthday. At the unveiling ceremony six months later, Willing handed the key to the clock tower to Edward Martin, mayor of Brighton, who asserted:

> … the generations yet to come will look upon this glorious memorial with pride and pleasure, and, bringing their minds back to this period, will feel additionally proud to dwell in a town where a gentleman of the magnificence and generosity of Mr Willing lived in the 19th century.[2]

Commemorative medals were handed out to spectators.[3] The clock tower is described by Nikolaus Pevsner as 'worthless', but the people of Brighton have retained a nostalgic affection for the clock and it represents the centre of modern Brighton.[4]

Notes
[1] frostbros.com/Contract/Jubilee (accessed 25 October 2010). [2] 'The Opening of the Jubilee clock tower', *Brighton Gazette and Sussex Telegraph*, 30 June 1888, p. 5. [3] The medals had, on one side: 'a representation of the tower, with the inscription "Willing's Clock Tower". On the reverse, encircled by "Presented to the town of Brighton 1887" was a crown and quartered shield bearing the emblems of England, Scotland, Ireland and Wales'. *Brighton Herald*, 30 June 1888, pp. 4–5. [4] Nairn and Pevsner (1965), p. 445.

Other sources
Arscott (2000), pp. 61 and 90.
Brighton Remembered: a Century of Pictures from the Archives of the Argus, Derby, 2002, p. 144.
Malcolm (1980), p. 58.
'Unveiling of the North street clock tower', *Brighton Herald*, 30 June 1888, p. 4.

Stanmer Park

At entrance to the Great Wood, visible to left of road to Stanmer House

The Frankland Memorial
Sculptor: unknown

Installed: June 1775
Materials/dimensions: Coade stone, 4.09 m high × 1.44 m wide × 1.44 m deep
Inscriptions (inscribed in roundel to front): TO THE / MEMORY OF FREDERICK FRANKLAND / E.S.O. MP. DIED MARCH / THE 8TH 1768 AGED 73 / THIS MONUMENT IS ERECTED / BY HIS EVER / AFFECTIONATE / AND MOST TRULY GRATEFUL / SON AND DAUGHTER / THOMAS LORD PELHAM / AND ANN HIS WIFE / JUNE 1775; (inscribed on base to front): HIC VITAM VIRTUS PIETASQUE (ORNAVIE?) ONESTAM JUSTA FIDE IN CHRISTO (PP ÆNUM?) DIGNUS (HAET?) / TP
Status: Grade II
Condition: fair (surface condition poor with pitting and erosion of the stonework. Latin inscription on base very difficult to decipher. Heads of tortoises on base broken off)
Commissioned by: Lord Thomas and Lady Ann Pelham, 1st Earl and Countess of Chichester
Owner/custodian: Brighton and Hove City Council

This classical-style large funerary urn is mounted on a column that is slightly concave and triangular in plan. It is decorated with a rope moulding, concave fluting, a swelling pattern of palm leaves and then roundels in a rectangular panel on each face. Two of the roundels enclose Classical figures and the third the inscription. The whole rests upon three tortoises standing upon a base with a Latin inscription and further decorative moulding.

Frederick Meinhardt Frankland was the Governor of the Bank of England. He was the son of Sir Thomas Frankland, 2nd Baronet Frankland and Elizabeth Russell. His daughter,

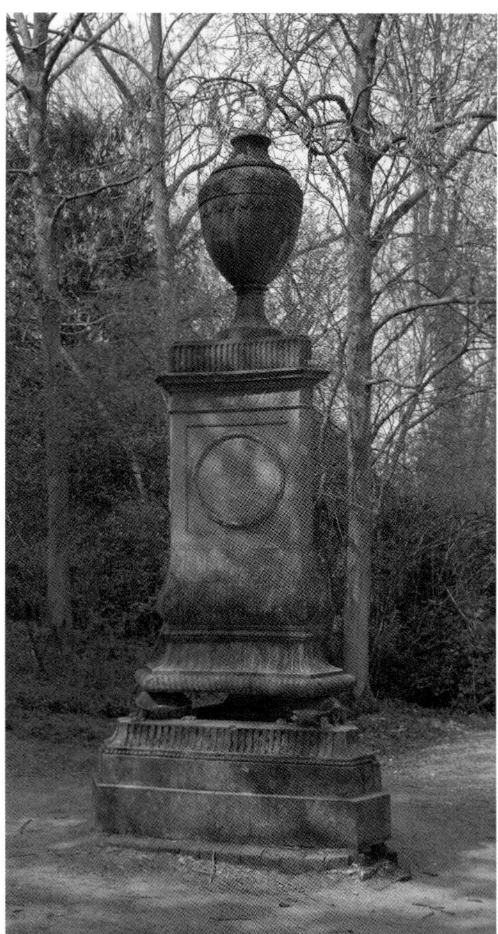

Unknown, *The Frankland Memorial*

Ann Frankland (c. 1735–5 March 1813), married Sir Thomas Pelham (1728–1805), 1st Earl of Chichester, owner of the Palladian style Stanmer House, designed by Nicholas Dubois, and the surrounding estate, where the monument to her father is sited.

Sources
Carder (1990), entry 175b.
Nairn and Pevsner (1965), p. 461.

Stanmer Park

In bushes at side of the Ranger's Yard; moved 1940 (formerly in vestibule of the Royal Pavilion and Brighton Museum and Art Gallery)

Captain Pechell Memorial Statue
Sculptor: Matthew Noble

Unveiled: February 1859
Materials/dimensions: Caen stone, 3.23 m high
Inscription: none visible on the figure; the
   pedestal on which it stood in the Royal
   Pavilion held the inscription: WILLIAM
   HENRY CECIL GEORGE PECHELL / CAPTAIN IN
   HER MAJESTY'S 77TH REGIMENT / ONLY SON
   OF VICE-ADMIRAL SIR GEORGE BROOKE
   PECHELL BARONET / M.P. FOR THE BOROUGH
   OF BRIGHTON / KILLED BEFORE SEBASTOPOL
   SEPTEMBER 3 1855 / IN THE NOBLE
   PERFORMANCE OF HIS DUTY WHILE LEADING
   HIS MEN IN / FRONT OF THE ADVANCED
   TRENCH NEAR THE REDAN / AGED 25 YEARS /
   ERECTED BY PUBLIC SUBSCRIPTION[1]
Status: not listed
Condition: very poor (badly weatherworn,
   eroded and covered in moss. Statue broken
   in several places; the head is broken off and
   is now missing. The hat (shako) that was in
   the figure's left hand is also broken off and
   discarded on the ground. Left arm broken
   off above the elbow. Some holes on the
   figure where the stone has been chipped
   away)
Commissioned by: Pechell Testimonial
   Committee
Funded by: Public Memorial Fund
Owner/custodian: Brighton and Hove City
   Council

The figure of Captain Pechell is dressed in the uniform of the Middlesex Regiment, with the right arm, that once held a sword, pointing forward, upwards and to the right. The left arm and hand were resting downwards holding Pechell's shako. The statue was carved, with the

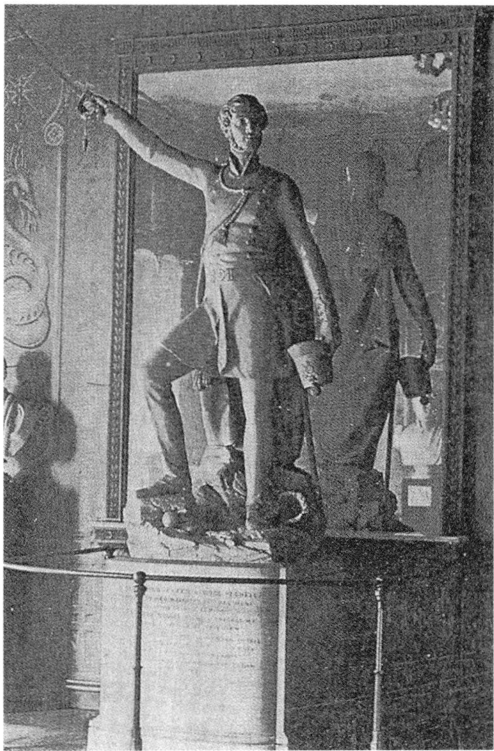

Matthew Noble, *Captain Pechell Memorial Statue*

exception of the right arm, from a single block of stone and represents Pechell in the act of leading his men in a charge.

Captain William Henry Cecil George Pechell was the only son of Vice-Admiral Sir George Brooke Pechell, Bart. and the Hon. Lady Katherine Annabella Pechell. George Brooke Pechell was MP for Brighton for over 25 years and the family had a particularly strong bond with the town. William Pechell was born at Castle Goring, Worthing, the family home, in May 1830. He was educated at Harrow and Sandhurst, entering the army in August 1848.[2] He was appointed a Captain in the 77th Regiment, fighting in the Crimea. After the assault on the Redan, Sebastopol, in June 1855, Pechell had refused an opportunity presented personally by Prince Albert to join the Royal Guards, which would have been 'the means of expediting his return to England'.[3] Pechell was killed before Sebastopol on 3 September 1855. He was buried temporarily by his regiment and his body was later returned to England in December of that year.

A well-attended public meeting was held in Brighton on Monday 24 September 1855 to determine the type of memorial suitable to commemorate Pechell. Laurence Peel, the proposer of the memorial, referring to the recent fall of Sebastopol, said that this good news had been unable to alleviate the pervasive sense of mourning in the town. The motion for a memorial was carried unanimously.

Matthew Noble, the London sculptor, was selected to make the statue. In various Pechell family documents the sculptor is given as Thorneycroft, but the Pavilion Committee minutes in 1859 confirm him as Noble, as do all newspaper articles, including the *London Illustrated News*. The two sculptors shared a studio during the time when the statue was constructed, which is possibly why there is some confusion.

There were suggestions that the memorial should be placed in the chancel of the Parish Church of Brighton (St Nicholas), near to the memorial to the Duke of Wellington.[5] On completion in February 1859, however, the statue was placed 'amongst the worthies' in the vestibule of the Royal Pavilion, which gave rise to criticism:

> The memorial statue of the son of our veteran Representative has arrived in Brighton, and occupies a place in the vestibule of the Pavilion. A most unfit receptacle, by the way, for such a work of art, both because it cannot be seen except to the greatest disadvantage, and because the Pavilion is an unsafe, and, therefore, improper place, in which to keep valuables of any kind … Some day, when it can be seen, Brighton will be proud of this statue.[6]

The statue was moved to the entrance hall of Brighton Museum in November 1914 and in 1930 to the southern end of the permanent art gallery; further discussions took place in 1930 about moving it to an outdoor position.[7] It was subsequently moved to Stanmer Park in 1940.[8] There were plans to take it to the Middlesex Regiment Museum, but these failed due to the difficulty of transporting a statue of such size and weight. It is now lodged in undergrowth in the Ranger's Yard at the park and has been severely damaged over the years by weather and several acts of vandalism.

Notes
[1] *Illustrated London News*, 19 February 1859.
[2] *Brighton Guardian*, 12 September 1855.
[3] *Brighton Herald*, 15 September 1855, p. 3.
[4] 'Extracts from the public journals relating to the death of Captain Pechell', *Castle Goring Archives 1547–1938*, West Sussex Records Office, Chichester.
[5] *Brighton Herald*, 29 September 1855, p. 3.
[6] 'Statue arrives in Brighton', *Brighton Herald*, 19 February 1859, p. 2. [7] *Brighton Pavilion and Library Committee Minutes*, 10 April 1930.
[8] *Brighton Museum Accounts*, 9 July 1940.

Other sources
'Fund to close January 1856', *Brighton Herald*, 5 January 1856.
'Town council accepts memorial', *Brighton Herald*, 8 January 1859.

Steine Gardens

Southeast corner of gardens, opposite York Buildings (originally in front of Carlisle House, near the Royal Pavilion; moved 1984 when the Pavilion grounds were remodelled)

Statue of Sir John Cordy Burrows
Sculptor: Edward Bowring Stephens

Unveiled: 14 February 1878
Materials/dimensions: statue: Sicilian marble on grey granite base approx. 2.4 m high × 70 cm wide × 70 cm deep; plinth 2.4 m high × 1.3 m wide × 1.3 m deep
Signature (on right-hand side of base): E.B. STEPHENS / 1878

Inscription (on front of plinth): SIR JOHN CORDY BURROWS KNT / THREE TIMES MAYOR OF BRIGHTON / ERECTED BY HIS FELLOW TOWNSMEN / AS A MARK OF THEIR ESTEEM / 1878
Status: Grade II
Condition: good (some discoloration and blackening of the surface)
Owner/custodian: Brighton and Hove City Council

John Cordy Burrows is depicted in contemporary dress, over which is his mayoral robe and chain of office. In a fairly informal

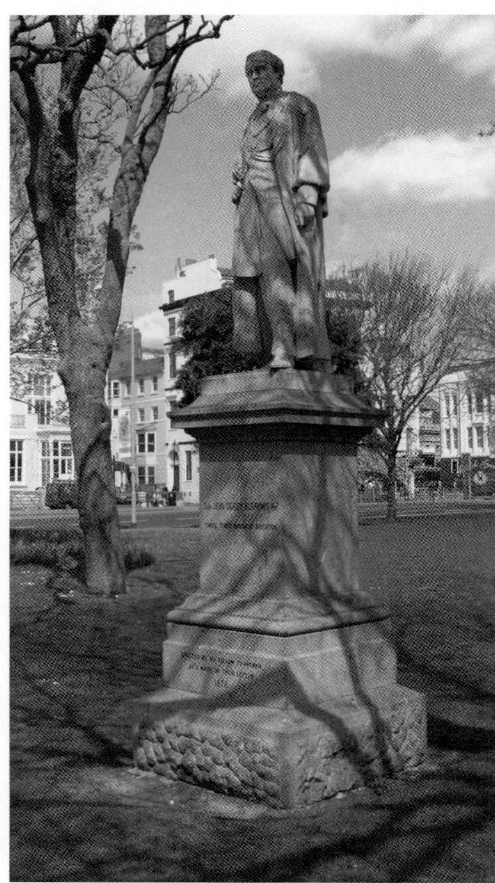

Edward Bowring Stephens, *Statue of Sir John Cordy Burrows*

pose, his right hand is placed on his hip, with the left resting at his side.

The cost of the statue, raised by a Memorial Committee, was over £700. It attracted favourable comment in the local press, which described it as, '[standing] out in its virgin whiteness in the damp and hazy atmosphere.'[1] The unveiling was accompanied by a specially composed ode, performed by members of the Brighton Sacred Harmonic Society who had also carried out Sir John's wish that they should sing over his grave.

Sir John had lived and practised in Brighton since 1837, having trained as a surgeon in Suffolk. He was elected an alderman to the first Borough Council in 1854, going on to serve as Mayor in 1857, 1858 and 1871. He was also responsible for the selecting the town's motto, *In Deo Fidemus*. The statue commemorates Sir John's many acts of philanthropy in the town; at the unveiling ceremony, Alderman Mayall listed his connections with the Literary and Scientific Institution (which he co-founded in 1841); the Working Men's Institute, the Steine Fountain (the plans for which he initiated); the Museum, Library and Picture Gallery, the Aquarium, the Children's Hospital and the 'great drainage scheme.'[2]

Notes
[1] *Brighton Gazette*, 14 February 1878. [2] *Brighton Herald*, 16 February 1878.

Other source
Carder (1990), entry 114d.

Victoria Fountain

Sculptor: William Pepper (the elder)

Architect: Amon Henry Wilds

Builders: Williams and Yearsley

Foundry: Eagle Foundry, Gloucester Road, Brighton
Unveiled: 24 May 1846
Materials/dimensions: fountain: cast iron, painted green with gilded decoration, on a

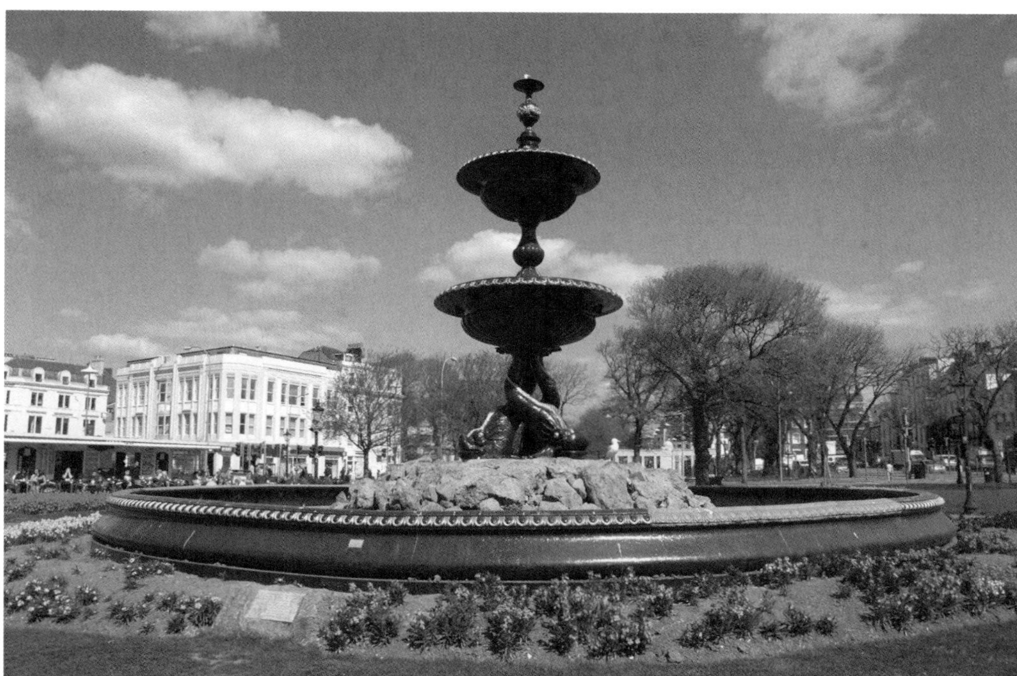

William Pepper, *Victoria Fountain*

base of Sarsen stones 9.7 m high × approx. 14.5 m diam.
Signature (base of basin, south side): A.H. WILDS / ARCHITECT
Inscriptions (plaque on south side): TO COMMEMORATE THE VISIT / OF / H.R.H. THE PRINCE OF WALES / PRESIDENT OF THE FOUNTAIN / SOCIETY / ON 25TH MAY 1995 / TO MARK THE RESTORATION OF / THE VICTORIA FOUNTAIN / WITH FUNDING BY BRIGHTON / COUNCIL / AND GRANT AID FROM / ENGLISH HERITAGE; (plaque on basin, south side): VICTORIA FOUNTAIN / RESTORED 1994 / BY DOROTHEA LTD / BUXTON DERBYSHIRE / Tel 0298 79121; (plaque on front of base, north side): FOUNTAIN INTERNATIONAL / PROMOTING THE HEALING / OF PEOPLE AND / COMMUNITIES / USING SPIRITUAL / AND EARTH ENERGIES. / FOUNDED HERE ON / ST. MICHAELS DAY 1981

Status: Grade II
Condition: good (the third basin and column were reinstated following restoration in 1990)
Commissioned by: John Cordy Burrows
Funded by: public subscription
Owner/custodian: Brighton and Hove City Council

The fountain has a cast-iron pool with egg-and-dart mouldings to the rim, in which stands a base of Sarsen stones found by workmen in the Steine in 1823. These support three intertwined hollow dolphins, with pumps inside, surmounted by two cast-iron basins, separated by a vase-shaped column, a motif also used as a finial at the top of the fountain.

After the Brighton Town Commissioners rejected the idea of erecting a fountain to honour the new Queen's accession in 1837, John Cordy Burrows placed a private commission with Amon Henry Wilds, who was responsible for much of Brighton and Hove's finest Regency architecture. With the aid of a public subscription of £1100, augmented by the proceeds of a night at the theatre, a concert at the Town Hall and a Grand Fancy Bazaar, the fountain was built in 1846 and unveiled to mark the Queen's 27th birthday.[1]

The inauguration of the fountain was marked with great ceremony. The proceedings were launched by a royal salute fired from the Pier Head at noon, the same time as the fountain was turned on. Specially commissioned music, including *Fountain Quadrilles* by Charles Coote, Burrows' son-in-law, was played. Local shops and businesses closed at 3 pm for the celebratory Fête Champêtre in the Royal Gardens, which concluded with fireworks.[2] The fountain quickly became a local landmark with coloured prints available at local booksellers.[3]

The surrounding area of the Steine was landscaped into public gardens for the erection of the fountain. The Sarsen stones, blocks of grey sandstone possibly deposited by glaciers, incorporated into the base of the fountain, were dug up by workmen digging a trench for a new gas main and it is thought that the name Steine, from the Scandinavian for 'place of stones', derives from their discovery.[4] The water from the fountain can be thrown up to between 20 and 30 feet and the reservoir at the bottom was originally filled with water lilies and goldfish. The dolphin figures were subsequently adopted as the Brighton Coat of Arms.

Prince Charles' visit to unveil the plaque to commemorate the restoration of the fountain in 1995 provoked a security alert when it became the focus of a protest about live animal exports from nearby Shoreham Harbour.[5]

Notes
[1] Carder (1990), entry 114e. [2] *Brighton Gazette*, 28 May 1846. [3] Ford (1981), p. 37. [4] School of Architecture (1987), p. 40. [5] *The Argus*, 25 May 1995.

Other source
Brighton Herald, 23 May 1846.

War Memorial

Architects: John W. Simpson and C. Kerridge Jnr

Letter carver: H. Cashmore

Unveiled: 7 October 1922
Materials/dimensions: main colonnaded altar: Portland stone, 4 m high × 3.6 m wide × 2.2 m deep; side colonnade: Portland stone, 3.2 m high × 11 m wide × 2.2 m deep; inscribed pillars: Portland stone faced with bronze, 2.3 m high × 80 cm wide × 80 cm deep
Inscriptions (back of central altar, facing north, in raised letters): WE CHEERED YOU FORTH NOBLE AND KIND AND BRAVE / UNDER YOUR COUNTRYS TRIUMPHING FLAG YOU FELL / IT FLOATS TRUE HEARTS OVER EACH QUIET GRAVE / BRAVE AND NOBLE AND KIND HAIL AND FAREWELL; (above columns, around top of south face, in carved letters): A GOOD LIFE HATH / ITS NUMBER OF DAYS / BUT A GOOD NAME SHALL / CONTINUE FOR EVER; (bronze plaque, back of the central altar, facing north): THIS MEMORIAL IS DEDICATED / TO THE / SERVICE MEN AND WOMEN / OF BRIGHTON / WHO GAVE THEIR LIVES IN / THE FIRST WORLD WAR 1914–1918 / THE SECOND WORLD WAR 1939–1945 / AND SUBSEQUENT CAMPAIGNS / THEIR NAMES ARE RECORDED / IN THE BOOK OF REMEMBRANCE / IN THE / PARISH CHURCH OF ST PETER
Status: Grade II
Condition: good
Owner/custodian: Brighton and Hove City Council

The memorial is designed in the form of a Roman water garden, with a large pool, to reflect the architecture, and a fountain in the centre. The water represents the Royal Navy and Merchant Navy and the memorial gardens represent the British Army and Royal Air Force.[1] At one end is a colonnade of four-sided stone columns in a stepped U-shape. At the centre is a semi-enclosed temple formed by a tall rectangular panel of stone filling the space between two columns and a roof surmounted by a small stone dome. Theatres of the First World War are carved in the stone panel facing the pond and on the inside of the temple space there is a metal inscription plaque and a stone altar table. The upper part of the dedicatory panel has a wreath and festoon of laurels.

In 1920 the Peace Celebration and War Memorial Sub-Committee of Brighton Council requested the Mayor to call a public meeting to decide on a permanent memorial and to invite subscriptions. Suggestions for a form of memorialisation that had a more practical application, such as an orphanage, had been rejected on the grounds that they '… did not meet the most essential requirement of a war memorial i.e. embodying in a permanent form the sacrifices of those who have fallen or suffered on account of the war'.[2] The council approached John W. Simpson PRIBA, requesting a design for a memorial that would cost around £5000 (later reduced to £3000). Another local architect, John L. Denman, later responsible for the designs of the Pylons marking the extension of the borough of Brighton, submitted his own plans for a memorial, which the council felt unable to adopt due to the projected cost. The plans and sketches for Simpson's scheme were put on public display in the Art Gallery and favourably received, particularly in light of the fact that the architect was an old Brightonian.[3] In 1921 the Appeal Sub-Committee sent copies of the appeal for subscriptions to '… private residents, to business firms and to professional people practising in the Borough'.[4] A notice board with a collecting box was placed at the site on the Old Steine, on which was recorded the weekly total collected. By the end of that year, an outline model was erected on the site, the Superintendant of Parks and Gardens had proposed a layout for the surrounding rose garden and the Borough Surveyor had been requested to supervise the removal of Sir

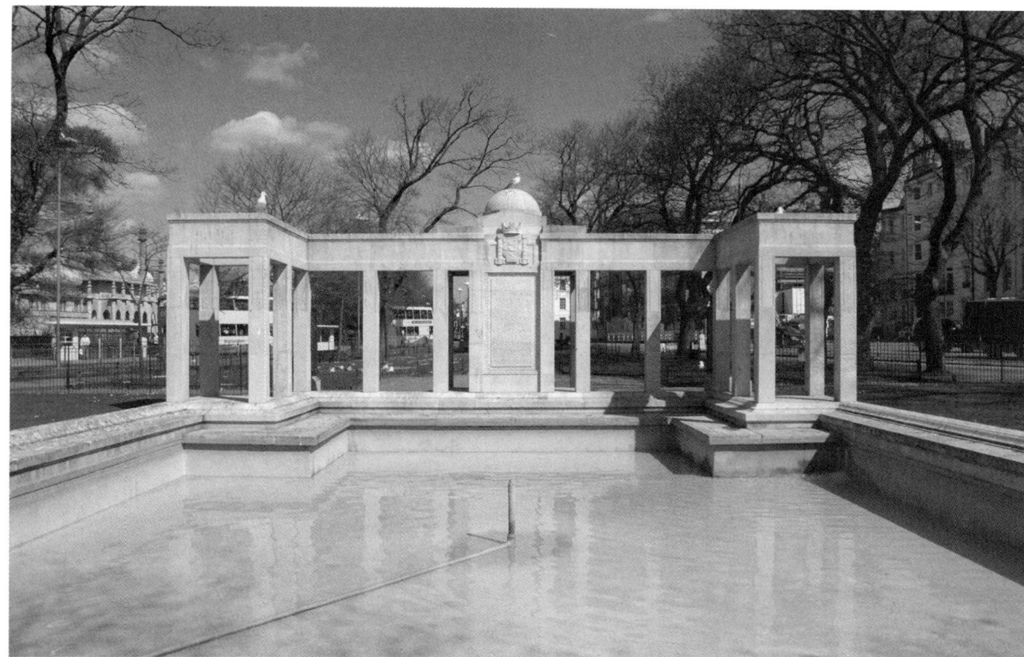

John W. Simpson and C. Kerridge Jnr, *War Memorial*

Francis Chantrey's statue of George IV, which originally stood on the site, to its present position near the north Gate of the Royal Pavilion.[5] The Sub-Committee's concern for the care and maintenance of the memorial, including the best ways to clean and light it and regulations concerning the laying of flowers and wreaths, continued until 1925.

The memorial was unveiled in 1922 by Admiral Earl Beatty and contains the names of 2597 men and 3 women from Brighton who lost their lives in the First World War. Facing the war memorial, at the northern end of the Steine is a plain pink granite obelisk, dated 1888, commemorating officers and men who fell in the Egyptian campaigns.[6] In 2010 a rough-hewn pink granite slab was placed behind the obelisk dedicated to all the citizens of Brighton, Hove and Portslade who have died in conflicts and on peacekeeping missions since the Second World War.

Notes
[1] Cooper, C., 'Lest we forget', *City News*, August–September 2004, p. 10. [2] Peace Celebration and War Memorial Sub-Committee Minute Book DB/B43/1, East Sussex Record Office, p. 26. [3] *The Argus*, 5 November 1921. [4] War Memorial Sub-Committee Minute Book DB/B43/2, East Sussex Record Office, np. [5] Ibid. [6] Carder (1990), entry 114f.

Other sources
A Pictorial and Descriptive Guide to Brighton and Hove, p. 61.
Brighton Herald, 15 October 1921.
Open Air Statues and Memorials, JLR6/5/87, Brighton History Centre.
UKNIWM ref. 16849.
'War memorial for Brighton', *The Argus*, 24 September 1921.

Western Road

CITY CENTRE

In front of Churchill Square Shopping Centre

Twins

Sculptor: Charlie Hooker

Unveiled: 3 September 1998
Materials/dimensions: carved and polished granite, etched bronze, cut and polished glass and audio-electronics. Orbs: 2 m diam; plinth and step seats: 2 m high × 2 m wide × 2.5 m deep. The granite used is of four colours: Imperial Green, representing Spring; Golden Summer, representing Summer; Imperial Red, representing Autumn; Bethel White, representing Winter
Signature (inscribed on bronze section of west facing quartile (Winter) westerly orb): Charlie Hooker 1998
Inscription (inscribed on bronze section of north facing quartile (Winter), westerly orb): TWINS / This sculpture uses solar energy to change / the volume levels of the sounds which / emanate from it. As the sun moves across / the sky it shines on different surfaces of the / sculpture, triggering music from two internal / sound systems. A surface is quiet when in / shadow and louder when in bright sunlight. / Each bronze panel shows a graph on which are / the sunshine recordings made at Churchill / Square during the 1997–98 building works. / (Similar recordings are taken daily by / weather forecasters across the world). / The graphs have been digitally translated / into music to produce twelve sound pieces, / one for each month of the year. / Each graph charts the sun's trajectory / during the various seasons and the types of / granite used in the sculpture represent the / four seasons. Autumn and Winter form one / 'twin', Spring and Summer the other.
Status: not listed

Charlie Hooker, *Twins*

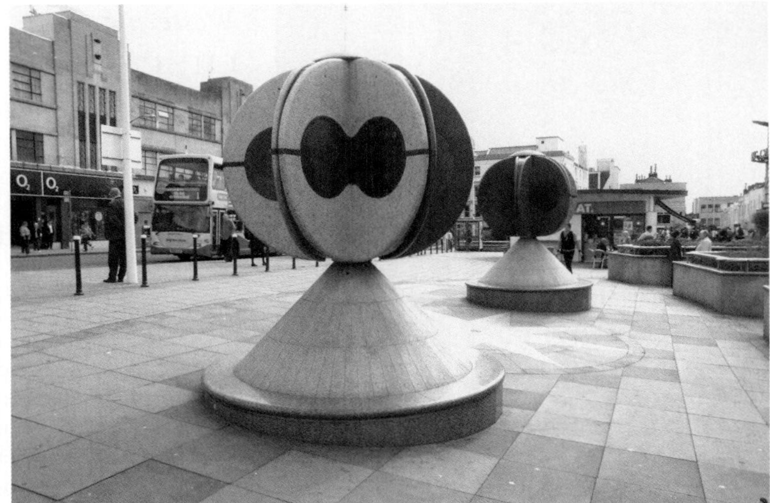

Condition: good (some minor graffiti; lighting and sound technology poorly maintained)
Commissioned and owned by: Standard Life Insurance Company

Twins is a site-specific and interactive work, formed of two sets of semicircular granite discs, sitting on cone-shaped bases with seating underneath. The centre of each face of the sculptures is formed by an etched bronze plaque. They result from the sculptor's ongoing interest in fusing art and science, particularly through the medium of meteorology. The passage of the sun across the sky triggers sounds that emanate from the sculptures, changing according to the time of day and the seasons. Hooker recorded sounds around Brighton for the year prior to the work being completed; they are stored electronically in circuits inside the sculptures and start to play as the sun comes out. The images on the plaques that form the surfaces are derived from Meteorological Office weather graphs recorded during the year the sculpture was being made and scanned into a computer. The sounds given out by the sculpture are a mixture of the Brighton sounds sampled by computer technology, governed by these graphs. They can be heard by people sitting close to the sculpture on the plinth seating. In the evening beams of light from inside each orb should meet across the distance of 5 m between each plinth.

The twinned pieces mark the entrance to a shopping mall, created by the remodelling of Churchill Square that entailed the demolition of William Mitchell's *Spirit of Brighton* that had stood in the plaza. The provisional budget for the project was £75,000, with the final cost close to £100,000. The local newspaper initiated a campaign against the pieces, which it nicknamed 'the orbs', and reported a rather bemused public reaction to their unveiling.[1]

Note
[1] Adams, M., 'Churchill Square's whispering sculptures', *The Argus* 2 September 1998.

Other sources
The Argus, 12 August 1997; 20 August 1997; 18 July 1998; 14 August 1998; 20 August 1998; 4 September 1998.
Brighton & Hove Leader, 28 August 1998.
Brighton & Hove News, August/September 1997; October 1998.
Charlie Hooker personal archive, Heathfield, 19 September 2007.
The Latest, Issue 30, nd, p. 6.
Mesquita, M. dos Santos, 'When art and science fuse well', *AGU Atmospheric Sciences*, vol. 1, 22 October 2007, pp. 1–3.
% For Art News, May 1997.

Station Road

Inside Buxted Park Estate, St Margaret the Queen Church, just inside gate

War Memorial

Architect: John Leopold Denman

Unveiled: c. 1920s
Materials/dimensions: top section including carvings: stone, 2.5 m high × 25 cm wide × 18 cm deep; base of obelisk: stone, 1.15 m high × 70 cm wide × 80 cm deep
Inscriptions (north face, base of obelisk): TO THE GLORY OF GOD / & IN GRATEFUL MEMORY / OF THOSE FROM / BUXTED CIVIL PARISH / WHO FELL IN THE GREAT / WAR FOR FREEDOM TRUTH / AND RIGHTEOUSNESS / 1914–1918 / "Their name liveth" / LIKEWISE THOSE WHO FELL / IN THE WORLD WAR / 1939–1945; (south face): ST MARGARETS (followed by the names of the fallen); (west face): HIGH HURSTWOOD (followed by the names of the fallen); (east face) ST MARY'S (followed by the names of the fallen); (around top of base): GREATER LOVE HATH NO / MAN THAN THIS THAT / A MAN LAY DOWN HIS / LIFE FOR HIS FRIENDS
Status: Grade II (listed 2007)
Condition: good (replacement parts on west and north faces; small chips and cracks remain on base)
Owner/custodian: St Margaret the Queen Church

The memorial has a square chamfered plinth, bearing the names of the fallen in two World Wars on each side, resting on a two-tier base with square blocks at each corner. From this rises a decorated lantern cross; at the top of the shaft are two carved figures of angels, each holding a shield to its chest. These support the lantern with carved reliefs depicting, on the west face St Margaret (canonised in 1250, around the time that the church was built) and

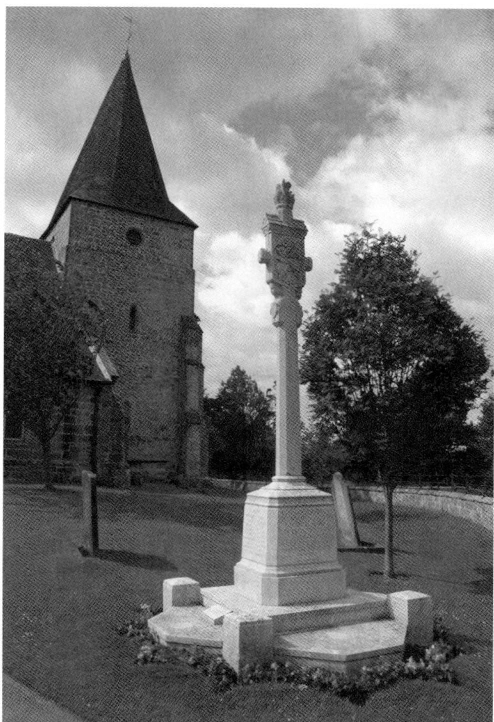

J.L. Denman, *War Memorial*

two children and on the north face St George killing the dragon. At the top of the shaft, above the lantern, sits a pelican feeding her young with her own blood, the symbol of sacrifice epitomised by the Passion of Christ.

The listing details describe the memorial as:

of unusual design, with detailed carvings delicately and skillfully executed. Prominently placed in the churchyard, it has group value with the Grade I listed Church of St Margaret the Queen, which in turn lies within the Grade II* registered Buxted Park.[1]

Note
[1] britishlistedbuildings.co.uk/england/east+sussex/ buxted (accessed 14 April 2011).

Other source
bhdchurches.org.uk/history (accessed 18 April 2011).

Fletching Common Road

Along path to right from Lane End Common car park

Meridian Marker

Stonemason: Percival Bridgman, Eastgate Wharf, Lewes

Unveiled: 10 October 1953
Materials/dimensions: stone, 1.3 m high × 60 cm wide × 60 cm deep
Inscriptions (to south face of pedestal): 1953 / THIS STONE / HAS BEEN ERECTED / ON / LANE END COMMON / IN THE / PARISH OF CHAIL / EY / NEAR THE / CENTRE OF SUSSEX / 159 FEET / ABOVE SEA LEVEL TO MARK THE POINT / WHERE THE / GREENWICH MERIDIAN / CROSSES THE MANOR / OF BALNETH
Status: not listed
Condition: good (but carved graffiti on the stone hemisphere)
Commissioned by: Ivor Grantham Esq. Lord of the Manor of Balneth (now known as Balneath)
Owner/custodian: Lewes District Council

The marker takes the form of a stone hemisphere atop a square inscribed pedestal. Through it runs a copper inset line marking the trajectory of the Greenwich meridian. When it was first erected, in the year of the coronation of Queen Elizabeth II, the monument stood in open land, but in the subsequent decades trees and shrubs have grown up around it, making it difficult to find. When the marker was rededicated in 2000 a decision was taken not to clean the stone, but to accept the weathering that had taken place.

At the original unveiling ceremony two local schoolchildren were chosen to walk down a whitewashed line indicating the meridian, while the Lord of the Manor stood with one foot in each hemisphere. After removing the Union

Jack that covered the stone, they were each given a silver crown and promised the Lord that they would return in 2000 to rededicate the marker. When Eric Taylor succeeded as Lord in 1995 he managed to trace the children and on 10 October 2000 the 1953 ceremony was re-enacted and the marker rededicated to the Queen.[1]

Note
[1] Dolan, G., TheGreenwichMeridian.org (accessed 14 April 2011).

Other source
waymarking.com/waymarks/ (accessed 14 April 2011).

A27 (Lewes Road)

Charleston farmhouse, near Firle

The painter Vanessa Bell first took out the lease on the farmhouse at Charleston in 1916, partly to be near her sister Virginia Woolf who rented houses at nearby Asheham and later Rodmell, but more urgently to provide work on the land for her lover Duncan Grant and his friend David Garnett, both conscientious objectors during the First World War. Vanessa's three children, Julian, Quentin and Angelica, lived there for a short while before returning to London after the war, when Charleston became mainly a holiday home. Many of the Bloomsbury group of writers and artists were regular visitors there. Bell and Grant had begun to decorate the interiors of the house as soon as they moved in, but when a longer lease was negotiated in the 1920s, more thoroughgoing alterations were undertaken. The layout of the garden was designed by the artist and critic Roger Fry around 1917 and included a pond in front of the house and a walled garden to one side. The house was taken over by the Charleston Trust in 1980 and extensively restored, both inside and out, and opened to the public. The house is Grade 2* listed. The garden was returned to Fry's original layout in 1986 by Peter Shepheard. It now contains a number of sculptures by Vanessa Bell's second son, Quentin, who first visited the house at the age of six.

In the garden, on the far side of the pond, facing the house

Leaning Female Figure

Sculptor: Quentin Bell

Constructed: 1954
Materials/dimensions: cement fondu; 2 m high × 55 cm wide × 56 cm deep
Condition: Good (leaning rectified by Cliveden Conservation workshop 1997)
Owner/custodian: Charleston Trust (gift of Vanessa Bell from the estate of Duncan Grant 1981)

This classically draped female figure, clearly influenced by ancient Greek sculptures, appears to rise from the reeds at the edge of the pond. Bell wrote 'She has no name … but has been mistaken for a ghost by at least one impressionable guest.'[1]

In the garden, by the pond, to the left of the house (original in the stable block)

Levitating Lady

Sculptor: Quentin Bell (facsimile made 2004)

Constructed: 2004 (original c. 1937)
Materials/dimensions: fibreglass; 70 cm high × 2.4 m wide × 36 cm deep
Condition: Good
Owner/custodian: Charleston Trust (gift of Quentin Bell)

This female figure, her body and face covered by drapery, lies horizontally, supported only by her long hair, which is anchored to a small brick plinth. This is an exact replica, made from the same material, as the original, which is currently in storage. Bell vividly remembered a performance by John Maskelyne and George Cooke, pioneer illusionists, that he witnessed as a child. Maskelyne's female assistant lay down and was covered with a sheet, then was made to levitate and apparently disappear.[2] Much later in life, levitation became a recurring theme in Bell's work.[3] One interpretation, known as 'The Dreamer', stood for many years (until it was displaced by a building extension) next to the Edward Boyle Library at the University of Leeds, where Bell was Professor of Fine Art 1962–67.

In the garden, at the end of the path leading away from the house to the orchard

Pomona the Lemon Gatherer

Sculptor: Quentin Bell

Constructed: 1954
Materials/dimensions: cement fondu with glazed terracotta apples; 2 m high × 50 cm wide × 58 cm deep
Condition: Good (some cracking and loss of cement from headdress due to inner rusting of ferrous armature[4])
Owner/custodian: Charleston Trust (gift of Vanessa Bell from the estate of Duncan Grant 1981)

Bell's classically dressed matron stands supporting a bucket full of apples on her head. In its monumentality, but also Bell's trademark playfulness, the statue is a good illustration of a whole range of sculptural influences, listed by Simon Watney as:

> … second century Greek Tanagra figures … Staffordshire fairings . ..the work of the sixteenth-century French sculptor Germain Pilon, especially his monumental standing female caryatids … [and] French eighteenth-century terracotta work, in particular the figures and reliefs of Clodion.[5]

Pomona was the ancient Roman goddess of fruit trees, gardens and orchards, particularly

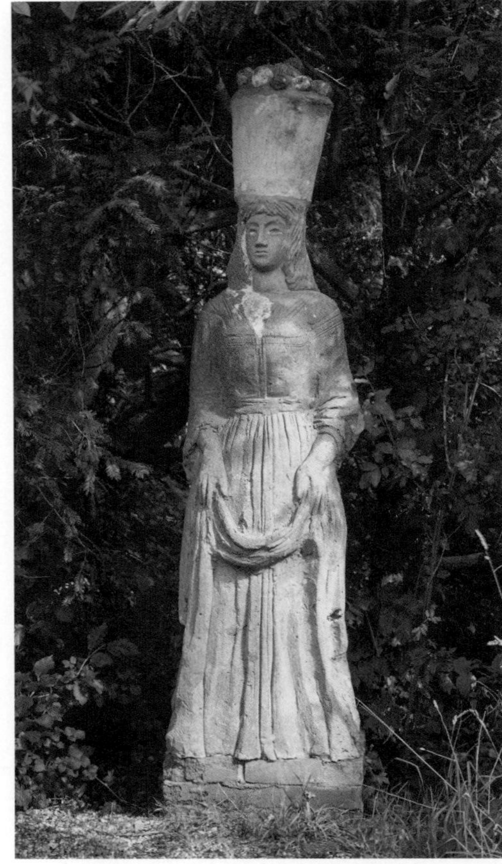

Quentin Bell, *Pomona the Lemon Gatherer*

associated with the apples that Bell has depicted her carrying, although in a wider sense, she symbolised fruitful abundance. David Mellor has suggested that, in his title for the piece, Bell was thinking of Duncan Grant's painting 'The Lemon Gatherers' (1910, currently in the Tate Gallery), 'with their massive baskets turning them into caryatids.'[6]

In the garden near the orchard, to the right and behind Pomona

The Spink
Sculptor: Quentin Bell

Installed: c. 1930
Materials/dimensions: carved brick; 2.8 m high × 94 cm wide × 92 cm deep
Condition: Good (pointing repaired)[7]
Owner/custodian: Charleston Trust (gift of Vanessa Bell from the estate of Duncan Grant 1981)

The female Sphinx emerges from her brick pedestal. Referring to the monument's popular

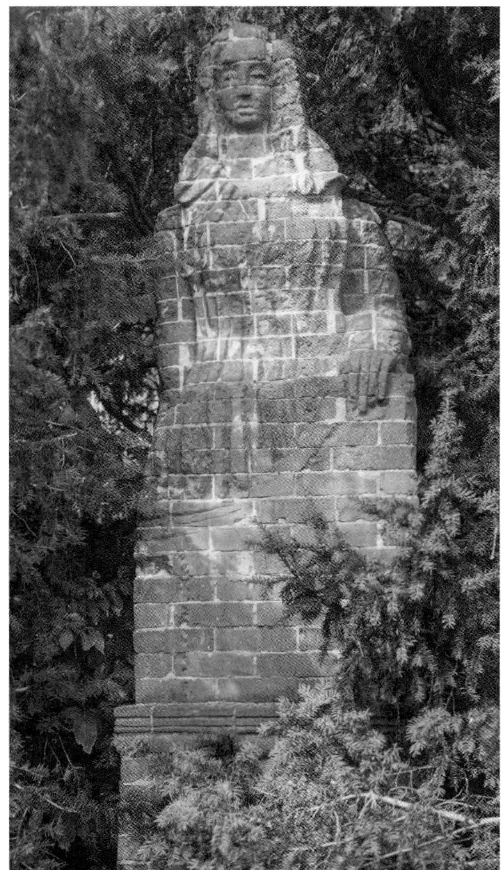

Quentin Bell, *The Spink*

name 'the Spink', Bell suggested that, '[t]he name has stuck rather better than the brickwork.'[8] He described how, after hearing about the brick sculptures of Vallombrosa, he constructed a monumental cube, from which he began to carve the figure. Having little experience with bricklaying, he encountered several problems with this medium:

> … nobody had told me how to choose my bricks … and I was forever running into the middle … which was so friable, so full of lumps of stone, anthracite, heaven knows what, that I was unable to make any shape out of it at all. It has now become one of the oddities of Charleston …[9]

Notes
[1] Bell, Q. and Nicholson, V., *Charleston: a Bloomsbury House and Garden*, London, 1997, p. 126. [2] Ibid., pp. 146–47. [3] Watney, S., 'Quentin Bell: potter', *Quentin Bell a Man of Many Arts*, Charleston, 1999, p. 32. [4] Cliveden Conservation Workshop report 1997, Charleston Archive. [5] Watney (1999), p. 36. [6] Mellor, D.A., 'Bell's fancies', *Quentin Bell a Man of Many Arts*, Charleston, 1999, p. 44. [7] Cliveden Conservation Workshop report 2004, Charleston archive. [8] Bell (1997), p. 145. [9] Ibid., p. 144.

Other source
Charleston database CHA/SC/40/41 & 41a/42/43.

CHIDDINGLY

Church Lane

South interior wall of Chiddingly Parish Church

The Jefferay Monument
Sculptor: William Cure II (and others)

Installed: 1612
Materials/dimensions: memorial: white marble veined in red, 3.7 m high × 3.3 m wide × 80 cm deep; figures: white alabaster, life size; base: white and red marble, 1.2 m high × 3.3 m wide × 80 cm deep
Inscriptions (on black marble tablet above figures): HERE LYE BVRIED THE BODIES: OF SR IOHN IEFFERAY, KNIGHT / LATE LORD CHEEFE BARON OF THE ESCHEQUER: AND OF / ALICE HIS FIRST WIFE SOLE DAUGHTER AND HEIRE OF JOHN / APSLEY OF LONDON GENT: AND OF DAME ELIZABETH THERE / SOLE DAUGHTER AND HEIRE: MARIED TO SR EDWARD / MOUNTAGU OF BOUGHTON IN THE COUNTY OF NORTHAMPTON / KNIGHT OF THE BATHE: BY WHOME SHEE LEFT ISSUE LIVINGE / ONE ONELY DAUGHTER ELIZABETH MARIED TO THE RIGHT / HONORABLE SR ROBERT BERTIE KNIGHT OF THE BATHE LORD / WILLUGBY OF WILLUGBY BEACKE AND ERSBY WHO HAVE / ISSUE NOW LIVINGE THREE SONNES: MOUNTAGU: ROGER: / AND PEREGRINE: AND ONE DAUGHTER, KATHERINE. / THE SAYD SR JOHN JEFFERAY DYED THE XXIIITH OF MAY: / 1578: ALICE HIS FIRST WIFE DIED THE ( ) MAY[1] / AND DAME ELIZABETH MOUNTAGU THERE DAUGHTER DIED THE: 6: OF DECEMBER: 1611: AT WHOSE REQUEST TO HER / SAID HUSBAND SR EDWARD MOUNTAGU IN MEMORY BOTH / OF HER DISCENT AND OFSPRINGE,: THIS MONUMENT WAS / ERECTED AND FINISHED: 1612.
Status: not listed
Condition: poor (Sir Edward Montagu's hand and sword pommel are missing, only part of the quillon remains. Dame Elizabeth is missing both her wrists and hands. From her neck at the back hangs the broken off remains of a cloak or cape. Corners of cushions broken off. The kneeling figure of Elizabeth has hands missing, coiffure is badly damaged and the right side of the face and shoulder is missing. The figure of Sir John Jefferay has remains of red paint in the folds of his garments. The monument was fully restored in 1996 with the aid of an anonymous donation and grants from the Sussex Historic Churches Trust and the Historic Churches Preservation Trust. On specialist advice no attempt was made to

replace the missing parts or restore the vanished colourings)[2]

Commissioned by: Sir Edward Montagu
Owner/custodian: Chiddingly Parish Church

The monument occupies the width of the wall in a bay extended out from the South aisle. The centre piece is of two reclining figures, Sir John Jefferay, Chief Baron of the Exchequer of Elizabeth I and MP at various times for Arundel and East Grinstead, in legal robes, above his wife Dame Alice, hands clasped in prayer, her head on an embroidered pillow and two standing figures, Sir Edward Montagu, their son-in-law, to the left and their daughter Dame Elizabeth to the right, with their granddaughter Elizabeth kneeling at the front. The figures stand within a large classical architectural structure with a plinth and moulded bases, the two standing figures within semicircular niches with diminishing fluted semicircular heads and each on a drum of stone

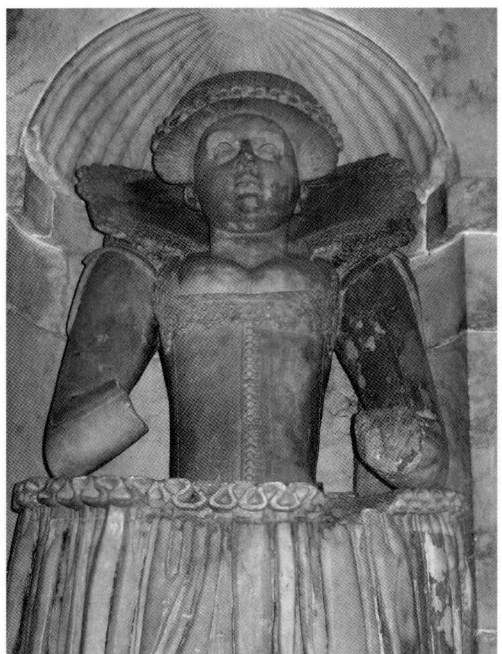

William Cure II, *The Jefferay Monument* **(detail)**

said to represent the cheeses that were placed before them as stepping stones as they walked to Church from their house at Chiddingly Place, as they were too proud to put their feet to the ground. At the top centre is a semicircular coffered arch containing a black tablet with the bearded figure of Death to the left in medieval costume holding a spade. On the right, a naked bearded old man with a cloak covering his loins, holding an hourglass in his left hand and a scythe in his right, signifies Time.

Although the sculpture has been attributed to William Cure II, from a famous family of sculptors who came from Amsterdam in 1541 and worked in England for three generations, it is currently believed that it was probably the work of more than one sculptor, as there are considerable variations in the quality of the carvings. The monument is thought to be one of only two examples of seventeenth-century funerary statuary with figures standing upright.[3]

Notes
[1] The date of death of Dame Alice is obliterated but recorded in 1862 as 28 May 1570. [2] Loosemore, J. (project manager) *Chiddingly Church: the Jefferay Monument of 1612 Restored 1996*, church leaflet, nd. [3] Loosemoore, J. and Burgis, J., *Chiddingly Church Guide*, Hastings, 1995, pp. 9–12.

Other sources
Llewellyn (2011), pp. 72–78.
Parish of Chiddingly archive, East Sussex Record Office, Lewes, PAR292.

Next to church car park

Spirit of the Village (The Chiddingly Millennium Sculpture)

Sculptor: Sue Nunn

Letter carver: Helen Mary Skelton

Installed: 2000
Materials/dimensions: carved centrepiece: oak bole with Dunhouse sandstone base, 1 m high × 55 cm wide × 55 cm deep; four

sculptures: oak, each 2.5 m high × 40 cm wide × 40 cm deep
Signature (around stone base): CHIDDINGLY MILLENNIUM OAK SCULPTURE Sue Nunn – Sculptor / SPIRIT OF THE VILLAGE 2000 AD
Inscriptions: (on wooden inscribed plaque attached to inner aspect of the fence surrounding the garden): CHIDDINGLY MILLENNIUM OAK SCULPTURE AND GARDEN This project has been made possible by generous grants, donations and support from: The Arts Council, / South East Arts, East Sussex County Council, Wealden District Council, Chiddingly Parish Council; Abbott / Joinery, Adams and Remers, American Express, Albourne Stone and Marble, Boron, Chandlers-BMW, / Cuprinol, Davies and Tate, Elphick and Son Ltd., Farley Farm, Farm Photographic, George Hammond Plc., / Jenners, Laughton Agriplant, Mark Caruthers Carpenter, Nigel Braden Architectural Designs and Consultancy, / P.B. Fencing, P. and P. Paving, Penrose Forest Products Ltd, Trencherlink, Ivan Vincent, C.B. Winter & Sons, / Wooden Wonders Ltd., Marilyn Ambroziak, Rex and Gill Bretten, Joyce and Ken Boulter, Sandi Cook, Peter / and Pam Dye, Kevin Hannah, Corin Hardy, Noel and Winnow Hardy, Dave and Barbie Harrison, Terry / Hungerford, Dawn Jackson, George Kennard, Edward and Jose Loosemore, Jeni Longley, Brenda and Jerry / Longley, David and Kay Miller, Tony and Ros Penrose, Andrew Smith. Peter Hamlin, Lord of the Manor of / Chiddingly, has provided an endowment to preserve the sculpture into the future. Underneath this plaque is a second one carrying a list of names of those who helped with the fencing and establishing of the garden; (on wooden inscribed plaque attached to inner aspect of the fence surrounding the garden): THE CARVED OAK BOLE / Here you will find: Two cheeses amongst the roots near Chiddingly Church denoting the story of the / Jefferay family

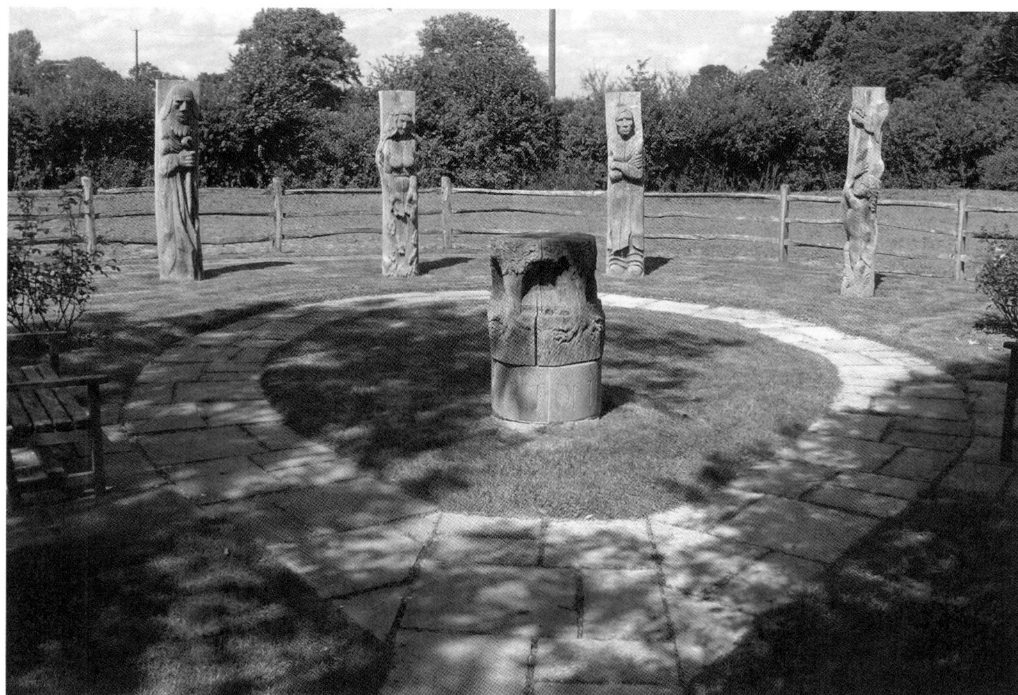

Sue Nunn, *Spirit of the Village (The Chiddingly Millennium Sculpture)*

The group of sculptures within a fenced garden was created to mark the Millennium and 'celebrate a rural way of life, sadly declining'.[1] At the centre stands an oak bole carved with five communal village buildings: church, village hall, shop, pub and school. They are surrounded by oak trees with symbols of local legends entwined in their roots. Encircling the central piece are four tall allegorical figures, or protective guardians, symbolising the seasons. An old man (Winter) holding a traditional Sussex shepherd's crook, represents wisdom; a woman (Autumn) holding oak leaves, represents compassion; Summer is symbolised by a young man, wearing a leather blacksmith's apron, representing strength and a young girl (Spring), dancing through bluebells while a hare leaps overhead, represents joy. The sculptures were all carved from a single 150-year-old oak tree.

Nearby stands a stone birdbath with GEORGE KENNARD 2000 carved into its base and HARMONY. TRANQUILLITY. PEACE inscribed around its bowl.

Note
[1] suenunnartist.co.uk (accessed 27 October 2010).

who lived at Place Farm during Tudor times and were reputed to walk to the Church / on "cheeses". An Onion Pie by the Village Hall symbolises the poisoning of William French by his / wife Sarah Ann, who added arsenic to his onion pie and was the last woman to be hanged in Lewes / Prison. A 16th Century Cannon near the school is a reminder that the Sussex Weald was the centre / of the Iron industry. There are many "hammer ponds" found locally from which the iron was cast, / linked to place-names such as Gun Hill and Furnace Lane. A Galleon represents the fleet that fought / off the Spanish Armada, -many locally-grown oaks were used to build ships. A Bottle Kiln by the / Six Bells Pub represents the early brick-making industry at the Dicker. Also to be discovered is a / motorbike, a more modern village legend, and by the Shop is a shoe last in memory of the Russell / and Bromley shoe business started by John Clifford Russell who lived in the village. You will also / see a swap – a smaller version of the scythe used locally since the earliest days of agriculture. A further wooden plaque carries the names of the Chiddingly Festival Committee and the Millennium Oak Advisory Group who oversaw the project and the carved logos of the main funders. Underneath several of the inscribed plaques are vertical plaques holding the names of all the residents of the village at the time of the Millennium

Status: not listed
Condition: good
Funded by: The Arts Council, South East Arts, East Sussex County Council, Wealden District Council, Chiddingly Parish Council and local firms and individuals
Owner/custodian: Chiddingly Parish Council

The Cross/Crowborough Hill

Outside shops at junction with Beacon Road

Statue of Sir Arthur Conan Doyle
Sculptor: David Cornell

Unveiled: 14 April 2001
Materials/dimensions: statue: bronze, 1.9 m high × 65 cm wide × 60 cm deep; plinth: stone, 40 cm high × 77 cm wide × 60 cm deep
Signature (back of coat, bottom right): David Cornell / 2000
Inscription (front of plinth): SIR ARTHUR CONAN

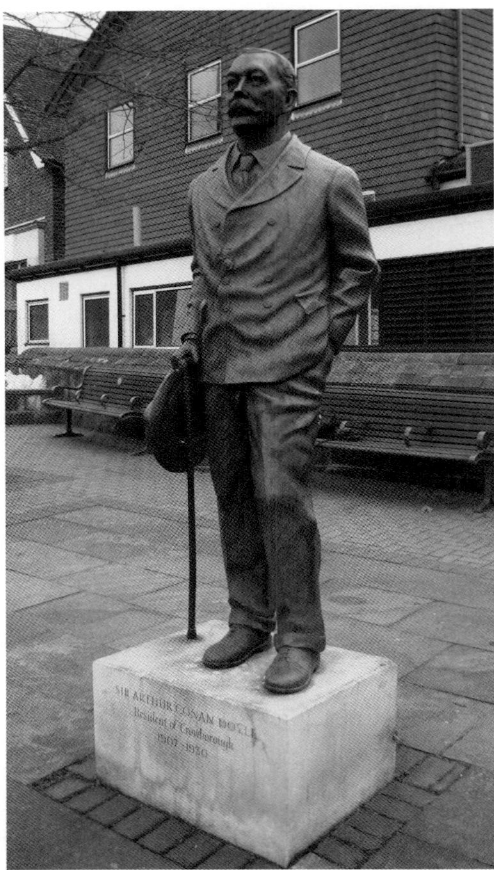

David Cornell, *Statue of Sir Arthur Conan Doyle*

DOYLE / Resident of Crowborough / 1907–
1930
Status: not listed
Condition: good (but metallic staining to
plinth)
Commissioned and owned by: Crowborough
Town Council
Funded by: the Town Council and donations
including from *The Daily Mail*

The full-length portrait sculpture depicts the
author standing in a casual pose, holding his hat
and stick in his right hand. It commemorates his
connection with the town of Crowborough,

where Conan Doyle spent the last 23 years of
his life at his house named Windelsham.
Members of the Conan Doyle (Crowborough)
Establishment initiated the fund-raising for the
memorial, having previously erected a memorial
plaque on Montargis Terrace, in the town
centre, in 1992. Mrs Georgina Doyle, wife of Sir
Arthur's nephew, unveiled the sculpture before
an audience that included admirers of the
author's work from Japan, America and
Europe.[1]

Note
[1] localauthoritypublishing.co.uk (accessed
28 February 2008).

Other source
'A brief history of the Conan Doyle (Crowborough)
    establishment', the-conan-doyle-crowborough-
    eastablishement.com (accessed 28 February
    2008).

DITCHLING

West Street (B2116)

*On traffic island at junction with Lodge
Hill Lane*

War Memorial
Designer: Eric Gill
Letter carver: Joseph Cribb

Installed: 1919
Materials/dimensions: Portland stone: base:
    30 cm high × 1.9 m wide × 1.9 m deep; base
    of obelisk: 53 cm high × 1.07 m wide ×
    1.07 m deep; obelisk: 2.6 m high × 52 cm
    wide × 52 cm deep
Inscriptions (encircling upper part of base of
    the obelisk): GREATER LOVE HATH NO / MAN
    THAN THIS THAT A / MAN LAY DOWN HIS LIFE
    / FOR HIS FRIENDS; (on east face of obelisk):
    REMEMBER (followed by the names of the
    fallen from the First World War, then '1914–
    1918'); (south face); REMEMBER (followed by

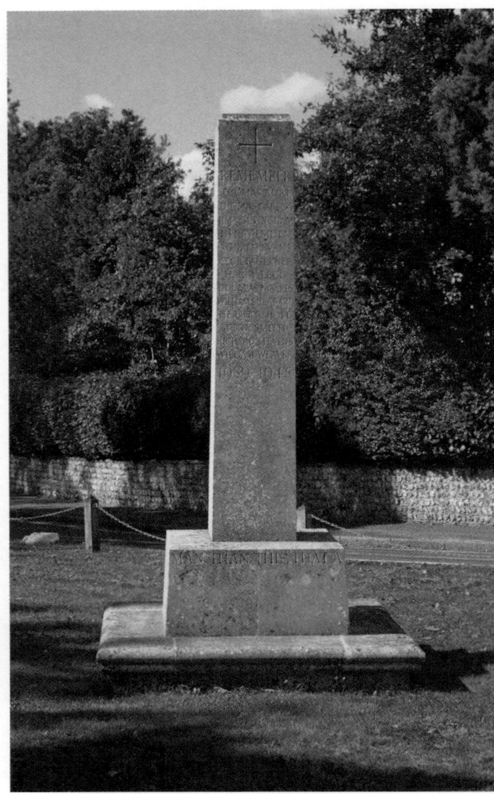

Eric Gill, *War Memorial*

the names of the fallen from the Second
World War, then '1939–1945')
Status: not listed
Condition: good (repair to northwest corner of
    base)

This simple square, tapering obelisk is sited at
the centre of a grassed and fenced triangular
traffic island. It relies for its effect on the
simplicity and elegant proportion of its incised
lettering.

Eric Gill came to live in Ditchling from his
home town of Brighton in 1907 and set up the
Guild of St Joseph and St Dominic there in
1920. Joseph Cribb was his assistant and a
fellow founder member of the Guild,

continuing his involvement, after Gill left in 1924, up until his death in 1967. Gill and Cribb's production of war memorials following the end of the First World War was prolific and includes the more pictorial example at South Harting.

Sources
Arscott, D. (1997), p. 85.
Cribb, R. and J. (2007), p. 77.
Ditchling Museum, Church Lane, Ditchling. There are undated photographs of the War Memorial and its unveiling ceremony in the Joseph Cribb collection.
Wilcox, T. (ed.), *Eric Gill and the Guild of St Joseph and St Dominic*, Hove, 1990.

EASTBOURNE

Borough Lane

OLD TOWN

Inside Manor Gardens

Eighteen Thousand Tides

Sculptor: David Nash (assisted by Walter Bailey)

Installed: August 1996
Materials/dimensions: recycled oak beach groynes: tallest, 4.04 m high; shortest 2.44 m high; circular base: shingle with recycled oak retaining wall, 8 m diam.
Inscription (on plastic plaque attached to base): Eighteen Thousand Tides 1996 / Recycled oak groynes from Eastbourne seafront / DAVID NASH / A sculpture commission by the Towner Art Gallery / Purchased through the Collection Scheme in partnership with the / Contemporary Art Society and funded by the Arts Council of England, / Contemporary Art Society, Eastbourne Borough Council, friends of the / Towner and the Towner Contemporary Art Fund Committee / Assistance has also been received from Posford Duvivier, J T Mackley / & Co. Ltd. And Serco Ltd. /

More information about the sculpture and David Nash is available at the / Towner Art Gallery & Local Museum, an Eastbourne Borough Council service
Status: not listed
Condition: good
Commissioned by: The Towner Art Gallery and Museum, Eastbourne
Owner/custodian: Eastbourne Borough Council

The sculpture consists of 10 recycled wooden columns, of varying heights, standing within a gravel-filled circle marked by a low wooden wall. Nash chose to use discarded groynes (posts that help to stabilise beach shingle) from the Eastbourne seafront for his piece. It was the first time that he had worked with sea-weathered timber, which he and Walter Bailey shaped and proportioned using a chainsaw. The precise location of each pillar within the circle was determined by a series of grids and canes. The groynes have been placed in concrete 'pipes' 1.5 m below ground level, to hold them in place underneath the shingle.

Nash wrote:

The relentless breathing of tides, the sea pressing against Eastbourne over twenty-five years, eighteen thousand breaths, has formed the timbers in this sculpture. … I have chosen ten images to place together working with proportion and number framed by a low wall to create a space that is uniquely of Eastbourne and is aesthetically and socially approachable on many levels, from the mysteries of 'number' – single, pair, trilogy, quartet, – to using the wall as a seat.[1]

The sculpture stands in the gardens of the eighteenth-century building that housed the Towner Gallery until 2008/9 when the gallery was relocated to a new building at Devonshire Park, College Road, Eastbourne.

Note
[1] *Eighteen Thousand Tides: A Sculpture by David Nash*, Towner Art Gallery and Local Museum pamphlet, Eastbourne, nd.

David Nash, *Eighteen Thousand Tides*

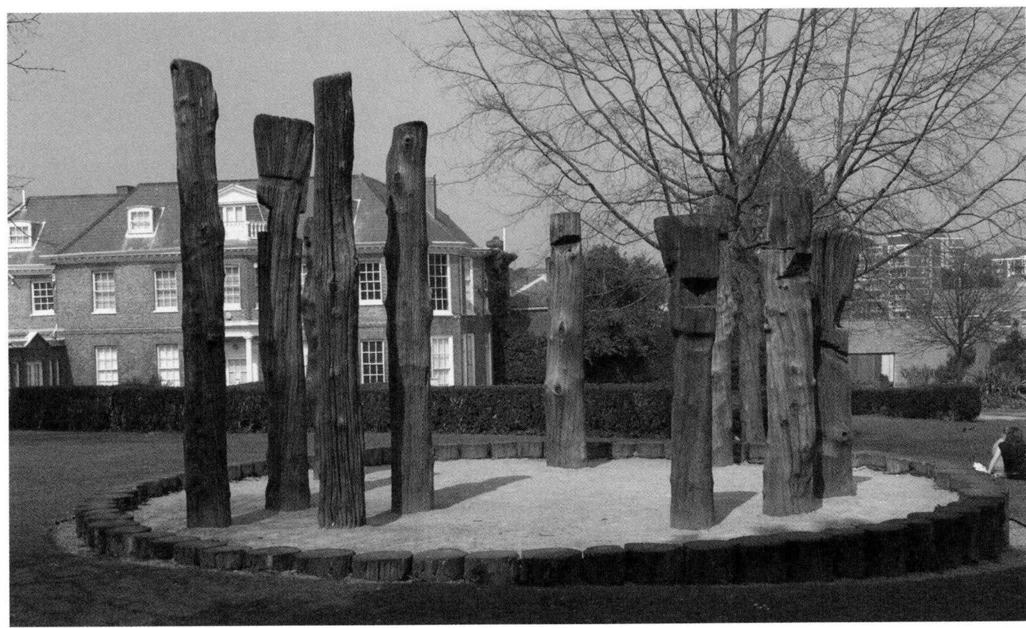

Ruth-Less Memorial

Designers: Kevin Watson and George Dixon

Unveiled: 13 May 1995
Materials/dimensions: Norwegian granite,
1.37 m long × 1.07 m wide
Inscriptions (underneath carved relief): In
memory of the crew of a B-24D Liberator
Bomber / No. 41–24282 BAR Y "RUTH-LESS"
/ of 506 Squadron, 44th Bombardment
Group, 8th. U.S.A.A.F. / Who all lost their
lives, when, / badly damaged by enemy
action and in very low cloud, / the aircraft
crashed here on February 2nd. 1944
(followed by names, hometowns and states

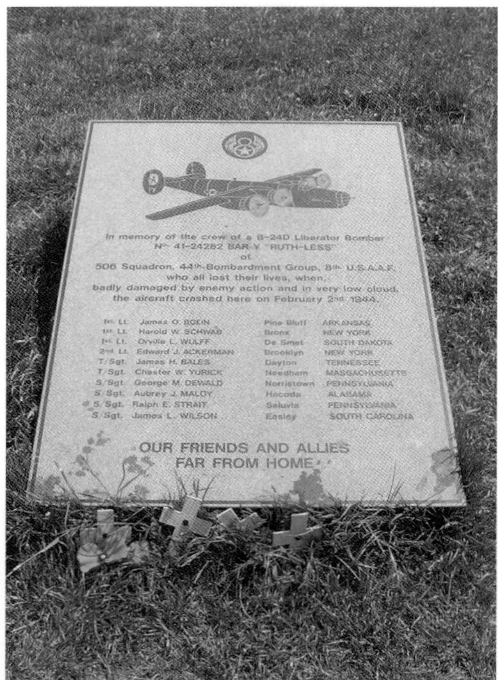

Kevin Watson and George Dixon, *Ruth-Less Memorial*

of the ten crew members who lost their lives.
Underneath the names): OUR FRIENDS AND
ALLIES / FAR FROM HOME
Status: not listed
Condition: good
Commissioned by: Ruth-Less Memorial Fund
Owner/custodian: Eastbourne Borough
Council

The rectangular memorial is set horizontally
into the grass of the Downs. The lettering is
polished and raised against a rough-hewn matt
finish, underneath a carved relief image of the
squadron insignia and the bomber.

Relatives of the dead airmen attended the
unveiling ceremony for which the monument
had been covered with an American flag and the
bloodstained folded hat of 1st Lt. Orville Wulff,
found in his breast pocket when he died. The
Royal Air Force Red Arrows display team flew
past in salute at the end of the ceremony.

Sources
Eastbourne Herald, 8 June 2007, p. 5.
Longstaff-Tyrell, P., *Front-line Sussex: Napoleon
   Bonaparte to the Cold War*, Stroud, 2000, p. 84.
Watson, K., *"Ruth-Less" and Far From Home*,
   Eastbourne, 2000, chapter 2.

Cavendish Place

SEAFRONT

*Junction with Elms Avenue, opposite the
Pier*

Royal Sussex Memorial

Sculptor: William Goscombe John

Foundry: A.B. Burton
Unveiled: 7 February 1906
Materials/dimensions: sculpture: bronze, 1.9 m
   high × 90 cm wide × 90 cm deep; pedestal:
   pink granite, 2.1 m high × 1.2 m wide × 1.2 m
   deep; plinth: pink granite, 1.68 m high ×
   1.68 m wide × 88 cm deep; stepped base: red
   granite, 3 m high × 3 m wide × 27 cm deep
Signatures: (on relief facing NE, bottom left):
   W. GOSCOMBE JOHN ARA; (on relief facing

SW, bottom right): W. GOSCOMBE JOHN ARA;
(statue base facing SW: A.B. BURTON.
FOUNDER / THAMES DITTON; (statue base
NE): W. GOSCOMBE JOHN SC. / 1906
Inscriptions (SE face of pedestal, bronze plaque
on sash): ROYAL SUSSEX REGIMENT
(underneath sash): TO THE / HONOUR AND
GLORY / OF / THE OFFICERS NON-
COMMISSIONED / OFFICERS AND MEN OF THE
2ND BAT- / TALION ROYAL SUSSEX REGIMENT /
FORMERLY 107 / REGIMENT / BENGAL /
INFANTRY WHO LOST THEIR LIVES / DURING
THE SERVICE OF THE BATT- / -ALION ABROAD
IN MALTA EGYPT / AND INDIA FROM 1882 TO
1902 / AND IN SPECIAL MEMORY OF THE CA- /
-MPAIGNS IN WHICH THE BATTALION / TOOK
/ PART / THE BLACK MOUNTAIN / EXPEDITION
OF 1888 AND THE TIRAH / CAMPAIGN OF
1897–98 THIS MEMORIAL / HAS BEEN
ERECTED BY THEIR COMRADES; (on NW face
of pedestal, bronze plaque on sash): 2ND
ROYAL SUSSEX REGIMENT; (underneath sash):
ROLL OF OFFICERS NON COMMISSIONED
OFFICERS AND / MEN WHO DIED WHILE THE
BATTALION WAS ON FOREIGN / TOUR OF
SERVICE FROM 21 JULY UNTIL 11 DEC. 1902
Followed by names of the fallen.
Status: Grade II*
Condition: fair (corrosion to bronze plaques,
   particularly names of the fallen on NW face.
   Metallic staining to pedestal on all sides, with
   significant chips and cracks to plinth and
   base)
Owner/custodian: Eastbourne Borough
Council

The memorial depicts a young officer of the
2nd Battalion of the Royal Sussex Regiment, in
an alert pose, with a drawn downward-facing
sword in his right hand and his left hand resting
on his hip. The uniform is of the Bengal
Regiment, one of the old regiments of the East
India Company. When the Company was
dissolved the regiment was taken over by the
Government and became the 107th regiment,
which in turn became the 2nd Battalion.

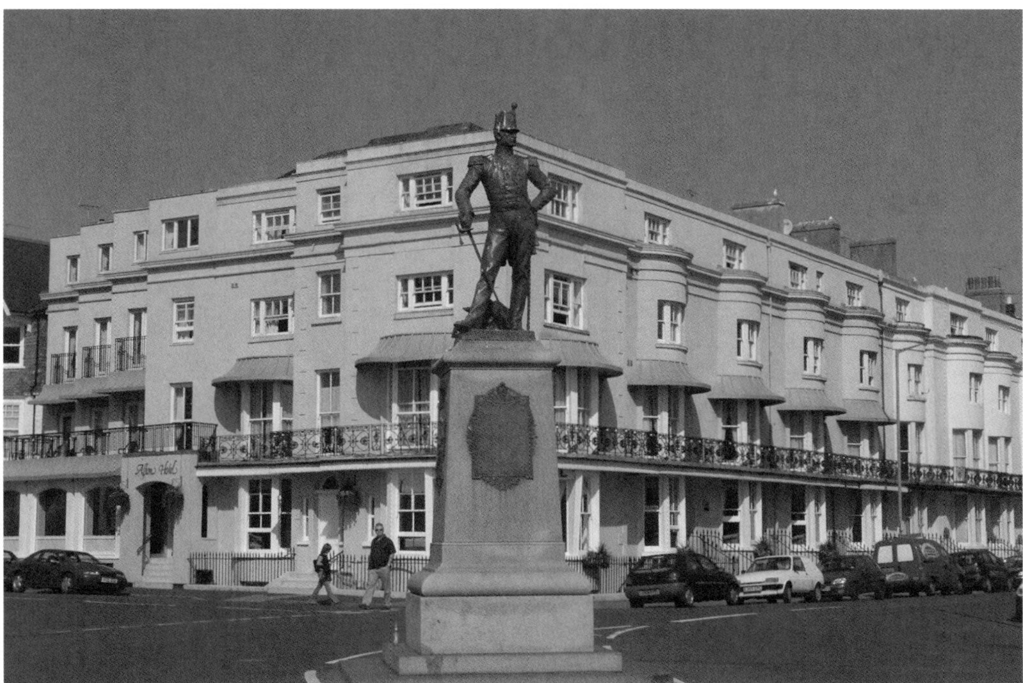

William Goscombe John, *Royal Sussex Memorial*

Below the statue, the pedestal has bronze plaques on all sides; the SW and NE faces have pictorial reliefs of soldiers in action; the SE and NW faces have inscribed plaques.

The statue was unveiled by the Duke of Norfolk, Lord Lieutenant of Sussex and a Major of the 2nd Battalion of the Royal Sussex Regiment, in the presence of a Guard of Honour, who had travelled on a special train from Chichester.

Sources
Eastbourne's Historic Street Furniture, Eastbourne Local History Society, 1986, p. 15.
Longstaff-Tyrell (2000), pp. 20 and 39–40.
Pearson, F., *Goscombe John at the National Museum of Wales*, National Museum of Wales, 1979, p. 86.

Devonshire Place
SEAFRONT

Facing the sea at the junction of Devonshire Place and Grand Parade

Statue of VII Duke of Devonshire
Sculptor: William Goscombe John

Foundry: E. Gruet, Paris
Unveiled: 17 August 1901
Materials/dimensions: statue: bronze, 1.5 m high × 1.7 m wide × 2 m deep; plinth: stone, 1.5 m high × 1.8 m wide × 2.3 m deep; stepped base: stone, 1 m high × 2.5 m wide × 3 m deep
Signatures (on left-hand side of base): W Goscombe John ARA sculptor London 1901; (to rear of the bronze base towards the right): E. GRUET JNE FONDEUR PARIS
Inscriptions (on the base, facing away from the sea): ERECTED BY THE VOLUNTARY SUB /

SCRIPTIONS OF INHABITANTS OF / EASTBOURNE IN COMMEMORATION / OF HIS GENEROUS INTERESTS IN ITS / WELFARE AND PROGRESS MD CCCCI / J A SKINNER J P CHAIRMAN; (on the base, facing the sea): WILLIAM / SEVENTH DUKE OF DEVONSHIRE / K.G P.C. D.C.L. F.R.S. / CHANCELLOR OF THE UNIVERSITY OF / CAMBRIDGE LORD LIEUTENANT OF / THE COUNTY OF DERBY BORN 27 / APRIL 1808 DIED 21 DECEMBER 1891
Status: Grade II
Condition: good (but surface treatment deteriorating)
Funded by: public subscription
Owner/custodian: Eastbourne Borough Council

William Cavendish, 7th Duke of Devonshire (1808–1891) who as 2nd Earl of Burlington, succeeded to the Dukedom in 1858, is represented in his robes as Chancellor of Cambridge University, depicted with great attention to embroidered details, cording and tasselling. He is seated in a flamboyantly curved chair, in an attitude of deep thought, an open book held dangling from his left hand. The pose accords well with the treasurer of the subscription fund's description of the Duke as, '… pre-eminently the friend of clever men … who seemed to have a happy knack of always selecting men of genius to serve under him …'.[1] Goscombe John's approach to his subject has been described as in a, '… strong, mature and personal style', with the depiction of his robes adding '… fluid movement and colour'.[2] Admiration for the Duke of Devonshire monument brought further commissions for similar compositions for its sculptor, including W.E.F. Lecky for Trinity College Dublin and Principal Viriamu Jones for University College, Cardiff (1906).[3] A plaster bust of the 7th Duke, a study for the final bronze, was executed in 1900 and the completed statue was awarded a gold medal at the Paris Salon of 1901, the first time that it had been given to a British

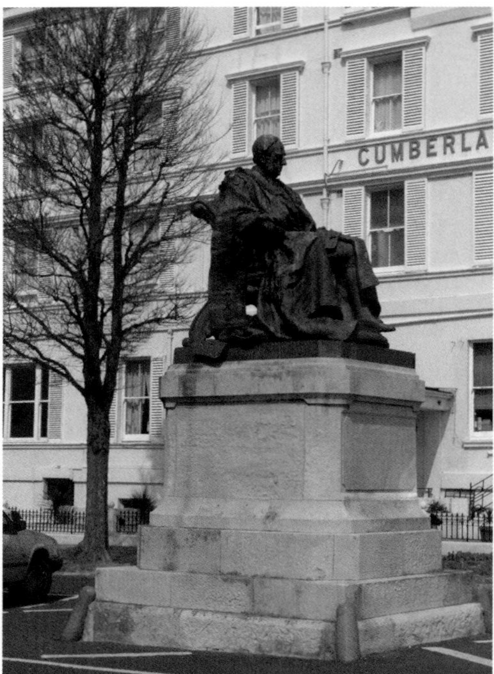

William Goscombe John, *Statue of VII Duke of Devonshire*

sculptor.[4] It was exhibited at the Royal Academy prior to its erection on the site and following its unveiling the local paper praised not only the skill of the sculptor, but also the efficiency of the local firm of masons who prepared the surrounding kerbing, largely due to their use of a steam sawing machine.[5]

The Duke is described as the chief benefactor and founder of modern Eastbourne and David Cannadine points to the town as, '… exemplifying all the benefits that accrue when a dukedom connected itself with a watering place.'[6] The statue was unveiled by the Marquis of Abergavenny, Lord Lieutenant of Sussex. In his speech, the 8th Duke of Devonshire remarked upon the fact that the statue was installed 10 years after the death of his predecessor, which he felt was evidence of the lasting respect and affection in which he was held. This justified an exception to his assertion that,

[I]n these days we have, I think, too many memorials. No man of prominence in any walk of life can scarcely depart without a proposal being made for the erection of a memorial to him in some form or another.[7]

Notes
[1] *Eastbourne Chronicle*, 17 August 1901, p. 5.
[2] Pearson (1979), p. 13. [3] Ibid. [4] Ibid, p. 80. The model is now in the Devonshire Hospital at Buxton. There is also a small bronze version of the statue in the Fitzwilliam Museum, Cambridge. [5] *Eastbourne Chronicle*, 17 August 1901, p. 5. [6] Cannadine, D., *Lords and Landlords: the Aristocracy and the Towns 1774–1967*, Leicester, 1980, p. 230. [7] *Eastbourne Chronicle*, 24 August 1901, p. 6.

Other sources
Eastbourne's Historic Street Furniture (1986), p. 14
Elleray, R.D., *Eastbourne a Pictorial History*, Chichester, 1995.
Koch, A. (ed.) *Academy Architecture and Architectural Review*, vol. 20, 1901.

Grand Parade

SEAFRONT

Lower Parade, underneath columns facing bandstand

John Wesley Woodward – Titanic Memorial

Sculptor: Charles Godfrey Garrard

Unveiled: 24 October 1914
Materials/dimensions: memorial: pink/grey granite, 76 cm high × 1.45 m wide × 9 cm deep; panels: bronze, 50 cm high × 34 cm wide × 2.5 cm deep
Signature (bottom of portrait relief, to right): C G GARRARD SC.
Inscription (left-hand panel): THIS TABLET IS ERECTED AS / A TRIBUTE TO THE SELF / SACRIFICE AND DEVOTION OF / JOHN WESLEY WOODWARD / (FORMERLY A MEMBER OF / THE EASTBOURNE MUNICIPAL / ORCHESTRA / THE DUKE OF DEVONSHIRE'S / ORCHESTRA / AND THE GRAND HOTEL EASTBOURNE ORCHESTRA), / WHO WITH OTHERS OF THE / HERO-MUSICIANS OF THE / SHIP'S BAND PERISHED IN / THE ATLANTIC THROUGH THE / SINKING OF THE WHITE STAR / LINER "TITANIC" / ON APRIL 15TH 1912. / "FAITHFUL UNTO DEATH"
Status: Grade II
Condition: fair (a piece of the bronze scrollwork above the violin is missing. There is metallic staining on the granite underneath the plaques. At some point it appears that the bronze has been varnished and is now discolouring)
Commissioned by: Arthur Beckett, newspaper publisher
Funded by: public subscription
Owner/custodian: Eastbourne Borough Council

The memorial takes the form of three bronze plaques set within an architectural granite wall tablet. At the centre is a portrait medallion of John Wesley Woodward, with a relief of a violin and scroll of music underneath. The left-hand plaque bears the inscription, while that on the right-hand side bears a relief depicting the sinking Titanic and lifeboats.

Woodward, 32 when he died, was born in West Bromwich, Staffordshire on 11 September 1879. He became well known as a cello player, leaving Oxford to join the Duke of Devonshire's band at Eastbourne, but that enterprise fell through around 1909, so he joined the White Star Line. Woodward and all

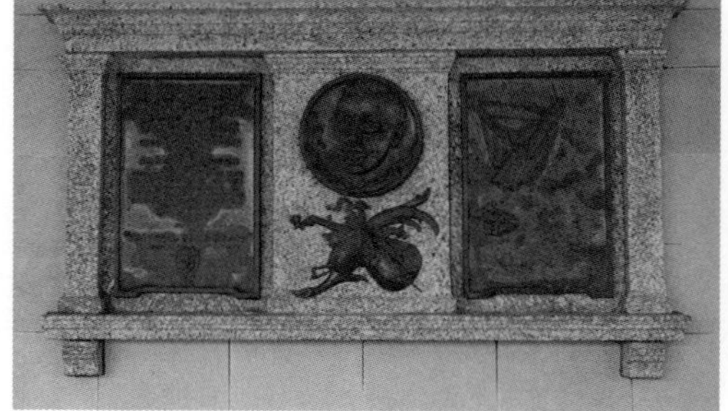

Charles Godfrey Garrard, *John Wesley Woodward – Titanic Memorial*

the other musicians on the ship perished in the sinking of the Titanic on her maiden voyage in 1912.

In raising support for a memorial to the popular local musician, the local newspaper referred to the fact that work on a memorial to a Belgian member of the orchestra had already begun and urged that Eastbourne's tribute should be 'of a graceful and artistic character, symbolical of music, and above all, with no funereal features about it'.[1] The memorial was unveiled by the opera singer, Clara Butt.

Note
[1] *Eastbourne Gazette*, 24 April 1912.

Other sources
encyclopedia-titanica.org/titanic-biography/john-wesley-woodward (accessed 5 October 2010).

King Edward's Parade
SEAFRONT

On the Western Lawns opposite the Grand Hotel

Statue of VIII Duke of Devonshire
Sculptor: Edward Alfred Briscoe Drury

Foundry: The Morris Singer Company Ltd, Frome
Unveiled: 24 October 1910
Materials/dimensions: statue: bronze, 2.60 m high × 90 cm wide × 1.1 m deep; pedestal: grey granite, 2.4 m high × 1.35 m wide × 1.35 m deep; stepped base: grey granite, 45 cm high × 1.95 m wide × 1.95 m deep
Signature (bottom left-hand side of base): A.DRURY ARA
Inscription (on pedestal, facing King Edward's Parade): SPENCER COMPTON / EIGHTH / DUKE OF DEVONSHIRE KG / CHANCELLOR OF THE UNIVERSITY / OF CAMBRIDGE LORD LIEUTENANT / OF THE COUNTY OF DERBY MAYOR / OF EASTBOURNE 1897–1898 BORN 23 JULY 1833 / DIED 24 MARCH 1908 /

ERECTED BY THE INHABITANTS OF EASTBOURNE / IN RECOGNITION OF HIS GREAT SERVICES TO / HIS COUNTRY AS A STATESMAN AND OF HIS / DEEP INTEREST IN THE PROSPERITY AND / WELFARE OF THE TOWN 1910
Status: Grade II
Condition: good
Funded by: public subscription
Owner/custodian: Eastbourne Borough Council

The statue portrays the Duke in the robes of Chancellor of Cambridge University. On his shoulder hangs the collar of the Order of the Garter, with a pendant of George V. He faces inland and holds a pince-nez in his right hand, as was his habit when addressing a public assembly. Immediately below the figure of the Duke, at the top of the pedestal, appears the Devonshire coat of arms in bronze, created, like the head and hands of the statue, by the *cir perdu* process.[1]

The site was considered to be particularly appropriate because the Duke had inherited the Parade from his father and gifted it to the town. The statue cost £1000 and was erected in recognition of the Duke's service as mayor and his contribution to the development of Eastbourne as a fashionable resort attracting eminent visitors, including the King. In this he had been continuing a family tradition that had begun with the development of the town in the 1850s; as David Cannadine has pointed out, '… the "Empress of Watering Places", the "Duke's Town", was almost entirely the creation of the House of Cavendish.'[2]

The statue was unveiled by the Duke of Norfolk, Lord Lieutenant of Sussex who experienced some difficulty with the procedure. The cloth draping the statue became lodged and the sculptor had to ask for assistance from two workmen who pulled at it violently, but only disclosed the top of the statue, whereupon one of the men ascended a ladder and completed the clearance of the torn material. The current

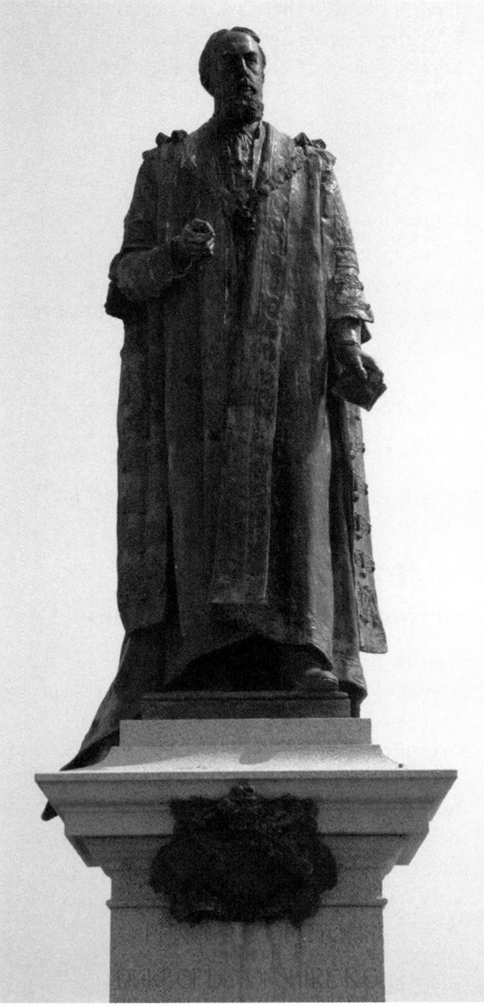

Edward Alfred Briscoe Drury, *Statue of VIII Duke of Devonshire*

Duke of Devonshire, nephew of the deceased and, like him, Mayor of the town, was then invited to accept the statue on behalf of the inhabitants. In his speech he stated that:

There were always many who desired that a memorial should be what was called "something useful"; but he thanked them [inhabitants of Eastbourne] sincerely for having decided that this memorial should take the form of a permanent monument, and he was glad to say that their selection of a sculptor had been attended with greatest possible success.[3]

Notes
[1] *Eastbourne Chronicle*, 28 October 1910.
[2] Cannadine (1980), p. 63. [3] *Eastbourne Chronicle*, op. cit.

Other sources
Eastbourne's Historic Street Furniture (1986), p. 15.
Elleray (1995).

Memorial Roundabout

TOWN CENTRE

Junction of Devonshire Place and Trinity Trees

War Memorial

Sculptor: Henry Charles Fehr

Unveiled: 10 November 1920
Materials/dimensions: statue: bronze, 1.8 m
  high; pedestal, granite, 3 m high
Inscriptions (bronze plaque, north face): WORLD
  / WAR / II; (underneath wreath): TO / THOSE
  WHO DIED / 1939. 1945 / WE / WILL /
  REMEMBER / THEM; (bronze plaque, south
  face): THE TRIBUTE OF / EASTBOURNE / TO
  HER GALLANT / SONS AND DAUGHTERS / WHO
  WERE FAITHFUL / UNTO DEATH / IN THE
  GREAT WAR / 1914–1918 / THEIR NAMES / ARE
  RECORDED / ON OAK TABLETS / IN THE TOWN
  HALL
Status: Grade II
Condition: good
Commissioned by: Mr Alderman O'Brien
  Harding J.P. Mayor of Eastbourne
Funded by: public subscription
Owner/custodian: Eastbourne Borough
  Council

The memorial depicts a bronze statue of the Angel of Victory, who appears to have just alighted and has one foot on the globe at the

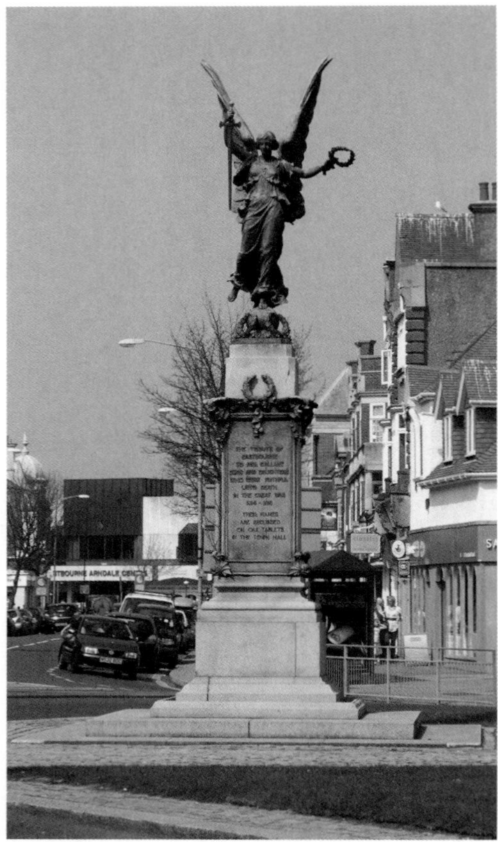

Henry Charles Fehr, *War Memorial*

summit of the pedestal. She carries in her right hand a down-turned sword, signifying peace, and in the left she holds out a wreath of laurel. Below the statue the stone pedestal bears bronze plaques carrying inscriptions to north and south, decorated at the top with scrolled leaf designs and wreaths, and at the bottom, fish motifs.

A feature of the proposed site was the 'Princess Alice' tree, which, like the Princess Alice Memorial Hospital, was named after the second daughter of Queen Victoria, who stayed in Eastbourne with her family for several weeks in the autumn before her death in 1878. The tree, which was becoming structurally unsound, was removed to make way for the war memorial.

Names and details of the fallen of Eastbourne were collected by Rev. H. Plume, M.A. As there were more than 1000 names they were carved on oak panels, produced by Messrs. G. Bainbridge & Son, to be erected in the Town Hall, rather than on the war memorial itself. The unveiling ceremony was led by General, Lord Horne, G.C.B., K.C.M.G. Over 4000 people attended, including the orphans of the fallen heroes. The next morning revealed the Memorial literally covered with flowers and tributes of affection and remembrance.

Sources
Forvague, H.W., *1883–1933 Municipal Eastbourne: Selections from the Proceedings of the Town Council*, Eastbourne, 1933, pp. 98–106.
londonancestor.com/newspaper/1882/0715/eastbourne -sussex (accessed 15 June 2012).
Surtees, J., *Eastbourne: a History*, Chichester, 2002.

Seafront Pathway to Health Project

The 'Pathway to Health' project in Eastbourne is one of four national health walk demonstration projects piloted by the British Heart Foundation and the Countryside Agency.[1] The pathway is along the five miles of promenade from Langney Point to Holywell featuring signs at regular intervals to act as markers so that walkers can identify their progress over time as they improve their speed and become fitter.[2]

Three sculptures were added to provide points of interest along the way. Each sculptor worked with a local community group to produce works that reinforce the health message in a light-hearted and contemplative way.

SEAFRONT

Between bandstand and lifeboat museum

Taking a Stone for a Walk
Sculptor: Jackie Brown

Constructed: December 2000

Materials/dimensions: east side uprights: white granite, 1.15 m high × 50 cm wide × 50 cm deep; west side uprights: white granite, 1.3 m high × 55 cm wide × 50 cm deep

Inscription (on stone tablet set into wall to the right of sculpture): TAKING A STONE FOR A WALK / BY JACKIE BROWN AND PARTICIPANTS / FROM THE BOURNE CENTRE / DECEMBER 2000 / A SCULPTURE CELEBRATING WALKING / AS PART OF THE PATHWAY TO HEALTH/ WALK PROJECT

Status: not listed

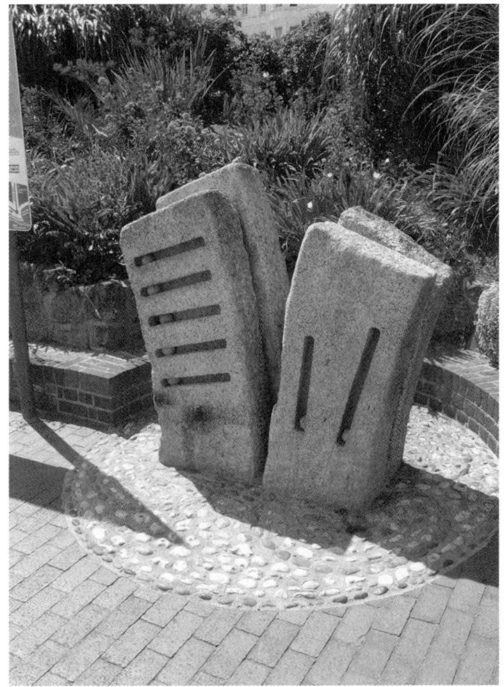

Jackie Brown, *Taking a Stone for a Walk*

Condition: good (some graffiti to top of inscribed tablet)

Owner/custodian: Eastbourne Borough Council

The four curving uprights have incisions with moveable granite balls set inside. The south-facing upright to the west has horizontal incisions. The upright to the east has a vertical incision. On the north face, the stone on the east hast a cruciform incision. The sculpture is set in a circular pebbled area that has a spiral motif.

Promenade

SEAFRONT

Sovereign Park

Fuel for the Fossil
Sculptor: Steve Geliot

Constructed: July 2000

Materials/dimensions: heart: concrete, 75 cm high × 85 cm wide × 35 cm deep; tallest upright: oak, 1.35 m high × 20 cm wide × 20 cm deep; shortest upright: oak, 83 cm high × 24 cm wide × 24 cm deep

Inscription (plaque on inscribed stone tablet on rock in front of south face): FUEL FOR THE FOSSIL / BY STEVE GELIOT AND PARTICIPANTS / FROM GENERATIONS ART PROJECT / JULY 2000 / A SCULPTURE CELEBRATING WALKING / AS PART OF THE PATHWAY TO HEALTH WALK PROJECT

Status: not listed

Condition: good (inscribed tablet weathered and chipped on edge)

Owner/custodian: Eastbourne Borough Council

The rough-hewn sculpture of a heart is set on 18 recycled wooden uprights of varying heights arranged in a rectangle emerging from the pebbled foreshore.

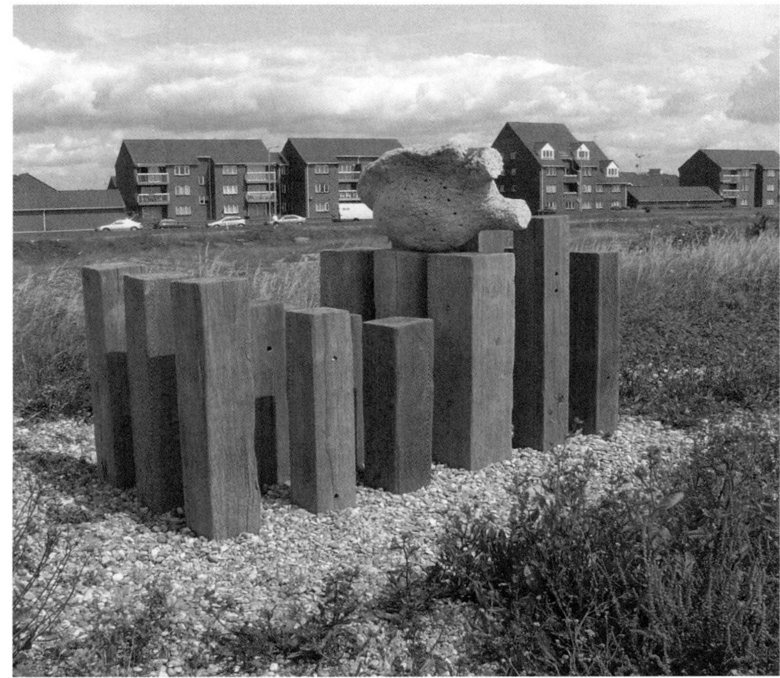

Steve Geliot, *Fuel for the Fossil*

Near the bowling greens and Treasure Island Fun Park

Young at Heart
Sculptor: Fleur Gray

Constructed: July 2000
Materials/dimensions: wood and metal, 1.5 m high × 1.5 m wide × 50 cm deep
Inscription (on inscribed stone tablet set into wall to right of the sculpture): YOUNG AT HEART / BY FLEUR GRAY / AND PARTICIPANTS FROM AGE CONCERN JULY 2000 / A SCULPTURE CELEBRATING WALKING / AS PART OF THE PATHWAY TO HEALTH / WALK PROJECT
Status: not listed
Condition: good (corner and edges of stone tablet chipped)
Owner/custodian: Eastbourne Borough Council

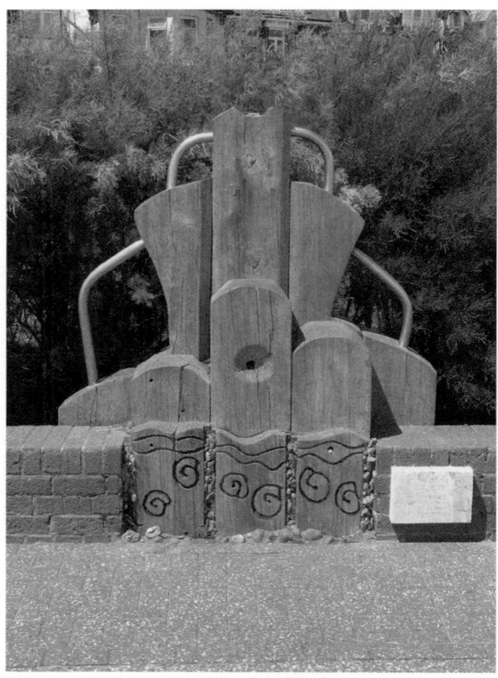

Fleur Gray, *Young at Heart*

Gray conducted six workshops with elderly people at the Venton Centre in Eastbourne, basing her sculpture on images and feedback from this group. She has described how the eight wooden pillars, with wavy lines representing both rippled tide lines and lines on the forehead, also recall the organs that used to be played in cinemas. They are of varying heights so that the eye levels of children sitting on the high ones are the same as older people sitting lower down, thus bridging the age gap. The metal bars reference aids for the elderly, but also the 'fountain of youth'. The spirals imagery combines the fossils found on the Seven Sisters cliffs nearby and the term for the elderly, 'old fossil'. The marble in the centre is to remind people not to lose their marbles, while the bird on the top is from the expression used for elderly women, 'She's a funny old bird'.[3]

Notes
[1] Fiddler, H., *Eastbourne's 'Pathway to Health' Walk Project: The Impact of the Signs on Walking Behaviour*, School of Healthcare Professions, University of Brighton, July 2001, p. 5. [2] *Eastbourne Herald*, 20 March 2003. [3] Fleur Gray, email correspondence.

Other source
Southlondonwomenartists.co.uk (accessed 29 October 2010).

South Street

On west wall of St Saviour and St Peter's Church Hall facing Spencer Road

Madonna and Child
Sculptor: Mark Batten
Architects: David Clarke and Frederick Ford

Installed: 1957
Materials/dimensions: stone, 1 m high × 56 cm wide × 10 cm deep
Signature (bottom right-hand corner): MARK BATTEN SC.

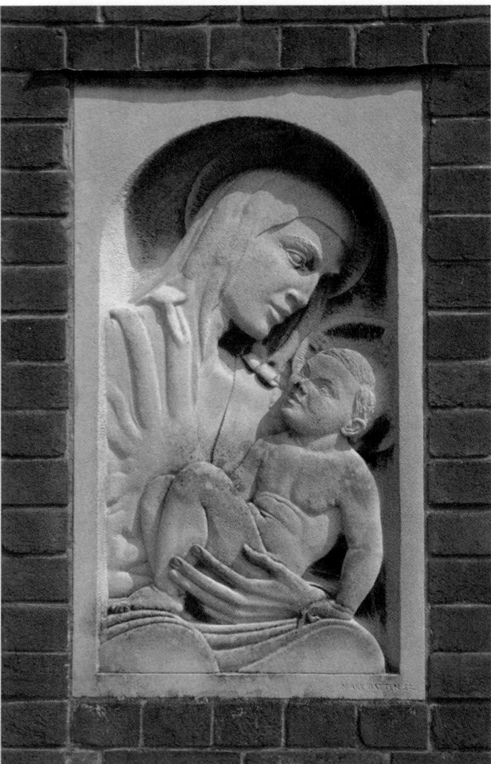

Mark Batten, *Madonna and Child*

Status: Main Church Grade B (equivalent to II*)
Condition: good
Commissioned by: a Church parishioner
Owner/custodian: St Saviour and St Peter's Church

This arched relief depicts a seated Madonna, cradling the infant Christ in her lap, balancing his body with a right hand of exaggerated proportions. Although both faces are identifiable as twentieth century, the relief has the monumental feel of early Renaissance paintings. The piece is carved into a stone rectangle on the façade of the church hall, a twentieth-century addition to the main church, which is Gothic Revival, designed by George Street RA in 1867.

Mark Batten, then president of the Royal Society of British Sculptors, worked direct onto the stone, from drawings approved by the architect and patrons, without the use of an intermediary maquette. He wrote:

> The problem solved here was that of making a work of vitality and significance without affronting the very proper desire to harmonize with the character of the architecture and the function of the building.[1]

Note
[1] *The Studio*, vol. 154, 1957, p. 191.

Other sources
Batten, M., *Direct Carving in Stone*, London, 1966.
Eastham, M., Review, *British Journal of Aesthetics*, reprinted 8 January 1990, p. 90.
C. Wroughton, correspondence, 21 October 2005.

FAIRWARP

B2026

Christ Church graveyard (western section)

Tomb of Frederick Gustav Jonathan Eckstein

Sculptor: Sir William Reid Dick

Installed: 1932
Materials/dimensions: angels (four identical): patinated bronze, 76 cm high × 93 cm wide × 15 cm deep; tomb: stone, 97 cm high × 90 cm wide × 2.16 m deep; stepped base: stone, 28 cm high × 1.3 m wide × 2.53 m deep
Signature (bottom right of bronze reliefs): RD/1932
Inscription (east face of tomb): IN / AFFECTIONATE MEMORY OF / SIR FREDERICK G.J. ECKSTEIN / BARONET / BORN 9TH APRIL 1857 / DIED 10TH JUNE 1930
Status: Grade II
Condition: good (but metallic staining to the stone from bronze angels. Bird guano to top of tomb. Cracks and corrosion to the stepped base)
Commissioned by: Eckstein family
Owner/custodian: Christ Church, Fairwarp

The stone sarcophagus sits on a plinth and has a moulded lid. The corners have bronze angels with wings unfurled and there are two bronze reliefs to the sides; on the south face depicting Sudanese plantation workers picking cotton and on the north face a bronze relief of a negro firing a machine gun in a scene from the First World War.

Sir Friedrich Eckstein was born in Germany and pioneered the development of South African gold mines together with his brother, Hermann, founder of the famous Witwatersrand mining house of H. Eckstein and Co. In 1887 he became Chairman of the Central Mining & Investment Corporation, but

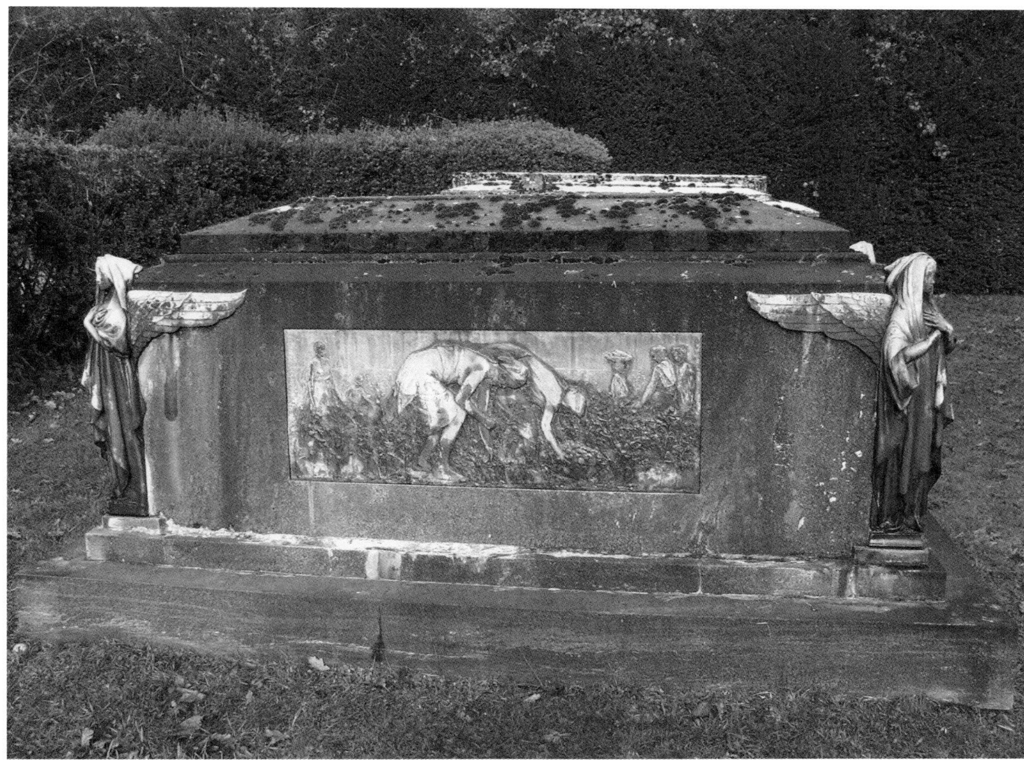

Sir William Reid Dick, *Tomb of Frederick Gustav Jonathan Eckstein*

was finally forced out of office by anti-German hysteria that broke out at the beginning of the First World War. From 1888 Eckstein lived in Johannesburg, where he had a grand house called Warrington Hall in the suburb of Doornfontein. He married Catherine Mitchell of Kimberley with whom he had a daughter, Herminie Beatrice and a son, Bernard Friedrich. Sir Friedrich moved to England in 1901, first to The Walsingham Hotel, Piccadilly and then to 18 Park Lane, London. He was granted British nationality in 1906. After renovating and extending Ottershaw Park in Surrey, he moved in 1919 to Oldlands Hall, Fairwarp where he died and was buried in 1930. His son and daughter are buried near to his tomb.

Monument to Herminie Beatrice Eckstein

Sculptor: Sir William Reid Dick

Executed: 1930
Installed: 1945
Materials/dimensions: statue: patinated bronze,
1.73 m high × 80 cm wide × 53 cm deep;
pedestal: stone, 50 cm high × 67 cm wide ×
53 cm deep
Signature (right side at base): Reid Dick 1930
Inscription (west face of pedestal): HERMINIE
BEATRICE / ECKSTEIN / BORN 19TH. JANUARY
1893 / DIED 14TH. MARCH 1945 / FARE THEE
WELL MY BEST BELOVED / YOU HAVE
BROUGHT MUCH HAPPINESS / INTO MANY
LIVES. THE REMEMBRANCE / OF YOU WILL
ALWAYS BE WONDERFUL

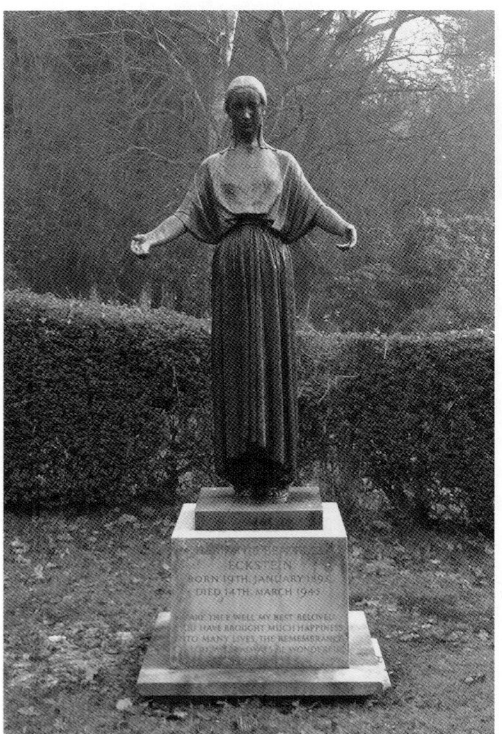

Sir William Reid Dick, *Monument to Herminie Beatrice Eckstein*

Status: Grade II
Condition: good
Commissioned by: Sir Bernard Eckstein
(brother)
Owner/custodian: Christ Church, Fairwarp

The monument comprises a standing figure of
the deceased as a young woman in ancient
Greek dress with outstretched arms. She faces
west towards the tombs of Frederick and
Bernard Eckstein, her father and brother.

Hermine Beatrice Eckstein laid the
foundation stone for the enlargement of Christ
Church in 1935. The early date of the statue
suggests either that this figure was selected as a
memorial before her death or that a favourite
piece of sculpture was used as a memorial
afterwards. Herminie Eckstein appears to be
erroneously spelt 'Hermione' in various sources.

Tomb of Sir Bernard Eckstein

Sculptor: Sir William Reid Dick

Installed: 1950
Materials/dimensions: tomb: stone, 1.05 m high
× 1 m wide × 2.25 m deep; base: stone, 15 cm
high × 1.3 m wide × 2.54 m
Signature: illegible, but Pevsner states that the
relief panels are signed and dated Reid Dick[1]
Inscription (east side): IN MEMORY OF / SIR /
BERNARD ECKSTEIN BART / BORN 2ND
NOVEMBER 1894 / DIED 10TH MAY 1948
Status: not listed
Condition: fair (detail to tomb is quite severely
weather worn. Many of the lead letters from
the inscription are missing)
Owner/custodian: Christ Church, Fairwarp

The sarcophagus has a moulded cross on top.
The north and south faces have sculptural relief
panels depicting dancing winged cherubs. The
west face of the tomb bears the Eckstein coat of
arms.

In his will, Sir Bernard Eckstein directed that
Sir William Reid Dick be asked to '… design
and erect a tomb … in keeping and in harmony
with the monument over his father's grave …'.[2]

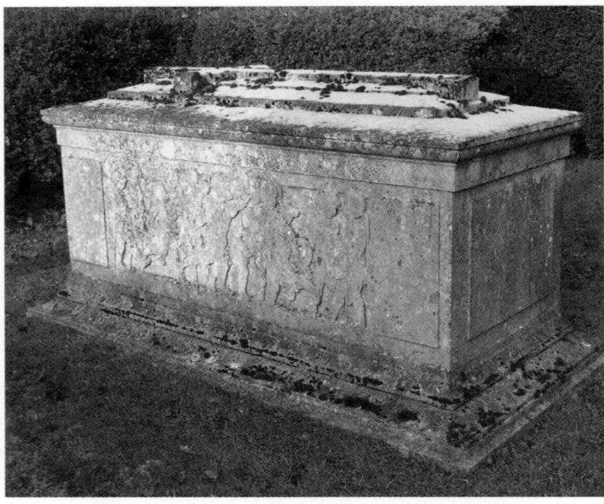

Sir William Reid Dick, *Tomb of Sir Bernard Eckstein*

The executors approved Reid Dick's design,
although his estimated cost of £7500 was
considered rather high and they requested
information about the cost of Frederick
Eckstein's grave, designed by Reid Dick in the
1930s, although '… admittedly, apart from
rising prices, your reputation as a sculptor is
now such as to prohibit any real comparison.'[3]

In the first months of 1950 Reid Dick
appears to have commenced work on the
monument, reacting with surprise to a letter
from the solicitors acting for the executors
informing him that the father of one of the
minor beneficiaries of Sir Bernard's will had
strongly protested against the cost of the work
and was threatening to make a court application
to prevent such expenditure. Again there was an
enquiry as to whether the costs could be
lessened.[4] Reid Dick protested that the work
was already nearing completion and stated
uncompromisingly that '… a memorial could
have been designed at a cost less than £7500, but
not by me …'.[5]

The problems were resolved without
recourse to the courts, although there remained
some quibbles about how the sculptor should
be paid and a delay in obtaining the required
permission from the Parochial Council for the
erection of the monument, which resulted in
Reid Dick having to insure the finished

memorial for three months at a cost of £20, before it could finally be erected in the Fairwarp churchyard.[5]

Notes
[1] Nairn and Pevsner (1965), p. 499. [2] Letter from executors of Sir Bernard Eckstein to Sir William Reid Dick, 29 October 1948, Tate Archive TGA 8110/4/17. [3] Ibid, 13 December 1949. [4] Letter from Middleton Lewis and Co., Solicitors, to Sir William Reid Dick, 15 March 1950, Tate Archive TGA 8110/4/17. [5] Pencil note from Sir William Reid Dick to Middleton Lewis and Co., 16 March 1950, Tate Archive TGA 8110/4/17. [6] Letters from executors of Sir Bernard Eckstein to Sir William Reid Dick, 4 and 31 July 1950, Tate Archive TGA 8110/4/17.

Other sources
johnathersuch.com/op_website/op_owners_text (accessed 3 January 2008).
Mapping the Practice and Profession of Sculpture in Britain and Ireland 1851–1951, University of Glasgow History of Art and HATII, online database 2011.

Falmer (South)

University of Brighton campus, Village Way, on grassy slope, outside Paddock Field Halls of Residence

Brighton Lights

Sculptor: Hamish Black

Unveiled: February 1998
Materials/dimensions: sculpture: rusted steel, 5.2 m approx. high × 2.1 m diam.; base: steel, 2.1 m diam.
Inscription (in cream-painted lettering around circular base): Brighton Lights by Hamish Black. Illuminated by Kim Howells M.P. Minister for Lifelong Learning. February 1998. Paddock Fields [*sic*] residences. University of Brighton in partnership with London & Quadrant Housing Trust
Status: not listed
Condition: good

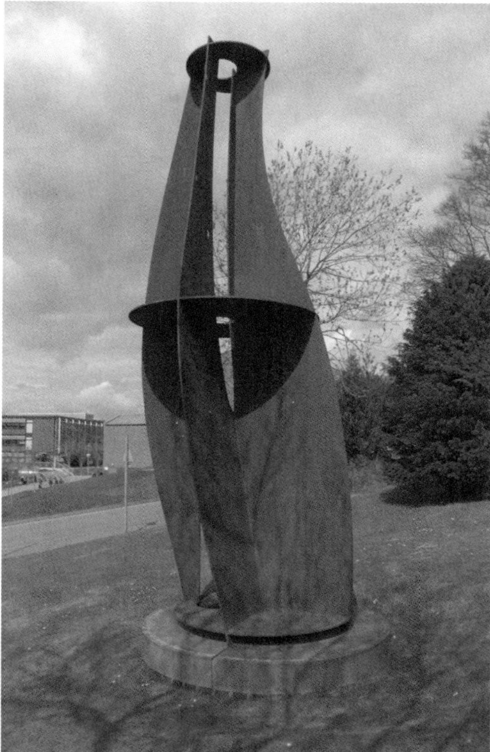

Hamish Black, *Brighton Lights*

Owner/custodian: University of Brighton

The sculpture is composed of cut-out shapes surrounding a vertical void that is filled day and night with light, its outer edges shaped by light waves.[1] A circular light fixture is set in the south facing semicircle of the base, so that the sculpture lights up through the middle.

The joint commissioners, London & Quadrant Housing Trust, are responsible for the day-to-day management of the University accommodation.[2]

Notes
[1] Hamish Black, email correspondence, 4 March 2013. [2] brighton.ac.uk/accommodation/halls/falmer (accessed 19 April 2012).

Other source
hamishblack.com (accessed 19 April 2012).

University of Brighton campus, Village Way, Great Wilkins Halls, at top of steps outside building A, at bottom of steps outside building B and on grassed area at back of building C

Pollen Forms

Sculptor: Steve Geliot

Installed: 2004 (planting by Fiona Atkinson)
Materials/dimensions: weathered oak: main group of three pieces: 90 cm high × 1 m wide × 90 cm deep; 80 cm high × 1.3 m wide × 70 cm deep; 1 m high × 70 cm diam.
Status: not listed
Condition: good (intentional cracking and weathering)
Commissioned and owned by: University of Brighton

Six carved round or oval forms are scattered across the grassy verges surrounding one of the University's Halls of residence. Their shapes were, 'inspired by pollen grains viewed by [a] scanning electron microscope.'[1] Geliot has emphasised his liking for 'scientific techniques [that] can reveal otherwise hidden elegant complexity'.[2]

Notes
[1] stevegeliot.com/archives (accessed 18 April 2012). [2] Ibid.

Other source
Steve Geliot, email correspondence, 19 April 2012.

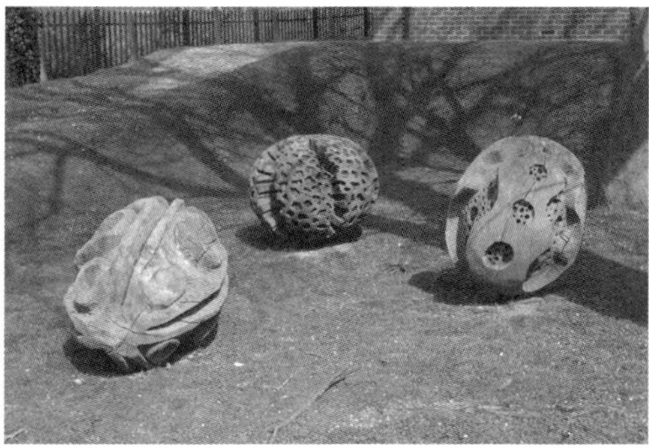

Steve Geliot, *Pollen Forms*

Hillside

Junction with London Road, on grassed area opposite the Freshfield (Village) Hall

War Memorial

Sculptor: Ernest George Gillick

Installed: 1920
Materials/dimensions: stone, sculptures and
    top of monument, 2 m high × 85 cm wide ×
    85 cm deep; shaft, 2.55 m high × 58 cm
Signature (base of north face of shaft): E.G.
    GILLICK / SC. 1920

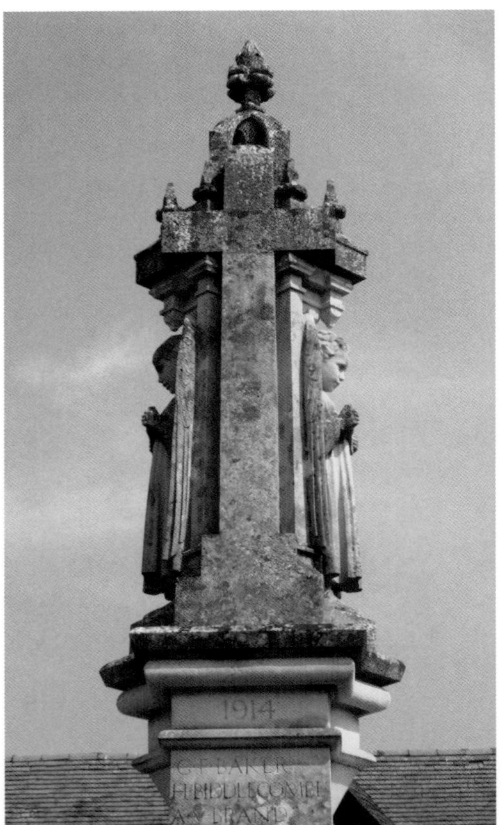

Ernest George Gillick, *War Memorial*

Inscription (around base, starting on west face):
IN REMEMBRANCE OF / MEN OF FOREST ROW /
WHO DIED FOR ENGLAND / IN THE GREAT
WARS
Status: not listed
Condition: good (but considerable biological
    growth all over)
Owner/custodian: Forest Row Parish Council

The stone shaft of the memorial is topped by a
Latin cross at the back with figures of children
depicted as angels at each side. The whole is
surmounted by a foliate finial. The children's
faces resemble photographs of Henry Douglas
Freshfield, son of the owners of Kidbrooke
Park, who died aged 14 on 16 September 1891.
His family funded the building of the village
hall, designed by J.M. Brydon in 1892 (rebuilt
in 1895 following a fire), as a memorial gift to
the people of Forest Row. It is appropriate that
the war memorial stands facing the Grade II
listed hall, as if incorporating several layers of
remembrance.

Sources
Byford, E.C., *A Centenary Celebration of Forest Row
    Village Hall 1892–1992*, Forest Row, 1992.
forestrowvillagehall.org/history (accessed 8
    December 2010).
UKNIWM ref. 17284.

Friston Hill

*The Selwyn (North) Transept, Parish
Church of St. Mary the Virgin (formerly in
the chancel)*

Monument to Sir Thomas Selwyn

Sculptor: Isaac James (attributed)

Installed: after 1613
Materials/dimensions: monument: alabaster and
    grey marble with gilding and painted
    decoration, 2.4 m high; base: 1.8 m wide ×
    50 cm deep

Inscription (on plaque behind kneeling figures):
DM / & / MEMORIAE SACRUM / THOMAE
SELWYN ARMIGERO (EX ANTI / QUA IN HOC
TRACTU SELWYNORUM/ORIUNDO FAMILIA)
VIRO (DUM VIXIT) EXI / MIA & PIETATE &
PROBITATE & COMITATE / SINGULARI & AD
GENTILUM & AMICORUM / SUBSIDIA SEMPER
PRONO. / EX ELIZABETHA CONIUGE HENRICI
GORING / A BURTON EQUITIS AURATI FILIA,
TRES / SUSCEPIT FILIOS (VERO TENERIS IN /
ANNIS LUCEM HANC AMISERE) & FILIAS SEX /
MARIAM NEMPE THO: WOODWARD LOCATUM
/ ELIZABETHAM THOME PARKER / ALICIAM
IOHANNI WODWARD / DOROTHEAM/ANNAM,
& BEATRICEM. / V. ANN.LXVII. ANIMAM
CHRISTO REDDI/DIT APUD FRISTON XVI
MARTII A. SALUTIS MDCXIII / EXPECTANT
EXUME HIC CONDITQ MAGNU / QUE UNIVERSI
EXPECTAMQ DIEM / L. M. P.MOER. /
ELIZABETHA CONIUNX (Sacred to the memory
of Thomas Selwyn Esquire (descended from
the ancient Selwyn family in this district) A
man (while he lived) distinguished for piety,
honesty and liberality and ever ready to
come to the aid of relatives and friends. By
Elizabeth his wife, a daughter of Henry
Goring of Burton, Knight, he has three sons
(who lost the light of this life in their tender
years) and six daughters, Mary, joined in
wedlock to Thomas Woodward, Elizabeth to
Thomas Parker, Alice to John Woodward,
Dorothy, Anne, Beatrice. He lived for 67
years and rendered his soul to Christ at
Friston on the sixteenth March in the year of
our salvation 1613. His remains hidden here
await the great day for which all men look.
Elizabeth his sorrowing wife placed this
stone in memory)
Status: not listed
Condition: good (some minor damage to
    kneeling figure, third from left on base)
Commissioned by: Selwyn family
Owner/custodian: Parish Church of St Mary
    the Virgin

The monument has two principal figures,

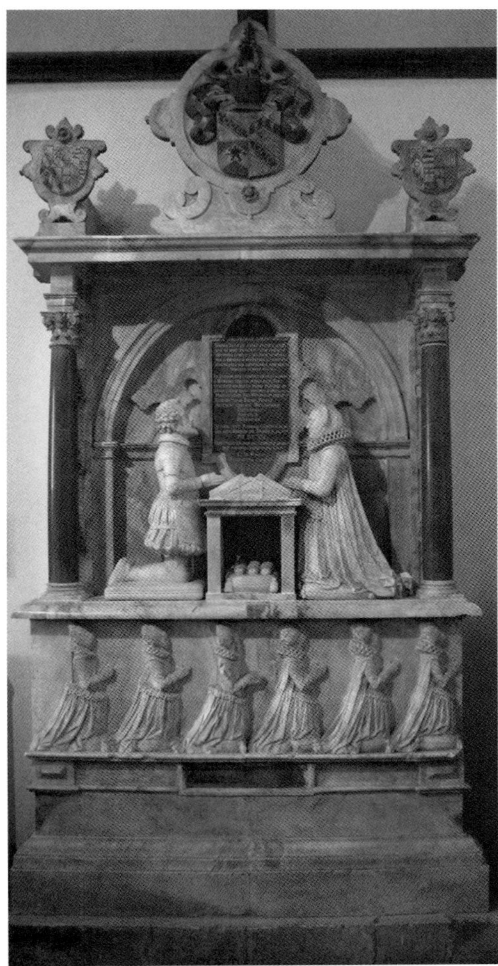

Isaac James (attrib.), *Monument to Sir Thomas Selwyn*

depicting Thomas and Elizabeth Selwyn, kneeling either side of a prayer desk with open volumes. Beneath the desk three infant corpses, referring to three sons who died in childhood, rest on a cushion; around the base, six kneeling figures depict six surviving daughters. The memorial is surmounted by three carved, painted and gilded armorial crests.

The Selwyn transept was built around the middle of the nineteenth century by Miss Anne Gilbert:

… for the purpose of providing additional seating accommodation, and also as a place to move two of the Selwyn Monuments, which up to that time had stood in the Chancel and considerably reduced its space.[1]

On the opposite side of the transept to the Thomas Selwyn monument is a large marble slab with shields of many quarterings surmounted by the crest of the family, a flaming torch held by lion's paws. On this monument is a record of Sir Francis Selwyn, his large family and the death of his son and heir, William Thomas, 'last of the ancient family'.[2] There are two further monuments to the Selwyn family in the church; a brass memorial on an oak base, originally inlaid in Sussex marble, in a blocked up doorway, on the south wall of the nave and a worn stone memorial beneath the carpet of the aisle.

Notes
[1] Evans, Rev. A.A., *Friston Parish Church: a Short Historical Account*, revised edn 2006, np. [2] Ibid.

Other sources
Evans, Rev. A.A., *The Selwyns of Sussex*, 1923, revised edn 2002.
Llewellyn (2011), pp. 139–40.

Eastbourne Road (A22)

Opposite Crockstead Hotel and Showground

Bow Bells Pelham Milestone
Sculptor: unknown

Installed: 1754
Materials/dimensions: cast iron on wooden support, 1 m high × 30 cm wide × 15 cm deep
Status: not listed
Condition: fair (old paintwork falling away; structure covered with ivy. Similar mileposts have five Bow bells, but there is no evidence that one has been removed from this one)
Commissioned by: Union Point to Langney Bridge Turnpike Trust
Owner/custodian: Wealden District Council

The milestone, located at the roadside, faces northeast. It bears a relief of a buckle at the top, representing the Pelham family, the number 46 underneath and a series of four bells on a bowed ribbon, decreasing in size towards the base. All the relief elements are painted black.

In 1356 at the battle of Poitiers a local knight, Sir John Pelham, together with Sir Roger De La Warr captured Jean the King of France and Sir John was given the King's belt buckle as a badge of honour. This badge can be seen on many churches and buildings in the area around Laughton, showing the influence and power of the Pelham family, who once owned much of the land in Sussex.

This is one of a series of Bow Bells milestones on the A22 between Hailsham and East Grinstead, the longest sequence of milestones in the country. Others can be found on the A26 between Uckfield and Lewes and between East Grinstead and Forest Row. They were erected by the Turnpike Trusts that were formed in the eighteenth century to improve roads. This type is known as a 'rebus' or puzzle milestone because of the visual reference to Bow Bells Church in the City of London from where most roads heading south were measured.[1]

Note
[1] Arscott, D. (1991), p. 46

Other sources
R. Caldicott (Milestone Society), email correspondence, 14 August 2007.
Haselfoot, A.J., *The Batsford Guide to the Industrial Archaeology of South-East England: Kent, Surrey, East Sussex and West Sussex*, London, 1978, pp. 84–87.
msocrepository.co.uk (accessed 20 December 2010).
Swinfen and Arscott (1984), p. 72.

Bethune Way

ALEXANDRA PARK

Boating Lake, southern end of park

Continuum

Sculptor: Rick Kirby

Unveiled: 20 May 2005
Materials/dimensions: welded stainless steel
    plates, 3.5 m high × 7 m deep
Status: not listed
Condition: good
Commissioned by: Hastings Borough Council,
    Arts Council South East, Hastings
    Greenway and the Southern Water
    Compensation Fund
Owner/custodian: Hastings Borough Council

Rick Kirby, *Continuum*

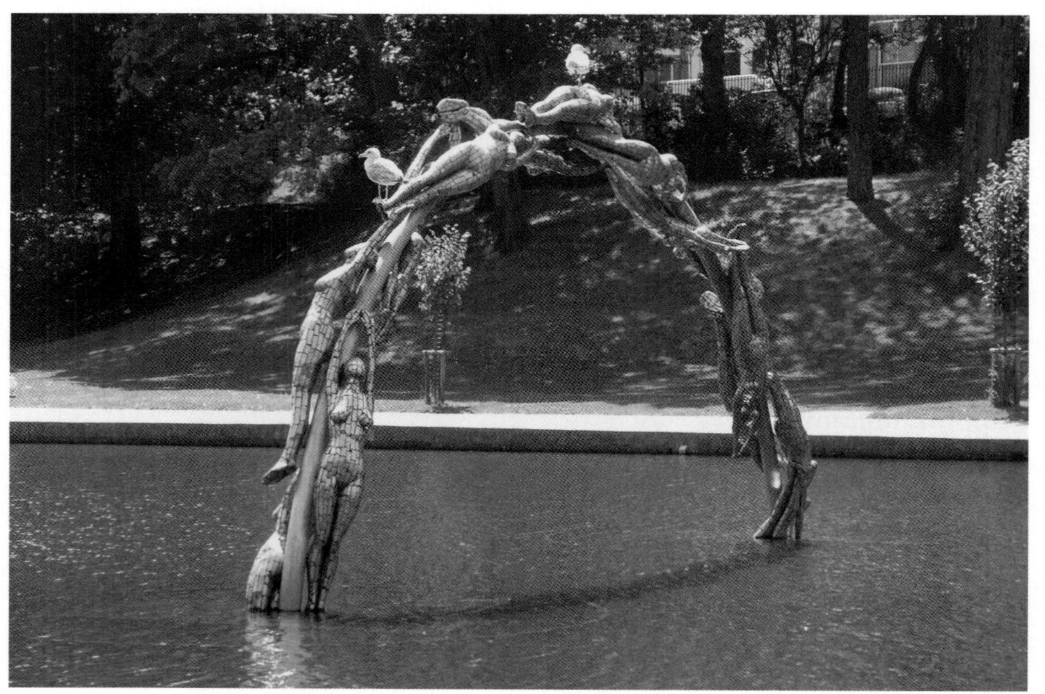

The sculpture forms an arch of intertwined diving female figures, emerging from, and disappearing into, the water, in the middle of the boating lake. The arch is high enough for boaters to row underneath. It is illuminated by underwater lights at night. The commission was advertised locally and nationally and attracted a large number of responses. The artists' brief stated:

> In the creation of the artwork the artist is invited to take into consideration the outstanding features of Alexandra Park: natural beauty, historic landscaping, lakes and streams, wildlife etc. They should also be aware of the ethos of the Greenway, promoting access to green spaces, healthy living, environmental awareness and alternatives to motorised transport. The proposed artwork may therefore [embody] the overall ethos of the park while firmly looking forward to modern Hastings.[1]

A panel consisting of representatives of the Friends of Alexandra Park, Better Braybrooke, Custodians of the Park and Hastings Young Persons' Council selected Kirby's design from a shortlist of six, believing that it was most effective at livening up the lake.[2] Its stylized nude female figures made up of many small metal plates are a constant theme of his public art.[3] To celebrate the installation of the sculpture a free boating evening was held on the lake on the evening of its unveiling.

Notes
[1] hastings.gov.uk/about/issue28_continuum (accessed 5 October 2010). [2] Ibid. [3] rickkirby.com (accessed 2 June 2011).

Other source
M. Hambridge (Public Art Development Officer, Hastings Borough Council), email correspondence, 31 January 2006.

Bethune Way/Lower Park Road

In Alexandra Park

War Memorial

Sculptor: Margaret Winser

Unveiled: 26 March 1922
Materials/dimensions: column: painted
    limestone, approx. 6 m high; statue: bronze:
    approx. 1.4 m high; base: stone with grassed
    areas: 6 m diam.
Signature (south-facing relief, bottom right):
    MARGARET WINSER / DSGNR & SC.
Inscriptions: (NE face, underneath relief, carved
    in black painted letters into stepped base of
    obelisk): ON LAND / BURMA NORTH AFRICA /
    GALLIPOLI / FRANCE PALESTINE; (NW face,
    underneath relief, carved in black painted
    letters into stepped base of obelisk): AT SEA /
    FAR EAST KOREA / SALONIKA / WEST AFRICA
    ITALY; (south face, underneath relief, carved
    in black painted letters into stepped base of
    obelisk): IN THE AIR / FALKLANDS /
    MESOPOTAMIA / EAST AFRICA BELGIUM;
    (south face, underneath top of obelisk):

COURAGE; (NW face, underneath the top of obelisk: VIGILANCE; (NE face, underneath top of obelisk): FORTITUDE; (on curved wall around back of monument, carved in blue painted letters): THEIR NAME LIVETH FOREVER MORE WE WILL REMEMBER THEM
Status: Grade II
Condition: good (in October 1990 the bronze plaques listing war dead were stolen. They were replaced in 1991, post Second World War names were added and the memorial was completely renovated)
Owner/custodian: Hastings Borough Council

The memorial design is described in the listing details of 2002 as comprising:

… a triangular chamfered limestone column (now painted) decorated with swags and shields of Hastings Borough, surmounted by a winged figure with a spear and wreath, symbolising Victory. Three bronze reliefs are set into the base of the column depicting all three armed services; the Army, symbolised by foot soldiers with rifles; the Navy by ratings in a warship moving a buoy and the RAF by an aviator in an aeroplane. Three steps are inscribed with the names of battles and theatres of war. A large polygonal plinth is inscribed with the names of the Fallen and originally contained flowerbeds but these have been cemented over.[1]

The memorial was built to commemorate some 1250 men from the Borough of Hastings who died in the First World War. A large crowd, estimated at over 10,000 people, assembled in the park to witness the unveiling by General the Earl of Cavan and dedication by the Lord Bishop of Chichester, the Right Reverend Winfrid Oldfield Burrows.[2]

The sculptor Margaret Winser's treatment of

Margaret Winser, *War Memorial*

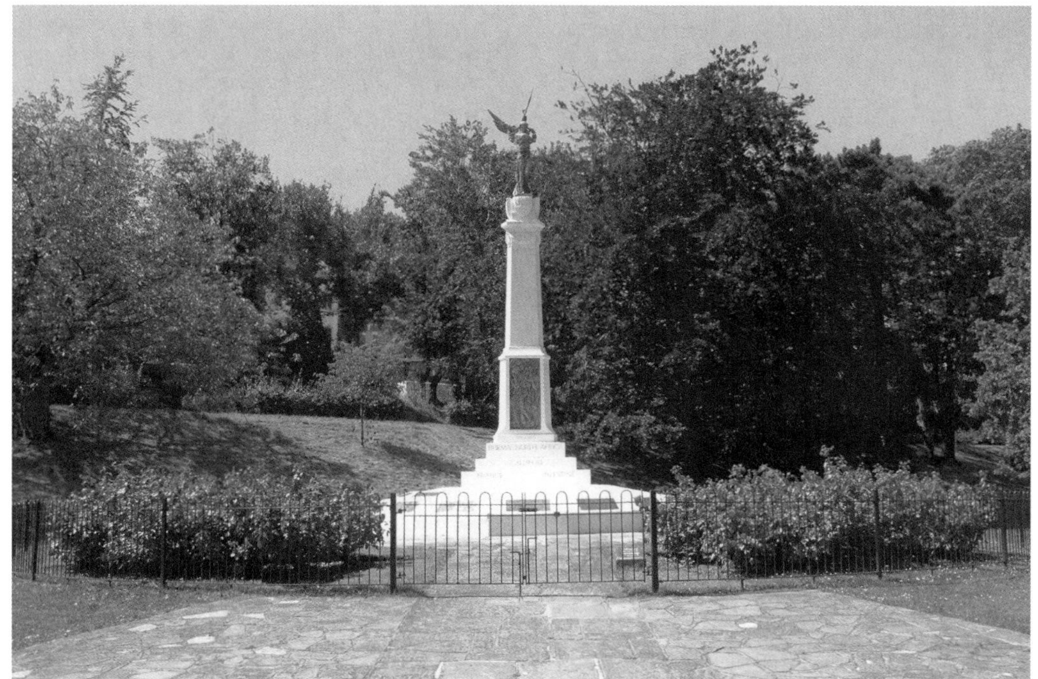

the figures is both realistic and dynamic. She was photographed in the local paper at work on the model of the memorial and in Alexandra Park inspecting the bronze figure shortly to be placed at the top.[3]

Notes
[1] *Planning (Listed Buildings and Conservation Areas) Act 1990: 33rd Amendment of the 3rd List of Buildings of Special Architectural or Historic Interest,* Hastings Borough Council Archive, 7 February 2002. [2] *Hastings and St Leonards Observer,* 25 March, 1 April and 2 December 1922. [3] Ibid., 4 and 8 February 1922.

Holmsdale Gardens
Summerfields Woods
The Greenspace Project

This project was run by the British Trust for Conservation Volunteers (BTCV, an organisation that works with people to improve their environment) to promote and improve green spaces in Hastings and St Leonards. Funding came from the Council's Smarten Up money, Hastings Regeneration Partnership, the Environment Agency, Biffaward and Arts Council England. Local residents helped select 10 sites around the borough and were involved with improvements to paths, steps and bridges and with the management of habitats.

One of the selected sites was Summerfields, a well-used semi-natural woodland with stream and ponds, which had suffered 30 years of neglect and disrepair. This part of the project benefitted from the Hendley Bequest, left by Miss Vera Hendley, a resident of Holmesdale Gardens at the time of her death, to ensure the upkeep and maintenance of Brisco's Walk, which runs the length of the northern side of the woods. It was the fifth local nature reserve declared by the council and the first to have an extensive art project associated with it, with the creation of four interconnected sculptures by Joc Hare, who describes himself as an arborist and sculptor and *Leaping Fish* by Leigh Dyer.

The revival of the Summerfields woods and

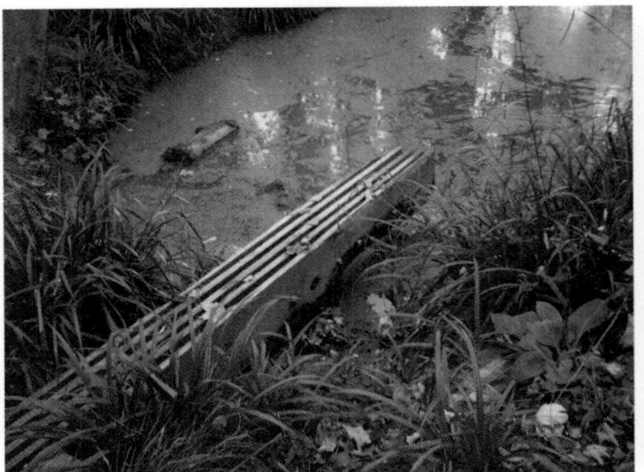

Joc Hare, *Weir Tree*

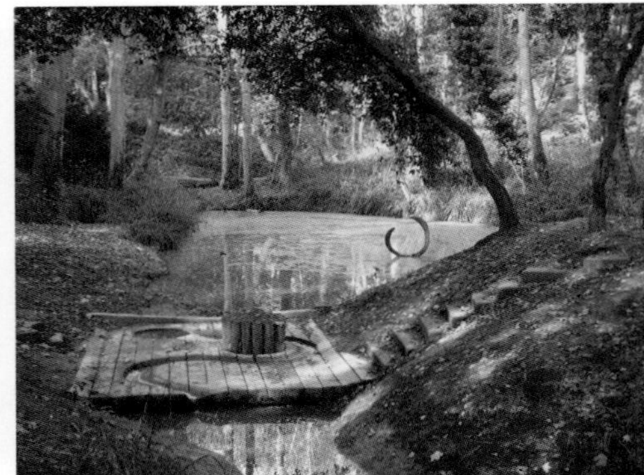

Joc Hare, *Hendley's Repose*

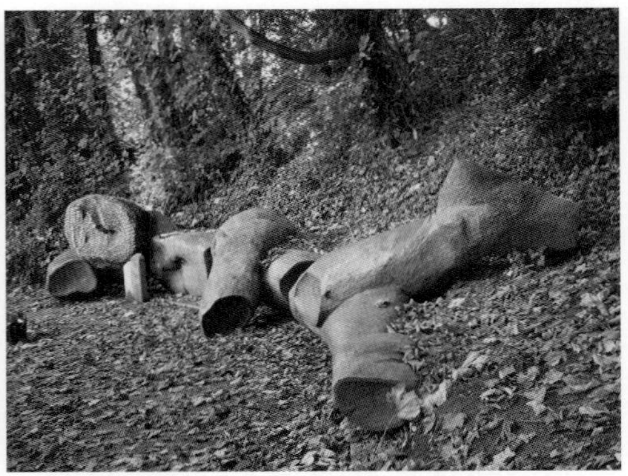

Joc Hare, *Jack*

ponds was celebrated in style on 16 June 2004; guests were led to the ponds from various meeting points by colourful costume-clad characters, courtesy of the Radiator Arts group. Singer Dessie Stefanov and musician Trevor Watts serenaded the 100-strong crowd as they wandered around the candlelit glen.

At the ponds in Summerfields Woods
Weir Tree
Sculptor: Joc Hare

Constructed: 2003
Materials/dimensions: 5 parallel panels, wood, 46 cm high × 6.38 m wide × 36 cm deep
Condition: good

The Weir Tree is an oak tree cut in lengthways strips. The water flows through it from one pond, as in a normal weir, and drops waterfall-like a foot or so into another pond

At the ponds in Summerfields Woods
Hendley's Repose
Sculptor: Joc Hare

Constructed: 2004
Materials/dimensions: base: wooden decking 17 cm high × 4.07 m wide × 3.18 m deep; circular uprights: wooden logs, 41 cm high × 86 cm wide × 82 cm deep; pool: wood and metal, 56 cm high × 79 cm wide × 79 cm deep
Condition: good

This piece, named after the local benefactress, consists of a wooden ford and log roll seat, with wooden steps up to a further seat at the end of the lower pond. The water rises up in a circular well within the ford and then meanders across the surface before falling into the next pool.

In Summerfields woodland near Gardens entrance
Jack
Sculptor: Joc Hare

Installed: May 2004
Materials/dimensions: painted wood, legs: 98 cm high × 3.3 m wide × 1.98 m deep; lower torso and thighs, 1.1 m high × 2.9 m wide × 1.12 m deep; head and upper torso, 1.42 m high × 3.94 m wide × 1.85 m deep
Signature (on torso): Jack / Joc Hare May 04 / www.logjam.net
Condition: good

This abstracted wooden figure is constructed from three cut and sculpted logs. It is reclining on its right-hand side just behind two old marker stones.

Sources
against-the dark.org accessed (15 December 2010).
bohemiawga.weebly.com/hbc-public-art (accessed 17 December 2010).
M. Hambridge (Public Art Development Officer, Hastings Borough Council), email correspondence, 31 January 2006.
hastings.gov.ukaccessed (15 December 2010).

Queen's Road

Queens Square, outside the entrance to Priory Meadow Shopping Centre

The Spirit of Cricket
Sculptor: Allan Sly

Unveiled: 6 June 1997
Materials/dimensions: patinated bronze, 3 m high × 1.8 m wide × 80 cm deep
Signature (on corner of base): Sly97
Inscription (on bronze plaque to the northwest of statue): "THE SPIRIT OF CRICKET" / Unveiled by HER MAJESTY THE QUEEN to celebrate the / opening of Priory Meadow Shopping Centre. / Priory Meadow Shopping Centre is built on the / site of the former Central Cricket and Recreation Ground / on which the game was enjoyed for over 130 years. / Commissioned by Boots Properties PLC. / Sculptor – Allan Sly FRBS 6th June 1997
Status: not listed

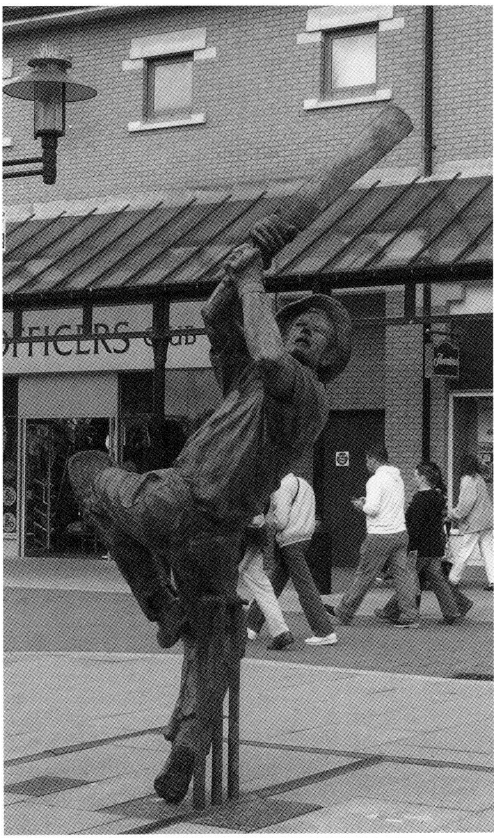

Allan Sly, *The Spirit of Cricket*

Condition: good
Commissioned by: Boots Properties Plc
Owner/custodian: BTW Shiells

The sculpture depicts a cricketer, wearing a sun hat and cricket pads, at the wickets, standing on one leg, bat raised in the air, turning in the direction of the ball he has just hit. The ball is set some 9 m high on the wall of a nearby shop.

The Ridge

BALDSLOW

In the grounds of Holmhurst St Mary, next to St Anne's House (formerly outside St Paul's Cathedral, London)

Statue of Queen Anne
Sculptor: Francis Bird
Architect: Sir Christopher Wren

Unveiled: 7 July 1713
Materials/dimensions: Queen Anne's statue: Sicilian marble, 2.5 m high × 1.2 m wide × 1 m deep; allegorical statues: Sicilian marble, 2 m high × 1.1 m wide × 70 cm deep; stepped base: stone: 1 m high × 5 m wide × 5 m deep; plinth: stone, 3 m high × 2.38 m wide
Status: Grade II*
Condition: poor (all lower group have faces and arms missing. Base is seriously damaged with cracks and breaks on all aspects. Queen Anne has arms and nose missing; much of the fine detail on her robes has eroded, leaving only faint tracery on the dress. Base has heavy moss all over, particularly to the east)
Commissioned by: Committee for St Paul's Cathedral

Due to the very poor condition of Bird's original sculpture, the following details of poses and iconography are taken from Philip Ward-Jackson's description of the exact replica executed by Malempre, which currently stands outside St Paul's cathedral:

> The Queen is represented standing, the crown on her head, the Order of St. George round her neck, and with the sceptre in her right hand and the orb in her left. Her sceptre is held pointing downwards. The Queen looks imperiously upwards and to her right. The statue has a substantial oval self-base.

> The plinth is also oval in general section, with an elaborate cornice, and four projections corresponding with the four surrounding allegorical figures. Between the projections are panels with frame mouldings. The whole structure stands on a circular platform with four steps, and is surrounded with a cast iron railing.

> To the front of the plinth stands a cartouche with the Royal Arms, which Britannia, to the left of it, supports with her left hand. With her right hand she supports a metal trident. Britannia looks upward to her left, and wears a laurel crown. She is amply dressed, with Minerva's breastplate adorned with a gorgon mask, worn as if it were a sash.

> France is seated with her eyes lowered towards her right. She is amply clad, and wears on her head a helmet with three fleurs-de-lis on the visor, surmounted by a plume sweeping backwards. Her right hand rests on a substantial truncheon, whose other end rests on the ground. With her right hand she steadies a large mural crown, which rests on her advanced left leg. Unlike Britannia, who is opposite to her at the front of the monument, she makes no physical contact with the cartouche bearing the Royal Arms.

> America is to the back of the monument on the north side. She looks upward to her right and wears a feathered headdress. Her body is naked, except for a feathered skirt and a drapery traversing her loins. The drapery folds about her right arm and hangs down between her legs. America's hair falls down upon her shoulders. She has a quiver of arrows at her back, supported by a strap, which appears over her left shoulder. In her left hand she holds a metal bow. Her right hand is raised and appears to have been clasping something, possibly an arrow. Her naked right foot rests on a severed, bearded male head, behind which stands a large lizard …

> Ireland is seated at the back of the monument on the south side. She is well draped but has a bare left breast. Her hair is loose and hangs down her back. A harp rests on her right thigh, which she supports with both hands.[1]

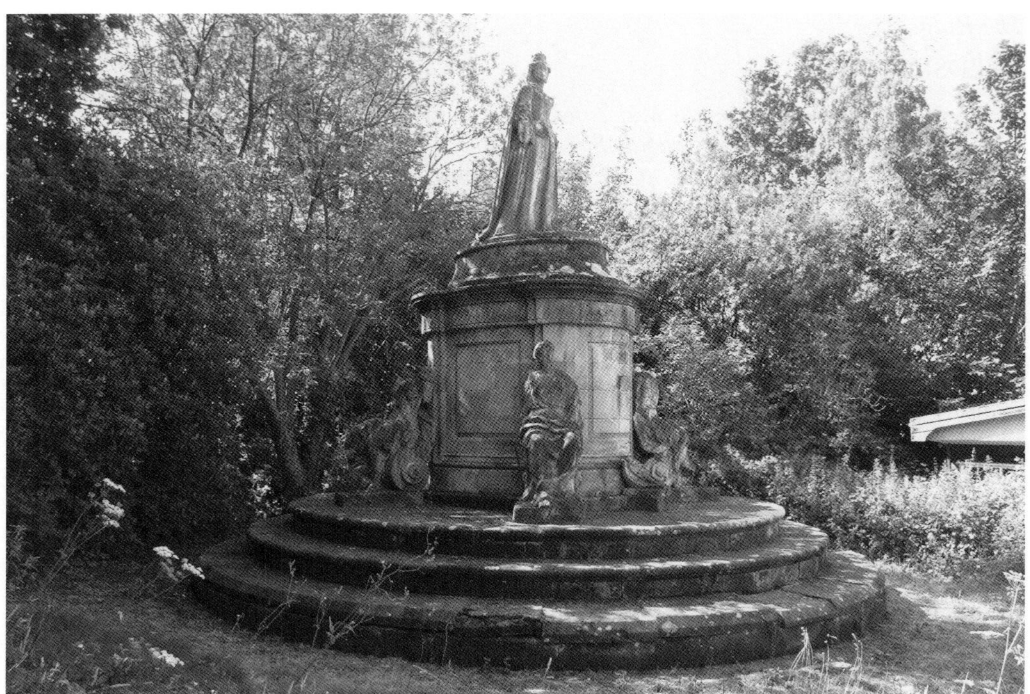

Francis Bird, *Statue of Queen Anne*

The statue by Bird was formerly sited in front of St Paul's Cathedral at the head of Ludgate Hill. Queen Anne saw herself as the inheritor of many of the attributes of Queen Elizabeth I and her image:

> … was promoted as a symbol of unity, first in the wake of the Union of England and Scotland in 1707 and then in celebration of national military victories in the War of the Spanish Succession.[2]

Following the signing of the Treaty of Utrecht in 1713, there was an ambitious scheme to erect 50 new churches in London, each with it own statue commemorating the queen.[3] This was abandoned following the Queen's death in 1714, but Bird, who had already executed much of the figurative sculpture on the cathedral, seems to have received the commission for the St Paul's statue around 1709.[4] Bird's statue,

within its enclosure, was intended to form part of the cathedral environs, although Sir Christopher Wren deviated from his original plan for a piazza and baptistery tower. Ward-Jackson describes the monument as '… the earliest example to survive in Britain of this baroque type … with radiating allegories…', suggesting that Bird had in mind examples in Rome and Paris.[5] Although the sculptural ensemble was, on the whole, well-received, the statue of the queen was both criticised and physically attacked, in 1743 and 1769, by delusional individuals, who caused considerable damage. Following public complaints to the Lord Mayor about its derelict condition, it was decided in 1886 to replace the damaged statue. The contract was given to Messrs Mowlem and Sons who employed Richard Belt for the work. After preparing plaster models, he apparently asked to be released from the employment and the artistic work was carried out by Monsieur Louis Auguste Malempre.

The original statue was placed in the care of the Cathedral trustees in 1887. It was discovered 18 months later, lying in the City stone yard by Mr Augustus J.C. Hare, a travel author, who wanted it for his estate at Holmhurst, near Hastings. He persuaded the Archbishop of Canterbury, the Bishop of London, and the Lord Mayor to allow him to transport it to his home by road, '… with the aid of twenty-eight horses, four trucks, four trolleys, and sixteen men.'[6] Hare provided a new plinth for the monument and replaced the missing parts, and expressed the hope that, '… they are enjoying the verdure and sea breezes after the smoke of the City.'[7] Since the late nineteenth century, however, the statues have lost the replacement parts, have continued to erode and are currently in a very dilapidated state.

Notes
[1] Ward-Jackson, P., *Public Sculpture of the City of London*, Liverpool, 2003, pp. 374–75. [2] Smith, N., *The Royal Image and the English People*, Cornwall, 2001, p. 134. [3] Ibid. [4] Ward-Jackson provides a detailed account of the commissioning, execution and critical reception of the statue. [5] Ibid. [6] Harper, C.G., 'Banished London', *Harmsworth Monthly Pictorial Magazine*, Vol. 2, No. 9, April 1899, p. 215. [7] Hare, A., *The Story of My Life*, London, vol. 6, 1900, p. 348.

Other sources
Arscott (1991), p. 21.
Darke, J. (ed.), *A User's Guide to Public Sculpture*, London, 2000, p. 34.
Dinsmore, J., *Statues and Memorials in Hastings and St. Leonards: a Report on Condition and Conservation Options*, Hastings, 1997, pp. 35–37.
Gunnis (1953), p. 53.
PMSA online database: Central London; CLCOL/x4; CLCOL215.
Swinfen, W., and Arscott, D., *People of Hidden Sussex*, Sussex, 1985, p. 27.

Junction with Trinity Street, outside the east end of Holy Trinity church

Waldegrave Memorial Drinking Fountain

Architect: Samuel Sanders Teulon

Stone carver: Mr Earp of London

Builder: Mr Howell
Unveiled: 26 May 1862
Materials/dimensions: base: stone, 14 cm high × 2.34 m wide × 2.24 m deep; inscribed panels: red granite (polished), 87 cm high × 78 cm wide; upper section: Portland stone, 2.1 m high × 87 cm wide × 87 cm deep; lower section and fountain: Portland stone, 2 m high × 1.48 m wide × 1.48 m deep
Inscriptions (south face): TO SARAH / COUNTESS OF WALDEGRAVE / IN GRATEFUL COMMEMORATION / OF THE CONSTANT SUPPORT / AFFORDED BY HER TO THE / RELIGIOUS AND BENEVOLENT / INSTITUTIONS OF THE BOROUGH AND NEIGHBOURHOOD; (east face): JESUS SAID / WHOSOEVER / DRINKETH OF THIS WATER / SHALL THIRST AGAIN / BUT WHOSOEVER DRINKETH / OF THE WATER / THAT I SHALL GIVE HIM / SHALL NEVER THIRST; (north face): ERECTED 1861 / BY SUBSCRIPTION / BY THE INHABITANTS OF / HASTINGS AND ST LEONARDS / INCLUDING / THE PENCE OF CHILDREN / AND YOUNG PERSONS / EDUCATED IN THE / NATIONAL SCHOOLS
Status: Grade II
Condition: poor (severe weathering; top of the spire missing; statues of the four evangelists missing from the canopy. No taps or cups at any of the fountains. Figure of Christ severely damaged). Conservation work was carried out in 1995
Funded by: public subscription
Owner/custodian: Hastings Borough Council

The fountain is in Gothic Revival style, with bowls on three sides (S, N and E), set on a single stepped curved base. Above each bowl is a carved red granite plaque set into the stone. Beneath a groined canopy and spire over the fountains are represented figures of Christ and the Woman of Samaria. The canopy is surmounted by richly carved finials and supported by four red granite columns. At the corners originally stood figures of the four evangelists. S.S. Teulon, who designed the memorial, was the architect of Holy Trinity church, the foundation stone of which was laid by the Countess of Waldegrave in 1857. It stands outside the east end of the church, but it is thought, based on photographic evidence, that it was relocated slightly when the vestry was added in 1892.[1]

Countess Waldegrave was born Sarah Whitear, daughter of the Rector of Hastings Old Town. She first married local landowner Edward Milward Jr who was Mayor of Hastings 20 times before his death in 1833. Then 13 years later she married William, Earl of Waldegrave, a senior naval officer and MP who died in 1859. The Countess laid the foundation stones of many of Hastings' churches and provided a public washhouse for the Old Town. The monument was planned as a tribute to her generosity and she was present at the opening ceremony, held on the Queen's birthday.

In 1995, council funds were allocated to the restoration of the fountain, although it was deemed too expensive to restore the water supply. Conservation work on the fountain, which then still possessed three of the evangelists' statues, was managed by WAS Chartered Architects of Uckfield and carried out by the Heritage Stone Restoration Company, of Sidcup Kent.[2]

Notes
[1] Saunders, M., *The Churches of S.S. Teulon*, London, 1982, p. 27. [2] WAS Chartered Architects, 96–98 High Street Uckfield. File: Countess Waldegrave Memorial HBC 95.147.

Other sources
The Argus, 20 August 1990, p. 9; 10 October 1995.
Dinsmore (1997), p. 3.
Hastings and St Leonards News, 30 May 1862.
Obituary, *Hastings News*, 25 April 1873.
Oxford Art Journal, London, 22 January 1916, p. 65.

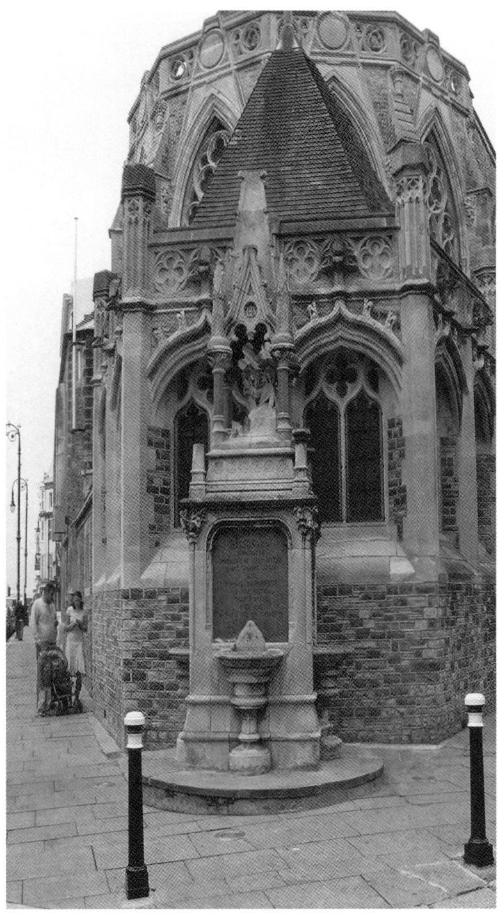

Samuel Sanders Teulon, *Waldegrave Memorial Drinking Fountain*

Southwest and southeast corners of the terrace

Lion and Unicorn

Sculptor: James Bubb (attributed)

Installed: mid-nineteenth century
Materials/dimensions: figures: limestone, 1.8 m
  high × 1.1 m wide × 1 m deep; plinths,
  concrete render over concrete and stone
  core, 2.4 m high × 1.2 m wide × 1.2 m deep
Status: not listed
Condition: poor (sculptures are very weathered,
  causing loss of detail to the carving, and in
  some areas blackened. Plinths have
  crumbling render and corroding armatures
  causing staining. Lion's tail and unicorn's
  horn are missing. Panels are splitting due to
  corrosion of armatures)
Owner/custodian: Hastings Borough Council

The lion stands at the western and the unicorn
at the eastern entrance of Robertson Terrace,
named after P.F. Robertson, MP for Hastings.
The figures, both standing on their hind legs,
holding heraldic shields, are taken from the
'Arms of Dominion' from the United Kingdom
Royal Coat of Arms. The lion represents
England and the Unicorn, Scotland. Their
plinths have carved floral panels stained pink,
on three sides. The heraldic unicorn is chained
as it was regarded in folklore as a very
dangerous beast, only tameable by a virgin.

It is thought that the sculptures were made
for Buckingham Palace as part of the second
phase of work carried out there by Decimus
Burton in 1850–51, but were surplus to
requirements and purchased by Patrick
Roberston, who installed them to denote
Crown ownership of the freehold of the land
on which his development stood.[1] They appear
in situ in a print of 1872. Although they have
been attributed to the sculptor James George
Bubb (?1781–1853) they do not appear in lists
of Bubb's known work.[2]

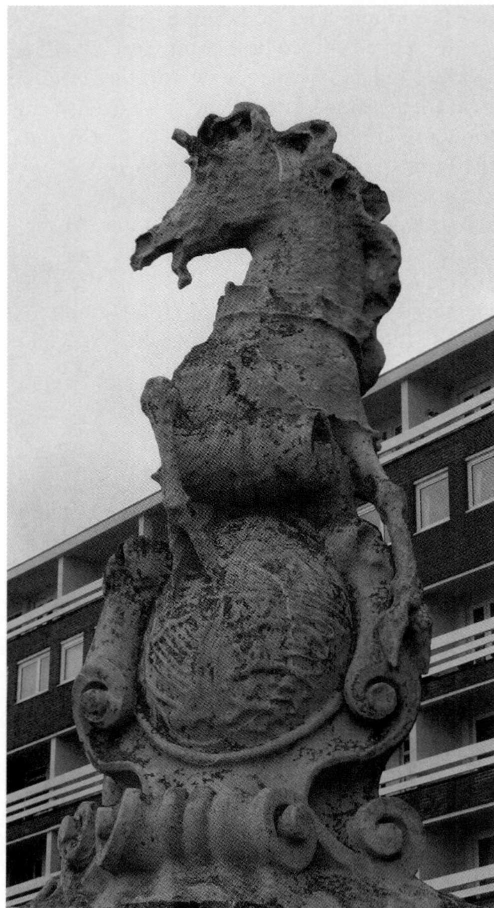

James Bubb (attrib.), *Lion and Unicorn*

Notes
[1] A. Scott (Old Hastings Preservation Society),
email correspondence, 11 November 2010; Alison
Hawkins (Keeper of Archives and Local History
Hastings Museum and Art Gallery), email
correspondence, 13 November 2013. [2] They are
attributed to Bubb in Dinsmore (1997) p. 6, but they
are not listed, for example, under Bubb's works in
Roscoe, I., Hardy, E. and Sullivan, M.G., *A
Biographical Dictionary of Sculptors in Britain 1660–
1851*, New Haven and London, 2009.

Other source
C. Francis (Burtons' St Leonards Society), email
correspondence, 4 and 7 November 2010.

SEAFRONT

Southern Side

Statue of Queen Victoria

Sculptor: Francis John Williamson

Unveiled: 31 December 1902
Materials/dimensions: statue: bronze, 2 m high
  × 1 m wide × 1 m deep; plinth: pink
  Peterhead granite (polished), 2.34 m high
Signature (on northwest side of base statue): F.J.
  WILLIAMSON. SC / ESHER 1902
Inscriptions (south face of plinth): VICTORIA R I
  / 1837 – 1901
Status: Grade II
Condition: fair (there is a hole in the bronze,
  approximately 3 cm across, on the front
  lower part of the Queen's robes, near the
  knee, where the statue was hit by a bullet
  from an enemy bomber in the Second World
  War. The statue was treated and repainted in
  November 1964)
Owner/custodian: Hastings Borough Council

The statue represents Queen Victoria at the
time of her first Jubilee in 1887. She is robed
and wearing a crown, standing with her hands
crossed, holding a sceptre in her right hand. She
stands upon an integral plinth bearing an
anthemion pattern. The statue was modelled
from sittings taken at Windsor Castle and the
Queen lent Williamson the jewels, robes, etc.,
to complete the work. It is a replica of an
original in marble that was placed in the
Examination Hall of the College of Surgeons. It
cost £844 15s, of which £787 10s was the
sculptor's fee. Williamson executed other
replicas for Londonderry, Rangoon, Perth,
Western Australia, King William's Town, South
Africa, Paisley, Scotland, Auckland and
Christchurch, New Zealand, and the North
West Province of India. At the time of the
Hastings unveiling, by the Marquis of
Abergavenny, Lord Lieutenant of Sussex,

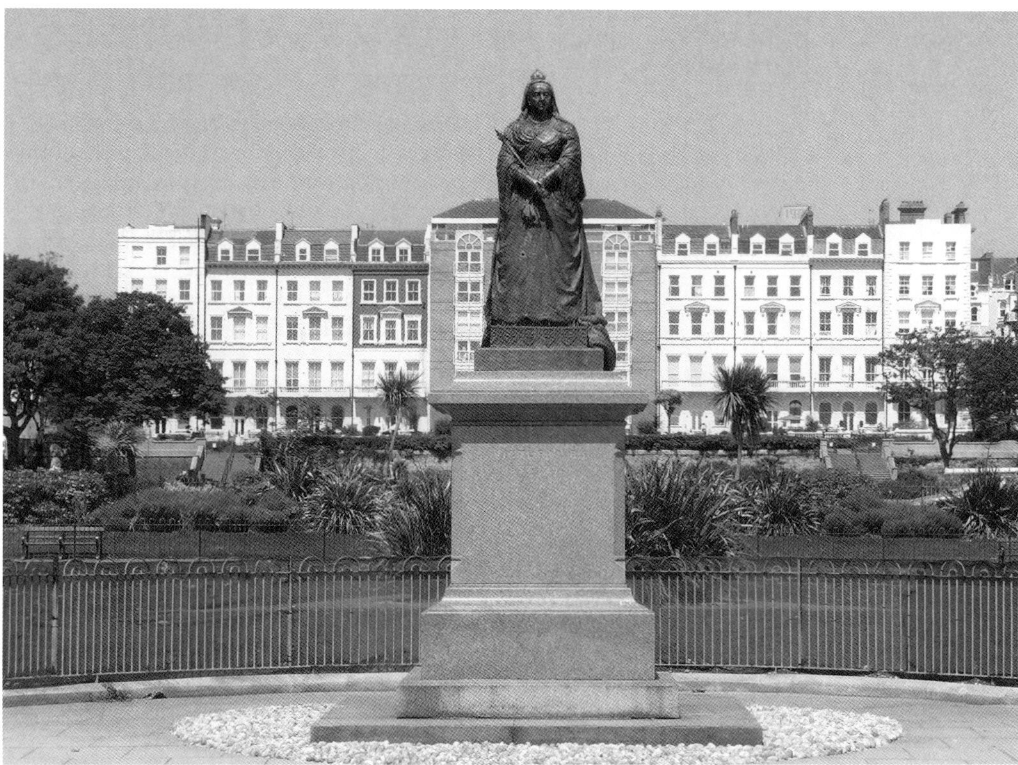

Francis John Williamson, *Statue of Queen Victoria*

Williamson stated, 'This is the only town in Sussex in which I have anything'.[1]

The memorial committee had debated how to commemorate the passing of the Queen. It had been thought that some building or object, beneficial to the poor or sick, would be more appropriate than a statue, but cost implications prevented this both in terms of initial outlay and in subsequent annual maintenance costs. When a statue had been decided upon and the commission given to Williamson, the late Queen's private sculptor, it was also hoped to transform Warrior Square Gardens with fountains, flower beds, etc., but local landowners would only give up the small strip of land on which the statue was subsequently placed.

Note
[1] *Hastings and St. Leonard's Observer*, 3 January 1903.

Other sources
Dinsmore (1997), p. 11.
Haines, P., *Hastings in Old Photographs: a Second Selection*, Sutton, 1991, p. 130.
Hastings Observer, 7 November 1964, p. 1.

White Rock
On esplanade to east of pier

Boer War Memorial
Designers: J.M. Whitehead and Sons Ltd

Unveiled: 6 May 1903
Materials/dimensions: red Aberdeen granite, bronze and gun metal, 5.4 m high × 1.95 m wide × 1.94 m deep

Inscriptions (on south face, in black painted carved letters, repainted in 1995): ERECTED BY THE / INHABITANTS OF THIS BOROUGH / TO THE MEMORY OF / THEIR BRAVE FELLOW TOWNSMEN / WHO FELL IN THE SOUTH AFRICAN WAR / 1899 TO 1902; (names of the fallen are inscribed on the other three faces)
Status: not listed
Condition: good (but large piece of step broken off at northwest corner. Small holes in granite of base on the west face underneath flags on east face. Some wind damage to south face (facing sea) and some corrosion evident to the bronze flags)
Owner/custodian: Hastings Borough Council

The memorial is in the form of a Corinthian column, which is surmounted by a ball finial on which sits a bronze flame. Crossed gunmetal flags, representing the Union Jack and the colours of the Royal Sussex Regiment, are draped near the base of the column. The column rests on an octagonal base, which, in turn, sits on a rectangular plinth, standing on two unpolished granite steps.

There were objections to the proposed site for the memorial, opposite the Grand Hotel, for various practical reasons and the present site was decided on afterwards. The total amount raised for the memorial was £335 10s, £150 of which was a grant from the Council's surplus on the Coronation celebrations and the remainder raised by church collections and individual contributions. The *Hastings and St Leonards Observer* stated that the monument would, '… help to wipe out the stigma – already partially removed by the Queen Victoria memorial in Warrior Square – that Hastings is a statueless and monumentless town'.[1] It was unveiled by Major General Sir Leslie Rundle. The planned date was 29 April 1903, but Major Rundle had to postpone until 6 May 1903.

The memorial was hit by lightning on 19 June 1974, causing so much damage that it had to be dismantled. It had been shifted forwards and sideways and was unstable. The lightning

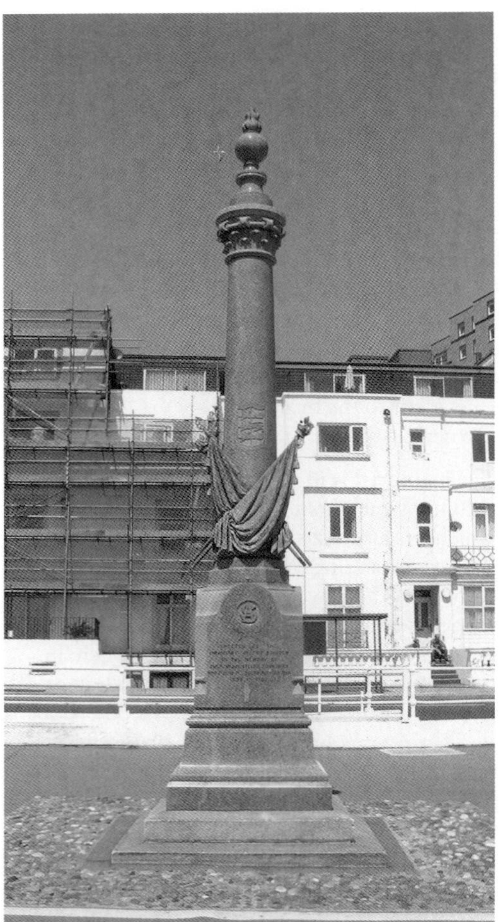

struck the copper flame at the top of the monument, causing it to fall, making a hole in the pavement. A sear mark was created down the front of the memorial. It was eventually restored and placed back in its original position in May 1976. A rededication service was held on 5 September 1976, attended by two survivors from the Boer War, 93-year-old Herbert Steele of Hastings and 95-year-old Archibald Bowers of Sutton-at-Hone, Kent.[2]

Notes
[1] *Peace Memorial: Supplement to the Hastings and St. Leonards Observer*, 9 May 1903. [2] *Hastings and St Leonards Observer*, 11 September 1976.

J.M. Whitehead and Sons Ltd, *Boer War Memorial*

Other sources
Dinsmore (1997), p. 12.
Evening Argus, 20 June 1974.
Hastings and St Leonards Advertiser, 12 March, 26 March, 9 April, 30 April, 7 May and 14 May 1903.

White Rock Road

SEAFRONT

White Rock Theatre (formerly known as White Rock Pavilion); on wall above main entrance and side walls

Eight Decorative Roundels

Sculptor: Gilbert Bayes

Architects: Charles Cowles-Voysey and Hugh Townshend Morgan

Commissioned: 1926 (the building was opened in 1928)
Materials/dimensions: Doulton stoneware, 91.5 cm diam.
Signature (to the right at bottom of each roundel): GILBERT BAYES 1926
Status: not listed
Inscription (on a plaque to the left of the entrance): This stone was laid by / Alderman Fellowes / April 7th 1926
Condition: good (roundels did not require

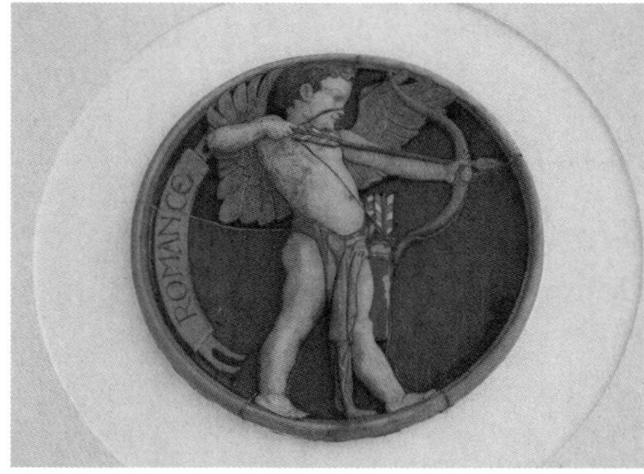

Gilbert Bayes, *Eight Decorative Roundels* (detail)

restoration when the building was repainted in 2012)
Owner/custodian: Hastings Borough Council

The roundels are glazed in blues, browns and greens, each one depicting a cherub symbolising an aspect of the arts and a banner with its title. They are arranged in a frieze, with Romance and Terpsichore (the Greek muse of dance and choral singing) on the west-facing side wall, Adventure and Drama to the west of the main entrance, Romance and Terpsichore again to the east of the entrance and Adventure and Drama repeated on the east-facing side wall. Influenced by the brightly coloured glazed terracotta roundels and reliefs produced by the Della Robbia family in fifteenth- and sixteenth-century Florence, they ornament a cream and white stuccoed building designed for seaside entertainment, described by Pevsner as in the 'Spanish Mission style of America'.[1]

Cowles-Voysey (1889–1981) was the son of the arts and crafts architect Charles Francis Annesley Voysey (1857–1941). According to Louise Irving, he was the first architect to appreciate the decorative potential in Bayes' designs for the Doulton pottery. The White Rock Pavilion was the second building for which he commissioned ceramic roundels, and the same designs were later used for St Christopher's nursery school on the Sidney Street estate, London.[2] *Drama* was also exhibited at the Arts and Crafts Exhibition Society in 1928 (with a price of £36 15s) and *Romance* at the Royal Academy in 1935.[3] Within Sussex, Cowles-Voysey again employed the motif of roundels symbolising the drama in his design of Worthing Assembly Hall (1933–34) and produced another seaside pavilion, the Denton lounge, on Worthing Pier (with John Brandon-Jones, 1959).

Notes
[1] Nairn and Pevsner (1965), p. 527. [2] Irvine, L., and Atterbury, P., *Gilbert Bayes Sculptor 1872–1953*, Shepton Beauchamp, 1998, p. 52. [3] Ibid., pp. 142–43.

Station Approach

At southern and northern entrances to old Heathfield railway tunnel accessed at bottom of Station Approach (to right) or via Millennium Green

Heathfield Tunnel Gates
Sculptor: Hamish Black

Installed: August 2001
Materials/dimensions: steel, each gate 7 m high × 2 m wide
Status: not listed
Condition: good
Commissioned, funded and owned by: Heathfield and Waldron Parish Council and Millennium Green Trust

The design of the gates was the result of workshops held by Hamish Black with pupils from Five Ash Primary School and students from Heathfield Community College. These were based on the original sectional drawing of the tunnel with the two vertical shafts and the diary of diggings to join the shafts and the excavations to either end. Each school viewed the results of the other's workshop and the result was a pile of photocopies from each student's work. This was then cut to the profile of the tunnel and the design came out as overlapping fan shapes within the arch. This image was rationalised by Black into four tones, which were achieved by bending the vertical steel strip at different angles. As he described it: 'by avoiding clichéd design processes we were able to design a completely original work'.[1]

The final design was presented to members of the Council and the Millennium Green Trust on 30 November 1999; work began in January 2000 and a formal opening ceremony occurred in July 2000, but the work was not completed until August 2001.

The tunnel is 250 m long and was opened on

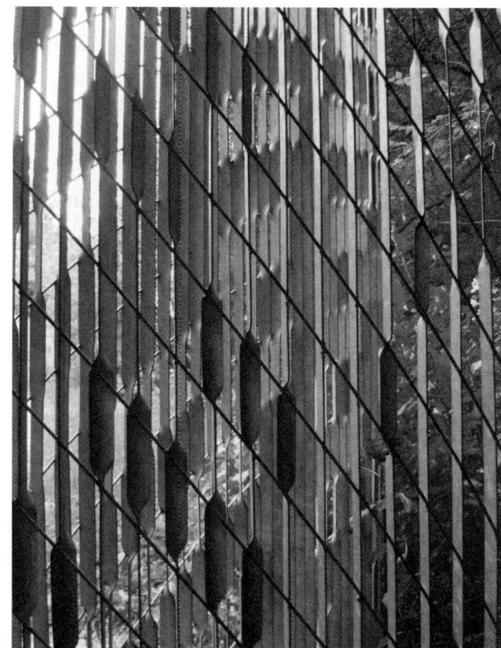

Hamish Black, *Heathfield Tunnel Gates*

3 April 1880 for the London, Brighton and South Coast Railway. The line was closed completely on 5 August 1968 by British Railways' Southern Region. It was restored for pedestrian and cycle use as part of a millennium project and a skateboard park was built in the cutting immediately south of the Tunnel. It was re-opened in January 2002. The tunnel links with the Sustrans cycle way Cuckoo Trail on which are six large steel pavilions mounted on access controls, also by Hamish Black.[2]

Notes
[1] Hamish Black, email correspondence, 2 December 2010. [2] Ibid., 30 November 2010.

Other source
wealden.gov.uk (accessed 1 November 2010).

Church Road

The Dacre Chapel All Saints Church

Monument to Thomas 8th Lord Dacre and Sir Thomas Fiennes
Sculptor: unknown

Installed: 1534
Materials/dimensions: painted Caen stone, Bonchurch stone and Purbeck marble, 4.7 m high × 3.2 m wide × 3 m deep
Status: not listed
Condition: fair (general weathering to stone work. Repainted, predominantly in strong reds and blues with gilding, c. 2000. Noses, fingers and thumb broken off some statuary. Edges of chest tomb broken on all sides)
Commissioned by: Dacre family
Owner/custodian: All Saints Church

The chest tomb is in late Gothic style, with the later addition of a cornice and niches. It bears the recumbent effigies of Thomas, 8th Lord Dacre (1470–1533) and his son, Sir Thomas Fiennes, who predeceased his father in 1528. They wear Milanese armour dating to about 1480, although their heads are bare. They lie side by side with their hands clasped together in prayer and their feet resting on animals, representing the Bull of the Dacre family and the Alant (wolf hound) of the Fiennes family.[1] Both sides of the chest are decorated with quatrefoil motifs, now picked out in red and above the arch facing the Chancel carved shields (the middle one bearing the arms and eagle crest of the Fiennes family) helmets and mantling make up the cornice.

The weathering on the north side of the tomb suggests that it may originally have been placed on the outside wall of the church before the addition of the chapel afforded greater protection from the elements.

The badly deteriorated tomb was restored in

1970 with funding from Mrs Elizabeth Dacre, widow of Air Commodore George Bentley Dacre, C.B.E., D.S.O. Brighton architect John Denman and Wilfred Scott-Giles, O.B.E., F.S.A. F.H.A., Fitzalan Pursuivant Extraordinary of the College of Arms, acted as consultants to the project and the work was executed by Herstmonceux resident and master mason, George Elliott, B.E.M.[2]

The restoration process revealed some original colouring of the shields and it was decided to repaint these, leaving blank those whose motifs could not be conclusively identified. The work also confirmed that the effigies were not originally those of Lord Dacre and his son. Their identity had long been in doubt since their tabards bear the arms of the Hooe family. It was established that they were initially carved to represent the half-brothers Hooe and subsequently altered. In Mary Tate's history of the church, she suggests that the figures might have come from Battle Abbey after its dissolution in 1539, when many of its tombs and carvings were sold off, and were bought and altered by the Dacre family, for financial reasons.[3]

Notes
[1] Tate, M. H., *All Saints Church Herstmonceux*, Herstmonceux, revised edn, 1978, pp. 6–8. [2] Ibid. [3] Ibid.

Other source
Llewellyn (2011), pp. 168–69.

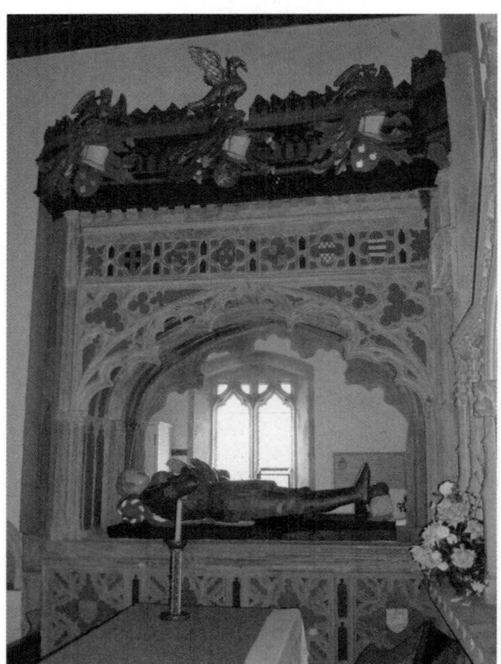

Unknown, *Monument to Thomas 8th Lord Dacre and Sir Thomas Fiennes*

HOVE

1A Connaught Road
Sediment and Cut
Sculptor: Ekkehard Altenburger

Installed: August 2004
Materials/dimensions: *Sediment*: Kilkenny limestone, 1.46 m high × 1.19 m wide × 56 cm deep; *Cut*: Kilkenny Limestone, with yellow and blue acrylic paint, 2.8 m high × 60 cm wide × 60 cm deep
Signature: *Sediment* (bottom left-hand corner, front face, in incised letters): "sediment" / E. Altenburger 2004; *Cut* (bottom left-hand corner, front face, in incised letters): "cut" / E. Altenburger 2004.
Inscription: *Cut* (bottom left-hand corner, below signature, in incised letters): These sculptures were / commissioned for the city of / Brighton & Hove by / KARIS DEVLOPMENTS LTD
Status: not listed
Condition: good
Commissioned by: Karis Developments Ltd under Percent for Art scheme

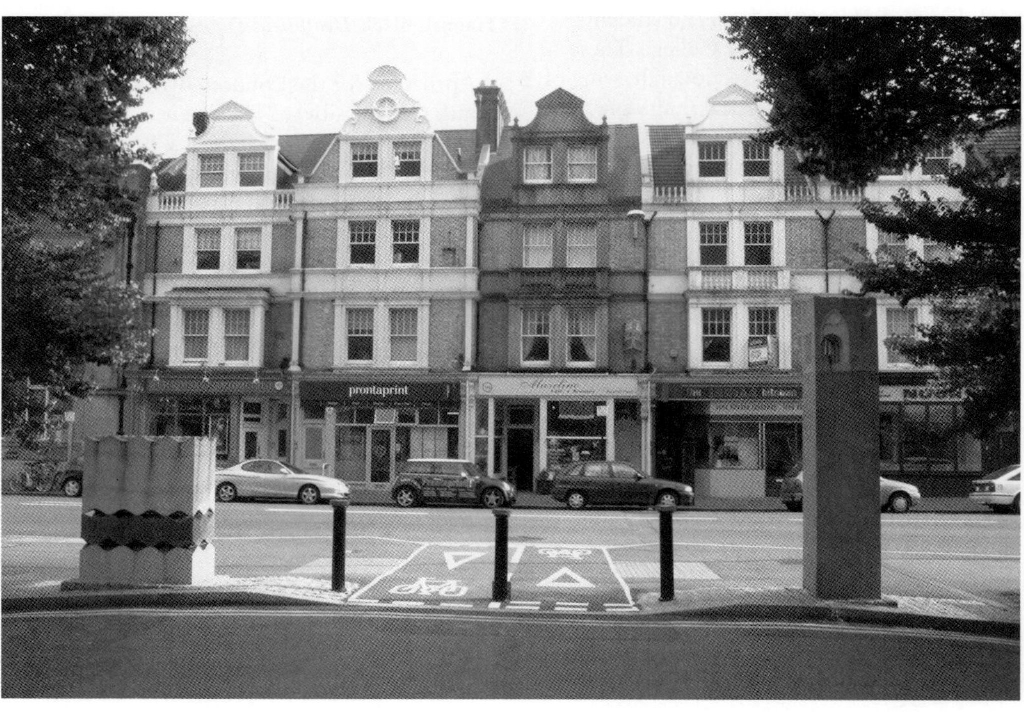

Ekkehard Altenburger, *Sediment and Cut*

The sculpture is formed of two parts, each using 1.2 tonnes of limestone. *Sediment* is a rectangular block, with undulating faces and a darker layer sandwiched between two lighter ones. *Cut* is a taller plinth shape standing opposite, with references to local architecture, including a church window and staircase, highlighted in colour, carved into the top section. The two pieces were inspired by the geology and later urban landscape of Brighton and Hove and were unveiled by Mayor Councillor Pat Drake. They face each other at the end of the road now inaccessible to traffic, marking the entrance to a property development that includes 40% affordable homes for local people.

Sources
altenburger.org.uk (accessed 18 April 2011).
City News (free magazine), October 2004.

Goldstone Crescent

Eastern edge of Hove Park

Fingermaze
Sculptor: Chris Drury

Landscape contractor: Drew Cane
Installed: 2006
Materials/dimensions: York stone set into lime mortar, 30 m wide × 37 m deep
Inscription (information plaque at tip of the design next to the path): Fingermaze / Chris Drury, 2006 / Stone & Lime Mortar / Giant fingerprint / incorporating a / Cretan labyrinth / Walking the labyrinth is / traditionally linked to / contemplation and renewal / – follow the / grass path from the / base of the sculpture / into the centre and back out again.
Status: not listed
Condition: good
Commissioned by: Brighton and Hove City Council for 'Eco-Brighton'
Owner/custodian: Brighton and Hove City Council

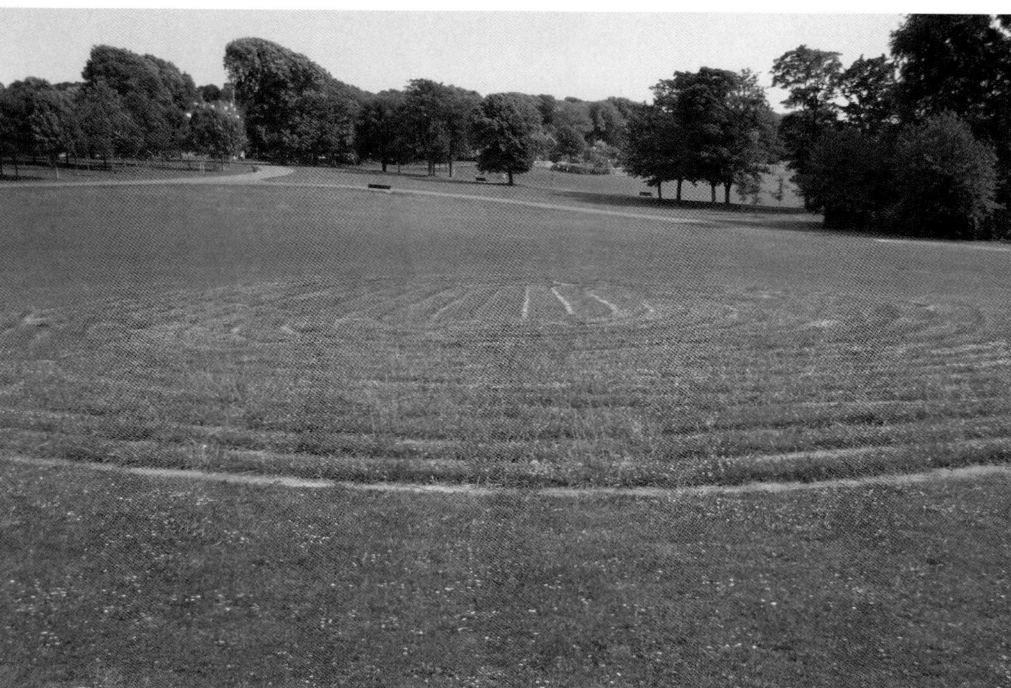

Chris Drury, *Fingermaze*

The labyrinth is based on a fingerprint with a Cretan maze pattern inserted into the central whorl. It is an ancient, mystical pattern containing a meandering path to the centre, which is often used to symbolise the journey through life. These patterns are mirrored in the nerve endings of our fingers, the way in which liquids and blood travel through the body, in the weather system in the sky and patterns in the solar system. Drury refers to these vortex patterns as 'a universal flow'.[1] They are a recurring theme within his work also exemplified by *The Heart of Reeds* in Lewes. Drury has explained, 'the work is a two-dimensional drawing until it is walked; then it becomes a sculpture.'[2]

The work was originally in Stanmer Park, where it was mown temporarily into the turf and then made as a permanent piece in York stone set into lime mortar in Hove Park. Lime mortar was chosen because its production uses less energy and leaves a smaller carbon footprint than cement. Over time the stones weather and weeds and grass creep into the gaps, making the outline more smudged and blurry, increasing the resemblance to real fingerprints.

'Eco-Brighton' was part of a two-year cultural programme in Brighton and Hove called 'Making a Difference', which aimed to transform the cultural life of the city. Chris Drury was selected from many artists who responded to a brief to produce a piece of art based around an environmental issue and to promote more sustainable ways of living.

Notes
[1] *Schools Resource Pack to Accompany Fingermaze in Hove Park*, Brighton and Hove, 2007. [2] Ibid.

Other source
Chaplin, E., 'My Lewes' (interview with Chris Drury), vivalewes.com (accessed 8 July 2011).

Grand Avenue

SEAFRONT

At junction with Kingsway

Statue of Queen Victoria

Sculptor: Thomas Brock

Unveiled: 9 February 1901
Materials/dimensions: statue: bronze, approx.
  3.5 m high × 1.5 m wide × 1.5 m deep;
  pedestal: grey Aberdeen granite, 3.48 m high
  × 2.6 m wide × 2.6 m deep
Signature (on base of statue, on bottom right
  east-facing corner): THOMAS BROCK SC; (on
  bottom left corner of each plaque): Thos
  Brock
Inscriptions (south face on base of plinth):
  ERECTED / BY THE INHABITANTS OF HOVE /
  TO COMMEMORATE THE SIXTIETH
  ANNIVERSARY / OF THE ACCESSION OF /
  QUEEN VICTORIA / JUNE 20 A.D. 1897; (north
  face on the lower section of the pedestal):
  BORN 24 MAY 1819 DIED 22 JAN 1901; (south
  face, circling the top part of the plinth
  anticlockwise): VICTORIA DEI GRA /
  BRITANNIAE REGINA FIDEI DEFENSOR / IND
  IMPERATRIX; (below east face bronze relief):
  EDUCATION; (below west face relief):
  COMMERCE; (below north face relief):
  SCIENCE AND ART; (below south face relief):
  EMPIRE
Status: Grade II
Condition: good (some metallic staining under
  bronze reliefs)
Funded by: public subscription
Owner/custodian: Brighton and Hove City
  Council

The standing statue of Queen Victoria is
depicted life-size, wearing royal regalia with
crown and veil, and facing south, towards the
sea. She holds a sceptre in her right hand and an
orb in her left. The orb is surmounted by the
winged figure of Victory, claimed by John
Sankey to be a reference to Antonio Canova's
Napoleon as Mars the Peacemaker (1802–06) in

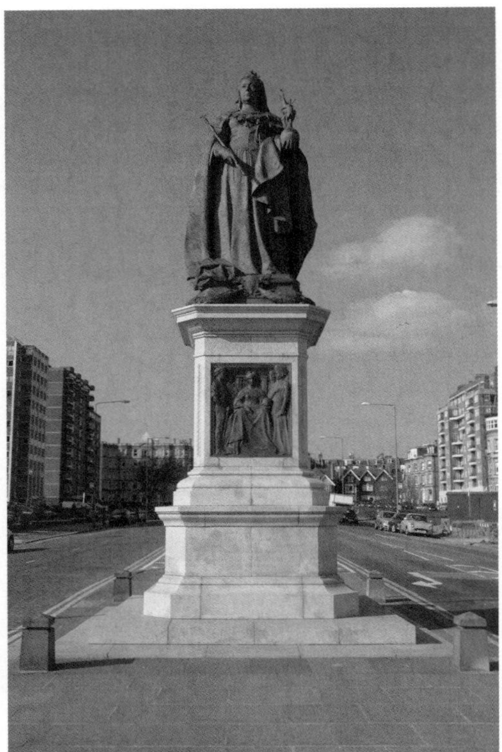

Thomas Brock, *Statue of Queen Victoria*

Apsley House.[1] Around the angle of the bronze
plinth are festoons of laurel and in front, a
cartouche bearing the letters: V.R.I. The dado
of the granite plinth is embellished with four
low-relief bronze panels illustrating the benefits
of Victoria's reign, with allegorical figures
representing Commerce, Education, Science
and Art, and Empire, that Brock was requested
to add to the statue. In the centre of the south-
facing panel (Empire) sits a female figure
holding a pair of scales in her right hand,
symbolic of Justice. In her left hand she holds
an orb. On her right stand figures representing
Canada and Australia; on her left, those
representing India and Africa. On the north-
facing panel (Science and Art) a central seated
female figure embraces a child who is sitting on
an anvil with an electrical machine in his hands.

Behind him stands a youth holding another
piece of machinery. On her left is a figure of a
boy with a palette and brush, with a mallet,
chisel and compasses at his feet. The east-facing
panel (Education) shows a mother, seated with
a book on her knees, teaching a child to read.
Standing behind them are three scholars of
different ages, engaged in study. In the
foreground of the west-facing panel
(Commerce) kneels an Eastern trader, with his
wares spread out in front of him, offering them
for sale to two merchants, who stand looking
down at the goods. Behind is a figure with a
vase in his hands; the sea is visible in the
background and a galley with sails set.[2]

The statue was commissioned to
commemorate the Queen's Jubilee in 1897,
described by the *Art Journal* as a '…
thanksgiving year for sculptors'.[3] The Hove
version was the fourth to be commissioned at a
cost of £3000. The Hove committee requested a
memorial '… of large proportions and of the
highest class.'[4] Accordingly, Brock made the
figure of the queen taller than the earlier
Worcester version and increased the impression
of height by including an elaborately carved
base set on the pedestal.[5] Very similar versions
were erected in the same period in Victoria
Park, Carlisle, Victoria Square Birmingham and
outside City Hall, Belfast, although Brock's
best-known work, the Queen Victoria
Memorial outside Buckingham Palace in
London (1911), shows the queen in a seated
posture.

Brock's monument was not completed until
the year of the Queen's death in 1901. It was
unveiled, on what was described as '… the great
Day of Mourning', by the Mayoress, Mrs
Colman, a week after Queen Victoria's funeral.[6]
It was a simple ceremony, as it was judged
inappropriate to have any speeches, but a
wreath was laid on behalf of the women of
Hove. Although they do not face each other,
Brock's Queen Victoria (seaward aspect) and
Frampton's and Lutyens' St George war
memorial (inland aspect) form 'punctuation

points' at either end of Hove's imposing Grand Avenue.

Notes
[1] Sankey, J., *Thomas Brock and the Critics: an Examination of Brock's Place in the New Sculpture Movement*, unpublished PhD thesis, University of Leeds, 2002, p. 174. [2] *Brighton Herald*, 9 February 1901. [3] Sankey, p. 170. [4] Ibid., p. 174. [5] Ibid. [6] *Brighton Herald*, 9 February 1901.

Top of avenue, on an island in the middle of the road

War Memorial: St George

Architect: Sir Edwin Lutyens

Sculptor: George Frampton

Unveiled: 27 February 1921
Materials/dimensions: statue: bronze, 1.22 m high; column and plinth: white granite, 5 m high; plinth: base: white granite 96.5 cm wide × 96.5 cm deep
Signature (bottom right-hand side of integral base): Frampton Sc.
Inscriptions (north face, bottom of column): MCMXIV / TO / MCMXIX; (north face, bottom of plinth): 1914–19 1939–45 / IN EVER / GLORIOUS MEMORY / OF / HOVE CITIZENS / WHO GAVE / THEIR LIVES / FOR THEIR / COUNTRY / IN THE / GREAT WAR / AND / WORLD WAR; (east face, bottom of column): MCMXXXIX / TO / MCMXLV (south face, bottom of column: MCMXIV / TO / MCMXIX; (south face, bottom of plinth): THEIR NAME / LIVETH / FOR EVERMORE; (west face, bottom of column): MCMXXXIX / TO / MCMXLV
Status: Grade II
Condition: good
Owner/custodian: Brighton and Hove City Council

The memorial takes the form of a bronze figure of St George in armour, sword in right hand, shield in left, set high on a Tuscan column, dado and plinth. Lutyens himself selected the site; his original suggestions of a cenotaph and then an

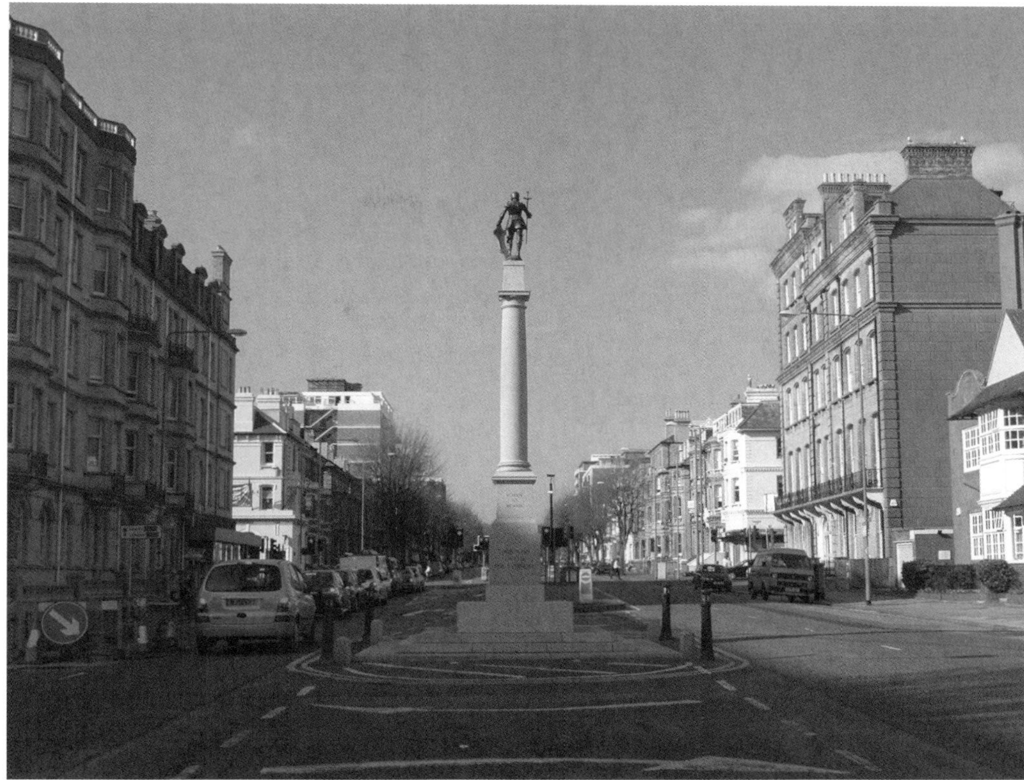

George Frampton, *War Memorial: St George*

obelisk were turned down in favour of the chosen design. Once this design had been decided upon, as Tim Skelton, in his work on *Lutyens and the Great War* states:

> The war memorial at Hove … went very smoothly with barely eleven months elapsing between the first suggestion for a memorial in 'Vestry Notes' in a local newspaper and the unveiling of a 20ft-high circular column surmounted by a bronze figure of St George holding a sword, somewhat dangerously, by the blade and sculpted by Sir George Frampton[1]

The memorial cost £1537 and was unveiled by Lord Leconfield. Mr J.O. Thomas represented Lutyens, who was in India working on the design and building of New Delhi. The local newspaper contained a stirring account of the unveiling:

> The huge flags that enveloped the memorial fluttered to the ground and the rays of the sun touched the figure of our patron saint as it stood in symbolic attitude with uplifted [*sic*] sword.[2]

In the caption to his illustration of the Hove memorial, Skelton modifies his attribution of the sculptor to '… from the studio of Sir George Frampton'.[3] There is no archival evidence of Frampton's direct involvement with the development of the memorial, indeed in most local histories the sculptor is not mentioned at all, with emphasis placed exclusively on the fact that it was Lutyens' design. The statue of St George appears to be a generic type, with variations, produced by Frampton for war memorials. The earliest example appears to be a memorial to Old Radleians who died in the Boer War, at Radley College chapel, dated 1903. Here St George holds a lance, instead of a sword, in his right hand.[4] The figure appears again, symbolising fortitude, in Frampton's design for a commemorative bronze plaque outside the house of the painter Sir Lawrence Alma Tadema (1836–1912), dated 1914.[5] Other examples of First World War memorials that incorporate similar figures of St George include a memorial to Francis L. Mond, RFA, RAF executed in 1918, now in the Imperial War Museum and war memorials in Fordham, Cambridgeshire (1921) and Maidstone (1922). All the figures bear some resemblance to Donatello's bronze statues of David, executed in the 1440s, in their pose, although they are clad in Renaissance-inspired armour.

The symbolic choice of St George, patron saint of England, for these memorials reinforces attributes of bravery, honour and chivalry with which he is traditionally associated. He was a soldier of the Roman Empire, venerated as a Christian martyr. He is associated with the story of George and the Dragon and is one of the Fourteen Holy Helpers. He is said to have been beheaded at Lydda in Palestine and 23 April was named as Saint George's day in 1222.

The inscription on the dado of the memorial was modified to include a dedication to the men and women of Hove who died in the Second World War as well as the Great War. No individual details are included, but 631 names were engraved by a Mr Hadlow on a series of brass tablets, framed in oak, mounted in the vestibule of Hove Public Library in Church Road.

Notes
[1] Skelton, T., *Lutyens and the Great War*, London 2008, p. 75. [2] *Brighton Herald*, 5 March 1921. [3] Skelton (2008), p. 169. [4] George Frampton, files of black and white photographs, FR/S18 a–b, Henry Moore Institute archive, Leeds. [5] Ibid., FR/M1 a–c.

Other sources
Brighton Herald, 26 February 1921.
buildingopinions.com accessed (3 October 2010).
Middleton, J., *Encyclopaedia of Hove*, Hove, vol. 15, 2003, pp. 9–10.
roll-of-honour.com/Cambridgeshire/Fordham (accessed 8 July 2011).

Norton Road

In front of the entrance to Hove Town Hall

The Juggler
Sculptor: Helen Collis

Installed: December 1995
Materials/dimensions: patinated bronze, with red pigment on firebrands; 2.74 m high
Signature (to outer aspect of right thigh): Collis
Inscription (white metal plaque in wooden frame to front of statue): 'The Juggler' / by Helen Collis / presented by / Dr Martin Hildyard / husband of Helen Collis, / and by Helen's family
Status: not listed
Condition: good
Owner/custodian: Brighton and Hove City Council

The sculpture depicts a male figure balancing high above the pavement on a unicycle supported by a small pyramidal plinth. His head, with sweptback hair, is turned towards his right and with his hands he is juggling firebrands. The piece is a replica of the sculpture that won Helen Collis the Sussex Arts Club Award for Visual Arts. It was the last work of the artist, who died of cancer in August 1995 at the age of 57. The work was presented to Hove in her memory by her husband and unveiled by Council Leader, Ivor Caplin. At the opening ceremony the piece was described as, '… a whimsical work and one that will put smiles on the faces of passers by.'[1] Its subject was particularly appropriate because the square outside the Town Hall in which it stands was intended as a venue for the performing arts during the Brighton Festival.

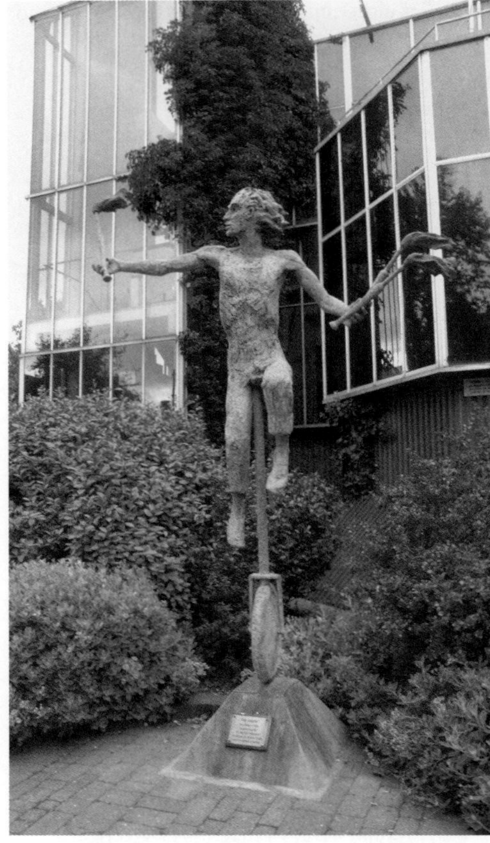

Helen Collis, *The Juggler*

Juggler was Hove's first new public work of art for 75 years. A replica of Canova's *Dancing Girl* (1805) stood outside the previous Town Hall until the building was destroyed by fire in 1966. It was removed to no. 3 Adelaide Crescent, Hove, but has since disappeared, leaving only the plinth remaining.

Note
[1] 'Helen's gift', *The Argus*, 15 December 2005, p. 13.

Other source
mybrightonandhove.org.uk (accessed 1 October 2010).

Abinger Place

Churchyard, Church of St John sub Castro, junction with Lancaster Street

Monument to Russian prisoners of war (Czar's Obelisk)

Designer: Philip Currey

Stonemason: John Strong

Installed: 1877
Materials/dimensions: obelisk: stone with red granite columns, 4.25 m high × 1.55 m wide × 1.55 m deep; stepped base; stone, 46 cm high × 2.5 m wide × 2.5 m deep
Inscriptions (east face): SACRED / to the Memory of / the Russian Soldiers / who died Prisoners / of War in Lewes / in the years / 1854 / 1855 1856; (west face): RAISED / by order of / His Majesty / the Emperor of / Russia / Alexander II / 1877 / THE MEMORIAL / was restored by the / Embassy of the USSR / 1957 / At the instance of the / Friends of Lewes / Society; (south face): These Lines / are transcribed from the first Memorial / Now save what here is laid / Soon will the Lord come / who has said / Those that on me believe / them will Raise to Eternal life; (north face, severely weatherworn): The / First Memorial / Placed over the Soldiers' Remains / by their Surviving / Comrades was a simple / Head Stone bearing the following inscription (indecipherable). The other four sides contain the names of the soldiers
Status: Grade II
Condition: fair (weather-worn with all-over biological growth; top of the cross broken off; crack to the top of the base on west side)
Commissioned by: Russian authorities
Owner/custodian: Church of St John sub Castro

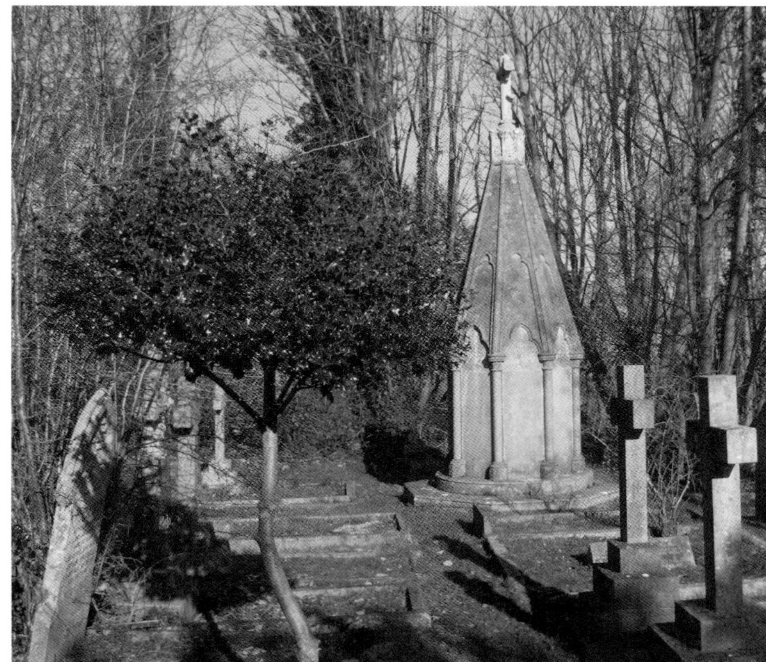

Philip Currey,
Monument to Russian prisoners of war (Czar's Obelisk)

The monument is in the neo-Gothic style, with an octagonal drum with marble shafts carrying cusped pointed arches and ribs to the pointed octagonal spire. An octagonal tabernacle above supports a cross. Four of the panelled sides contain dedicatory inscriptions.

During the Crimean War, 300 Finnish prisoners were brought to Lewes as prisoners of war. They were conscripts to the Russian army (Finland being a substate within the Russian empire), captured during the joint British and French strike on Bomarsund fortress in 1854. While the officers were billeted around the town, the ordinary soldiers were held in the old Naval prison. Locals and tourists visited the prisoners, who made toys for them to buy.[1] Twenty-eight of them died, mostly from tuberculosis. An opera, *The Finnish Prisoner*, by local composer Orlando Gough, with libretto by Stephen Plaice, based on the story behind the monument, was staged in Lewes in September 2007.[2]

Notes
[1] Interlocking wooden puzzles made by the prisoners may be seen in the Anne of Cleves House Museum in Lewes. See Arscott (1991), p. 63.
[2] Coleman, N., 'Chorus in a car park', *The Guardian*, 10 September 2007, p. 26.

Other source
sussexparishchurches.org (accessed 18 October 2010).

Cockshutt Road

In the grounds of Lewes Priory, on the site of the Battle of Lewes

Lewes Memorial (The Helmet)

Sculptor: Enzo Plazzotta

Foundry: The Morris Singer Company Ltd
Installed: 1964
Materials/dimensions: sand-cast aluminium, 4.5 m high
Inscriptions (underneath the pictorial elements of the frieze): NOW ENGLISHMEN, READ ON ABOUT THIS BATTLE FOUGHT AT LEWES'

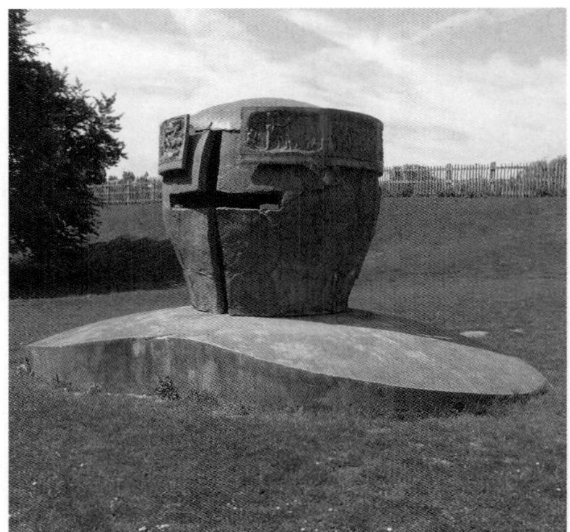

Enzo Plazzotta, *Lewes Memorial (The Helmet)*

WALLS. BECAUSE OF THIS YOU ARE ALIVE / AND SAFE. REJOICE THEN IN GOD / LAW IS LIKE FIRE, FOR IT LIGHTS AS TRUTH, WARMS AS CHARITY, BURNS AS ZEAL. WITH THESE VIRTUES / AS HIS GUIDES, THE KING WILL RULE WELL; (plaque on base): PRESENTED TO THE PEOPLE OF LEWES / BY THEIR MEMBER OF PARLIAMENT / SIR TUFTON BEAMISH, M.C. / TO MARK THE 700TH ANNIVERSARY / OF THE BATTLE OF LEWES / FOUGHT ON THE 14TH MAY 1264 / AND UNVEILED BY / THE DUKE OF NORFOLK, E.M., K.O. / DESIGNED AND EXECUTED BY / ENZO PLAZZOTTA

Status: not listed
Condition: good
Commissioned by: Sir Tufton Beamish
Owner/custodian: Lewes Town Council

The abstracted shape of the sculpture, created by the lost wax process, suggests a medieval helmet, incorporating a cross to symbolise the role of the church and the bravery of those who fought in the Battle of Lewes. The helmet is crowned by a frieze in bas-relief, depicting eight scenes from contemporary chronicles about the battle. The words around it are taken from 'The Song of Lewes', a long and complex Latin poem written by an unknown churchman.

The battle was fought in 1264 towards the west of the town between a rebel army, seeking freedom from the absolute rule of the monarchy, led by Simon de Montfort and the barons and the forces of Henry III. De Montfort won a famous victory, taking Henry prisoner and occupying Lewes.

Sources
Christopher, A., *The Battle of Lewes Memorial*, Lewes, 1966.
Strachan, W.J., *Open Air Sculpture of Britain: A Comprehensive Guide*, London, 1984.

Cuilfail Tunnel Roundabout
North end of tunnel, on roundabout

Cuilfail Spiral
Sculptor: Peter Randall-Page

Unveiled: 3 October 1983
Materials/dimensions: sculpture: Portland stone, 3.6 m high; plinth: brick, 60 cm high
Inscriptions (on brick wall on Phoenix Causeway, opposite the sculpture): SCULPTURE BY PETER RANDALL-PAGE / CUILFAIL SPIRAL / UNVEILED ON / 3RD OCTOBER 1983 / BY / J.R. LOVILL C.B.E. / CHAIRMAN - ASSOCIATION OF COUNTY COUNCILS / MEMBER - EAST SUSSEX COUNTY COUNCIL / COMMISSIONED BY EAST SUSSEX COUNTY COUNCIL / SOUTH EAST ARTS / MOUNTFIELD ROADSTONE LTD. / THE SPIRAL RELATES TO THE FOSSIL FORMS FOUND IN THE CHALK THROUGH WHICH THE TUNNEL PASSES
Status: not listed
Condition: good
Commissioned by: East Sussex County Council, South East Arts and Mountfield Roadstone Ltd
Owner/custodian: Lewes Town Council

Seven segmented blocks of stone are arranged in a spiral form, resting on a brick plinth. The sculpture marks the entrance to the Cuilfail road tunnel cut through the chalk cliffs, opened in 1980 in an area that was previously occupied

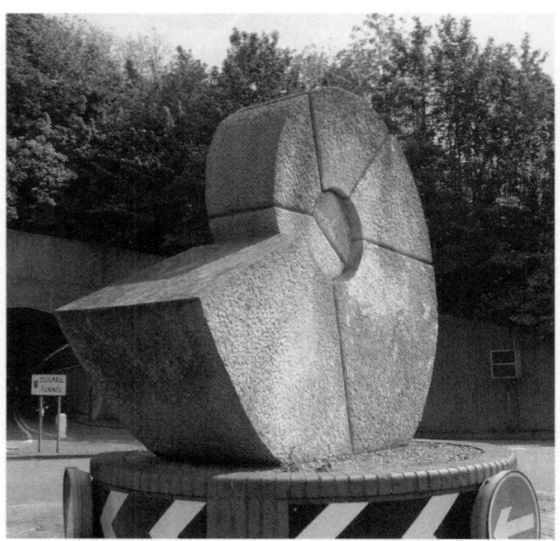

Peter Randall-Page, *Cuilfail Spiral*

by wharves and factories. Its design is suggestive of a snail (its local nickname) or an ammonite fossil, many of which are found in the location. The title *Cuilfail* is Celtic for 'Paul's Retreat', named by developer Isaac Vinall after a hillside near a holiday home in Oban in Scotland.

Sources
Gammon, A., *Historic Lewes*, Lewes, 1995.
geolocation.ws (accessed 19 August 2011).
Peter Randall-Page Sculpture and Drawings 1977–1992, Leeds, 1992, pp. 25, 77.
Strachan (1984).

High Street
Town Hall

Between 1999 and 2007, Lewes Town Hall was the venue for four important temporary exhibitions of sculpture. The inaugural exhibition focused on a sculpture that had a close relationship to the town: *The Kiss* by Auguste Rodin. The life-size marble version of this iconic piece, now in the possession of the Tate Gallery, was commissioned in 1900 by Edward Perry Warren, an American who had come to live in Lewes House in 1890. Warren was a lover of the arts and collector, who was a friend of Rodin. The sculptor completed Warren's piece in 1906 and it was installed in the coach house of Lewes House due to its size and weight. In 1914 Warren offered it for public display in the Town Hall, where it remained for nearly two years. In the year of Rodin's death (1917), however, the Borough Council requested that it be taken back on the grounds that its subject might be considered 'undesirable' and it was returned to the coach house where it stayed until Warren's death in 1928. Having changed hands several times between then and 1939, it was eventually loaned to the Tate and purchased by the gallery in 1955 for £7500. Following strenuous efforts by a group of local residents to 'bring *The Kiss* home', the Tate loaned the sculpture to be shown in an exhibition in the newly refurbished Assembly Room in Lewes Town Hall, where it had originally been on display. *The Kiss* was exhibited together with other Rodin pieces relating to the same theme, in marble, bronze, terracotta and plaster, lent by the Victoria and Albert Museum and the Musée Rodin as well as the Tate.

Following the popularity and success of the Rodin exhibition, Sculpture Exhibitions Limited organized *A Sculptor's Development: Anthony Caro* in 2001, which comprised not only a retrospective exhibition in the Town Hall but also a series of educational workshops in which Caro:

> … collaborated with people from East Sussex – children, students, teachers, non-specialists and professionals – to create a project that examines his development as an artist and some of his working methods.[1]

Even more ambitious was a collaboration, partly funded by the European Union, between the Town Hall, the Chateau-Musée de Dieppe, Charleston farmhouse, the Crypt Gallery, Seaford and the Thebes Gallery, Lewes, on a Henry Moore exhibition *Land + Sea*, in 2004. The Town Hall showed pieces on the theme of 'Land', exploring landscape as a source of inspiration for Moore and the siting of his sculptures within it. The project again had a strong educational remit, with students from Sussex and Northern France participating in workshops conducted by sculptors Hamish Black, Marcus Cornish and Didier Lebas.

The final exhibition of the series was *With the Grain: Wood Sculpture by David Nash* in 2007. The sculptures on show charted Nash's career from 1976, demonstrating his intimate relationship with his most frequently used material. As with the preceding exhibitions, Sculpture Exhibitions Limited emphasized its educational value through schools workshops involving the sculptor.

Note
[1] *A Sculptor's Development: Anthony Caro*, exhibition leaflet, Lewes, 2001.

Other sources
Hawksworth, M., *The Kiss Comes Home*, Meridian TV, 1999.

Henry Moore Land + Sea, exhibition leaflet, Lewes, 2004.
hqinfo.blogspot.co.uk/2011/10/jm-archive-rodin-in-lewes (accessed 19 April 2012).
Rose, C., *"I am much inclined to it" the Story of Lewes House*, Lewes, updated edn 2007.
With the Grain: Wood Sculpture by David Nash, exhibition leaflet, Lewes, 2007.

Junction with Market Street

War Memorial

Sculptor: Vernon March

Unveiled: 6 September 1922
Materials/dimensions: approx. 8.5 m high × 2.2 m wide × 3.7 m deep
Signature (on right-hand side of plinth, below shield, in carved letters): VERNON MARCH SC.
Inscriptions (underneath winged figure): LIBERTY; (on shield): IN MEMORY OF / THE MEN OF LEWES / WHO DIED / FOR THEIR

Vernon March, *War Memorial*

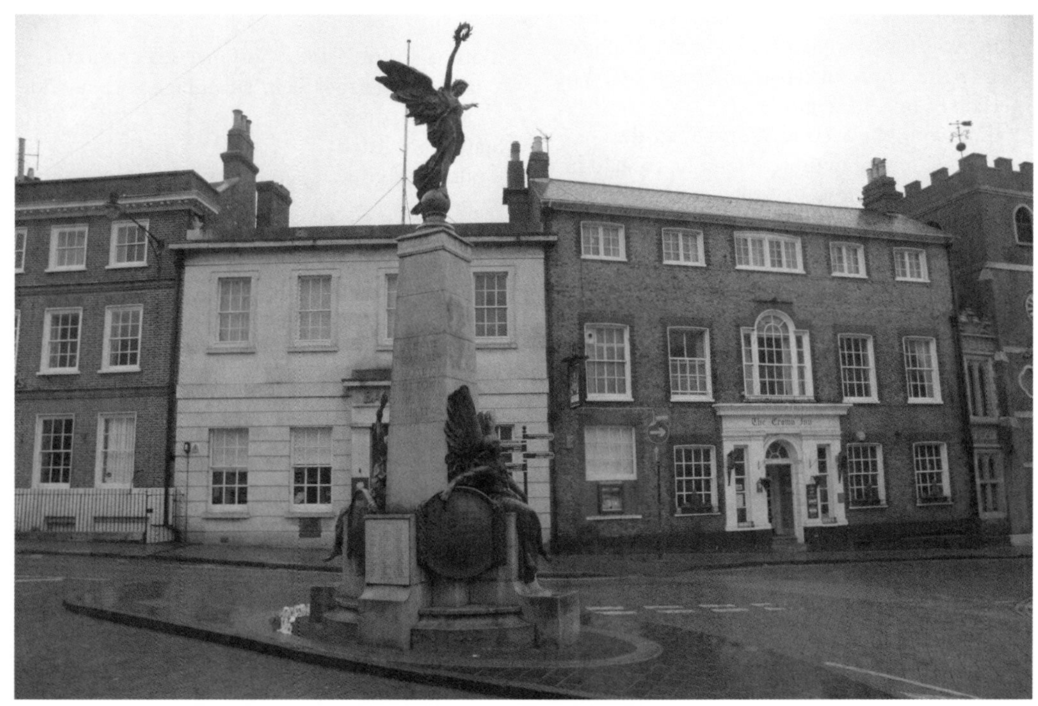

COUNTRY / AND FOR MANKIND / IN THE
GREAT WAR / 1914 – 1918; (on the obelisk):
"THIS / WAS / THEIR / FINEST / HOUR"; (also
on obelisk): LIKEWISE / REMEMBER / THOSE
OF / THIS TOWN / WHO GAVE / THEIR LIVES /
IN THE WAR / 1939–1945
Status: Grade II
Condition: good (some parts replaced)
Owner/custodian: Lewes Town Council

The tall, square stone cenotaph rise from a low,
wide plinth and is topped by a winged female
figure, standing on a globe, holding aloft a
wreath. Low stone piers on each side with oval
shields carry the names of the fallen, held by
one winged female figure to the east and one to
the west.

Vernon March's design was chosen, by
Edward Prior, Slade Professor of Fine Art at
Cambridge University, as the winner of an
open competition from a field of 35 entries. The
bronze figures were cast in the garden of the
March family in Farnborough in Kent. The
model for the face of Victory, the uppermost
figure, was Barbara Jean Kelly, who lived next
door to the family of artists and sculptors, who
specialised in war memorials.[1]

Following the Second World War, the
Borough Council invited the public to send in
names of the fallen so that they could be added.
By 21 July 1950, only 42 names had been
received; these were inscribed on a small
commemorative plaque and a quotation from
Winston Churchill's 'Finest Hour' speech was
added to the shaft. In 1977, the Town Council
once again considered the matter and the
Reverend John Hopgood MA and Councillor
Dr Graham Mayhew JP undertook research to
collect the names of the town's Second World
War dead. One hundred and twenty-six names
were inscribed on two panels on the north and
south faces. The Memorial was re-dedicated on
Sunday 1 March 1981 in the presence of over
100 relatives and representatives from the
armed forces.

The siting of the memorial in the middle of
the high street, where the upper and lower parts
of the town meet, ensures its continued
function as a focal point within the community;
in addition to its importance in Remembrance
Day ceremonies, it is also the congregation
point for the Lewes Bonfire Societies, for
'bonfire prayers' on 5 November every year.

Note
[1] Leith, A., 'The War Memorial: a familiar face at
the top of the hill', *Viva Lewes*, November 2007,
p. 45.

Source
Elliston, R.A., *Lewes at War 1939–1945*, Seaford,
(revised edn) 1999, p. 195.

St Anne's Crescent

Above entrance to County Hall

County Hall Relief
Sculptor: William Mitchell
Architect: Jack Catchpole

Unveiled: 31 October 1968
Materials/dimensions: polymerised concrete
tinted bronze–green, 2.5 m high × 12 m wide
× 30 cm deep
Status: not listed
Condition: good (covered with anti-pigeon
netting)
Owner/custodian: East Sussex County Council

The rectangular relief is constructed from 11
separate panels of abstract shapes, pierced by 5
narrow double-height coloured glass windows
in shades of blue and green and extends across
the length of the entrance above the doors.

The new County Hall building, which cost
£1m, brought together council departments that
had previously been scattered over 17 different
sites in Lewes. Mitchells' relief accentuates the
central part of a group of three comparatively
tall buildings, with a lower connecting link. The
flint work is designed to reflect the architecture
of St Anne's Church, which stands nearby, and
brown Sussex bricks were used to represent the

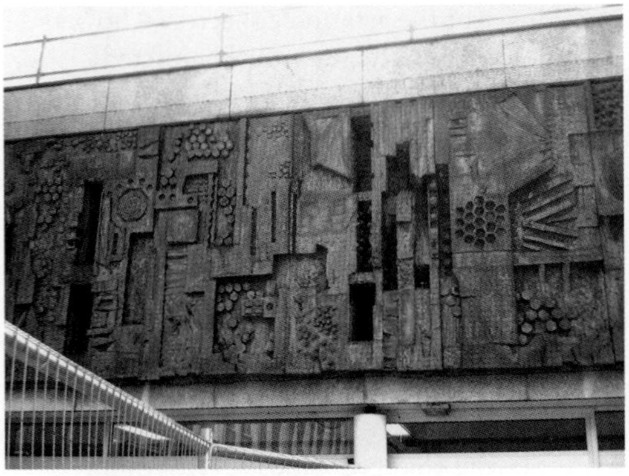

William Mitchell, *County Hall Relief*

Wealden clay. Despite these historical
references, the building was seen as
uncompromisingly modern, a quality
reinforced by the materials and style of the
sculpted relief.

County Hall was opened by the Duchess of
Kent, in the car park, decorated for the occasion
with chandeliers, a red carpet and blue and
white drapery, as the fourth wing that would
contain the council chamber was not yet
finished. It was dedicated by the Bishop of
Chichester assisted by the rector of St Anne's
church.

Sources
The Argus, 31 October 1968 and 1 November 1968.
Brighton and Hove Herald, 1 November 1968.
britishpathe.com/record.
William Mitchell, telephone conversation, 2
December 2010.
Pearson, L. (2007), pp. 116–37.

Styles Field

*Set in triangular flowerbed on piazza
outside library*

Sculpture of Thomas Paine
Sculptor: Marcus Cornish

Unveiled: 4 July 2010
Materials/dimensions: statue: sandstone, 1.3 m

high × 45 cm wide × 57 cm deep; plinth: red brick with flint panels on three sides and limestone panel with inscription: 50 cm high × 66 cm wide × 70 cm deep
Inscription (carved into limestone tablet on plinth): THOMAS / PAINE / 1737–1809
Status: not listed
Condition: good
Commissioned and funded by: an anonymous Lewes resident
Custodian: Lewes District Council

The figure of Thomas Paine is depicted, dressed in shirt and breeches, kneeling and holding a book in his left hand. His appearance closely corresponds with his description on his arrival in Lewes, aged 32 as '… a slim man of medium height with vibrant dark eyes.'[1] The figure emerges from the block of sandstone with his head turned enquiringly to the left. The fact that the sculpture is carved from a single block of stone, the back and sides of which are left in a roughened, unfinished state, suggests the symbolic emergence of mankind from the darkness of superstition into the knowledge of the Enlightenment. The statue was unveiled on American Independence Day by Tony Benn, vice-chairman of the Tom Paine Society, who said, '[w]henever I think of Lewes, I think of Tom Paine, and whenever I think of Tom Paine, I think of Lewes.'[2]

Thomas Paine (1737–1809) was born in Thetford in Norfolk to a mixed Anglican/Quaker family and was apprenticed to his corset-maker father following an interrupted period of study at Grammar School. He left home at 16 to serve briefly as a privateer, before returning to his trade in London and Sandwich. He qualified as an excise man, but was dismissed and worked in London as a schoolteacher. It was again as an excise man that he arrived in Lewes in 1768. He found an intellectual home in the thriving county town that was republican in outlook and accommodated a range of dissenting religious groups. As well as a practical

involvement in the governance of the town, Paine also attended the White Hart Evening club and often won the 'Headstrong' debating prize. He married his landlord's daughter, Elizabeth Ollive, in 1771, but the couple formally separated three years later.

Paine was elected spokesman for his fellow excise men to present their case for increased wages and improved conditions, in a bid to reduce corruption in the service. The early model for unionisation presented in his pamphlet 'The Case of the Officers of Excise' (printed in Lewes in 1772) failed to convince Parliament and Paine was again dismissed. Having been introduced to Benjamin Franklin by a former tutor to George III, Paine left Lewes for America in 1774. His support for the American Revolution and independence from the United Kingdom took the form of two pamphlets 'Common Sense' (1776) and 'The

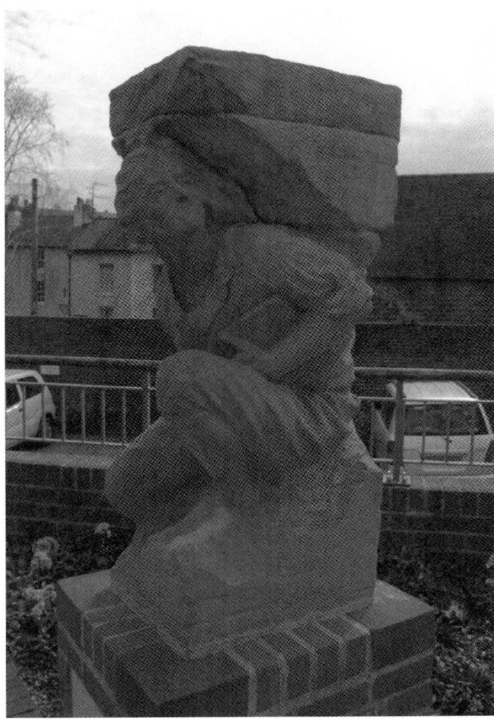

Marcus Cornish, *Sculpture of Thomas Paine*

American Crisis' (1776–83), the publication of which earned him the nickname of 'the father of the American Revolution'. The measure of his deep-rooted influence on American politics was indicated by the fact that President Obama quoted from his work in his inauguration speech in 2009. During the 1790s Paine lived in France and was deeply involved in the French Revolution, publishing *The Rights of Man* in 1791 and *The Age of Reason* in 1793–94. The latter book earned him notoriety because of its attack on organised religion and advocacy of freethinking.

The anonymous donor of the sculpture felt strongly that Lewes should commemorate Paine's association with the town and was already an admirer of Marcus Cornish's work. The local sculptor created the piece from paintings and prints of Paine. He said of his work:

> The idea was to have a record and a presence [of Thomas Paine] because people are very proud of [him] to have been here. It may not be everybody's cup of tea, what he was thinking and writing about, but I think he was an original thinker and somebody trying to do good for society.[3]

Cornish's sculpture features in 'The Tom Paine Trail' that marks significant places in the town connected with his six-year residence there.

Notes
[1] *The Tom Paine Trail*, Lewes District Council, nd.
[2] bbc.co.uk/news (accessed 12 April 2012). [3] Ibid.

Other source
Michele Brooker (librarian at Lewes Library), interview, 12 April 2012. There is a series of photographs of the installation and unveiling of the statue.

High Street

*North side, opposite Middle House Hotel
(previously outside Mayfield Primary
School, moved postwar)*

Village Sign
Designer: Geoffrey Webb

Unveiled: 27 July 1922
Materials/dimensions: sign and weathervane:
  painted and gilded metal, 2.5 m high × 70 cm
  wide × 20 cm deep; post, wood, 2.7 m high
Inscriptions (on west face): MAIDS FIELD; (on
  post facing south): FOLLOWING A SPEECH / BY
  HIS ROYAL HIGHNESS / THE DUKE OF YORK /
  AT THE ROYAL ACADEMY / IN 1920 ON THE
  REVIVAL OF VILLAGE SIGNS, / THE DAILY MAIL
  ORGANISED / A VILLAGE SIGNS COMPETITION
  / AND EXHIBITION, OFFERING / A TOTAL OF
  £2200 IN PRIZES. / TEN AWARDS WERE MADE
  AND / THE DESIGN FROM WHICH / THIS SIGN
  WAS CONSTRUCTED / SECURED SECOND PRIZE
  £500
Status: not listed
Condition: fair (general weathering; on east side
  a short section of one of the pincer handles is
  missing, caused by the collapse of the sign,
  which hit a nearby bus shelter)
Commissioned and funded by: *The Daily Mail*
  newspaper

The sign is a double-sided cut-out panel, its
west face depicting a maiden holding a
beribboned nameplate with two female children
holding garlands of flowers, including the rare
spiked rampion that is peculiar to the parish
and found only in East Sussex. The east face
bears the same image but with the addition of a
male child, sat in front of the maiden. Around
the pole just underneath the sign, the legend of
the tenth-century St Dunstan holding the devil
by the nose with a pair of pincers is depicted.
The ends of the cornice bear the shields of the

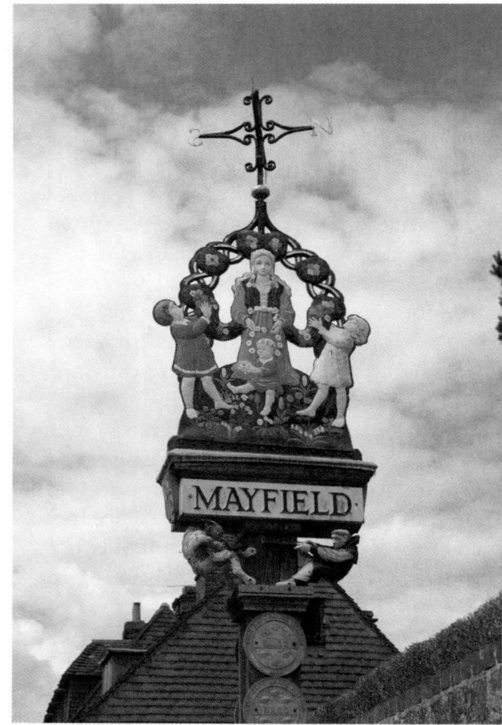

Geoffrey Webb, *Village Sign*

Archbishops of Canterbury, the diocese of
Chichester, St Dunstan and Archbishop Islip,
who built the Old Palace.

This is the oldest surviving, most famous,
tallest and most decorative village sign in
Sussex, and refers to the alleged original name
of the village, Maid's Field. Interest in village
signs was promoted by the Prince of Wales
(soon to become King Edward VII) and his
wife, Princess Alexandra, who commissioned
early ones, some of which survive, for the
Sandringham estate. The first were in 1912 to
commemorate the coronation of George V.
Royal interest in the signs continued and in
1920 Prince Albert, Duke of York, later to
become King George VI, at a Royal Academy
banquet, urged, on behalf of his fellow
motorists, a revival of the tradition of marking
the entrance to a village in this way, '… a

welcome guide to a visitor in a strange land.'[1]

Following the prince's speech, *The Daily
Mail* ran a competition for new designs and
mounted an exhibition of the 525 entries at
Australia House in the Strand. *The Builder*
magazine published an extensive review of the
competition entries, with illustrations of the
three prizewinners and the runner-up.[2]
Geoffrey Webb, who came from East
Grinstead, was awarded second prize for his
Mayfield design in 1920.

The *Daily Mail* had informed the village that
they would pay for the construction and
erection of the sign, but it was not installed
until 1922, when it was unveiled by the
chairman of the Parish Council (and High
Sheriff of Sussex), Stanley Dennis. The delay
was due to arguments over the site and the
parish council's preoccupation with the
construction of a war memorial at that time.
The sign was later moved, as it was not
adequately visible to traffic entering the village
and was cleaned in 1925 and renovated in 1930.

Notes
[1] *The Builder*, 7 May 1920, p. 542. [2] *The Builder*,
22 October 1920, p. 455.

Other sources
Arscott (1991), p. 44.
Chapman, B., *The Village Signs of Sussex*, Lewes,
  2006, pp. 101–02.
Mayfield Local Historical Society, *Mayfield: Ancient
  Wealden Village*, Mayfield, 2005, p. 8.
Sellens, F., 'Where they wanted it to be in 1920', *The
  Courier*, 24 January 1997; 'Amy's prize sign of the
  times', *The Courier*, 1 August 1991.

*St Dunstan's Church, in nave, suspended
above altar*

The Resurrection Spirit
Sculptor: Maggi Hambling

Installed: 2013
Material/dimensions: thin gauge, mirror-
  polished steel, approx. 1.3 m wide
Inscription (on metal plaque on wall to right of
  nave): "The Resurrection Spirit" (2013) / by

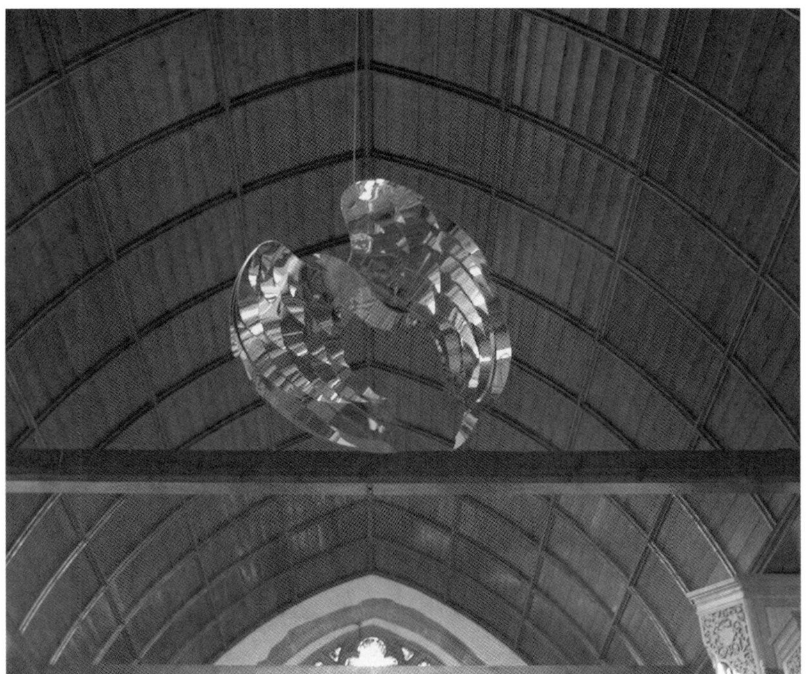

Maggi Hambling CBE / in loving memory of Walter Podger (1927–2008) / loyal servant and benefactor of this Church
Status: not listed
Condition: good
Owner/custodian: St Dunstan's Church

The fragile-looking, shining bird with angel's wings, which soars above the nave, 'caught in a moment of flight', is a metaphor for 'the hope, meaning and essence of the resurrection.'[1] It was commissioned by Father Nigel Prior, who decided to spend some of the nearly £1m legacy left to the church in 2010 by his sacristan, Walter Podger, a retired banker, on a work of contemporary art to commemorate him.[2] Nathaniel Hepburn, curator of the nearby Mascalls Gallery, aided the vicar in the choice of Hambling, for whom it was the first commission for a piece of sculpture in a church.[3]

Hambling said she wanted her piece to 'encourage the eye to rise from the altar to the sky', and hopes it will 'unify the spiritual life' of the twelfth-century building's interior and surroundings.[4] She describes herself as an 'optimistic doubter' on the subject of death, but for many years has produced a painting or drawing, often of the crucifixion, on Good Friday, which she regarded as the most miserable day of the year during her childhood.[5] Her visualisation of the resurrection was consecrated by the Bishop of Chichester on Advent Sunday and hangs above the newly commissioned altar table, made of oak by Simon McLay, with stainless steel panels also designed by Hambling and engraved by Stewart Alston.[6]

Notes
[1] culture24.org.uk/art/sculpture (accessed 2 June 2013). [2] Kennedy, M., *The Guardian*, 29 March 2013. [3] culture24.org.uk.; *The Argus*, 29 March 2013 [4] Ibid. [5] Kennedy (2013). [6] stdunstansmayfield.org.uk (accessed 2 June 2013).

Station Road

Colkins Mill Church, on grass verge, to the right, in front of church entrance gate

Martyrs' Memorial
Sculptor: unknown

Unveiled: October 1950
Materials/dimensions: stone, 1.3 m high × 50 cm wide × 50 cm deep
Inscriptions (on the open book): THY WORD / IS TRUTH; (south face, base of memorial): erected 1950; (south face): IN GRATEFUL MEMORY / OF THE PROTESTANT / MARTYRS OF MAYFIELD / & ROTHERFIELD 1556–7; (west face): Burnt at Mayfield 1556 / JOHN HART, THOMAS / RAVENSDALE AND TWO / MEN NAMES UNKNOWN; (north face): Burnt at Lewes 1557 / ALEXANDER / HOSMAN / of Rotherfield; (east face): Burnt at Lewes 1557 / WILLIAM MAYNARD / THOMASINA WOOD / both of Mayfield
Status: not listed
Condition: good (but inscriptions severely worn and difficult to read)
Commissioned by: Deacons and Members of Colkins Mill Congregational Church

The square-stepped base of the south-facing memorial is surmounted by a sculptural depiction of wooden staves issuing flames lapping around a central column. On top of the column is a square inscribed block on which rests an upright open book.

The memorial is dedicated to the six Protestant martyrs of Mayfield and one of Rotherfield, victims of the so-called Marian persecutions carried out in England and Wales during the reign of Mary I of England (1553–58). Under pro-Catholic legislation anyone judged guilty of heresy against the Catholic faith was burned at the stake, an unusual form of execution in England, but one used by the Spanish Inquisition during the reign of Mary's husband Philip.

It is situated on what is supposed to be the

nearest possible spot to the original site of the burnings, actually on the other side of Station Road. Four people were burnt to death in Mayfield on 23 September 1556. Their names were John Hart, Thomas Ravensdale and two others, a shoemaker and a leather worker, whose names were not recorded. More burnings took place in Lewes on 23 June 1557 including William Maynard and Thomasina Wood of Mayfield and Alexander Hosman of Rotherfield.[1] The memorial was unveiled by G.W.J. Cole, Esq. M.C. and was dedicated by the Rev. Canon Ferguson.

Note
[1] There is also a monument to the Protestant martyrs, erected in 1901, on Cliffe Hill, on the Cuilfail estate, Lewes. See publicsculpturesofsussex.co.uk.

Other sources
Mayfield Historical Society (2005), pp. 6–7.
Mayfield Newsletter, no. 344, September 2006.
Stoneham, E.T., *Martyrs of Jesus: The Story of the Sussex Martyrs of the Reformation*, Burgess Hill, second edn 1952, p. 46.
F.W.R. Wallis, correspondence, 8 August 2008.

NETHERFIELD

B2096 Darwell Hill

Inside a gated clearing in the trees, next to Doctor's Cottage

Polish Airmen's Memorial
Designer: Stanislaw Jozefiak

Unveiled: 28 May 2001
Materials/dimensions: memorial: dark grey bricks, 3.2 m high × 1.45 m wide × 45 cm deep; plaque: bronze, 90 cm high × 62 cm wide × 1 cm deep; base: stone, 10 cm high × 1.5 m wide × 86 cm deep
Inscription (on plaque affixed to front): HERE ON 27/28 MAY 1941 / A WELLINGTON BOMBER / NZ-N OF 304 POLISH SQUADRON / CRASHED AFTER BOMBING THE FRENCH / PORT OF BOULOGNE WHERE IT HAD BEEN / HIT AND BADLY DAMAGED / CREW WHO DIED / F/LT. KUSZCZYNSKI BRONISLAW (PILOT) / P/O. WOROCZEWSKI JAN STANISLAW (PILOT) / F/O. WIECZOREK CEZARY (NAVIGATOR) / SGT. DROZDZ JOZEF (AIR GUNNER) / DROWNED IN THE LA MANCHE CANAL / CREW WHO SURVIVED / SGT. NILSKI JOZEF (W/OP. AIR GUNNER) / SGT. JOZEFIAK STANISLAW (W/OP. AIR GUNNER) / BALED OUT
Status: not listed
Condition: good
Commissioned by: Stanislaw Jozefiak
Owner/custodian: Rother District Council

A stepped path and gate lead up to the memorial to Polish airmen whose plane crashed on the site. It takes the form of an upright, stepped rectangle of brick with rounded edges. On the front is a large bronze plaque with an engraved Polish eagle and the names of the dead and two survivors. Above the plaque is a bronze cut-out of a flying eagle. The monument is surmounted by a small metal crucifix.

The Wellington 1C bomber R1392 NZ took off from the 304 Polish Squadron at Syerston for a bombing raid on Boulogne. The plane was hit by anti-aircraft guns shortly after releasing its payload and started to spiral out of control. The rear gunner, Jozef Drodz, baled out over the channel and was never found. The pilot regained control, but soon after the plane caught fire. Two further crew members managed to bale out, but those remaining were killed when the plane crashed at Darwell Hole. They are buried in the Polish Air Force cemetery in Newark, Nottinghamshire.

In 2000 Stanislaw Jozefiak, one of the crew members who had baled out and landed at Hatfield near Tunbridge Wells, travelled from his home in Derbyshire to attend a memorial service at Chailey to honour three Polish combat squadrons. With the help of David Martin he was able to locate the exact site where his plane had crashed into a large oak tree that still stood on the site. He decided to build a

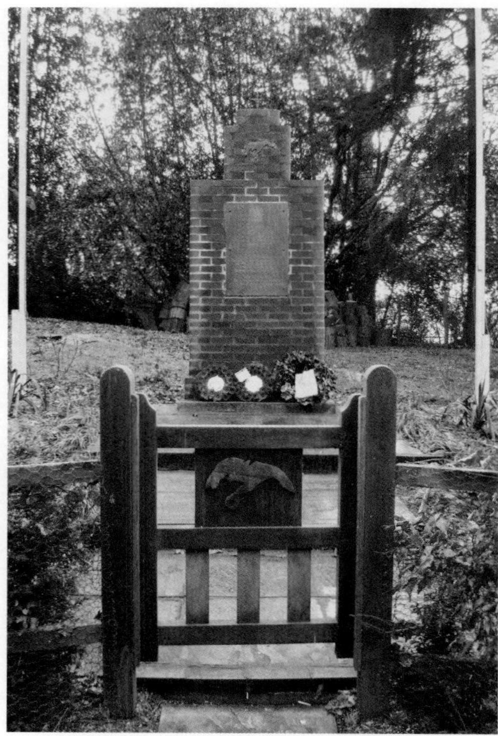

Stanislaw Jozefiak, *Polish Airmen's Memorial*

memorial to his fallen friends and came down to the site on frequent occasions, building the monument little by little. It was completed on the anniversary of the crash on 28 May 2001.[1]

Note
[1] Rowland, D., *Survivors: True Stories of Airmen who Crashed – and Lived to Tell the Tale*, Peacehaven, 2004, pp. 81–87.

Chapel Street

In middle of road, junction of Chapel Street and Fort Road

The Look Out

Designer: Darren Woodley

Artist: Carol Havard

Metalworks: GW Ironworks
Unveiled: 1 July 2006
Materials/dimensions: sculpture: galvanised
    steel, 3.5 m high × 1.65 m wide × 1 m deep;
    plinth: concrete with mosaic, 46 cm high ×
    1.57 m wide × 1.57 m deep
Inscription (on steel plaque to front of
    sculpture, in black painted incised letters):
    The 'Look Out' was designed / by Darren
    Woodley (aged 12)/ Manufactured by GW
    Ironworks. / With thanks to:- / Newhaven
    Town Council, South Downs CVS, / NCDA,
    Travis Perkins, Tideway School, /
    Newhaven Fort and Awards for All. /
    Unveiled by Mayor Rod Main on / Saturday
    1st July 2006
Status: not listed
Condition: good (but evidence of rough repairs
    and paint on upper part of plinth almost
    entirely peeled away)
Commissioned by: South Downs Council for
    Voluntary Service and Newhaven Town
    Council
Funded by: Awards for All lottery grant
    (£4800)
Owner/custodian: Newhaven Town Council

A male figure constructed from open-work
metal mesh faces northwest, on 'look out',
standing in a depiction of the crow's nest of a
boat. The structure stands on a square plinth,
the sides of which are decorated in a pictorial
mosaic with various maritime motifs. The
whole is on a traffic island surrounded by a low
perimeter fence. The design had to be approved

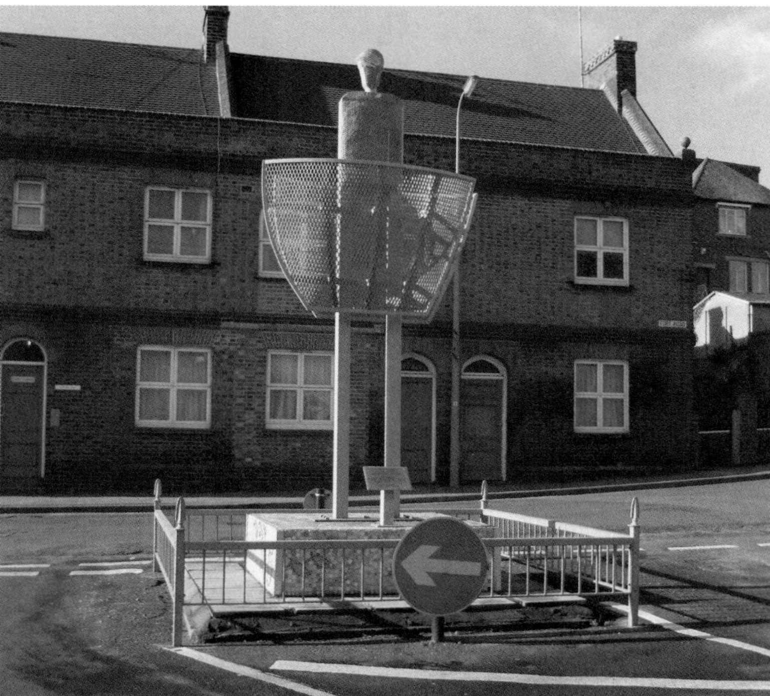

Darren Woodley,
The Look Out

by the highways authority to make sure that it
would not obscure the views of drivers at a
busy road junction, hence its height.

Tideway School pupil Darren Woodley won
the competition to design a sculpture to reflect
the town's maritime history. There were 11
entries in all from local young people and
residents were invited to choose their favourite.
Many locals helped to make the mosaic plinth
for the sculpture at a series of workshops led by
local artist Carol Havard, including one at the
Fish Festival at the end of May.

The site for the sculpture had become
available after the town's war memorial was
moved to the Memorial Gardens site at South
Way to join the Canadian and Maritime
Memorials there. The creation of the new
sculpture was part of a project coordinated by
Jackie Blackwell of South Downs Council for
Voluntary Service as a way of encouraging
young people to participate in the regeneration
of their town. The unveiling was included in
Exposed, a mini youth music festival, on the
West Quay.[1]

Note
[1] *Newhaven Town Council Newsletter*, Issue 3, July
2006.

Other source
Newhaven Town Council Annual Report, 2006–07.

The Drove

Inside entrance to Sainsbury's Superstore

Bridge

Sculptor: Hamish Black

Executed: 1994
Materials/dimensions: cast iron on mirrored
    background, 1.5 m high × 4.8 m wide ×
    23 cm deep
Signature: (bottom right of sculpture): BRIDGE /
    Hamish Black / 1994

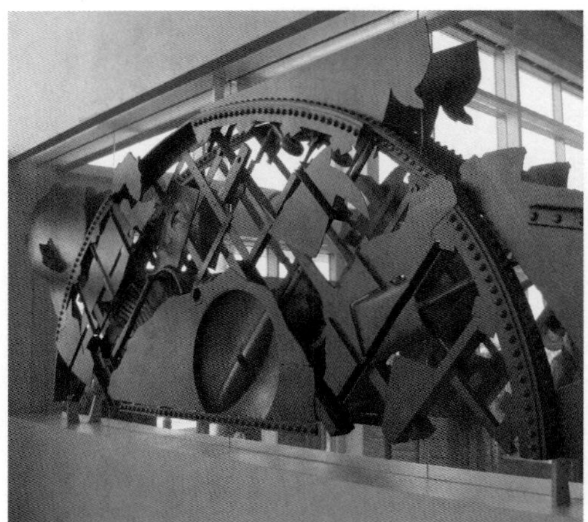

Hamish Black, *Bridge*

Status: not listed
Condition: good
Commissioned and owned by: J. Sainsbury plc

The latticework semicircular sculpture is affixed to the wall with a mirrored backing, reflecting its reversed image. It resembles half of a large cogwheel with cast shapes of tools and other objects such as a spanner, pitchfork and spade. Hamish Black has said of this piece:

> [It] can be read different ways, a bridge shape made from a whole range of forged steel and iron utilitarian objects, a superstructure seen through the cut-away surface, like a Haynes auto manual.[1]

The fact that the retail development in which the sculpture is sited is near to the swing bridge at the entrance to Newhaven harbour (opened in 1974) is reflected in its title.

Note
[1] Hamish Black, email correspondence, 30 November 2010.

Meeching Rise/Church Hill

NE corner of churchyard of St Michael's Church

Monument to HMS Brazen

Sculptor: not known

Materials/dimensions: top section of obelisk: ashlar, 5 m high × 75 cm wide × 75 cm deep; lower section of obelisk, ashlar, 2.5 m high × 1.25 m wide × 1.25 m deep; stepped base: ashlar, 1 m high × 3.1 m wide × 3.1 m deep
Inscription (on panel on SE face): THE FRIENDS OF / CAPTN. HANSON / CAUSED THIS MONUMENT / TO BE ERECTED / AS A MARK OF THEIR ESTEEM / FOR A DESERVING OFFICER / AND A VALUABLE FRIEND. / IT WAS THE WILL OF HEAVEN / TO PRESERVE HIM / DURING FOUR YEARS VOYAGE / OF DANGER AND DIFFICULTY / ROUND THE WORLD, / ON DISCOVERIES, WITH CAPTN. VANCOUVER / IN THE YEARS 1791. 1792. 1793. 1794. / BUT TO TAKE HIM FROM US / WHEN MOST HE THOUGHT HIMSELF SECURE. / "The Voice of the Lord is upon the Waters"; (on panel on SW face): NAMES OF / THE OFFICERS LOST, / JAMES HANSON ESQR. / COMMANDER / JAMES COOK / LIEUTS / JOHN DENBRY / PATRICK VENABLES / MIDSHIPMEN / JAMES HANWELL / JOHN BRAUGH PURSER / ROBERT HILL SURGEON / THOMAS WHITFIELD BOATSWAIN ROBERT AALDER YAWRLE GUNNER / JOHN TEAGUE CARPENTER; (on panel on NW face): SACRED / TO THE MEMORY / OF / CAPTN. JAMES HANSON / THE OFFICERS, AND COMPANY / OF HIS MAJESTY'S SHIP BRAZEN; / WHO WERE WRECKED / IN A VIOLENT STORM / UNDER THE CLIFF /BEARING FROM THIS PLACE S.W./ AT 5 O'CLOCK A.M. JANRY. 20TH. A.D.1800. / ONE OF THE CREW ONLY SURVIVING / TO TELL THE MELANCHOLY TALE, / BY THIS FATAL EVENT, THE COUNTRY, ALAS! WAS DEPRIVED, / OF 105 BRAVE DEFENDERS AT A TIME, WHEN IT / MOST REQUIRED THEIR ASSISTANCE. / THE REMAINS OF MANY OF THEM / WERE INTERRED NEAR TO THIS SPOT / BY THE DIRECTION OF / THE LORDS COMMISSIONERS OF / THE ADMIRALTY. / "The Waters saw thee O God"; (on panel on NE face): THE BRAZEN / HAD BEEN ORDERED / TO PROTECT / THIS PART OF THE COAST / FROM THE INSOLENT ATTACKS OF THE ENEMY; / AND ON THE EVENING / PRECEEDING THE / SAD CATASTROPHE, / HAD DETAINED A FOREIGN VESSEL, WHICH / WAS PUT UNDER THE CARE OF / THE MASTER'S MATE, A MIDSHIPMAN, / 8 SEAMEN, AND 2 MARINES; / WHO WERE THEREBY SAVED / FROM THE FATE OF THEIR / COMPANIONS; (on top step of base, facing SE, inlaid lead letters): THIS MONUMENT WAS RESTORED / BY LOUISA, WIDOW OF THE ABOVE CAPTN. JAMES HANSON. R.N. / OCTOBER 1878
Status: Grade II
Condition: fair (biological growth all over; railings rusting; base cracked and crumbling. Weather wearing to detailed carving of the obelisk. Restored in 1878. Parts of the old inscription still faintly visible underneath the newer slate panel)
Commissioned by: The friends of Captain Hanson
Owner/custodian: Church of St Michael, Newhaven

The obelisk has carved dolphins set within architectural motifs at the bottom of each face. On each side of the plinth are slate panels set into arched recesses, with designs of seaweed and shells, above and dolphins below. The panels are engraved with details of the shipwreck.

HMS *Brazen* was a captured French 18-gun sloop-of-war, formerly *L'Invincible General Bonaparte*. Its captain, James Hanson, had previously served under Captain Vancouver on his celebrated voyage of 1791–94, when he circumnavigated the world and charted part of North America. The ship departed from Portsmouth on 16 January 1800, with 117 men to protect the waters between St Helen's on the

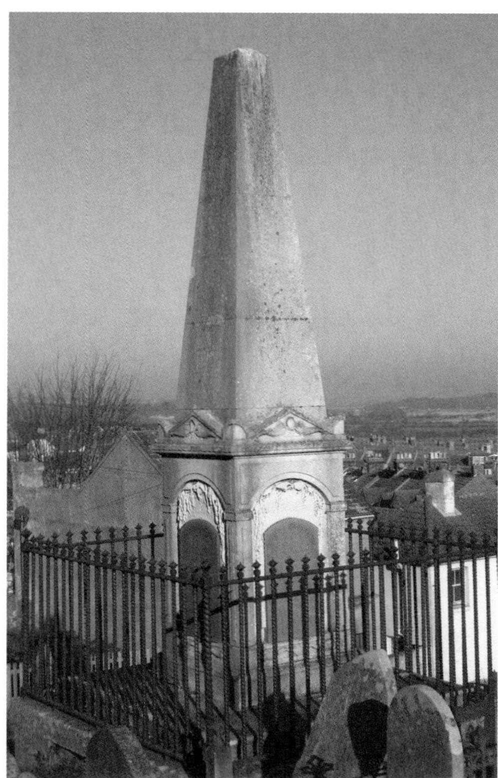

Unknown, *Monument to HMS Brazen*

Isle of Wight and Beachy Head. It foundered on rocks a few hundred yards off the coast of Newhaven on 26 January. Civilians tried to save the crewmen using cliff-top cranes that had been given by the Royal Humane Society, but they could not reach survivors unless they were at the foot of the cliff. Ultimately, only one man survived, Jeremiah Hill, who had been carried to the shore clinging to wreckage. The dead were buried in various nearby churchyards but 10 bodies were never recovered. The disaster prompted Newhaven to commission a lifeboat, which was installed in the harbour in 1803.

Source
Thornton, N., *Sussex Shipwrecks*, Newbury, 1988, pp. 70–75.

South Way

War Memorial Garden, near west side of Swing Bridge: formerly at junction of Chapel Street and South Road (moved 2006)

HM Transports Memorial
Designer: C.T. Hooper

Erected: c. 1920

Materials/dimensions: obelisk: stone set with grey granite panels, 2 m high × 90 cm wide × 90 cm deep; ball and lantern: stone, metal and glass, 1 m high × 50 cm wide × 50 cm deep; stepped base with corner posts: stone 40 cm high × 2.8 m wide × 2.8 m deep

Inscriptions (southeast face): THIS / MEMORIAL / IS ERECTED TO THE MEMORY / OF THE CAPTAINS, OFFICERS / AND SEAMEN, OF H.M. TRANSPORTS / WHO LOST THEIR LIVES WHILST / SAILING FROM THIS PORT / DURING THE GREAT WAR, / 1914 TO 1918, / AND ALSO IN COMMEMORATION / OF THE VALUABLE SERVICES / RENDERED BY THE MERCANTILE / MARINE OF THE UNITED KINGDOM DURING THE WAR; (on small concrete flowerpot below): PRESENTED BY / WOMEN'S SECTION / BRITISH LEGION / NEWHAVEN; (granite panels show the names of the fallen)

Status: not listed

Condition: fair (small chips to all sides of the obelisk. Render is coming away from the stone in places on all four sides. The lantern appears defunct. Some gaps between the stones of the base where the render has fallen out)

Owner/custodian: Newhaven Town Council

The obelisk sits on a square base of three steps with rough-hewn posts at each corner that hold chains surrounding the memorial. Each face has an inset grey granite inscribed panel with black painted lettering and an oval carved panel near the top which bear, on the SE face, an anchor, on the NW face, a life ring, on the SW face, a ship's wheel and on the NE face, a ship's propeller. Surmounting the obelisk is a stone sphere supporting a round glass lantern.

The port of Newhaven fulfilled a crucial function during the First World War, when it served as the principal departure point for ships

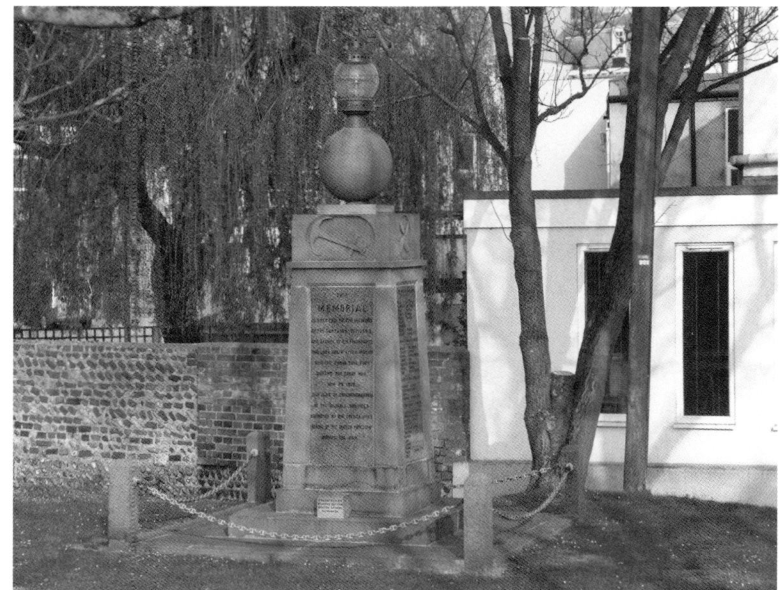

C.T. Hooper, *HM Transports Memorial*

carrying supplies to France. Eleven ships and about 100 seamen were lost in enemy attacks. Their sacrifice was commemorated at the end of the war, when Newhaven Urban Council commissioned the council surveyor, C.T. Hooper to design two memorials, one dedicated to the men of the Mercantile Marine and the other to the men of Newhaven who perished during the fighting. They continue to act as a focus for the annual Remembrance Day services.[1]

Note
[1] newhaventowncouncil.gov.uk/newhaven-history (accessed 2 September 2011).

West Quay

On grassed area, next to pedestrian walkway

Nesting Cormorant
Sculptor: Christian Funnell

Installed: 2002
Materials/dimensions: sculpture: banded steel and chain link fencing, 80 cm high × 50 cm wide × 1 m deep; post: recycled wooden groyne, 2.4 m high × 28 cm wide × 40 cm
Status: not listed
Condition: good (some oxidisation visible to the steel)
Owner/custodian: Newhaven Town Council

This sculpture of a cormorant, with its neck extended, sits facing east towards the harbour, in a nest made from chain link fencing. The nest is perched on top of a tall wooden groyne and has nine metal feathers lodged inside it.

Next to car park at the beginning of the pedestrianised area

Newhaven Cormorant
Sculptor: Christian Funnell

Unveiled: 15 May 2003
Materials/dimensions: sculpture: galvanised and

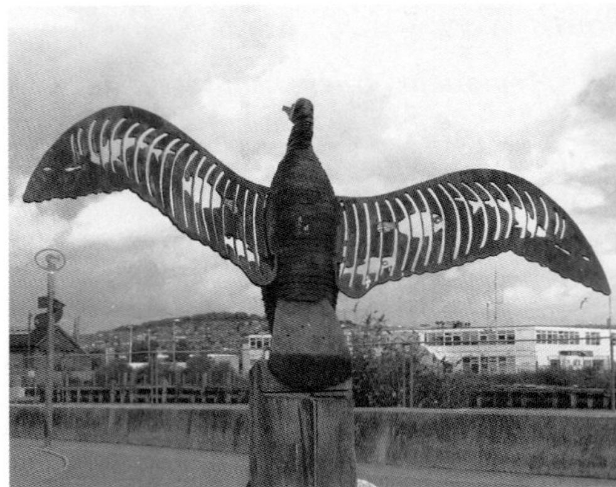

Christian Funnell, *Newhaven Cormorant*

painted steel, 2 m high × 2.4 m wide × 40 cm deep; pedestal: wood (beach groyne), 1.9 m high × 45 cm wide × 45 cm deep; base: brick topped by stone slabs, 4 m
Signature (wooden plaque at base of pedestal): CHRISTIAN / FUNNELL.com / 077998833000
Inscription (metal plaque on north face of base): This tribute to the heritage and future of Newhaven / was unveiled by / His Royal Highness The Duke of Kent KG / on the occasion of his visit to Newhaven / 15th May 2003
Status: not listed
Condition: good (some graffiti)
Commissioned by: Lewes District Council
Owner/custodian: Newhaven Town Council

The cormorant stands with wings, incorporating cut-out designs of fish, outstretched. The figure is set on a circular base topped with stone slabs, inset with four uplighters, forming a seat. The pedestal is made from an old beach groyne. The whole is sited in a pedestrianised area also containing bicycle clamps and decorative stone balls. To the eastern rim there is a seat constructed similarly to the sculpture base.

In 2001 the sculptor originally placed a similar piece, made from tyres on a steel frame, on a platform in the harbour waters, where it remains. Funnell, a keen windsurfer, who lives in Newhaven, enjoys making sculptures that connect with the sea. He stated:

> It amused me to make a sculpture of a bird with outstretched wings in the tradition of the American eagle etc. because cormorants on the river look like they are imitating it when they stand next to it drying their wings.[1]

The original piece was installed without permission, but when local councillors saw it, they liked it and commissioned the pieces now on the West Quay.

Note
[1] Christian Funnell, email correspondence, 3 October 2007.

NORTHIAM

Church Lane
The Frewen Chapel, Parish Church of St Mary

Monument to Anne Frewen
Sculptor: William Behnes

Installed: 1844
Materials/dimensions: white and grey marble, 2.2 m high × 1.25 m wide × 30 cm deep
Signature (to bottom right of outer aspect of plinth): W. BEHNES / SCUR. LONDON
Inscriptions (to front of plinth in black painted incised letters): IN THE VAULT BENEATH LIES THE BODY OF / ANNE, THE WIFE OF THOMAS FREWEN, ESQRE. OF BRICKWALL. / SHE WAS THE ELEVENTH OF TWELVE CHILDREN OF WILLIAM WILSON CARUS WILSON, ESQRE. M.P. / BY HIS WIFE MARGARET, DAUGHTER AND SOLE HEIR OF BENJAMIN SHIPPARD, OF NATLAND / AND WAS BORN AT HER FATHERS SEAT, CASTERTON HALL, WESTMORELAND, JULY 19TH. 1803. / SHE DIED AT BRICKWALL, AT THE BIRTH OF HER SIXTH CHILD, (A STILLBORN FEMALE INFANT) FEBRUARY 18TH.

1844, / LEAVING FIVE YOUNG CHILDREN, MARY, SELINA, JOHN, LATON, AND ELEANOR, / TO DEPLORE THE LOSS OF A TENDER MOTHER. / HER DISPOSITION, NATURALLY MILD AND GENTLE, WAS IMPROVED BY A RELIGIOUS EDUCATION, / AND IT PLEASED GOD IN HIS INFINITE MERCY, TO CALL HER IN EARLY YOUTH TO A SAVING KNOWLEDGE OF HIMSELF. / HER RELIGIOUS PRINCIPLES WERE DEEP-SEATED BUT UNOBTRUSIVE, AND THOUGH SHE FELT STRONGLY, / SHE WAS DIFFIDENT IN HER PROFESSION LEST THROUGH THE INFIRMITY OF HUMAN NATURE, / RELIGION MIGHT BE DISGRACED BY AN INCONSISTENT WALK. / FOR HER STATION IN LIFE, SHE WAS VERY MODERATE AND SELF-DENYING, / AND EVER READY TO MINISTER TO THE TEMPORAL AND SPIRITUAL WANTS OF HER FELLOW CREATURES. / IN PROSPERITY SHE WAS MEEK AND HUMBLE, PATIENT AND UNCOMPLAINING IN ADVERSITY AND IN SICKNESS, / AND RESIGNED IN THE HOUR OF DEATH: HER LAST WORDS WERE "THY WILL BE DONE!" / THOMAS FREWEN ESQRE. ERECTS THIS MONUMENT / TO COMMEMORATE HER MANY EXCELLENCIES, AND HIS OWN IRREPARABLE LOSS. / THOU ART GONE TO THE GRAVE, WE NO LONGER BEHOLD THEE, / NOR TREAD THE ROUGH PATHS OF THE WORLD BY THY SIDE; / BUT THE WIDE ARMS OF MERCY ARE SPREAD TO ENFOLD THEE, / AND SINNERS MAY HOPE, SINCE THE SINLESS HAS DIED. / "WHAT SHALL SEPARATE US FROM THE LOVE OF CHRIST? SHALL TRIBULATION, OR PERSECUTION, / OR DISTRESS, OR NAKEDNESS, OR FAMINE, OR PERIL, OR SWORD; NAY, IN ALL THESE THINGS WE / ARE MORE THAN CONQUERORS, THROUGH HIM THAT LOVED US." / "QUICQUID EX ILLA AMAVIMUS, QUICQUID MIRATI SUMUS MANET"; (on banner underneath shield at base of plinth in incised letters); MUTARE NONEST MEUM (It is not mine to change, the Frewen family motto)

Status: not listed
Condition: good

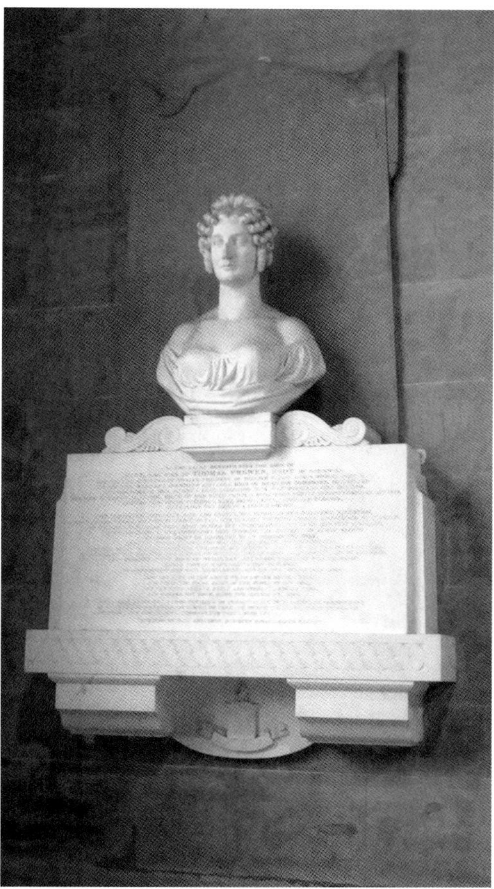

William Behnes, *Monument to Anne Frewen*

Commissioned by: Thomas Frewen (her husband, whose own memorial is also in the chapel)
Owner/custodian: Frewen family

The portrait bust of the deceased shows her with a contemporary hairstyle and suggestion of modern dress. The bust surmounts an architectural inscribed plinth with a voluted top and the whole is set against a grey marble panel with shaped corners.

The architect Sidney Smirke extended the church and designed the Frewen Chapel, built above the Frewen Mausoleum in 1845, in soft, porous sandstone. It contains memorials to members of this family who have been associated with the local community since the Elizabethan era and whose connection continues to be maintained. Anne Frewen's husband, Thomas, is commemorated by a marble and mosaic Gothic-style monument, erected c. 1870.

Sources
Green, A., *A Short Guide to the Parish Church of St Mary, Northiam*, nd.
Llewellyn (2011), pp. 239–44.
Nairn and Pevsner (1965), p. 574.

OVINGDEAN

Greenways

On exterior wall above chapel of Blind Veterans UK Brighton Centre (formerly St Dunstan's National Centre)

Winged Victory
Sculptor: Julian Phelps Allan OBE
Architect: Francis Lorne

Installed: 1939
Materials/dimensions: reconstituted concrete, 6.1 m high
Status: not listed
Condition: good (considerable biological growth, some minor repairs to back of base)
Commissioned and owned by: St Dunstan's

An art deco-style figure emerges from the blocks of concrete, with wings suggested by carving on the side faces. The features are androgynous, but the title Winged Victory confirms her gender as female.[1] She holds the insignia of St Dunstan's, a national charity, founded in 1915 by Sir Arthur Pearson, owner of *The Evening Standard* newspaper, to help blind ex-Service men and women and their families. Simon Rogers has suggested a link between the Victory and the Angel of Mons, a

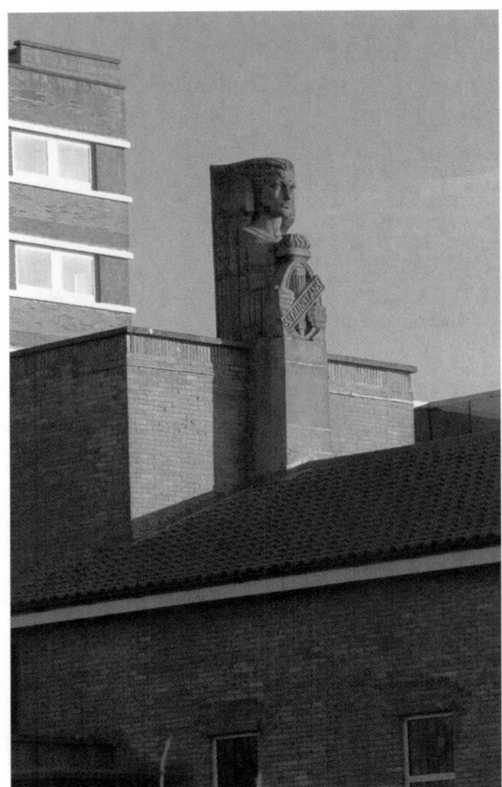

Julian Phelps Allan, *Winged Victory*

spectral figure, who, according to legend, appeared to British soldiers during the Great War and forbade the Germans from advancing further. The Angel was adopted in promotional material for St Dunstan's in the early days of the war, depicted leading a blind man from the trenches.[2] Rogers argues that the myth of the Angel was incorporated into the figure of the Winged Victory, which adorns an otherwise blank brick wall, above the chapel roof of the purpose-built St Dunstan's building designed by Francis Lorne in 1939. It was deliberately located outside London in anticipation of further casualties resulting from the Second World War.

While working on the piece, the sculptor, who changed her name from Eva Dorothy to Julian Phelps, wrote, 'It is rather an adventure, especially as no one knows whether the floor of my studio will hold it!'[3] In an ironic twist of fate, she herself was registered blind in 1974. In the course of her long career (she died aged 103) Phelps completed many private and public commissions, including the tombstone of Emily Pankhurst.

There is photographic evidence of a large bust (presumably of Sir Arthur Pearson) on the roof at the front of the St Dunstan's building prior to the 1960s.[4]

Notes
[1] The most famous example is the Winged Victory of Samothrace, the second-century BC marble sculpture of the Greek goddess Nike (Victory) in the Louvre. [2] Rogers, S., 'Angel of the knight', *St Dunstan's Review*, April 1997, pp. 8–9. [3] *St Dunstan's Review*, June 1999, p. 15. [4] Terry Sinnott (local historian), correspondence, 23 September 2007; *The Argus*, 22 September 2007.

Other sources
Robert Baker (archivist, St Dunstan's Collections & Archives), email correspondence, 20 April 2012.
Troak, M., *Pioneer Days at Peacehaven: a Trip Down Memory Lane*, Telscombe, 2007.

PATCHAM

Patcham Downs

North of Patcham Court Farm (Braypool Lane exit off A27)

Chattri Monument
Architect: Sir Swinton Jacob
Designer: E.C. Henriques

Builder: William Kirkpatrick Ltd, Manchester
Materials/dimensions: dome and columns: white Sicilian marble, 8.94 m high; total area: 12.19 m × 18.28 m
Inscription: TO THE MEMORY OF ALL THE INDIAN SOLDIERS WHO GAVE THEIR LIVES IN THE / SERVICE OF THEIR KING-EMPEROR IN THE GREAT WAR THIS MONUMENT ERECTED ON THE SITE / OF THE FUNERAL PYRE WHERE THE / HINDUS AND SIKHS WHO DIED IN HOSPITAL AT BRIGHTON PASSED / THROUGH THE FIRE IS IN GRATEFUL ADMIRATION AND BROTHERLY AFFECTION DEDICATED
Status: Grade II
Condition: good
Commissioned by: The India Office and Sir John Otter, Mayor of Brighton (1916)
Owner/custodian: Brighton and Hove City Council

The Chattri, which means umbrella in Hindi, Punjabi and Urdu, is an octagonal, domed monument, the dome supported by eight pillars; three granite blocks cover the concrete cremation slabs. Its design symbolises the protection offered to the memory of the dead. The designer was an architectural student from Mumbai, who undertook the work without a fee.

During the First World War, 12,000 Indian soldiers who were wounded on the Western Front were hospitalised at sites around Brighton, including the Royal Pavilion.[1] The Chattri stands in memory of all Indian troops, but is particularly associated with the 53 Hindu and Sikh soldiers who died locally and whose remains were cremated at this spot. The cremations took place at around one per week for the duration of the Indians' stay, the first on 31 December 1914 and the last on 30 December 1915.

The original idea for a memorial is attributed to Lieutenant Das Gupta of the Indian Medical Service, who approached the mayor of Brighton, John Otter, in August 1915 for permission to erect a memorial on the site where the cremations took place. The mayor embraced the idea with great enthusiasm and became the driving force behind it. Otter proposed two memorials: one to be erected on the ghat, or cremation site; the other, in the town, of a more general nature to commemorate the link with the Indians (now the southern gateway to the Pavilion, paid for by subscriptions raised in India by Sirdar Daljit Singh). The India Office and Brighton Corporation each bore half of the cost of erection, but Brighton alone is responsible for ongoing care and maintenance. Gardens were laid surrounding the monument, with four miniature avenues of red and white rose trees pointing north, south, west and east and the whole area turfed. The final cost of the entire scheme was £4964, which included £1117 spent on a caretaker's cottage (since demolished).

The Chattri was unveiled by Edward, Prince of Wales in 1921, but the first public service of commemoration (the British Legion Pilgrimage) did not take place until 18 September 1932. Following numerous complaints from walkers and visitors about the condition of the memorial, in 1939, on the advice of the India Office, the Imperial War Graves Commission undertook a thorough

survey and drew up a plan for maintenance that involved a reduction in the area of land covered (originally two acres) and other measures. Brighton Corporation finally agreed to undertake the work in 1942. The pilgrimage was resurrected in 1951, taking place annually until 1999 when the British Legion decided that they could no longer maintain the ceremony. Hearing of its demise, Davinder Dhillon, a local Sikh teacher, undertook its stewardship and it has continued to be held annually on the third Sunday in June since 2000, with representatives of the Undivided Indian Ex-Service, the Brighton and Hove Hindu Elders Group, members of the armed forces and police, the mayor and local people in attendance. The Chattri was chosen as the site of Anish Kapoor's *C-Curve* sculpture during the 2009 Brighton Festival.

Note
[1] A small exhibition, using paintings, archive photographs, contemporary accounts and film footage to tell the story of the building's use as a military hospital, opened in a first floor room of the Pavilion in 2010.

Other sources
A Pictorial and Descriptive Guide to Brighton and Hove, p. 94.
The Argus, 18 August 1997.
Beevers, D. and Roles, J. (1993), p. 224.
Brighton Gazette, 8 December 1920 and 2 February 1921.
Brighton Herald, 5 February 1921.
Carder (1990), entry 122h.
chattri.com (accessed 1 October 2010).
Collis (2010), pp. 58–59.
Longstaff-Tyrrell (2000), p. 36.

Horsham Avenue

At bottom of avenue, on cliff top, facing the sea

George V Memorial: Silver Jubilee Prime Meridian Monument
Architect: R. Jones

Unveiled: 10 August 1935
Materials/dimensions: white stone and York stone, 6.1 m high; sphere and rod, copper and bronze
Inscriptions: (south face): PEACEHAVEN / KING GEORGE V MEMORIAL / ERECTED BY THE INHABITANTS IN THE / YEAR 1936 TO COMMEMORATE THE / BENEFICENT AND ILLUSTRIOUS REIGN / OF THEIR BELOVED-SOVEREIGN (1910–1936) / AND TO MARK PEACEHAVEN'S POSITION ON / THE PRIME MERIDIAN OF GREENWICH; (immediately underneath the above): In Celebration of the / International Prime Meridian Centenary / 1884–1984 / This plaque was unveiled by the Mayor of Peacehaven / Councillor Alfa Clayton / 26 June 1984; (at base): THIS STONE WAS LAID / ON MAY 30TH 1936 BY / C.W. NEVILLE ESQ. THE / FOUNDER OF PEACEHAVEN / (IN THE YEAR 1919); (on north

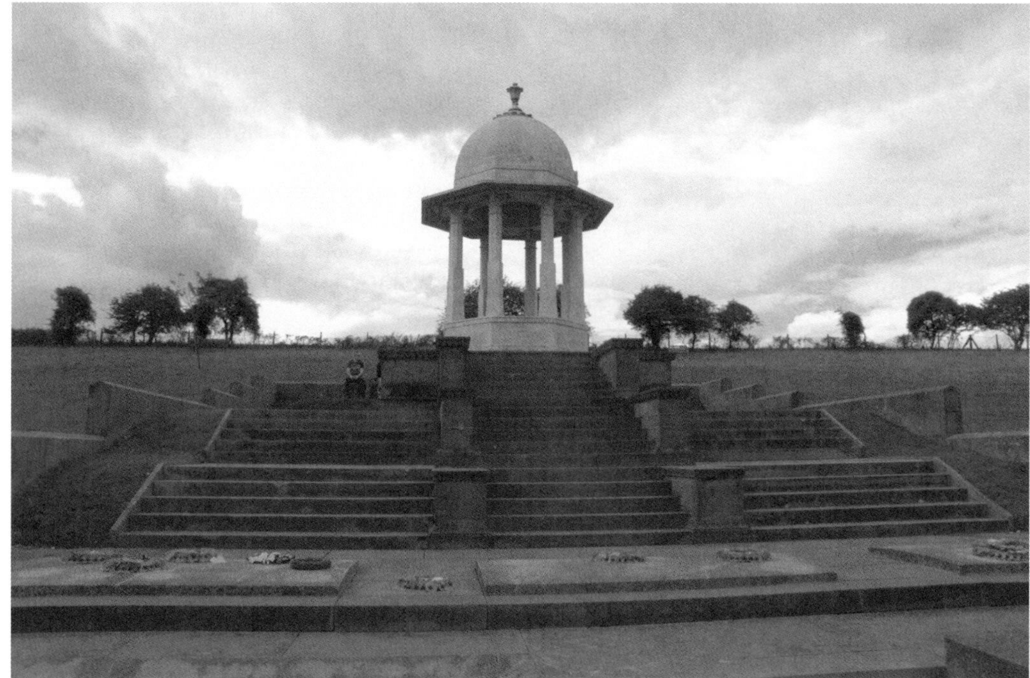

E.C. Henriques, *Chattri Monument*

face): DISTANCE FROM THIS POINT (followed by a list of many world destinations and their distances)
Status: not listed
Condition: good
Funded by: public subscription
Owner/custodian: Peacehaven Town Council

This memorial drinking fountain is a tall rectangular structure, with architectural details, surmounted by a copper globe with a bronze rod pointing to the North Star. The lower part has two opposing arched openings above semicircular drinking basins. The south face bears the inscriptions. Below the memorial the meridian line runs through a concrete channel across the grass. The drinking fountain replaced an earlier wooden structure with a large star

and four distance signposts, erected by Commander Davenport RN, who established the exact point where the Greenwich Meridian passes through Peacehaven. The new one, overlooking the sea, cost £300. It was unveiled by Charles William Neville, the founder of Peacehaven, during celebrations held for the Silver Jubilee of King George V. Neville had bought the surrounding land during the First World War and 'laid out a grid of streets and building plots, advertising a new "garden city by the sea".'[1] The monument has been moved inland on two occasions due to cliff erosion.

Note
[1] Arscott (1991), p. 59.

Other source
Poplett, B., *Peacehaven: a Pictorial History*, Chichester, 1993, np, figs 122–126.

R. Jones, *Monument to George V*

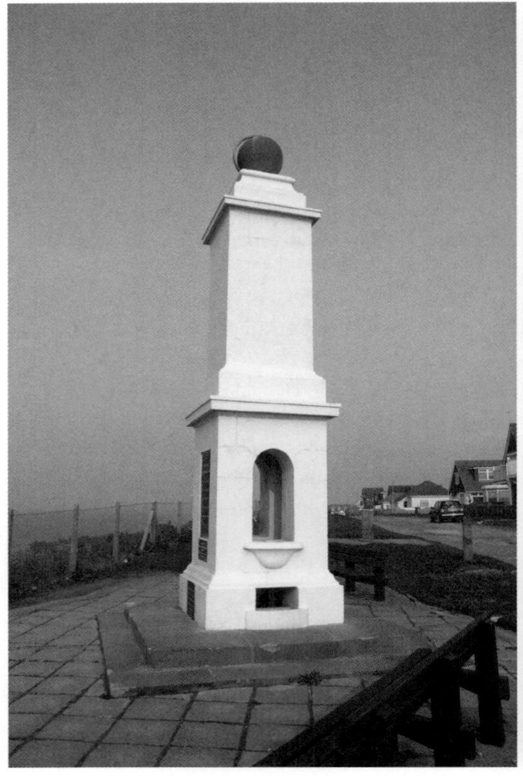

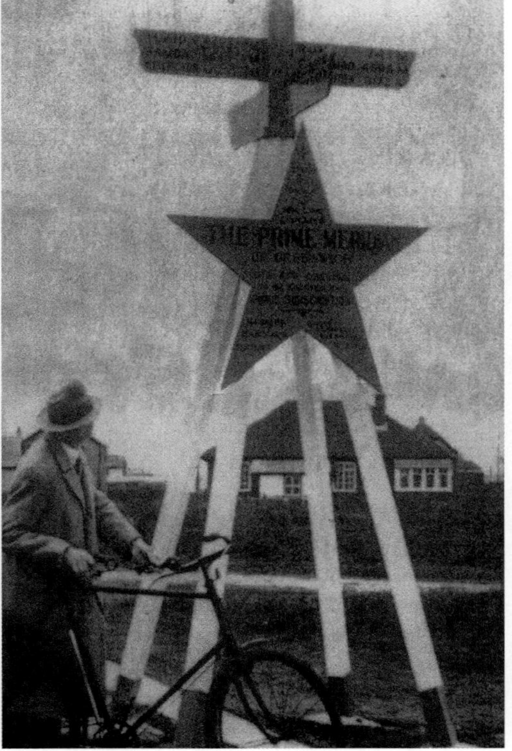

Eastbourne Road

Top of drive the Bernhard Baron Cottage Homes (possibly previously located at Southdown Hall)

The Diplock Stag
Sculptor: unknown

Materials/dimensions: statue: cement, painted buff colour, on metal armature, 1.95 m high × 1.3 m wide × 40 cm deep; plinth: brick with flint panels, 1.45 m high × 1.5 m wide × 67 cm deep
Inscriptions (to front of plinth): THESE COTTAGE HOMES WERE ERECTED IN 1937 / UNDER A TRUST CONTAINED IN THE WILL OF CALEB DIPLOCK / OF POLEGATE WHO DIED ON THE 23RD MARCH 1936 / ON THE 21ST JUNE 1944 IT WAS DECIDED BY THE HOUSE OF LORDS (AFFIRMING THE DECISION OF THE COURT OF APPEAL) / THAT THIS TRUST WAS VOID FOR UNCERTAINTY IN ITS WORDING / IN SEPTEMBER 1945 THE PROPERTY WAS PURCHASED BY THE / SOCIETY OF FRIENDS (QUAKERS) WITH THE AID OF / CONTRIBUTIONS INCLUDING A SUBSTANTIAL GRANT FROM / THE BERNHARD BARON TRUST IN RECOGNITION OF WHICH / THE DWELLINGS ARE HEREBY RE-NAMED THE BERNHARD BARON COTTAGE HOMES
Status: not listed
Condition: good (restored c. 2006 following damage from vehicle impact, some surface lifting on right-hand antler)
Owner/custodian: Bernhard Baron Cottage Homes

The stag stands alert atop a rectangular plinth and forms the focal point of the main drive up to the complex of flint and brick cottages. It is claimed that the sculpture was created, on site, over a wire armature, by a local plasterer at the time of the erection of the cottages. Residents

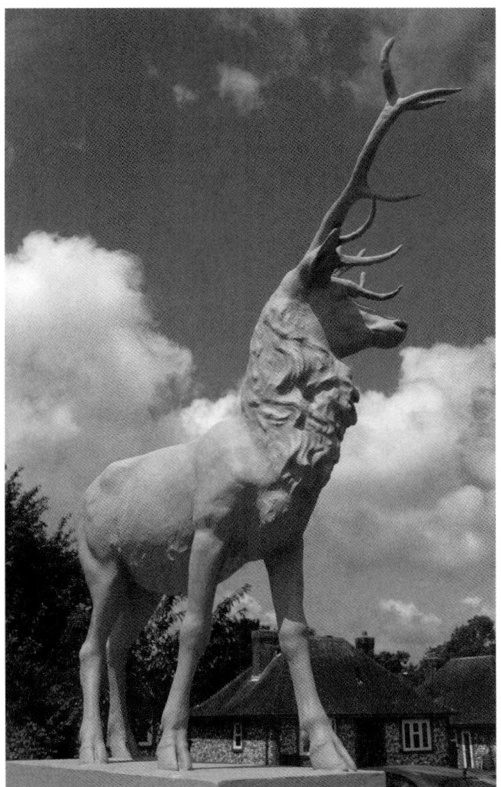

Unknown, *The Diplock Stag*

apparently recalled seeing him sitting astride its back making the antlers, although doubts have been cast about the practicality of sitting on 'green' concrete. Another story is that the stag came from Southdown Hall, the nearby Diplock family home, possibly from the garden, or from an archway over the main drive leading from the High Street. It is known that the Diplocks had garden ornaments imported from France soon after the house was built and it is possible that this is the origin of the sculpture; an almost identical stag was placed over an arch at Charborough Park, Dorset, in 1841. It is also understood that the Stag was used in the design of beer labels for Diplock's brewery.[1]

The 12 Diplocks Cottages in Polegate were built in 1936 as a memorial to Caleb Diplock, a wealthy resident and landowner. They were built for the poor and needy living within three miles of the Parish Church. The first residents were elderly evacuees who had been made homeless in the Second World War. They were put up for sale in 1945 following the successful contesting of Diplock's will by distant relatives. With the generous help of the Bernhard Baron Trust, the cottages were purchased and renamed after the wealthy director of the Carreras Tobacco Company and philanthropist. Under the Trusteeship of the Religious Society of Friends (Quakers) the cottages are for those in need, of any religion or political opinion, providing this is not made a nuisance to others.

Note
[1] Bernhard Baron Cottage Homes, bbch.co.uk (accessed 15 October 2010).

Other source
Swinfen and Arscott (1985), p. 117.

Church Square

Parish Church of St Mary the Virgin, wall of north transept

Monument to John Woollett

Sculptors: Samuel Manning and John Bacon (the Younger)

Installed: after 1819
Materials/dimensions: white marble, 2.55 m high × 1.15 m wide × 11.5 cm deep
Signatures (on base of plinth, left-hand side, in incised letters): J.BACON, INVT; (on base of plinth, right-hand side, in incised letters): S.MANNING, FT.
Inscriptions (at base of relief, in incised black painted letters): THY GENTLE ARM, BENEVOLENCE, SUSTAINS / OUR FAINTING HOPE, THY BALM OUR LIFE REGAINS; (on plinth, in incised black-painted letters): SACRED TO THE MEMORY OF / JOHN WOOLLETT, ESQR. / LATE OF THIS TOWN; / WHO DEPARTED THIS LIFE ON THE XXIIIRD. OF MARCH / MDCCCXIX, / IN THE LXTH. YEAR OF HIS AGE. / HIS LAMENTED REMAINS ARE DEPOSITED / IN THIS CHURCH; (on left-hand page of open book, in incised letters): CTS (ACTS); (on right-hand page of book): CHAP x. / A just Man / And one / That / Feared God / VER 22
Status: not listed
Condition: fair (hand missing from raised arm, cracks to bottom of anchor and piece missing from anchor ring; cracks to arched frame and chips to plinth where monument has been secured to wall with metal pins)
Commissioned by: Woollett family
Owner/custodian: Parish Church of St Mary the Virgin

The sculptural relief, commemorating a local solicitor and benefactor, features two female

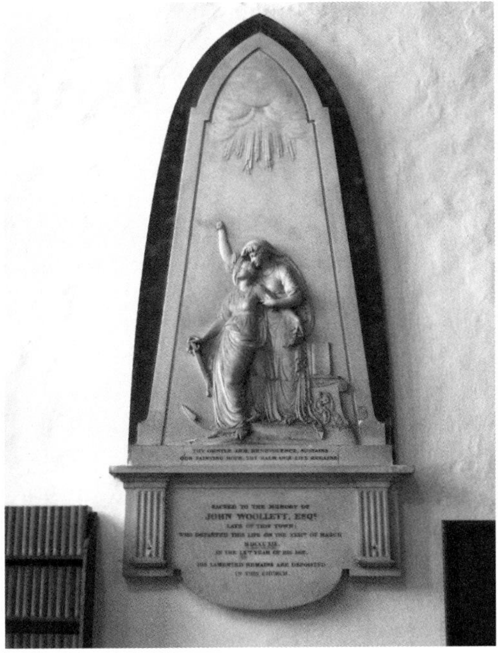

Samuel Manning and John Bacon, *Monument to John Woollett*

figures. The one to the rear (representing Hope) holds the left arm of the front figure (representing Benevolence) and indicates heavenward with her raised right arm. Clouds are depicted above her from which emanate rays of light. The figure at the front leans back against the rear figure, resting her right arm on an anchor and has flowers in her left hand. Behind the two figures is a scrolled plinth that has a sculptural relief of a male figure giving a drink to another male figure lying on the ground, possibly illustrating the story of Cornelius and St Peter from the Acts of the Apostles, referred to in the inscription on the bible directly above.

Samuel Manning was a pupil of John Bacon the Younger and they later went into partnership as monumental masons. Most of the work was carried out after Bacon had virtually retired and so it was Manning who did most of the designing and carving on the memorials. Much of the success of the business was due to the name Bacon and most of the memorials produced by the firm are regarded as inferior. Gunnis, however, regards the Woollett monument as one of their better pieces.[1]

Note
[1] Gunnis (1953), pp. 31–32.

Other sources
Holloway, W., *The History and Antiquities of the Ancient Town and Port of Rye in the County of Sussex*, London, 1847.
Llewellyn (2011), pp. 288, 299.

Harbour Road

The Church of the Holy Spirit, far side of churchyard

Mary Stanford Memorial

Sculptor: James Wedgwood

Unveiled: 19 November 1931
Materials/dimensions: stone, 3.67 m high ×
 1.25 m wide × 45 cm deep
Inscriptions (above statue): WE HAVE DONE

THAT WHICH WAS OUR DUTY TO DO; (plaque on front of plinth): TO THE MEMORY OF / THE SEVENTEEN BRAVE / MEN, THE CREW OF THE / MARY STANFORD LIFE- / BOAT, WHO PERISHED IN / A HEAVY GALE WHILE / GALLANTLY RESPONDING / TO THE CALL FOR HELP / FROM THE S.S. ALICE OF / RIGA ON THE MORNING OF / THE 15th NOVEMBER 1928.
Status: not listed
Condition: good
Commissioned by: Royal Society of British Sculptors (open competition)

A tall cruciform arched monument is set on a three-stepped base at the head of a large collective grave that holds the remains of the lifeboat crew. Above the inscription tablet, within a shallow niche, stands the figure of a lifeboat man, his head bowed, wearing a sou'wester and lifejacket and holding a coil of rope in his right hand. Plaques to each of the lost crewmen are set into the base around a central gravelled area.

The cost of a new lifeboat for Rye Harbour was met in 1916 by a legacy in memory of Mary Stanford, after whom the boat was named. Twelve years later, the boat was launched in a southwest gale to go to the aid of the small steamer *Alice* of Riga, laden with a cargo of bricks, that had been in collision with the larger German vessel *Smyrna*. News was received that the crew of the *Alice* had been rescued by another vessel and the recall signal was fired three times. Apparently the crew of the lifeboat did not see it. As the boat was returning to harbour she was seen to capsize and the whole of the crew perished. On 20 November 1928 the funeral of 15 crew members was held; one further body was later washed ashore at Eastbourne and one was never found. The memorial was unveiled three years later by Lord Blanesborough.

All the men's dependants were pensioned by the Royal National Lifeboat Institution (RNLI), with the local fund raising over

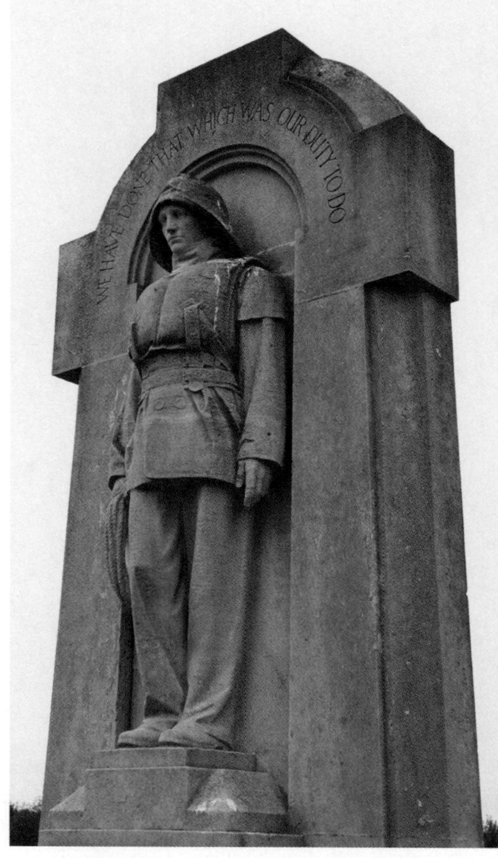

James Wedgwood, *Mary Stanford Memorial*

£35,000. In addition to Wedgwood's monument, a memorial tablet made of Manx stone was presented to Rye Harbour by the people of the Isle of Man and a memorial stained glass window was placed in nearby Winchelsea church.

Sources
Arscott (1991).
Hutchinson, G., *The Mary Stanford Disaster: the Story of a Lifeboat, November 15th, 1928*, 1984.
Thornton (1988), pp. 114–19.

Strand Quay

On Winchelsea Road Roundabout

The Spirit of Rye
Sculptor: Ron Dellar

Builders: students of Hastings College
Installed: 2000
Materials/dimensions: wall: red brick, 2 m high
× 8.35 m wide × 75 cm deep; relief: stone,
75 cm high × 2.6 m wide × 2 cm deep
Signatures (names carved into various bricks):
GARY. D. 99/ DYLAN. P. / PERCY ELDRIDGE /
DAZ POOLEY
Inscription (bronze plaque set into stone at base
of wall): THE SPIRIT OF RYE / Designed by
Ron Dellar / Erected by Students of the

Ron Dellar, *The Spirit of Rye*

Hastings College of Arts and Technology /
Sponsored by Rother Environmental Group
and Rye Conservation Society / 2000 AD
Status: not listed
Condition: poor (covered with graffiti and
vegetation)
Commissioned by: Rother Environmental
Group & Rye Conservation Society
Owner/custodian: Transco

The curved, wedge-shaped stone relief depicting
a female profile with flowing hair contrasts with
the red brick wall into which it is set. The
surface of the wall has flowing lines of moulded
brick along its length, echoing the shapes of the
relief. At the bottom of the wall is a narrow
pebbled area separating the sculpture from the
pathway. The site was the place where day
labourers used to line up to be chosen for work.[1]

In February 2012, the sculptor, dismayed at
the state of neglect of the wall, approached Rye
Conservation Society and Rother Environmental
Group to seek their support in restoring the
sculpture. He pointed out that it was the only
piece of public art in Rye and the only lasting
marker of the Millennium.[2] He also suggested
that the Town Council take over ownership of
the wall, as the company that owned the land
no longer exists.[3] The council debated his
request but the costs involved presented
considerable problems in implementing this plan.

Notes
[1] 'Calls to restore the Spirit of Rye', *Rye and Battle
Observer*, 3 February 2012. [2] Ibid. [3] The gas
transporting company Transco has been incorporated
into National Grid.

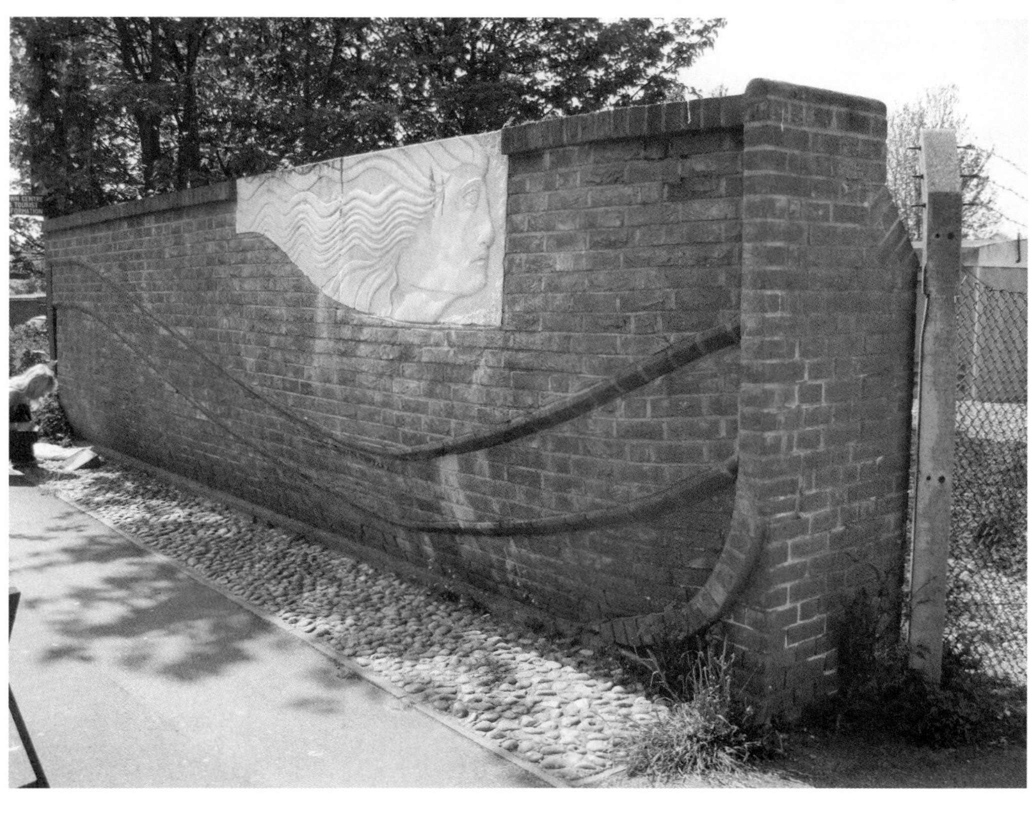

ST LEONARDS-ON-SEA

Grand Parade

On Promenade opposite Marine Court

Stream
Sculptor: Esther Rolinson

Builders: Sutton Vane Associates
Installed: March 2002
Materials/dimensions (each of seven columns):
steel base, blue glass upper, 3.5 m high ×
36 cm wide × 36 cm deep
Status: not listed
Condition: good
Commissioned by: Hastings Borough Council
and South East Arts
Owner/custodian: Hastings Borough Council

Reflecting Esther Rolinson's background in
both performance and fine art, this site-specific
light installation comprises a series of seven
steel and blue glass columns, extending along
the promenade for some 40 m. At night, the
columns illuminate in sequence with blue light
creating a 'wave' to echo the movement of the
sea.

The project was realised by the independent

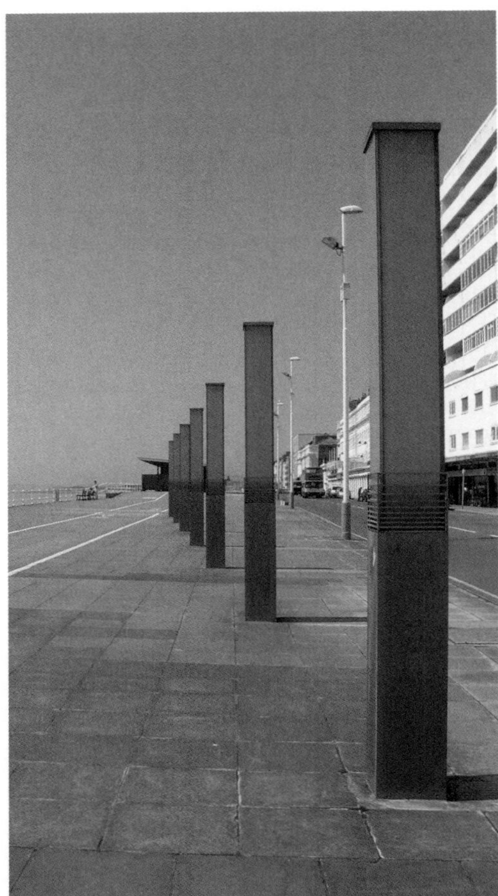

Esther Rolinson, _Stream_

lighting design consultancy Sutton Vane Associates (established in 1995) that covers all areas of commercial and residential architectural lighting design, from lighting master plans for cities to schemes for museums and leisure attractions, exhibitions and specially commissioned light art. Rolinson again used glass and an animated light sequence for _Align_ (2006), set into the entrance piazza and steps of Lewes public library.

Sources
insitearts.com (accessed 8 December 2010).
sva.co.uk (accessed 8 December 2010).

Grosvenor Crescent/Sea Road

In West Marina Gardens (moved 1953, previously in the Brassey Institute, Hastings, then Hastings Museum)

Harold and Edith

Sculptor: Charles Augustus William Wilke

Created: 1875
Materials/dimensions: statue: marble, 84 cm high × 1.35 m wide × 87 cm deep; plinth: brick core with concrete render, 76 cm high × 1.83 m wide × 1.22 m deep
Inscription: the original integral marble base had the inscription (now completely eroded): Edith finding the body of Harold on the battlefield of Hastings.
Status: not listed
Condition: poor (the sculpture is severely weathered and virtually none of the carved surface remains. Prominent features, such as noses and fingers, and the detail of Harold's chain mail armour, are now lost or eroded. Soil and sand have become deposited in the crevices of the carving. The fingers of Harold's left hand, the toes of his left foot and the end of his axe handle are lost. The corners on the eastern side of the plinth are gone)
Owner/custodian: Hastings Borough Council

The sculpture shows King Harold II and his common-law wife Edith (commonly known as Edith Swan-Neck). Harold lies dying on his back, holding an axe in his right hand, and the figure of Edith is hunched over him, holding up his head towards her face.

Harold died at the battle of Hastings in 1066. It is said that his body was terribly mutilated by the Norman army and they refused to surrender it to his mother, even for his body weight in gold. Folklore has it that Edith Swan-Neck walked through the carnage of the battle and identified Harold by marks on his body

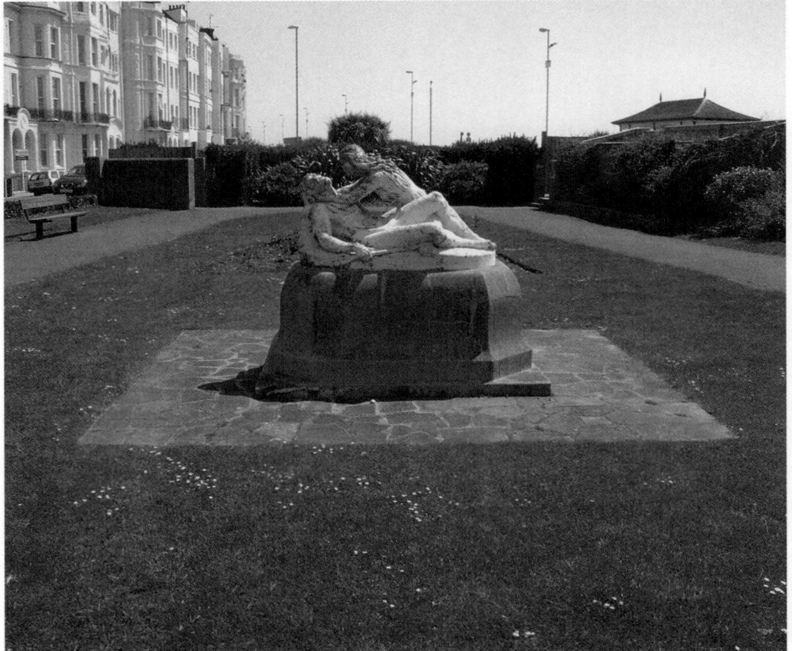

Charles Augustus William Wilke, _Harold and Edith_

known only to her. Another interpretation is that she was captured by William's troops and forced to identify the body so that they could be sure that Harold was dead. The confirmation of his death marked the turning point in the battle, as it severely demoralised Harold's army. The identification of the body and collection of body parts allowed the monks at Waltham Abbey to give Harold a Christian burial.

The statue of Harold and Edith was commissioned in the 1870s by Lord Brassey MP, who had employed Wilke to sculpt busts and allegorical portraits of several members of his family.[1] He had requested that it be placed in the proposed new Town Hall, which was never built. Subsequently, the siting of the sculpture, at one time stored in the ice rink in Cambridge Road, proved something of a problem for the town. It was exhibited on the first floor of the Brassey Institute, but in 1928 it was moved to St John's Place with the rest of the contents of the museum and originally displayed inside the building.[2] There appears to be no record of when the decision was taken to move the sculpture outside to the museum grounds; it is likely to have been due to shortage of interior space, which, as the curator J. Manwaring Baines pointed out in 1938, was a problem resulting from the fact that St John's had originally been a domestic dwelling.[3] The sculpture was again re-sited in 1953 when a new access road, cutting across the museum grounds, was constructed for the Royal East Sussex Hospital.[4] The hospital management committee paid for its removal to its present position, where it was provided with a new concrete plinth and surrounding crazy paving. Reports of the move in the local paper indicate that the piece was not very highly regarded by that time, as they state that the sculptor was 'unknown'.[5] Exposure to the sea air and weather resulted in severe erosion of the marble surface, returning it to a crystalline state in places and eradicating the fine surface detail, particularly in the figures' costumes, that is evident in black and white postcards of the sculpture produced in 1908.[6] In 1995 the sculpture was included in a review of all the statues in the borough of Hastings. Concern was expressed about its poor condition, but it appears to have been too late to take remedial action.[7]

Notes
[1] Wilke sculpture file, Hastings Museum Archive.
[2] Ibid. Notes by Victoria Williams, curator.
[3] *Hastings and St Leonards Museum Association Report*, 1938–39. [4] Education Committee minutes, 18 December 1952 and 22 January 1953. [5] *Hastings Evening Argus*, 23 February 1953. [6] Hastings Museum Archive. [7] Ibid. Correspondence January–March 1995.

Other sources
Dinsmore (1997), p. 4.
Ron Fellowes, correspondence with Robert Meek of the *Hastings Observer*, 2 May 2007.
Heather Grief (Hastings Local History Group), email correspondence, 9 June 2009.
Hastings and St Leonards Observer, 3 October 1953.
Hastings Evening Argus, 29 October 1953.

TICEHURST

Pashley Road

Pashley Manor Gardens

Mr and Mrs James Sellick are the owners and inhabitants of Pashley Manor. The house has a Tudor front built in 1550 by Sir Thomas May, and a Queen Anne rear added in 1720. It is timber-framed and Grade I listed. It is set in 11 acres of award-winning gardens. The estate can be traced back to 1262, when the de Passele family built a moated manor and held the estate until 1453, when it was sold to the forebears of Anne Boleyn, who used it as a hunting lodge. It is believed that Anne Boleyn stayed here as a child. The Boleyn family held the manor until the execution of Anne. The present owners have been developing and replanting the gardens, with the advice of Antony du Gard Pasley, since 1981 and opened them to the public in 1992. Evidence of gardening at Pashley has been found from the sixteenth century and the park contains oak trees that are over 500 years old.

Jubilee Courtyard
Diana the Huntress

Sculptors: Students from the Accademia, Florence

Constructed and installed: c. 1985
Materials/dimensions: statue: sandstone, 1.65 m high × 50 cm wide × 40 cm deep; plinth: sandstone, 50 cm high × 46 cm wide × 46 cm deep
Status: not listed
Condition: good (but some weather wearing to the finer detail. Covered in moss and other biological growth)
Owners/custodians: Mr and Mrs James Sellick

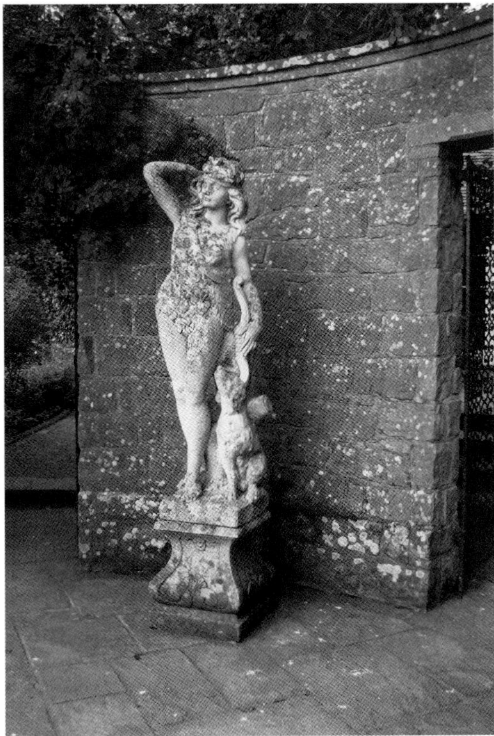

Students from the Accademia, Florence, *Diana the Huntress*

This figure of a semi-naked Diana dressed only in a short vestment of oak leaves is sculpted from a single piece of sandstone. The goddess has long wavy hair and wears a half-moon and serpent headdress. In her left hand she holds a bow; her right arm is raised over her right shoulder as she reaches for an arrow from a quiver. At her left foot sits an alert hunting dog, with his head raised towards his mistress.

In Roman mythology, Diana was the goddess of the hunt, being associated with wild animals and woodland, and also of the moon. In literature she was the equivalent of the Greek goddess Artemis. Along with her main attributes, Diana was an emblem of chastity. Oak groves were especially sacred to her.

In front of the Doric Temple, on a small island in the middle of the moat
Anne Boleyn
Sculptor: Philip Jackson

Installed: before 2003
Materials/dimensions: coloured resin, 1.8 m
    high × 90 cm wide × 80 cm deep
Status: not listed
Condition: good
Commissioned and owned by: Mr and Mrs
    James Sellick

The statue of Anne Boleyn, with hooded, bowed head and hands clasped in front of her at waist level, in a pose suggestive of an acceptance of her fate, stands on an island overlooking the lake. She was the second wife of King Henry VIII of England and was queen consort from 1533 until 1536. She was the mother of Queen Elizabeth I of England. The sculptor made the statue especially for the present owners because of the historic connection between the original house and the Boleyn family. The island on which the statue stands marks the site of this house, built in 1262.

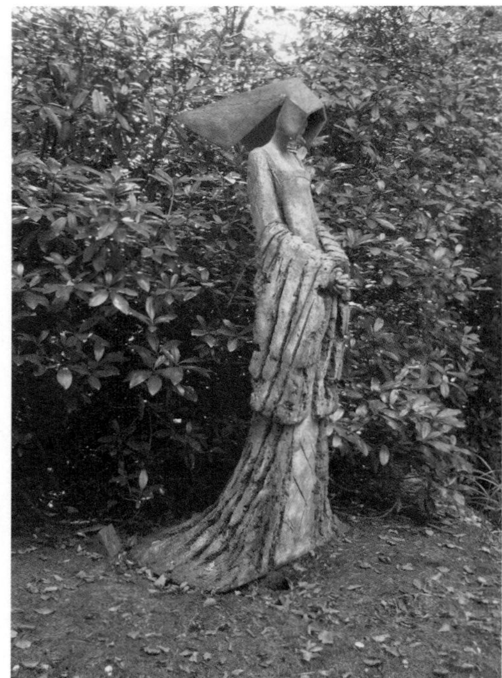

Philip Jackson, *Anne Boleyn*

In the Victorian greenhouse
Eos
Sculptor: Neal French

Purchased and installed: 2008
Materials/dimensions: press moulded terracotta,
    1.1 m high × 38 cm wide × 26 cm deep
Status: not listed
Condition: good
Owners/custodians: Mr and Mrs James Sellick

The goddess Eos is depicted with simplified features, her right arm extended around the back of her head and her left arm curved over the top. It was specifically modelled as a garden piece and is one of an edition of seven. The mottled surface of the terracotta gives an aged appearance, suggesting ancient sculpture.

Eos is, in Greek mythology, the Titanic goddess of the dawn, who rose from her home

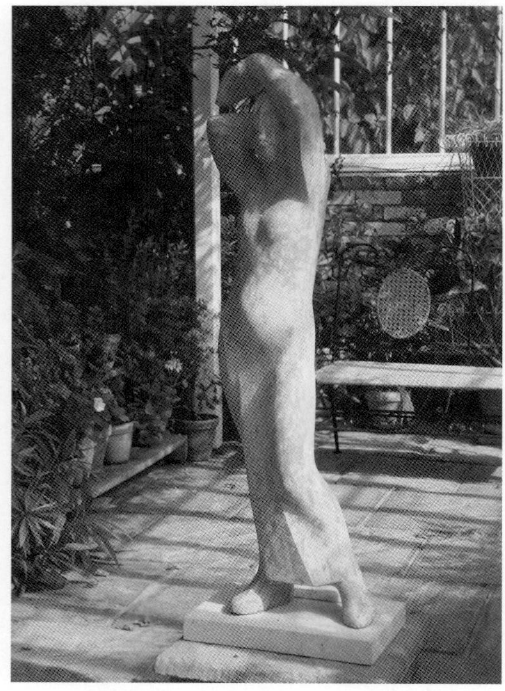

Neal French, *Eos*

at the edge of Oceanus, the ocean that surrounds the world, to herald her brother Helios, the sun.

Sources
Sellick Family, *Pashley Manor Gardens Through the Seasons*, Norwich, 2003.
Kate Wilson (Pashley Manor Gardens), email correspondence, 12 June 2008.

WARBLETON

Church Hill

Warbleton Parish church, north wall, in a bay behind the organ

Monument to Sir John Lade
Sculptor: Michael Rysbrack

Commissioned: after 1720

Materials/dimensions: white and variegated marbles, 4 m approx. high × 2 m wide × 22 cm deep

Inscription (below portrait bust): Here lyes interred the body of Sʳ JOHN LADE of Sᵗ SAVIOURS SOUTHWARK Barᵗ the fifth Youngest Son of THOMAS LADE / SOMETIME OF THIS PARISH GENT. He was five times chosen Member of Parliament for the Borough of SOUTHWARK where he lived / from fourteen Years Old to the day of his Death, he was a Justice of the Peace for more than 30 Years for the counties / of Y [*sic*], SUSSEX, KENT and MIDDLESEX, one of the Deputy Lieutenants of the Borough of SOUTHWARK and of the / Lieutenancy of the City of LONDON, in all which posts he behaved himself with great integrity. His Candour, Courage, / Zeal and Skill, rendered him remarkable in all his acts of Power, A Friend to Monarchy, and the established Church / of England, yet without Acrimony to Dissenters A true friend to those unto whom he professed Amity, and altho' / he lived in Party times, could never be biased against his Judgement either by Place, Power or Honour: But as a / true Englishman despised all for what he thought the good of his Country. He dyed a Bachelor in the 30. day of July 1710 / aged 78 years; and After having done great Favours to his Friends / and Relations he left the Bulk of his Estate to the / Grandson of his Eldest Brother JOHN INSHIP, now JOHN LADE Esqʳ who in Gratefull remembrance thereof to his Memory / has erected this Monument

Status: not listed

Condition: good

Owner/custodian: St Mary's church

The informality of the portrait bust, with its fleshy face, without a wig, and with open shirt and casual drapery, demonstrates Rysbrack's skill at capturing a likeness. The architectural surround uses different coloured marbles to good effect and Pevsner particularly praises the 'skilful floral decoration'. He deplores the fact that the memorial is hidden away behind the organ, maintaining that, '[I]t ought to be set in a worthier position. Sussex has little like it.'[1] Although supporting the opinion of Rysbrack's contemporaries that he was, '… an acknowledged master of the portrait bust',[2] the Lade monument has little of the baroque drama of the Powlett monument in West Grinstead (see entry) and does not appear in Gordon Balderston's list of works by Rysbrack.[3]

Notes
[1] Nairn and Pevsner (1965), p. 620. [2] Eustace, K., *Michael Rysbrack Sculptor 1694–1770*, Bristol Museum and Art Gallery, 1982, p. 14. [3] Roscoe, Hardy and Sullivan (2009), p. 1079.

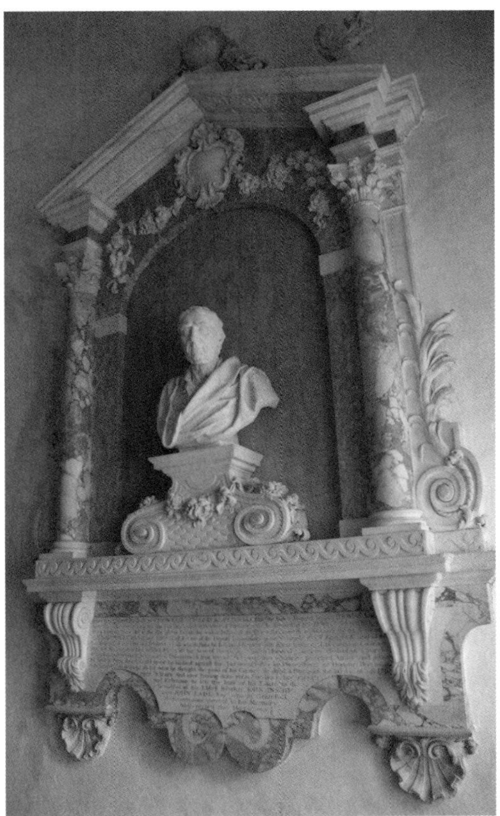

Michael Rysbrack, *Monument to Sir John Lade*

The Street

On Windover Hill

The Long Man of Wilmington

Sculptor: unknown

Installed: currently thought to be eighteenth century

Materials/dimensions: painted concrete blocks, 72.5 m high × 35.5 m wide

Status: not listed

Condition: good (the terracettes, horizontal ripples in the turf, change constantly as the soil is rolled downhill by weathering and animal activity. The concrete blocks vary in condition but are repainted annually)

Owner/custodian: Sussex Archaeological Society

The outline of a male figure, marked out in white painted blocks, is set into the hillside on a 28 degree slope. In each hand he holds either lances, staves or spears or uprights possibly representing portals. They are almost symmetrical, giving the illusion of an unfinished rectangular frame. Both legs are now turned to the east but the feet were originally wider apart and both facing outwards, as seen in a photograph of 1874. The figure is naked and featureless, but early drawings indicate that he was originally clothed, with facial features and a helmet-shaped head. The figure's proportions only appear correct from the air due to elongation to counteract foreshortening. It is possible that the sightline should be from the old yew tree (400 AD) in Wilmington churchyard. This was a focus of pagan religious activity before the church was built.

The Long Man is the largest of the British Giants at over 70 m (Cerne Abbas is 55 m). There have been many suggestions for the figure's identity, including: Beowulf, a Saxon warrior or haymaker, Wotan, Baldur, a Roman

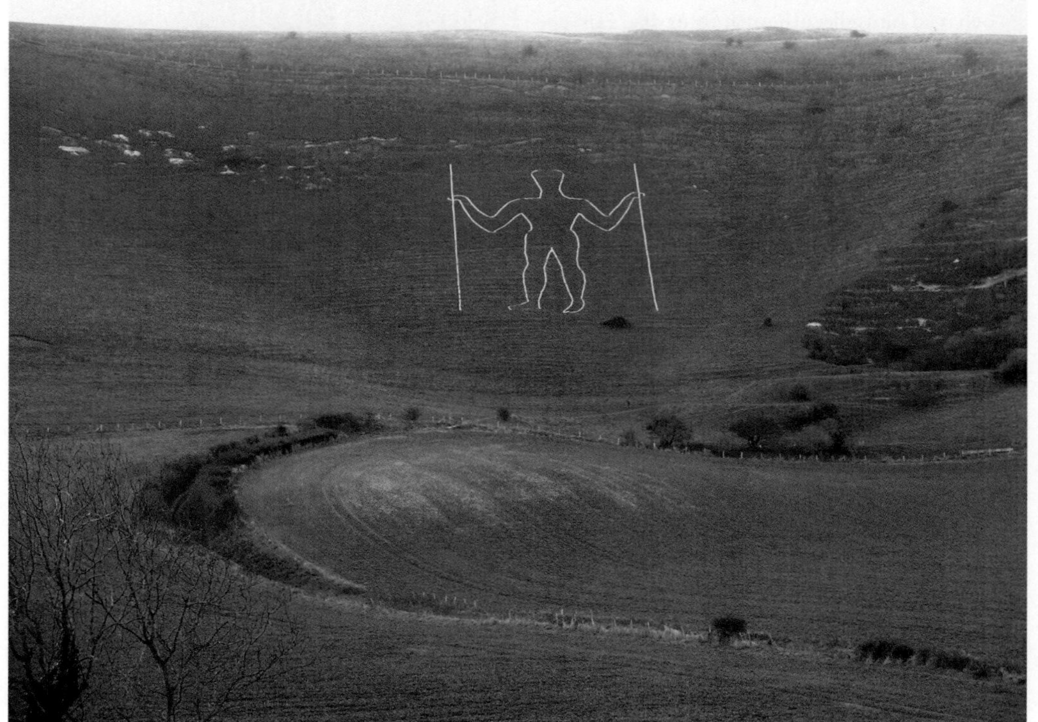

Emperor, Dodman (a ley line surveyor), the fighting man badge of King Harold, Herne the Hunter, Samson, the Herald of the Harvest and St Peter.

The monument was traditionally assumed to be Neolithic, but this has been called into question, primarily because it is not mentioned in any early documents. The earliest written reference to the figure is in 1779. It is therefore suggested that it is in fact a Georgian Folly. A drawing from 1710 has been discovered by surveyor John Rowley and another, by Sir William Burrell, is dated 1766. The earliest known photograph of it was taken in 1874.

Nevertheless, many people still feel that it possibly originated in prehistory, as its monumentality and iconography suggest a Neolithic site of which there is a high concentration at the eastern end of the South Downs. One of the main problems in

Unknown, *The Long Man of Wilmington*

identifying the figure's origins is that it is not the original chalk but is now an assemblage of white painted concrete blocks that were placed there in 1969. In 1874 it was outlined in yellow bricks. The figure was painted green in the Second World War to prevent Germans using it as a navigation aid. The site was handed over by the Duke of Devonshire to the Sussex Archaeological Trust in 1925. The chalk grassland around the Long Man of Wilmington is designated a Site of Special Scientific Interest (SSSI), being lowland calcareous grassland.

Sources
Castleden, R., *Ancient British Hill Figures*, Seaford, 2000.
Sussex Past: the Long Man of Wilmington, Sussex Archaeological Society leaflet, Lewes, nd.

Withyham Road (B2110)

The Sackville Chapel, Parish Church of St Michael and All Angels

The Sackville Chapel was added to the church by the 5th Earl in 1624. On 16 June 1663, the church had been largely destroyed after a lightning strike. The heat generated was so great that even the bells melted. The original Sackville monuments were completely destroyed. The church was rebuilt, but was not reopened until 1672 and the rebuilding of the Sackville Chapel was not completed for another eight years. The chapel is unusual in that it does not come under the jurisdiction of the Bishop but is privately owned by the 11th Earl De La Warr, who is patron of the church.[1] The monument to the Honourable Thomas Sackville is set in the centre of the large chapel, enclosed by railings thought to be original, with other monuments to the Sackville family affixed to the walls. The dramatic, Baroque-influenced three-dimensionality of Cibber's masterpiece contrasts with the restrained repertory of neoclassical forms that appear in the nineteenth-century reliefs. The church was given a Grade I listing because of the monuments.

Monument to the Honourable Thomas Sackville and the 5th Earl and Countess of Dorset
Sculptor: Caius Gabriel Cibber

Erected: 1678 (original monument, pre-1624, destroyed by fire 1663)
Materials/dimensions: white and black marble, 1.93 m high × 2.63 m wide × 3.68 m deep
Inscriptions (on east side, in carved letters):
This Monument was design'd to be Erected / before the decease of ye Rt Hon Richard / Earl of Dorset Father of this Youth / who

departed this life ye 27th of August / in the year of our Lord God 1677 / And in ye 55th year of his age, And ye / Rt Hon Frances Countess Dowager of / Dorset Relict of the said Father / And Mother of the said Youth / Erected the same to perpetuate ye memory / of her Husband and Son in the year / of our Lord 1678; (on west side, in carved letters): STAND NOT AMAZ'D (READER) TO SEE US SHEAD / FROM DROWNED EYES VAINE OFFERINGS TO YE DEAD / FOR HE WHOSE SACRED ASHES HERE DOTH LYE / WAS THE GRAT HOPES OF ALL OUR FAMILY / TO BLAZE WHOSE VERTUES IS BUT TO DETRACT / FROM THEM, FOR IN THEM NONE CAN BE EXACT. / SO GRAVE AND HOPEFULL WAS HIS YOUTH / SO DEARE A FREIND TO PIETY AND TRUTH / HE SCARCE KNEW SIN BUT WHAT CURST NATURE GAVE, / AND YET GRIM DEATH HATH SNATCH'D HIM TO HIS GRAVE. / HE NEVER TO HIS PARENTS WAS UNKEIND / BUT IN HIS EARLY LEAVEING THEM BEHEIND / AND SINCE HATH LEFT US AND FOR ERE IS GON / WHAT MOTHER WOULD NOT WEEPE FOR SUCH A SON. / MAY THIS FAIRE MONUMENT THEN NEVER FADE / OR BE BY BLASTING TIME OR AGE DECAY'D / THAT THE SUCCEEDING TIMES TO ALL MAY TELL / HERE LIETH ONE THAT LIV'D AND DIED WELL. / HERE LYES THE THIRTEENTH CHILD AND SEAVENTH SON / WHO IN HIS THIRTEENTH YEARE HIS RACE HAD RUN. / THOMAS SACKVILLE

Status: Grade I

Condition: fair (crack to top left-hand corner of south-facing relief; second step facing east cracked in three places)

Owner/custodian: Earl De La Warr

A stepped base supports a large black and white marble sarcophagus upon which reclines the figure of the young Hon. Thomas Sackville, with his left hand resting on a skull, signifying that he predeceased his parents. To the back of him is the figure of his father, Richard, 5th Earl of Dorset, kneeling on the top step of the base with his gaze directed towards the statue of his

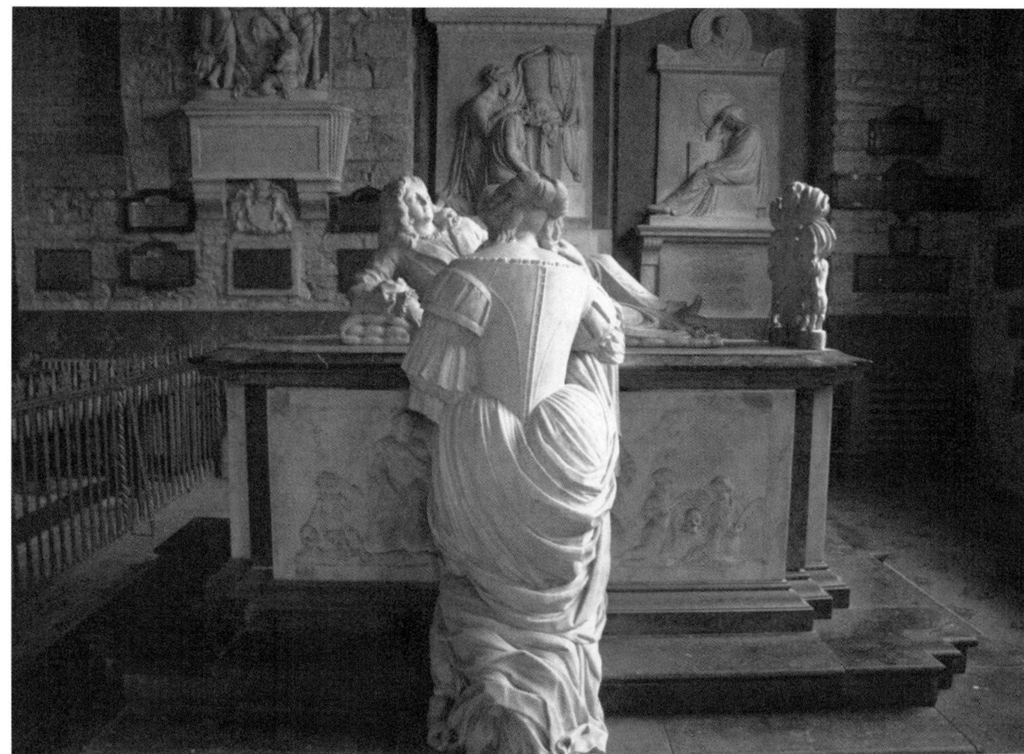

Caius Gabriel Cibber, *Monument to the Honourable Thomas Sackville and the 5th Earl and Countess of Dorset*

wife. In front of the reclining figure is the figure of the Hon. Thomas Sackville's mother, Lady Frances Sackville, kneeling on the top step of the base, her right hand leaning on the sarcophagus and supporting her head. The figures of mother and father appear transfixed with grief. At each end of the tomb is an inscribed panel and, at the feet of the reclining figure on the east side, a large upright sculptural relief of the Sackville coat of arms. On each side of the sarcophagus are sculptural reliefs of the other children, six sons and six daughters. Pevsner states that Cibber's monument was, '… different from any seen in England up to that time, inspired clearly by the Italian Baroque, perhaps by way of Holland.'[2]

The Honourable Thomas Sackville was only 13 when he died in 1675 at Samur on the river Loire in France. The 5th Earl, his father, had intended to erect a monument to his memory, but he died himself within two years and eventually it was Lady Sackville who erected the monument to her husband and her other children. The contract for the monument can still be seen in the Sackville archives; dated 1677, it states that the work should be: 'Substantiall rare and Artificially performed' and was to be finished in 10 months. Cibber was to be paid £350, and the monument was to be to 'Ye well liking of Mr. Peter Lilly [*sic*] his Majesty's painter, or any other Artist who shall be desired to give their Judgement thereof'.[3]

Monument to John Frederick 3rd Duke of Dorset

Sculptor: Joseph Nollekens

Erected: 1802
Materials/dimensions: white and dark grey marble, 2.45 m high × 1.4 m wide × 25 cm deep
Signature (to front bottom right): Nollekens FI 1802
Inscription (underneath relief in carved letters): JOHN FREDERICK DUKE and EARL OF DORSET; / Earl of Middlesex, Baron of Buckhurst, and Baron of Cranfield; / Knight of the Most Noble Order of the Garter: / Lord-Lieutenant and Custos-Rotulorum of the County of Kent, and City of Canterbury; / Vice-Admiral of the Coasts of the said County and Steward of Stratford upon Avon. / He was Ambassador to the Court of France. And Steward of HIS MAJESTY's Household. / He died in the Year 1799 the 19th. Day of July in the fifty fifth Year of his Age; / And was buried near this Place: / To whose Memory this is offered, with the utmost Gratitude, Affection and Honor / By his Widow ARABELLA DIANA
Status: Grade I
Condition: good
Commissioned by: Arabella, Duchess of Dorset
Owner/custodian: Earl De La Warr

This sculpted relief with three figures is affixed to the north wall of the chapel. It shows two cherubs, one standing to the left, one seated in front, who drape garlands over a lidded urn on which is a portrait relief of the 3rd Duke. Another cherub stands to the right. In his left hand is an upturned torch and he supports his head with his right arm and hand on the urn. The figures sit on a plinth that holds an inscription to the front.

John Frederick Sackville, 3rd Duke of Dorset (25 March 1745–19 July 1799), was the son of Lord John Philip Sackville and Frances Leveson-Gower. He married Arabella Diana

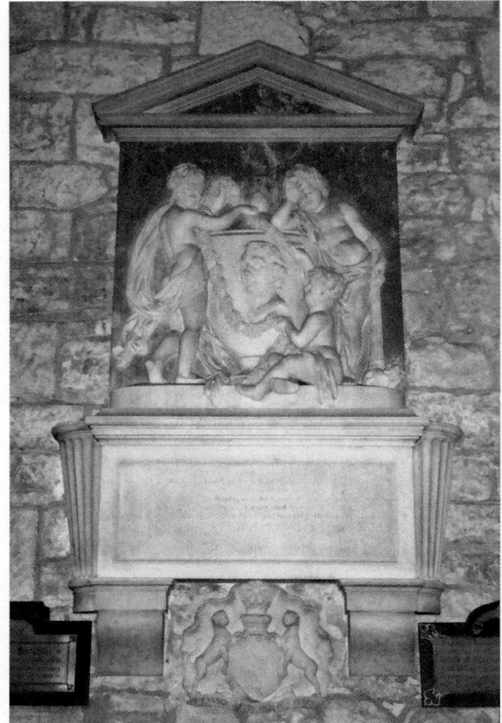

Joseph Nollekens, *Monument to John Frederick 3rd Duke of Dorset*

Cope (1768–1 August 1825), daughter of Sir Charles Cope and Catherine Bisshopp. The 3rd Duke was the last British Ambassador to France before the revolution of 1789 and became a close friend of Queen Marie Antoinette.

Monument to George John Frederick 4th Duke of Dorset

Sculptor: John Flaxman

Erected: 1815
Materials/dimensions: white and dark grey marble, 2.7 m high × 1.68 m wide × 25 cm deep
Signature (to east side in carved letters): FLAXMAN. / R.A. / SCULPTOR.

Inscription (underneath relief, in carved and gilt letters): UNDER THIS MARBLE ARE DEPOSITED / THE REMAINS / OF GEORGE JOHN FREDERICK DUKE OF DORSET, / WHO WAS KILLED BY A FALL FROM HIS HORSE / IN THE VICINITY OF DUBLIN, / ON THE 14TH DAY OF FEBRUARY A.D. 1815, / HAVING JUST ATTAINED THE AGE OF 21 YEARS. / IN THE HIGHEST RANK HE WAS HUMBLE. / AMIDST THE TEMPTATIONS OF YOUTH / HIS MORALS WERE EXEMPLARY: / HIS REASON STRENGTHENED BY EARLY CULTURE, / HIS MIND ENLIGHTENED BY KNOWLEDGE, / HIS MANNERS FORMED BY BENEVOLENCE, / HIS VIRTUES FOUNDED ON RELIGION, / RENDERED HIM / THE DELIGHT OF HIS FRIENDS, / THE HOPE OF HIS COUNTRY. / HIS PREMATURE DEATH / WAS BY TWO NATIONS / DEPLORED AS A PUBLICK CALAMITY. / BUT TO THOSE WHO LOVED HIM, / HIS VIRTUES SUPPLY A CONSOLATION: / THEY SORROW. BUT NOT AS WITHOUT HOPE: /FOR THROUGH THE MERCY OF THEIR REDEEMER. THE SPIRITS OF JUST MEN MADE PERFECT / SHALL MEET TO PART NO MORE.
Status: Grade I
Condition: good
Commissioned by: Arabella, Duchess of Dorset
Owner/custodian: Earl De La Warr

This relief monument is also mounted on the north wall of the chapel. A portrait medallion of the Duke in contemporary dress appears above a seated, mourning, classically draped figure symbolising his mother. Her right arm supports her head as she leans against an urn. The relief sits on a base that is inscribed to the front.

George John Frederick Sackville, 4th Duke of Dorset (15 November 1793–14 February 1815) was the only son of John Frederick Cranfield Sackville, the 3rd Duke of Dorset and Arabella, Duchess of Dorset. As he died unmarried, the titles passed to Charles Sackville Germain, 2nd Viscount Sackville (1767–1843), the son and heir of George Germain, 1st

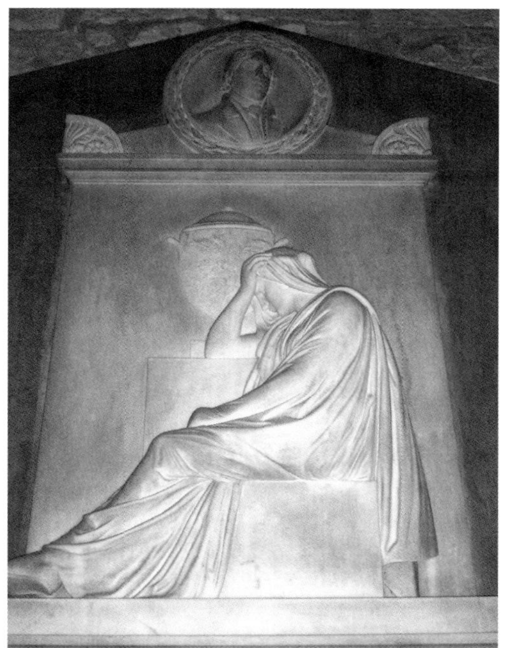

John Flaxman, *Monument to George John Frederick 4th Duke of Dorset*

Viscount Sackville. Charles Sackville Germain thus became the 5th Duke of Dorset. When he subsequently died on 29 July 1843, the Dukedom of Dorset became extinct.

Monument to Arabella Duchess of Dorset

Sculptor: Sir Francis Leggat Chantrey

Commissioned: 1828
Erected: 1831
Materials/dimensions: white and dark grey
    marble, 2.85 m high × 1.6 m wide × 36 cm
    deep
Signature (to eastern side, in carved letters):
    CHANTREY.SC.
Inscription (to front of monument, underneath
    relief, in carved letters, painted black): TO
    THE MEMORY OF / ARABELLA DIANA DUCHESS

OF DORSET, / THE HOURS OF HER LAST
ILLNESS WERE FEW AND HER DEATH SUDDEN, /
BUT HER SORROWING DAUGHTERS HAD THE
CONSOLATION OF KNOWING / THAT SHE WAS
NOT UNPREPARED TO MEET IT, / FOR IN HER
WAS ALL THE PIETY OF A CHRISTIAN /
EXTENSIVE CHARITY TO THE INDIGENT / AND
CONSTANCY IN EXERCISING THE DUTIES/
WHICH ADORN AND RENDER HAPPY
DOMESTIC LIFE. / SHE DIED AUGUST 1ST. 1825
IN THE 58TH YEAR OF HER AGE.

Status: Grade I
Condition: good
Commissioned by: Lady Mary Sackville,
    Countess of Plymouth and Lady Elizabeth
    Sackville, Countess De La Warr
Owner/custodian: Earl De La Warr

This sculpted relief depicting the Duchess's two grieving daughters is set against a dark grey marble background under a canopied top decorated with neoclassical motifs. The two female figures wear classical drapery and have skilfully carved neoclassical hairstyles. They kneel, weeping, in front of a draped urn supporting themselves with their left arms. This motif is described by Whinney as '[a] much favoured design' of Chantrey.[4] As Lieberman points out, Chantrey was never paid the full amount for the commission (£829 2s 6d), but did not press the Duke of Dorset for the balance of over £200, due to his social position.[5]

Arabella was the daughter of Sir Charles Cope and Catherine Bisshopp. She was the widow of John Frederick Cranfield Sackville, 3rd Duke of Dorset and later married Lord Whitworth. Her two daughters, who commissioned the monument, were Lady Mary Sackville, Countess of Plymouth (30 July 1792–20 July 1864) and Lady Elizabeth Sackville-West, Countess De La Warr (11 September 1795–9 January 1870).

Notes
[1] This entry is included with kind permission and support from the Earl and Countess De La Warr.
[2] Nairn and Pevsner (1965), p. 638. [3] Countess De La Warr and Innes-Smith, R., *The Sackville Chapel*, Withyham, 1993, p. 3. [4] Whinney (1964), p. 223.
[5] Yarrington (1991), p. 233.

Other sources
Countess de La Warr, correspondence, 11 February 2008, 9 September 2008.
Llewellyn (2011), pp. 410–13.
Sackville-West, R.W., *Historical Notices of the Parish of Withyham in the County of Sussex, With a Description of the Church and Sackville Chapel*, London, 1857.
Smith, J.R., *Historical Notices of the Parish of Withyham*, London, 1857, pp. 58–100.

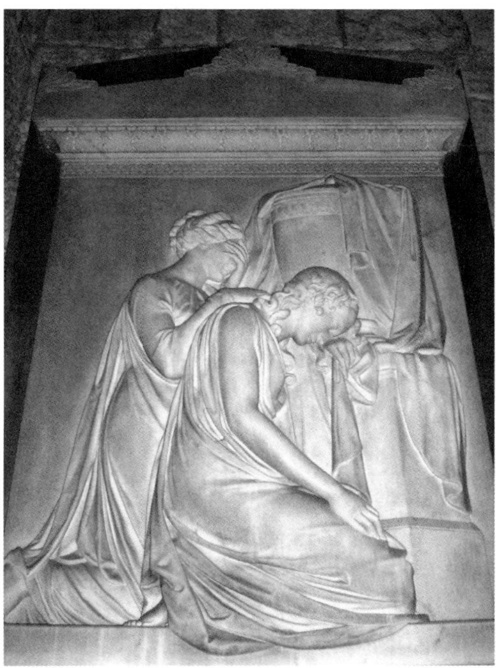

Sir Francis Leggat Chantrey, *Monument to Arabella Duchess of Dorset*

AMBERLEY

Church Street

Eastern wall of churchyard, St Michael's Church

Tomb of Edward Stott
Sculptor: Francis Derwent Wood

Installed: 1918
Materials/dimensions: monument: stone, 3 m

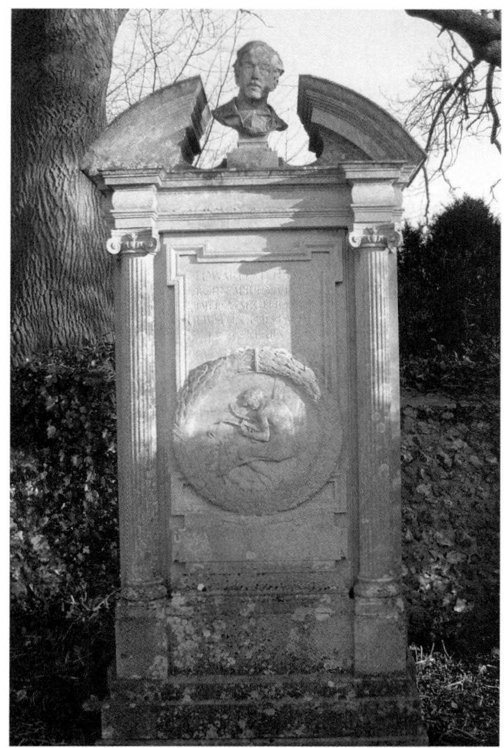

Francis Derwent Wood, *Tomb of Edward Stott*

high × 1.35 m wide × 65 cm deep; bust: stone, 55 cm high × 35 cm wide × 35 cm deep
Inscription (above medallion): EDWARD STOTT ARA / BORN APRIL 25, 1855 / DIED MARCH 19, 1918 / LIVED IN THIS PARISH / 30 YEARS / BY HIS WORKS / YE SHALL KNOW HIM
Status: not listed
Condition: good (but some weathering and small area at northern corner of arch to side of bust broken off)
Owner/custodian: St Michael's Church

The west-facing monument is classical in style, with ionic columns and a broken pediment enclosing a portrait bust of the deceased. The columns frame a stone slab bearing an inscription and a wreathed medallion with a relief of Orpheus with his lute. Orpheus was believed to be one of the chief poets and musicians of antiquity, and the inventor of the lyre.

The Lancashire-born painter Edward Stott lived in Amberley where he painted scenes of English rural life, influenced by Millet and Bastien Lepage. He was a founder member of the New English Art Club in 1886. Stott, a bachelor, left most of his money to the Royal Academy for travelling scholarships.[1]

Tomb of Francis Derwent Wood
Sculptor: Francis Derwent Wood
Architect: Sir Edwin Lutyens

Installed: 1926
Materials/dimensions: whole monument: stone and bronze, 1.85 m high × 1.7 m wide × 31 cm deep; relief: patinated bronze, 60 cm high × 1 m wide × 10 cm deep

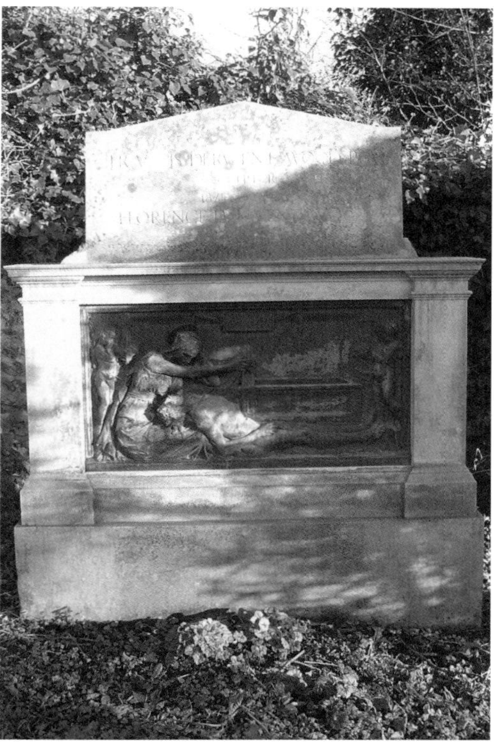

Francis Derwent Wood, *Tomb of Francis Derwent Wood*

Signature (bottom right-hand corner of relief): F. DERWENT WOOD. 1909.
Inscriptions (top section): FRANCIS DERWENT WOOD R.A. / SCULPTOR / 1871 + 1926 / FLORENCE DERWENT WOOD / 1873 + 1969; (on banner at top of relief): PASSVS ET / SEPVLTVS EST ('He suffered and was buried' from the Credo)
Status: not listed
Condition: fair (stone blocks broken on both

sides at the top of the monument. Damage caused during the theft of two 15–18-inch statuettes of muses that were taken in the 1980s)[2]

Owner/custodian: St Michael's Church

The tomb is a rectangular box shape with classical pilasters at the corners. It is surmounted by a geometric panel bearing the inscription. Set within the façade is a bronze relief panel, which is a copy of the *Pietà* that Wood originally carved for All Saints Church (later the Russian Orthodox cathedral) in Ennismore Gardens, London and which was exhibited at the Royal Academy in 1910.

In addition to his reputation as a sculptor, Wood is known for his pioneering work constructing masks for the facially disfigured during the First World War.

Notes
[1] lbhf.gov.uk (accessed 4 November 2010). [2] Tim Locker, correspondence, 30 November 2010; David Thornley (vicar of St Michael's church) correspondence with Mrs Locker (granddaughter of Derwent Wood), 22 April 1991.

Other sources
Alexander, C., 'Faces of war', *Smithsonian Magazine*, February 2007.
Greenacombe, J. (ed.), *Survey of London*, Knightsbridge, vol. 45, 2000, pp. 186–90.
Times Past, Storrington and District Museum, issue 23, Spring 2006, p. 2.

BOGNOR REGIS

High Street

At the junction with London Road, opposite Abbey National Building Society

Sun Sculpture

Sculptor: Pete Codling

Unveiled: 19 March 2008
Materials/dimensions: painted copper with gold leaf, 7 m high × 1.5 m wide × 1 m deep
Signature: (on base, SE face): Pete C 08

Status: not listed
Condition: good (some scratched graffiti on base)
Commissioned by: The Art and Regeneration Partnership for Bognor Regis and Littlehampton
Funded by: Arts Council England South East, Arun District Council, Bognor Regis Town Marketing Group, Littlehampton Town Centre Action Group, West Sussex County Council and Single Regeneration Budget (SRB)
Owner/custodian: Bognor Regis Town Council

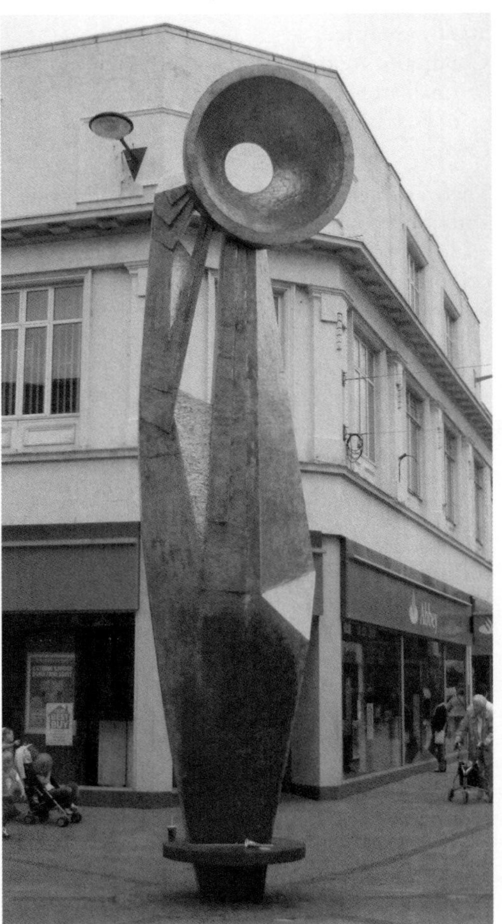

Pete Codling, *Sun Sculpture*

The sculpture consists of a large upright variable-width shaft, painted turquoise and gold to depict the rays of the sun, surmounted by a large sun-like gold-painted disc. At its base is an integral round seat. The sculpture faces southeast and is situated in a pedestrianised shopping area.

Bognor Regis is recorded as being one of the sunniest places in Britain, so the sun was a natural subject for the commission brief given to the sculptor in January 2006. He was also asked to reflect Bognor's history as a famous seaside resort. The sculpture is inspired by ancient sun masks, the story of Icarus, the interpretation of dreams and local history, including the modern seaside tradition of the International Bognor Birdman. It was the first piece of public art in Bognor since a fountain was installed to celebrate Queen Victoria's Diamond Jubilee in 1897 and was part of the Arts and Regeneration project for Bognor Regis and Littlehampton, for which £65,000 Arts Council funding was awarded. Other commissions for the scheme included Richard Farrington's Bathing Machine in Bognor Regis Museum and Matthew Fedden's railings for the historic weather station on the seafront.

Codling believes that public art should be a celebration of the future as well as of the past, and organised a series of workshops for local people to ensure their input into the project. He also worked on the design with students from Bognor Regis Community College and University College Chichester. Other public sculptures in the region by the same sculptor include Woolston Millennium Garden in Southampton and the Arundel Street Precinct in Portsmouth.

Sources
arun.gov.uk/cgi-bin/buildpage.pl?mysql=4468 (accessed 11 October 2010).
Lord, F. (ed.), *Public Art and Artists' Commissions in West Sussex*, West Sussex Arts Partnership, Chichester, 2008, p. 28.

Victoria Drive

On the west wall, above the entrance to the Parish Church of St Wilfrid (relocated 1977 and 2008)

Christ Ascendant

Sculptor: Uli Nimptsch

Unveiled: 7 May 1964 (Ascension Day)
Materials/dimensions: bronze, 2.5 m high × 1 m wide × 50 cm deep
Status: not listed
Condition: good
Commissioned by: Miss Helen Dey CBE
Owner/custodian: Parish Church of St Wilfrid

The sculpture depicts the figure of Christ ascending to heaven, with one foot still touching the earth and his arms raised above his head. The sense of movement is enhanced by the diagonal thrust of the legs and the swirling drapery surrounding the body.

Statues of Christ ascendant are far less common than those depicting Christ crucified or glorified. The donor of this sculpture, at one time a Matron of St Bartholomew's Hospital in London before retiring to Bognor, had a seven and a half year battle to have the design accepted and installed. Professor Thomas Monnington and colleagues in the Royal Academy recommended the commission go to Uli Nimptsch, whose previous work included an over life-size statue of David Lloyd George in the House of Commons, completed in 1963; a commission originally awarded to Sir Jacob Epstein, but transferred to Nimptsch on Epstein's death in 1959.

The sculpture has been relocated twice since its original installation in the church, which itself has never been completed. In 1977 it was moved from its commanding position over the altar to a rather obscure site in the South Transept following the closure of St John the Baptist Church in London Road (demolished 1972). Fixtures and fittings were transferred to St Wilfrid's, including a reredos with a

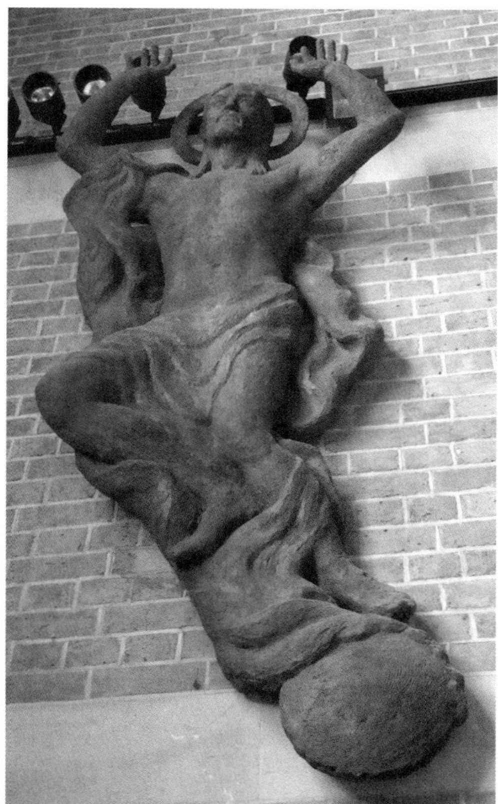

Uli Nimptsch, *Christ Ascendant*

removable canopy that was installed over the altar and necessitated the removal of Nimptsch's sculpture. In 2008 the statue was returned to a more prominent position on the west wall, high above the entrance. It was rededicated on Ascension Day, 21 May 2009.

Source
wilfrid.com/church/statue (accessed 11 October 2010).

Church Walk

Martlet Centre, opposite St John's Church

Stone Garden

Sculptors: Jane Sybilla Fordham and David Parfitt

Installed: 1996
Materials/dimensions: central feature: 2.14 m high × 1 m approx. diam. On cruciform cobblestone base
Inscription (on rectangular granite plaque, on west-facing perimeter wall): illegible, apart from date (1996) at bottom
Status: not listed
Condition: good
Commissioned and owned by: Mid Sussex District Council

This composite sculpture landscape consists of 10 large tree- and plant-carved forms, surrounded by low brick walls, positioned within a 30-metre-long ground scheme derived from knot work parterres. Various other motifs and decorative stonework adorn the walls including small sculptural pieces embedded into the brick that were made by local residents in sculpture workshops run by the artists at the Market Place as part of the Mid Sussex Community Arts Festival. Some of the pieces reflect the design and colours of St John's church opposite. David Parfitt described his approach as:

> … reversing the Capability Brown approach; where he used natural forms as a setting for architecture, I'm using the architectural environment of the precinct as a foil for an expression of natural forms.[1]

This was the first public art project commissioned by Mid Sussex District and was officially opened by District Councillor Mrs Anne Jones.

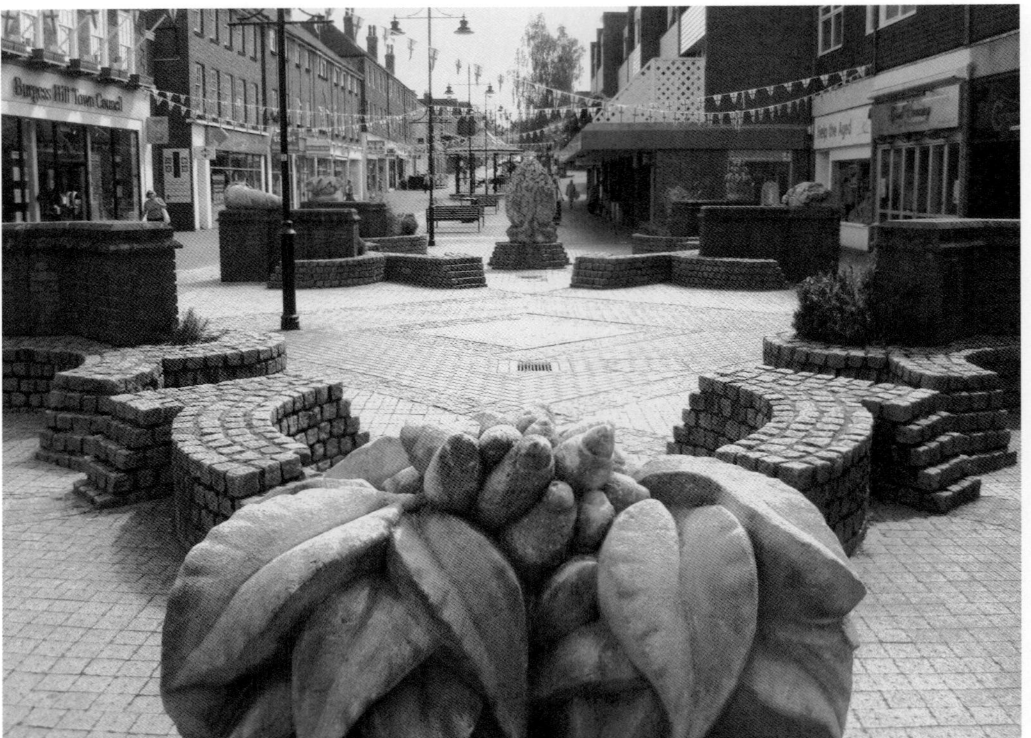

Jane Sybilla Fordham and David Parfitt, *Stone Garden*

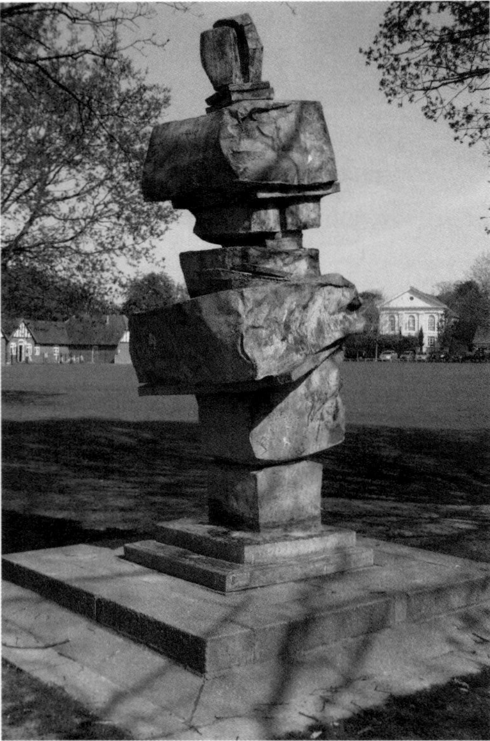

Sean Crampton, *Figure of Stability*

Note
[1] Stallwood, J., 'An interview with David Parfitt', *About Town* (Burgess Hill Council magazine), September 1996, p. 17.

Other sources
Frederic M. Avery (Burgess Hill Local History
    Society), email correspondence, 19 April 2011.
creative-process.com (accessed 11 January 2011).
David Parfitt, email correspondence, 18 April 2011.
janesybillafordham.com (accessed 11 January 2011).

Lower Church Road

In St Johns Park/recreation ground (formerly in Martlets Shopping Centre, Lower Church Walk)

Figure of Stability

Sculptor: Sean Crampton

Executed: 1971
Materials/dimensions: bronze and copper,
    3.3 m high × 1.35 m wide × 1.15 m deep
Signature (on middle section of northwest face):
    SC71
Status: not listed
Condition: good (but some graffiti to northwest
    face)
Owner/custodian: Mid Sussex District Council

The abstract sculpture is formed of stacked variable-sized blocks representing sand-blown rocks in the desert. It weighs two tons and originally had an internal framework filled with sand (which was not replaced when it was moved) to support the heavy-gauge copper covering.

The statue was unveiled in 1972 to mark the opening of the new Martlets Shopping Centre and the suggestion for its form came from the Managing Director of the developers, The Land and House Property Corporation, who was a keen rock climber. At its unveiling, local people were unenthusiastic, as they could discern no connection with the town and its history.[1] The piece was moved in 1993 to its present site, where the open parkland was considered to be more in keeping with its subject.

Note
[1] Frederic M. Avery (Burgess Hill Local History Society), email correspondence, 24 April 2011.

Broyle Road

Chichester Festival Theatre and Minerva Theatre, Oaklands Park

Chichester Festival Theatre was opened in 1962 under the direction of Sir Laurence Olivier. It was designed by Philip Powell and Hidalgo Moya and was built during 1960–61. It is now a Grade II* listed building. Powell has been described as, 'one of the masters of British post-war modernism' and was the designer of iconic works such as the Skylon for the Festival of Britain in 1951 and the Osaka Expo Pavilion in 1970.[1]

The theatre was the idea of a local ophthalmologist, Leslie Evershed-Martin, who raised the £105,000 needed through private fundraising, public subscription and commercial sponsorship. Between 1962 and 1965 Olivier established at Chichester the founding actors of his National Theatre Company. The classical themes of most of the sculptures that enhance the theatre complex accord with Evershed-Martin's vision of a return to the theatre of the Greeks, where the community would gather to debate topical issues and celebrate holidays.[2]

A fringe festival became established in a large marquee erected opposite the Festival Theatre. The Minerva Theatre, designed by Kenzie Lovell, in 1982, stands today on the old site and keeps alive its tradition of exploring new and exciting work. It was opened in April 1989 under the direction of Sam Mendes.

In the foyer of the Festival Theatre

Faces of Olivier

Sculptor: Lawrence Holofcener

Unveiled: 5 May 1985
Materials/dimensions: bronze, 70 cm high × 1 m wide × 7 cm deep
Signature (underside of bottom right-hand edge): L Holofcener / 1984
Inscriptions (underside of bottom left-hand edge): Laurence / OLIVIER; (bronze plaque attached to wall below relief): A tribute to / Laurence Olivier / from his / Colleagues and Friends / in America and Britain. / 5 May 1985 Sculptor: Lawrence Holofcener
Status: not listed
Condition: good
Owner/custodian: Chichester Festival Theatre

The wall-mounted sculptural relief comprises 28 small bronze busts depicting Laurence Olivier as various theatre characters that he played. A large photograph of Olivier is above the sculpture and below there is an explanatory diagram of the various roles depicted.

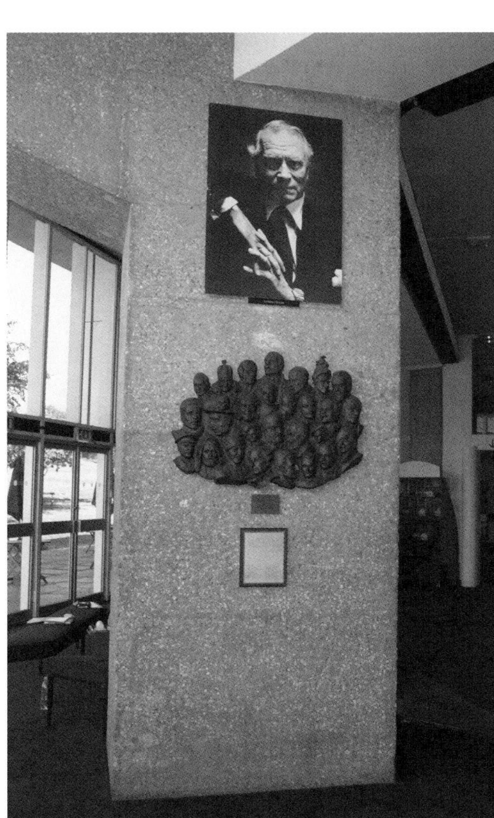

Lawrence Holofcener, *Faces of Olivier*

Outside entrance to Festival Theatre

Spartacus

Sculptor: Tom Merrifield

Foundry: Meridian Bronze
Constructed: 1984
Installed: 1988
Materials/dimensions: statue: patinated bronze, 2.4 m high × 60 cm wide × 90 cm deep; base: patinated bronze, 83 cm high × 1 m wide × 80 cm deep
Signature (on base, in script): © T Merrifield 2/9
Status: not listed
Condition: good
Owner/custodian: on permanent loan to

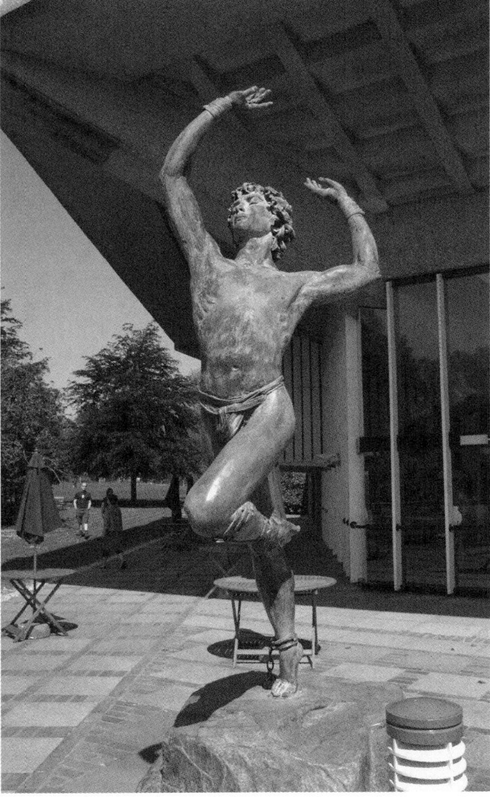

Tom Merrifield, *Spartacus*

Chichester Festival Theatre by the artist

The life-size nude figure is of a dancer in the role of Spartacus, leader of a slave uprising against the Roman republic, from the ballet by Khachaturian (1903–1978) and was inspired by a performance by the Bolshoi Ballet in London. Merrifield's own career as a dancer was terminated when he broke his leg. His presentation of the sculpture occurred following a chance meeting with John Gale, then Director of the Chichester Festival Theatre.

On the patio of the Minerva Theatre (previously outside the Festival Theatre)

Oedipus

Sculptor: Trude Bunzl

Installed: 1984 (presented by Mr K. and Mrs Reidl, sister-in-law of the sculptor)

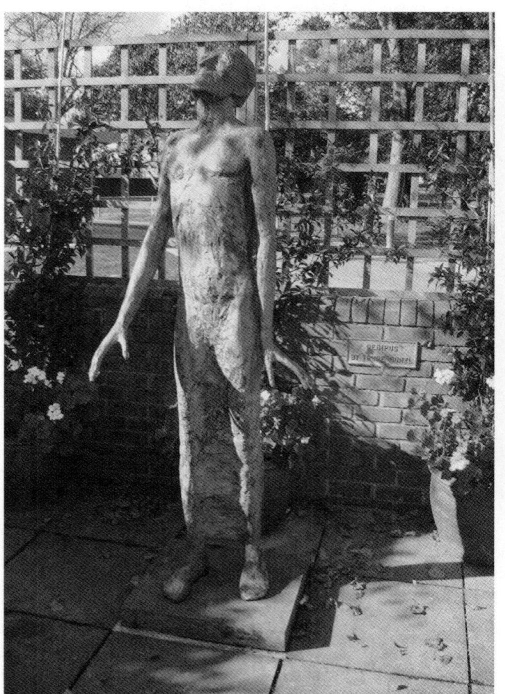

Trude Bunzl, *Oedipus*

Materials/dimensions: patinated bronze, 1.95 m high × 70 cm wide × 50 cm deep
Inscription (bronze plaque affixed to the wall at the back of the statue): OEDIPUS / TRUDE BUNZL
Status: not listed
Condition: good
Owner/custodian: Chichester Festival Theatre

The sculpture depicts Oedipus as a semi-draped figure with his head raised and outstretched hands by his side. In the Greek myth Oedipus fulfilled a prophesy by the Oracle, unknowingly murdering his father and marrying his own mother, who, on discovering this, killed herself. When Oedipus learnt the truth he blinded himself with brooches from her gown. The tension in the posture portrays Oedipus just after he has carried out this act.

Bunzl's sculpture was moved shortly after its installation to make way for Tom Merrifield's *Spartacus*.

Outside foyer of the Minerva Theatre

Minerva

Sculptor: Philip Jackson

Installed: 1997
Materials/dimensions: patinated bronze, 1.6 m high × 1.75 m wide × 95 cm deep
Signature (base of right arm of cloak): JACKSON
Inscription (on side of base): LESLIE EVERSHED-MARTIN / CBE SB ST. J. (1903–1994) FOUNDER OF / CHICHESTER FESTIVAL THEATRE
Status: not listed
Condition: good
Commissioned by: Minerva Theatre
Owner/custodian: Chichester Festival Theatre

The larger than life-size sculpture represents a cloaked and hooded Minerva reclining on a simple bronze bench atop a rectangular brick base. She supports herself with her arm. The left hand and arm are outstretched towards a

Philip Jackson, *Minerva*

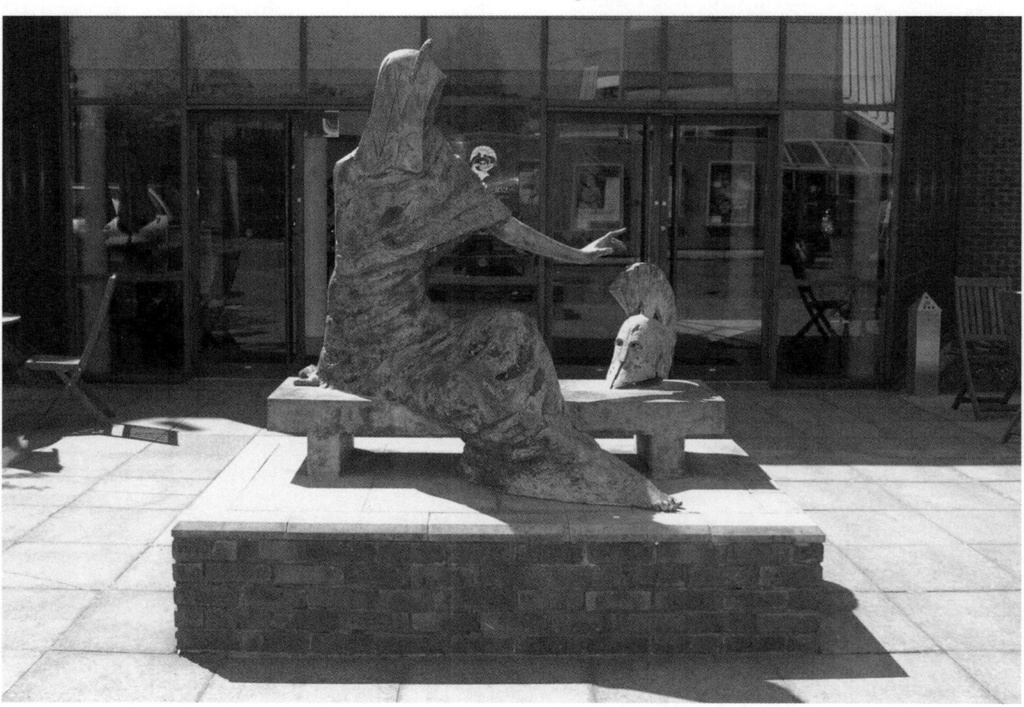

warrior's helmet at the far edge of the bench.

Minerva was the Roman Goddess of crafts, poetry and wisdom and is known as the inventor of music. The Romans believed that Minerva was not born in the usual way, but emerged fully grown and wearing armour, from the head of Jupiter. The sculpture was commissioned to commemorate the founder of the Chichester Festival Theatre and was unveiled by Carol Evershed-Martin.

Notes
[1] Stansfield Smith, C., 'City architecture', in Foster, P. (ed.), *Chichester and the Arts 1944–2004: a celebration*, Chichester, 2004, p. 37. [2] Hewitt, P., 'Leslie Evershed – Martin and Chichester Festival Theatre', in Foster (2004), p. 96.

Other sources
cft.org.uk (accessed 12 November 2010).
holofcener.com/faces (accessed 12 November 2010).
The Walter Strachan Collection (WJS/13), John Rylands University Archive, Manchester.
Williams, G., 'Public sculpture', in Foster (2004), pp. 177, 180–81.

Canon Lane
Chichester Cathedral

The building of the present Cathedral was begun in 1076 and consecrated to the Holy Trinity in 1108. Thus Transitional and Early English work was added to the original Romanesque, and in subsequent centuries there was additional building in the Decorated and Perpendicular styles. There is little external sculpture, other than a series of gargoyles, some medieval and some more recent additions, on the exterior drains and a corbel table on the south transept, re-cut in 1932 to include recognisable heads of King George V and Lloyd George. This device has been repeated in more recent work on the main entrance, either side of which are stone bosses bearing portraits of Queen Elizabeth II and Prince Philip.

Originating with the inspired patronage of Walter Hussey, Dean from 1955 to 1977, the Cathedral has become well known for its collection of contemporary art and design, including an altarpiece, *Noli Me Tangere*, by Graham Sutherland (1960), a tapestry designed by John Piper for the high altar (1966), a stained glass window by Marc Chagall (1978), a polyphant stone and beaten copper font (1983) by John Skelton, who also completed a Virgin and Child in 1988, and works by Geoffrey Clarke, Cecil Collins, Patrick Proctor and Ceri Richards. Hussey's own collection is now housed in Pallant House Gallery.

Outside Cathedral entrance, in West Street
St Richard
Sculptor: Philip Jackson

Unveiled: 15 June 2000
Materials/dimensions: statue: bronze, 2.8 m high × 95 cm wide × 1.2 m deep; pedestal: Trevone granite, blue Welsh slate and Portland limestone; 4 m high × 1.2 m wide × 1.4 m deep
Signature (on the base): JACKSON
Inscriptions (in middle of base, St Richard's prayer): THANKS BE TO THEE / MY LORD JESUS CHRIST / FOR ALL THE BENEFITS / WHICH THOU HAST GIVEN / ME. FOR ALL THE PAINS / & INSULTS WHICH THOU HAST BORNE FOR ME. / O MOST MERCIFUL REDEEMER / FRIEND & BROTHER. MAY I / KNOW THEE MORE CLEARLY / LOVE THEE MORE DEARLY & FOLLOW THEE MORE NEARLY; (on stone slab in front of statue): THIS STATUE OF ST. RICHARD / WAS A GIFT FROM THE FRIENDS / OF CHICHESTER CATHEDRAL TO / MARK THE MILLENNIUM. IT WAS / SCULPTED BY PHILIP JACKSON & / DEDICATED BY THE RT. REVD. ERIC / KEMP. BISHOP OF CHICHESTER / ON THURSDAY 15TH JUNE 2000
Status: not listed
Condition: good
Commissioned by: The Friends of Chichester Cathedral
Owner/custodian: The Dean and Chapter of Chichester Cathedral

Philip Jackson, *St Richard*

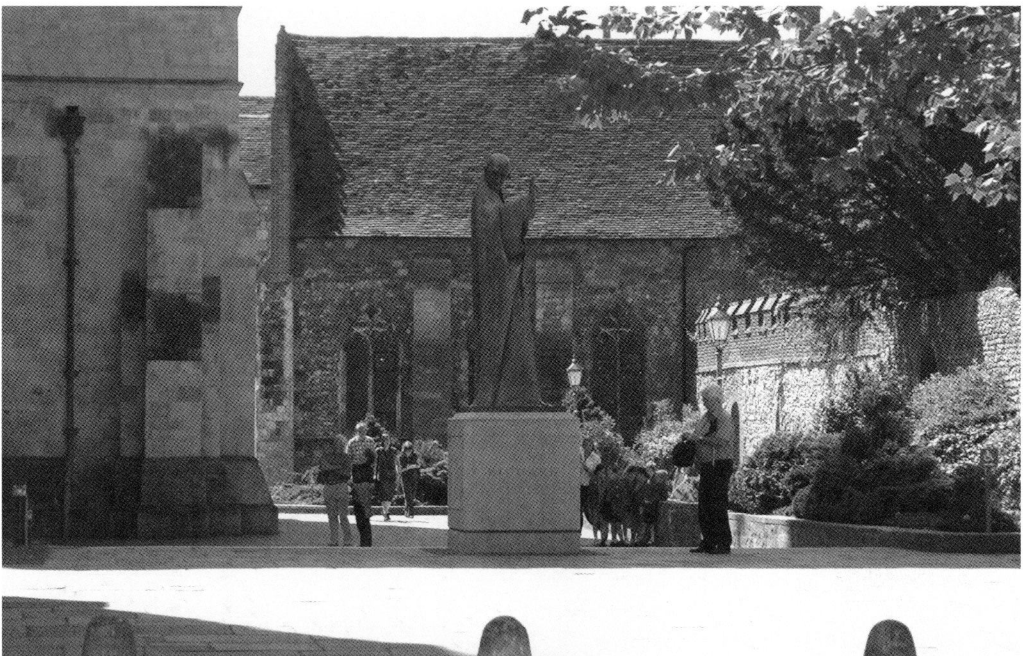

Philip Jackson's sculpture portrays a cloaked St Richard with his head turned to the right and right arm extending through the opening of the cloak with the hand raised in blessing. In his left hand he holds a scourge, symbol of self-discipline. St Richard was the first Bishop of Chichester; on his death, his heart was buried in Dover and his body taken back to Chichester. Three years later, on 22 January 1262, he was canonised. On 16 June 1276, in the presence of King Edward I, Queen Eleanor, the Archbishop of Canterbury and other bishops, and a great crowd of people, his body was moved to the shrine behind the high altar of the cathedral, where it became a place of pilgrimage and prayer for the people of Sussex.

Jackson was also commissioned to execute a 1.2 m high bronze statue of Christ in Judgement sited above the Lady Chapel and unveiled in 1998.

Inside Cathedral set into wall of south choir aisle, either side of tomb of Robert Sherburne
Lazarus Panels
Sculptor: unknown

Executed: probably first half of twelfth century
Materials/dimensions: Purbeck limestone, each
    panel 1.38 m high × 1.37 m wide
Status: not listed
Condition: good
Owner/custodian: The Dean and Chapter of
    Chichester Cathedral

Nairn describes these Romanesque panels as '… the most memorable things in the cathedral.'[1] He suggests that they were part of a twelfth-century choir screen and were re-used as building stones behind the choir stalls until they were rediscovered in 1828 and installed in their present position. The panels illustrate the story of Lazarus as described in chapter 11 of the gospel of St John. The first shows Christ arriving at Bethany, greeted by Martha and Mary, the sisters of the dead Lazarus. The second shows the raising of Lazarus from the

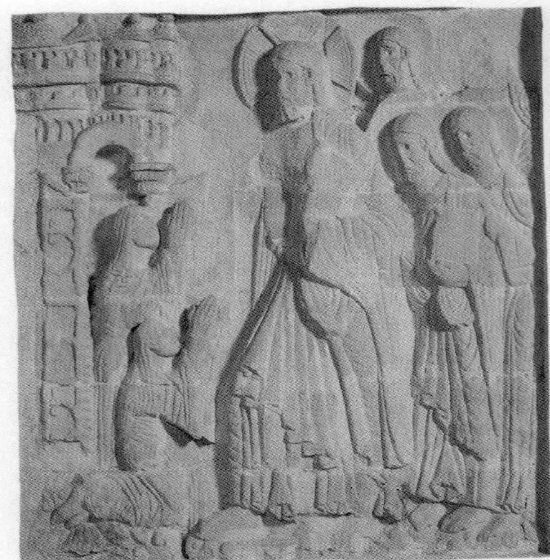
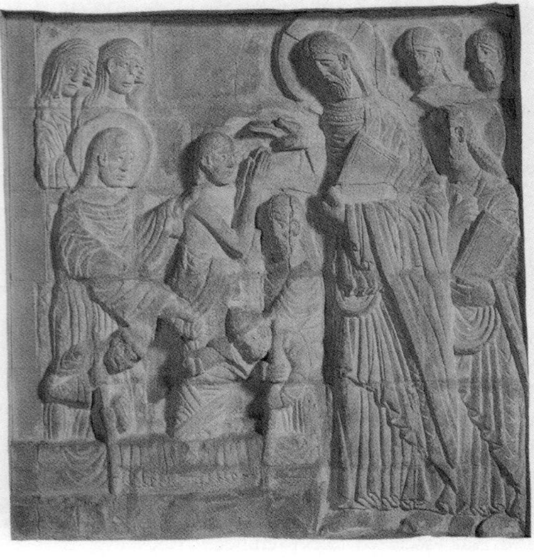

Unknown, *Lazarus Panels*

tomb. There is great expressiveness in the carving of the faces of the key characters in the story, which would originally have had coloured inlay set into the eyes.

On west-facing wall, St Clement's chapel, South Aisle
Monument to Agnes Cromwell
Sculptor: John Flaxman

Commissioned: 1798
Materials/dimensions: marble: 1.42 m high ×
    61 cm wide × 6 cm deep
Signature (bottom left-hand corner): FLAXMAN /
    R.A. / SCULPTOR
Inscription (on pediment): COME THOU
    BLESSED; (below relief): SACRED TO THE
    MEMORY OF AGNES SARAH HARRIET, /
    DAUGHTER OF HENRY CROMWELL ESQ.
    CAPTAIN R.N. / AND MARY HIS WIFE / WHO
    DIED ON THE 30TH DAY OF NOVEMBER 1787 /
    IN THE 18TH YEAR OF HER AGE
Status: not listed
Condition: good
Owner/custodian: the Dean and Chapter of
    Chichester Cathedral

The memorial is in the shape of a stele (Greek or Roman funerary slab) with its edges tapering upwards. The classically draped Miss Cromwell is depicted in relief, her hands clasped together in prayer, looking heavenwards, with three angels assisting her, two clasping her body around the hips and a third leaning over her, pointing the way. Nairn comments on its '… free flowing design, which is … a faint echo of Blake.'[2] A related drawing and two plaster models are in the collections of University College London and Flaxman's accounts for the monument, including transportation and mounting of the monument in the cathedral in 1800, survive.[3]

On his return from Italy in 1794, a large part of Flaxman's sculptural practice was devoted to the designing of memorials to the dead, which he treated as 'sermons in stone', believing that the congregation who viewed them should be inspired by the virtues of the deceased and share in a universal sense of loss.[4] The sculptor was an active member of the Swedenborgian New Church in London, which deeply affected the iconography of his memorials. Emanuel Swedenborg (1688–1772) believed that death was a transition from the 'natural' to the spiritual being, a process in which angels, with

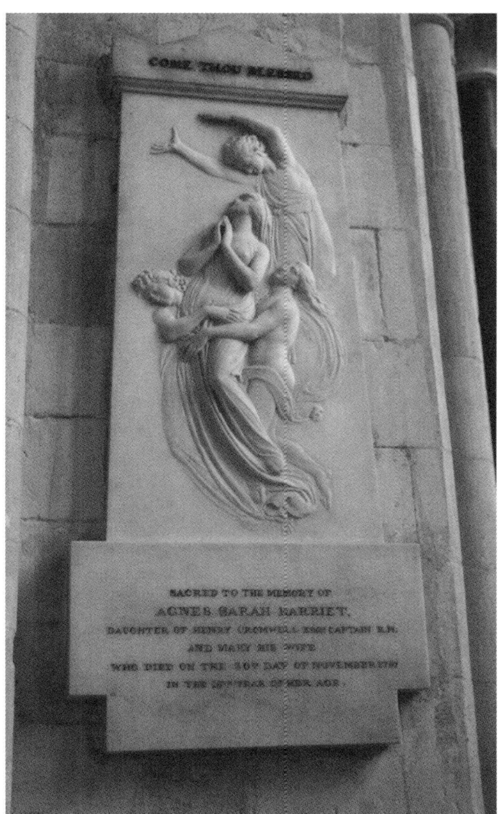

John Flaxman, *Monument to Agnes Cromwell*

all the attributes they had possessed when alive, were guardians and protectors of the living, guiding them towards the spiritual universe, as visualised in the Cromwell monument.[5]

Flaxman provided eight other memorials in the cathedral, including those to William Collins (1795), Jane Smith (1796), Francis and Bridget Dear (1803) and Sarah Udny (died 1811). Of this group, the Cromwell monument shows the most delicate and refined modelling. A signed late replica was included on the monument to Mrs Elizabeth Ann Kensall (died 1837) in Holy Trinity Church, Fareham.[6]

End of north aisle to left of main entrance
Sir William Huskisson Memorial
Sculptor: John Edward Carew

Installed: 1832
Materials/dimensions: statue: marble, 2.1 m high × 92 cm wide × 92 cm deep; pedestal: marble, 1.4 m high × 92 cm wide × 92 cm deep
Inscriptions (on front of pedestal): TO THE MEMORY OF / THE RIGHT HONOURABLE / WILLIAM HUSKISSON, / FOR TEN YEARS ONE OF THE REPRESENTATIVES OF THIS CITY / IN PARLIAMENT, / THIS STATION HE RELINQUISHED IN MDCCCXXIII, / WHEN YIELDING TO A SENSE OF PUBLICK DUTY / HE ACCEPTED THE OFFER OF BEING RETURNED FOR LIVERPOOL, / FOR WHICH HE WAS SELECTED ON ACCOUNT OF / THE ZEAL AND INTELLIGENCE DISPLAYED BY HIM /IN ADVANCING THE COMMERCIAL PROSPERITY OF THE EMPIRE / HIS DEATH WAS OCCASIONED BY AN ACCIDENT NEAR THAT TOWN / ON THE XV OF SEPTEMBER MDCCCXXX / AND CHANGED A SCENE OF TRIUMPHANT REJOICING / INTO ONE OF GENERAL MOURNING / AT THE URGENT SOLICITATION OF HIS CONSTITUENTS / HE WAS INTERRED IN THE CEMETERY THERE / AMID THE UNAFFECTED SORROW OF ALL CLASSES OF PEOPLE. / GIFTED WITH EXTRAORDINARY NATURAL ABILITIES/ HE CULTIVATED THEM WITH UNREMITTING APPLICATION / AND MATURED THEM BY LONG REFLECTION AND EXPERIENCE / HE EARLY DEVOTED HIMSELF TO THE SERVICE OF HIS COUNTRY / AND WAS CALLED TO SOME OF THE HIGHEST OFFICES OF THE STATE / WHICH HE FILLED ALIKE WITH HONOUR TO HIMSELF / AND ADVANTAGE TO THE PUBLICK. / THE INHABITANTS OF CHICHESTER AND ITS NEIGHBOURHOOD, / DEEPLY REGRETTING HIS UNTIMELY LOSS, / HAVE CAUSED THIS STATUE TO BE ERECTED / TO RECORD TO POSTERITY / THEIR ADMIRATION OF HIS TALENTS AND INTEGRITY / AS A STATESMAN, / THEIR RESPECT AND AFFECTION FOR HIS PRIVATE CHARACTER / BORN MDCCLXX DIED MDCCCXXX.
Status: not listed
Condition: good (but missing little finger of left hand and cement repairs to base)
Commissioned by: Third Earl of Egremont
Funded by: public subscription
Owner/custodian: the Chapter of Chichester Cathedral

The taller than life-size standing figure, dressed in the robes of a Roman senator, is set on a large square plinth. His right arm is pointing downwards and to the right with palm open and the left hand holds a scroll. William Huskisson was secretary to the treasury under

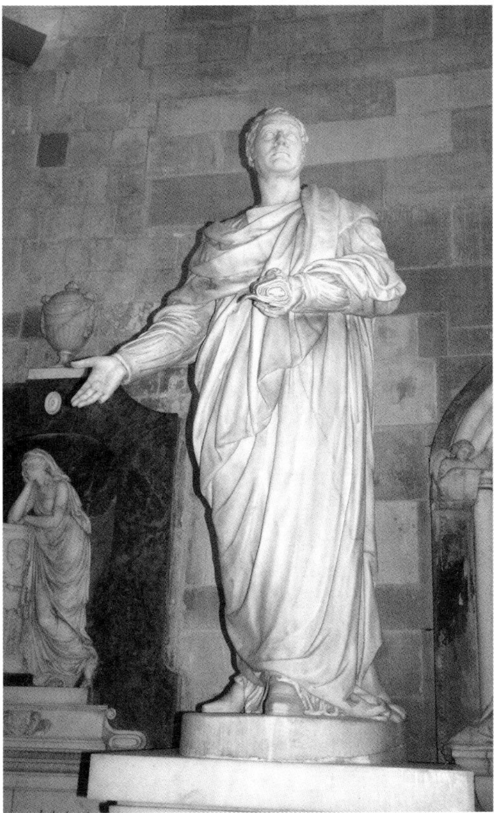

John Edward Carew, *Sir William Huskisson Memorial*

William Pitt 1804–06 and established a reputation as one of Britain's leading economists. He was elected MP for Chichester in 1812 and was given responsibility for the proposed Corn Laws by Lord Liverpool, who made him President of the Board of Trade in 1822. He refused to serve in the government of the Duke of Wellington, becoming one of the leading reformers in the Tory party and an advocate of Catholic Emancipation. He supported the construction of the railways and was invited to attend the official opening of the Liverpool and Manchester railway on 15 September 1830. He was run over and killed by George Stephenson's steam locomotive, the *Rocket*, because he had not taken sufficient care before crossing the track to start a conversation with the Duke of Wellington. He lived for a few hours after the accident, was lucid enough to dictate and sign a codicil to his will, and met his end with dignity.

During the court case that Carew brought against the executors of the third Earl (see Petworth entry), the sculptor claimed that Egremont insisted that there should be a statue of Huskisson, rather than the proposed commemorative tablet, in the cathedral. Carew estimated that the statue had cost £2000 and alleged that the Earl had not made up the difference between this sum and the £350 that had been raised for the tablet by public subscription.[7]

Notes
[1] Nairn and Pevsner (1965), p. 157. [2] Ibid, p. 160. [3] *John Flaxman: Line to Contour*, Ikon Gallery Birmingham, 2013, p. 75; Croft-Murray, E., 'An account book of John Flaxman R.A.', *Walpole Society*, vol. XXVIII, Oxford, 1940, p. 61. [4] Ibid. [5] *John Flaxman 1755–1826 Master of the Purest Line*, Sir John Soane's Gallery, London, 2003, pp. 17–18. [6] Croft-Murray (1940). [7] *Report of the Trial* (1840), p. 8.

Other sources
cathedralsplus.org.uk (accessed 16 December 2010).
Foster (2004), pp. 175–77.
Gunnis (1953), pp. 78–80.
Matthew, H.C.G. and Harrison, B. (eds.) *Oxford*

Dictionary of National Biography, vol. 28, Oxford, 2004, pp. 974–80.
philipjacksonsculptures.co.uk (accessed 16 December 2010).
Swinfen and Arscott (1985), p. 60.

College Lane

University of Chichester Bishop Otter Campus

A college for training school masters was established as a memorial to William Otter, former Bishop of Chichester, in 1840. After more than a century as a successful teacher training college and a number of changes of name, the institution became the Chichester Institute of Higher Education in 1995 and in 1999 gained degree-awarding powers in its own right, becoming University College Chichester. The original college buildings were in Gothic Revival style, but much of the ambience of its twentieth century successor is due to the work of the architectural firm of Bridgewater, Shepheard and Epstein in the 1950s and 1960s.

The college has had a longstanding commitment to art education and to developing a collection of contemporary art that would inspire and inform students. This was initiated in 1947 when Eleanor Hipwell, head of art for the Bishop Otter College, acquired three paintings from an exhibition held at the Victoria and Albert Museum. The building up of the collection was pursued with determination by the principal Miss K.E. Murray and Hipwell's successor, Sheila McCririck. They succeeded in acquiring quality work with inadequate monetary resources, supported by Bishop Bell, Chairman of the Bishop Otter College Council, and Walter Hussey, who arrived as the new Dean at Chichester Cathedral in 1955. Their legacy has been a sensitivity to the enhancement of college buildings, the Otter Art Gallery and the placement of sculpture around the campus.

Corridor (cloisters of the old building)
Mother and Child
Sculptor: Willi Soukop

Executed: c. 1947
Materials/dimensions: Polyphant stone, 53 cm high × 28 cm wide × 25 cm deep

The sculpture depicts a mother sitting with her knees raised, supporting a child in her lap and cradling his body with her arms. The heads of the two figures are turned towards each other, lightly touching.

The small sculpture, placed upon a wooden plinth attached to the wall at eye level, has a presence that goes beyond its size. Its smooth, simplified shapes and 'primitive' treatment of the facial features reflect the approach of the German expressionist sculptor Ernst Barlach

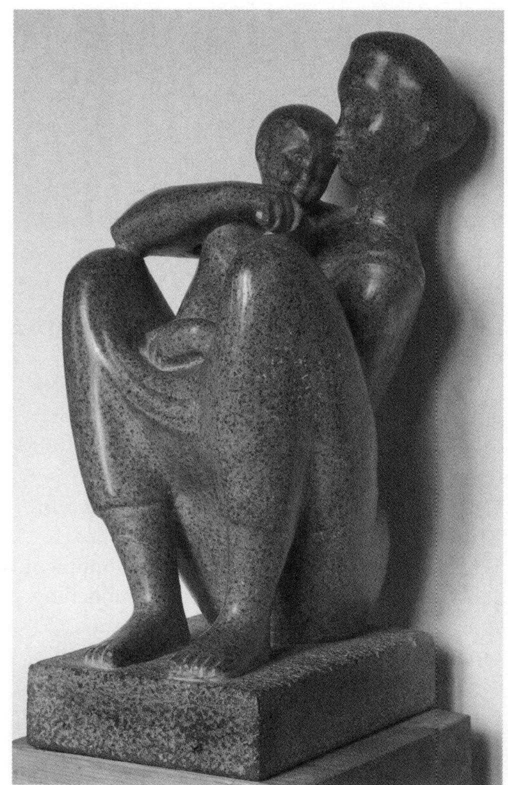

Willi Soukop, *Mother and Child*

(1870–1938), one of Soukop's acknowledged influences. Soukop summarised his empathy with his materials early in his career when he wrote:

> The most satisfying results I have achieved followed when there existed a relation of 50% material and 50% myself. Away from the block of wood or stone … I find it impossible to create sculpture.[1]

Western gable over entrance to the chapel

Cross Theme

Sculptor: Geoffrey Clarke

Architect: Peter Faulkner Shepheard
Builders: Robert Marriott Ltd
Unveiled: 21 March 1962

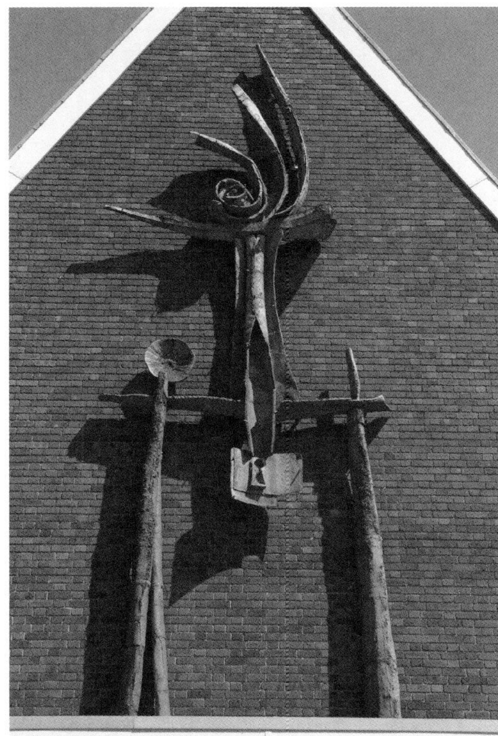

Geoffrey Clarke, *Cross Theme*

Materials/dimensions: cast aluminium, 9.15 m high
Status: not listed
Condition: good
Owner/custodian: University of Chichester

The sculpture's large abstracted forms, described as 'spiky', are an interpretation of the theme of the crucifixion.[2] As well as the central figure of Christ suffering on the cross, it also depicts the two thieves who were crucified with him. The sculpture contains a nugget of glass, a symbol of the eye of God.

The College Chapel was built in 1962 and has an unusual cruciform design partly dictated by the funding available (£13,000). The western gable over the entrance was considered an appropriate location for a sculpture. Geoffrey Clarke had been commissioned for pieces in Chichester Cathedral and was therefore asked to create the sculpture for Bishop Otter College. 'Illumination; inspiration; light; kindling of mind and spirit; vision' were words used by Clarke to describe his feelings about the piece, which was unveiled by Roger Wilson, Bishop of Chichester, during the Chapel's dedication ceremony.[3]

Facing the chapel

Axis Mundi

Sculptor: John Skelton assisted by Reuben Walters

Unveiled: 6 October 1990
Materials/dimensions: French limestone, 2.75 m high × 2.8 m wide × 50 cm deep
Signature (on south face, bottom left-hand corner, carved vertically): John Skelton 1988
Status: not listed
Condition: good
Owner/custodian: University of Chichester

Two large, roughly columnar blocks, one horizontal set on top of one vertical, form a Tau Cross (named after the Greek letter it resembles). The axis mundi (axis of the world)

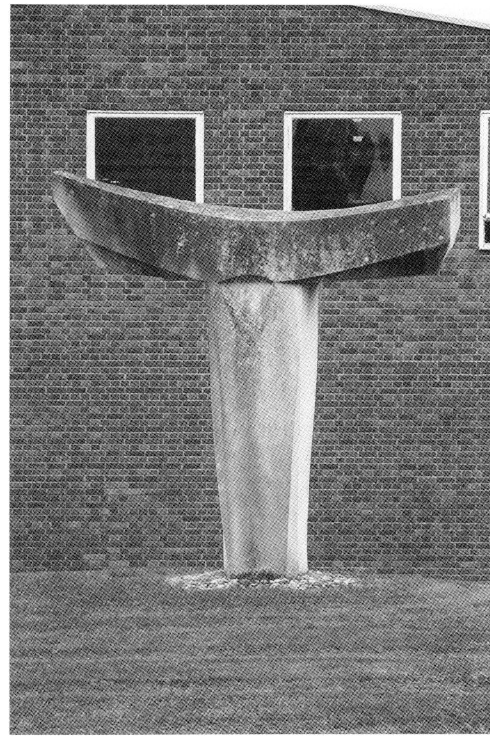

John Skelton, *Axis Mundi*

in religion and mythology is the world centre and/or the connection between heaven and earth. The vertical block represents life and the horizontal the afterlife, at the same time symbolising the conflict and interaction of male and female forces.

John Skelton spent a year as artist in residence at the college from October 1989 and the sculpture was made to commemorate its 150th anniversary. It was unveiled on Graduation Day in the autumn of 1990, when Skelton's daughter Rebecca graduated from the college, and dedicated by Archdeacon William Filby.

Murray Relief
Sculptor: Peter Hodgkinson

Constructed: 1993
Materials/dimensions: stone, with bronze
 inserts, 1.22 m high × 77 cm wide × 28 cm
 deep
Inscription (on bronze plaque on wall below
 relief): MISS K M E MURRAY / PRINCIPAL 1948–
 70 / ONE MUST WAIT UNTIL THE EVENING TO
 KNOW HOW SPLENDID THE DAY HAS BEEN / –
 SOPHOCLES / SCULPTOR PETER HODGKINSON
 RCA
Status: not listed
Condition: good (cleaned January 2011)
Commissioned by: trustees of Bishop Otter
 College
Owner/custodian: University of Chichester

The relief depicts abstracted organic forms,
symbolising life and growth, in high relief
against a textured background. One of the small
bronze inserts, which punctuate the surface,
represents a seed within two halves of a stone
pod; the other has the appearance of an ancient
archaeological find.

The piece was commissioned to
commemorate the work of Miss Elizabeth
(Betty) Murray as Principal of the College. It is
an unusual example of the sculptor's work,
which is more commonly directly
representational, as in his sculpture of Sir Tom
Finney, the footballer (2004) and the Chorley
Pals War Memorial (2010).

Notes
[1] Letter from Soukop to unknown recipient,
December 1939. W. Soukop papers 2003/5 box 1,
Henry Moore Institute archive, Leeds. [2] Foster
(2004), p. 190. Williams records the title of the piece
as *Crucifixion*. [3] 'Two teachers' training colleges: 1,
Chichester', *The Architectural Review*, vol. 132,
November 1962, p. 358.

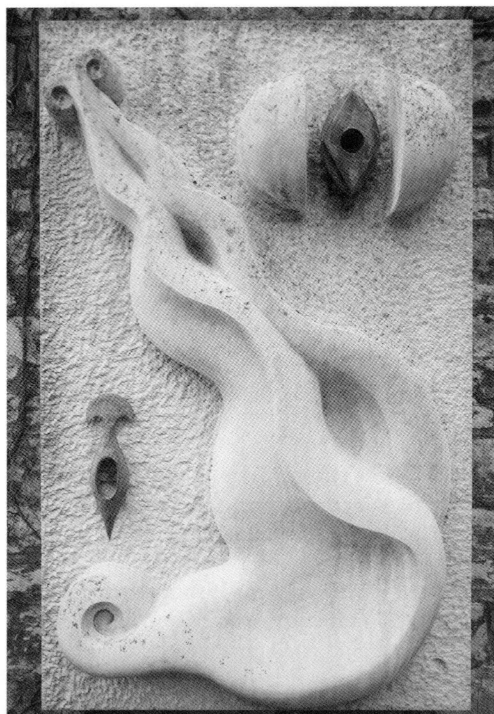

(above) Peter Hodgkinson, *Murray Relief*

(right) Yvonne Hudson Rusbridge,
Minerva Tile Relief

Other sources
Bailey, C., 'John Skelton obituary', *The Guardian*, 3
 December 1999.
James, N.P., 'John Skelton: Axis Mundi', *Cv/Visual
 Arts Research*, London, vol. 55, 2005, pp. 20–23.
Parkin, M., 'Obituary: Willi Soukop', *The
 Independent*, 9 February 1995.
Powers, A., 'Obituary: John Skelton', *The
 Independent*, 6 December 1999.
Brian Rigby (Honorary Curator, Otter Gallery
 University of Chichester), email correspondence,
 27 June 2007; meeting, 28 January 2011.
Strachan (1984).
Warne, H. and Brighton, T., *A Portrait of Bishop Otter
 College: Chichester 1839–1990*, Chichester, 1992.

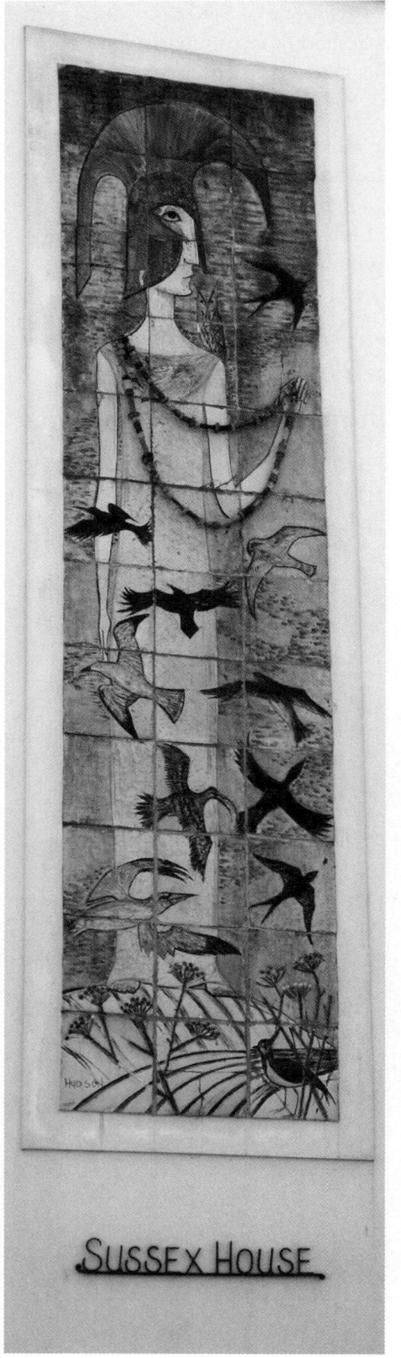

Junction of Crane Street and North Street

High up on north wall of Sussex House

Minerva Tile Relief
Sculptor: Yvonne Hudson Rusbridge

Installed: 1966
Materials/dimensions: ceramic with oxidised
    coloured glazes, 3.5 m high × 90 cm wide
Signature (bottom left-hand corner): HUDSON
Status: not listed
Condition: good
Owner/custodian: unknown

The panel is mounted on the wall above the title
SUSSEX HOUSE (which currently houses several
West Sussex County Council services) in
applied metal lettering. It comprises 36 ceramic
tiles, with raised surfaces and sculptural
elements, which were fired at 1300°C in
Hudson Rusbridge's own kiln.[1] A stylised head
of Minerva is shown in profile. She has a
columnar body with elongated head and
plumed helmet. There is an owl perched on her
shoulder and her gaze tracks the flight of a
departing Swift. There is a Lapwing at her feet
and other birds fly around her, including
Chough, Crow, Herring Gull, Curlew, Bittern,
Kestrel, Sparrow Hawk, Cormorant and
Swallow. She holds out her left arm, on which is
hung one end of a freestanding necklace of
ceramic beads. Although the classical theme
relates to the Minerva Theatre (opened 1982)
and Philip Jackson's sculpture of the goddess
(1997), Rusbridge's relief predates them and
appears to have been specifically designed for
the building on which it is sited.

Note
[1] Foster (2004), pp. 187–89.

Other source
David Rusbridge (artist's son), email correspondence,
    28 January 2009.

East Row

*Junction with Little London, outside
Chichester District Museum*

The Symbol of Discovery
Sculptor: John Skelton

Architect: Stanley Roth
Installed: 1963
Materials/dimensions: Kirkstone Westmoreland
    green slate, 2 m high × 60 cm wide × 25 cm
    deep; jewel: gold leaf set in Perspex
Inscriptions (plaques set into cobbles at front):
    Symbol Of / Discovery / Westmorland slate
    / John Skelton / Unveiled in 1963 by Sir
    Charles Wheeler PRA / Museums present to
    the world the precious offerings of the earth
    JS

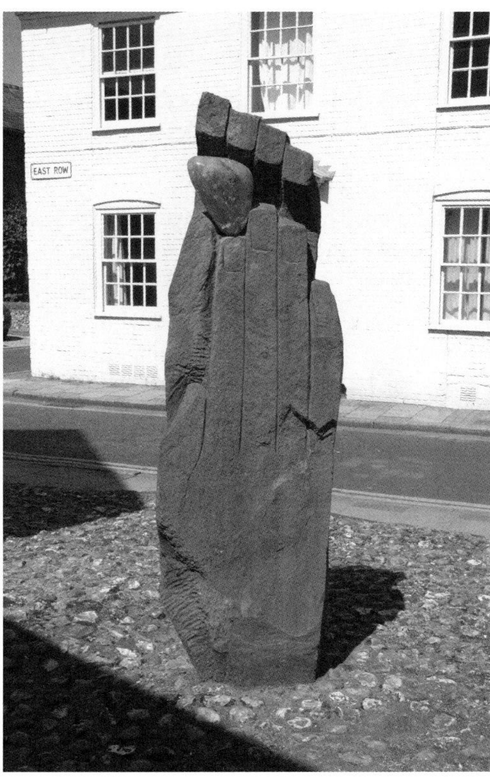

John Skelton, *The Symbol of Discovery*

Status: not listed
Condition: good
Commissioned by: Stanley Roth
Owner/custodian: Chichester City Council

The sculpture depicts two hands cradling a
man-made jewel. As Gaynor Williams has
described it, it is:

> [c]onstructed around the idea of a
> 'fragment', the form of the work has its roots
> in the discovery of antique remains, an idea
> that in the Romantic period became a
> symbol of loss. One of Henry Fuseli's most
> famous works shows a male figure bereft and
> weeping over the beauty of a large carved
> antique fragment. This metaphor for the lost
> totality, a vanished wholeness, looks back to
> the holy relics of saints, and Skelton's work
> draws on this tradition.[1]

The sculpture was commissioned by Stanley
Roth to stand on the forecourt of the Museum
and was unveiled at its opening. An explanatory
plaque made of blue slate, inscribed by Skelton,
is embedded into the cobble surround in front
of his work.

Note
[1] Foster (2004), p. 183.

6 Market Avenue

*Enclosed courtyard inside Chichester Law
Courts*

Helping Hand of Justice
Sculptor: John Skelton
Architect: Stanley Roth

Installed: 1973
Materials/dimensions: Normandy limestone,
    90 cm high × 90 cm wide × 80 cm deep
Status: not listed
Condition: good
Owner/custodian: Chichester Law Courts

The sculpture has been carved directly into a
cube of limestone. It depicts a child's hand,

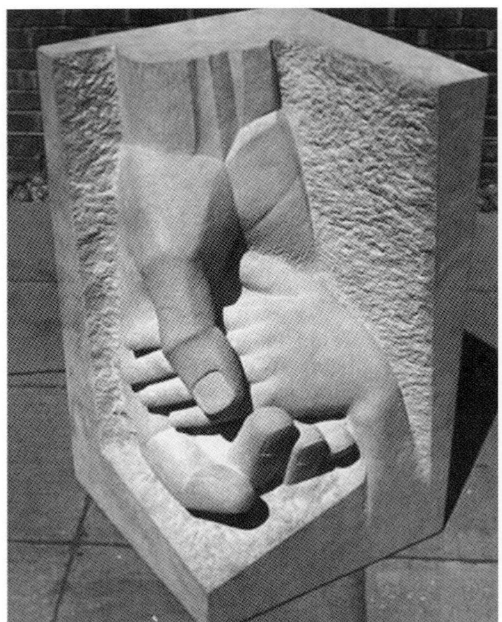

John Skelton, *Helping Hand of Justice*

modelled on that of his daughter Helen Mary, resting in the palm of an adult's hand. Skelton commented that the work was 'directed equally to those giving help and seeking it'.[1]

Note
[1] Foster (2004), p. 184.

Other source
Strachan (1984).

Market Avenue

St Richard's Catholic Church, above main entrance

Crucifix

Sculptors: Philip Lindsey Clark and Michael Clark

Executed: 1962–63
Materials/dimensions: bronze, 3 m high × 2 m wide
Status: building Grade II

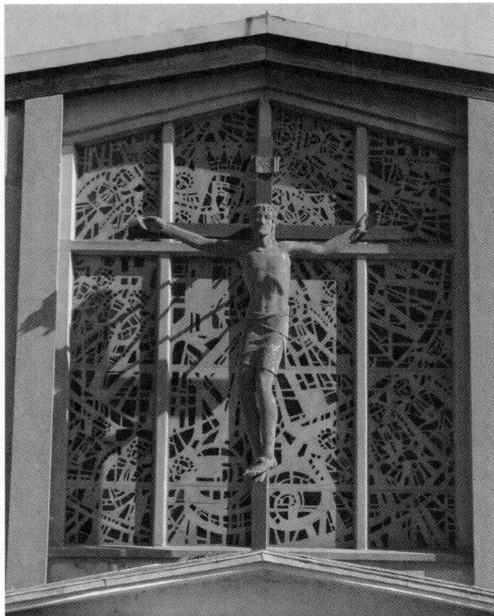

Philip Lindsey Clark and Michael Clark, *Crucifix*

Condition: good
Commissioned by: Father Langton-Fox (worked at the church 1959–65)
Owner/custodian: St Richard's Church

The figure of the crucified Christ, with its crosshatched texturing, has the simplified directness of early Christian or primitive sculpture. The father and son team who made it specialised in ecclesiastical work. The crucifix, placed above the entrance door of the church, is set against a striking window in Loire glass depicting Mary, Queen of Heaven. The 62 panels of glass, also commissioned by Langton-Fox, who had close links with Chartres, home of Loire glass, in 1962, are the primary reason why the church was listed in 2007.

Sources
Parish of Chichester with The Witterings, correspondence, 12 June 2008.
Vail, A., *The Shrines of Our Lady in England*, Leominster, 2004.

Market Place

Junction of North, South, East and West Streets

Market Cross

Sculptor (original bust of Charles I): Hubert le Sueur (fibreglass copy: Derek H. Rollings)

Architect: unknown

Clockmakers: Gilbert and Johnston, Crawley
Installed: 1501 (clock 1904)
Materials/dimensions: Market Cross, Caen stone approx. 9.42 m diam. × approx. 11.6 m high; bust of Charles I (original) gilded bronze, 95 cm high × 65 cm wide × 30 cm deep
Inscriptions (niche on south face, long since eroded away): DAME / ELIZABETH FARRINGTON / RELICT OF / SIR RICHARD FARRINGTON / BARONET / GAVE THIS CLOCK / AS AN HOURLY MEMENTO / OF HER GOOD WILL / TO THIS CITY / MDCCXXIV / GEORGE HARRIS MAYOR; inscription added in 1746 (now faded): THIS BEAUTIFUL CROSS / ERECTED BY / EDWARD STORY / BISHOP OF CHICHESTER / WHO WAS ADVANCED / TO THAT DIGNITY / BY EDWARD IV MCCCCLXXV / WAS FIRST REPAIRED / IN THE REIGN OF CHARLES II / AND NOW AGAIN / IN THE TWENTIETH YEAR / OF OUR PRESENT SOVEREIGN / GEORGE II MDCCXLVI / THOMAS WALL MAYOR / AT THE SOLE EXPENSE OF CHARLES DUKE OF RICHMOND / LENOX AND AUBIGNY; inscription placed in clock chamber 1904: IN COMMEMORATION / OF THE CORONATION OF / KING EDWARD VII / THIS CROSS WAS REPAIRED / BY PUBLIC SUBSCRIPTION 1903–4 / PEYTON TEMPLE MACKESON / MAYOR; (on gilded bronze plaque at base of original bust): CAROLUS REX aet XXXVII
Status: Grade I
Condition: good (but some erosion of stone carvings)

Commissioned by: Bishop Edward Story
  (1422–1503)
Owner/custodian: Chichester District Council

The Cross is an open arcaded octagon with
buttress piers at the angles terminating in finials
carrying iron standards. The space between the
arcade wall and the central column, that carries
a lantern, is roofed by an elaborate vaulted
tierceron ceiling with bosses of foliage and fruit.
The pennants on the finials contain the coats of
arms of Bishop Story, Henry VI, Lady
Farrington and the City of Chichester. The
carvings depict; on the north face, two wide-
mouthed gargoyles; on the northeast face, an
inverted winged monster, a sea horse and a
goat; on the southeast face, a double-headed
eagle and a stallion; on the south face, a sheep
and a salmon; on the southwest face, a deer, a
wyvern (a winged two-legged dragon with a
barbed tail), a camel and a winged lion.

The Cross is one of the few in Britain that
still stands on its original site. By the indenture
dated 28 December 1501, Bishop Edward Story
paid £10 to the Mayor and Corporation of
Chichester for the ground on which it was
built, replacing a much earlier wooden version.
No record exists of how it was built or how
much it cost. Each face of the structure has a
niche that originally contained statues,
probably of bishops, as there is evidence of a
bishop's mitre carved into each one. Major
damage was done to the angels and statues of
bishops in December 1642, during the Civil
War.

In the niche facing West Street there is a life-
sized bust of Charles I by Hubert Le Sueur, one
of a number of versions, executed in c. 1637 and
presented to the city by Charles II '… in
recognition of its role as a monarchist
stronghold during the Civil War'.[1] The original
belongs to Chichester City Council and was on
loan to Pallant House Gallery from 2000; it is
currently (2013) on long loan to Tate Britain.

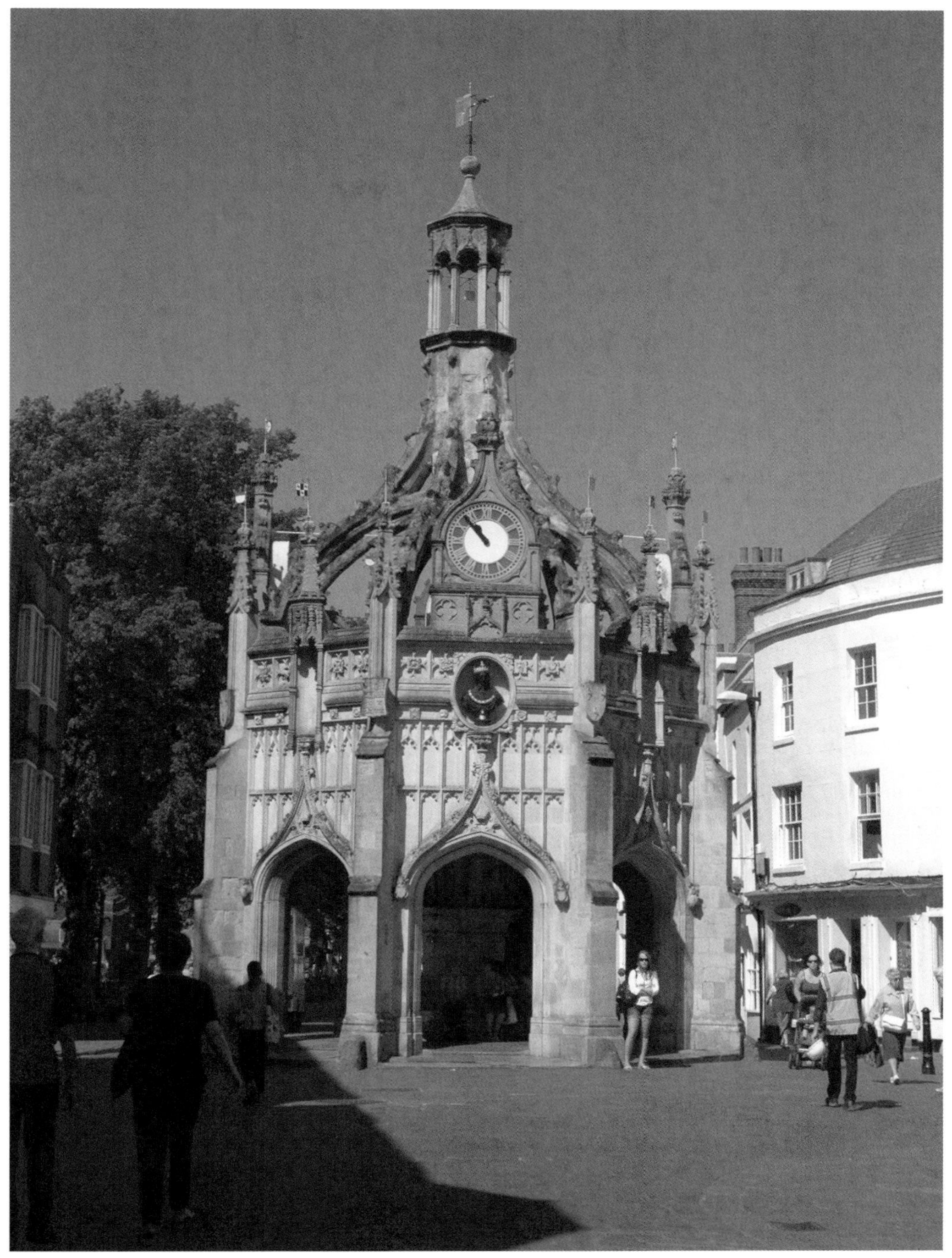

Hubert le Sueur, *Market Cross*

On the Market Cross is now a fibreglass copy cast by Derek H. Rollings of Chichester in 1978.

In 1689 the Protestant William and Mary were proclaimed King and Queen at the Cross following the flight of James II. In 1724 a clock was added on three sides, given by Lady Farrington. The decision to have only three dials was much criticised. In 1746 it was removed at the personal expense of Charles, 2nd Duke of Richmond, and replaced with one that had four dials. A striking clock, now powered by electricity, was installed in 1904. On three of the dials the figures are made from cast iron but the dial facing North Street is much more intricate and may date from the eighteenth century. In 1928, the Cross was 'rendered' in the name of restoration and badly damaged by the process, which obscured many of the carvings. Repairs were again made in the 1950s and in 1978–80 when the rendering was removed. The Cross was listed in July 1950; it is also a scheduled monument under the Ancient Monument Areas Act 1979 (as amended by the National Heritage Act 1983).[2]

Notes
[1] Pallant House records CHCPH 1176. We are grateful to Simon Martin, Collections Manager, and Sarah Norris of Pallant House library for help with this entry. [2] Foster, P. (ed.), *A Jewel in Stone: Chichester Market Cross 1501–2001*, Otter memorial paper no. 15, Chichester, 2004.

Other sources
Arscott, D., *Curiosities of West Sussex: a County Guide to the Unusual*, Market Drayton, 1993, p. 2.
Whinney (1964), p. 36.

9 North Pallant

Pallant House Gallery

In 2006 an extension to the existing Grade One-Listed Queen Anne townhouse of 1712, was opened to the public. It was designed by Long & Kentish architects in association with Colin St John Wilson (1922–2007), architect of the British library (finished 1997) with the primary intention of displaying the loan of his important collection of British art, mainly from the 1960s and 1970s. Other sculptures by Paolozzi currently on display in the British Pop Art gallery include *Standing Figure* (1957), *Crash Head* (1970) and *Newton after Blake* (1993–94), a maquette for the bronze sculpture outside the British Library.

Right-hand corner of courtyard
Bride of the Konsul
Sculptor: Eduardo Paolozzi

Constructed: 1962
Materials/dimensions: bronze, 1.98 m high × 58 cm wide × 51 cm deep
Inscription (on small metal plaque immediately in front of sculpture): Eduardo Paolozzi 1924–2005 / Bride of the Konsul / 1962 / Bronze / Wilson Loan
Status: not listed
Condition: good (some weathering)

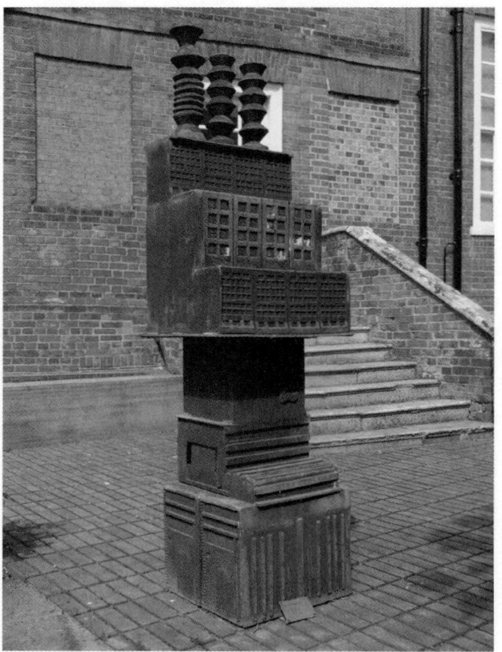

Eduardo Paolozzi, *Bride of the Konsul*

Owner/custodian: Pallant House Gallery (Wilson Gift through the Art Fund 2006)

The sculpture consists of three Brancusi-style columns on stepped vertical blocks with geometric surface patterning, resembling a high-rise block of flats. The number 2, welded to the base, is a reminder that it originally stood outside Colin St Jon Wilson's house at number 2 Granchester Road, Cambridge. It is the companion piece to *Konsul*, produced in the same year and currently in the Tate Britain collection. It is suggested that Paolozzi's machine aesthetic, already established in the 1950s was refined by his familiarity with German engineering and industrial development, which he observed while a visiting professor at the Hochschule für Bildende Künst, Hamburg (1960–62). It also refers to the futuristic imagery of Fritz Lang's *Metropolis* (1927), one of the sculptor's favourite films. Like *Artificial Sun* (below) the sculpture is linked to a series of screenprints, in this case a book, *Metafisikal Translations* published in 1962.[1]

Left-hand corner of courtyard
Artificial Sun
Sculptor: Eduardo Paolozzi

Constructed: 1964
Materials/dimensions: non-corrosive aluminium, 2.4 m high × 1.4 m wide × 1.1 m deep; central disk: 90 cm diam.
Inscription (on small metal plaque immediately in front of sculpture): Eduardo Paolozzi 1924–2005 / Artificial Sun / 1964 / Aluminium / Wilson Loan
Status: not listed
Condition: good (some weathering)
Owner/custodian: Pallant House Gallery (Wilson Loan 2006)

The sculpture sits on a flat integral base; concentric circular disks and an S-shape are welded onto four uprights with geometric

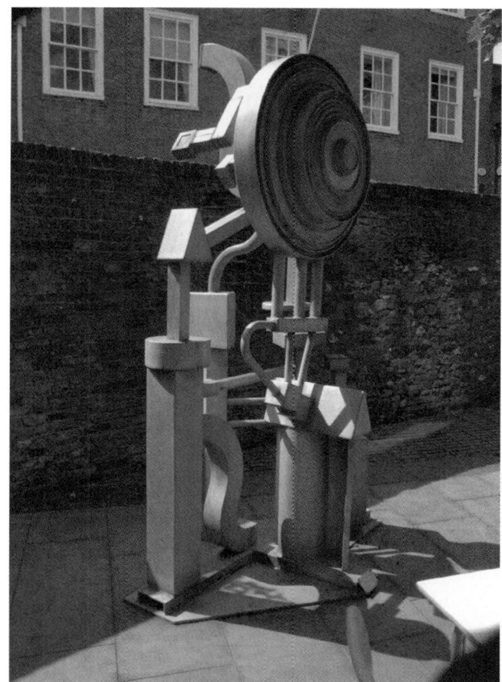

Eduardo Paolozzi, *Artificial Sun*

shapes, centring the weight of the sculpture towards its top. The piece takes its title from the first of a series of 12 screen prints in the portfolio 'As Is When', 'which in turn refers to the life and writings of the Austrian born philosopher Ludwig Wittgenstein.'[2] Paolozzi described his drawing upon Wittgenstein's works as, '… a kind of combined autobiography.'[3] Four of these screenprints were gifted to the gallery, where they can be found in the British Pop Art room, by Colin Wilson.

The title *Artificial Sun* arose from Paolozzi's longstanding interest in science fiction writing, particularly the work of J.G. Ballard, where man's ability to recreate our natural source of heat and light can be read as reflecting both optimism and pessimism.[4] Paolozzi's fascination with modern technology, clearly referenced in his works of the 1950s and 1960s,

was reinforced by his collaborations with engineering firms. He provided free-hand sketches that were translated into blueprints for the production of models before the sculptures were cast in metal. *Artificial Sun* is made of the type of aluminium commonly used in aircraft manufacture.[5] Another version, currently in a private collection, was executed in stainless steel in 1964.

Notes
[1] Sanger, A., entry on tate.org.uk, 2009 (accessed 14 August 2012). [2] Simmons, J., 'Artwork of the month' talk, Pallant House Gallery, 29 August 2012. [3] Ibid. [4] Ibid. See also 'Speculative illustrations: Eduardo Paolozzi in conversation with J. G. Ballard and Frank Whitford', *Studio International*, vol. 182, 1971, pp. 136–43. [5] Ibid.

Other source
Pallant House database, ID codes CHCPH1480 and CHCPH1481.

Spitalfield Lane

St Richard's Hospital

The original building at St Richard's Hospital was erected in 1938–39 by West Sussex County Council. It had 194 beds for elderly and infirm people, but at the beginning of the war in 1939, the Government declared it an Emergency Medical Service General Hospital. By 1940, 10 hutted wards were added, taking the number of beds to 400. It continued to enlarge in the postwar period and serves an area of around 400 square miles. The hospital attained NHS Trust status in 1994 and in April 2009 it merged with two other hospitals, Worthing and Southlands, in Shoreham-by-Sea, to become Western Sussex Hospitals NHS Trust.
The Art for St Richard's scheme was initiated in 1994–95, with the driving forces Geoff Metcalfe

Vincent Gray, *One Criterion* (see next page)

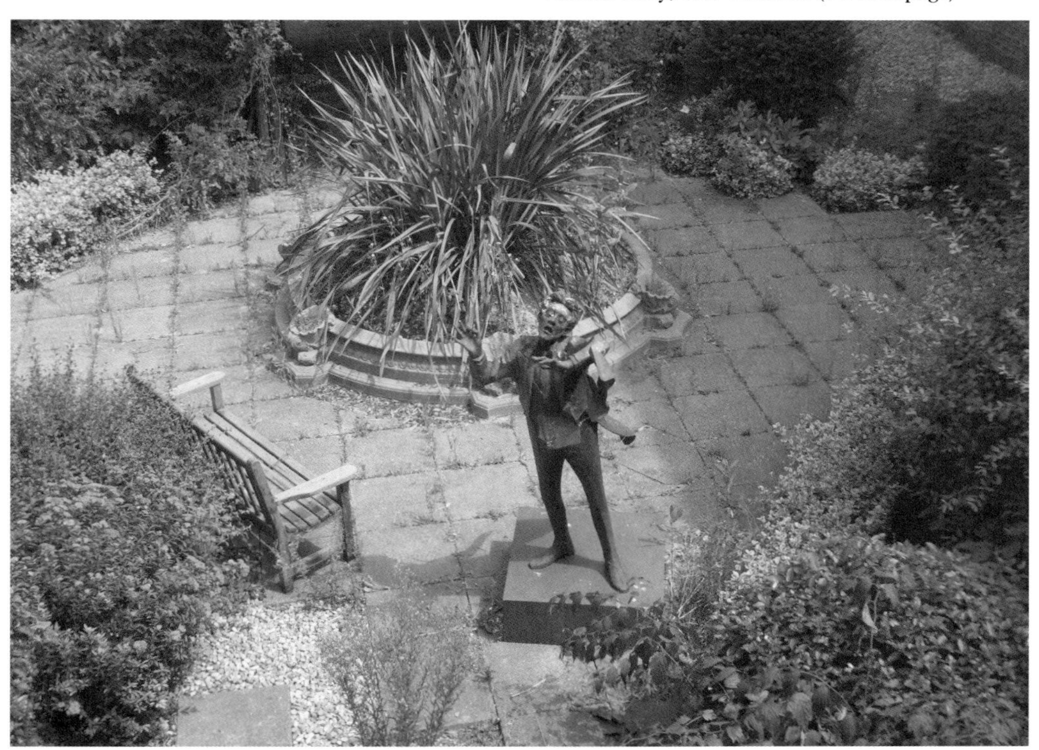

and his late wife Amanda, who founded
Artplace, a consultancy and advisory service for
art in hospitals and worked on a similar project
at Worthing Hospital. One of their innovations
is six-monthly changes of exhibitions, of mainly
two-dimensional work, within St Richard's. The
funding for the scheme comes predominantly
from the hospital's League of Friends, with
contributions from the hospital budget usually
in connection with building projects.[1]

The commissioning of sculpture was given
great impetus by the construction of the new
main wing, opened in December 1996, which
incorporated a series of themed courtyards,
particularly suited to displaying three-
dimensional art. They make reference to
Chichester's past, as in the Roman, eighteenth-
century and cloister courtyards and to its
geographical situation, with titles such as
Seashore and Grandstand.

One Criterion

Sculptor: Vincent Gray

Installed: 1996
Materials/dimensions: statue: resin, 1.85 m high
    × 1.1 m wide × 1.2 m deep; base: resins,
    30 cm high × 90 cm wide × 90 cm deep
Signature (to outer aspect of right heel): GRAY
    1996
Status: not listed
Condition: good
Owner/custodian: on long-term loan from the
    sculptor

The life-sized statue is of the composer and
conductor Leonard Bernstein, dressed in tails,
waistcoat and bow tie, in the act of conducting
an orchestra. A piece of music is suspended at
waist level as if falling to the floor. Vincent
Gray has explained that he took the title from
Bernstein's response to an interview question.
When asked what were the principles by which
he judged a piece of music, he replied; 'One
criterion … does it exalt me?'[2]

Seashore courtyard

The Seashore

Sculptor: Libby Tribe

Installed: unknown
Materials/dimensions: wood with resin spheres
    and found objects (tallest post): 1.3 m ×
    10 cm wide × 10 cm deep; (shortest post):
    9 cm high × 25 cm wide × 25 cm deep
Status: not listed
Condition: fair (one post is pushed over and the
    sphere is missing from another)
Owner/custodian: St Richard's Hospital

The series of 45 roughly carved square posts is
arranged in three rows and set into a
semicircular shape. On top of each post is a
sphere of resin with found objects relating to
the seashore set inside. The piece encloses a
pebbly beach-like space, with informal planting
at the back.

Libby Tribe, *The Seashore*

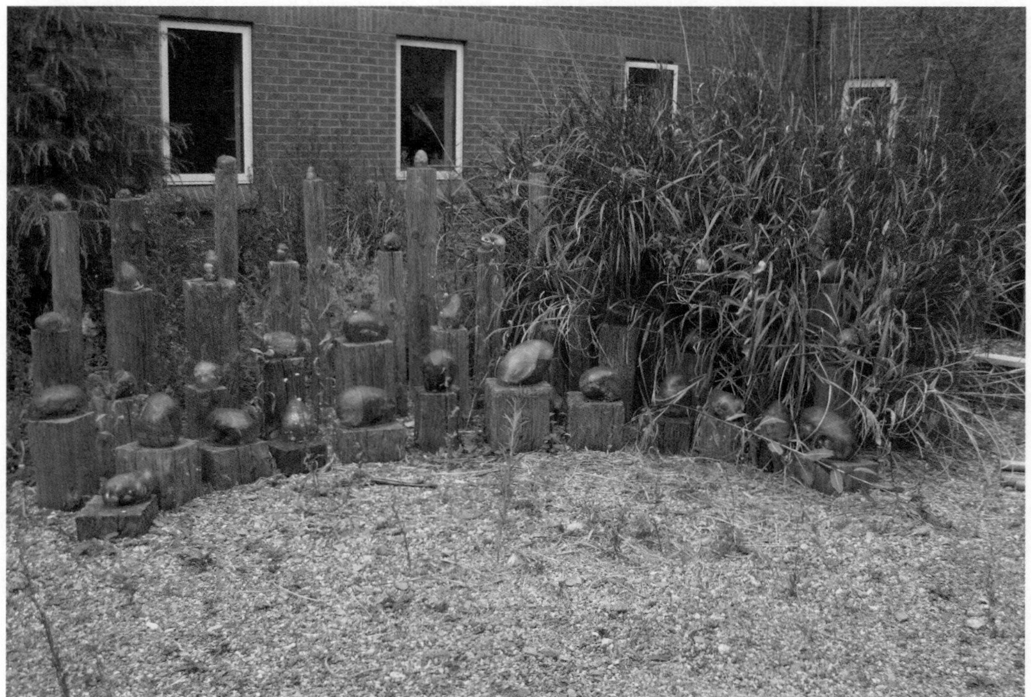

Junction of Out Patients Department corridor

Two Men on a Bench

Sculptor: Giles Penny

Executed: (original bronze) 1994
Materials/dimensions: fibreglass and resin
    coloured blue, sculpture: 1.85 m high ×
    1.78 m wide × 1.7 m deep; integral base:
    13 cm high × 1.88 m wide × 1.99 m deep
Status: not listed
Condition: good (but small hole in surface of
    left arm of figure facing the Out Patients
    Department)
Owner/custodian: St Richard's Hospital
    (donated by Art for St Richard's)

The large sculpture depicts two monumental
nude male figures sitting in slumped positions
facing away from each other with their hands in
their laps at either end of a geometric bench, as
in a hospital waiting room. The original 1994
sculpture was in bronze, in an edition of 10.

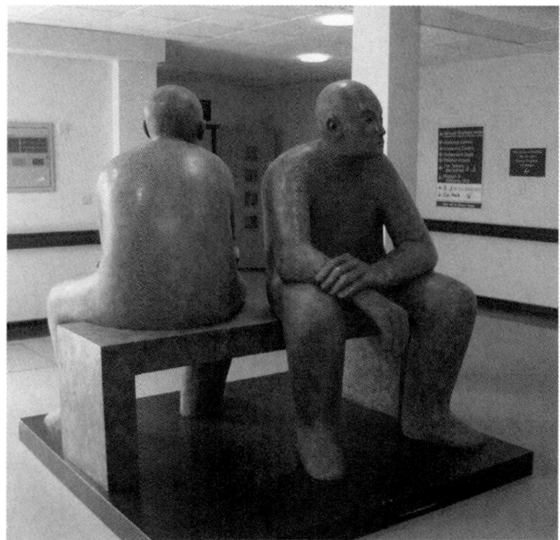

Giles Penny, *Two Men on a Bench*

One of the originals can be seen at Canary Wharf, where it was first placed as part of the exhibition, *Shape of the Century*. It can be found just south of Cabot Square, at the bottom of Cubitt Steps by the side of Mackenzie Walk.

Ground-floor corridor facing west
The Tree of Life
Sculptors: Chris Rutter and Evelyn Bennett

Installed: 1997
Materials/dimensions: polychromed concrete over welded steel armature, 1.85 m high × 2.05 m wide × 40 cm deep
Status: not listed
Condition: good
Owner/custodian: St Richard's Hospital (donated by Art for St Richard's)

The sculpture was inspired by the forms and colours of nature and the landscape. Stylised figures of the sun, a tree and a flower decorate a tree-like form. It was created in response to the theme suggested by Art for St Richard's for the ground floor of the hospital; 'Gardens and Downs'. A companion piece, *Moon Tree*, by

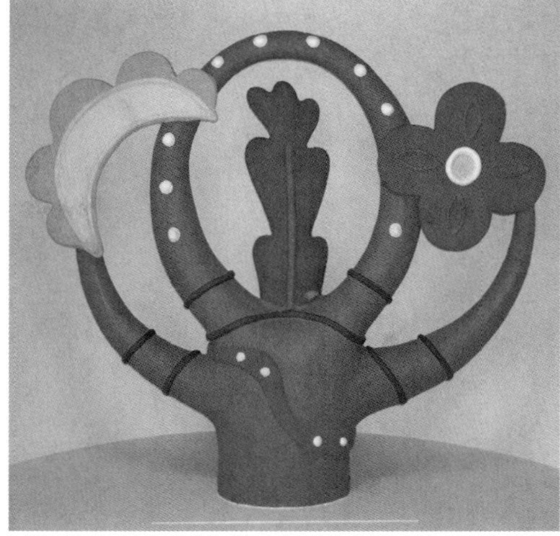

Chris Rutter and Evelyn Bennett, *The Tree of Life*

the same sculptors, of similar proportions and bright colours, was installed at the first-loor corridor junction in the same year.

Opposite the Roman courtyard
Mr Noah Reliefs
Sculptor: Giles Penny

Installed: 1996
Materials/dimensions: each relief: painted plaster, 33 cm high × 23 cm wide × 2.5 cm deep
Signature (to bottom left of each relief): G.P. 96

Giles Penny, *Mr Noah Reliefs*

Status: not listed
Condition: good (fourth relief repaired 2008)
Owner/custodian: St Richard's Hospital

The four reliefs depict the biblical story of Noah and the Ark in bold and simplified shapes, which give them monumentality despite their small size.

Waiting area of the Women and Children's Unit
Mother with Children
Sculptor: Marion Lyon

Installed: late 1950s
Materials/dimensions: bronze, 65.5 cm high × 32 cm wide × 23 cm deep; polished wooden pedestal, 60 cm high × 48 cm wide × 48 cm deep
Signature (to rear of base): Marion Edie (sculptor's maiden name)
Status: not listed
Condition: good
Owner/custodian: St Richard's Hospital

The sculpture depicts a mother holding a baby in her left arm and the hand of a child, who stands to her left, with her right hand. The bulk of their bodies contrasts with their small abstracted heads in a manner characteristic of much figurative sculpture of this period. The model for the sculpture was exhibited at the Royal Academy in 1958, described as 'group for welfare clinic'.[3]

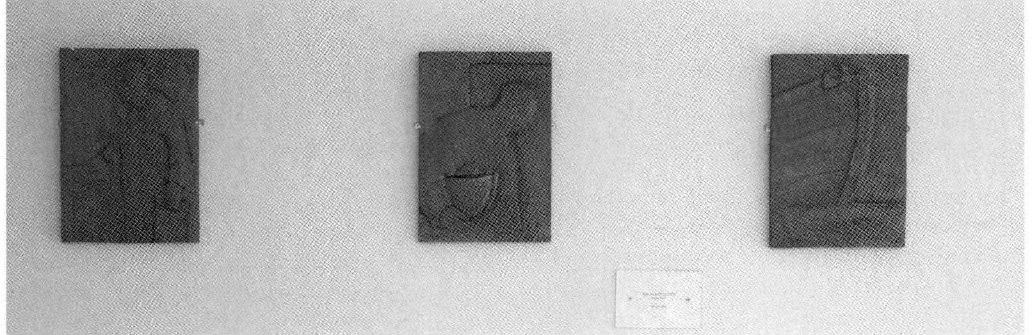

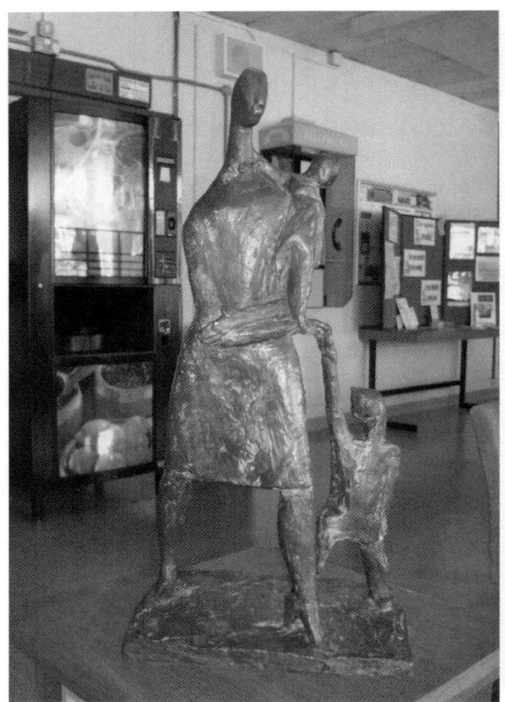

Marion Lyon, *Mother with Children* (see previous page)

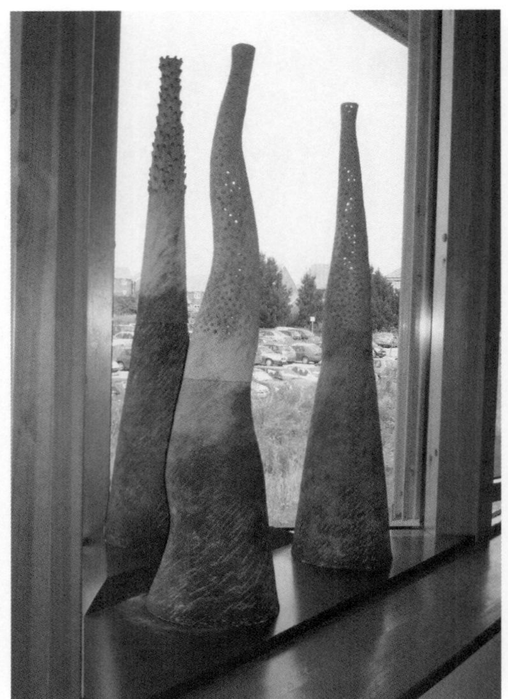

Nancy Angus, *Three Conical Forms*

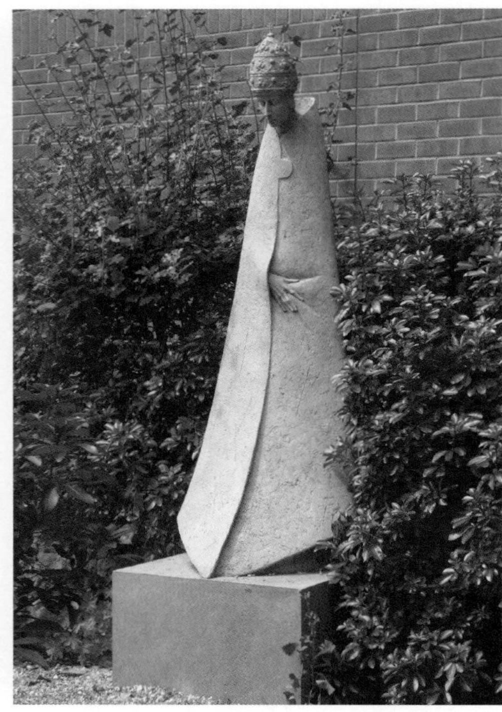

Philip Jackson, *Pope Joan*

On diagonal window ledge outside Bosham and Selsey Wards
Three Conical Forms
Sculptor: Nancy Angus

Installed: 1999
Materials/dimensions: blue glazed ceramic, each
   90 cm high × 20 cm wide × 20 cm deep
Status: not listed
Condition: good
Owner/custodian: St Richard's Hospital

This group of three asymmetrical conical forms all have textured bases with pierced and decorated upper parts reminiscent of natural forms such as seedpods or pine cones.

Cloister courtyard
Pope Joan
Sculptor: Philip Jackson

Installed: 1999
Materials/dimensions: resin (edition of five,
   original in bronze), 2.33 m high × 71 cm
   wide × 61 cm deep
Status: not listed
Condition: good
Owner/custodian: on long-term loan from
   sculptor

This elongated female figure is depicted in papal robes and triple crown. Her expression is serene with slightly androgynous features. Her right hand is seen emerging from the robe with fingers outstretched, covering her pregnancy.

There is no evidence that Pope Joan ever existed, but popular legends were circulating from the thirteenth century. One version states that she lived around 1100 and was a very talented woman, who dressed as a man, became notary to the Curia, then cardinal and finally pope. One day she went out on horseback, gave birth to a son and was then bound to the tail of a horse, dragged round the city, stoned to death by the mob, and was buried at the place where she died. Another version has it that she came to Rome, where she taught science, and thereby attracted the attention of learned men. She enjoyed the greatest respect on account of her conduct and erudition, and was finally chosen as pope, but, becoming pregnant by one of her trusted attendants, she gave birth to a child during a procession from St Peter's to the Lateran, somewhere between the Coliseum and St Clement's. There she died almost immediately, and it is said she was buried at the same place.

Sea Change

Sculptor: George Cutts

Installed: 1996 (edition of 6)
Materials/dimensions: stainless steel, 10 m high
 × 5 cm wide × 5 cm deep
Status: not listed
Condition: good
Owner/custodian: St Richard's Hospital
 (donated by Art for St Richard's)

George Cutts explores the contrast between the inorganic material of stainless steel and the movement of natural forms. Two thin poles, driven by electric motors, slowly revolve, catching the light and the shape between them changes. The space between the poles can seem almost fluid like water and the optical illusion created sometimes suggests that the poles are waving and not rotating, in imitation of kelp swaying with the movement of the waves, as observed by the sculptor during scuba diving trips. The movement has also been described as having, '… a mesmerising quality, much as the tune of the snake charmer's flute mesmerises the cobra'.[4] This effect was disliked by many of the patients looking out of the surrounding ward windows and so it was stopped. The sculpture is now static.

Shangri-La courtyard

Fluke

Sculptor: Walter Bailey

Installed: 1997
Materials/dimensions: carved oak, 3 m high ×
 1.3 m wide × 65 cm deep
Status: not listed
Condition: good
Owner/custodian: St Richard's Hospital
 (donated by Art for St Richard's)

The central piece of the sculpture is carved from a forked branch of an ancient oak tree, carved to represent the tail, or fluke, of a whale as it dives into the depths of the sea and is surrounded by three smaller blocks of wood carved with a scroll motif and a circle of rough-hewn rocks. The whole assemblage sits in the centre of concentric circles of small pebbles and slate that depict ripples in water. The wood comes from a tree that fell in the severe gales that swept the south of England on 15/16 October 1987.

Walter Bailey, *Fluke*

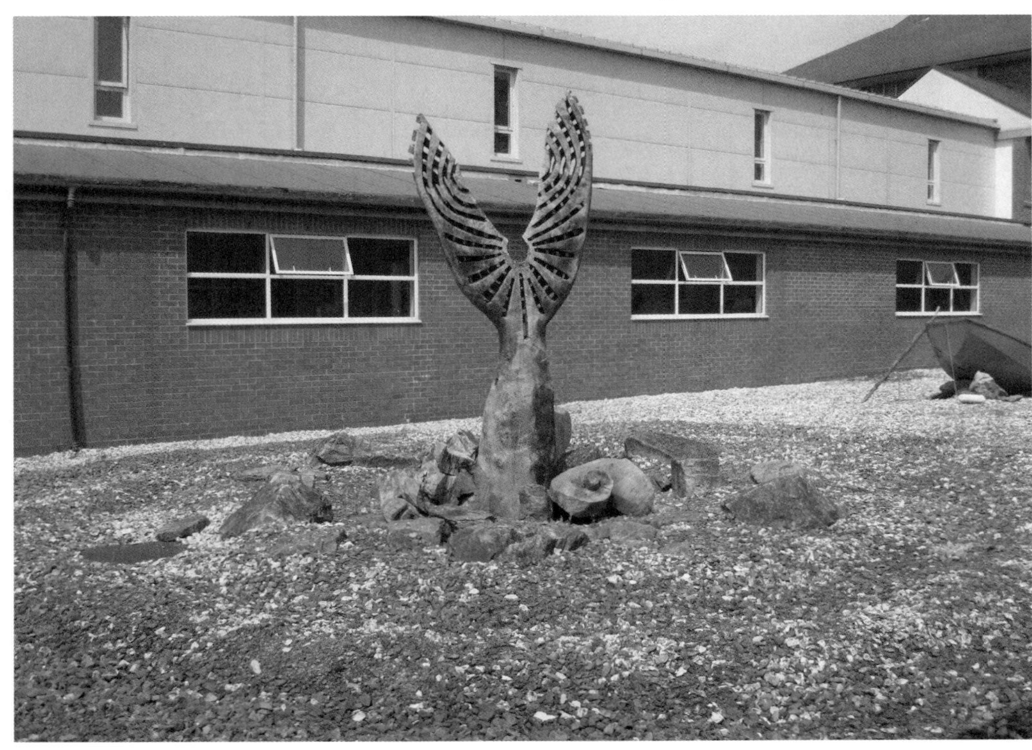

George Cutts, *Sea Change*

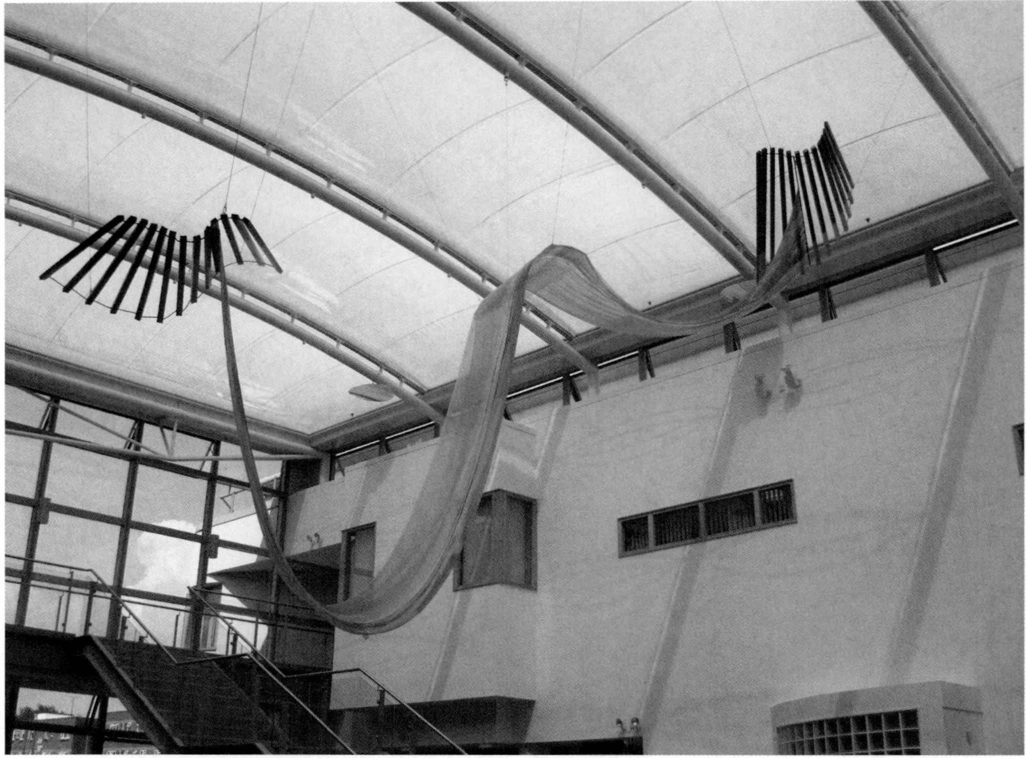

Hanging from ceiling of reception area of the Chichester Treatment Centre

Jan Blake, *Shoreline*

Shoreline

Sculptor: Jan Blake

Installed: 2005
Materials/dimensions: painted silk organza, wood and steel tension wire, 5.7 m wide × 1.2 cm deep
Status: not listed
Condition: good (in 2008, the existing and damaged painted silk was replaced with a new piece completed by the artist at the time of the original commission)
Owner/custodian: St Richard's Hospital

This sculpture hangs above the atrium of a waiting area. It consists of approximately 8 m of silk organza, painted in soft blues, yellows and greens, looped from a series of slatted wooden frames resembling beach decking. The whole structure is suggestive of the sea on the shoreline.

Jan Blake explains that her work:

… has developed from flat hand painted silk hangings to dynamic sculptural structures influenced by my designs for theatre productions; in particular dance and physical theatre. These structures, stretched with painted silk organza, transform spaces both public and domestic in scale. They have the effect of theatre transformation cloths i.e. images appear and disappear as the available light changes giving a continually changing picture according to viewpoint. The space and its use becomes the 'script' from which the ideas evolve.[5]

Notes
[1] Geoff Metcalfe, telephone conversations, 10 and 14 February 2011. [2] Vincent Gray, email correspondence, 2 December 2010. [3] *Royal Academy Exhibitors 1905–1970*, vol. III, Yorkshire, 1978, p. 6. [4] *British Contemporary Sculpture at Goodwood*, Cass Sculpture Foundation, 2002/03, p. 44. [5] ukonline.co.uk/janblake99 (accessed 23 December 2010).

Other sources
Christine Brooker (PA to Director of Planning, Royal West Sussex NHS Trust), email correspondence, 17 September 2008.
Vincent Gray, correspondence, 3 December 2005.
Foster (2004), pp. 191–3.
sculpture.org.uk (accessed 4 January 2011).
vincentgray.co.uk accessed (15 November 2010).
westernsussexhospitals.nhs.uk/about-us/st-richards-hospital/ (accessed 4 January 2011).
fieldartprojects.com (accessed 4 January 2011).

COCKING

Cocking Hill

On open ground behind Lamberts Yard and car park

Cocking History Column

Sculptors: Cocking History Group with Juliet Crawford and Philip Jackson

Constructed: 1999–2005
Unveiled: 15 April 2005
Materials/dimensions: bronze and Portland stone, 4.57 m high × 4 m wide × 4 m deep
Signatures: each of the bronze plaques has the initials of the member of the local community who made it. The two bronze parish maps have the initials JTC in the bottom right-hand corner
Inscription (west face of the plinth): THE PARISH / OF / COCKING / AD 2000
Status: not listed
Condition: good
Funded by: Heritage Lottery Fund (£21,532) and Nationwide Building Society (£1500)
Owner/custodian: Cocking Parish Council

The column, inspired by Trajan's column in Rome, weighs three-quarters of a ton, and is decorated with 48 low-relief bronze panels depicting episodes from local history that spiral downwards around it. They tell the story of the village chronologically, through images and text, from the Bronze Age at the top to the Millennium at the bottom. Between the panels a narrow ribbon of national history giving context to the Cocking events twists around the column. Two bronze relief parish maps, made by Juliet Crawford, are inset into the stone base, facing north and east. There is a lead-wrapped time capsule beneath the column.

The piece was created as part of Cocking's Millennium celebrations and the West Sussex Parish Maps Project. The Cocking History Group was planning the production of a paper map, but local resident and sculptor Philip Jackson suggested this more ambitious project. He taught 28 volunteers, who worked at home, the art of working in wax for low-relief modelling and letter carving. The panels were cast at Lasham in Hampshire.

The column was unveiled by Lady Cowdray, one of the modellers, and blessed by Cocking's vicar, Colin Bradley.[1] It won a prestigious Sussex Heritage Award, the ceremony for which took place at the De La Warr Pavilion, Bexhill on Thursday 6 July 2006.

Note
[1] Leslie, K., *A Sense of Place: West Sussex Parish Maps*, Chichester, 2006, pp. 60–62.

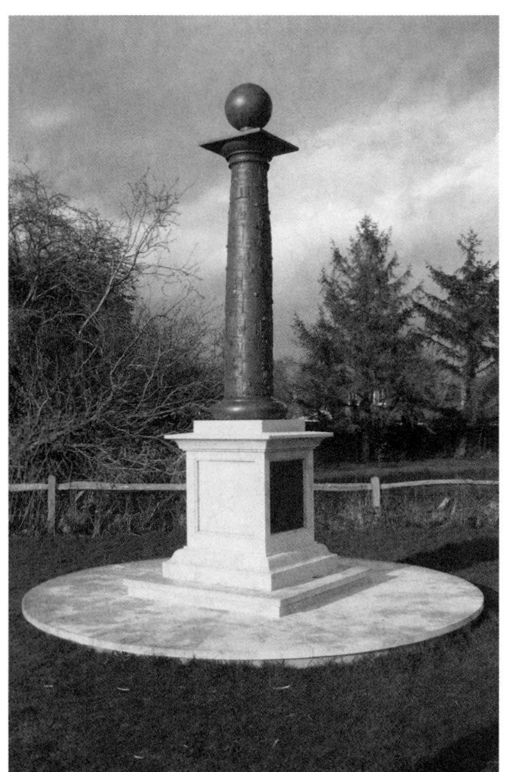

Cocking History Group, *Cocking History Column*

CRAWLEY

The Boulevard
Foyer of Town Hall

Bust of Alf Pegler
Sculptor: David Cornell

Unveiled: 15 May 1999
Materials/dimensions: bronze, 65 cm high × 55 cm wide × 30 cm deep
Signature (underneath left shoulder): David Cornell Sc.
Inscriptions (plaque to front of base): Cllr. A E PEGLER OBE. DL. / 1924–1996; (underneath right shoulder): ALF PEGLER OBE. DL
Status: not listed
Condition: good
Owner/custodian: Crawley Borough Council

The one-and-a-quarter life-size portrait bust of Councillor Alf Pegler is set on a large upright square plinth. The piece has a relaxed air, depicting Councillor Pegler in a fairly informal suit and tie.

On the front of the bust's wooden plinth is a framed information sheet about Pegler's career. He was widely known as 'Mr Crawley', serving as Leader of the Council for 18 years and as Mayor 1982–84. He was also a member of the West Sussex County Council from 1958 and was made a Deputy Lieutenant of West Sussex in 1982. He was awarded an OBE for services to housing and made a Freeman of the Borough in May 1995.

David Cornell was also commissioned to complete the first life-size statue of Sir Arthur Conan Doyle in nearby Crowborough.

Source
davidcornell.com (accessed 16 November 2010).

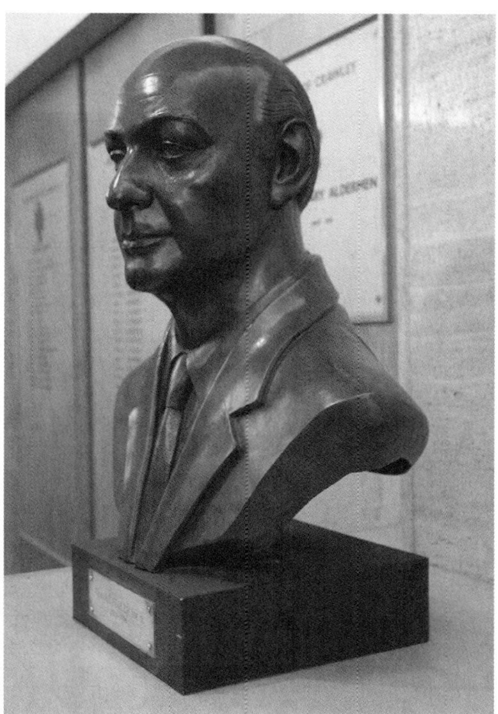

David Cornell, *Bust of Alf Pegler*

The Broadway

On wall above entrance to TJ Hughes store

Family Group
Sculptor: Richard Browne

Installed: 1959
Materials/dimensions: sculpture: bronze, 2 m
  high × 1.5 m wide × 50 cm deep; back slab:
  concrete, 3 m high × 2 m wide
Inscription (on black circular plaque
  underneath the sculpture, near to shop
  entrance): CRAWLEY ARTS COUNCIL / THE /
  ABOVE SCULPTURE, / 'FAMILY GROUP'
  ERECTED / IN 1959 AS A SYMBOL OF /
  CRAWLEY NEW TOWN, IS BY / SUSSEX
  SCULPTOR RICHARD / BROWNE / (1921–1990)
  / AWARDS FOR ALL
Status: not listed
Condition: good (covered with netting to avoid
  guano damage)
Owner/custodian: not known

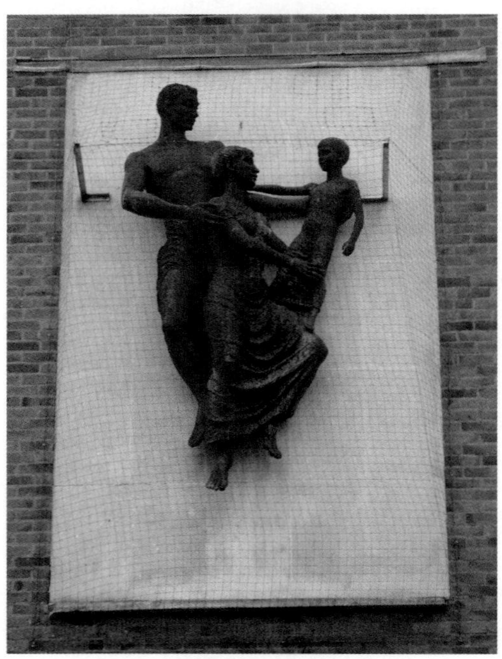

Richard Browne, *Family Group*

The composite sculpture depicts a standing man
and woman facing a small boy, who is perched
on the mother's knee. They all wear abstracted
drapery of an indeterminable period. The
sculpture is placed high up on the façade of the
building that was once the Cooperative Society
shop. The piece symbolises the enlarged
community of Crawley, which was designated a
New Town in 1947, when it had a population
of 9500, but had grown to over 50,000 by 1959
when the sculpture was erected.

Source
Crawley Arts Council, *The Crawley Heritage Trail*,
2007.

Hawth Avenue

*On roundabout opposite Weald Drive
outside the entrance to the Hawth Theatre*

Flying Spiral
Sculptor: Ray Smith

Installed: 2001
Materials/dimensions: Corten (self-weathering)
  steel, 5 m high × 3 m wide × 25 cm deep
Status: not listed
Condition: good
Commissioned and owned by: Crawley
  Borough Council

The sculpture takes the form of a large red and
rusted steel spiral ending with an abstracted
flying figure, arms outstretched. It faces
southwest and northeast in the middle of a
grassed, planted roundabout. The artist has
described the piece in the following way:

> There are three broad elements to the work.
> They are a (Celtic) spiral, a human figure
> with arms outstretched and by association,
> the ideal of a plane taking off. The link
> between the figure and the idea of the plane
> calls to mind the playground games where
> children run around with outstretched arms.
> The resulting form lends itself to a number
> of possible interpretations.[1]

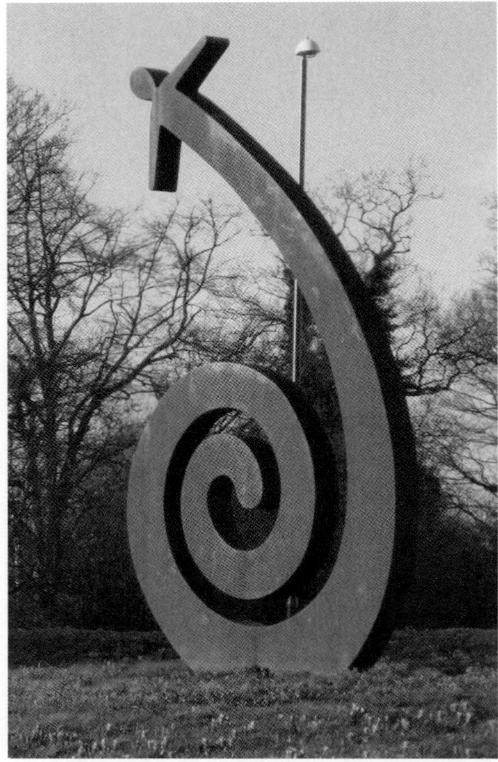

Ray Smith, *Flying Spiral*

The sculpture was the first artwork to be
commissioned for Crawley's 'Art on
Roundabouts' scheme as a result of the
Council's public art policy and strategy,
commissioned in 1995.

Note
[1] crawley.gov.uk (accessed 17 November 2010).

Other source
Lord (2008), p. 26.

Gateway to High Street

Sculptor: Kate Maddison for Chrysalis Arts Ltd

Builders: Colas Ltd

Unveiled: 11 December 1999

Materials/dimensions: steel plate hand cut and painted with blue enamel (tallest section): 2.85 m high × 1.25 m wide × 9 cm deep; (shortest section): 1.25 m high × 1.25 m wide × 9 cm deep

Signature (plaque attached to each section, bottom right): CHRYSALIS ARTS LTD / THE ART DEPOT, ASQUITH INDUSTRIAL ESTATE, / ESHTON ROAD, GARGRAVE, NORTH YORKSHIRE BD23 3SE

Inscriptions (bronze plaque attached a low, planted wall opposite the Golden Tree sculpture at the south end of High Street): HIGH STREET / CONSERVATION AREA IMPROVEMENTS / Opened 11th December 1999 / by / David Dewdney – Chairman / Highways And Transport Committee / West Sussex County Council and / Councillor Brenda Smith – Chair / Environment Committee / Crawley Borough Council / Jointly Funded and Designed By / West Sussex County Council / and Crawley Borough Council / Public Artwork – Chrysalis Arts Ltd /Main Contractor – Colas Ltd

Status: not listed

Condition: good

Owner/custodian: Crawley Borough Council

Five curvilinear steel frames on each side of the road form a low gateway to the regenerated area of the High Street. Each section contains cut-out silhouette images that refer to Crawley's past, present and future. The sections stand in a heavily planted base and recede in height towards the north.

The design of the gateway was part of an extensive £1.2 million regeneration project initiated in 1998 by Crawley Council and West Sussex County Council. Chrysalis Arts were commissioned to collaborate with council planners and engineers to refurbish the High Street. Artist Kate Maddison developed a concept based upon the town's historic importance for travellers as the halfway point between London and Brighton. Her designs also refer to the architecture of the High Street, particularly the older buildings, formed from arched timbers. Maddison and Antonia Stowe organised workshops for local people to help create images for the gates and also gathered footprint patterns from Saturday shoppers.

Chrysalis Arts designed and commissioned the fabrication of all the artwork street furniture, which included: 20 cycle racks, eight removable barriers, 11 seats, 20 gateway panels, 7 tree planters, 7 double lampposts, 19 single lampposts, 12 illuminated bollards and 102 bronze cast footprints.

This part of the High Street refurbishment scheme was completed in 1999 and a further commission was undertaken in 2000 by Charlwood developers. This involved a series of artwork railing panels, based on the same High Street design concept, for the frontage of a new building at the southern end.[1]

Note
[1] chrysalisarts.org.uk/projects_crawley (accessed 27 October 2012).

Other source
Crawley Arts Council (2007).

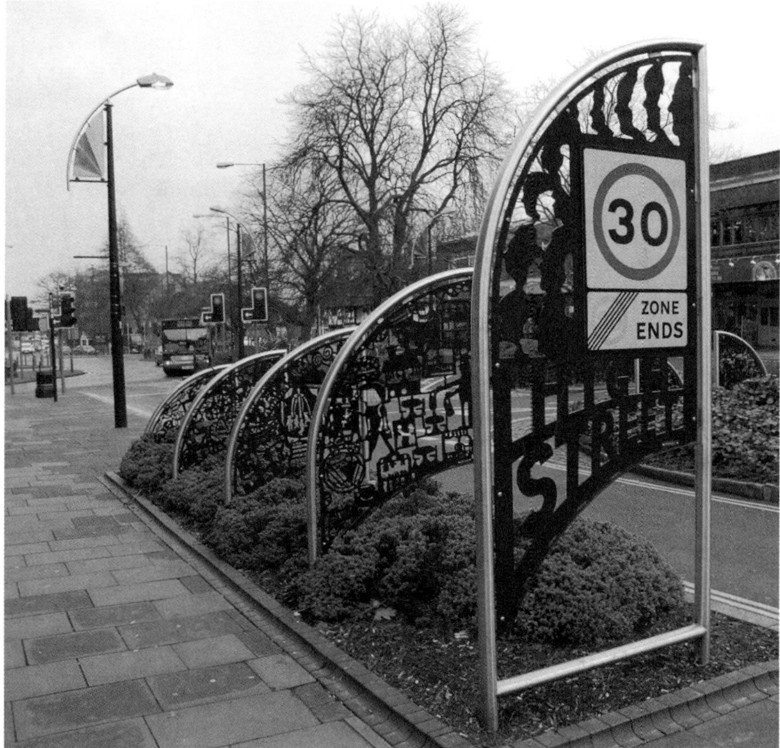

Kate Maddison,
Gateway to High Street

South end at junction with Ifield Road

The Golden Tree
Sculptor: Joss Smith

Installed: 2006

Materials/dimensions: sculpture: bronze, 2.9 m high × 1.6 m wide × 60 cm deep; pedestal: black granite, 87 cm high × 74 cm wide × 74 cm deep; acorn cup base: York sandstone, 49 cm high × 1.87 m wide × 1.87 m deep

Inscription (plaque to south face, in front of sculpture): GOLDEN TREE / JOSS SMITH –2006 / The artwork stands on the site of the town's old market cross at a time when Crawley / was an ancient junction and market place within the Weald covered once by dense / Forests. / The charcoal from these forests was used to create early iron tools such as the axe / head depicted within the bronze section of the sculpture many of which have been / found locally. / The black Granite Anvil represents the local history of iron working in the area. / The base is a York Sandstone Acorn cup to depict the Jurassic limestone under the / area and the fact that Crawley was once forest. / The sculpture is topped by two crows to remind us that Crawley was originally called / Crow Lea – a place of crows.

Status: not listed

Condition: good

Owner/custodian: Crawley Borough Council

The sculpture is in three sections; a base textured with overlapping triangular scales to represent an acorn cup; a central anvil-shaped plinth and a bronze axe-shaped sculpture atop of which are depicted two crows. The concept and iconography of the piece are comprehensively outlined in its inscription. This sculpture stands at the opposite end of the High Street to the gateway and was the final element of the refurbishment scheme.

Sources
Crawley Arts Council (2007).
Crawley Borough Council, *Public Art Supplementary Guidance Note 11*, March 2003.
crawley.gov.uk (accessed 27 October 2011).

Queens Square

In the Martlets shopping area

Martlets Tree
Sculptors: Peter Parkinson and Richard Quinnell

Installed: October 1999

Materials/dimensions: sculpture: metal, 4.5 m wide × 4.5 m deep; octagonal base with integral seating: stone, 2.5 m wide × 2.5 m deep

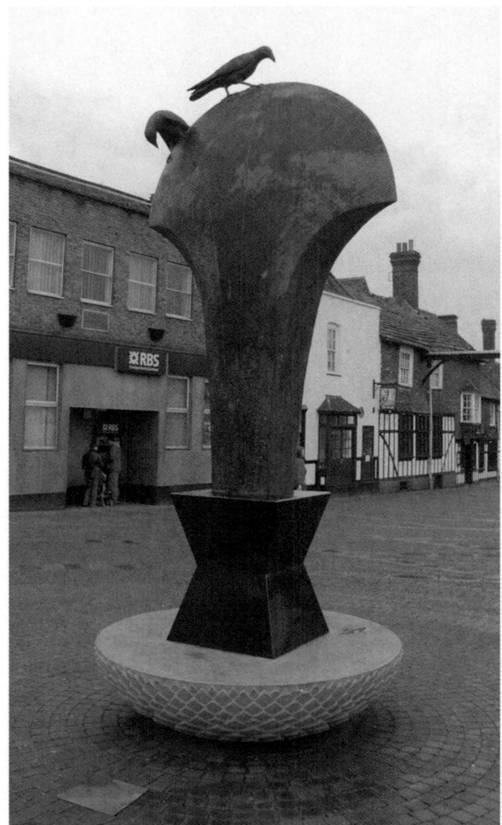

Joss Smith, *The Golden Tree*

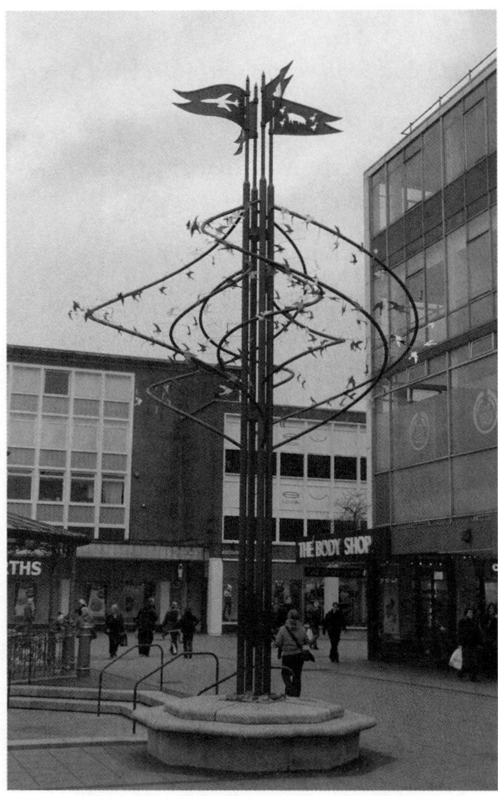

Peter Parkinson and Richard Quinnell, *Martlets Tree*

Inscription (plaque to east side): THE MARTLETS TREE / 1999 / DESIGNED BY PETER PARKINSON / MADE BY RICHARD QUINNELL / GENEROUSLY SUPPORTED BY SCOTTISH WIDOWS / WITH GRANT AID FROM SOUTH-EAST ARTS / THE WORK IS A CELEBRATION OF THE HERALDIC ORIGIN OF THE STREET NAME 'THE MARTLETS' / THE MARTLET, A MYTHICAL HERALDIC BIRD, FEATURES ON THE 13TH CENTURY COAT OF ARMS / OF THE NORMAN De ARUNDEL FAMILY, GREAT SUSSEX LANDOWNERS, AND HENCE ON / THE COATS OF ARMS OF BOTH CRAWLEY AND WEST SUSSEX COUNTY COUNCIL / THE IMAGES ON THE TREE SYMBOLISE ACTIVITIES OF HISTORICAL IMPORTANCE / TO THE PROSPERITY OF THE

Status: not listed
Condition: good
Commissioned and funded by: Scottish
Widows Insurance Company and South East
Arts under the Percent for Art scheme
Owner/custodian: Crawley Borough Council

The sculpture has four tapering staves, each
bearing a pennant with a cut-out pictorial
design bearing symbols of Crawley's history (as
detailed in the inscription), forming a central
shaft. From each stave a stylised branch swirls
around the top half of the sculpture, bearing
over 100 shiny cut-out depictions of the
mythical martlet bird loosely attached so that
they move and shimmer with the breeze.

Source
Crawley Arts Council (2007).

Tilgate Drive

*Tilgate Park, at entrance to Nature Centre
(formerly elsewhere in the park)*

Lion

Sculptor: Christian Funnell

Installed: 2000
Materials/dimensions: steel, painted green,
1.65 m high × 60 cm wide × 3.2 m
Signature (on upper surface of tail): C.F. 00.
Status: not listed
Condition: good (green paint later addition)
Owner/custodian: Crawley Borough Council

The north-facing large lion is sculpted from
interlacing strips of steel, with cut-out shapes of
butterflies around its mane. The sculpture
formerly acted as a way marker in the park, but
now stands on two railway sleepers set into the
ground outside the nature centre, home to over
500 animals of 95 species, ranging from cows

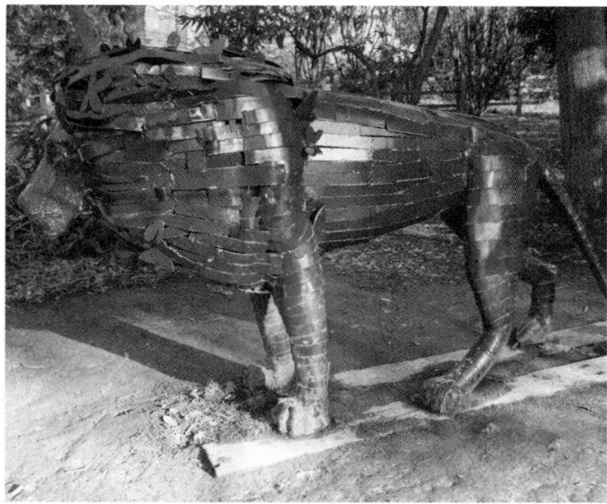

Christian Funnell, *Lion*

and cranes to frogs and pheasants. Funnell's
sculpture was one of the first of Crawley's 'Art
in the Greenway' projects.

Source
adrawingaday.co.uk/christianfunnell/ (accessed 16
November 2010).

*Tilgate Park, next to path, approximately 230 m
from lake*

Conduit and Continuum

Sculptor: Will Glanfield

Installed: 2001
Materials/dimensions: English oak, each
upright: 1.8 m high × 58 cm wide × 7 cm
deep; bench: 1.65 m high × 2.6 m wide ×
90 cm deep
Status: not listed
Condition: good
Funded by: Arts Council Regional Lottery
Award
Commissioned and owned by: Crawley
Borough Council
Conduit is composed of five curved wooden
uprights and *Continuum*, a sculptural bench of
similar design, is located 100 m away across the
parkland. The bench is visible through the holes
in the wooden uprights, on the faces of which
are carved leaves. The five native trees

represented are Common Oak, Hawthorne,
Goat Willow, Alder and Scots Pine.
Glanfield has stated that:

Both pieces reflect and transform the theme
of the other, and should be considered
together. These pieces are inspired by
thoughts on continuity, layerings and
accumulations, and aspiration in nature.
Continuum reflects the same completed
form of *Conduit* in its central element.[1]

Note
[1] willglanfield.co.uk (accessed 17 November 2010).

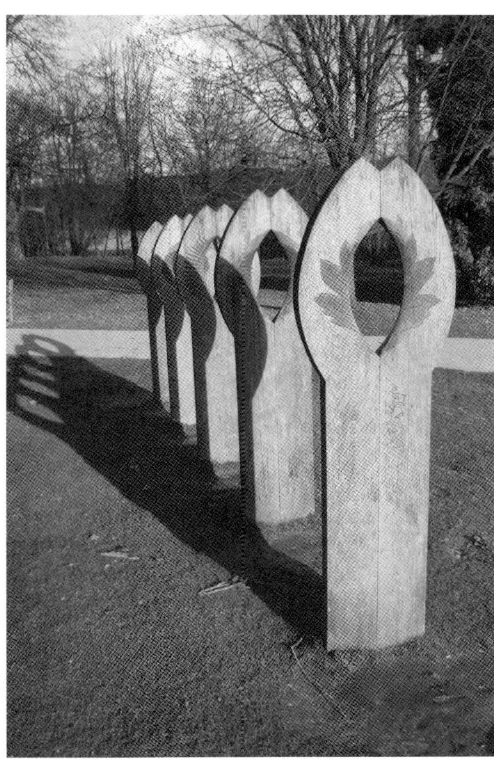

Will Glanfield, *Conduit and Continuum*

Gatwick Airport

North Terminal, within spiral ramps at each end of departure lounge

Slipstream and *Jetstream*
Sculptor: William Pye

Installed: 1988
Materials/dimensions: mirror-polished stainless
    steel, each cone 4 m high × 6.8 m diam.
    Overall diam. 8.4 m
Status: not listed
Condition: good
Commissioned by: Gatwick Airport Ltd
    through the Design Working Group
    comprising representatives of BAA, the
    Conran Design Group and architects YRM
Owner/custodian: Gatwick Airport

The twin sculptures are asymmetrical cones,
with off-centre apexes. Their titles refer to both
water and flight:

> …with connotations of jet and rocket
> propulsion and vapour trails, wakes and
> washes, reinforcing the imaginative
> suggestions born of the formal combination
> of nose cones and moving water.[1]

Each has been constructed from 46 steel sheets
fastened to a wigwam-like structure of wooden
ribs. Water is supplied to the cones from two
500-gallon tanks, suspended from the floor
joists below each piece, by means of two
pumps, at a rate of 500 gallons per minute. The
water flows in a thin film down the surface of
each sculpture, exploiting the effect of 'lamina
flow' by which surface tension creates rhythmic
wave patterns. It runs off the cones into shallow
circular pools, which in turn overflow at the
edges, giving the illusion that the cones are
floating on flat discs of water. Pye has stated
that his inspiration came from his observation
of patterns of rainwater running down a road in
the Black Mountains in mid Wales.[2]

The new north terminal at Gatwick airport
was opened by HM the Queen on 18 March

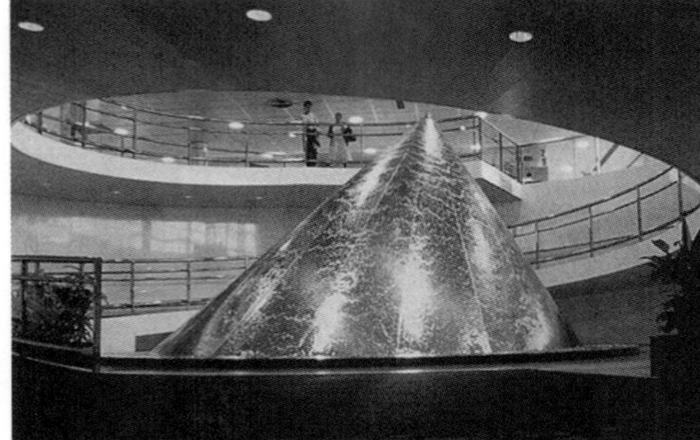

William Pye, *Slipstream*

1988. Passengers departing from the terminal
walk down the ramps that encircle the
sculptures, which ensures that they are seen by
thousands of people every day.[3] They received
considerable critical acclaim and received
awards from the Wapping Arts Trust (for the
best site specific commission of 1988) and the
association of Business Sponsorship of the Arts
(for the best commission of new art in any
medium 1988).[4]

Throughout his career, William Pye has
explored the use of flowing water in sculpture.[5]
He provided an additional sculpture, entitled
Aquabar, for the North Terminal departure
lounge in 2003. It comprises three transparent
vessels of different diameters, where water rises
and falls in programmed cycles. As the water
rises an air-core vortex forms in each vessel and
water finally overflows the perimeter edge to
ripple down the vertical sides.

Notes
[1] Pye, W., *Water Sculpture at Gatwick Airport*,
London, 1988. [2] Ibid. [3] williampye.com (accessed
22 April 2013). [4] See, for example, Glancey, J.,
'Terminal shopping', *RIBA Journal*, vol. 95, no. 6,
June 1988, pp. 26–29. [5] An interesting example, in
East Sussex, of Pye's use of water within the
landscape can be found at Clinton Lodge gardens,
Fletching, which may be visited through the National
Garden scheme open days. http://www.clintonlodge
gardens.co.uk (accessed 22 April 2013).

Other source
Daniele Harwood (assistant to William Pye), email
    correspondence, 17 April 2013.

Church Platt

Parish Church of Holy Trinity

The present church originated with a small
chapel in the thirteenth century, which was
extended in the succeeding two centuries. In the
sixteenth century the Sergison (or mortuary)
chapel was built adjoining the north chapel and
was gifted to the church in 1888. The architect
G.F. Bodley restored the church in 1855–56 and
the interior was magnificently decorated with a
painted ceiling and stained glass by his pupil
C.E. Kempe, who lived in nearby Lindfield.

To left of main altar
Monument to Charles Sergison
Sculptor: Thomas Ayde[1]

Constructed: 1734
Materials/dimensions: white and grey marble,
    3.8 m high × 2.17 m wide × 70 cm deep
Signature (on edge of portrait medallion): Tho.
    ADEY. SCULPT. IT.
Inscription (on left-hand side of panel on base):
    Near this Place lyeth Interred ye Body of /
    CHARLES SERGISON Esqr. Of Cuckfield Place,
    / who departed this life Novr. ye 26th. 1732
    Aged 78. / He was initiated into ye Civil
    Government / of the Royal Navy in the Year
    1671, / as a Clerk in one of His Majesty's
    Yards, / & laudably Served through Several
    Offices / till the Year 1719 (namely 48 Years)
    / 35 of which as a Principal Officer and /
    Commissioner to the Satisfaction of / the
    Several Kings and Queens, and their /
    greatest Ministers, and all his Superiors, /
    about which time the Civil Government / of
    the Navy being put into Military hands, / he
    was esteem'd, by them, not a fit person / to
    serve any longer; (right-hand side of panel
    on base): He was a Gentleman of great
    Capacity & Penetration / exact Judgment, /
    close Application to Business / Strict

Integrity: / These Virtues compleatly
qualify'd him for t/y [that] Post which he so
well fill'd, so long enjoy'd / In those who
serv'd under him. Merit alone recommended
/ Fidelity and Diligence were rewarded, /
which gain'd him Respect, Esteem and
Honour. / He serv'd his Country in several
Parliaments, where like a true Patriot, / he
consulted only ye real Interest of ye Nation,
without any particular views of his own. / In
private Life He observ'd Justice & Probity /
was Affectionate to his Relations / Peaceable
to his Neighbours / Kind and Beneficent to
his Servants / And in every Station an
Honest Man
Status: not listed
Condition: good

On the sarcophagus is a seated female figure,
with swirling baroque drapery, symbolising
truth, looking at her reflection in a hand mirror
that she holds in her right hand. Her left hand
rests on the top of a large medallion with a
profile relief portrait of Charles Sergison that is
supported on her raised left knee. To her left a
naked seated cherub helps support the
medallion, a memorial form made popular by
James Gibbs.[2] At the top of the back slab is a
white marble relief of the Sergison coat of arms.
The whole rests on a tomb-like pedestal that
has an inscribed panel to the front.

Charles Sergison purchased Cuckfield Park
in 1691, the same year that he was granted the
coat of arms with a dolphin crest, and it
remained in the family until 1968. By 1800 the
Sergison family owned 41 properties in
Cuckfield. Sergison was, aged 17, a junior in
one of the naval dockyards and became Chief
Clerk to John Pepys, the brother of the diarist.
He rose to become one of the four Principals in
control of the navy and he served for 48 years
under William III, Queen Anne and George I.
He was aggrieved by being forced to retire at 65
years old. During his retirement he collected
folios of Minutes of the Navy Board, now
known as The Sergison Papers and published

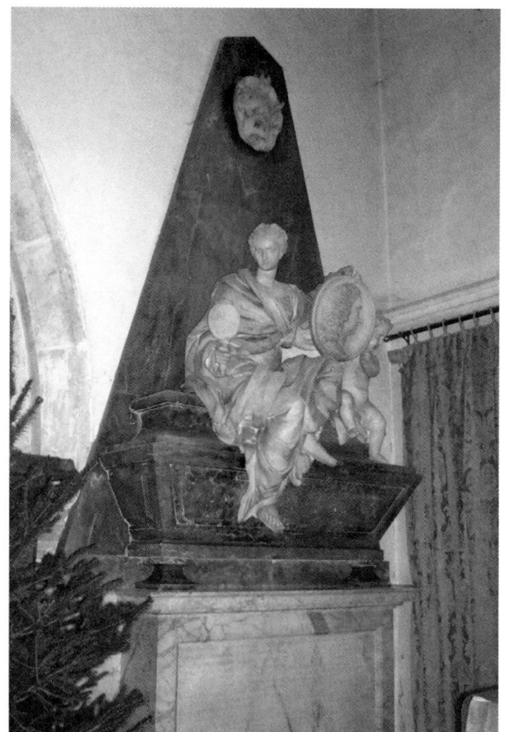

Thomas Ayde, *Monument to Charles Sergison*

by the Naval Records Society. His papers are
now in the Royal Maritime Museum in
Greenwich.

Sergison's will directed that his body, '… be
decently interred in my burying place in the
chancel of the parish church', and '… a
monument be set up on the north side of the
chancel'.[3] The Rev Daniel Walter who
dominated Cuckfield for nearly half a century
(1713–61), refused permission for the erection
of the monument overshadowing the altar but
Sergison's heir called a vestry meeting and
enlisted the support of several inhabitants to
overturn his decision.[4]

There is a monument to Sergison's daughter-
in-law, Mary Ann, who died in 1804, designed
by Richard Westmacott, over the north door of
the church. It depicts a woman weeping over an

urn, in Westmacott's, '… early "severe" style …'.[5]

South aisle, southeast corner
Monument to Captain Percy Burrell
Sculptor: John Bacon (the younger)

Installed: 1810
Materials/dimensions: white and grey marble,
3 m high × 1.55 m wide × 17 cm deep
Signature (bottom right): J. BACON, Junr.
Sculptor, / LONDON, 1810
Inscription (underneath figures): SACRED TO
THE MEMORY OF PERCY BURRELL. / CAPTAIN
IN THE SIXTH REGIMENT OF DRAGOON –
GUARDS, / FOURTH SON OF SIR WILLIAM
BURRELL BART. OF KNEPP IN THE COUNTY OF
SUSSEX. / AND SOPHIA ELDEST DAUGHTER OF
SIR CHARLES RAYMOND BART. / THIS GALLANT
OFFICER WAS BORN ON THE 5TH OF JULY
1779, / AND AT THE ILLCONCERTED AND
FATAL ATTACK ON BUENOS-AYRES ON THE
5TH OF JULY 1807, / AFFORDED AN EXAMPLE
OF THAT SELF DEVOTION, SO FREQUENT IN
THE MILITARY ANNALS / OF HIS COUNTRY:
FOR WHILST LEADING THE COLUMN OF
DISMOUNTED CAVALRY / AFTER THE
UNTIMELY FALL OF HIS SUPERIOR OFFICER LT.
COL. KINGTON. AND / WHILST IN THE ACT OF
ENCOURAGING BY HIS INTREPID EXAMPLE /
THE EXERTIONS OF HIS MEN, WHO WERE
EXPOSED TO A MOST DESTRUCTIVE FIRE, / HE
WAS MORTALLY WOUNDED BY A MUSKET
SHOT. / THUS FELL IN THE CAREER OF HONOR
AND THE PRIME OF LIFE, / THIS BRAVE AND
ACCOMPLISHED GENTLEMAN, REGRETTED
AND LAMENTED / BY ALL WHO KNEW THE
EXCELLENT QUALITIES OF HIS HEART AND
MIND. / AND BY NONE MORE TRULY THAN HIS
FELLOW SOLDIERS. / HIS TWO SURVIVING
BROTHERS HAVE CAUSED THIS MONUMENT TO
BE ERECTED. / AS A TRIBUTE OF RESPECT TO
DEPARTED WORTH. / AND A MOURNFUL
TESTIMONY OF THEIR FRATERNAL AFFECTION.
Status: not known
Condition: good (but small chip to the right of

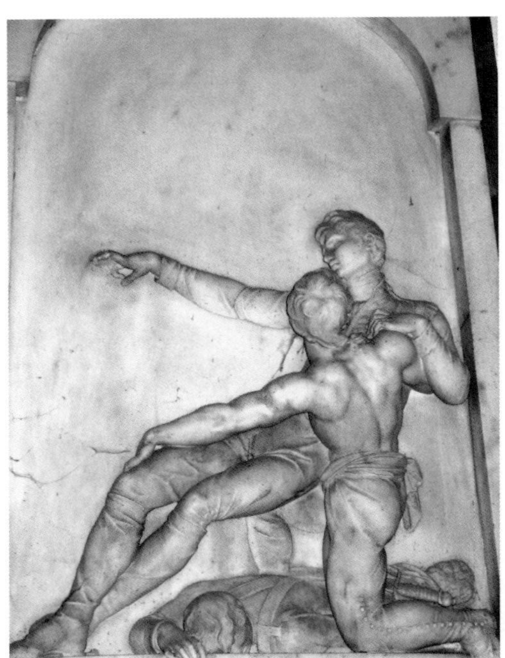

John Bacon, *Monument to Captain Percy Burrell*

signature and crest at base of monument is cracked across its full width)
Commissioned by: two surviving brothers of Percy Burrell
Owner/custodian: Parish Church of Holy Trinity

The sculptural relief of three male figures is set upon a large rectangular base that bears an inscribed panel, underneath which is the family coat of arms surrounded by a lion skin. The whole structure is surmounted by an urn in relief. The figures depict a scene from the assault on Buenos Aires in 1807. One figure lies dead, face down on the ground. Another is on one knee supporting the dying or dead figure of Percy Burrell in his arms.

The inscription criticises the army command for its handling of the battle in which Burrell was killed.[6]

There are 13 monuments in the church to members of the Burrell family, who made their fortunes as ironmasters and later lived in Cuckfield at the Elizabethan Ockenden House.[7]

Western porch, above door to clock tower
Kennedy War Memorial
Sculptor: Fillipo Lovatelli (attributed)

Installed: c. 1936
Materials/dimensions: white, honey-coloured and grey marble, 1.5 m high × 1.8 m wide × 20 cm deep
Inscriptions (left-hand panel, inscribed in gilt letters): TO MY BELOVED SON PAUL ADRIAN / THE RIFLE BRIGADE BORN 11 DEC 1886 / KILLED AT FROMELLES 9 MAY 1915 / THIRD SON OF SIR JOHN. G. KENNEDY K.C.M.G. / FILI MI, FILI MI, QUIS MIHI TRIBUAT UT EGO / MORIAR PRO TE, FILI MI, FILI MI? (My son, my son, would that I had died for thee, my son, my son, II Samuel 18:33 Vulgata.); (middle panel, inscribed in gilt letters): TO MY DEARLY LOVED SON ARCHIBALD EDWARD / CAPTAIN 93RD ARGYLL & SUTHERLAND HIGHLANDERS / BORN 7 SEPT. 1878 KILLED AT LE CATEAU / 26 AUG. 1914 ELDEST SON OF SIR JOHN. G. / KENNEDY. K.C.M.G. / THE LORD KNOWETH THEM THAT ARE HIS; (right-hand panel, inscribed in gilt letters): TO MY DARLING SON JOHN PATRICK FRANCIS / THE RIFLE BRIGADE BORN 28 SEPT. 1891 / KILLED AT VILLERS BRETONNEUX 24 APRIL 1918 / YOUNGEST SON OF SIR JOHN G. / KENNEDY K.C.M.G. / CAUSA ALIIS VITA CUR FRUERENTUR ERAT; (underneath, in one line extending across all three panels in gilt letters): IN THANKFUL REMEMBRANCE OF THEIR LIVES AND PROUD REMEMBRANCE OF THEIR DEATH. THEIR LOVING MOTHER
Status: not listed
Condition: good
Commissioned by: Sir John G. Kennedy, KCMG and Evelyn Adela Bootle-

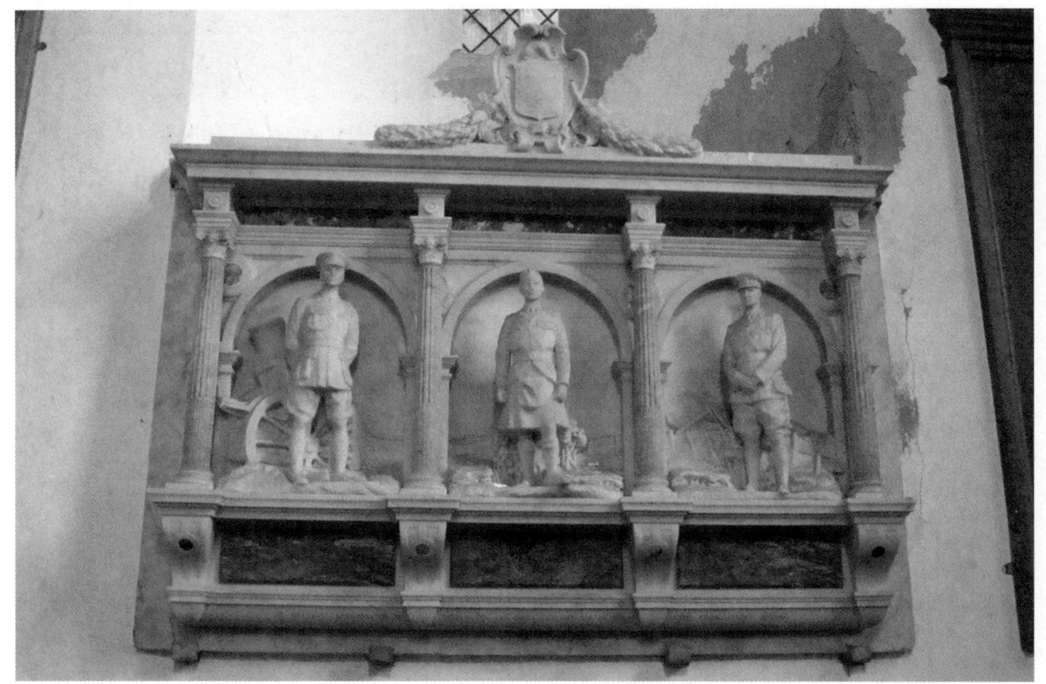

Fillipo Lovatelli (attrib.), *Kennedy War Memorial*

Wilbraham (parents)
Owner/custodian: Parish Church of Holy
Trinity

This memorial to three brothers killed in the
First World War takes the form of a large
architectural wall-mounted panel, supported by
four carved brackets, between which are panels
bearing the inscriptions, and supported by the
Kennedy family crest. Rising above these are
four Corinthian columns, which separate three
arched panels from which project three-
dimensional full-length portrait sculptures of
the Kennedy brothers, each depicted in
uniform, against a battlefield setting.

Paul Adrian Kennedy is named on the
Ploegsteert Memorial, near Ypres, Belgium and
has no known grave. He was 28 years old.
Archibald Edward Kennedy is buried in Le
Cateau Military Cemetery near Cambrai. He
was 35 years old. John Patrick Francis Kennedy
is buried in Crucifix Corner Cemetery, Villers-
Bretonneux on the Somme. He was 26 years
old.

The Faculty of the Diocese of Chichester,
granting permission to Lady Kennedy to erect
the memorial to her sons, describes it as '…
measuring approximately seven feet by five feet
… to the design of Lovatelli of Rome.'[8] The
finished piece, however, bears no signature.

Notes
[1] 'Adey' is spelled 'ADYE' in most sources; see
Whinney (1964), p. 127; Gunnis (1953), p. 15.
[2] Whinney (1964). [3] Wright, M., *A Chronicle of
Cuckfield*, Cuckfield, 1991 edn, p. 125. [4] Ibid.
[5] Busco (1994), p. 131. [6] Arscott (1997), p. 50.
[7] *Parish Church of Holy Trinity Cuckfield*,
Cuckfield, revised edn, 2005. [8] West Sussex Record
Office Par 301/4/51. Count Fillipo Lovatelli was a
flamboyant figure in Roman society during this
period; see *New York Times*, 24 and 26 February
1922.

Other source
masonicgreatwarproject.org.uk (accessed 15 October
2012).

Petworth Road

*Priory Church of St Mary, in chapel at east
end of south aisle (previously in the
Montague Chapel, St Mary Magdalene and
St Denys Parish Church, Midhurst, moved
1851)*

Monument to Sir Anthony Browne
Sculptor: Garret Johnson (attributed)

Installed: sixteenth century
Materials/dimensions: marble and alabaster,
painted and gilded, 3.45 m high × 3 m wide ×
1.95 m deep
Inscriptions (above middle arch, plaque with
inset lead letters): HERE LYETH YE BODYE OF
YE RIGHT HONORABLE / ANTHONIE BROWNE
VICOUNT MOUNTAGUE CHIEFE
/STANDARDBEARER OF ENGLAND & KNIGHT OF
YE / HONORABLE ORDER OF YE GARTER
WHEREOF HE WAS / ANCIENST AT HIS DEATH &
ONE OF YE HONORABLE / PRIVYE COUNCELL
TO QUEEN MARIE WHO AS HE / WAS NOBLYE
DESCENDED FROM YE LADYE LUCYE / HIS
GRANDMOTHER ONE OF YE DAUGHTERS & CO-
/ HEYRES OF LORD JOHN NEVILL MARQUES
MOUN- / TAGUE SO HE WAS PERFECTLY
ADORNED WITH ALL / YE VIRTUES OF TRUE
NOBILITYE & IN YE 66 YERE OF HIS AGE HE
ENDED HIS LYFE AT HIS HOWSE AT / HORSLEY
IN SURREY YE 19 OF OCTOBER 1522 & IN YE 34
YERE OF YE RAIGNE OF OURE MOST /
SOVERAIGNE LADY *Q* ELIZABETH; (front of
sarcophagus, on left-hand plaque with inset
lead letters): HERE LYETH YE BODIE OF YE
LADYE JANE RATCLIFFE ONE OF / YE
DAUGHTERS OF ROBART EARL OF SUSSEX WHO
ENDED / HER LYFE AT COWDRY Ao Do 1552
YE 22 OF JULYE & WAS OF YE AGE OF 20
YEARES & YE FIRST WYFFE OF ANTHONY /
VICOUNT MOUNTAGUE HERE BURYED BY
WHOME HE HAD ISSUE / ONE SONNE ANTHONY
BROWNE ESQUIER DECEASED & HERE /

LIKEWISE BURIED WHICH ANTHONY WAS
FATHER UNTO AN- / THONY VICOUNT
MOUNTAGUE NOW LIVINGE * HE HAD ALSO /
BY HER ONE DAUGHTER MARYE BROWNE YET
LIVINGE WHO / WAS MARIED FIRST TO HENRY
WRYTHEOSTEY EARLE OF / SOUTHAMPTON &
AFTER TO SR THOMAS HENEAGE / KNIGHT
VICE-CHAMBERLAN TO *Q* ELIZABETH & ONE
OF YE HONORABLE / PRIVIE COUNCELL; (front
of sarcophagus, middle plaque with inset lead
letters): THIS HONORABLE MAN IN YE YERE
1553 WAS / IMPLOYED BY Q MARIE IN AN
HONORABLE / AMBASSAGE TO ROME WITH
DOCTOR THYRL- / BIE BISSHOPE OF ELYE
WHICH HE PERFORMED / TO HIS GREATE
HONOR & COMMENDATION/ & YE SECONDE
YERE AFTER HE SERVED Q / MARIE AS HER
MAJESTIES LIEUTENANT / OF YE ENGLISH
FORCES AT YE SIEGE OF ST. QUINTINES* / IN YE
YERE 1559 Q ELYZABETH SENT / HIM
AMBASSADOUR INTO SPAINE TO KINGE /
PHILIPP & LIKEWISE 1565 & 1566 TO YE
DUCHES / OF PARMA THEN REGENT OF YE
LOWE / COUNTRIES ALL WHICH HE EFFECTED /
BOTH WISELYE & HONORABLYE TO YE SERVICE
OF GOD HIS PRINCE & COUNTRIE; (front of
sarcophagus, right-hand plaque with inset
lead letters): ANTHONY VICOUNT MOUNTAGUE
TOOK TO HIS / SECONDE WYFFE MAGDALEN
DACRE ONE OF YE / DAUGHTERS OF WILLIAM
DACRE KNIGHT LORD / DACRE, GRAYSTOCK &
GYLESLAND, & LORD WARDEN / OF YE WEST
MARCHES OF ENGLAND FOR ANEMPSTE
SCOTELANDE, BY WHOME HE HAD ISSUE *5*
SONNES / PHILIPP WILLIAM SR. GEORGE
BROWNE KNIGHT, / THOMAS & HENRYE & *3*
DAUGHTERS, ELIZABETH / MABELL, & JANE
WHEROF PHILIPP WILLIAM / THOMAS &
MABELL DEPARTED THIS / LYFF BEFORE THEIR
FATHER; (brass inscribed plaque with painted
letters, affixed to wall to right of tomb): THE
MONUMENT IN MEMORY OF SIR ANTHONY
BROWNE / FIRST VISCOUNT MOUNTAGUE K.G. /
WHO DIED 19TH. OCTOBER 1592 AGED 65 /
FORMERLY STOOD OVER THE FAMILY VAULT IN
THE / CHANCEL OF THE PARISH CHURCH OF

Status: not listed

Condition: fair (when the monument was
moved, due to lack of space in the Midhurst
church, in 1851, it was severely damaged and
altered. It was not originally a mural tomb
but was surrounded by iron railings and a
large obelisk stood at each corner. The plinth
was also severely reduced and the placement
of the three figures altered. The small statue
on the right of the sarcophagus is missing its
head, hands and the corner of the base. The
ram at the foot of the recumbent figures has
its collar chain chipped and nose damaged.
The small statue to the back of the kneeling
figure is broken in half. The painted surfaces
show signs of wear)

Commissioned by: the Montague family

Owner/custodian: Priory Church of St Mary

The monument to Anthony, Viscount
Montague and his two wives occupies the east
end of the church. It is in two stages; the higher,
eastern one has three semicircular arches
supporting a slab on which, before a cubical
block bearing his epitaph, kneels the effigy of
the viscount, bareheaded, bearded, and wearing
a ruff and the mantle and collar of the Order of
the Garter over armour. On the lower stage,
west of this, on a chest tomb, rest the effigies of
his two wives, Jane Ratcliffe and Magdalen

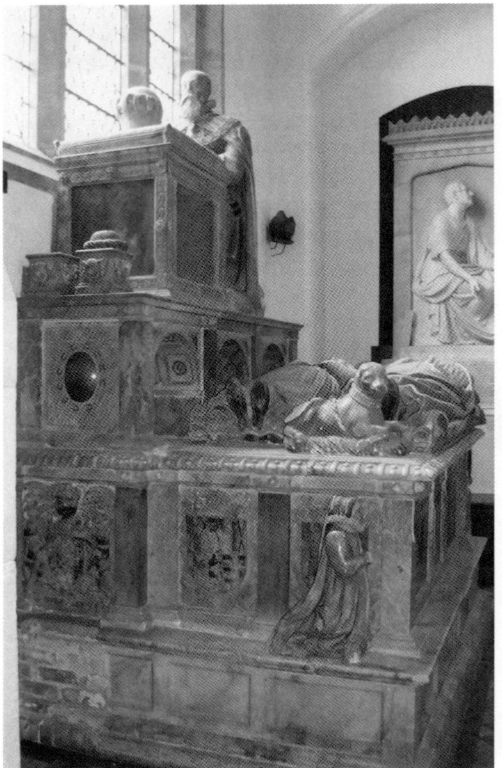

Garret Johnson (attrib.), *Monument to Sir Anthony
Browne*

Dacre, in mantles and kirtles; on the front of
this tomb are their epitaphs and at each end are
small kneeling effigies of their descendants.[1]

Sir Anthony Browne was Chief Standard-
Bearer of England, and was created Lord
Montague by Queen Elizabeth, who was his
guest for a week at Cowdray Park in Midhurst,
one of England's most important early Tudor
houses, that was partially destroyed by fire in
1793.[2]

To the right of the Browne monument, in
twin niches, are wall-mounted monuments to
Elizabeth Mary Poyntz, only sister of the last
Lord Montague and her husband William
Stephen Poyntz. They are conventional white
marble neoclassical seated relief portraits; that

of Lady Elizabeth, mourning the drowning of
their two sons, was completed in 1839 by
Francis Chantrey and that of her husband by
Raffaele Monti in 1848.

Notes
[1] Salzman, L.F. (ed.), 'Easebourne', *A History of the
County of Sussex: Volume 4: The Rape of Chichester*,
London, 1953, pp. 47–53. [2] cowdray.org.uk
(accessed 3 November 2010).

Other source
yeoldesussexpages.com/churches (accessed 6 April
2008).

EASTERGATE

Nyton Road

*On roundabout at junction with Fontwell
Avenue and Barnham Road*

War Memorial

Sculptor: Morris Harding

Unveiled: 19 December 1920

Materials/dimensions: upper section including
lion: stone, 2.6 m high × 69 cm wide × 1.7 m
deep; lower section: stone, 80 cm high ×
87 cm wide × 1.75 m deep

Signature (on upper section of northern face in
carved letters): MORRIS-HARDING. R.B.S. SC. /
LONDON. 1920

Inscriptions (within carved wreath underneath
lion's paws to western face, in Art Nouveau
script): FOR / VALOUR (carved letters to
western face, underneath wreath): ERECTED
TO / THE GLORIOUS / MEMORY OF / THE MEN
OF / EASTERGATE / WHO LAID /DOWN THEIR /
LIVES FOR / THEIR COUNTRY / IN THE GREAT /
WAR 1914–1918

Status: Grade II

Condition: good (but slight chipping to parts of
each side)

Owner/custodian: Eastergate Parish Council

The catafalque-shaped monument is built of
solid blocks, six courses in height, with the top

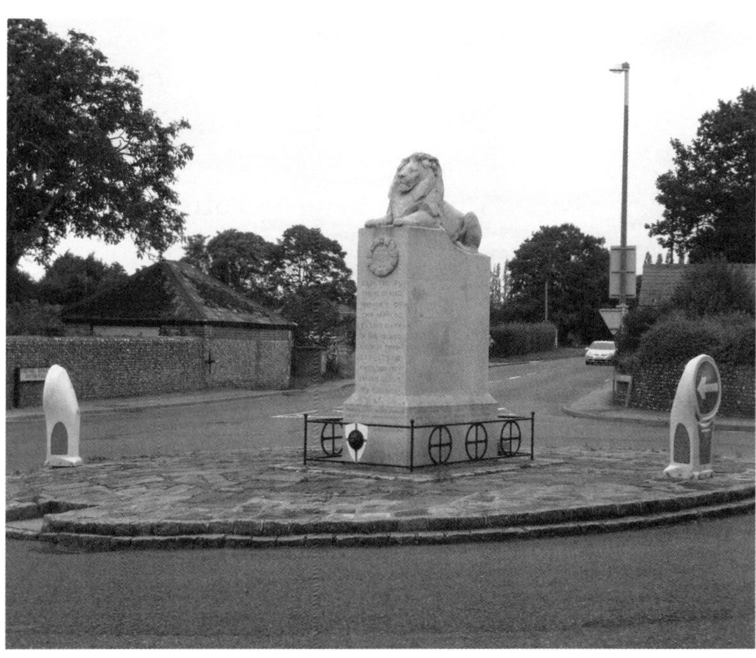

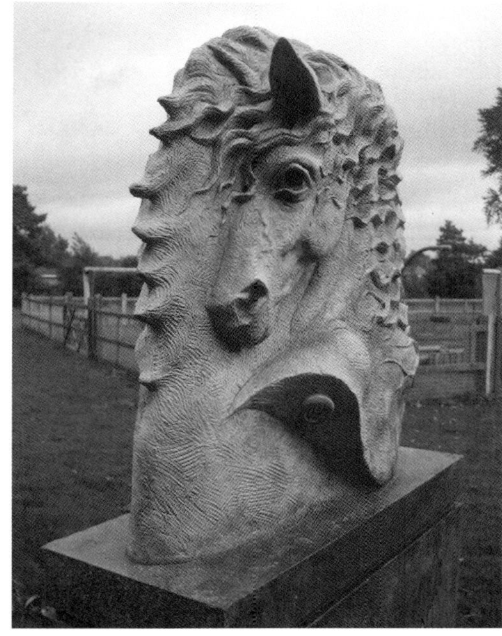

(left) Morris Harding,
War Memorial

(right) Vincent Gray,
*Memorial to Lucy and
Rebecca Hassell*

course shaped to represent a mound on which a full-sized lion sits, facing west The figure is ruggedly modelled, with a realistic touch in the tail hanging down over the monument at the rear. Harding established a reputation for his animal modelling, which he further developed in his major work at St Anne's cathedral in Belfast. He became a member of the Society of Animal Painters in 1921.[1]

A dedicatory inscription is carved to the front (west) of the memorial underneath a wreath, with names of the fallen carved into the sides of the lower section. The memorial was unveiled by the Duke of Richmond and Gordon. The listing details describe it as '… a dignified piece of symbolism, somewhat in the manner of Lutyens, highly original in concept and imaginatively sited'.[2]

New names of the fallen from the Second World War were added to the upper section of the northern face in 2008. The memorial was originally surrounded by a chain hung from 10 German gun barrels, which were removed for scrap in 1940. They have been replaced in the last few years by low metal railings around the base.

Notes
[1] belfastcathedral.org/heritage/artists-and-sculptors (accessed 16 October 2012). [2] britishlistedbuildings. co.uk (accessed 18 November 2010).

Blackboy Lane

Next to Fishbourne Club and Fishbourne Pre-School

Memorial to Lucy and Rebecca Hassell

Sculptor: Vincent Gray

Unveiled: 3 June 2007
Materials/dimensions: sculpture: glass-reinforced plastic (GRP), 63 cm high × 64 cm wide × 22 cm deep; pedestal: GRP, 1.25 m high × 70 cm wide × 26 cm deep

Signature (underneath neck of horse on north side): VG; (underneath neck of horse on south side): 07
Inscriptions (carved into plinth on south side): QUEM DI DILIGUNT / ADOLESCENS MORITUR (Whom the gods love dies young) / Herein are held treasured thoughts / of Beckie and Lucy; (carved into plinth on north side): SILENTIUM AMORIS (the silence of love) / Together in our hearts we remember / two spirits entwined for eternity; (inscribed on silver and black plaque in front of plinth on south side): IN / LOVING MEMORY / OF / two sisters / LUCY ALICE HASSELL / born 22 May 1993 / REBECCA AMY HASSELL / born 29 June 1990 who were tragically lost in a car accident / 15th. October 2005; (inscribed on silver and black plaque in front of plinth on north side): This sculptured memorial by Vincent Gray ARBS / was commissioned by / Eva Parker-Knight / and funded by monies raised from a / dance tribute show performed and aided / by Beckie's and Lucy's close friends

Status: not listed
Condition: good
Commissioned by: Eva Parker-Knight (friend of the sisters)
Funded by: friends and family
Owner/custodian: Hassell family

A tall, rectangular inscribed pedestal is surmounted by a sculpture of two horses' heads, facing in opposite directions with manes streaming behind. The design was chosen to reflect the girls' love of horse riding. Their mother said:

> … it shows that although they were separate people they were also united and shows them running free. We like to think of them as riding across the back of the Downs.[1]

Inside the pedestal was placed a time-capsule containing letters, photos and trinkets from friends and family of the two girls. The whole piece is coloured in a light and dark blue and set into a circular base of broken blue slate on a grassed area next to a children's play park. In this area are two memorial plaques, one at the base of each of the two inscribed sides of the pedestal. Adjacent to the memorial statue is a wooden bench with another inscribed plaque. The memorial was unveiled by the Duchess of Richmond and around 100 people attended to light candles and lay roses.

Note
[1] 'Sculpture unveiled in memory of sisters', *West Sussex Gazette*, 4 June 2007.

Other source
'Tributes to two special angels', *The Argus*, 25 October 2005.

Goodwood Estate

The original Goodwood House was built in the seventeenth century by the 9th Earl of Northumberland, whose main home was nearby Petworth. Following additions to the brick Jacobean house by Colen Campbell, it was sold to the 1st Duke of Richmond and passed down through the family, becoming more classicised in appearance in the eighteenth century due to remodelling by Matthew Brettingham. Following a fire at Richmond House in London in 1791, two large Regency-style wings were added in order that the extensive collections of art treasures amassed by the 2nd and 3rd Earls could be accommodated in their Sussex country house. The interiors have been restored to their original Regency splendour by the current Duke.

A number of accomplished marble portrait busts, mainly of previous Dukes of Richmond, are displayed in the principal rooms. These include two by Joseph Nollekens (1737–1823)[1] and one by Henry Weekes (1807–1877).[2] There are also some copies after the antique, most notably a half-length of the Apollo Belvedere by Joseph Wilton (1722–1803), commissioned for Richmond House. In the drawing room is a marble group of two dogs by Ann Seymour Damer (1749–1828), half-sister of the 3rd Duchess.[3]

The Goodwood estate comprises nearly 12,000 acres, some of which continue to be farmed, while 180 acres have been turned into a Country Park open to the public, in which a hotel and country club are sited. The first private race meeting was held by the 3rd Duke in 1801, who then turned it into a permanent fixture. The estate also accommodates the aerodrome, formerly a Second World War fighter station and subsequently a private airfield and the motor racing circuit, founded by the 9th Duke in 1948.

Claypit Lane
Goodwood Motor Circuit and Aerodrome

On grassed area next to the Aero Club
Statue of Douglas Bader
Sculptor: Kenneth Potts

Unveiled: 9 August 2001
Materials/dimensions: bronze, 2.08 m high × 1.22 m wide × 94 cm deep
Signature (on upper surface of integral bronze base, on back of statue in carved letters): Kenneth Potts 2001
Inscription (on upper surface of the integral bronze base, on front of the statue in raised letters): WING COMMANDER DOUGLAS BADER DSO & BAR DFC RAF / FLEW HIS LAST MISSION FROM THIS AIRFIELD 9TH AUGUST 1941
Status: not listed
Condition: good (but biological growth to base and northeast corner chipped)

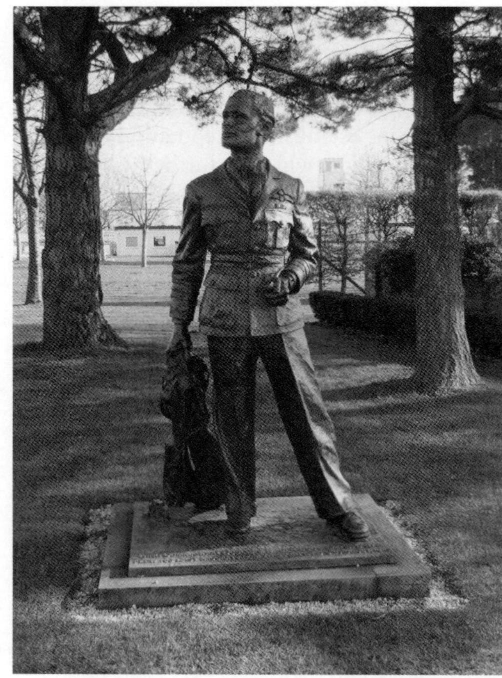

Kenneth Potts, *Statue of Douglas Bader*

Commissioned by: the Earl of March (owner of
the Goodwood estate)
Owner/custodian: Goodwood Motor Circuit

This one-and-a-quarter life-size statue of the
war hero, Douglas Bader, who died in 1982,
faces west towards the airfield. He holds a pipe
in his left hand and a flying helmet in his right
and looks at the sky, watching for weather and
returning pilots. This is the only sculpture of
the subject; it is claimed that once when Bader
was invited to sit for a sculptor, he replied, 'not
bloody likely'.[4] His widow, however, said at the
unveiling, 'It's very good. It captures the spirit
of Douglas. He never wanted a statue but now
they've done it I think he would be quite
pleased.'[5]

The ceremony took place exactly 60 years to
the day after Bader flew from Goodwood (then
known as RAF Westhampnett) on his last
wartime mission. Later that morning he was
rammed by a German fighter and had to
parachute into Northern France, where he was
taken prisoner. He spent the rest of the war as a
prisoner of war, making several escape bids
from the notorious Colditz Castle.

Douglas Bader was a charismatic figure who
had lost both legs in a flying accident some
years before the war; despite this disability, he
displayed flying skills and leadership qualities
of the highest order, which made him a
household name during and after the war. He
was subsequently knighted for his work with,
and for, disabled people. The statue stands
outside the flying school at Goodwood as a
permanent tribute.

Facing the pits area, next to the Aero Club

Statue of Mike Hawthorn and Lofty England

Sculptor: David Annand

Installed: September 2005
Materials/dimensions: 2.1 m high × 1.75 m wide
× 2.05 m deep
Inscriptions (on south face of base, in carved

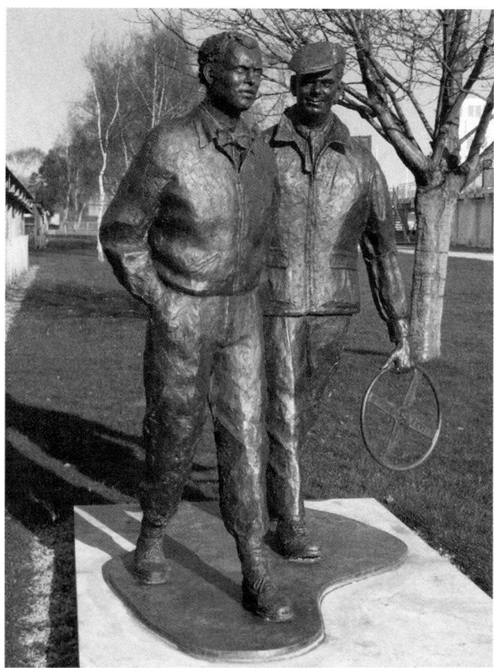

David Annand, *Statue of Mike Hawthorn and Lofty England*

letters): MAY THEIR NAME LIVE FOREVER /
David Annand Sculptor; (on east face of base
in carved letters): Mike Hawthorn 1929–1959
'Lofty' England 1911–1995 / First British
World Champion 1958 Jaguar Competition
Manager 1949–56; (on north face of base in
carved letters): Supporters R Alcock, J
Butterworth, Members of the J.D.C. XK
Register / E-type. Register, J.L.C, Jaguar
Club of Denmark; (on west face of base in
carved letters): Appeal Benefactors. Ron Lea,
John Pearson, Nigel Webb / Benefactors:
Jaguar Cars Ltd. Lucas Huni. Ole Sommer.
Clive Brandon. The Earl of March.
Status: not listed
Condition: good
Commissioned by: The England Hawthorn
Memorial Trust
Funded by: public and private donations
Owner/custodian: Goodwood Motor Circuit

The figures of racing driver Mike Hawthorn
and his trainer Lofty England, on a shallow
stone base, appear to stride across the lawns.
Hawthorn holds his helmet in his left hand. The
right hand of the England statue rests on
Hawthorn's left shoulder and he holds the
steering wheel from a Jaguar car in his left.

Hawthorn, driving a Ferrari, became
Britain's first Formula One World Champion
in 1958. He was killed in his Jaguar Mark 1
saloon in an accident on Thursday 22 January
1959. The accident took place at the Hog's
Back, on the A31 between Farnham and
Guildford. His car, going at high speed, lost
control in severe crosswinds and hit a tree. He
was buried on 28 January 1959 at West Street
Cemetery in Farnham. Ironically, Hawthorn
was already dying from kidney disease. He had
retired from motor racing after his Formula
One win, upset by the loss of close friends and
traumatised by the 1955 Le Mans race disaster
where at least 80 spectators had been killed
when Pierre Levagh's Mercedes crashed into
the crowd.

Approximately £70,000 was collected in
donations, including a new X-type Jaguar car
that was raffled over many events. The statue
was unveiled at the 2005 Goodwood Revival
race meeting and dedicated by Lord March.

Kennel Hill

Outside the Kinrara Pavilion, Goodwood Racecourse

Horse

Sculptor: Elisabeth Frink

Unveiled: 29 July 1980
Materials/dimensions: patinated bronze, 2.24 m
high × 72 cm wide × 2.5 m deep
Signature (carved into rear right of base): Frink
1980
Inscriptions (stone plaque on face of brick
plinth, underneath front of horse, in carved
letters): ELISABETH FRINK C.B.E R.A / JULY

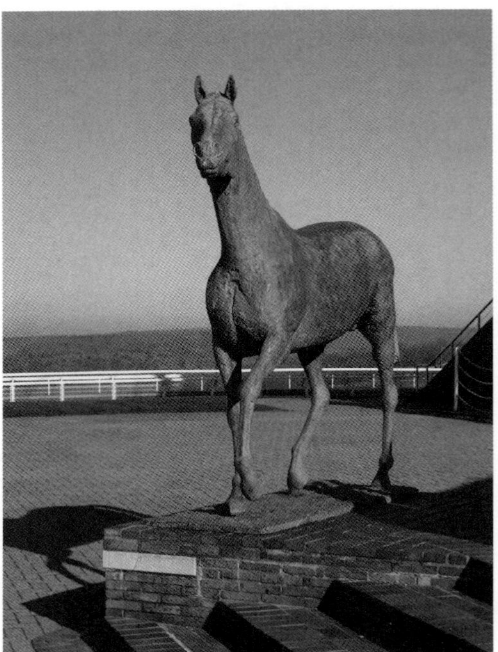

Elisabeth Frink, *Horse*

1980; (stone plaque on northwest face of plinth): HER MAJESTY THE QUEEN OPENED THIS GRANDSTAND ON JULY 29TH 1980
Status: not listed
Condition: good (but staining and cracks to both inscription plaques)
Commissioned by: The Earl of March
Owner/custodian: Goodwood Racecourse

High up on the Sussex downs, this full-size statue of a standing horse faces southwest and is mounted on a brick plinth built into steps leading up to the modern brick-built Pavilion, next to the Richmond enclosure of the racecourse. The sculpture is Frink's only truly life-like representation of a horse, for which she was paid £30,000. Frink's biographer, Stephen Gardiner, describes it as, '… as near a photographic likeness as an academic painting by Alfred Munnings …'.[6] Although the horse's left leg is lifted as if it were about to break into a gentle trot, and it wears an alert expression,

Gardiner claims that it lacks the energy and vitality of Frink's earlier treatments of this subject, particularly her small *Horse and Rider* of 1969.[7]

Notes
[1] Gunnis (1953, pp. 278–79) lists a bust of the Duchess of Richmond dated 1812 and an undated bust of the Duke. [2] Gunnis (1953, p. 419) records a bust by Henry Weeks of the 5th Duke of Richmond, dated 1845. [3] Baird, R., *Goodwood: Art and Architecture, Sport and Family*, London, 2007. [4] 'Statue captures the spirit of war hero', *Hereford Times*, 16 August 2001. [5] 'Memorial to Spitfire ace', *The Argus*, 10 August 2001. [6] Gardiner, S., *Frink: the Official Biography of Elisabeth Frink*, London, 1998, pp. 216–17. [7] Ibid.

Other sources
Elisabeth Frink: 1930–1993, Sculptures, Graphic Works, Textiles, Salisbury Festival, 1997, p. 59.
mikehawthorn.org.uk (accessed 10 November 2007).

New Barn Hill

Cass Sculpture Foundation

Established by private collectors Wilfred and Jeannette Cass, whose house is in the grounds, the Cass Sculpture Foundation is a charity, recognised internationally as the home of twenty-first century British sculpture.[1] Wilfred was born in Berlin and comes from the famous Cassirer family; his great uncle, Paul Cassirer, was the most important dealer for Impressionist painters in Europe. Upon his retirement from Moss Bros in 1992, Wilfred and Jeannette moved from London to West Sussex, where they co-founded The Cass Sculpture Foundation (previously known as Sculpture at Goodwood) in 1992. Over the next year, they visited some 30 sculpture parks around the world before deciding upon the style, aim and design of their own estate. Long-term friends of Henry Moore and Elisabeth Frink, Wilfred and Jeannette sold their own personal collection, which they had bought directly from the artists, to fund the creation of their sculpture park.

In February 2006, the Foundation moved from its existing offices in the founders' house to its own purpose-built Foundation Centre within the woodland of the sculpture estate. The building was designed by Studio Downie Architects, the practice that had already designed the Visitor Gallery in 1994. Wilfred was awarded the CBE in the Queen's Eightieth Birthday Honours List, in June 2006, for services to Art.

The Foundation commissions, displays, promotes internationally and sells monumental sculptures to a diverse range of buyers from around the world, from private collectors, to individual enterprises, to public spaces, to the business community. Over 160 monumental sculptures from over 120 British artists have been commissioned in the last 15 years. Thus it continues to provide support and promotion for contemporary British sculpture as well as a unique aesthetic experience for its many visitors.

Based in the heart of West Sussex, the Foundation occupies 26 acres of unspoilt ancient woodland within which over 70 regularly changing monumental works by over 50 carefully selected British sculptors, at all stages of their careers, are on display. Each year the Foundation commissions 12–15 large-scale sculptures and numerous smaller works. It covers the costs of casting or fabrication of each new work, which encourages artists to realise sculptures that would otherwise be beyond their financial reach. When a sculpture is sold the Foundation receives back its financial outlay and a percentage to cover its overheads, the major proceeds going to the artist.

The Foundation Centre is the home for an extensive reference library and an archive, which comprises sketches, final drawings, maquettes and other materials created by the sculptors during the commissioning process. Differing approaches to making drawings are evident in the collection; some are original plans of a technical nature, some are visions, others are reflections about sculpture.

Entrance to Cass Sculpture Foundation

Gate

Sculptor: Wendy Ramshaw

Installed: 2001
Materials/dimensions: aluminium, 4 m diam. ×
   3 cm deep (edition of 8)
Status: not listed
Condition: good
Commissioned by: Cass Sculpture Foundation

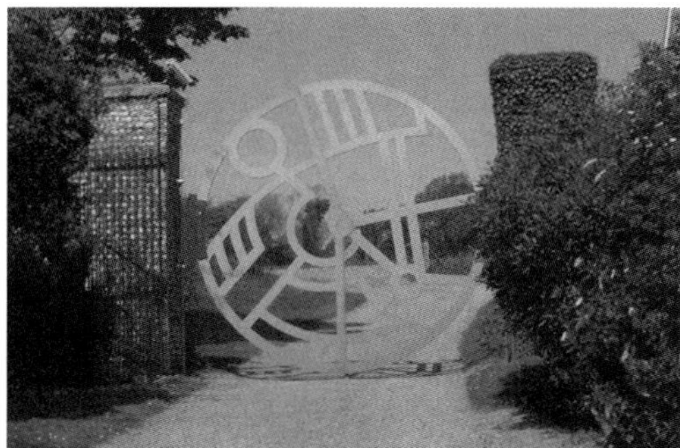

Wendy Ramshaw, *Gate*

Gate marks the entrance to the sculpture estate
and thus is one of the few permanent pieces on
the site. Its abstract circular form incorporates
the number five to represent the first five years
of the foundation. Ramshaw, best known as a
jeweller, designed a key ring for an Open Day
to mark this anniversary and Gate is a scaled-up
version of this. The change of scale, from the
4.5-cm key ring to the sculpture, is almost 100-
fold, but the forms have been little altered,
other than to accommodate a roughly central
opening. The larger of the circular motifs
represents the hole or loop to attach keys to the
ring. The matte finish of *Gate* complements the
greys of the flint walls between which it stands
and the design is enriched by the play of
shadows. There is no manual opening
mechanism, to preserve the purity of the design;
Gate is opened either by remote control or
telephone instruction from the Foundation
Centre.

Note
[1] Cass Sculpture Foundation, Goodwood, nr.
Chichester, West Sussex PO18 0QP. Open to the
public during summer and autumn.

Other sources
Cass Sculpture Foundation, *British Contemporary
   Sculpture at Goodwood 02/03*, Goodwood, 2003,
   p. 114.
ramshawwatkins.com (accessed 12 October 2010).
sculpture.org.uk (accessed 12 October 2010).
Thorpe, J. and P., 'Sculpture park', in Foster (2004),
   pp. 222–25.

St Joseph's Way

The Orchards Shopping Centre

A Family Outing

Sculptor: John Ravera

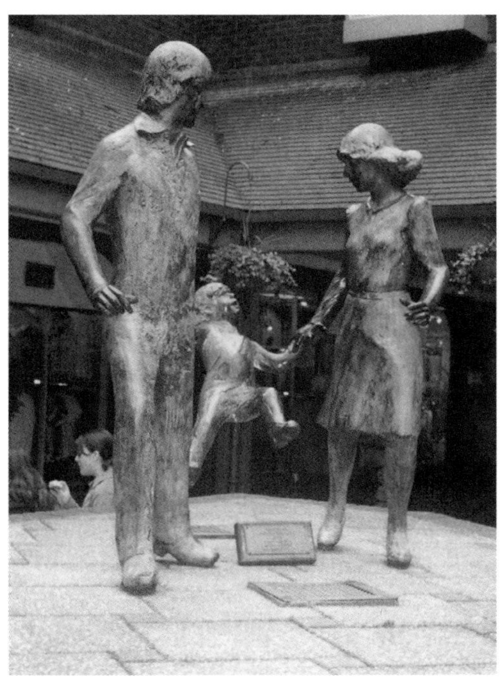

John Ravera, *A Family Outing*

Installed: 1985
Materials/dimensions: bronze, 1.64 m high ×
   1.46 m wide × approx. 1 m deep
Status: not listed
Condition: good
Commissioned and owned by: Norwich Union
   Insurance Group

The sculpture shows a man and woman in
contemporary dress, holding the hands of a
child who they are swinging between them.
Very similar family groups by the same
sculptor, with slight variations in pose, were
installed in the same year as the Haywards
Heath version in shopping centres in Solihull
and Bexleyheath.

Source
PMSA records, vads.ac.uk (accessed 3 November
   2011).

Blackhorse Way Forum

*Pedestrianised area opposite Sainsbury's
Superstore and Beales*

The Horsham Heritage Sundial

Sculptors: Edwin Russell and Lorne McKean, assisted by Damian Fennell

Foundry: Atelier Foundry
Unveiled: 24 October 2003
Materials/dimensions: sundial; bronze, 1.8 m
   high × 2.75 m diam.; base: marble, 36 cm
   high × 4.05 m diam.
Signature (western edge of sundial): ATELIER
   FOUNDRY
Inscriptions (bronze plaque on base, facing
   north): THE HORSHAM HERITAGE SUNDIAL /
   UNVEILED BY HER MAJESTY THE QUEEN / 24
   OCTOBER 2003 / COMMISSIONED BY
   HORSHAM DISTRICT COUNCIL / SCULPTURE
   AND DESIGN BY LORNE MCKEAN AND EDWIN
   RUSSELL, WITH DAMIAN FENNELL / THE
   SUNDIAL IS THE START OF THE DISTRICT-WIDE

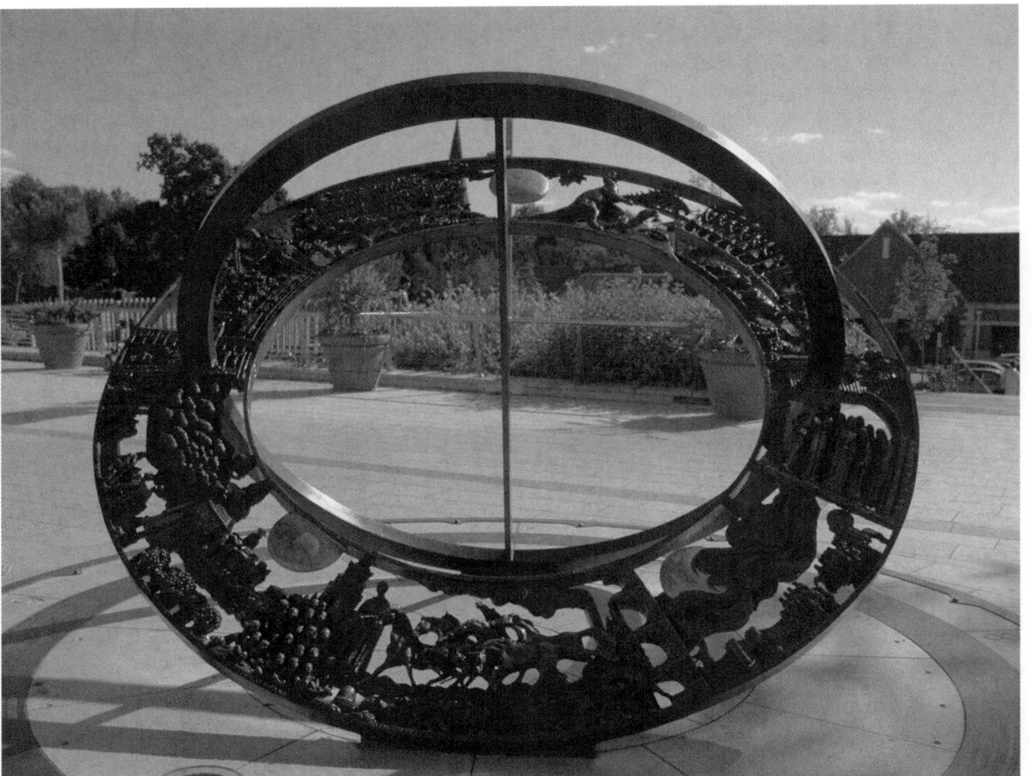

originally intended to be viewed through a glass panel, which did not form part of the realised design. The sundial, which took a year to make and cost £160,000, was unveiled by H.M. Queen Elizabeth II.

The inscription on the relief is from the Percy Bysshe Shelley (1792–1822) poem, *Adonais: An Elegy on the Death of John Keats* (1821) stanza 52:

> The One remains, the many change and pass;
> Heaven's light forever shines, Earth's
>   shadows fly;
> Life, like a dome of many-coloured glass,
> Stains the white radiance of Eternity,
> Until Death tramples it to fragments. – Die,
> If thou wouldst be with that which thou dost
>   seek!
> Follow where all is fled! – Rome's azure sky,
> Flowers, ruins, statues, music, words, are
>   weak
> The glory they transfuse with fitting truth to
>   speak.

The creation and installation of the sundial was part of the expansion of Horsham town centre, to create the Forum in the space between Blackhorse Way and Sainsbury's supermarket. The redevelopment began in 2002 at a cost of £22m and provided a new multi-storey car park, affordable housing, a refurbished bus station, recreational space and more retail outlets.

Notes
[1] Lord (2008), p. 28. [2] hiddenhorsham.co.uk (accessed 10 November 2011).

Other sources
'Illuminating tales from a sundial', *News Release*, Horsham Museum, 17 February 2005.
'The sculptured world: a retrospective exhibition of Lorne McKean and Edwin Russell', *News Release*, Horsham Museum, 5 April 2005.

HERITAGE TRAIL AND IS ALSO THE HOME OF / HORSHAM DISTRICT'S TIME CAPSULE WHICH HOUSES OBJECTS SELECTED AND VOTED ON BY GROUPS AND / INDIVIDUALS ACROSS THE DISTRICT AS BEING THE MOST REPRESENTATIVE IN THE YEAR 2000; (bronze plaque on base, facing south): HORSHAM DISTRICT COUNCIL WOULD LIKE TO THANK / THE FOLLOWING FOR MAKING THE SUNDIAL POSSIBLE / J SAINSBURY DEVELOPMENTS LTD / SAINSBURY'S SUPERMARKETS LTD / ALLDERS DEPARTMENT STORES LTD; (on sundial pictorial relief, in raised letters): THE ONE REMAINS / THE MANY CHANGE AND PASS (Shelley)

Status: not listed
Condition: good
Commissioned and owned by: Horsham District Council

This sundial is in the form of a three-dimensional pierced bronze ring with relief sculptures and lettering depicting the history of the Horsham District in the manner of a medieval chronicle. Detailed historical background information was provided by Jeremy Knight, curator of Horsham Museum.[1] Local references include: dinosaur remains at Rudgwick and Southwater, the influence of the Saxons and Romans, the Bronze Age at Chanctonbury Hill, St Cuthman at Steyning, myths and legends of the forests, the Quakers, Shipley Mill and Hilaire Belloc, the Knights Templar, the Carthusian Monastery at Cowfold, Percy Bysshe Shelley and his cat.[2] It sits on a marble base that is set with another encircling bronze text ring describing the narrative depicted on the sculptural relief. Buried within the plinth is a time capsule,

Pirie's Place Shopping Centre

Pirie's Donkey and Cart
Sculptor: Lorne McKean

Installed: 1993
Materials/dimensions: patinated bronze, 1.6 m
   high × 1.05 m wide × 3 m deep
Signature (on the harness on the hind leg of the
   donkey): L.McK. 1992
Inscriptions (on harness under the donkey's
   neck): JANITA / BORN 1972; (bronze plaque
   on wall facing sculpture): WILLIAM PIRIE /
   this sculpture / by Lorne McKean is for the /
   enjoyment of the users of / Pirie's Place. It
   depicts / William Pirie, who was /
   Headmaster of Collyers / from 1822–1869,
   during which / time he became a familiar /
   figure travelling around / Horsham with his
   donkey / & cart. He bought property / in
   Horsham, and built 15 / cottages on this site
   / naming it Pirie's Place, from / which this
development / takes its name.
Status: not listed
Condition: good
Owner/custodian: Horsham District Council

A life-size statue of William Pirie, sitting in his
realistically modelled donkey cart, faces north,
in the courtyard at the entrance to the shopping
centre. It is designed for children to climb and
sit upon.

The sculpture was one outcome of major
investment in the town of Horsham that
included the commissioning of artworks for its
public spaces, which had been lacking until
1990. Lorne McKean and her husband Edwin
Russell created four pieces, starting with the
Swan Fountain, followed by *Pirie's Donkey and
Cart*, *Roundels of Life* on the war memorial in
the Carfax and finally the *Horsham Heritage
Sundial* in 2003.

Sources
horshamsociety.org (accessed 10 November 2011).
lornemckean.com

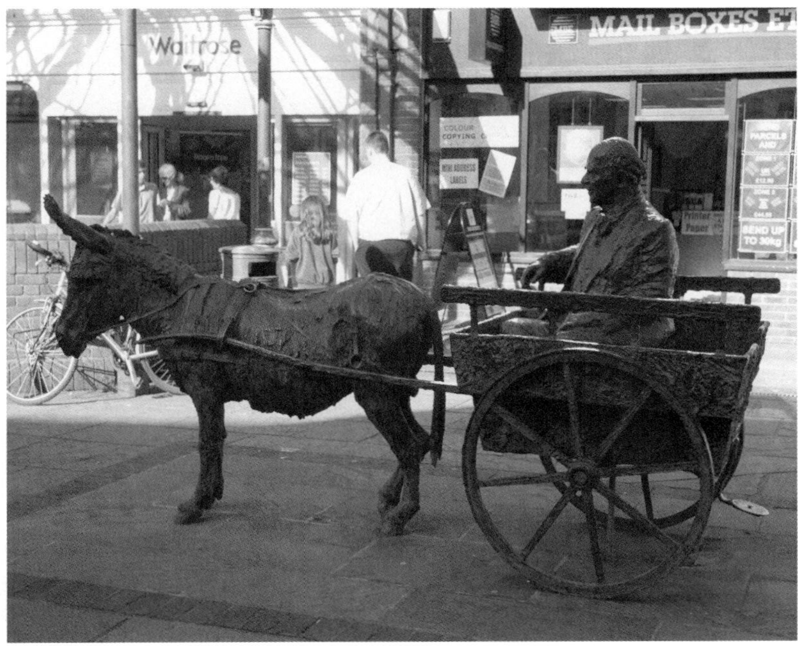

Lorne McKean, *Pirie's
Donkey and Cart*

*Horsham Park, in centre of Horsham in
Bloom Millennium Maze*

The St Leonard's Forest Dragon
Sculptor: Hannah Holmes Stewart

Installed: 2000
Materials/dimensions: bronze, 1.2 m high ×
   1.15 m wide × 90 cm deep
Signature (at the bottom of wing): Hannah
   Holmes 2000
Inscriptions (carved into stone plaque set in
   front of sculpture): Horsham in Bloom / THE
   / ST. LEONARD'S FOREST / DRAGON / by
   /Hannah Holmes / sponsored by / BALLAST
   plc SOUTH EAST / and / ROYAL SUN ALLIANCE
   / May 2001
Status: not listed
Condition: good
Commissioned by: Horsham in Bloom
Funded by: Ballast plc South East and Royal
   Sun Alliance
Owner/custodian: Horsham District Council

This sculpture of a seated dragon with wings
folded, its tail curled around the upper part of
its neck as it turns to look at the viewer, sits
upon a large natural rock, surrounded by an
open sandy area. It is sited in the centre of a
children's maze in an enclosed garden in the
park.

The committee of 'Horsham in Bloom'
wanted the Maze to be a lasting marker of the
move into a new Millennium. It was created in a
previously neglected area of Horsham Park,
using money and labour supplied by local
businesses as well as individual volunteers.
They were keen to have a local theme, so the
maze incorporates the myths and legends that
are well known in the Horsham Area. St
Leonard's Forest lies on the northern outskirts
of the town and for generations people believed
that it was home to a dragon. The stories about
the dragon brought St Leonard to the forest
where he confronted the beast. In the fight

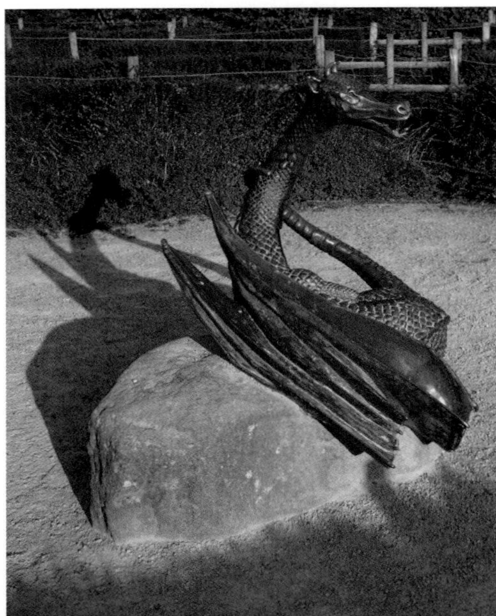

Hannah Holmes Stewart, *The St Leonard's Forest Dragon*

blood was spilled, and where it fell, patches of lilies-of-the-valley, which still bloom every year, sprang up.

The planting in the four main flower beds at the corners of the maze continues the theme of stories associated with the locality, with one reflecting the link between Sussex and myths of fairies, another legends of smugglers and highwaymen, a third planted like the seashore and the final one referencing the dragon's lair.

Sources
hannahstewartsculpture.co.uk (accessed 21 December 2010).
horshaminbloom.org.uk (accessed 21 December 2010).

In the centre of Park House Garden, Horsham Park

Sungod
Sculptor: John Skelton

Installed: 1991
Materials/dimensions: sculpture: stone, 90 cm high × 20 cm wide × 65 cm deep; base: brick and tile, 40 cm high × 4 m wide × 65 cm deep
Inscriptions (motto is spelled out on the face of each of the blocks with numbers inscribed): VIII VII VI V IIII III II I XII XI X IX VIII VII VI V IIII / HO RA S N ON NU M E RO N I SI SE R E N AS; (metal plaque on upper face of base): "I COUNT NOT THE HOURS UNLESS THEY BE HAPPY" / SUNGOD BY JOHN SKELTON
Status: not listed
Condition: good (but evidence that the gnomon was broken off about midway down; repair is clearly visible)
Owner/custodian: Horsham District Council

This sundial stands on a brick and tile circular base set in the centre of a garden. Its gnomon (the indicator that casts the shadow) takes the form of a stylised bearded male face. The numbers, in Roman numerals, are inscribed on the tops of stone blocks set onto the base and the motto, spelt out in groups of one or two letters, is carved into their outside faces .The sundial replaced an earlier model in Park House Garden.

Source
Salt, D., *Memorials, Monuments and Modern Memorabilia of Horsham*, Horsham, 2nd edn, 2000, p. 1.

John Skelton, *Sungod*

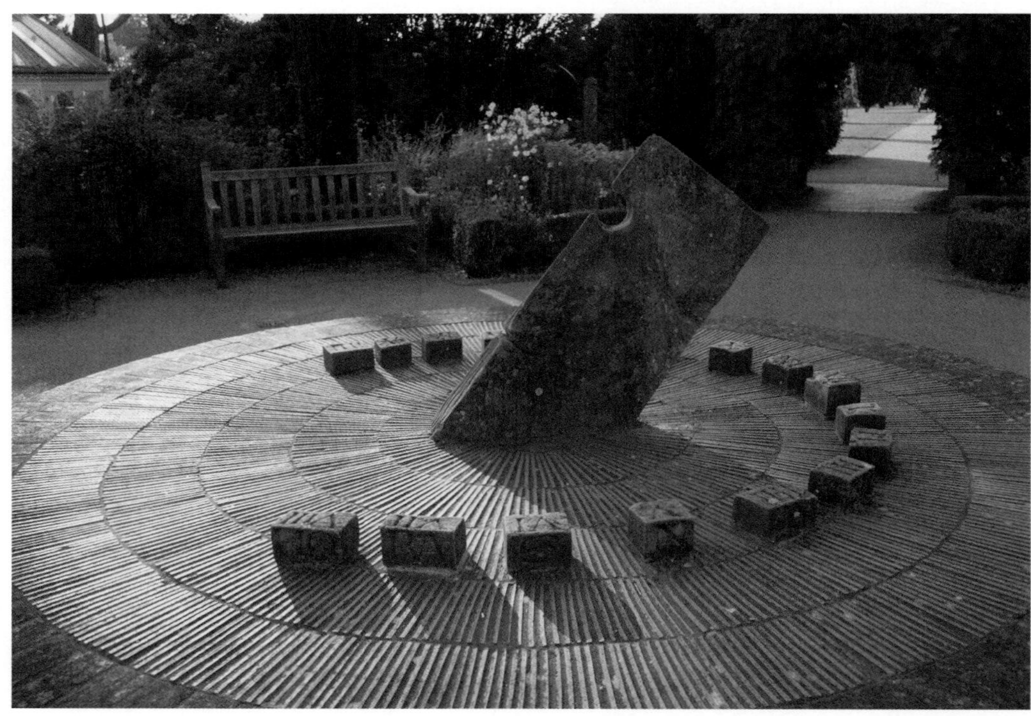

West Street

In the centre of the pedestrianised area at the junction with Springfield Road

Cosmic Cycle (The Rising Universe)

Sculptor: Angela Conner

Unveiled: 13 November 1996
Materials/dimensions: satellite arms and bowl: polished concrete, 13.72 m diam.; large sphere and shaft: concrete and steel, 8.54 m high
Inscription (inscribed plaque on top of the bowl on southeast side): "COSMIC CYCLE" / WATER IS SHELLEY'S ELEMENT. IT FLOWS THROUGH HIS POETRY. IT DRAWS HIM / TO ITSELF. TRAGICALLY, IN THE MEDITERRANEAN ACCIDENT WHICH ENDS HIS LIFE IN WATER / THE SOURCE OF LIFE ON THIS PLANET, THERE IS ALSO DEATH / IN MY SCULPTURE, A NEW, COSMIC SHAPE, LIKE LIFE ITSELF, EMERGES FROM ITS SHELL. / WATER ANIMATES IT. BY SHEER WEIGHT (EVENTUALLY 6 TONS) IT PRESSES THE FORM DOWN AGAIN / UNTIL, WITH A MIGHTY BREAKING OF WATERS IT IS FREE TO RISE AND BEGIN AGAIN. SHELLEY, / HORSHAM'S POET OF LIBERTY KNEW THAT THERE IS A CYCLE TO ALL THINGS, LINKING ATOM AND / COSMOS IN ONE RECURRING PATTERN / ANGELA CONNER
Status: not listed
Condition: good (some chipping and cracking to all the four smaller bowls on the ends of the satellite arms. Water supply restricted)
Commissioned and owned by: Horsham District Council

The large circular fountain bowl is set in a circular paved area with four radiating arms. In the centre of the bowl stands a large spherical sculpture that, with the action of water, moves up and down a central shaft. The sphere fills with water, pushing it down the shaft. When the weight of water reaches 6 tons, the water is

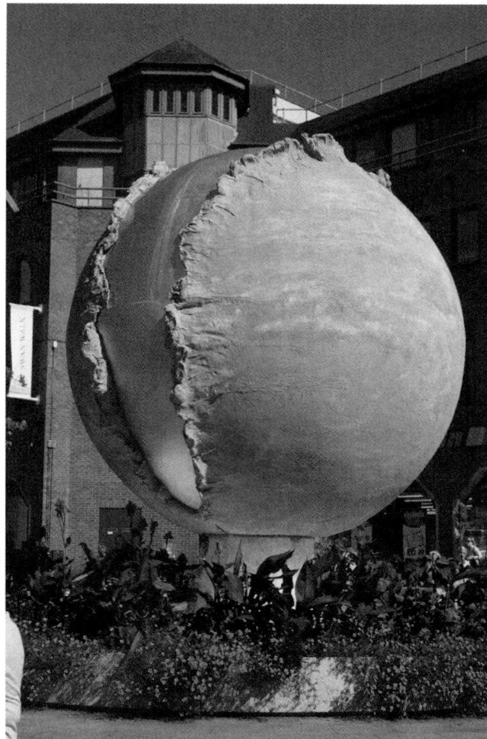

Angela Conner, *Cosmic Cycle (The Rising Universe)*

released at force into the bowl. On the ends of each of the radiating arms is a smaller bowl with smaller spheres that revolve with the action of circulating water.

This fountain is occasionally known as the Shelley Fountain. The poet's family home, Field Place, is nearby and in 1992 a Shelley Gallery and Library were established at Horsham Museum to mark the bicentenary of his birth. The creation of the fountain, within a new shopping centre, provided a more public tribute. 'The Rising Universe' refers to Shelley's poem *Mont Blanc* (1816), in which he aimed to imitate what he called 'the untameable wildness and inaccessible solemnity' he had experienced at the mountain and from which the sculptor drew her inspiration.[1] At the unveiling

ceremony members of Horsham Symphony Orchestra played a new work by composer Martyn Harry, also inspired by Mont Blanc.

The sculpture became a local landmark, to the extent that it featured in a montage of local images in the opening sequences of the BBC's regional news programme. It has, however, been dogged with technical problems, which did not appear to have been resolved by a major overhaul in 2005. In 2009 the District Council engaged in a public consultation over what should happen to the fountain. There were three options: to fully repair it, to lock the mechanism in a static position or to remove it. The first option was finally adopted and the repaired fountain was reopened in May 2010, but failed to function properly, allegedly due to a faulty weld. The Horsham Society reported that '[A]s of March 2011 the fountain is working to restricted hours and on a slower cycle.'[2]

Notes
[1] horsham.gov.uk (accessed 19 September 2007).
[2] *Horsham Society Newsletter*, June 2010 (updated October 2010 and March 2011), horshamsociety.org (accessed 10 November 2011).

Swan Square, inside Swan Walk Shopping Centre (temporarily removed 30 September 2007)

Swan Fountain

Sculptor: Lorne McKean

Installed: 1990
Materials/dimensions: sculpture: blue patinated bronze, 3 m high × 2.18 m wide × 3 m deep; pool: black ceramic tiles, 77 cm high × 2.18 m wide × 3.9 m deep
Inscription (bronze inscribed plaque on top of the pool behind swans): SCULPTURE IN BRONZE / BY LORNE MCKEAN / COMMISSIONED BY NORWICH UNION / 1990
Status: not listed
Condition: good
Commissioned and owned by: Norwich Union Life Insurance Society

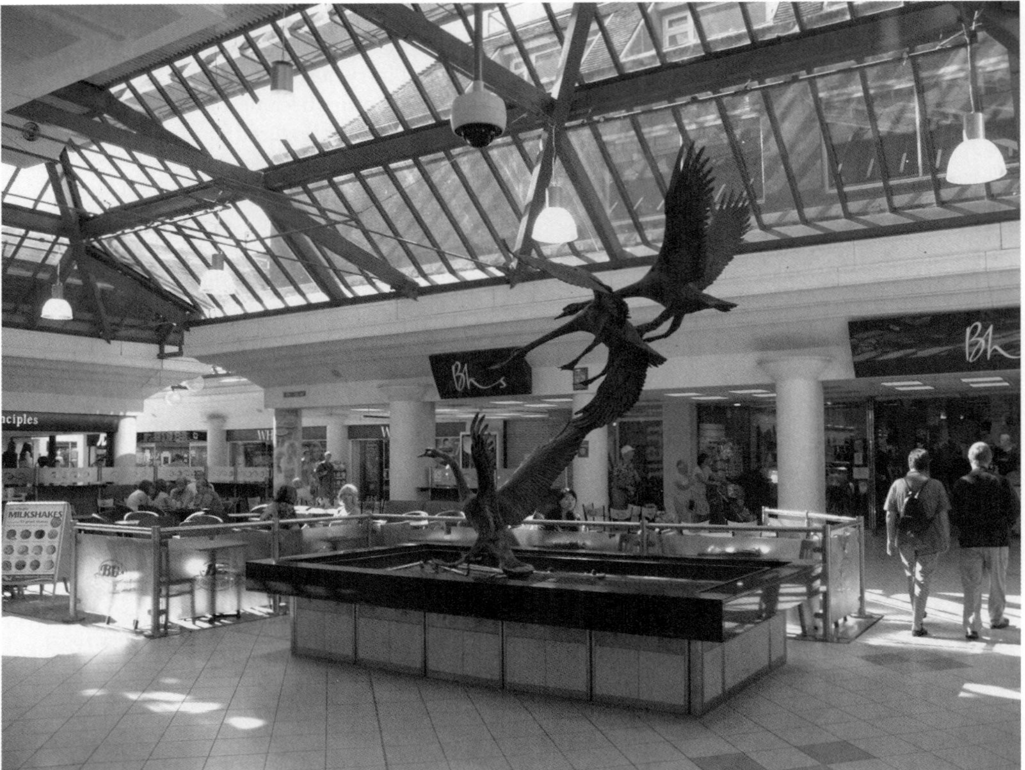

Lorne McKean, *Swan Fountain*

This dynamic group sculpture shows three swans landing on water. It is set in a black-tiled pool that holds a water feature. The piece was Horsham's first public work of art, sited in an eating area of the Shopping Centre.

Following an environmental and safety review, the sculpture was removed on the instructions of the management of Swan Walk who said the move would make the shopping centre more environmentally friendly and cut down water wastage. This provoked a public outcry (including a campaign by the Chair and members of the Horsham Society) with protesters describing the removal as 'political environmental correctness gone mad.'[1] It subsequently emerged that the sculpture was removed to gain a little more retail space. Swan Walk management eventually bowed to public pressure, agreed to renovate the swans and returned them to their original position in September 2008.

Note
[1] 'Feathers fly as swans "walk" to stop water wastage', *West Sussex Gazette*, 2 October 2007.

Other sources
hiddenhorsham.co.uk (accessed 22 November 2010).
Horsham Society Newsletter, October 2007; January 2009.
horshamsociety.org (accessed 10 December 2011).
'Swans on the move', *West Sussex Gazette*, 21 September 2007.

Lavant Road

St Nicholas Church, in niche in north wall (formerly in church vault)

Monument to Dame Mary May
Sculptor: John Bushnell

Installed: 1676
Materials/dimensions: white, grey and black marble, 80 cm high × 1.42 m wide × 46 cm deep
Inscription (on cartouche set into wall below reclining figure): Here / Lies the Body of Dame Mary May second wife to S[R] / John May of Raughmere, the only surviving Sister & sole Heir to S[R] / John Morley of Brooms & Daughter to S[R] John Morley of Chichester / son to S[R] Edward Morley a second Brother of the Family of Halnaker Place / Piously contemplating ye uncertainty of this life, among other solemn Prep / arations for her funeral Obsequies, shee erected this monument in ye / time of her life in ye year of Our LORD 1676. She departed / this life in ye year of Our LORD 1681 in ye 41st year of her age
Status: not listed
Condition: good
Owner/custodian: St Nicholas Church

The effigy of Lady May was sculpted during her lifetime and shows her reclining on her right side, propped up by pillows underneath her right arm and with her left hand on her raised left knee. The pose suggests a deathbed and, as is clear from the inscription was intended as a *memento mori*.[1] The figure is almost identical to that of Jane, Lady Marlborough on her tomb at Ashburnham (1675, see entry).[2] Lady May commissioned her monument when she was a widow aged 36 and it has been suggested that she sought advice from her late husband's uncle, the architect

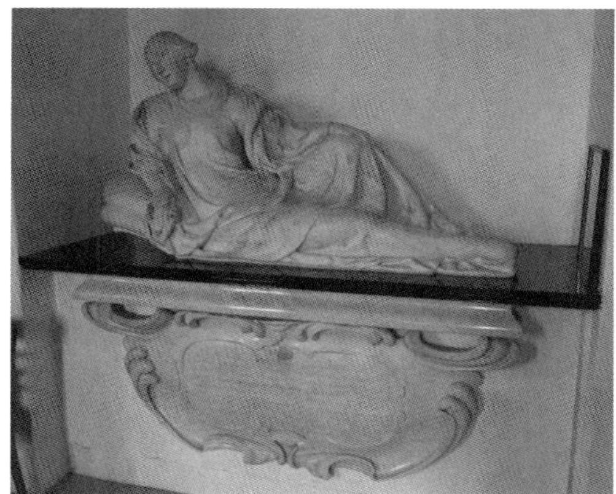

John Bushnell, *Monument to Dame Mary May*

Hugh May (1622–1684), who had connections in Lavant and Chichester and was an advocate of the baroque style in England.[3] The portrait was regarded as a good likeness, although there has been later debate as to whether the pockmarked surface of her face represents an accurate depiction of a woman who had suffered from smallpox, an act of vandalism, or a deterioration of the marble.[4]

Lady May's monument was originally placed in the chancel of the church, above the family vault. It appears to have been moved to the south wall of the nave in the late eighteenth century and in 1871 was removed to the vault under the chancel floor, to make way for an additional window.[5] It remained inaccessible to the public until 1981, when access to the vault was constructed and in 1987, during a further extension of the church, the sculpture was cleaned and installed in a specially built niche between the north aisle and the new extension.

Notes
[1] Bayley, Rev. T.D.S., 'Lady Mary May's monument in mid-Lavant Church', reprinted from *Sussex Archaeology Collections*, vol. CVII, 1969. [2] A drawing of the monument by Samuel Hieronymous Grimm, executed around 1780 (now in the British Library) shows the central figure flanked by shell-shaped lamps (symbolising immortality), lying on a shelf supported by ornate brackets, with the cartouche decorated with a winged cherub below. [3] Bayley (1969). [4] Ibid. [5] Ibid.

Other sources
Esdaile, K.A., 'John Bushnell', *Walpole Society*, vol. XV, 1926–27; vol. XXI 1932–33.
lavantchurches.net (accessed 20 June 2013).
Roscoe (2009), pp. 174–76.

LITTLEHAMPTON

Pier Road/Arun Parade

Along river walkway between the Look and Sea! Centre and the Oyster Pond

Six Oyster Waymarkers

Sculptors: Brian Fell and Gordon Young with students from Littlehampton Community School

Unveiled: 11 July 2007
Materials/dimensions: granite and metal, 1 m
    high × 68 cm wide × 50 cm deep
Status: not listed
Condition: good
Commissioned by: Arun District Council
Funded by: Arts Council England and
    Littlehampton Town Council
Owner/custodian: Littlehampton Town
    Council

Each waymarker consists of a low metal column with a circular metal plaque on top. The outer aspect of the plaque is decorated with a large oyster shell motif. In the centre is set a granite circle with incised letters bearing a different fish recipe on each marker. These are designed so that rubbings can be taken of the recipes. The waymarkers were created and placed along the river walk to reflect the historical use of the Oyster Pond, which was made in the late eighteenth century to store the oysters brought ashore as the trade flourished.

The design and installation of the waymarkers was intended to promote the local identity of the town and formed part of the

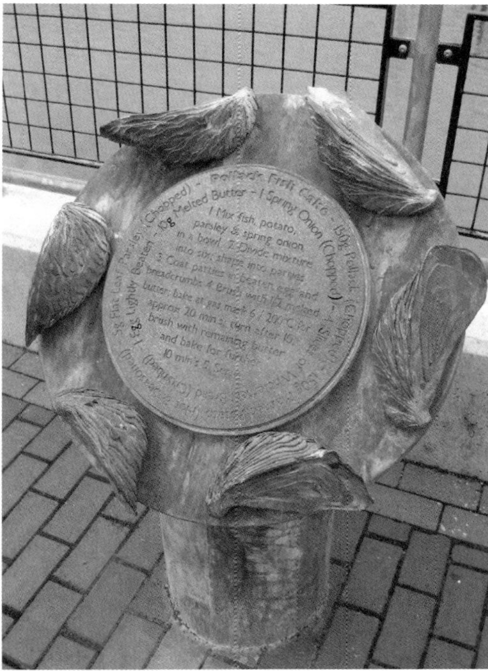

Brian Fell and Gordon Young, *Oyster Waymarker*

Arts and Regeneration project for Littlehampton and Bognor Regis. Gordon Young spent a day with the students and staff at Littlehampton Community School as they worked with, and cooked, various types of locally caught fish, making recipes, drawings, poems and other written work. The recipes were collected in *The Oyster Pond Littlehampton Fish Recipe Book*, which was launched at the same time as the unveiling of the waymarkers.

Source
arun.gov.uk (accessed 11 January 2011).

Surrey Street

In garden next to public car park

River Circle

Sculptor: John Thomson

Builders: MJF Welding, Southampton
Installed: 2004
Materials/dimensions: 316L Stainless steel, 3.8
 m high × 3.8 m wide × 2.1 m deep
Status: not listed
Condition: good
Commissioned and owned by: Arun District
 Council
Funded by: South East England Development
 Agency (SEEDA) and Bellways Homes

The *Circle* is formed of eight curved interlocking jigsaw-like panels welded together. The panels have 'cut-out' representations of various marine flora and fauna found in the area based on research involving local and national experts in the field. Set into the brick base is a bronze sculptural relief that depicts similar designs. It is sited on the banks of the river Arun, where it enters the sea, and was part of a government initiative to revitalise a former industrial site. The sculpture forms the central focus of a new square, which is part of a development that has preserved the historic buildings as well as providing new housing, a Youth Hostel and a Sea Life Centre, thereby contributing to the regeneration and economic life of Littlehampton.

The design was selected in a national competition and uses 316L stainless steel, which is specified for marine and hostile environments. Structural calculations were supplied by Fast Calc of Portsmouth. It exemplifies Thomson's interest in non-traditional sculptural materials and processes. A series of workshops with local youth groups provided the imagery for a number of permanently installed metal panels located adjacent to the main sculpture, as well as large-scale printed banners for a local community centre. As Thomson has stated:

> [t]his part of the project was designed to inform and give 'ownership' of the work to the local community. I also gave public lectures that provided an insight into technical and aesthetic aspects of the project'.[1]

Note
[1] creaddm.solent.ac.uk (accessed 21 October 2010).

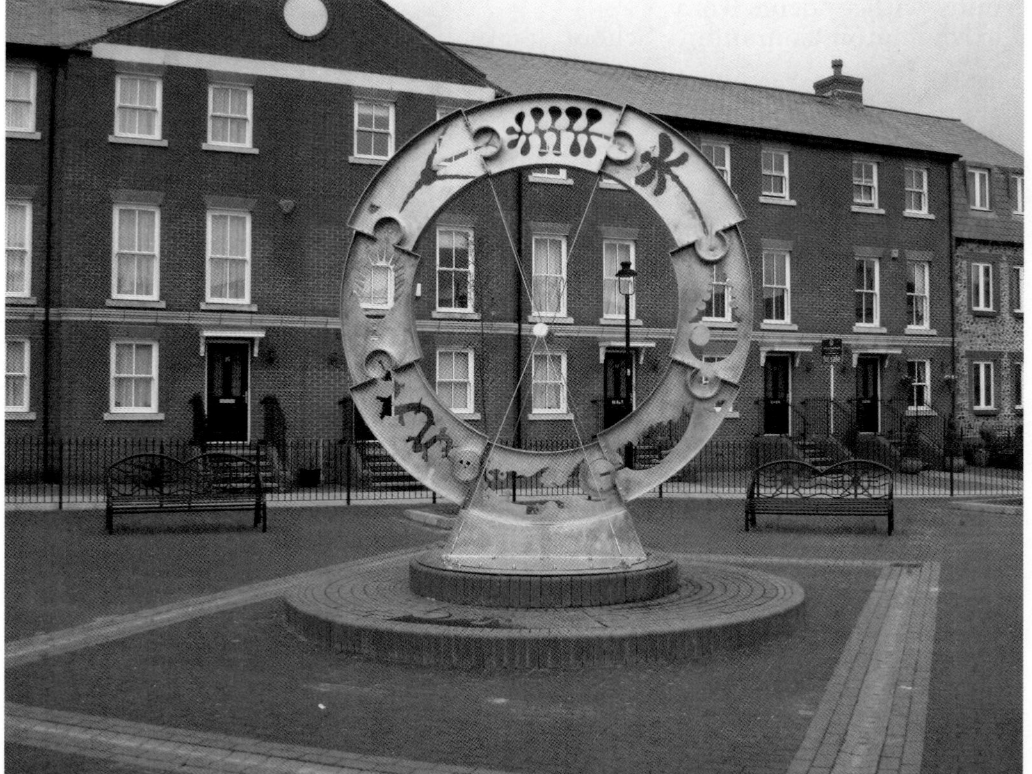

John Thomson, *River Circle*

Liphook Road

North interior wall of the Parish Church of St Peter (previously in a church in south of France)

Seven Deadly Sins

Sculptor: unknown

Installed: 1906 (created c. 1300)
Materials/dimensions: marble heads set into
 hard volcanic rock, 50 cm high × 1.44 m
 wide × 10 cm deep
Inscriptions (plaque underneath sculpture):
 THIS BAS-RELIEF IS A FINE EXAMPLE / OF OLD
 ITALIAN WORK. AND ITS DATE / IS ABOUT 1300
 A.D. IT REPRESENTS / THE SEVEN DEADLY SINS
 AND IS CARVED / OUT OF A HARD VOLCANIC
 ROCK, THE MONKS' FACES BEING OF MARBLE.
 IT ONCE BELONGED TO A CONVENTUAL

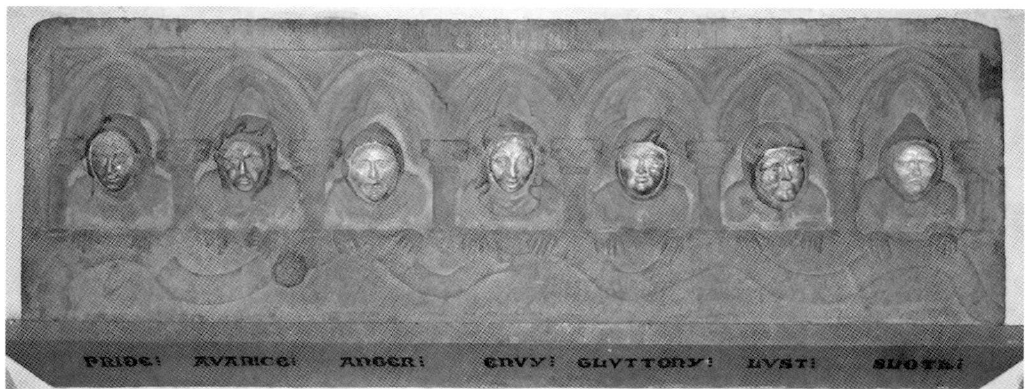

Unknown, *Seven Deadly Sins*

CHURCH IN THE SOUTH OF FRANCE. AND WAS / PRESENTED TO LYNCHMERE CHURCH IN 1906. / J.WIPPELL & CO.LTD. EXETER & LONDON; (on a tablet beneath the sculpture, underneath each of the figures): PRIDE: AVARICE: ANGER: ENVY: GLUTTONY: LUST: SLOTH:

Status: not listed
Condition: good
Owner/custodian: Church of St Peter

Each of seven Gothic trefoil arches contains the carved face of a monk, his expression depicting the impact of one of the seven deadly sins. All are clean-shaven except the face of 'Sloth'.

The seven deadly sins, also known as the capital vices or cardinal sins, are a classification of vices that were originally used in early Christian teachings to educate and instruct followers concerning fallen man's tendency to sin. The firm of J. Wippell of Exeter referred to in the inscription are Clerical Outfitters and Church Furnishers, established in 1789. They also specialise in restoration and repair work and were responsible for re-installing the piece.

Sources
Salzman (1953), pp. 67–70.
Swinfen and Arscott (1984), p. 11.
wippell.co.uk (accessed 20 October 2010).

MIDHURST

Bepton Road

Over entrance to the Divine Motherhood and St Francis of Assisi Roman Catholic Church

Madonna and Child

Sculptor: Sean Crampton

Architect: Guy Morgan and Partners (1957)

Installed: c. 1965
Materials/dimensions: patinated bronze, 3 m high × 1.5 m wide × 30 cm deep
Inscription (on underside of Madonna's robe, to right): 62 SC
Status: not listed
Condition: good
Owner/custodian: The Divine Motherhood and St Francis of Assisi Roman Catholic Church

The figure of Christ, depicted as a young boy with arms outstretched, stands in front of his mother, who rests her hands on his shoulders. The sculpture faces northeast in a shallow niche between brick pillars; immediately below it, set into the door lintel, is a bronze papal tiara and the keys of St Peter. The two figures confront

the visitor to the church with a directness and gravitas, that, together with the marked stylisation of their robes, invokes Byzantine sculpture.[1]

Note
[1] The church possesses incomplete correspondence that suggests that a Professor Guyatt submitted a proposal for a Madonna and Child to be placed on the tympanum in 1962. This may have been Richard Guyatt (1914–2007), Professor of Design at the Royal College of Art (see Obituary, *The Independent*, 29 October 2007).

Other source
Fr Peter Johnstone, email correspondence, 16 February 2011.

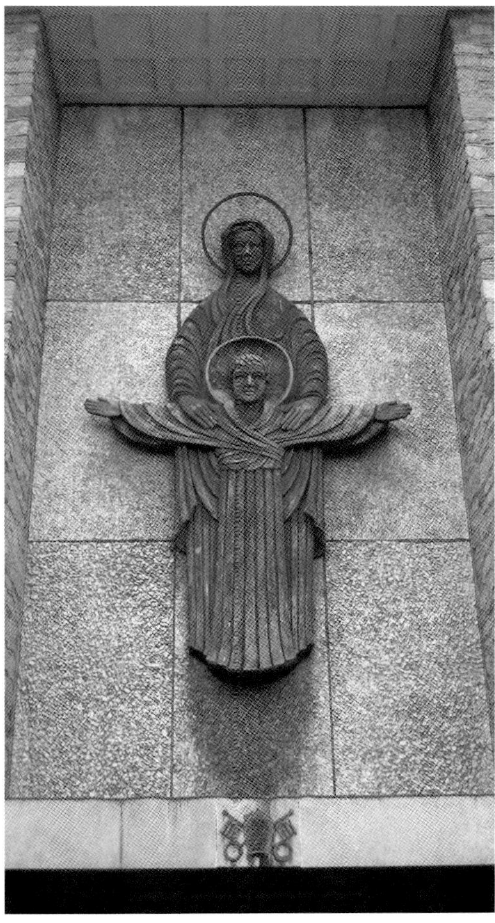

Sean Crampton, *Madonna and Child*

Church Street
Parish Church of St Mary the Virgin

In the Baptistery
Monument to the Percy Family
Sculptor: John Edward Carew

Installed: 1837
Materials/dimensions: white, black and grey
  marble, 4.85 m high × 2.44 m wide × 74 cm
  deep
Signature (carved letters, on right-hand side of
  plinth): J.E. CAREW. SCULPTOR FECIT / Proh
  Pudor Academiae / Non Academicus (Ah!
  to the shame of the Academy not an
  Academician)[1]
Inscriptions (carved letters immediately below
  sculpture): IN THIS CHANCEL WERE BURIED /
  HENRY PERCY 9TH. EARL OF
  NORTHUMBERLAND 1632. / LADY DOROTHY
  DEVEREUX, HIS WIFE. 1619. / LADY LUCY
  PERCY, COUNTESS OF CARLISLE. HIS
  DAUGHTER. 1660. / ALGERNON 10TH. EARL.
  HIS SON. 1668. / LADY ANN CECIL, HIS WIFE.
  1637. / LADY ELIZABETH HOWARD. HIS
  SECOND WIFE. 1704. / LADY ANN PERCY. LADY
  STANHOPE, HIS DAUGHTER. 1654. / JOSCELINE
  11TH. EARL. HIS SON. 1670. LADY ELIZABETH
  WRIOTHESLEY, HIS WIFE. 1698. / HENRY EARL
  OF OGEE. 1680. / AND OTHERS OF THE FAMILY
  OF PERCY WHICH AT THE DEATH OF
  JOSCELINE / BECAME EXTINCT IN THE MALE
  LINE. / THIS MONUMENT WAS ERECTED TO
  THEIR MEMORY / BY THEIR DESCENDANT
  GEORGE BART. OF EGREMONT / IN THE YEAR
  1837 THE 86TH OF HIS AGE. / MORTUIS
  MORITURUS; (carved letters at base of
  monument): IN THE CHURCH WAS BURIED
  JOSCELINE DE LOUVAIN / WHO MARRIED
  AGNES. THE HEIRESS OF THE PERCY FAMILY. /
  HE WAS BROTHER TO QUEEN ADELICIA / WHO
  AFTER THE DEATH OF HER HUSBAND HENRY
  THE FIRST / GAVE TO HIM THE HONOR AND

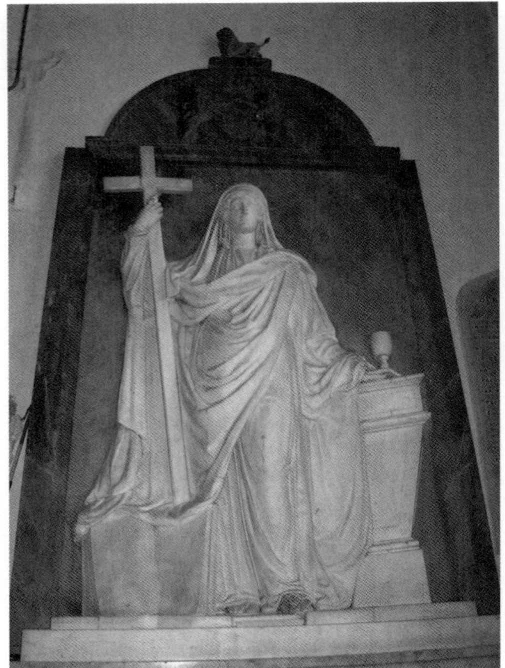

John Edward Carew, *Monument to the Percy Family*

MANOR OF PETWORTH A PART OF HER DOWRY
  / WHICH GRANT WAS CONFIRMED TO THE
  FAMILY BY HENRY THE SECOND
Status: not listed
Condition: good
Commissioned by: George, 3rd Earl of
  Egremont
Owner/custodian: Parish Church of St Mary
  the Virgin

This collective monument to the Percy family,
ancestors of the Wyndhams and founders of
Petworth House and estate, faces west. A large
sarcophagus is built into the wall, surmounted
by a classically draped female figure, representing
Faith, holding a large cross in her right hand
and her left resting on an urn. Above the figure
is the Percy coat of arms. It was erected in
memory of his ancestors by the Earl of
Egremont just before his death in 1837, aged 86.

The Irish sculptor Carew was employed by
Lord Egremont at Petworth for several
commissions, from 1823 to 1837. Carew felt at
the time that his talents were not generally
recognised, hence the inscription at the top of
the plinth.

In the Baptistery, underneath the organ
(previously behind the High Altar)
Madonna and Child
Sculptor: John Flaxman

Executed: unknown (Flaxman's work for Lord
  Egremont at Petworth House dates from the
  1820s)
Materials/dimensions: white marble, within
  grey/brown marble frame, 85 cm high ×
  76 cm wide × 8 cm deep
Status: not listed
Condition: fair (a crack runs fully across the
  medallion through the face of the Madonna
  and across the neck and arm of the child)
Owner/custodian: Parish Church of St Mary
  the Virgin

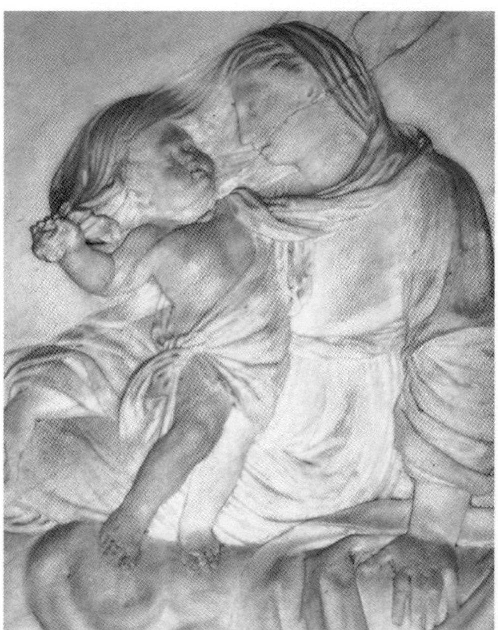

John Flaxman, *Madonna and Child*

A finely carved medallion relief of a Madonna and child is set into a rectangular marble frame, affixed to the wall facing east. The Virgin is seated on cloud-like forms, with the Christ child standing on her lap, tugging at her veil. The lively interaction between the two figures belies Nairn's description of the piece as, '[s]mall, dainty and Wedgwood-like …'.[2]

West side of nave (formerly in the centre of the chapel)
Monument to the Earl of Egremont
Sculptor: Edward Hodges Baily

Installed: 1840
Materials/dimensions: statue: white marble, 1.6 m high × 78 cm wide × 1.45 m deep; pedestal: white marble, 1.38 m high × 1.05 m wide × 1.55 m deep
Signature (on northern face of pedestal): E.H. BAILY. R.A. / FACIEBAT / LONDINI / 1840

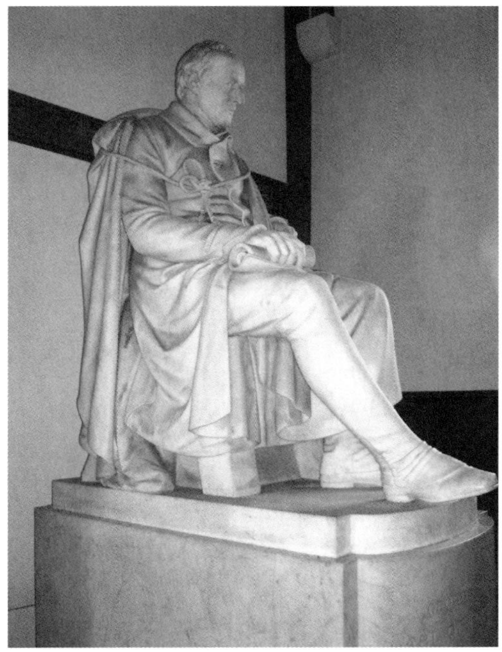

Edward Hodges Baily, *Monument to the Earl of Egremont*

Inscriptions (to front of pedestal in carved letters): GEORGE O'BRIEN / EARL OF EGREMONT / BORN DECR. 18. 1751 / DIED NOVR. 11. 1837. / FILII. POSUERE.
Status: not listed
Condition: good
Owner/custodian: Parish Church of St Mary the Virgin

The large seated statue of George O'Brien, Earl of Egremont, wearing contemporary dress, with a large cloak tied loosely across his shoulders, is by the same sculptor as the statue of Nelson In Trafalgar Square (1842). He faces east, holding a scroll in his right hand and the fingers of his left hand closed around a flat oblong object, possibly an eyeglass.

The 3rd Earl inherited Petworth House and estate in 1763 and for the following 74 years established a significant reputation as a collector, particularly of neoclassical sculpture and patron of artists such as J.M.W. Turner. He was also responsible for the redesigning of the church in 1827–1829.

Notes
[1] *The story of Petworth Parish Church*, nd.
[2] Nairn and Pevsner (1965), p. 295.

Other sources
A Walk Around St Mary's Petworth, nd.
Gunnis (1953), pp. 34, 80.
sussexparishchurches.org (accessed 23 November 2010).

Petworth House

Petworth house is home to one of the most important collections of sculpture in the country, or, more accurately, two collections: one of ancient marbles from classical Greece and Rome and the other of works by prominent British neoclassical sculptors of the early nineteenth century. They represent the collecting passions of father and son, Charles, 2nd Earl of Egremont (1710–63) and his heir George, the 3rd Earl (1751–1837), although sadly Charles did not survive to see his precious pieces displayed in his country home. When

George, aged 12, inherited the title, most of the ancient marbles acquired by his father in the 1750s and 1760s remained in the packing cases in which they had been shipped from Rome. The 3rd Earl unpacked and arranged this collection, which Cornelius Vermeule has claimed was, '… scientifically and aesthetically superior to the typical cargoes shipped from Rome in the eighteenth century' and equal to that of the Earls of Leicester at Holkham Hall in Norfolk.[1] His interest in contemporary sculpture came later and he patronized what John Kenworthy-Browne has described as '… the second generation of English neo-classical sculptors', including John Flaxman, Richard Westmacott, Francis Chantrey and John Edward Carew, rather than their predecessors, Joseph Nollekens, John Bacon and Thomas Banks.[2]

The house into which these collections were introduced, and its owners, the Percy family, were already well established as a focus of cultural patronage. The 10th Earl of Northumberland (1602–1668), having been brought up in scholarly surroundings by his bibliophile father, enjoyed a distinguished military and diplomatic career until the Civil War, when his fortunes diminished. As part of the circle around Charles 1st he acquired a taste for architecture, became a patron of Van Dyck and a collector of Old Masters and antique statuary. Thus, in the 1630s, were formed the foundations of the Petworth picture collection.

The creation of a palace fit to display the increasing collections was the work of Charles Seymour, 6th Duke of Somerset (1662–1748), who married into the family in 1682 and used his wife's money to rebuild the house. He was nicknamed the Proud Duke and his ambitious architectural scheme, modelled on the Palace of Versailles, is thought to have been designed by Daniel Marot. The ambience of the house and its estate are described by Nairn as '… proud and patrician, scorning false ostentation but not afraid of extreme richness when richness is needed.'[3] The work was largely complete by

1702 and the Duke employed the royal craftsmen in the rebuilding and refurbishing of the house, the most notable achievement being the magnificent carved room by Grinling Gibbons. His formal gardens were remodelled by 'Capability' Brown in the 1750s by the Duke's grandson, the 2nd Earl of Egremont (1710–63), the politician and collector whose antique statues remain on display in the house.

George O'Brien Wyndham, 3rd Earl of Egremont, agriculturalist, philanthropist and keen racehorse owner, surpassed all his ancestors in his patronage of the arts and passion for collecting. Indeed, the painter John Constable described Petworth as '… that house of art.'[4] Egremont's particular enthusiasm was for contemporary art and he invited many artists to stay at the house, including J.M.W. Turner, who executed a series of paintings of its interiors and parkland. In his desire to accommodate the growing Petworth art collections and display them to best advantage, Egremont remodelled and rearranged almost every room, including the Carved Room and his father's North Gallery that was extended twice, in 1824–25 and 1825–27. The collection of neoclassical sculpture that was to be displayed there has been compared by Kenworthy-Browne to '… the other post-Napoleonic collections, the most famous and best of which are at Woburn Abbey and Chatsworth.'[5] Unlike his contemporaries, Egremont encouraged artists working in England rather than in Rome and was closely involved with his chosen sculptors in choices of subject and composition. Philip McEvansoneya describes this aspect of his patronage as seeing himself '… as a contributor to the creative process.'[6] His collection lacks the cohesion of Woburn's heroic or mythological subjects or Chatsworth's concentration on the works of Canova and his followers. Kenworthy-Browne has, however, identified a connecting concept related to '… England, English poetry, to rural life or to pastoral literature.'[7] He credits Egremont with beginning a revival of 'ideal' or poetical works in England through his commissions.

What has been described as 'the golden age' of Petworth came to an end with the 3rd Earl's death, with his successors making few changes, although Egremont's grandson, the 2nd Lord Leconfield (1830–1901), commissioned Anthony Salvin to make considerable alterations, principally at the south end of the house and in the Carved Room. In 1947 Charles, 3rd Lord Leconfield (1872–1952) gave the house and park with an endowment to the National Trust, thus ensuring their permanent preservation. Members of the family continue to live there.

The North Gallery
Vermeule recommends the Petworth collection as,

> … one of the few … groups of statues, busts and reliefs still exhibited with little change in its neo-classical setting, in a gallery with niches and pictures on the walls beyond or in the no less formal but warmer and more intimate rooms of the house.[8]

The gallery was built to display the collection of antique marbles of the 2nd Earl of Egremont, which had been put together in Rome with the advice of the painter Gavin Hamilton and '… architect, decorator and antiquities dealer' Matthew Brettingham, who performed the same roles at Holkham Hall.[9] The South Corridor, the earliest part of the gallery, was formed by him between 1754 and 1763 by glazing over an open cloister at the north end of the house, to provide an arcade or *loggia*, such as those used by the ancient Romans and their Italian successors to display sculpture. Like the long rectangular galleries of Roman *palazzi* and museums, it displays around 70 statues and busts (the major part of the collection), the former in niches or on plinths and the latter on wall brackets or consoles.

The putting together of such a collection required not only substantial funds (the considerable cost of packing and transport had to be added to the purchase price) but also the ability to negotiate the stringent export controls exercised by the Papacy in Rome. The imperative to ensure that the papal collections, now displayed in the Capitoline Museum and in the Vatican, contained the most outstanding examples of classical sculpture meant that the Pope only granted licences for excavations within the Papal States to a small number of privileged dealers, in exchange for payment and a share of the finds. Some of the principal Italian families were also occasionally willing to sell statues and other antiquities from their ancestral collections. One such was Cardinal Alessandro Albani, a collector and dealer whose collections rivalled those of the Pope. Hamilton and Brettingham, who acted on behalf of the 2nd Earl, were part of the sophisticated Albani circle in Rome, which was a considerable advantage in easing the restrictions on excavation and export. Equally important, it gave them an introduction to Albani's librarian, the great art historian and expert on antiquity, Johann Winckelmann. The Petworth collections include at least one piece with an Albani provenance (*Statue of an Amazon* in the north gallery) and there were other acquisitions from famous Roman collections, including that at the Palazzo Barberini.[10]

Following the practice of the time, in response to collectors who did not wish to purchase 'incomplete' statues, Hamilton and Brettingham employed experienced restorers of excavated fragments, including Pietro Pacilli (1716–1773) and Bartolomeo Cavaceppi (1716–1799).[11] The latter's published account of his work, the *Raccolta* (1768–72), includes engravings of two statues restored for 'Milord Egremont' still in the North Gallery (*Ganymede with an Eagle* and *Agrippina as Ceres*).[12]

The collections continued to grow even after the death of the 2nd Earl in 1763, with the final shipment from Italy, which included a statue of

Silenus, arriving two years after his demise. At this time the gallery had only just been completed and the niches on the southern wall were still being filled 10 years after its construction. The 3rd Earl added restored Roman pieces, and two Greek masterpieces to this inheritance.[13]

Central Corridor, North Gallery
As Marjorie Trusted points out, marble sculptures, which formed the major part of most important eighteenth-century collections of antiquities were often, '… large and heavy … [and] therefore needed adequate display space … for this reason country houses rather than town houses in London, were generally the preferred location.'[14] The expansion of the collections required the 3rd Earl to plan significant extensions to the gallery at Petworth; the top-lit Central Corridor was added in 1824–25, immediately followed by the Square Bay, with all the work completed by October 1827. The fact that the Earl did not directly employ an architect suggests that he played a substantial role in the design of the expanded gallery. Christopher Rowell suggests that he was influenced by Sir John Soane's Dulwich Picture Gallery (1817), the first public gallery in England, and sought the architect's advice as he had done on previous occasions in connection with his plans for Petworth.[15] The Earl also sought the advice of at least three artists: the painter Thomas Philips and sculptors Sir Francis Chantrey and John Edward Carew. He left the practical execution of his ideas to the Petworth building yard under the supervision of Thomas Upton, the Clerk of Works.

Brettingham's colour scheme for the South Corridor was grey–blue, but, following the 3rd Earl's extensions, the expanded galleries were painted white, although this colour was beginning to be regarded as unsuitable for sculpture galleries as it made antique sculpture look dingy. During the 1991–93 restorations the galleries were returned to their 1873 colour scheme of dark red, which, together with green,

was considered more suitable for the display of marble sculpture, being considered by Ruskin to accentuate its contours. It should also be remembered that the sculptures would have been viewed in natural daylight, or, as the 2008 exhibition *The Return of the Gods* reminded its audience, with the dramatic highlighting of candles.[16]

The impetus for the extensive redevelopment of the galleries was the 3rd Earl's already expanding collection of contemporary sculpture. The present sculpture arrangement in the North Gallery (devised in 1991–93) was designed to restore that conceived by the 3rd Earl, other than the two massive groups by Carew rescued from ignominy in the tearoom. It was taken from a unique ground plan of the 3rd Earl's statue deployment drawn up in 1835 by H.W. Philips.

His first commission for what Kenworthy-Browne has classified as 'poetic' sculpture, was to John Flaxman for a *Pastoral Apollo* (1813–25) followed by his masterpiece *St Michael Overcoming Satan* (c. 1817–26) around which the Square Bay was built. The figure of Satan, as described by Milton, exerted a considerable fascination for Egremont. In 1819 he encouraged Francis Chantrey to turn away from his habitual portraits to produce an ideal work: 'a capital figure of Satan, with something of his original brightness'.[17] Chantrey, who eventually abandoned the commission, felt keenly the competition with Flaxman and his failure 'was destined to tease the sculptor, more or less as long as he lived'.[18]

A plaster model of a figure of Satan, subsequently destroyed, was part of the many commissions to the Irish sculptor John Edward Carew, employed almost exclusively by Lord Egremont from the 1820s. This former assistant of Richard Westmacott had come to the notice of the Earl in 1813 and developed a reputation, as described by Haydon in 1826, as 'perhaps the best cutter of marble in England … as rapid as lightening [*sic*] with his chisel, but idle in thought, preferring the chat of a gossiping

Coffee House to the glory of fame'.[19] Egremont encouraged Carew's inclination towards heroic and massive sculptural groups, often suggesting a subject and occasionally cancelling a commission when it did not accord with his own conception.

By 1831 the sculpture galleries were essentially complete and Egremont employed only Carew. The sculptor moved to Petworth in 1835 and was also provided with a studio in Brighton, where Egremont had a house. In 1837, the year of Egremont's death, Carew was working on a large group of Prometheus, while his patron was busy constructing a new dining room for the tenants (currently the tearoom). When he installed Carew's colossal sculpture there he christened it the Promethean Hall. It now stands in the North Gallery from which the 3rd Earl had moved Carew's *Venus, Vulcan and Cupid* to stand at the opposite end of the Promethean Hall. This second gallery, doubling as a tenants' hall and incongruously hung with cattle pictures, was clearly intended as a museum of Carew's sculpture, but the enterprise was curtailed by the 3rd Earl's death. The Square Bay of the North Gallery now contains almost all of Carew's commissioned sculptures, many of which were placed there in 1835.

Carew had devoted the greater part of his career as a sculptor to executing commissions for Lord Egremont, for which, he claimed, he was not always adequately recompensed. When he failed to receive an expected legacy from his patron, he brought a court case against the Earl's executors, claiming £50,000 in back payment. Fellow sculptors Westmacott and Chantrey appeared as witnesses for Carew, verifying his status as a sculptor of merit and providing estimated values for the works executed for the Earl. Carew's lawyer excused his client's lack of proper accounting on the ground that, '… like other men of genius [he] is not a man of the world.'[20] On the production of Carew's bank pass book and the Earl's accounts, however, the court case collapsed and two years later the sculptor was declared insolvent. As Rowell has pointed out, the proceedings of the trial remain as a rare record of sculptural practice in early nineteenth-century England.[21]

North Gallery, Square Bay
Adonis and the Boar
Sculptor: John Edward Carew

Executed: 1823–25/1826
Materials/dimensions: statue: white marble, 2.2 m high; wooden plinth: 97 cm high
Signature (on base underneath left hind leg of boar): J.E. CAREW, 1825
Condition: good

The sculpture illustrates the Greek myth of Adonis' fatal wounding by a boar. His right hand is raised holding a broken staff; the other part of the broken staff is lodged in a boar held by the muzzle by Adonis's left hand.

Carew remembered this as his first commission from Lord Egremont. It was a companion piece to the Arethusa, which the 3rd Earl had bought in 1823. The Adonis is on a larger scale and was valued by Carew at £1500. During the case bought by Carew against the Earl's executors, however, it was valued by Westmacott at £2000–£2500.[22]

North Gallery, Central Corridor
Arethusa
Sculptor: John Edward Carew

Executed: 1824
Materials/dimensions: statue: white marble, 1.4 m high; wooden plinth: 1 m high
Signature (to left of base near the dog's hind legs): J.E. CAREW. 1824.
Condition: fair (gouge on integral base between the legs. Small chips to left foot, inner calf and below letters of title)

Arethusa, a water nymph, is shown wearing a thin, draped shift-like garment. Her head is turned to the right as if listening. Her right arm and fingers are raised. A greyhound stands to her left side and her left hand rests on its head.

This was the first work by Carew to be acquired by the 3rd Earl. He visited Carew's London studio in the Edgware Road in 1823 to see the statue as a work in progress. At this time, Carew was still working for Sir Richard Westmacott. The statue, dated 1824, was shown in that year at the British Institution of which Lord Egremont was a Director. It was valued at '700 to 800 guineas' by Westmacott during Carew's court case.[23]

North Gallery, Central Corridor
Athleta Britannicus (The British Athlete)
Sculptor: John Charles Felix Rossi

Executed: 1828
Materials/dimensions: statue: white marble, 1.98 m high; wooden plinth: 1 m high
Signature (outer aspect of column): C. ROSSI. R.A. /MDCCCXXVIII
Inscription (front of base): ATHLETA BRITANNICUS
Condition: good (fingers of the right hand all broken and subsequently repaired)

The over life-sized statue depicts a prize-fighter, arms raised and prepared for a fight. He wears tight-fitting shorts and sandals. Although demonstrating a classical idealisation of physique and facial features, it was probably based on a contemporary boxer.[24]

Trusted suggests that Rossi's statue may have been designed as a response to Canova's severely classical figures, *Pugilists* (1801) in the Vatican.[25] Rossi would have seen these works during the three years he spent in Rome as the recipient of a Royal Academy travelling scholarship awarded in 1785, at the same time as that to fellow sculptor John Deare.

The production of Rossi's statue put him

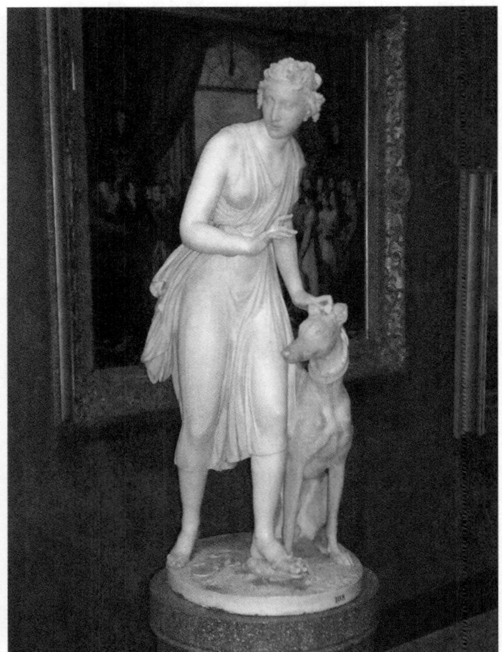

John Edward Carew, *Adonis and the Boar*

John Edward Carew, *Arethusa*

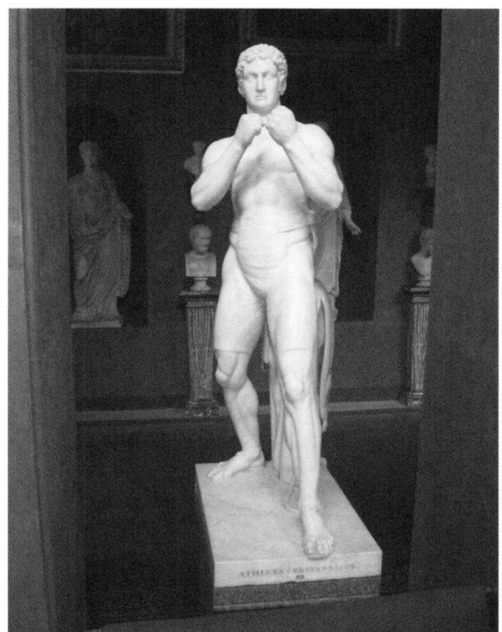

John Charles Felix Rossi, *Athleta Britannicus (The British Athlete)*

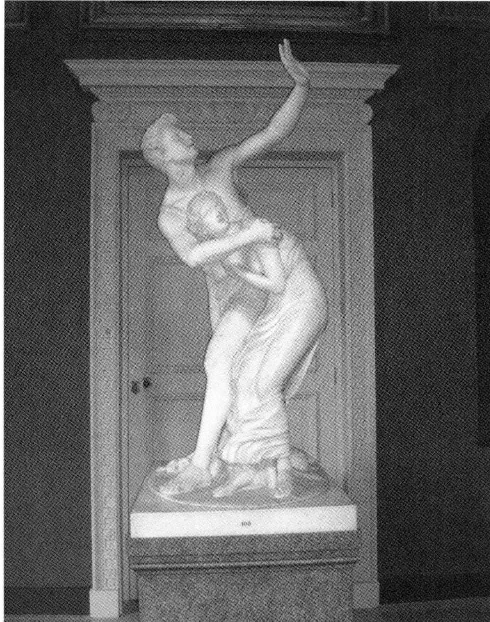

John Charles Felix Rossi, *Celadon and Amelia*

under severe financial strain, but, unusually, Lord Egremont was unsympathetic to his plea for more money in 1826. The sculptor appears to have offended his patron by forgetting the niceties of rank in his application.[26] The marble was shown at the Academy in 1828 as *The Pugilist* and was widely admired, particularly for the fact that it was cut from a single piece of marble. J.T. Smith described it as, '… truly vigorous and masterful …'.[27]

North Gallery, South Corridor
Celadon and Amelia
Sculptor: John Charles Felix Rossi

Executed: c. 1821
Materials/dimensions: statue: white marble, 2 m high; wooden plinth: 85 cm high
Inscription: (side of base, at left): CELADON AND AMELIA
Condition: good

The naked figure of Celadon looks skyward and holds up his left hand in an attempt to 'hold back' the lightning bolt. His right arm is wrapped around a cowering, semi-naked Amelia in a protective gesture. She gazes towards the lightning with an expression of fear.

The subject is taken from James Thomson's set of poems, *The Seasons* (1730) and depicts the moment in 'Summer' when Celadon and Amelia, the 'matchless pair' of lovers, are overtaken by a thunderstorm and Amelia is struck dead by lightning. They were on the point of entering a cottage, and this may explain why this position in the gallery (recorded in 1835, two years before the 3rd Earl's death) was chosen, in front of the false door. The group is not signed or dated, but was exhibited at the Royal Academy in 1821. Kenworthy-Browne points out that the piece is unlike any other known work by Rossi and that the dramatic pose sets it apart from contemporary

neoclassical sculpture. He suggests that the sculptor may have been influenced by William Blake or Henry Fuseli, who had drawn a sequel to this scene that was engraved in 1802.[28]

North Gallery, Central Corridor
Nymph and Cupid
Sculptor: Sir Richard Westmacott

Executed: c. 1827
Materials/dimensions: statue: white marble, 1.55 m high; wooden plinth: 1.03 m high
Condition: good

The nymph has her right arm raised at the elbow while looking over her right shoulder at Cupid who is 'held prisoner' by a ribbon that she holds in her right hand.

Exhibited in 1827 as *Cupid Made Prisoner*, this group is typical of the mythological works produced by Westmacott during the 1820s under the influence of contemporary Italian

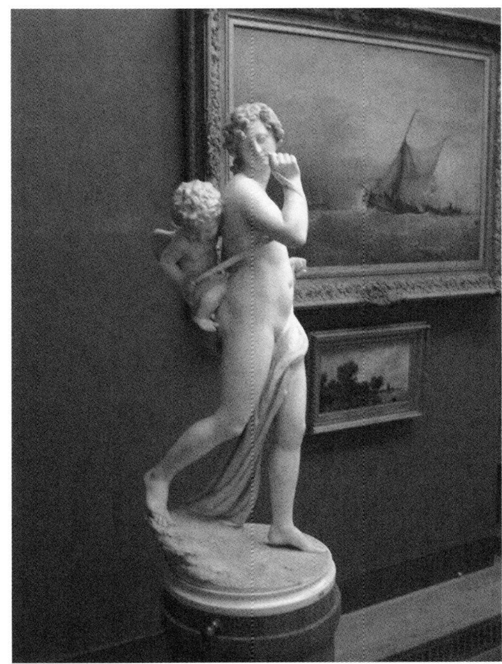

Sir Richard Westmacott, *Nymph and Cupid*

sculpture, particularly the work of Canova. It most closely resembles the Italian sculptor's *Three Graces* at Woburn Abbey and *Naiad and Cupid* then at Carlton House, both of which were *in situ* by the time Westmacott was working on this piece.[29] Whinney, although stating that the group is '… competently designed with a long spiral movement', also points to a lack of 'frank sensuality' in comparison with Canova.[30] Westmacott's group is the focal point of the enfilade on the west side of the house.

North Gallery, South Corridor
Pastoral Apollo
Sculptor: John Flaxman

Executed: 1825
Material: statue: white marble, 1.85 m high;
    wooden plinth: 1.06 m high
Signature (underneath dog's right hind leg):

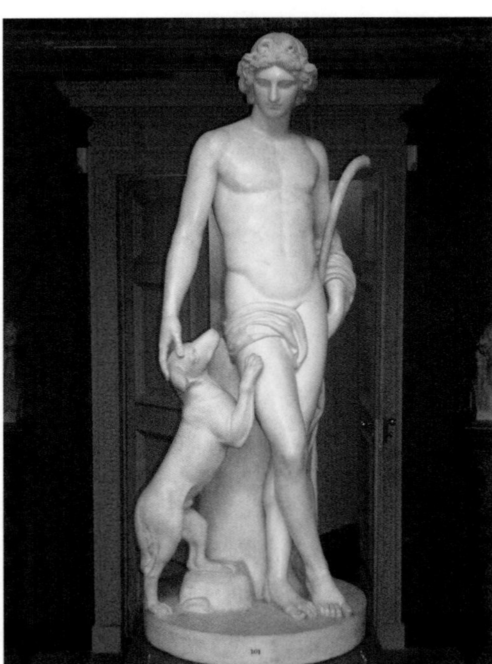

John Flaxman, *Pastoral Apollo*

J. FLAXMAN. R.A. 1825
Condition: good

The god Apollo is seen in his traditional role as protector of shepherds. Supported by his left arm, a Shepherd's crook extends to the floor behind him. A dog on its hind legs has the right paw on Apollo's right thigh and he reaches down to pat the dog's head with his right hand.

Lord Egremont's first payment for this piece was made in 1813; in total it cost him 900 guineas. A model was exhibited at the Royal Academy in 1814 and the finished marble in 1824. It was then returned to Flaxman's studio, McEvansoneya suggests for some refinements, which explains the fact that it is dated 1825.[31] The piece is often overlooked in favour of Flaxman's *St Michael Overcoming Satan*, but it represents the beginning of Egremont's commissioning of 'poetic' sculpture and a return to such subjects on the part of the sculptor after his earlier work for Thomas Hope and the Earl of Bristol in the 1790s.

North Gallery, Square Bay
Prometheus and Pandora
Sculptor: John Edward Carew

Executed: 1835–37 (unfinished)
Material/dimensions: statue; white marble, 2.7
    m high; plinth: Portland stone, 1.37 m high
Inscription (wooden plaque attached to base at
    the front): Prometheus/Pandora
Condition: fair (Pandora has broken fingers and
    thumb on right hand, third finger missing at
    knuckle; repair to big toe on Prometheus's
    left foot)

A naked Pandora sits on a draped block with her right knee raised. Prometheus stands to her right with his right arm raised aloft and in his hand an incompletely carved object. According to Greek myth, Prometheus created the first man from clay and stole fire from Zeus to give to mankind. In retribution, Zeus opened a box belonging to Pandora, Prometheus' sister-in-

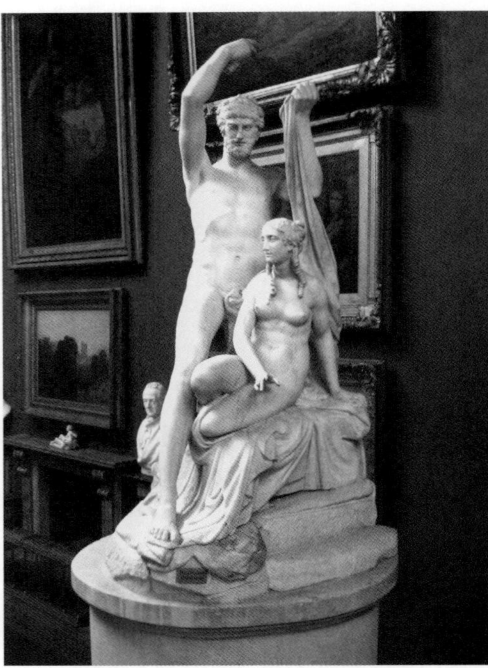

John Edward Carew, *Prometheus and Pandora*

law, thus releasing all the evils of the world with the exception of hope.

Work on the sculpture, for which Carew was paid £4000, began around 1825 and it remained unfinished after the 3rd Earl's death in 1837, when the sculptor became embroiled in the ultimately unsuccessful case against his patron's executors.

North Gallery, Central Corridor
Seated Venus
Sculptor: Richard Williams (after Joseph Nollekens)

Executed: c. 1823
Materials/dimensions: statue: white marble, 80
    cm high; wooden plinth: 96 cm high
Condition: good (large piece broken out of the
    grey base underneath the marble at the left-
    hand corner)

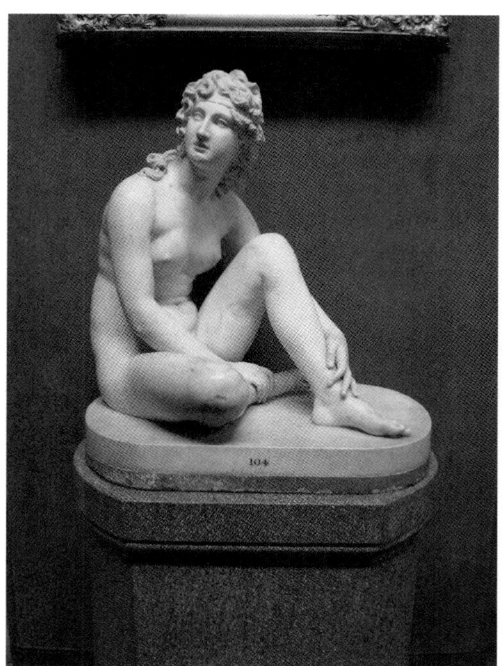

Richard Williams, *Seated Venus*

A naked seated Venus has her left knee raised with her right foot underneath. The pose is said to have been adopted by the model while getting dressed after a sitting.

Lord Egremont bought Nollekens' (1737–1823) plaster *Seated Venus* (private collection) at his posthumous studio sale in 1823. It was the only one of the sculptor's four Venuses that had not been produced using marble. The plaster version had originally been ordered by Lord Carlisle and placed in Castle Howard, but had subsequently been returned. Egremont gave the plaster to J.C.F. Rossi, in order for him to make a marble copy, as a memorial to the deceased sculptor, that did not in any detail depart from the Nollekens original. This presented difficulties due to the intricacy of the undercutting and Rossi had to invent new tools for the job that was entrusted to his assistant, Richard Williams. Perhaps due to its small size, the sculpture was not originally placed in the gallery but in a domestic room where it was drawn by Turner '… overlooking a vase of flowers.'[32]

North Gallery, Square Bay
St Michael Overcoming Satan
Sculptor: John Flaxman

Executed: 1826
Materials/dimensions: statue: white marble, 3.5 m high; wooden plinth: 1.26 m high
Signature (underneath Satan's left hand): J. FLAXMAN, R.A. 1826
Inscription (on back of base, below the serpent): THIS GROUP WAS EXECUTED IN 1826 BY JOHN FLAXMAN, R.A. / A MAN WHO PRESENTED THE MOST STRIKING EXAMPLE OF THE / PREEMINENCE OF THE MENTAL OVER THE CORPOREAL FACULTIES / OF HUMAN NATURE, IN THE UNION OF THE GREATEST DEBILITY / AND DISPROPORTION OF FRAME WITH THE STRONGEST ENERGY / OF CHARACTER, WITH THE MOST EXALTED SENTIMENTS OF HONOR / WITH A HEART ACTUATED BY UNIVERSAL BENEVOLENCE / AND WITH A SUBLIMITY OF GENIUS OF WHICH THIS WORK REMAINS / A SPLENDID MONUMENT HARDLY SURPASSED BY THE MOST / CELEBRATED PRODUCTIONS OF ANCIENT TIMES AND CERTAINLY / NONE OF HIS OWN.
Condition: good

A naked St Michael is about to plunge a long spear, held in both hands, into the body of a cowering Satan, whose body transforms into a serpent from the hip downwards. The piece was developed through at least two plaster models, both now in the Victoria and Albert Museum, one small-scale (c. 1891) and the other full-size, exhibited at the Royal Academy in 1822. Alterations from the original pose suggest that Flaxman responded to advice from Lord Egremont to make St Michael's line of sight '… more closely focussed on the wound he was inflicting on the devil.'[33] Both patron and sculptor admired Raphael's painting of St Michael, that Flaxman would have seen in the Louvre during one of several visits to Paris, and Egremont suggested that he use it as inspiration for his composition. Creating an equivalence to painting in a sculpture represented challenges that Flaxman relished, particularly the technical feat of, '… making in stone a figure alighting from flight.'[34]

The sculpture was ordered before April 1817 and finished in 1826, the year of the sculptor's death. It was carved, apart from the spear, from a single block of marble at a cost of £3500. The North Bay was designed for this work and it was the subject of two Turner watercolours, '… where it is turned slightly on its rotating plinth – a timely reminder that sculpture should not always be seen from the same point of view.'[35] Egremont's rationale for displaying the Flaxman piece and his other neoclassical commissions juxtaposed with antique sculpture was made clear in his remark to Westmacott that:

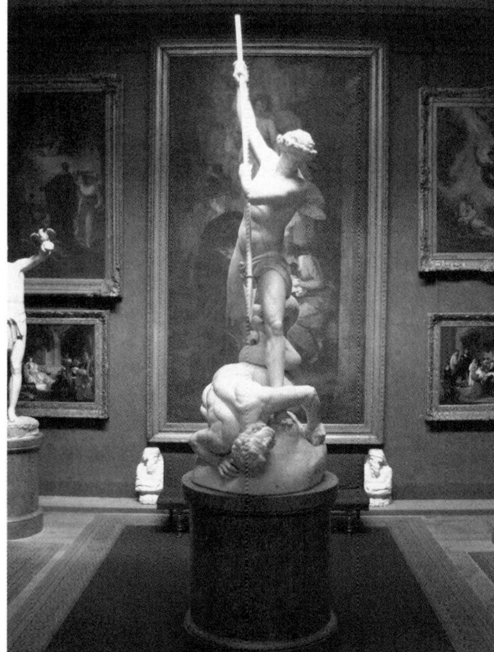

John Flaxman, *St Michael Overcoming Satan*

... it could be of great use to our sculptors to see themselves and to show others their works side by side with the ancients for the purpose both of deriving instruction and improvement and of inspiring confidence to themselves and to those thought to be their employers.[36]

The Dream of Horace
Sculptor: Sir Richard Westmacott

Executed: 1823
Materials/dimensions: relief: white marble, 138 m high × 1.85 m wide; frame: wood with gilding, 1.6 m high × 2.1 m wide
Condition: good

The three figures of a semi-naked Venus, helmeted Minerva and Apollo, with a lute, arch over the sleeping figure of a naked young boy (Horace), who is surrounded by a bear, doves and serpents. The subject is taken from Horace's *Ode to Calliope* (the Muse of Epic Poetry). The gods protect the boy not only from wild animals but also from attacks from barbarian tribes who, for Horace, included cruel Britons. The face of Venus (far left) was taken from 'the mistress of some man about in society', but the sculptor refused to reveal her identity.[37]

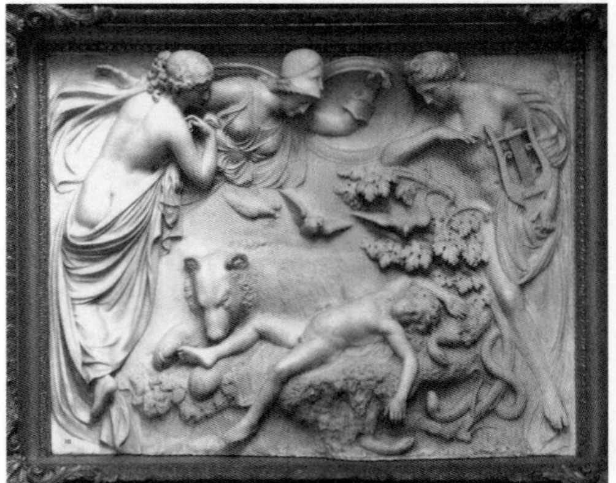

Sir Richard Westmacott, *The Dream of Horace*

The subject of Westmacott's relief is unusual, and is likely to have been chosen by his patron. It was exhibited at the Academy in 1823, just after completion, and subsequently installed in its present position within a blocked-up window at the west end of the North Gallery. Nicknamed 'Westmacotteles' by Egremont because of his addiction to all things Greek, the sculptor was a regular visitor to Petworth in the 1820s, and probably advised his host on matters of display, given his responsibility for the presentation of sculpture at the British Museum.

North Gallery, Square Bay
The Falconer
Sculptor: John Edward Carew

Executed: 1827–29
Materials/dimensions: statue: white marble, 2.27 m high; wooden plinth: 105 cm high

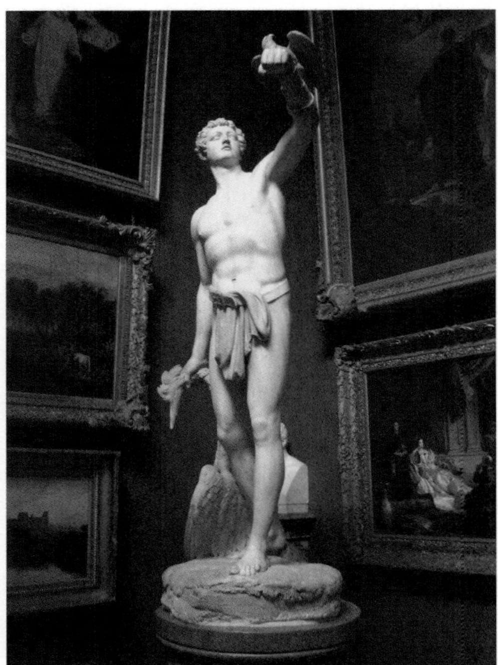

John Edward Carew, *The Falconer*

Condition: fair (tip of swan's beak missing and crack above the break)

The falconer, naked apart from a loincloth and belt, has a falcon perched on his outstretched left arm. In his right hand, he holds the neck of a dead swan.

Unlike Carew's other ideal statues, it apparently has no literary or mythological source and may have originally been intended for the Duke of St Albans, Grand Falconer of England.[38] It was admired by Francis Chantrey and the Duke of Devonshire.[39] Carew had completed the piece before his move from London to Brighton in 1831, and it was installed at Petworth in 1829. In 1835 it stood at the west end of the Central Corridor, was moved to the Audit Room after about 1865, and returned to the North Gallery in 1992.[40] It was valued by Westmacott at 1500 guineas at the court case brought by Carew.[41]

North Gallery, Square Bay
Venus, Vulcan and Cupid
Sculptor: John Edward Carew

Executed: c. 1827/28–31
Materials/dimensions: statue: white marble, 1.9 m high; plinth: Portland stone, 1.8 m high
Signature (left-hand corner of base in front of Cupid's right leg): J.E. / CAREW. / 1827
Inscription (on front of anvil): AITNA
Condition: fair (left arm of Cupid possibly has a previous repair. Marble cracked on the anvil between the 'A' and the 'I)

Vulcan, the god of fire, is seated on his anvil, its inscription referring to Etna, the volcano in Sicily. He rests his right hand on his hammer. His wife, Venus, stands behind him with her left hand resting on his right shoulder. Her son, Cupid, whose wings Vulcan forged, stands to the left of Vulcan and looks up towards his face.

Carew stated that he began work on this colossal group 'about 1827 or 1828' and that it was completed before 1831; however, his

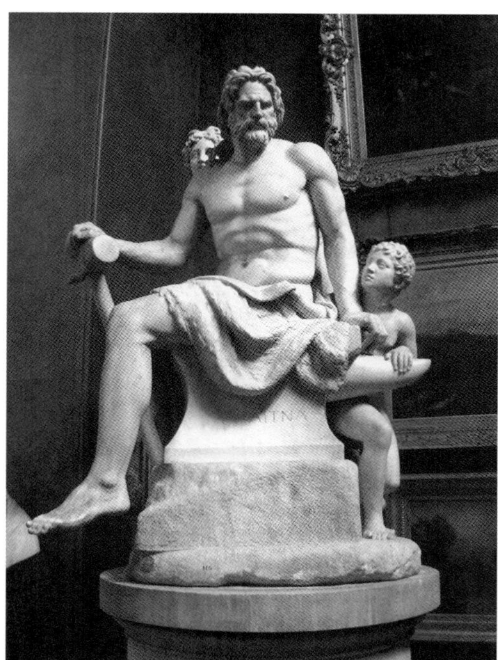

John Edward Carew, *Venus, Vulcan and Cupid*

assistant remembered that it was made in London and finished by 1828.[42] It was valued at £4000–£5000 by Westmacott during the court case proceedings.[43] Kenworthy-Browne believes that Carew's piece fails to attain Egremont's poetic ideals, being, '… more like the commonplace family of a blacksmith than a party of top gods'.[44]

This statue and the *Prometheus and Pandora* were originally positioned in niches at either end of the Audit Room (currently the tearoom) where they were placed on the present Portland stone pedestals supplied for £83.18s.2d.[45] The two statue groups were moved to the square bay in 1992.

Bust of King William III

Sculptor: Honoré Pellé (attributed)

Commissioned: c. 1724
Materials/dimensions: white marble; 1.9 m
    approx. high × 95 cm approx. wide × 35 cm
    approx. deep
Condition: fair (some weathering; repair to the
    nose)
Owner/custodian: Petworth estate

Nairn describes this large, flamboyant bust as, '… one of the best pieces of Baroque sculpture in England.'[46] The sculptor was clearly influenced by Bernini's bust of Louis XIV at Versailles (1665). He portrays a patrician figure glancing to his right, with an elaborately curled wig and drapery swirling around his upper arms and torso. Christopher Rowell suggests that this is the '… marble head representing the late King William' purchased by the 6th Duke of Somerset for £6 in 1724.[47] Whinney conjectures that it may in fact be a portrait of James II.[48]

The Duke employed a number of Huguenot émigrés from France, of whom Pellé was one; he also executed two signed busts of Charles II, now at Burghley House (1682) and the Victoria and Albert Museum (1684).[49]

Although created earlier, the bust was placed on the exterior wall of the sandstone Town Hall commissioned by the 3rd Earl of Egremont in 1793. The building was extended westward in 1869 and given to the town by John Wyndham in 1959. It was restored in 1995, but a replica bust was already in place by 1993.[50] The original was removed and placed inside Petworth House to prevent further weathering.

Notes
This entry has been produced with the generous support and permission of Petworth House and the National Trust. Much of the text has originated from the 1997 guidebook. The 3rd Earl of Egremont's

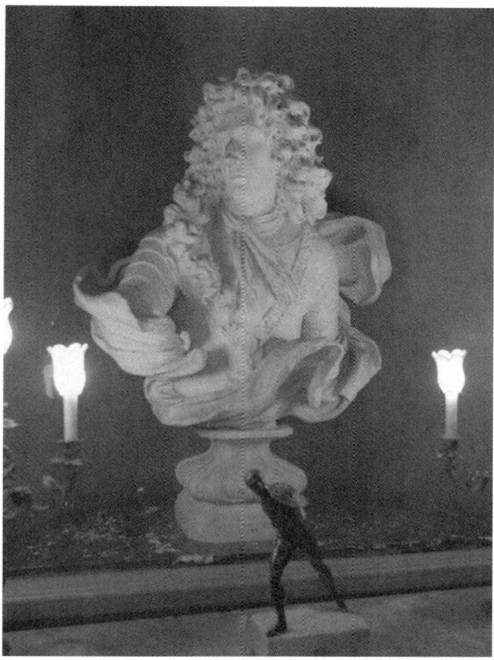

Honoré Pellé (attrib.), *Bust of King William III*

executors burnt most of his personal papers, so there is little surviving material relating to his patronage of art. There still exist, however, a mid-eighteenth-century *List of Statues and their Locations in Petworth and London* (PHA 11003) and a summary valuation of the sculpture in both locations of the same period (PHA 11001). There is also a mid-nineteenth-century catalogue of pictures, statues and books at Petworth (PHA 5308). These may be accessed through the West Sussex Record Office at Chichester.

[1] Vermeule, C., 'The ancient marbles at Petworth', *Apollo*, vol. CV, May 1997, p. 340. [2] Kenworthy-Browne, J., 'The Third Earl of Egremont and neo-classical sculpture', *Apollo*, vol. CV, May 1977, p. 367. All the contemporary sculptures are listed under 'Modern Statues' in the mid-nineteenth century handwritten *Catalogue of Pictures, Statues and Books in Petworth House and Offices* (PHA 5308). [3] Nairn and Pevsner (1965), p. 301. [4] Rowell (1997), p. 4. [5] Kenworthy-Browne (1977), p. 367. [6] McEvansoneya, P., 'Lord Egremont and Flaxman's "St Michael overcoming Satan"', *Burlington Magazine*, no. 143, 2001, pp. 351–59. [7] Kenworthy-Browne (1977), p. 368. [8] Vermeule

(1997). The care and attention paid to the placing of the antique statues is clear from the mid-eighteenth century lists, which include notes on the gallery stating, 'one wanting for the chimney' and a list of 'busts not yet placed' (PHA 11003). The 3rd Earl's papers also include a mid-eighteenth century design for a pedestal for the marble Hall, to be made of black and white marble (PHA 8039). [9] Ibid. [10] PHA 11003 includes a Young Nero bought for 200 crowns and a Youth with a Phrygian Cap, for 30 crowns, from the Barberini collection. [11] Ibid. There are numerous pieces listed as 'bought of Cavaceppi'. [12] Rowell (1997), pp. 79–80. [13] J.E. Carew restored arms head and legs to an 'ancient statue of Bacchus from Rome'. *Report of the Trial* (1840), p. 18. [14] Trusted (2008), p. 7. [15] Rowell (1997), p. 35. [16] Trusted (2008). [17] Kenworthy-Browne (1977), p. 370. [18] Ibid. [19] Rowell (1997), p. 89. [20] *Report of the Trial* (1840), p. 5. [21] Rowell (1997), p. 89. [22] *Report of the Trial* (1840), p. 5. [23] Ibid. [24] Trusted (2008), p. 31. [25] Ibid. [26] Kenworthy-Browne (1997), p. 371. [27] Ibid. [28] Ibid. [29] Ibid., p. 372. [30] Whinney (1964), p. 215. [31] McEvansoneya (2001), p. 351. [32] Kenworthy-Browne (1977), p. 372. [33] McEvansoneya (2001), p. 352. [34] Ibid. [35] Kenworthy-Browne (1977), p. 370. [36] McEvansoneya (2001), p. 357. [37] Kenworthy-Browne (1977), p. 372. [38] Rowell (1997), pp. 4–6. [39] Kenworthy-Browne (1977), p. 372. [40] Rowell (1997), p. 46. [41] *Report of the Trial* (1840), p. 5. [42] Rowell (1997), p. 46. [43] *Report of the Trial* (1840), p. 5. [44] Kenworthy-Browne (1997), p. 373. [45] Mr Burgess, 'a marble man at Tillington', was called as a witness during the court proceedings brought by Carew against the 3rd Earl's executors. He recalled having sold Carew Portland stone pedestals for the Prometheus Gallery at Petworth. [46] Nairn and Pevsner (1965), pp. 296–97. [47] Rowell (1997), p. 22. [48] Whinney (1964), p. 245. [49] Roscoe (2009), p. 969. [50] Information board, Leconfield Memorial Hall.

London Road/A23

Newtimber Holt (up path near Pyecombe Service Station)

Newtimber Giant

Sculptors: Sue Nunn and Alice Fox (with students from the University of Brighton and members of the Hillview Family Centre, Moulsecoomb)

Installed: May 2005
Materials/dimensions: wood, mixed media and plants, 27.43 m long
Status: not listed
Condition: good
Commissioned and funded by: Community–University Partnership in Practice (CUPP, University of Brighton) and the National Trust

This site-specific piece shows a giant female figure, constructed solely from materials found at the location, lying on her back within a wooded copse. New vegetation has established itself within the open framework of the figure.

This was the first of three pieces created on National Trust land near Brighton in May 2005, 2006 and 2007.[1] Each year, students from the Faculty of Arts at the University of Brighton, together with local artists and a group of women from a community arts group on a nearby council estate, worked together for two weeks. The sculptures emerged from the joint experiences of two very different groups of people and the forms suggested by the landscape, local history and the materials on hand. Their size and capacity for growth indicate the achievement of their makers in placing their own mark on the landscape. They represent an ongoing partnership and what can be achieved through creative, inclusive, collaborative working.

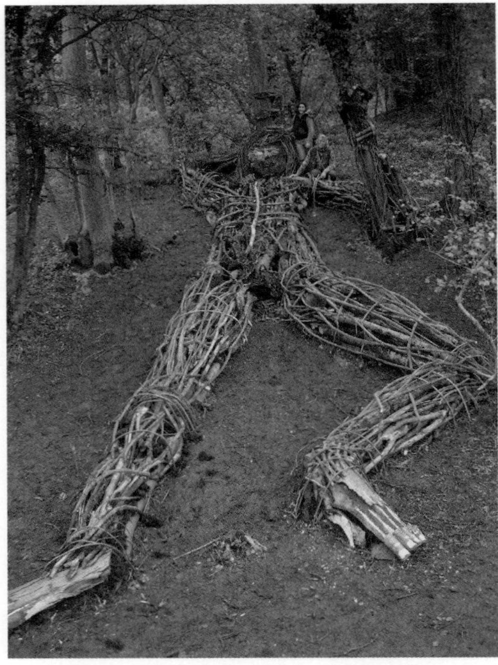

Sue Nunn and Alice Fox, *Newtimber Giant*

The request for this project came from a National Trust warden who attended a presentation on the Access to Art Project (inclusive arts for people with complex learning disabilities) and saw the potential for groups to work within areas of National Trust land. The works were part of a vision of building a natural sculpture trail across the Sussex Countryside.

Note
[1] The other two were *Saddlescombe Spiral* (2005, Saddlescombe) and *Sleeping Dragon* (2007, Stanmer Park, Brighton, since disappeared).

Other sources
artsresearch.brighton.ac.uk (accessed 5 January 2011).
Millican, J. with Fox, A. and Nunn, S., 'Art in the Woods: an Exploration of a Community/University Environmental Arts Project', in *Community–University Partnerships in Practice*, Leicester, 2007.

Habin Hill

Next to path leading to the Parish Church of St Bartholomew

War Memorial
Sculptor: William D. Gough
Architect: Sir John Ninian Comper

Unveiled: 28 August 1920
Materials/dimensions: scrolled base of obelisk: stone, 60 cm high × 80 cm wide × 80 cm deep; obelisk and cross: stone, 4.5 m high × 55 cm wide × 35 cm deep; base: stone, 1.58 m high × 73 cm wide × 73 cm deep
Inscriptions (in carved letters across two sides of the triangular aspect facing the road): IN MEMORIAM A.D. 1914–1919 (followed by the names of the fallen); (underneath this): ANNO DNI. 1939–1945 (followed by the names of the fallen)
Status: not listed
Condition: good
Owner/custodian: Parish Church of St Bartholomew

This ornate stone war memorial has a rectangular base built into the church wall to show a triangular aspect facing west towards the road. An obelisk with a scrolled base sits on this base, with, at its middle, a carved figure of St George slaying the dragon with decorative finials above. At the top of the obelisk is depicted a crucifixion scene. The base bears the names of the fallen and an inscription in low relief.

St George, patron Saint of England and associated with bravery, honour and chivalry, is commonly found in the iconography of war memorials. The architect, Sir Ninian Comper, wrote in 1948 to the Vicar of Rogate, 'I have always liked the Rogate cross, the best of many I have designed – partly I think because I heard the gypsies liked it!'[1]

Note
[1] Le Pla, P., *The Parish Church of St. Bartholomew Rogate*, Rogate (revised edn), 2003, p. 11.

B2145 Chichester Road

On roundabout at the entrance to Selsey, junction of Manor Road

Kanagawa
Sculptor: William Pye

Foundry: Nautilus Fine Art Foundry (now Zahra Modern Art Foundries)
Constructed: 2000
Installed: 2007 (edition of 3)
Materials/dimensions: patinated bronze, 2 m high × 4.3 m wide × 3.6 m deep
Signature (to lower edge): CAST BY NAUTILUS (N) William Pye/2000
Status: not listed
Condition: good
Commissioned and funded by: Graham Pye (housing developer) and Coastal West Sussex Partnership
Owner/custodian: Selsey Town Council

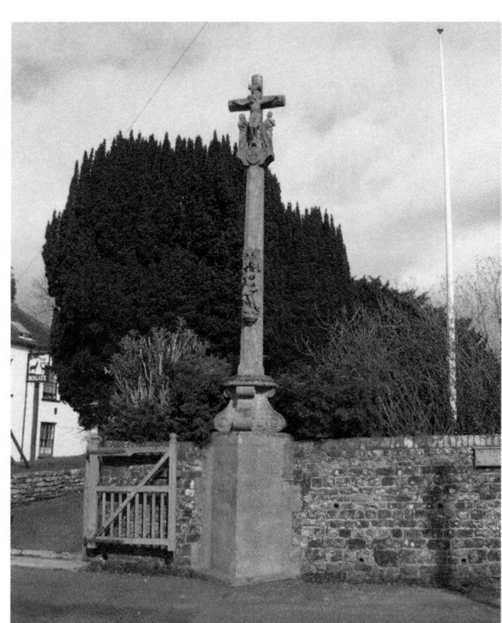

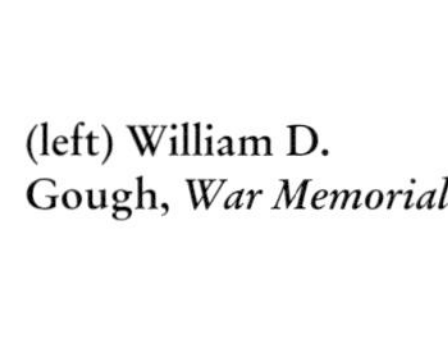

(left) William D. Gough, *War Memorial*

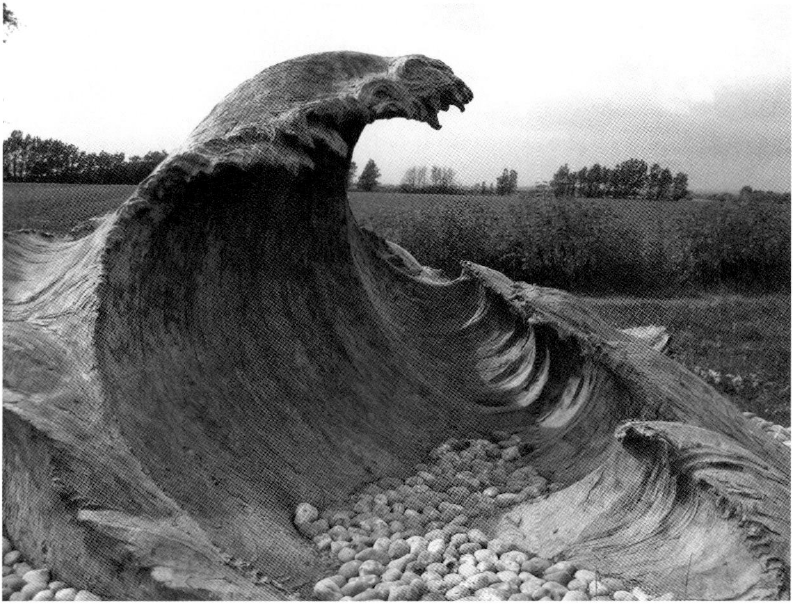

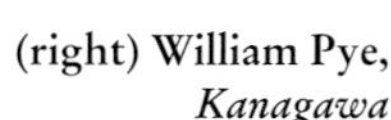

(right) William Pye, *Kanagawa*

The large bronze sculpture of a giant wave faces oncoming traffic on a roundabout and was intended to mark the entrance to the town, referencing its connection with the sea. Pye took his inspiration from the famous Katsuhika Hokusai (1760–1849) wood-block print *The Great Wave off Kanagawa*.

The sculptor had been invited to participate in one of the *Small Is Beautiful* exhibitions at Flowers East Gallery in London, and on seeing massive waves crashing on the Long Island shore where he was staying that summer, was prompted to use the impression as the subject for a small sculpture that was subsequently enlarged. He was fascinated by the process of depicting the energy and movement of water in a clay model and then translating it into the durable medium of bronze.[1] The Selsey sculpture is made of 2.5 tonnes of bronze and the final cost was £60,000. It was purchased from the Cass Foundation at Goodwood.

The sculpture, which it was hoped would be illuminated at night, was welcomed as part of the Selsey High Street Vision to improve the appearance and character of the site. There was, however, some local criticism that the disastrous earthquake and subsequent tsunami that devastated Kanagawa, in the greater Tokyo area, in 1923 rendered the title and subject of the work inappropriate to a seaside town potentially threatened by rising sea levels.[2]

Notes
[1] *British Contemporary Sculpture at Goodwood* (02/03), p. 94. [2] 'Revealed: Selsey's new £60,000 sculpture', *West Sussex Gazette*, 6 July 2007.

Old Shoreham Road
Ropetackle Development

This development regenerated a part of Shoreham, along the banks of the river Adur, which had lain derelict for the previous 35 years. Planned and constructed between 1999 and 2006, it provides nearly 200 homes, an arts centre, a series of public open spaces and a riverside walk. The commissioning of public art was an integral part of the redevelopment scheme, coordinated by lead artist Steve Geliot who worked with Adur District Council, Berkley Homes, P.R.C. Fewster, South East England Development Agency (SEEDA) and Arts Council England. He invited seven additional artists[1] to contribute works exploring the history, geology and ecology of the site; selected pieces are listed below; all were commissioned by the consortium and are unlisted. Running concurrently with the commission was an Artists and Schools programme in which Anna Twinam-Cauchi worked with students at Boundstone Community College to create new works, inspired by the Ropetackle site and its artworks, for sites in the school grounds. Local guitarist Richard Durrant worked with students and staff at Kings Manor School to produce original compositions also inspired by the site. Both projects were documented by digital media artist Malcolm Buchanan-Dick.[2]

Outside Ropetackle Arts Centre, Riverside Walk
Barnacle Trees

Sculptor: Steve Geliot

Landscape architect: Andrew Morton, P.R.C. Fewster

Installed: 2005
Materials/dimensions: four shafts: stainless steel, 10 m high, embedded in wooden bases, illuminated by fibre optics
Condition: good

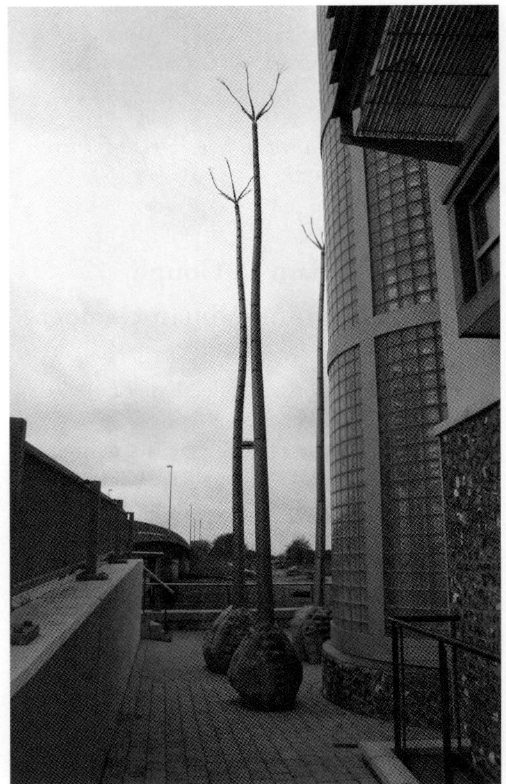

Steve Geliot, *Barnacle Trees*

The sculpture is composed of three tall, waving shafts ending in fringed branches that rise from irregularly shaped bases made from small blocks of wood encrusted with barnacle shapes. The subject matter refers to the diverse microscopic flora and fauna of the river Adur on which it is sited; the shapes are based on magnified images of estuary microorganisms.

Lenses
Sculptor: Amanda Hopkins

Installed: 2005
Materials/dimensions: 14 optical lenses, each 9
   cm diam., mounted on metal bases
Condition: fair (seven lenses vandalised and
   replaced 2008)

The series of lenses is placed at intervals along a balustrade that separates the outer edge of the development from the river shore. Some are incorporated within the steel hawsers that form part of the balustrade and others on top of its supporting wooden posts.

Amanda Hopkins originally trained as a psychologist and was initially inspired by the expansive skies and quality of light at Ropetackle. After learning about the history of early film and photographic studios nearby, she developed the idea for *Lenses*, encouraging the viewer to examine close up the detail of the landscape.

Unwinding
Sculptor: Teresa Martin

Installed: 2005
Materials/dimensions: cast iron and bronze
   resin, 2.24 m high × 4.0 m at widest part
Condition: good

The sculpture is a hollow rounded cone-shaped structure, pierced with zigzag slits to reveal the interior. Although abstract in form, it draws upon key elements in the immediate landscape; the patterns on the riverbed created by tidal action, the play of light on water, the vegetation on the riverbank, the shapes created by the processes of erosion and silting. Martin also makes reference to the recent archaeological excavation at Ropetackle, likening the internal cavities of the highly textured surface of her work to the smugglers' tunnels running under the town.

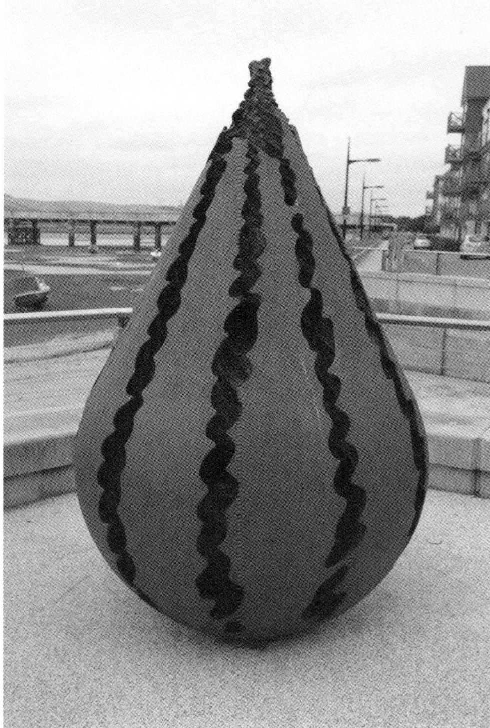

Amanda Hopkins, *Lenses*

(right) Teresa Martin, *Unwinding*

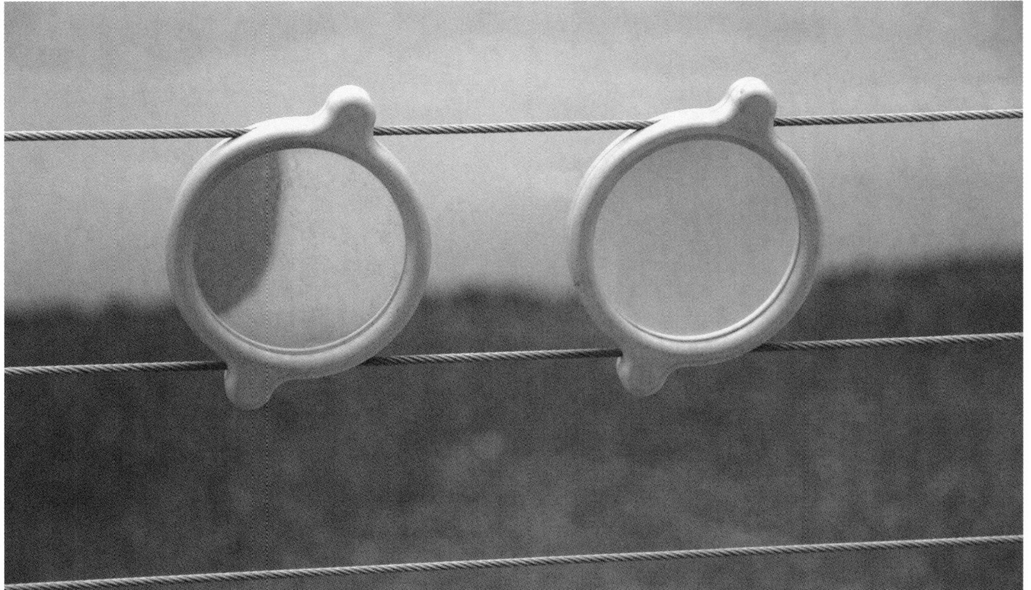

Carved Wooden Sculptures
Sculptor: Anna Twinam-Cauchi

Installed: 2005
Materials/dimensions: found wooden posts;
   tallest 1.36 m high; shortest 40 cm high
Condition: good

The shaped wooden posts, carved from salvaged sea defence timber donated by Shoreham Port Authority, are grouped together in eight sets of twos and threes along the sea wall. The pieces emphasise the shapes and textures created by weathering. Using a similar approach, Twinam-Cauchi had also designed 28 oak and elm bollards for the seafront development in Brighton in 1999.

Notes
[1] Geliot has produced many public sculptures in

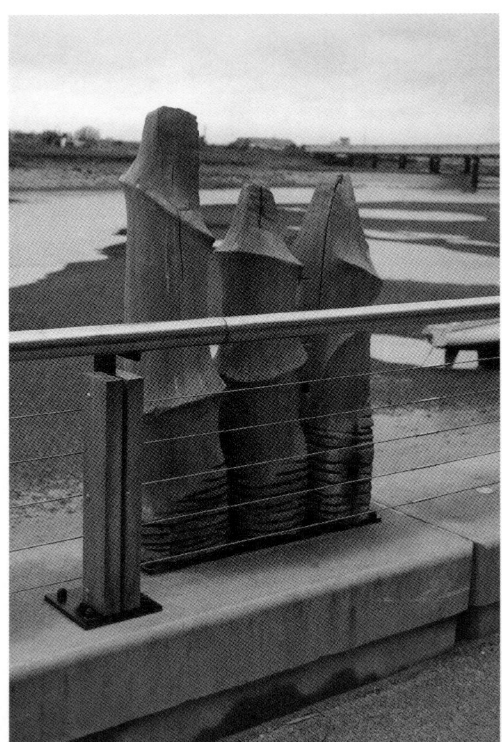

Anna Twinam-Cauchi, *Carved Wooden Sculptures*

Brighton and East Sussex; he was also lead artist for the New England development, Brighton and Arts Coordinator for the Royal Sussex County Hospital. The other artists involved at Ropetackle were: Steven Follen, Paul Harrington, Amanda Hopkins, Teresa Martin, Jon Mills, Rachel Reynolds and Anna Twinam-Cauchi. [2] Lord (2008), p. 5.

Other sources
'Art by the river: sculpture at Ropetackle',
    adur.gov.uk (accessed 11 November 2010).
Teresa Martin (sculpture tutor, City College,
    Brighton and Hove), correspondence, November
    2008.
Seeda News, 15 September 2004; 25 January 2005;
    seeda.org.uk/news_&_events (accessed 25
    October 2007). Seeda's land and property assets
    were transferred to the Homes and Communities
    Agency at the end of 2011 and the agency
    dissolved.

Church Hill

Church of St Mary, in south aisle next to window (formerly in a recessed tomb in the chancel where the organ is now)

Effigy of Anthony St Leger of Binstead

Sculptor: unknown

Installed: 1539
Materials/dimensions: oak, 40 cm high × 1.56 m
    wide × 54 cm deep
Status: not listed
Condition: fair (tips of fingers missing. Cracks
    down front of face and chest and below
    elbow of right arm. Tip of shoe on left foot
    broken off)
Owner/custodian: Church of St Mary

The effigy of Anthony St Leger Esq. of Binstead depicts the deceased in plate armour associated with the Wars of the Roses, with his hands on his chest, palms together in prayer. His head, with collar length hair, rests slightly to the right on a helmet.

St Leger died in 1539 and requested in his will to be interred in Slindon Parish Church before a picture of the Virgin Mary that no longer exists and is thought perhaps to have been a mural or stained glass window.[1] This is the only existing example of a wooden effigy in Sussex. The tomb chest on which the effigy lay has disappeared. The figure was removed from its former site in the church when the organ chamber was relocated. A protective metal herse (an arrangement of iron straps derived from a portcullis) was erected around it in 1990 to ensure security. Nairn describes it as, '…

Unknown, *Effigy of Anthony St Leger of Binstead*

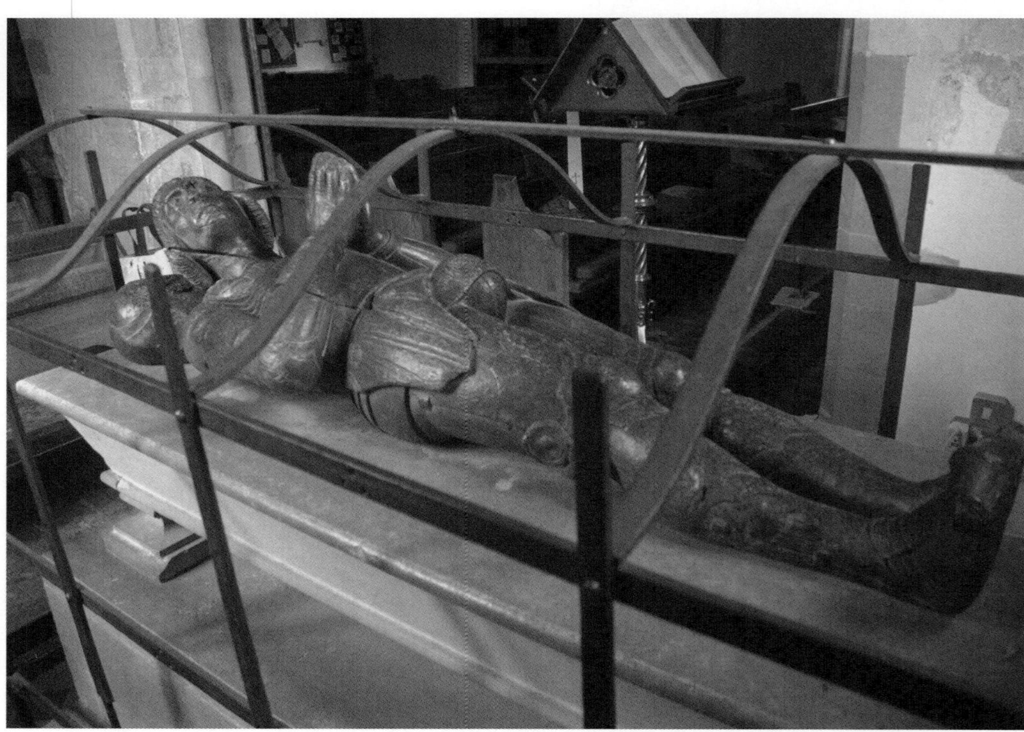

admirably modelled, alert and inquiring and individual. Worth any number of mechanical effigies.'[2] The writer and historian Hilaire Belloc (1870–1953), whose mother lived in Slindon, wrote a poem (aged 9) entitled *The Nameless Knight*, about the tomb.[3]

Notes
[1] *The Church of St Mary, Slindon*, leaflet, nd.
[2] Nairn and Pevsner (1965), p. 327. [3] Foster, A., *Aspects of the Religious History of Slindon Since the Reformation*, Slindon, 2013, np.

Other source
Swinfen and Arscott (1984), p. 124.

St Richard's Catholic church, on wooden bracket on east wall

Monument to Anthony James Radcliffe
Sculptor: Bertel Thorwaldsen

Commissioned: after 1814
Materials/dimensions: marble, 77.5 cm high × 75.5 cm wide × 5 cm deep
Inscriptions (at top of central pillar on relief): REQUIESCAT / IN PACE; (at base of central pillar): D O M / THE FAITHFUL WHO VISIT THIS CHAPEL ARE HUMBLY ENTREATED / TO PRAY FOR THE REPOSE OF THE SOUL OF THE LATE / ANTHONY JAMES RADCLYFFE EARL OF NEWBURGH / WHO DEPARTED THIS LIFE NOVEMBER THE XXVIII MDCCCXIV / HE DIED AS HE LIVED RESPECTED AND BELOVED BY ALL WHO KNEW HIM / THESE LINES ARE INSCRIBED BY HIS AFFLICTED WIDOW / ANNE NEWBURGH
Status: church Grade II
Condition: good (chip to base of relief)
Owner/custodian: St Richard's church

This small relief depicts, on either side of a central pillar bearing an urn, a kneeling praying female figure and an angel, the 'genius of death', with head bowed, holding an extinguished torch and poppy heads, symbolising sleep and death.[1]

The '… severe, Hellenising style …' of the

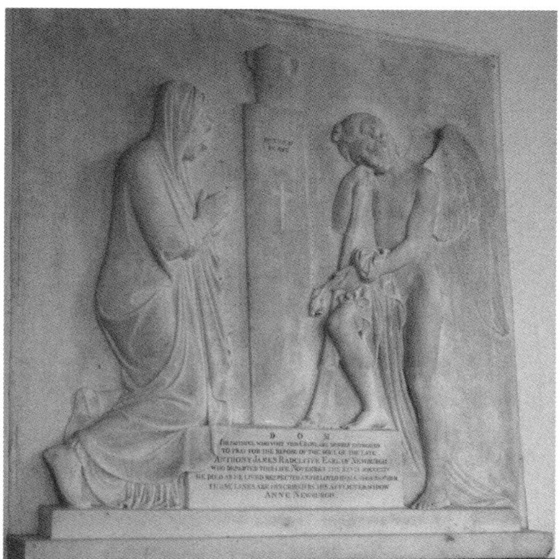

Bertel Thorwaldsen, *Monument to Anthony James Radcliffe*

Danish sculptor Thorwaldsen was popular with English patrons, including the 6th Duke of Bedford, the 6th Duke of Devonshire and the banker and connoisseur Thomas Hope, who regarded him as a rival to Antonio Canova and John Flaxman.[2] Most of his commissions were for portrait busts or sculptures of classical subjects and he produced few funerary monuments; this is one of only three in England.[3]

Both Gunnis (1953) and the English Heritage listing details (2005) state that the sculpture is signed, but there is no visible signature. The Thorwaldsen museum in Copenhagen has confirmed that it is by Thorwaldsen and that he did not sign his sculptures.[4]

Notes
[1] Roscoe (2009), p. 1262. [2] Ibid. [3] Nairn and Pevsner (1965), p. 326. [4] We are grateful to Mr John Moor, of St Richard's Church, for this information.

Reynolds Lane
Junction with School Hill and Park Lane

Village Sign
Designer: unknown

Installed: 2000
Materials/dimensions: oak, 2.8 m high × 60 cm wide × 28 cm
Inscriptions (bronze plaque on north face of post, in black painted incised letters): THIS SIGN WAS DONATED BY / THE SLINDON PUDDING CLUB / AND DEPICTS THE SHAPE & SIZE / OF THE BAT AND WICKET / THAT WAS FIRST USED IN / SLINDON IN 1731; (on east and west faces of post and cross bar, in carved letters): SLINDON 2000.
Status: not listed

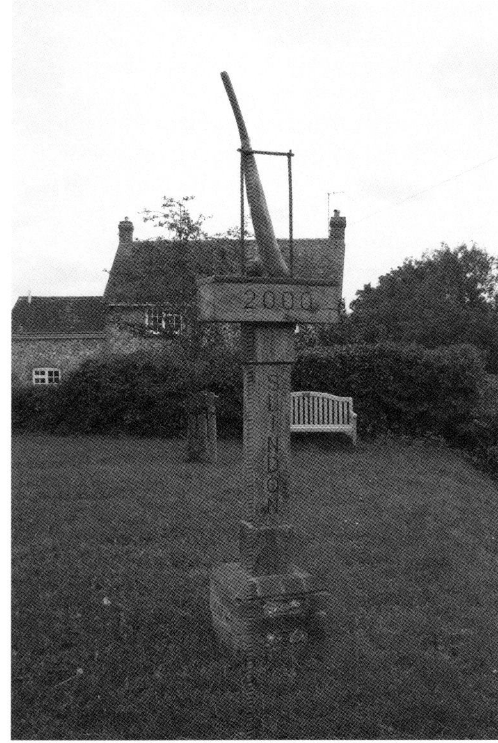

Unknown, *Village Sign*

Condition: fair (black paint of inscription
wearing in places. Post split badly on eastern
side due to weather)
Commissioned and funded by: Slindon
Pudding Club
Owner/custodian: Slindon Parish Council

This sign at the entrance to the village depicts a
crick (predecessor of the present-day cricket
bat, similar to a hockey stick, but heavier and
longer), ball and wicket resting on a wooden
cross piece atop a wooden post resting on a
brick base.

It commemorates the fact that Slindon can
claim to have the oldest cricket club in
continuous existence, having originated in the
seventeenth century with the Duke of
Richmond at Goodwood Park. He developed a
team of players, including Slindon residents,
largely from his estate workers and local
landowners. The Duke also developed the first
set of rules governing the playing of the game
that became the subject of a formal agreement
in 1744. Richard Newland and his brother and
nephew were key to the development of cricket
in Slindon. The Common with its clay surface
on fast-draining gravel provided a level and fast
pitch allowing more accurate play than the
usual downland turf. When the Duke was
summoned by the King to help suppress the
Stuart rebellion in Scotland, Newland and his
fellow players formed their own club.

Sources
slindon.com (accessed 5 January 2011).
Swinfen and Arscott (1984), p. 124.

The Street/Cow Lane

*South transept of the Church of St Mary
and St Gabriel, next to the Cowper family
tomb*

Madonna and Child
Sculptor: Karin Jonzen

Installed: 1985
Materials/dimensions: statue: patinated bronze
resin, 85 cm high × 48 cm wide × 40 cm
deep; plinth: wood, 86 cm high × 47 cm wide
× 47 cm deep
Status: not listed
Condition: good
Commissioned and owned by: Church of St
Mary and St Gabriel

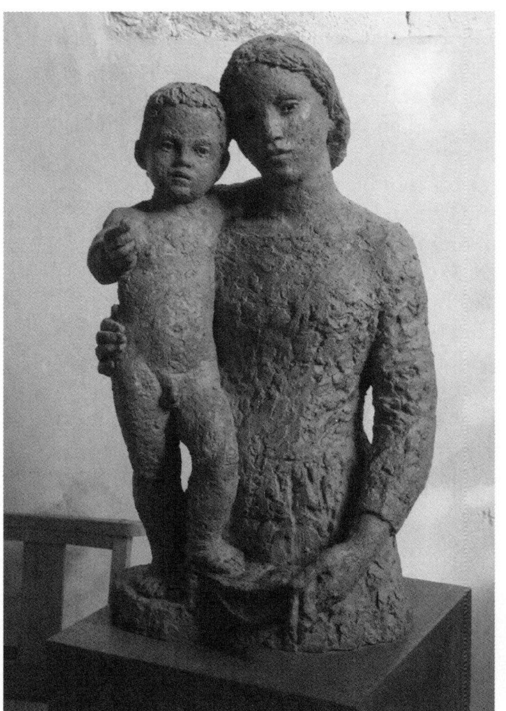

Karin Jonzen, *Madonna and Child*

In this contemporary interpretation of the
theme, the standing figure of the Christ child
leans against the torso of the Madonna. The
statue was commissioned to replace a
fourteenth-century Spanish wooden Madonna
and Child that had been stolen from the church.
Jonzen's earlier treatment of the theme was
criticised as representing 'a watered down
"children's corner" kind of Christianity'.[1]

Note
[1] Conlay, I., 'The religious theme, such a brave
experiment', *The Catholic Herald*, 15 August 1958,
p. 7.

Other sources
Lucie-Smith, E., 'Karen Jonzen: obituary', *The
Independent*, 2 February 1998.
St Mary and St Gabriel Harting: a Brief Guide,
church leaflet, nd.

Churchyard of St Mary and St Gabriel

War Memorial
Sculptor: Eric Gill

Unveiled: 3 March 1921
Materials/dimensions: obelisk: Portland stone,
5.33 m high × 53 cm wide × 53 cm deep;
base: Portland stone, 62 cm high × 1.2 m
wide × 1.2 m deep
Inscriptions (on northeast face): AND / THUS /
THEY DIED / LEAVING / THEIR DE- / ATHS FOR
/ AN EXAMPLE / OF A NOBLE / COURAGE /
AND A MEMORIAL / OF VIRTUE / NOT ONLY /
UNTO YOUNG / MEN BUT / UNTO ALL / THEIR
/ NATION / II MACC.VI.31
Status: not listed
Condition: good (cracks over base)
Commissioned by: Rev A.J. Reeves of South
Harting
Owner/custodian: Church of St Mary and St
Gabriel

The tall slender obelisk, surmounted by a cross,
has bas-relief carvings around the lower sides,
depicting the patron saints of England, Ireland,
Scotland and Wales: to the southeast, St
George; northeast, St Patrick; northwest, St

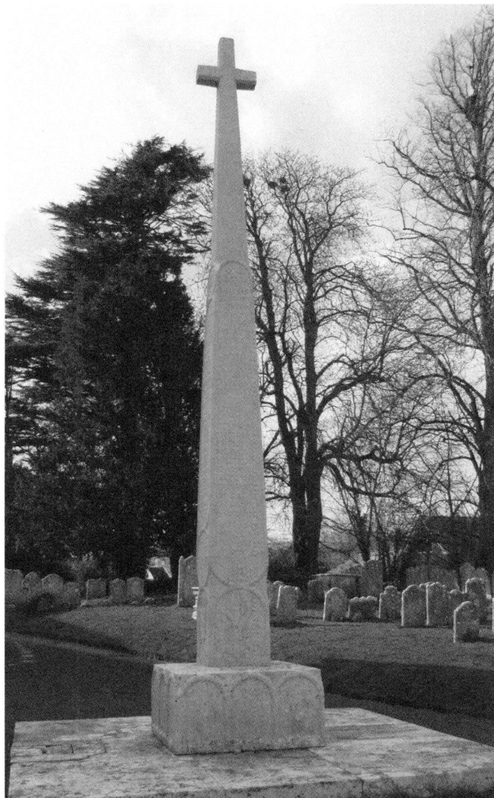

Eric Gill, *War Memorial*

Andrew; southwest, St David. Arched panels bear 35 names of those from South Harting who died in the First World War.

Gill was commissioned in 1919 (this was job no. 708 in his ledgers) and spent a total of 34 days working on the memorial, over the following two years. He made preliminary drawings with Desmond Chute and worked on carving the stone with his assistant Hilary Stratton. The total cost was £450 and the cross was dedicated on 3 July 1921 by the Venerable Archdeacon of Chichester.[1]

Note
[1] Collins, J., *Eric Gill: the Sculpture, a Catalogue Raisonné*, London, 2006, p. 115.

Vicarage Lane

Opposite the Church of St Andrew, at the entrance to St Cuthman's field

Statue of St Cuthman
Sculptor: Penelope Reeve

Installed: 2000
Materials/dimensions: Portland stone, 1.5 m high × 1.8 m wide × 1.4 m deep
Signature (carved into stone at base, facing south): PENELOPE REEVE / 2000
Inscription (carved into stone at base, facing east): ST. CUTHMAN / BUILDER
Status: not listed
Condition: fair (according to local newspapers, the sculpture has been repeatedly vandalised since its unveiling; evidence of replacement of nose)
Commissioned by: Millennium Celebration Group Steyning 2000
Owner/custodian: Steyning Parish Council

St Cuthman, patron saint of Steyning, is depicted sitting on a stone block gazing to the right in the direction of St Andrew's Church. His right foot rests on a depiction of the 'Steyning Stone' (the original was discovered in 1938 and is in the porch of the church; it may have been the centrepiece of pagan worship on the site where the church now stands). Behind the right leg of the statue is a bag of builder's tools. According to legend, St Cuthman was an Anglo-Saxon shepherd who built a wheelbarrow in which he moved his ailing mother around with him, until eventually his wheelbarrow collapsed as he reached Steyning, whereupon he settled and built his Church. After the Norman Conquest his relics were transferred to the Abbey of Fécamp in Normandy.

The field in which the statue stands was purchased by public subscription, organised by

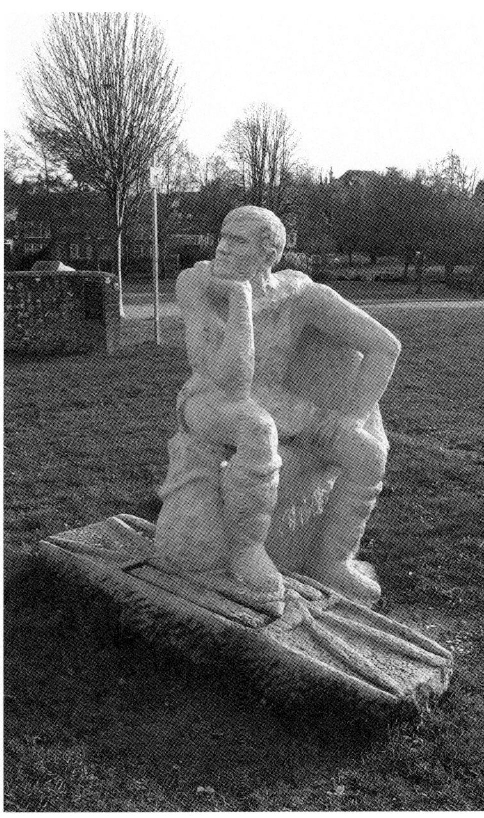

Penelope Reeve, *Statue of St Cuthman*

the Steyning Society, to be preserved as a public open space in 1966. Steps in the churchyard wall leading down to the field and the commissioning of the statue, which cost £9000, were funded by the local community to celebrate the Millennium.

Sources
chidhamandhambrook.info (accessed 12 December 2010).
Ford, H., *Steyning Conservation Area Guide*, Steyning, revised edn, 2003, p. 30.

Church Street/School Lane

St Mary's Church, on south wall, above door

Monument to Henry Hollis Bradford

Sculptor: Richard Westmacott

Commissioned: after 1816
Materials/dimensions: white marble; 1.5 m approx. high × 1.75 m approx. wide × 25 cm approx. deep
Signature (on bottom right-hand corner): WESTMACOTT (followed by illegible place name)
Inscription (on central tablet above regalia): TO THE MEMORY OF / SIR HENRY HOLLIS BRADFORD / KNIGHT COMMANDER / OF THE MOST HONOURABLE MILITARY ORDER OF THE BATH, / AND LIEUTENANT COLONEL / OF THE FIRST OR GRENADIER REGIMENT OF FOOTGUARDS. / THIS MONUMENT IS ERECTED / BY HIS COMPANIONS IN ARMS, / THE WITNESSES OF HIS VALOUR, / AND SHARERS OF HIS SOCIAL HOURS. / HE DIED AT LA VACHERIE NEAR LILLIERS IN FRANCE, / ON THE 17TH SEPTEMBER 1816, / IN THE 36TH YEAR OF HIS AGE / AND WAS BURIED IN THIS CHURCHYARD
Status: not listed
Condition: good (part of the sword handle broken)
Owner/custodian: St Mary's church

Below an Egyptian-style sarcophagus in relief is a 'still life' depicting Colonel Bradford's regimental colours, his plumed helmet and sword, circled with a laurel wreath, symbolising victory and valour. It is a skilfully composed example of the way in which, 'Westmacott and other sculptors of the period … personalized their memorials with attributes or emblems relating to the deceased's life.'[1]

On north wall, above door

Monument to Major Hugh Falconer

Sculptor: Richard Westmacott

Commissioned: after 1827
Materials/dimensions: white marble on grey slate; 2 m approx. high × 1 m approx. wide × 10 cm approx. deep
Inscription (below relief): SACRED TO THE BELOVED MEMORY OF / MAJOR HUGH FALCONER, / WHO SERVED MANY YEARS IN THE 71ST HIGHLAND REGIMENT / AND ON THE STAFF IN INDIA AND IN EGYPT WITH ZEAL AND HONOUR. / HE WAS BORN AT INVERNESS N.B. ON THE 12TH OF JUNE 1770, / AND DEPARTED THIS LIFE AT BRIGHTON ON THE 23RD OF JANUARY 1827. / A BRAVE SOLDIER, A FAITHFUL FRIEND, AND IN EVERY RELATION OF LIFE / A JUST, HONOURABLE AND GOOD MAN. / ALSO IN AFFECTIONATE REMEMBRANCE OF MARY, ELDEST DAUGHTER OF THE ABOVE / SHE DIED AT BOULOGNE SUR MER IN FRANCE / ON THE 8TH OF FEBRUARY 1825 IN THE 17TH YEAR OF HER AGE / THIS LITTLE MEMORIAL OF HER EARLY AND RARE VIRTUES IS PLACED IN THE VILLAGE WHICH SHE LOVED, AS AN INCENTIVE TO YOUTH / TO FOLLOW SO BRIGHT, SO SWEET AN EXAMPLE, / FOR TRUTH, INTEGRITY, AND HUMILITY WERE THE GUIDES / OF HER PURE AND INNOCENT LIFE; (on separate tablet below main memorial): IN MEMORY ALSO OF EIZABETH RELICT OF THE ABOVE / BORN NEAR BRADFORD / WHO DEPARTED THIS LIFE AT BRIGHTON FEBRUARY 4TH 1841 IN THE (illegible) YEAR OF HER LIFE
Status: not listed
Condition: good
Owner/custodian: St Mary's Church

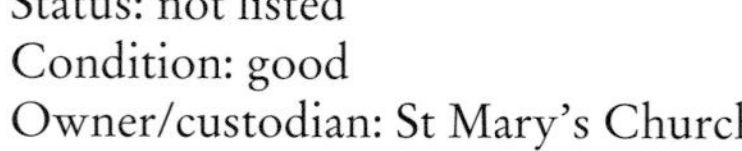

Richard Westmacott, *Monument to Henry Hollis Bradford*

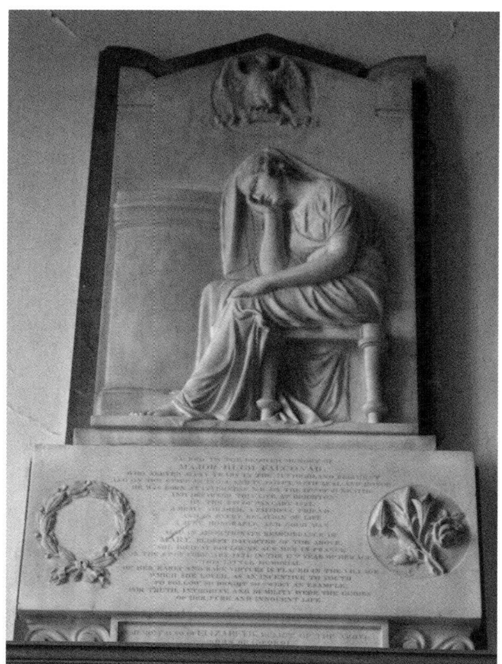

Richard Westmacott, *Monument to Major Hugh Falconer*

In this relief, Westmacott employs the common nineteenth-century memorial motif of the classically draped woman seated mourning next to a tomb. As Busco comments, she is '… intended to evoke inconsolable widows …' found in ancient Greek and Roman literature.[2] Westmacott used an identical composition in his memorial to Thomas Philip Bagge (died 1827) in St Mary's Church, Stradsett, Norfolk.[3] Only the symbolic motifs above and below the figure differ; in the Falconer relief a pelican, symbolising piety, appears above the mourner's head and either side of the inscription tablet are roundels formed of a laurel wreath to the left and to the right roses and lilies, symbolising purity, no doubt considered particularly appropriate in commemorating the life of Major Falconer's young daughter.

Notes
[1] Busco (1994), p. 131. [2] Ibid., p. 128. [3] Ibid., p. 133.

Off Steyning Road
St George's Church, west end of south wall

Monument to William Powlett
Sculptor: Michael Rysbrack

Commissioned: after 1746
Materials/dimensions: white and grey marble, 4.2 m approx. high × 2.4 m wide × 50 cm deep
Signature (left-hand corner, below figure): M: L RYSBRACK. Fecit.
Inscription (on panel below sculptures): To the memory of WILLIAM POWLETT Esqr. Late of ST LEONARD'S FOREST, / who departed this life the 2d day of May Anno Domini 1746,

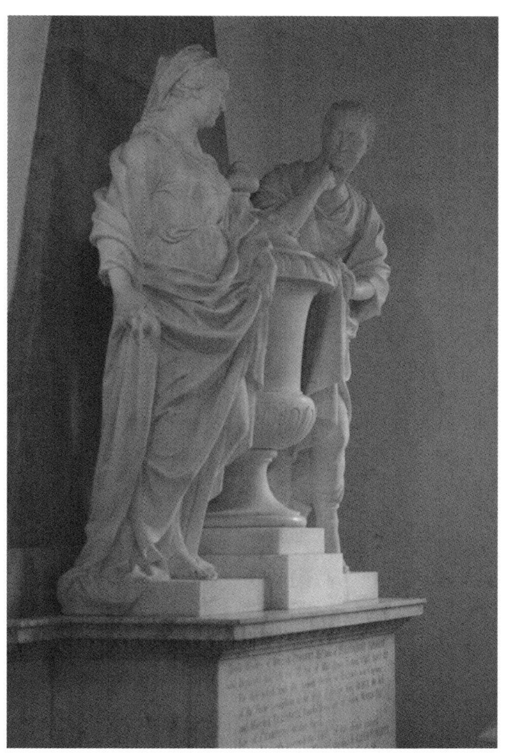

Michael Rysbrack, *Monument to William Powlett*

Aged 63 / He descended from the Antient family of BASING, was Captain / of the Horse Grenadiers in the reign of the King GEORGE the first, and Marryed ELIZABETH fourth Daughter of JOHN WARD Esqr. / late of CHAMPIONS in this Parish. / Here also lyeth interred the Body of the above named / ELIZABETH POWLETT late wife of the said WILLIAM POWLETT, / who Departed this life the 14th day of June 1753 Aged 66
Status: not listed
Condition: good
Owner/custodian: St George's church

William Powlett left instructions to his brother for: 'Five hundred pounds to be laid out on a monument for me and my dear wife'.[1] In Rysbrack's composition the loving interaction of the classically draped, over life-sized figures of the deceased, as they face each other across the urn upon which they lean, conveys a sense of human drama far removed from the mourning figures of the neoclassical monuments of the following century.[2] As Matthew Craske points out, '… both figures [are] the equal object of the viewer's attention' and the monument was 'designed as a tribute to the pair rather than at the behest of one as a tribute to the other.'[3]

South wall
Monument to Sir Merrick Burrell
Sculptor: Nathaniel Smith

Commissioned: after 1787
Materials/dimensions: white and light and dark grey marbles, 3.8 m approx. high × 2 m wide × 30 cm wide
Inscription (below portrait bust): To the Memory of / SIR MERRICK BURRELL, of West Grinsted [*sic*], Sussex, Bart. / Son of Peter Burrell, of Beckenham in Kent Esqr. / By his wife Isabella, / Daughter of John Merrick, of Stubbers in Essex Esqr. / He was born the third day of April, in the year 1699. / Lived respected and beloved / Eighty-eight Years. /

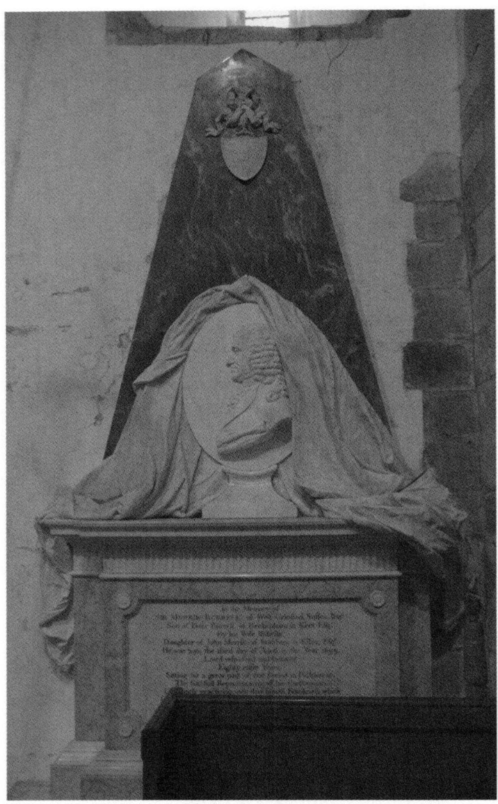

Nathaniel Smith, *Monument to Sir Merrick Burrell*

Sitting for a great part of that Period in Parliament, / the faithfull Representative of his Constituents, Constantly practicing, with that honest Frankness which / Compleats the true Character of an English Gentleman, / Those Virtues which adorn / A Man and a Christian.

Status: not listed
Condition: good
Owner/custodian: St George's church

The left edge of the portrait medallion of the deceased is covered by finely rendered drapery that flows down the sides of its supporting shelf. Smith was pupil and assistant to Louis Francois Roubiliac (c. 1705–62) and as Roscoe *et al.* point out, this memorial, '… derives from Roubiliac's Harvey monument at Hemstead in Essex (1758).'[4]

In addition to his political career, Sir Merrick Burrell also served as Governor of the Bank of England 1758–60.[5] He was created a baronet in 1766.

Notes
[1] Craske, M.J., *The London Trade in Monumental Sculpture and the Development of the Imagery of the Family in Funerary Monuments of the Period 1720–1760*, unpublished PhD thesis, Queen Mary and Westfield College, London, 1992, p. 98. [2] Roscoe (2009), p. 1081. [3] Craske (1992). [4] Roscoe (2009), p. 1152; Whinney (1964), p. 266. [5] Roberts, R. and Kynaston, D. (eds.), *The Bank of England: Money, Power and Influence 1694–1994*, Oxford, 1995, p. 248.

WORTHING

Chapel Road

Junction with Stoke Abbott Road

War Memorial

Designers/builders: JM Whitehead and Sons Ltd

Foundry: A.B. Burton
Stonemason: Francis Tate
Unveiled: 11 April 1921
Materials/dimensions: statue: bronze, 1.82 m high; pedestal: Portland stone faced with marble, 4.57 m high
Signature (bottom left-hand face of base): A.B. Burton/Founder/Thames Ditton
Inscriptions (southwest face): THIS MEMORIAL / WAS ERECTED BY PUBLIC SUBSCRIPTION / RAISED THROUGH THE WORTHING GAZETTE / IT WAS UNVEILED BY / FIELD MARSHALL SIR WILLIAM ROBERTSON BART. G.C.B. / ON 11TH APRIL 1921; (northeast face): OUR GLORIOUS DEAD / 1914–1918 / DUTY NOBLY DONE; (northwest face): OTHER CONFLICTS / STANFORD R.U. / LOVETT G.K. / PEARCE J.E.; (bottom of plinth): ALSO IN MEMORY OF / THOSE WHO FELL IN THE WAR / 1939—1945.

Names of the dead are listed on all four faces
Status: not listed
Condition: good
Funded by: public subscription raised by *The Worthing Gazette*
Owner/custodian: Worthing Borough Council

The architectural pedestal is surmounted by a life-size bronze figure of a soldier in full kit, representing Victory, with his right arm raised holding a helmet and his left hand holding a rifle. In 1919 the local newspaper launched the Worthing War Memorial Gazette Shilling Fund; it had decided to spearhead the campaign for a memorial after the Council's scheme was abandoned.[1] The War Memorial Committee commissioned Whitehead and Sons Ltd to make a bronze figure for £550 and four bronze

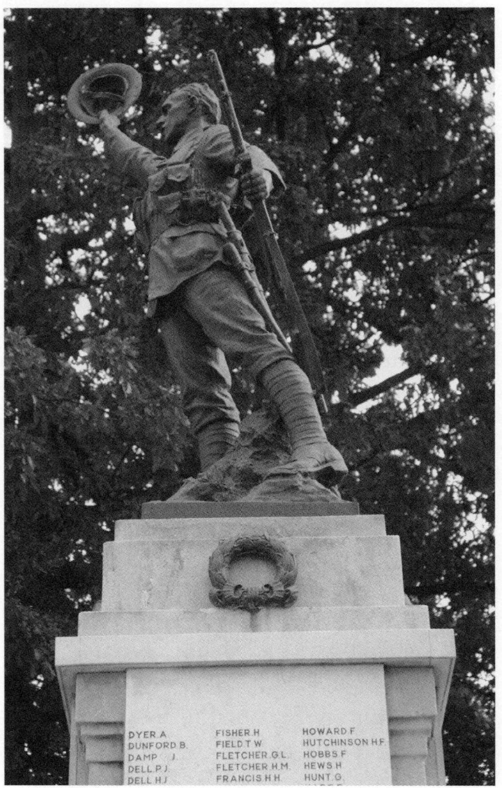

JM Whitehead and Sons Ltd, *War Memorial*

wreaths. No individual artist can be credited with the design of the figure as the company made it clear that the artists in its design department worked as a collective and that probably more than one was responsible.[2] The same figure was ordered for Stafford, Ebbw Vale, Chertsey, Truro and Edward Street Post Office in London.[3] The pedestal was designed by Frank Roberts, the Borough Surveyor and Engineer for Worthing, and supplied for £400 by Francis Tate, a local monumental mason, of Carrara Marble Works in North Street.

Field Marshal Sir William Roberts, who also presided at the opening ceremony for the war memorial at Chichester, unveiled the memorial. Excess funds from the public subscription were given to Worthing Hospital for its Maternity Extension fund, regarded by many local residents as another memorial to commemorate the war. The war memorial was moved slightly in 1933 when the new Town Hall was built. Names of the dead from the Second World War were later added to the base.

Notes
[1] Reasons for the Council's reluctance to organise the fundraising remain unclear, but may be related to the reported response of one councillor, approached for a donation, who noted that, although he was willing to contribute, he had already subscribed to two other Worthing memorials. The Council was represented on the Gazette's committee and was always intended to become the ultimate custodian of the memorial. 'The unveiling of the war memorial', *Worthing Gazette*, 6 April 1921. [2] Longstaff-Tyrell (2000), p. 37. [3] Potter, S. and Wilcox, T. (eds), *Public Art in West Sussex*, Chichester, 1995, p. 22.

Other sources
'Unveiled by a distinguished soldier', *Worthing Gazette*, 13 April 1921.
worthing.gov.uk (accessed 19 October 2010).

Liverpool Gardens

Top of rear colonnade, Montagu Shopping Centre

Desert Quartet

Sculptor: Elisabeth Frink

Unveiled: 13 June 1990
Materials/dimensions: Desert Quartet I: bronze, 1.3 m high × 1.24 m wide × 87.6 cm deep; Desert Quartet II: bronze, 1.28 m high × 1.16 m wide × 76.2 cm deep; Desert Quartet III: bronze, 1.27 m high × 1.15 m wide × 76.2 cm deep; Desert Quartet IV: bronze, 1.22 m high × 1.09 m wide × 80 cm deep
Status: Grade II*
Condition: good
Commissioned by: the Avon Group, Worthing
Owner/custodian: Worthing Borough Council

Elisabeth Frink, *Desert Quartet*

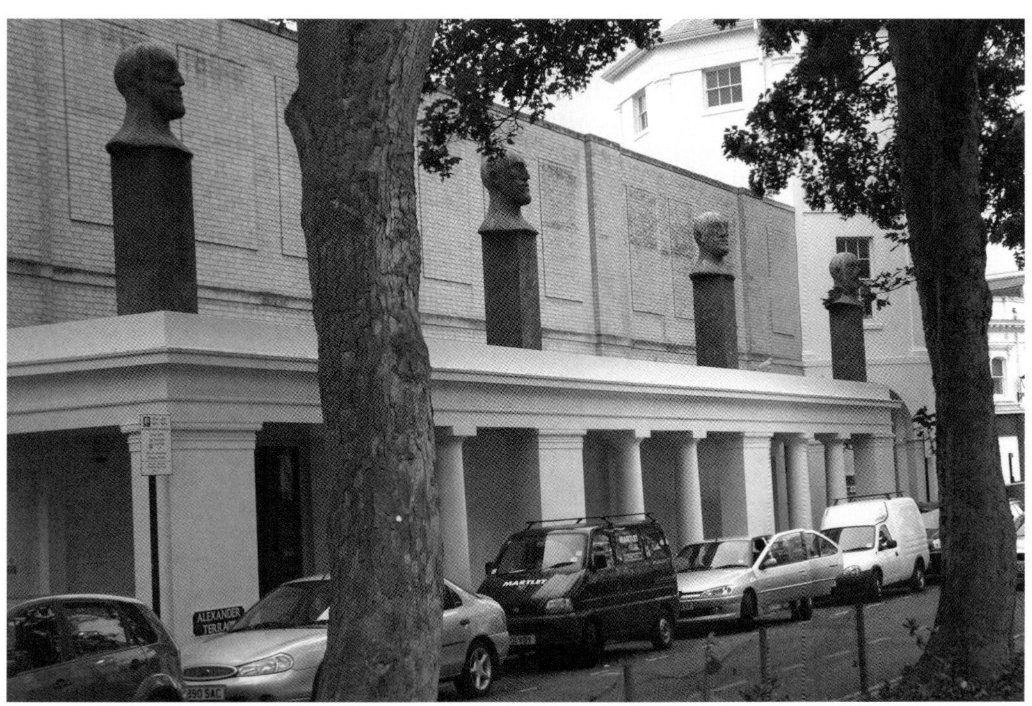

The four monumental male heads, with large staring eyes, are mounted on plinths on top of an architectural colonnade, set against a yellow brick façade. They are depicted without hair, their surface enlivened with rhythmic marks cut into the original plaster model with a chisel. The inspiration for the pieces came from a visit to the Tunisian Desert, with the original plaster of the heads reflecting the whiteness of the sand.[1] As Edward Lucie-Smith has stated, they 'radiate authority' in a way that is comparable to 'late antique representations of Roman Emperors', despite the fact that they are purely symbolic and not intended to depict a recognisable individual.[2] As with other large-scale busts, Frink was aiming to recreate the classical concept of the 'ideal'.

The commission was awarded in 1985 and Frink worked closely with the architect of the Montague Centre, Graham Excell. Due to ill health, however, Frink could not finish the original composition of horses and dogs that she was working on for the site and offered the heads, her penultimate work, instead. Each one is in an edition of six. They were unveiled by Peter Palumbo, chair of the Arts Council, to a mixed critical reception from residents of the town, some claiming that they were 'too sombre' or did not relate to the culture or history of the town.[3] By the time of Frink's death in 1993 the value of the piece was estimated at £2 million.

In 2007 local developer Humphrey Avon, who originally commissioned the sculptures, obtained planning permission to remove them and replace them with a piece that he claimed more closely resembled Frink's original plans for the site. He had already organised a competition with a first prize of £10,000 and chosen a winner, whose identity was not revealed. However, objectors insisted that Avon had gifted them to the Town Centre and that the original planning permission had stipulated that they were to be 'permanently placed on site'.[4] The Worthing Society, the PMSA, the Twentieth Century Society and others petitioned the Department of Culture, Media and Sport (DCMS), via English Heritage, to list the sculptures to prevent their removal. In May 2007 the sculptures and their supporting loggia were listed as Grade II*, with the DCMS acknowledging, '... the immense local and national value of this work ...'.[5] This was the first time that a public sculpture had been listed despite a rule that normally excludes works that have been executed less than 30 years previously.

Notes
[1] Gardiner (1998), p. 267. [2] Lucie-Smith (1994), pp. 67–69. Lucie-Smith dismisses the suggestion that the heads are idealised self-portraits. [3] 'Dame causes a stir', *Worthing Herald*, 15 June 1990, p. 1; 'Heads symbol of society', *Worthing Herald*, 22 June 1990, p. 10. [4] PMSA message board Summer 2007, pmsa.org.uk (accessed 17 May 2007). [5] Ibid.

Other sources
The Argus, 8 March, 15 May and 21 June 2007.
Elisabeth Frink: 1930–1993 (1997), pp. 31, 47.

Frink's Desert Quartet Receives Unprecedented Listing, artistsandmakers.com (accessed 21 June 2007).
Lucie-Smith, E., *Elisabeth Frink: Recent Sculpture and Drawings*, London, Fischer Fine Art, 1989.
Lydiate, H., 'Who owns Elisabeth Frink?, *Art Monthly*, no. 306, May 2007, p. 41.
'Montague sculptures unveiling', *Worthing Herald*, 1 June 1990, p. 5.
worthingfirst.org.uk (accessed 21 June 2007).

Lyndhurst Road,

Worthing Hospital

Worthing's first hospital was a dispensary created in 1829 in Ann Street. A new dispensary was set up in 1845 in Chapel Road, which, when enlarged in 1860, became known as the Worthing Infirmary and Dispensary. It moved to the current site in Lyndhurst Road in 1882 and was given the name Worthing Hospital in 1902.

Since then it has developed into a medium-sized District General Hospital with approximately 500 beds. The hospital is currently run by Western Sussex Hospitals NHS Trust, which also manages Southlands Hospital in Shoreham-by-Sea and St Richard's Hospital in Chichester.

In 1995 the Worthing and Southlands Hospital Art Project was registered as a charity by Chief Anaesthetist Roger Edwards, an accomplished amateur sculptor, and arts administrator Amanda Metcalfe. Their objective was, '[t]o help relieve the sickness of patients ... by improving, enhancing and maintaining the fabric of the said hospitals.'[1] The scheme was financed by a £140,000 private donation and South East Arts and the organisers mainly chose the work of artists known to them.[2] The charity was dissolved in 1999, but the hospital has continued to enliven its interior courtyards, corridors and waiting areas with works of art, with a continuing emphasis on sculpture, through a combination of private and public funding. In the Children's Centre, opened in 2001, there has been a focus on light-hearted

and entertaining works such as the wall pieces created by Anna Biddulph in 2003; *Octopus* made from plastic tubing and suckers and *Crocodiles* made from painted wooden clothes pegs, card and buttons.

Outside main building, to left of entrance
Worthing Spiral
Sculptor: Peter Randall-Page

Installed: 1997
Materials/dimensions: sculpture: Pakistan Golden Limestone, 89 cm high × 89 cm wide × 89 cm deep; base: Bodmin granite, 44.5 cm high × 1.35 m wide × 1.33 m deep
Status: not listed
Condition: good
Commissioned and owned by: Worthing and Southlands NHS Trust

The smooth honey-coloured spiral shell form, with some cross-hatching on its surface, stands on a contrasting grey rough-textured circular base, set within a small garden, approached by a winding gravel path. The planting around the

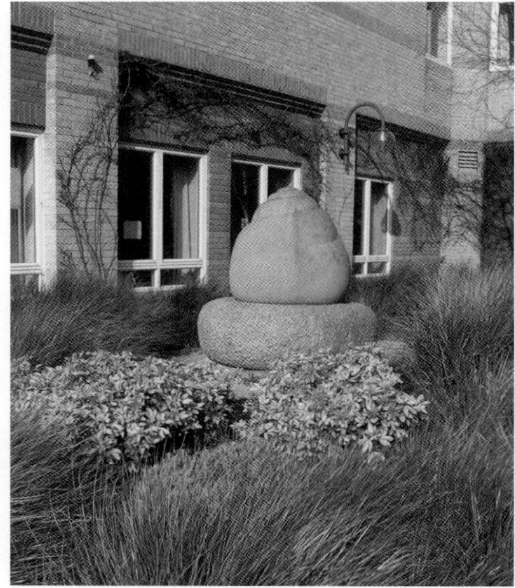

Peter Randall-Page, *Worthing Spiral*

sculpture is mainly grasses, suggestive of the seashore. The garden was intended to provide a quiet area for visitors to the hospital and the commission included two benches, designed by Steve Gelliot, which disappeared between late summer 2007 and March 2008.

In the centre of the pond, inner courtyard, just beyond main entrance
Care and Trust
Sculptor: Mary Cox

Installed: 1998
Materials/dimensions; bronze: figure of child, 1.25 m high; figure of mother, 1.67 m high
Inscription (plaque in front of sculptures): "CARE AND TRUST" / IN APPRECIATION OF THE WORK / OF / LYN WYATT JP.DL / FROM HER FAMILY AND FRIENDS / SCULPTED BY / MARY COX–1997

Status: not listed
Condition: good
Commissioned by: family and friends of Lyn Wyatt
Owner/custodian: Worthing and Southlands NHS Trust

The figure of a mother (symbolising care) and her daughter (symbolising trust), each standing on an individual paving stone in the centre of a goldfish pond, face each other, arms outstretched. The animated poses of the figures, including the movement of their clothing, with the girl springing forward from one foot, are intended to express the closeness of the family bond. Mary Cox is known for her sculptures of children, many of which are based on her own family.[3]

Mary Cox, *Care and Trust*

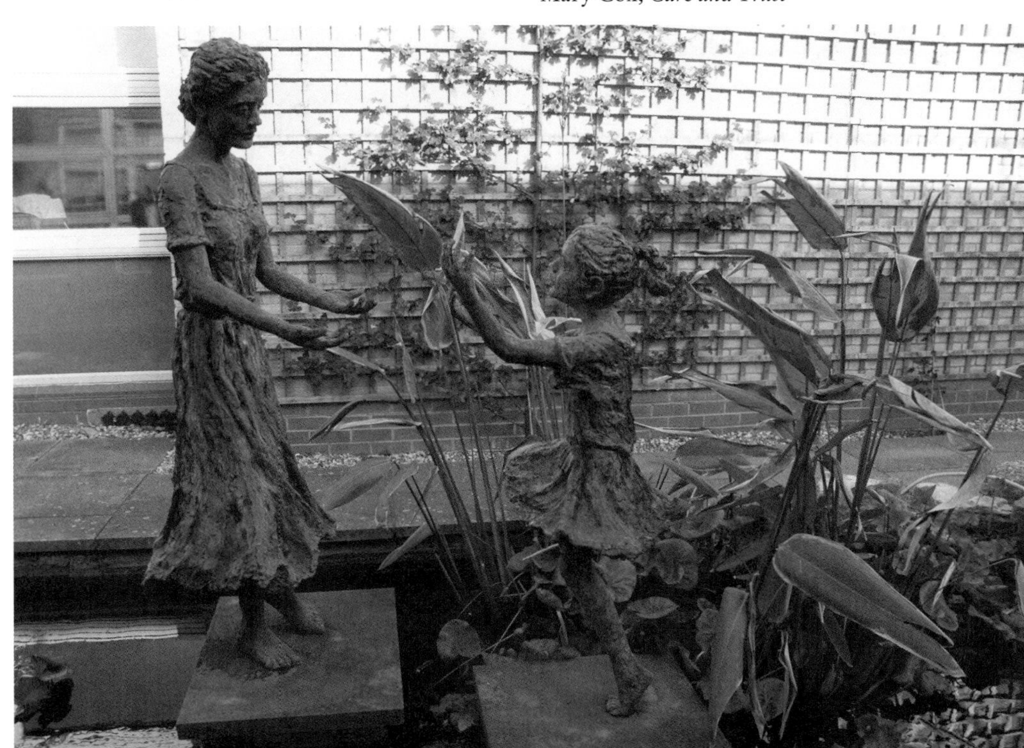

Lie Back and Relax
Sculptor: Reece Ingram

Installed: 1996
Materials/dimensions: charred elm, 1.5 m high
Inscription: (on plaque on right-hand corner of base): LIE BACK AND RELAX / 1996 / REECE INGRAM / this seal, in charred elm, has clearly enjoyed an excellent / lunch and is relaxing on the crest of a wave / By kind donation of Eschmann Equipment / Worthing & Southlands Art in Hospital Project
Status: not listed
Condition: good
Commissioned by: Worthing and Southlands NHS Trust Art in Hospitals Project and Eschmann Equipment
Owner/custodian: Worthing and Southlands Hospitals NHS Trust

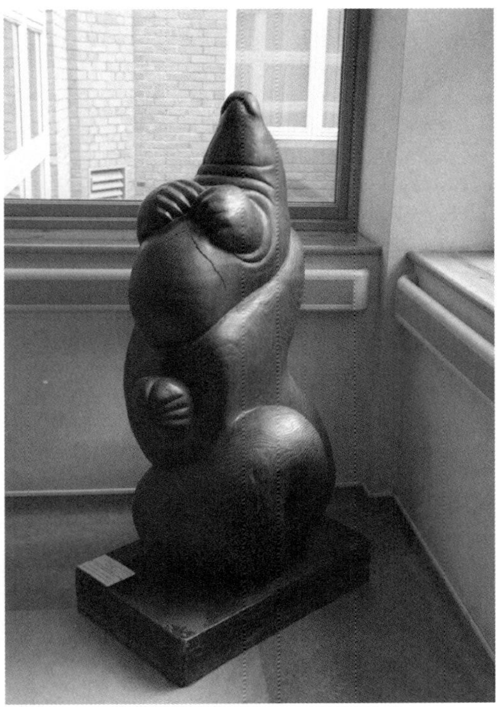

Reece Ingram, *Lie Back and Relax*

The seal's rounded forms emphasise the contours and grain of the wood from which it is made. Reece Ingram trained briefly as a taxidermist before attending Brighton Polytechnic in the 1980s. He has remained fascinated by animal forms and the tactile nature of materials. The public aspect of his work is also important, enabling him to explore new environments.

Inner courtyard, east wing
Penguins
Sculptor: Ian Nutting

Installed: 2002
Materials/dimensions: rusted sheet metal, tallest sculpture 2 m high; shortest 1 m high
Status: not listed
Condition: good
Owner/custodian: Worthing and Southlands Hospitals NHS Trust

Eleven penguins (10 adult, one baby), of cut and shaped scrap metal, are grouped around a central water feature, in a paved and pebbled courtyard. The stones and water reference their natural habitat and Nutting conveys individuality and animation despite his rather uncompromising material.

First floor, east wing
The Future – Hope and Compassion
Sculptor: Walter Bailey

Unveiled: 12 October 2000 at Worthing High School, South Farm Road
Materials/dimensions: charred oak, 2 m high
Status: not listed
Condition: good
Commissioned by: HSBC Invoice Finance (UK) Ltd, Worthing Borough Council and Worthing schools
Owner/custodian: Worthing and Southlands Hospitals NHS Trust

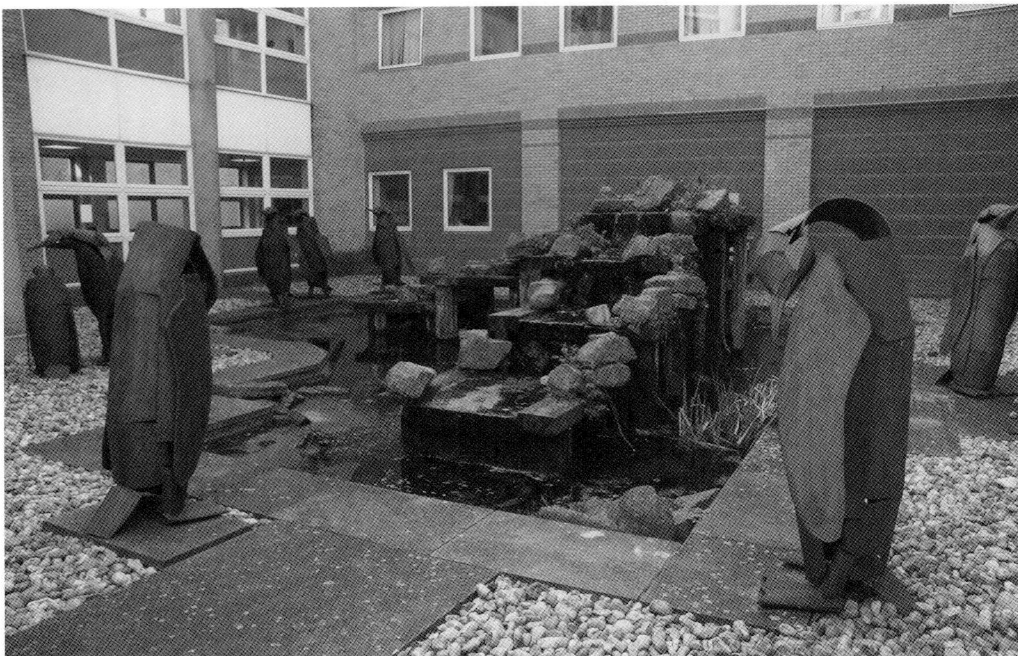

Ian Nutting, *Penguins*

Walter Bailey, *The Future – Hope and Compassion*

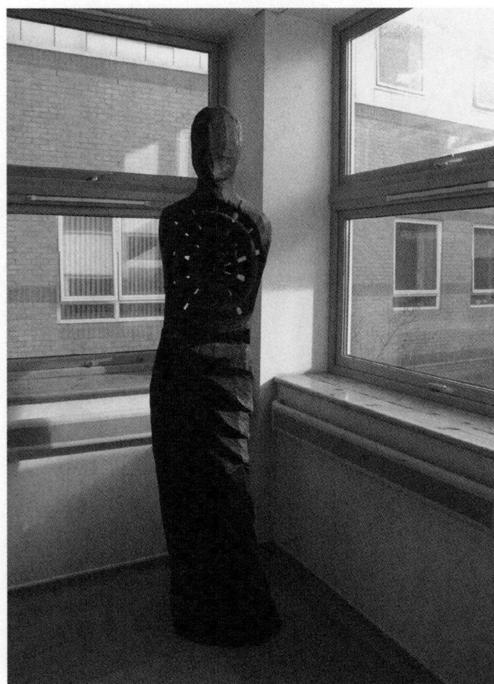

The sculpture depicts a female figure, standing directly on the floor. She is armless and featureless, her thorax pierced with a circular pattern. It was a Millennium sculpture carved from a single oak tree, using a chainsaw, created by Walter Bailey and local school children. It was intended to be '… a celebration of the open heart'.[4] Although a local newspaper claimed that it was one of a group of sculptures intended for the children's ward,[5] Bailey himself stated that it was always intended as a single piece and was to have been sited at the new main entrance to the hospital, which was never built.[6]

Notes
[1] charitycommission.gov.uk (accessed 18 January 2011). [2] Roger Edwards, retired Consultant Anaesthetist, interview, 15 May 2008. [3] marycox.co.uk (accessed 12 January 2012). [4] 'King of the chainsaw', *Worthing Herald*, 12 October 2000, p. 27. [5] Ibid. [6] Interview with Roger Edwards (2008).

Other sources
courcoux.co.uk/sculptors/nutting (accessed 7 May 2008).
Peter Randall-Page, correspondence, April 2008.
reeceingram.co.uk (accessed 10 June 2008).
walterbailey.co.uk (accessed 10 June 2008).

Marine Parade

SEAFRONT

West wall of the Denton Lounge at landward end of the Pier

Four reliefs

Sculptor: Laurence Henderson Bradshaw

Installed: c. 1960
Materials/dimensions: concrete, each relief 1.53 m high × 1.32 m wide × 10 cm deep
Signatures: (on the two central panels at bottom right hand corner): LAURENCE BRADSHAW (date indecipherable)
Inscriptions (bottom of panel second from left): MINERVA; (along right-hand side of panel third from left): NEPTUNE
Status: building Grade II
Condition: good (cleaned and restored late 2008/early 2009)
Owner/custodian: Worthing Borough Council

The four wall-mounted panels are spaced along the west wall of the Denton Lounge overlooking the beach. They have incised decoration, with the two end panels bearing the same dolphin and trident motif. The two central panels bear profile heads facing each other. The first is of Minerva, the Roman goddess of wisdom and mental activities, and also the protective deity of the arts and crafts, who granted talents to mankind; she is accompanied by an owl, symbol of wisdom. The second depicts Neptune, Roman god of water and the sea, together with a miniature female figure, possibly Amymone, daughter of Danaus, whom he rescued from a satyr and taught the art of creating springs.

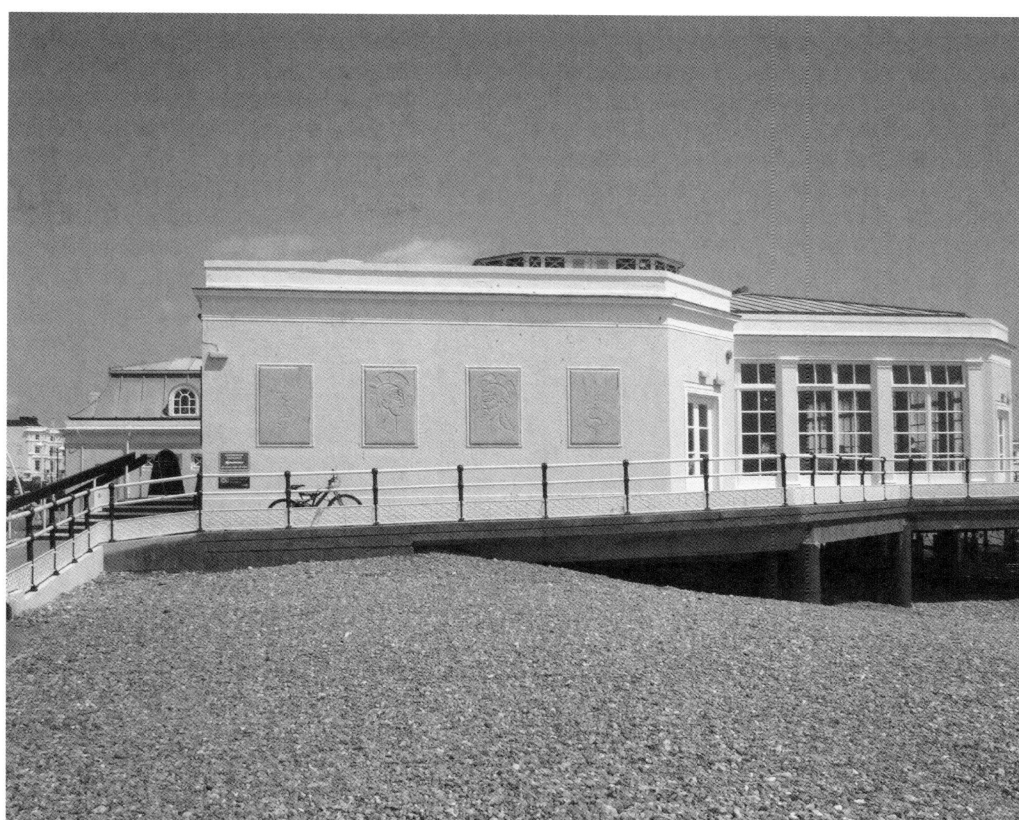

Laurence Henderson Bradshaw, *Four reliefs*

The architect of Denton Lounge was John Brandon-Jones (1908–1999), who worked with Charles Cowles Voysey (and Bradshaw) on Worthing Town Hall and Assembly Hall in 1933–34 and took over his architectural practice in 1954.[1] Bradshaw provided three tragic masks for the façade of the Assembly Hall in 1935. His best-known work is the memorial to Karl Marx in Highgate cemetery (1956). There is no mention of the reliefs in local newspaper accounts of the opening of the Denton Lounge in 1959, but the Bradshaw archive contains three photographs of the Minerva relief dated 1960.[2]

Notes
[1] Powers, A., 'Obituary: John Brandon-Jones', *The Independent*, 11 May 1999. [2] Laurence Henderson Bradshaw Archive (1899–1978), Henry Moore Institute, Leeds. Photograph album BR/P1. The back of one photograph is inscribed 'WORTHING PAVILLION [*sic*] ONE OF FOUR PANELS 1960 ARCH. BRANDON-JONES'. There are also two photographs of fish and tridents.

Other sources
Mrs Eileen Bradshaw, Braintree, Essex, interview, 4 October 2008.
Lindey, C., 'The man who moulded Marx', *The Morning Star*, 4 April 2007, p. 9.
Potter and Wilcox (1995), p. 24.
Seddon, J., 'From Worthing to Highgate and back: the career of Laurence Henderson Bradshaw (1899–1978)', *Sculpture Journal*, vol. 19.2, 2010, pp. 234–40.

At the seafront end of Steyne Gardens, in the middle of a sunken planted garden (originally on an island in the boating pool at the back of the Aquarena swimming pool)

Triton Fountain
Sculptor: Benjamin Hancocks
Designer: William James Bloye

Builders: Paine Manwaring Green Ltd and
  Landbuild Ltd
Executed: 1968
Unveiled: 8 May 2007
Materials/dimensions: patinated bronze, 1.3 m
  high × 1.3 m wide × 80 cm deep
Inscription (on green acrylic plaque with white
  letters affixed to low wall at back of
  fountain): STEYNE GARDENS / The Gardens
  were presented to the town in 1900 by the
  Dowager Lady Maria Georgiana / Loder.
  Widow of Sir Robert Loder DL.J.P. Baronet.
  / The sunken garden was laid out as a scented
  garden for the blind by the three Rotary
  Clubs of Worthing to commemorate / the
  75th Anniversary of Rotary International in
  1980. / The garden was refurbished in 2007
  by Worthing Borough Council as part of its
  'Greening / the Borough' Strategy and
  incorporates the 'Triton' fountain designed
  by William James / Bloye (1890–1975) the
  eminent civic sculptor and lecturer at
  Birmingham College of Art. / 'Triton' was
  given to Worthing by May Elizabeth
  Hancocks in 1968 to commemorate the /
  work of her husband Benjamin Hancocks
  A.R.C.A. (Lond) R.B.S.A. a fellow lecturer
  of Bloye in Birmingham. / 'Triton' was
  unveiled on 8th May, 2007 by the Mayor of
  Worthing Councillor Major Tom Wye M.B.E.
  / and the Cabinet Member for Culture,
  Leisure and Sport Councillor Paul High.
Status: not listed

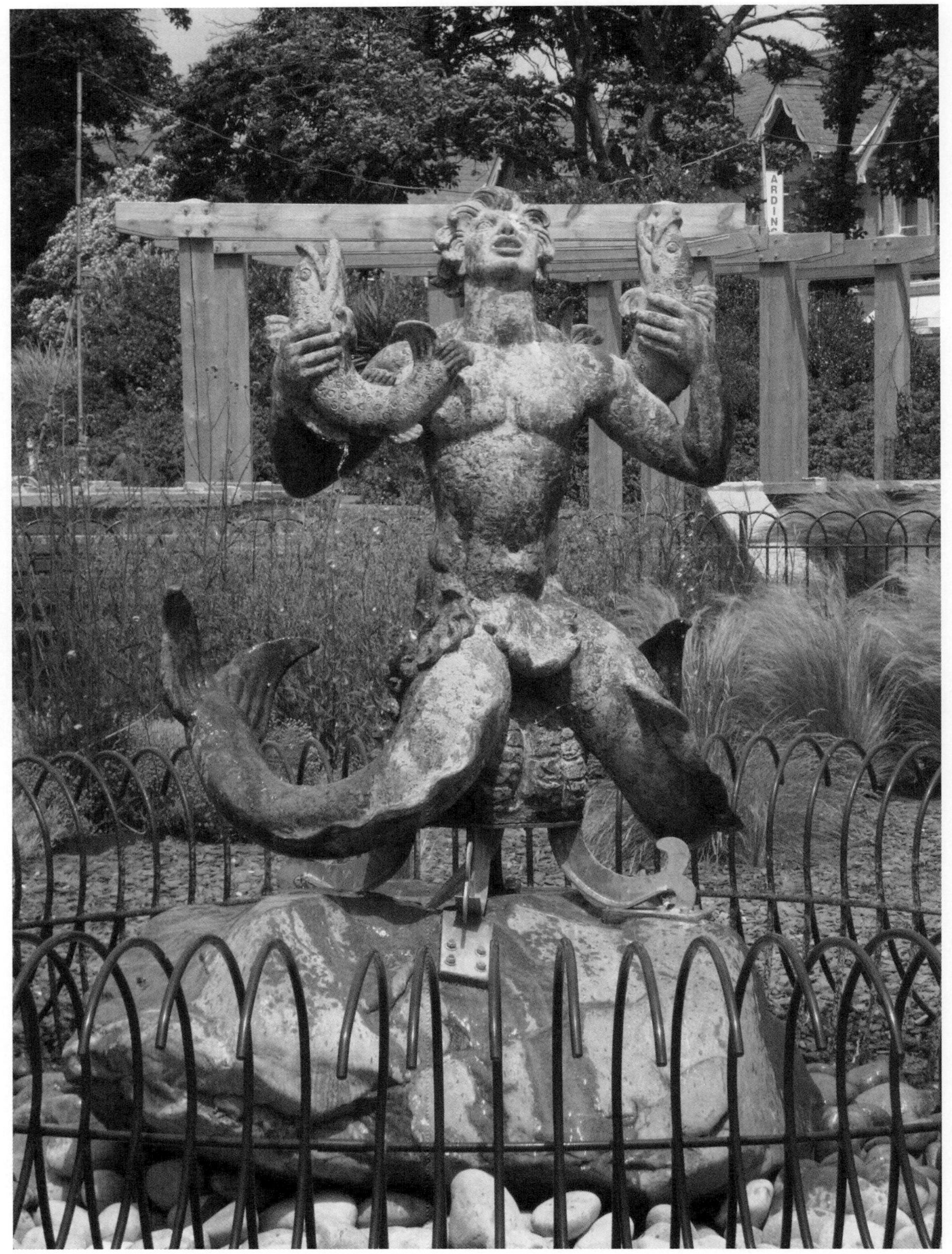

Benjamin Hancocks, *Triton Fountain*

Condition: good
Commissioned by: May Elizabeth Hancocks
Owner/custodian: Worthing Borough Council

The fountain depicts a Triton holding a fish in each hand, with water trickling from his elbows. He faces south towards the promenade and is seated on a galvanised steel base atop a rough-hewn rock.

According to Greek mythology, Triton was the son of Poseidon and Amphitrite, god and goddess of the sea. He is usually represented as a merman, having the upper body of a human and the tail of a fish. Triton's special attribute was a twisted conch shell, on which he blew to calm or raise the waves.

Benjamin Hancocks was the designer of the Triton figure in the centre of the fountain, creating a quarter-size clay model. He and his wife May were living in Worthing at the time, but he died in 1962, before the sculpture could be scaled up to full size and then cast, although it is unclear if there was ever the intention to produce a full-size bronze. His widow commissioned the cast sculpture, at a cost of £10,000, presumably through William Bloye, who designed the complete fountain. She gave it to the town in memory of her late husband, when it was placed in the middle of the boating lake at the Aquarena swimming pool.[1] When this became defunct, the sculpture languished in a Council depot until a new site could be found. In 2007 when the Steyne Gardens were given a £70,000 facelift, the fountain was provided with a new base and piping and installed in its present position.

Note
[1] Robin Norton (Ben Hancocks' great nephew), email correspondence, 20 February 2012.

Other sources
Norton, R.D.W., *Benjamin (Ben) Hancocks 1888–1962 British Artist (Sculpture/Oil/Watercolour/Drawing)* Woodstock, 2003, p. 8.
'Triton fountain has emerged', westsussextoday.co.uk (accessed 19 June 2008).
Worthing Council press release, 4 May 2007, worthing.gov.uk (accessed 19 June 2008).

Stoke Abbott Road

North elevation, facade of Assembly Hall

Three Tragic Masks

Sculptor: Laurence Henderson Bradshaw

Architects: Charles Cowles Voysey with John Brandon-Jones

Installed: 1935
Materials/dimensions: Empire (artificial) stone, 1.02 m high × 90 cm wide
Status: building Grade II
Condition: good
Owner/custodian: Worthing Borough Council

Three medallions with wave-shaped bases depicting heads in relief modelled on antique tragic masks are mounted on the two-storey red brick modernist building above the first floor windows.[1] They were made by James Longley and Co Ltd of Crawley for £120.[2] Longley also executed a number of Bradshaw's designs for decorations and fittings for the interior of the Assembly Hall. Two relief medallions in the entrance remain, but incised wall decorations for the dining room have been painted over.[3]

Notes
[1] 'Listed buildings in Worthing', Worthing Borough Council, worthing.gov.uk/cgi-bin/htm (accessed 22 November 2007). Laurence Henderson Bradshaw Archive (1899–1978) Henry Moore Institute, Leeds. BR/M11 Cuttings Book 1920–83, G/1–4. [2] Letter from Norman Longley, James Longley and Co. Ltd, Building Contractors, Steam Joinery Works, Crawley, Sussex, 27 July 1934, Bradshaw archive, Henry Moore Institute, Leeds, cuttings book no. 13, 53/1994/A/1/4. [3] Seddon (2010), pp. 234–40.

Other sources
Mrs Eileen Bradshaw, Braintree, Essex, interview, 4 October 2008.
Lindey (2007), p. 9.

Laurence Henderson Bradshaw, *Three Tragic Masks*

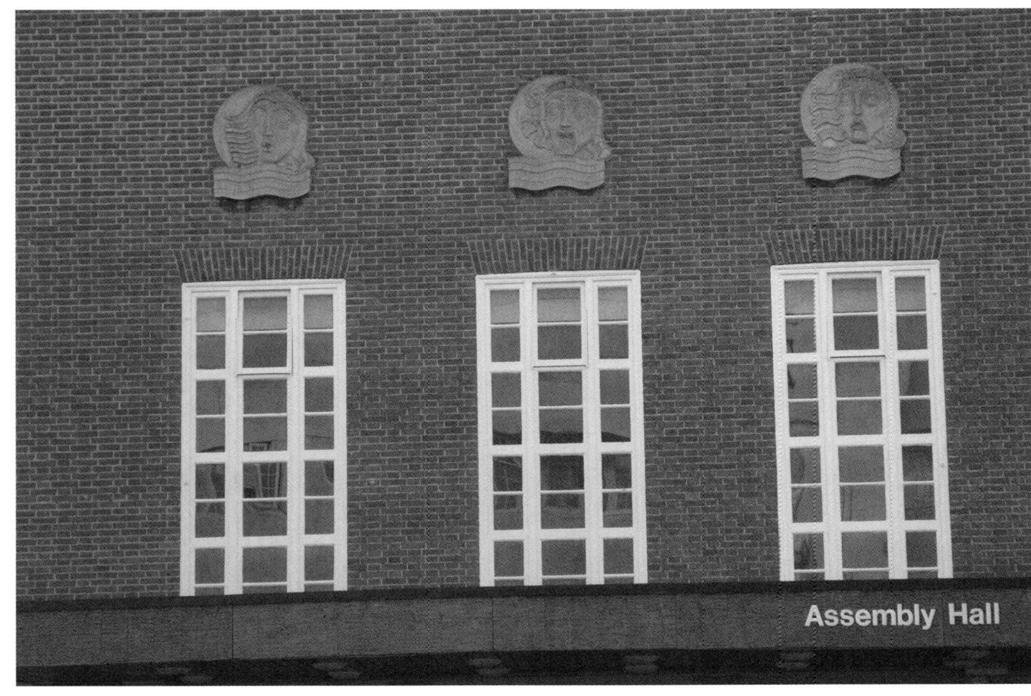

On the beach, opposite Anscombe Road

Waterwise Sculpture Garden
Sculptor: Tom Leach
Designer: John Marder

Builders: Adur & Worthing Services
Installed: 2006
Materials/dimensions: main sculpture: old
    wooden groyne, 1.6 m high × 1.3 m wide ×
    90 cm deep
Status: not listed
Condition: good
Commissioned by: Worthing Borough Council
    and Southern Water
Owner/custodian: Worthing Borough Council

The garden was commissioned to help raise
awareness of ways of conserving water. John
Marder, a freelance horticulturalist and garden
designer provided plans for a shingle garden of
800 m², with loose paths and variable-sized
wooden posts all carved from old beach
groynes. On the western side is a single carved
sculpture from similar wood. At various points
there are carved wooden information boards
about the project and the plants, which are all
species that require little water to survive.

The Parks and Engineering Sections of
Worthing Borough Council assisted with the
design and the garden was built with the help of
students from Oak Grove College; Elm Grove
First School; West Park First and Middle
Schools; Our Lady of Sion School, Worthing.
The project cost £50,000.

Source
worthing.gov.uk/worthingsservices/leisureandculture
    (accessed 19 October 2010).

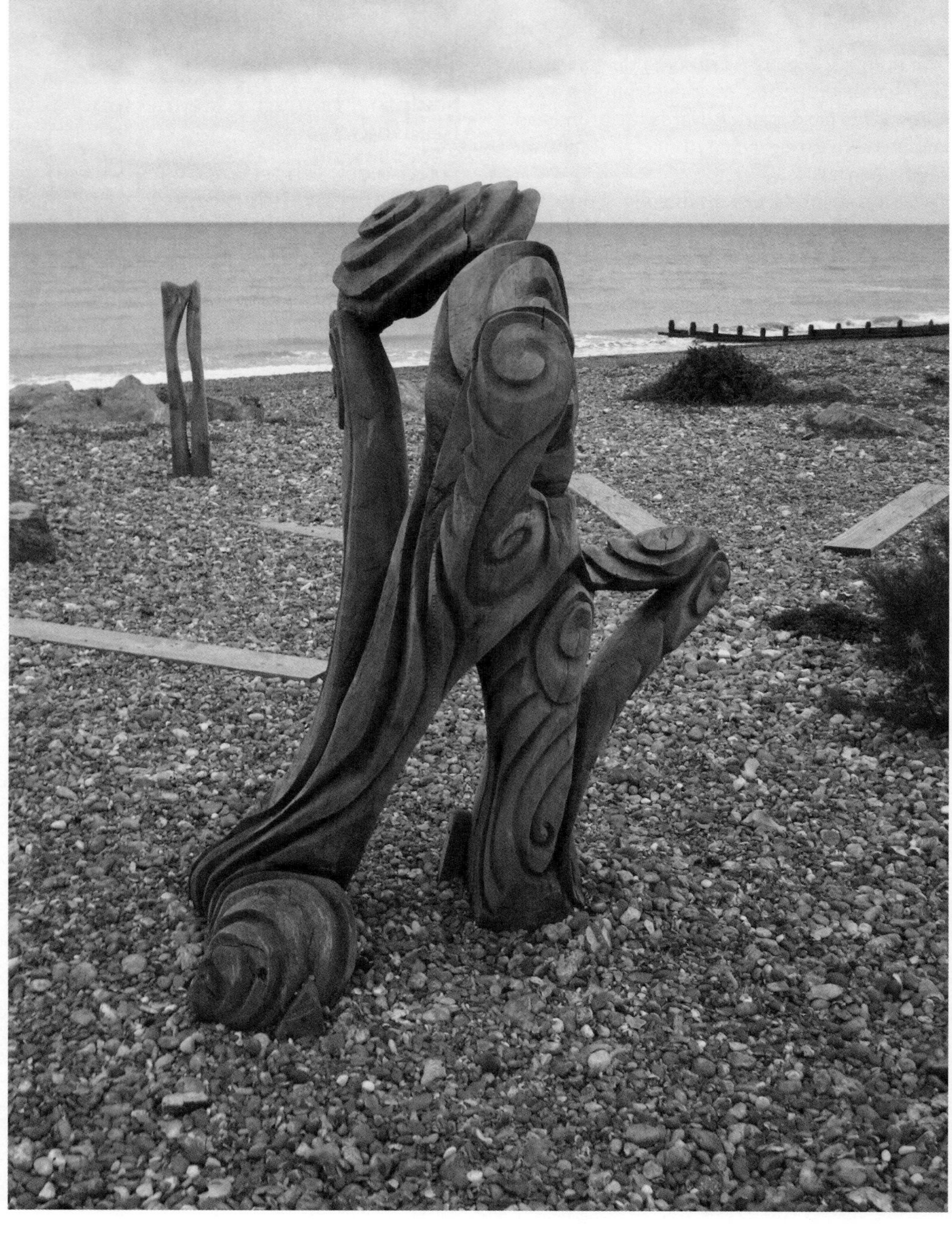

Tom Leach, *Waterwise Sculpture Garden*

Borde Hill Lane

Borde Hill House (moved 2007, formerly in the rose garden and the Italian garden)

The Bride (also known as the Veiled Lady)

Sculptor: Antonio Tantardini

Executed: mid 1800s
Materials/dimensions: sculpture: marble, life-size; octagonal base: marble, 76 cm high × 61 cm wide
Signature (on round plinth near right foot): ANTO. TANTARDINI F. MILANO
Status: not listed
Condition: good (but crack on left foot and to the veil at rear)
Owner/custodian: Borde Hill House

The female figure stands on a shallow plinth in a dramatic swooning pose with baroque style drapery swirling around her legs and feet. Her left arm is raised over the head; her right hand clutches the veil covering her face.

The statue was purchased from the Milan-based sculptor by the great great grandfather of the present owner of Borde Hill House, together with portrait busts of himself and his wife. The sculptures were originally displayed in his house at Binstead on the Isle of Wight and moved to Borde Hill when the house was purchased by his son in 1892.[1] The house is a Tudor mansion built by Sir Stephen Borde in 1598.

Borde Hill Gardens are set in 200 acres of Grade II* listed parkland and woodland with a

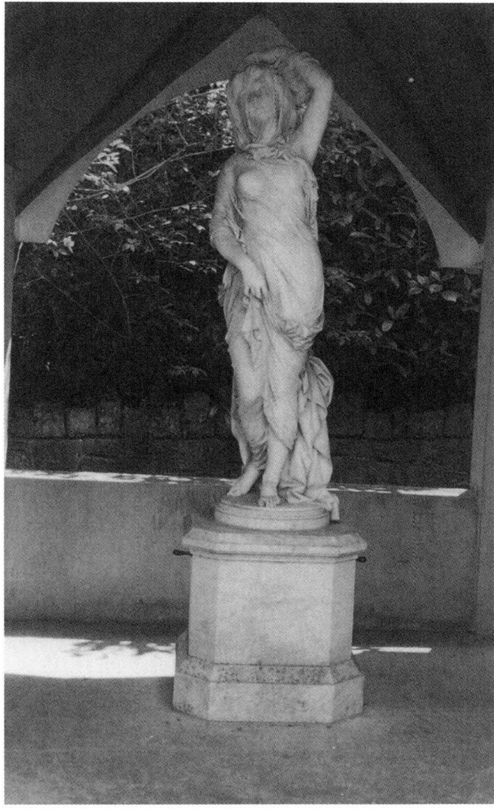

Antonio Tantardini, *The Bride*

nationally important collection of trees and shrubs. *The Bride* occupied various positions within the gardens, latterly placed under a brick and tile shelter, formerly the fern house. In 2007 the statue was moved inside the house to prevent it from further weathering. As only the gardens are open to the public, it is therefore no longer publicly accessible, although the gardens remain the setting for temporary selling exhibitions of outdoor sculpture throughout the season.

Note
[1] Andrewjohn Stephenson Clarke (present owner of Borde Hill House), telephone conversation, 14 November 2012.

Other sources
'Antonio Tantardini: obituary', *The New York Times*, 29 March 1879.
Borde Hill Gardens Guidebook, nd. c. 1980s.
Harrison, L., *A Sussex Guide: 20 Sussex Gardens*, Alfriston, 2007, p. 17.

Western Road

Churchill Square in front of Chartwell Court

The Spirit of Brighton

Sculptor: William George Mitchell

Unveiled: 11 October 1968
Demolished: 1992
Materials/dimensions: sand-blasted concrete, 9.15 m high
Commissioned by: Brighton Council
Owner/custodian: Standard Life Investments

The sculpture formed a large rectangular block with patterned and textured panels rising from a sculpted rockery base planted with shrubs with tumbling water features. At the time it was one of the biggest cast concrete sculptures in existence. William Mitchell said that he wanted to suggest that Brighton had a history that went back beyond its nineteenth-century association with the Prince Regent by invoking the

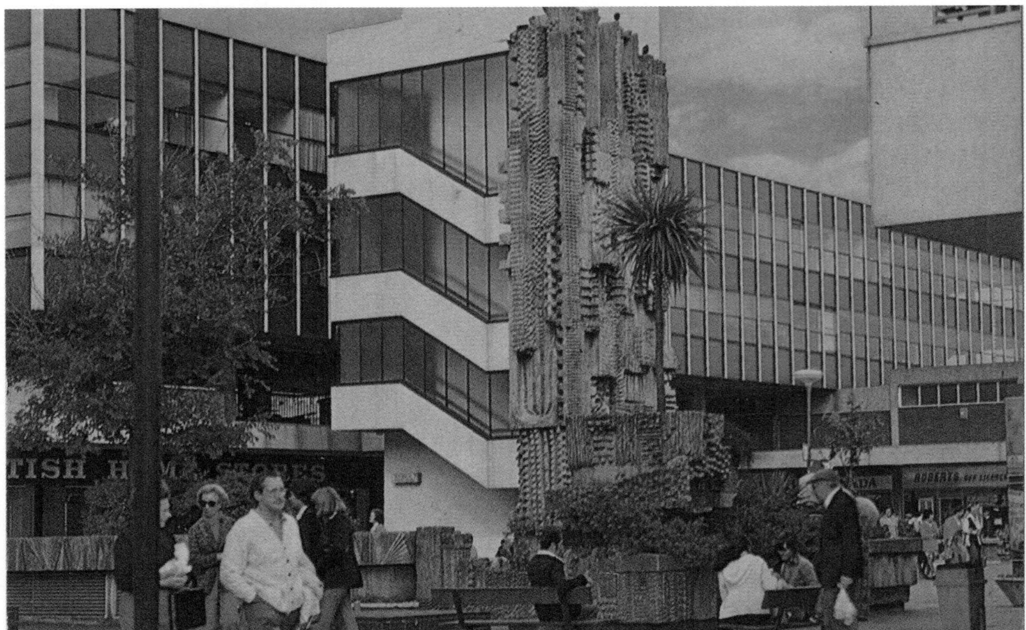

William George Mitchell, *The Spirit of Brighton*

Norman past of Sussex.[1] However, many people felt that his sculpture had the appearance of an ancient Aztec structure and it was originally to be lacquered, including pieces of gold mosaic meant to catch the sun. In the evenings the sculpture was floodlit.

The Spirit of Brighton stood in the centre of the original 15-acre Churchill Square shopping centre, named after the former Prime Minister who was a Freeman of Brighton. The idea of the redevelopment, that involved the demolition of a Regency street and two seventeenth-century cottages, was mooted in 1935 but not carried out until the 1960s. It was planned, at a cost of £9m, by Sir Hugh Casson, Brighton's Consultant Architect, and Russell Diplock Associates in conjunction with Myton Ltd, a member of the Taylor Woodrow Group. The centre was formally opened on 11 October 1968 by Mayor Thomas Taylor, followed by the opening of the lower level in 1972.

As an open and often windswept piazza, the design of Churchill Square came under frequent criticism and there were arguments about the maintenance of the planting around the sculpture and its water feature.[2] The sculpture was demolished by Standard Life Investments in 1992 and replaced with a bandstand as a temporary measure before commencement of the development of the Square in 1996. It is alleged that *The Spirit of Brighton* was broken up for hard core during the building of the new covered shopping mall that opened on 4 September 1998, with Charlie Hooker's sculpture *Twins* at its entrance.

Notes
[1] William Mitchell, telephone conversation, 1 December 2010. [2] Ibid.

Other sources
Collis (2010), pp. 63–64.
mybrightonandhove.org.uk (accessed 30 November 2010).
School of Architecture (1987), p. 87.

Junction of Robertson Street and Priory Road

On the site of Priory Bridge, which crossed Priory Stream

Prince Albert Memorial Clock Tower

Designer: Edward A. Heffer

Sculptor: Edwin Stirling

Builder: Mr Pattenden, Hastings
Stonemason: James Cowley
Metalworkers: Hart and Son, Hastings
Clockmakers: Thwaites and Reed, Clerkenwell
Installed: 1864
Demolished: November 1973
Materials/dimensions: Portland stone, granite, oak, 19.81 m high × 4.57 m diam. at base of tower; 2.43 m diam. at clock chamber
Inscription (immediately above the oak entrance door on a stone ribbon): Erected to Albert the Good, in the year of our Lord 1862
Commissioned by: Hastings Corporation
Funded by: public subscription

The tower was designed in the Gothic perpendicular style, with an entrance through an oak door on the west side. On the east side, a massive granite drinking basin was fixed. In a niche above the gable on the south side was a statue of Prince Albert in his robes as Knight of the Garter, with carved shields, on the north, east and west sides; on the south side the panelling was filled by the arms and supports of his Royal Highness. Above the clock chamber was an octagonal turret, with pierced quatrefoils of alternate design, for the chimes, and a plain spire with ornamental terminal and gilded vane, with the letter A incised, completed the whole. Tapering cast iron stands with wrought iron filigree decoration stood on stone

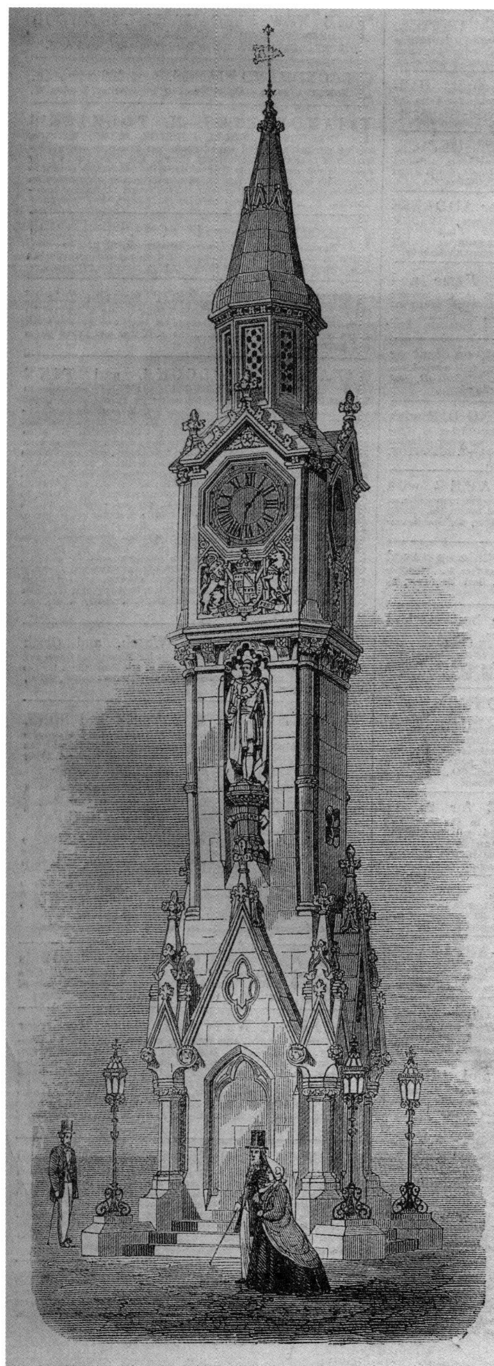

bases at each corner and between them four steps. The clock was illuminated by gas, and arranged to light automatically at 9 pm each evening.

Following Prince Albert's death in December 1861, Queen Victoria wrote to the Mayor of London expressing her desire for a memorial and he subsequently wrote to all Boroughs in the country requesting contributions. Hastings Corporation decided that they would divide donations between a national and local memorial, for which a clock tower was decided upon as most appropriate. As a result of a competition with a 10-guineas prize, Edward Heffer's design was selected and the statue of Prince Albert arrived from Liverpool on 3 July 1863. The foundation stone was laid on 10 November 1862, the 21st birthday of the Prince of Wales, Prince Albert's son. In a cavity in the stone, a bottle was placed containing a parchment, which read:

> Prince Consort Memorial. The foundation stone of this clock tower, erected in commemoration of the esteem and regard entertained by the inhabitants of this Borough towards his late Royal Highness, the Prince Consort, was laid by Thomas Ross esquire, Mayor of Hastings, on Monday the tenth day of November 1862.[1]

Moving of the memorial was proposed several times following the Second World War, usually for reasons of traffic congestion following continual development of the town; redevelopment plans in 1952 even suggested demolition. Arsonists set fire to the clock's woodwork in the early hours of Saturday 28 April 1973 and the clock was damaged and the surrounding stone cracked. On Monday 18 June 1973 another smaller fire broke out. Following this, serious faults were discovered and there was little opposition to Hastings Council's decision, taken on 11 October 1973, to demolish the tower as soon as possible. The

Edwin Stirling, *Prince Albert Memorial Clock Tower*

process began on Sunday 17 November 1973 and took two weeks. The demolishers broke the bottle with the parchment, did not understand its importance and threw it away.

Albert's statue was bought for £50 by a local resident, Miss Skelton, to be displayed in the Floral Hall/greenhouses in Alexandra Park. On inspection in 2007 it was standing under a tarpaulin, facing west, in a greenhouse in the gardeners' yards. Two of the lamps and columns stand outside Hastings Museum and Art Gallery in Bohemia Road. Inside the gallery, the Council has stored the drinking fountain bowl, the weather vane, some clock workings and a wooden door.

Note
[1] *Illustrated London News*, 2 January 1864, p. 13.

Other sources
Hastings Local History Group, *The Albert Memorial: an Illustrated History*, revised ed. 2004.
Prideaux, W.R.B., 'Statues and memorials in the British Isles', *Notes and Queries*, 14 January 1911, pp. 22–24.
Seddon, J., 'Landscape with statues: recording the public sculpture of Sussex' in S. Ewing *et al.* (eds) *Architecture and Field Work*, London, 2010, pp. 65–71.

BEXHILL-ON-SEA

Marina

Roof of the De La Warr Pavilion

'Hang on a Minute Lads, I've Got a Great Idea'

Sculptor: Richard Wilson

Installed: 7 July 2012
Dismantled: 1 October 2012
Materials/dimensions: full-size replica of a
    single decker bus
Commissioned and funded by: principal
    sponsor Eddie Izzard, part of London 2012
    Festival (The Cultural Olympiad); supported
    by Arts Council England and The Henry
    Moore Foundation

Wilson's installation was inspired by Michael
Caine's last line in the final scene of the classic
1969 film *The Italian Job* (directed by Peter
Collinson) in which British bank robbers steal
gold bullion in Turin and escape over the Alps
in a red, white and blue bus. It was a replica of
the twin-axle Harrington Legionnaire,
originally made in Brighton in the 1960s. The
sculptor used the whole building as the plinth
for the bus, which teetered on the edge of the
roof, tilting randomly due to a hydraulic
mechanism constructed on the underside.

    Wilson was asked by the late Alan Haydon,
director of the gallery, to install a piece on the
roof, to follow Antony Gormley's *Critical Mass*
(2010), comprising 60 casts of the artist's body,
the first ever sculpture to be installed on this
site. An exhibition of Wilson's drawings and
models for the project took place in the gallery

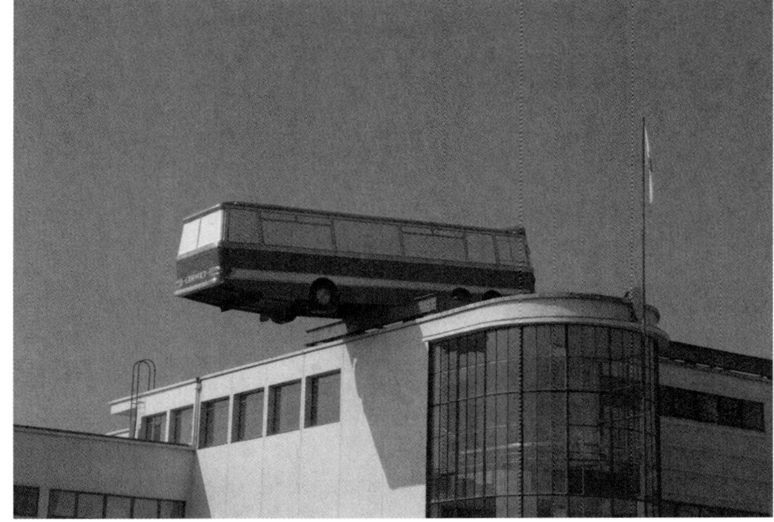

Richard Wilson, *'Hang on a Minute Lads, I've Got a Great Idea'*

below. He commented that his piece had:

> … very little to do with aesthetics, it is to do
> with fighting the weather conditions because
> if we put a coach on the roof it is going to
> want to blow off. So we've got to anchor it
> down.[1]

He said it was appropriate it should be part of
the Cultural Olympiad since the work was a
metaphor 'about the absolute limits of
anything.'[2] The colours of the bus were also
seen as a kind of 'flag-waving' for the British
Olympic team competing in London that
summer. Wilson hoped to sell the bus after it
was removed from the roof, believing that it
had potential as a form of advertisement.

Notes
[1] Brown, M., 'Artist Richard Wilson hangs out
"Italian Job" bus to teeter on Bexhill Pavilion', *The
Guardian*, 3 July 2012. [2] Ibid.

Other sources
Bexhill Observer, 4 July 2012.
dlwp.com/event/richard-wilson2 (accessed 13
    September 2012).

Cooden Sea Road

Outside Cooden Beach Hotel

Shredded Wheat Big Ben

Sculptor: Michelle Reader, assisted by Steno Vitale

Unveiled: 20 February 2008
Materials/dimensions: sculpture: British wheat
    sheaf reeds on wood and metal frame, 5 m
    high × 80 cm wide × 80 cm deep; base:
    wood, 35 cm high × 2.5 m wide × 2.5 m deep
Commissioned by: Nestle and General Mills
    Cereal Partners UK
Owner/custodian: Bexhill in Bloom

The sculpture was a scaled-down replica of the Palace of Westminster clock tower housing the clock's bell, named Big Ben, in London. It was commissioned by the manufacturers of Shredded Wheat breakfast cereal as one of eight models representing eight UK regions; the others were: Blackpool Tower, created by Su Blackwell; Edinburgh Castle, by Laura Antebi; the Giant's Causeway, by Jo-Anne Hatty; Shakespeare's Birthplace, by Iris Bertz; Snowdon, by Dave Cushley; the Angel of the North, by Sarah Walton; and the Eden Project, created by Emma Churchill. Big Ben was voted the landmark that best represented the southeast region and also Great Britain as a whole when the models were shown in the

Land of Wheat and Glory exhibition held for one day (1 October 2007) in Leicester Square in London in association with British Food Fortnight.

The artist, who works extensively with recycled materials and also produces theatrical props, said of her work:

> Simple materials have a wide creative scope for individual interpretation and wheat has proven to be a malleable material. Working with a material grown by British farmers seemed befitting to transform such an iconic British landmark as Big Ben.[1]

The sculpture was secured for Bexhill by Sandra Melvin, chair of Bexhill in Bloom, and erected outside the Cooden Beach Hotel with the permission of its owner James Kimber. It was added to a tour of local clocks as a tourist attraction. At the time of its installation it was estimated that it would withstand at least one year of wind and rain next to the sea. It has since disappeared.

Note
[1] Information board at unveiling ceremony, 20 February 2008.

Other sources
Bexhill on Sea Observer, 20 January 2008.
Hastings Observer, 18 January 2008.
londonnet.co.uk/news/2007/oct (accessed 8 December 2010).

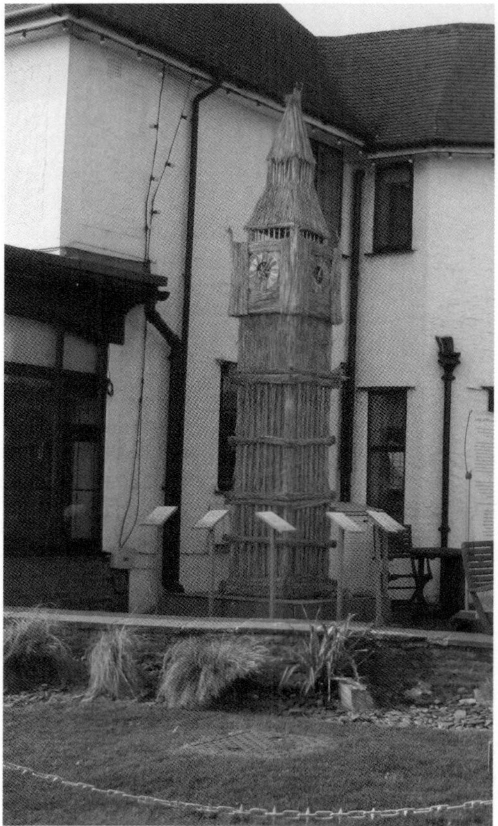

Michelle Reader, *Shredded Wheat Big Ben*

BRIGHTON

Lewes Road

Parking spaces, east side of The Level

Memorial to Rob Needham
Creators: family and friends

Installed: 25 September 2005.
Materials/dimensions: N registration Vauxhall Astra Car, sleeping bags, flowers, paper messages, tributes

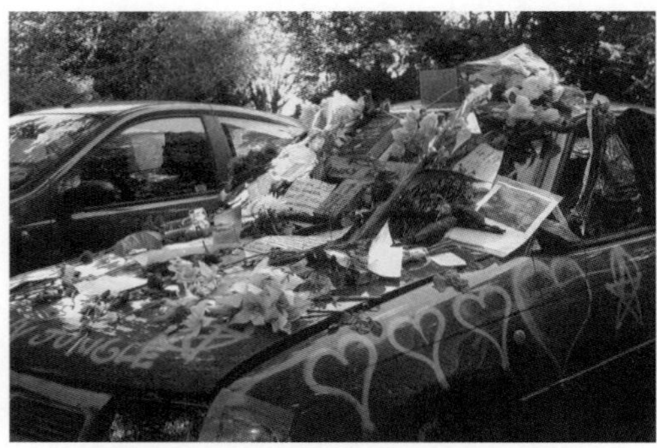

Family and friends, *Memorial to Rob Needham*

Inscriptions (various written inscriptions, including on passenger side of car body): never hurt noone [*sic*] loved by everyone / sleep tight my old mate / love Jung Jung (?)

This temporary memorial to 'Punky Rob' (Rob Needham, 1972–2005) grew up around a dilapidated car where he slept when he had nowhere else to go. Following his death from a heroin overdose at the West Pier Project, Regency Square, Brighton on 25 September 2005, it quickly became a focus of grief and anger at the tragedy of his death and was eventually completely covered with graffiti, floral and written tributes. 'Punky Rob' was a popular local figure, who played in a number of punk and heavy metal bands and was widely known through his busking. His funeral took place on 13 October 2005. The memorial was taken down towards the end of October, but the organic way in which it had developed and grown was recorded in a website, punkyrob.fotopic.net, that also includes documentation of his musical achievements, messages and commemorative events.

Sources
Conversation with the sister of the deceased at the site, 20 October 2005.
Kwintner, A. 'A fond farewell to Punky Rob', *The Argus*, 11 October 2005.

Patcham Downs

C-Curve

Sculptor: Anish Kapoor

Installed: May 2009
Materials/dimensions: mirror-polished stainless
steel, 2.2 m high × 7.7 m wide × 30 cm deep

In 2009, Anish Kapoor was invited by the new
chief executive of Brighton Festival, Andrew
Comben, to become the Festival's first guest
director. During the first three weeks of May
that year, Kapoor installed a trail of six works
throughout the city, as one critic put it,
'[turning] the hedonistic seaside town into his
personal playland.'[1] The pieces included *The
Dismemberment of Jeanne d'Arc* at the Old
Municipal Market (specially commissioned for
the Festival) and *Blood Relations* in the Fabrica
Gallery. Two works occupied outdoor public
spaces: *Sky Mirror* in Pavilion Gardens and *C-
Curve* high up on the Downs above Patcham.
Both sculptures have been exhibited in a variety
of settings, in a sense 'de-materialising',
reflecting back both the surrounding landscape

and the viewers of the work. *C-Curve*,
essentially a long, curved mirror, was reached
on foot after a mile-long trek from the road.
Although he made little reference to the fact,
the site was very near to the Chattri, site of
Indian funeral rites (see entry), which has some
significance in view of Kapoor's country of
birth. The sculpture attracted 10,000 visitors,
fascinated by the visual tricks it played as a
rather more troubling version of the trick
mirrors once found on seaside piers. It was
characterised as:

> [A] panopticon that surveys the view and
> plays tricks with your body as you attempt
> to understand how it has suddenly managed
> to segment the landscape into a triptych or
> redefine a patch of grey sky as a lake into
> which you see yourself tumbling headfirst.[2]

Notes
[1] Conrad, P., *The Observer*, 3 May 2009. [2] Ibid.

Other source
brightonfestival.org/2009 (accessed 29 July 2013).

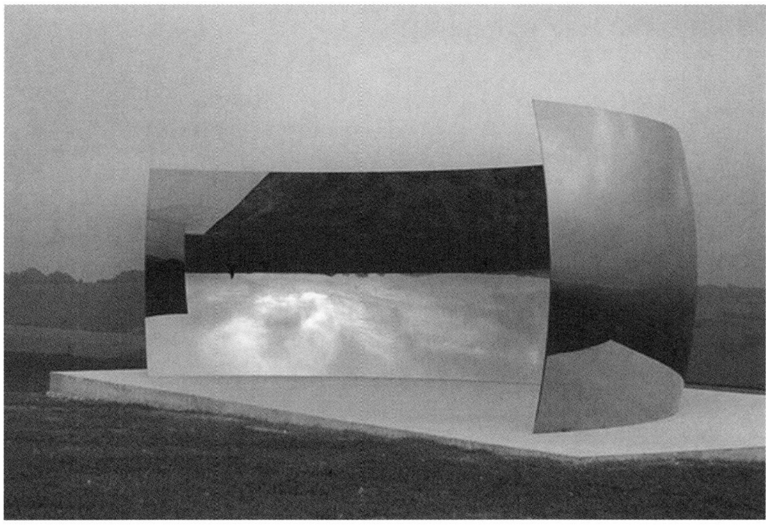

Anish Kapoor, *C-Curve*

Brighton Road

*Southwest corner of Beach House Park
(removed 2007) formerly on A27
roundabout, Arundel, during Arundel Arts
Festival*

Murmurations

Sculptor: Chris Blade

Installed: 2005
Materials/dimensions; stainless steel, each pole
6 m high
Funded by: Chris Blade

The sculpture was formed of a series of 12
stainless steel seagulls atop poles 6 m high. The
birds moved and reacted to the environment,
whether wind, the light from cloud, sun or sky.
Chris Blade, at the time a lecturer in three-
dimensional design at Northbrook College,
Worthing, stated of his piece:

> Although seagulls have some bad press
> locally they are at their most beautiful and
> graceful when flying free and soaring.
> Masters of their environment, the seagull
> sculpture presents a contrast to the
> commuters who are static and earthbound.[1]

This sense of the freedom of flight also
related to his own love of paragliding. The
creation of the sculpture began with
photographs of seagulls in flight, followed by
drawings and then laser-cut outline shapes of
the birds, with one side polished and the other
left matte to create a positive/negative effect.
Murmuration is more commonly used as a
collective noun for starlings, particularly when
they circle in flocks at dusk; as the title for this
sculpture, it reflects the kinetic qualities of the
piece.

Blade proposed the sculpture, which cost
him about £2000 to produce, as a temporary
installation on a roundabout on the approach

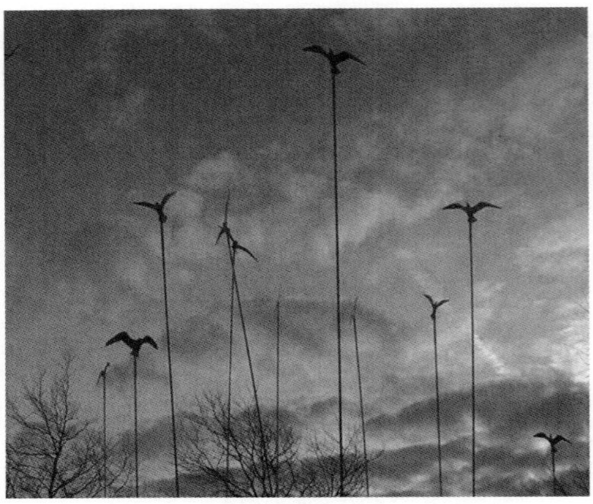

Chris Blade, *Murmurations*

road to Arundel during its annual arts festival.
Soon after its erection, individual birds began to
go missing. At the end of the festival the
sculptor approached the Sussex arts group
RAG (Revolutionary Arts Group) for help in
finding another temporary or permanent home
for his work. Worthing Borough Council's
parks team and curators at Worthing Museum
and Art Gallery agreed to relocate the sculpture
at the southern end of Beach House Park. The
theft of individual sculpted seagulls continued
and in 2006 the sculpture was in such a bad
state of repair, the council decided to dismantle
it. Due to a breakdown of communication, the
remains were not returned to their creator, who
was away working as a travel photographer,
and have subsequently disappeared.[2]

Notes
[1] artistsandmakers.com (accessed 11 December
2010). [2] Chris Blade, telephone conversation, 13
December 2010.

Other source
The Argus, 8 December 2006.

Abbreviations

A/F/P RBS	Associate/Fellow/President Royal Society of British Sculptors
A/F RIBA	Associate/Fellow Royal Society of British Architects
AWG	Art Workers' Guild
CGLAS	City and Guilds of London Art School
RA	Royal Academy of Arts
RCA	Royal College of Art
RSA	Royal Society of Arts
SPS	Society of Portrait Sculptors

Julian Phelps Allan (1892–1996)
Sculptor. Born Millbrook, Southampton. Trained at Westminster School of Art and the RA Schools (1922–25). Awarded the Landseer scholarship in 1923 and an RA gold medal in 1925. She studied in Florence under Libero Andreotti in 1926. She changed her name from Eva Dorothy Allan to Julian Phelps Allan in 1929. During the 1930s she travelled to Yugoslavia and met the sculptor Meštrovi in Zagreb 1936. She returned to Yugoslavia and Serbia in 1954 to study Byzantine frescoes. Allan exhibited at the RA in 1929–38, 1946 and 1949, and at the RSA from 1947. She executed bas-reliefs at Lambeth, Maudsley and other hospitals, private homes, public gardens, schools, colleges, art galleries, concert halls, cemeteries, convents and monasteries in England and Scotland. ARBS 1937; FRBS 1947; OBE.

Sources: Obit. *St Dunstan's Review*, June 1999; Charnot, M., Farr, D. and Butlin, M., *Modern British Paintings, Drawings and Sculpture*, London, 1964.

Ekkehard Altenburger (b. 1966)
Sculptor. Brought up on the German/Swiss border. In the 1980s he was apprenticed to a stonemason and worked on the restoration of the cathedral of Schwäbisch Gmünd. Altenbuurger studied sculpture at the Hochschule für Künst in Bremen (1991–95 and 1997–98, under Yuji Takeoka), Edinburgh College of Art (1995–96) and Chelsea College of Art, London (1998–99). Since 1995 he has been based in the UK, producing site-specific pieces for public and private clients here, throughout Europe and in America. He created sculptures for Queen Elizabeth Hospital in Gateshead (2005), Guatemala City Museum of Contemporary Art (2010) and Harlow Arts Trust (2010). He exhibited at SKULPTUR in Museum Rehmann, Switzerland, at 'Sculpture at Glyndebourne' in 2011 and at the RA 2011 and 2012. RBS.

Sources: saatchionline.com; artist's website.

Nancy Angus (b. 1958)
Ceramicist. Born Bath. Studied at Salisbury College of Art (1974–75), Bath Academy of Art (1976–77), South Glamorgan Institute of Art (1976–77), South Glamorgan Institute of Higher Education (1997–80), and University of Brighton (1999–2001). Based in Brighton. Awarded a Crafts Council Setting Up Grant (1985) and a South East Arts Travel Award (1986). She hand-builds pots, painting the surfaces with slips to create a dry quality, which is reminiscent of frescoes or tomb paintings. She has shown in numerous solo and group exhibitions in Europe and America, including *The New Spirit in Craft and Design*, a Crafts Council touring exhibition (1987), *Contemporary British Ceramics* in Los Angeles (2003) and in galleries in Paris, Zurich and Vienna. She completed a commission of five pots for British Rail in 1988 and her work is in several public collections, including the North West and South East Arts craft collections, Lotherton Hall, Leeds, Huddersfield Art Gallery, the Walker Art Gallery, Liverpool and the RSA.

Sources: Makers' files, University of Brighton; artist's website.

David Annand (b. 1948)
Sculptor. Trained Duncan of Jordanstone College of Art, Dundee. Based in Kilmany, Fife. After teaching in secondary schools for 14 years, Annand became a full-time sculptor. The majority of his works are public commissions and include many life-like sculptures of human figures and animals, such as *H'Nae Day Sae Dark* (1989) in Perth. Annand has received numerous awards for his work, including the Royal Scottish Academy's Latimer Award, the Benno Schotz Award and the Sir Otto Beit Medal from the RBS for *Deer Leap* (1987).

Source: nationalgalleries.org.

Walter Bailey (b. 1960)
Sculptor. Born Sunderland. His father was a fisherman and he attributes his appreciation of the elements and natural materials to early experiences at sea. Trained working with David Nash 1988–91. Most of his sculptures are directly carved in wood, often using a chainsaw and fire. They explore patterns of movement and the interaction between human beings and the natural cycle. He creates site-specific work for rural and urban landscapes, both in Britain and abroad. Key commissions in the UK have included *The Dunblane Memorial*

commissioned by NAPE (1998); *Origins* at Kew Gardens (2004); Amnesty International HQ (2007); external sculpture for Chippendale's former workshop in St Martin's Lane, London (2010); and a 7-year collaboration to create wood sculptures and glass design for Hamilton Assoc. Architects (subsequently Robin Partington Architects) for Park House, Oxford Street, London (2012). In 2002 Bailey was awarded the Enkū Grand Award by Gifu Prefecture in Japan. He lives and works in rural East Sussex and has work in public and private collections around the world. ARBS.

Sources: artist; axisweb.org; fourthdoor.co.uk.

Mark Wilfrid Batten (1905–1993)
Born Kirkcaldy, Scotland. Attended Beckenham and Chelsea Art Schools, and began experimenting with stone carving in 1927, although he did not exhibit until 1936, after a period spent in masons' yards in Cornwall, where he learned to carve granite. In 1939 he collaborated with Eric Gill, but usually worked alone in an isolated studio at Christian's River, Dallington, East Sussex. He was passionate about direct carving in stone, attributing its revival to Gill in the first decade of the twentieth century. He published *Stone Sculpture by Direct Carving* in 1957, revising the text under the new title *Direct Carving in Stone* in 1966. It remains one of the few manuals on the subject. PRBS 1956–61. Awarded Gold Medal for Sculpture by the Société des Artistes Français at the Paris Salon in 1977 for *Mountaineer*, his last non-commissioned sculpture.

Sources: Obit. *The Independent*, 20 January 1993; britishmuseum.org

Quentin Claudian Stephen Bell (1910–1996)
Painter, sculptor, potter, art historian, writer. Born London, the younger son of Vanessa and Clive Bell and brought up among the artists and writers of the Bloomsbury Group. After leaving school at 17 he toured Europe with the art critic Roger Fry and studied painting in Paris and Rome. He became a member of the Euston Road School in the 1930s. In 1935 he went to the Burslem School of Art in Staffordshire to acquire the technical knowledge to make pots, believing that pottery was essentially a form of sculpture. He collaborated with his mother and Duncan Grant on a series of murals at Berwick church, near the family home at Charleston. His career in art education began at Kings College Newcastle in 1952, continuing with professorships at Leeds University (1962–67), Oxford University (Slade professorship 1964–65) Hull University (1965) and Sussex University (1967–75). He published widely on topics as diverse as fashion, the Pre-Raphaelites, John Ruskin, the history of art education and 'bad' art. He completed an authoritative biography of his aunt, Virginia Woolf (1972). After retirement he concentrated on producing ceramic pieces. With his wife Olivier and sister Angelica Garnett, Bell helped to establish the Charleston Trust that ensured the preservation of the family home decorated by Vanessa Bell and Duncan Grant, which now displays several of his own pots and sculptures.

Source: Obit. *The Independent*, 18 December 1996.

Evelyn Bennett (b. 1964) and Christopher Rutter (b. 1961)
Evelyn Bennett trained as a printed textiles designer at Winchester College of Art and the RCA and has since worked as a designer of textiles and ceramics for companies such as Habitat, Esprit, Marks and Spencer, French Connection and George Davies. She has worked in Germany, Italy and Zimbabwe. She was awarded The South East Arts Travel Bursary to Mexico.
Christopher Rutter trained at Wimbledon College of Art and CGLAS as a stone carver and gained his MA in the School of Architecture at East London University. He has worked as an architectural carver on a wide variety of old and new buildings including Westminster Abbey, Ely Cathedral and King's College chapel and the Fitzwilliam Museum, Cambridge. He received a Henry Moore Trust Award to work at Portland Sculpture Park, the McColl Arts Foundation Travel Award to Zimbabwe and craftsmanship awards for his stone carving work, such as some of the new figures for the West Front of Westminster Abbey. Rutter and Bennett have worked closely together since 1994, making large-scale sculpture for a number of locations including Chichester, Hastings and Swindon Hospitals and 'Sculpture at Goodwood'. They have been awarded a South East Arts Direct Support Grant for incorporating digital technology into their work. In 2005 they were awarded a Leonardo da Vinci Fellowship to work at Cyprus College of Art and in 2006 a merit medal in the International Sculpture competition of the Beijing Olympics. They have exhibited widely in the UK and in Berlin, where they completed a residency at BBK Bethanien in 2012.

Source: artists' website.

Hamish Black (b. 1948)
Sculptor. Born Braintree, Essex. Studied at Eastbourne School of Art (1965–67), North East London Polytechnic (1967–70) and the Slade (1970–72). Based in East Sussex. Early works were made using equipment and materials in his father's forge, then, at 16, he started full-time art studies. After finishing his postgraduate studies, Black held regular part-time lecturing posts at BA and MA degree level; this sustained a studio that enabled the completion of a succession of public and private commissions in UK and Europe. His working method is as a constructor; a solo exhibition at the Kapil Jariwala gallery, London (1999) showed his catholic approach to materials, ranging from metal to paper, and to scale, ranging from very large to small and intimate. Black exhibits regularly, and is represented in

public and private collections in Britain and Europe. FRBS.

Sources: Cass Sculpture Foundation; artist's website.

Christopher Blade (b. 1963)
Designer, glass artist, travel photographer. Studied glass-making and design at Staffordshire University (1982–85) and RCA (1985–87). Founded his own business in a small studio next to the Royal Festival Hall in 1988. He worked for 20 years as a designer and craftsman, specialising in batch-produced furniture, jewellery, ceramics, glass and interior design. From 2006 he has worked as a photographer for a British Adventure Travel company. He has designed and managed many hundreds of glass production projects for clients including: Akzo Nobel, International Paint; Royal Victoria Infirmary, Newcastle; Ford Aerospace; Entrepreneurs' Forum, Newcastle; and Spey Whisky. In 2010 he acted as consultant to develop a sculpture of a stag's head to be cast in lead crystal for Glenfiddich Whisky displays in airports worldwide. Currently Senior Manager of Enterprise, Commissioning and the Glass Studio at the National Glass Centre, University of Sunderland, UK.

Source: artist's website.

Jan Blake
Sculptor, textile and installation artist. Born London. Trained as a specialist art teacher at Bath Academy of Art, graduating in 1968, then taught in secondary schools for nine years before taking a postgraduate course in Theatre Design at the Slade in 1981. In the same year she gained an Arts Council Award for Theatre Design. She spent 12 years working internationally as a freelance designer for drama, ballet, contemporary dance and opera companies. In 1994 she moved to Bristol to develop her work for public spaces. Her background in theatre design has greatly influenced her approach. She uses mainly silk organza painted with procion dyes to clad and drape within metal sculptures that have evolved from naturally occurring shapes and patterns. Recent commissions have included *New Leaf* (2005) at the Department for the Environment, Farming and Rural Affairs (DEFRA), London; *Life Boat* (2009) at Bristol Heart Institute (with sculptor Rob Olins) and *Gust* (2011) for the Radiotherapy department, Clatterbridge Cancer Care, Aintree, Liverpool. *Genie* (2011) and *Zig-Zag* (2013) explore the nature of patterns and transformations that evolve during the process of building a new transparent material from cardboard. *Zig-Zag* was used as part of a commission with Aune Head Arts at Dartington in association with EVA Sound Art Radio to create a sound piece for radio made from the percussive sounds of six dancers' feet on the floor in response to this moving sculpture.

Sources: artist's website; axisweb.org.

Nigel Boonham (b. 1953)
Sculptor. Born Aldershot, Herts. Trained in portrait sculpture and large-scale figurative pieces working as assistant to Oscar Nemon. His distinguished portrait subjects have included Lord Runcie (1981), Diana Princess of Wales (1991) and Dame Cicely Saunders (2001). He designed the Basil Hume Memorial Garden and statue in Newcastle upon Tyne, in 2002. He has also worked on complex sculptural projects, most notably on the refurbishment of the sanctuary at St Mary's Cathedral, Sydney, for which he carved the Entombed Christ altar (consecrated 2008), marble statues of the Risen Christ and Mary Magdalene (2010) and provided models for woodcarving and designs for furniture and six Presbytery screens. He has exhibited annually at the RBS since 1996, at the RA in 1975 and 1976 and the National Gallery, London in 1981 and 1995. FRBS 1983; PRBS 2004–09.

Sources: artist's website; rbs.org.uk; debretts.com.

Lawrence Henderson Bradshaw (1899–1978)
Sculptor, painter and engraver. Born Wallasey. Trained at Liverpool School of Art with the painter William Penn 1916–17. Following the First World War he worked with Frank Brangwyn. Some of Bradshaw's earliest surviving sculptural work consists of two bas-reliefs and banners depicting scenes from the life of St Philip Neri for Brompton Oratory made in 1926–27. During the interwar period he established a reputation for architectural sculpture, especially on civic buildings, such as the Guildhall at Cambridge (1935–37), Watford Town Hall (1933–40), Worthing Assembly Hall (1935–36), Leyton Police Station, London (1939) and Winchester Town Hall (1957). During the Second World War Bradshaw served as official war artist for the Norwegian government. After the war, the number of architectural commissions began to dwindle; in 1952 he submitted an unsuccessful proposal for a sculptural screen at the front of the Time-Life building in New Bond Street. He had been an active member of the British Communist Party since the 1930s and in 1955 gained the commission for the Marx memorial in Highgate cemetery, his most widely known work. The 1960s and 1970s were devoted to his prolific practice as a sculptor of portrait busts, including prominent political and cultural figures, such as Harry Pollitt, Colin Wilson and Hugh MacDiarmid, and to his painting.

Sources: Bradshaw Archive, Henry Moore Institute, Leeds; Lindey (2007).

Percival Bridgman
Stonemason. Apprenticed in 1899 to the family firm of C.F. Bridgman (formerly May and Parsons) of Eastgate Wharf, Lewes, whose history goes back to the eighteenth century. They were involved in general building and repair work as well as the erection and maintenance of tombstones in the many churchyards of East and West Sussex.

Sources: East Sussex Record Office (BRN01-98); tombstones.webs.com.

Jackie Brown (b. 1958)
Sculptor. Trained Southend College of Technology (1974–76) and Preston Polytechnic (1976–79). Gained a North East Arts Award in 1997. Brown's work explores the relationship between the domestic interior and the natural world. She is interested in mundane everyday processes like sorting, stacking, folding and dusting, which gain greater significance when they are seen in the landscape and captured moments of history are revealed. She has exhibited widely in group and solo shows in Britain and the United States and received commissions for public art projects from Cambridge County Council (*Over 100: The Beech Tree Project 1991*); Waverly Borough Council, Surrey, in conjunction with the Wildlife Trust (Frensham Common, 1998) and Eastbourne Council, the British Heart Foundation, the Countryside Agency and the University of Brighton (Eastbourne seafront 2000). She is a member of South London Women Artists.

Sources: artist; southlondonwomenartists.co.uk.

Richard Browne (1921–1990)
Sculptor. Born London. Studied at Wimbledon School of Art 1948–52, then the Slade 1953. Lived and worked in Old Heathfield, Sussex. Noted for his portraits, including Dame Alicia Markova (1961) given to the National Portrait Gallery 1992. He created figures of Hope and Justice for Guildford Cathedral and has work at City University, London, Crawley and Hemel Hempstead (*Growth* 1977). FRBS; President SPS.

Source: Buckman, D., *Artists in Britain Since 1945*, Bristol, 2006 edn.

Romany Mark Bruce (b. 1960)
Sculptor and painter. Born Ireland. Came to England in 1978 to study law. Moved to Brighton in 1989. He developed an interest in photography and was given the opportunity to experiment with sculpting, studying with Teresa Martin. He had his first exhibition in the Brighton Festival in 1992. He developed his style to deconstruct the human form, including the use of shattered windscreen glass to explore the space and light around it. His sculptures are collected in the USA, Australia, Hong Kong and the Middle East, and all over Europe. Bruce has for many years devoted much of his time to fundraising for HIV charities and is a Trustee of the Sussex Beacon, HIV/Aids Care Centre in Brighton.

Source: artist's website.

Trude Bunzl (1904–1982)
Sculptor. Born Amsterdam and studied medicine, but was more interested in music and poetry, from which she drew her subject matter. She emigrated to England and in 1958 studied sculpture under Bernard Meadows at Chelsea School of Art. She also took courses at St Martin's School of Art and showed in group exhibitions. Solo exhibitions were held in London in 1966, 1971 and 1972, at the Westcott Art Centre in 1967 and in Vienna in 1968. Examples of her work are to be found throughout England, Austria and Israel; best known are the Sophocles-inspired *Oedipus Rex* for Chichester Theatre, a head of Moses (inspired by Schoenberg's Moses and Aaron) and *Listening to Music*, a sculpture dedicated to Gustav Mahler.

Source: *Bénézit Dictionary of Artists*, Oxford, 2006.

John Edward Carew (1785–1868)
Sculptor. Born Tramore near Waterford, Ireland. He became an assistant to Richard Westmacott in London c. 1809. In 1822, the Earl of Egremont persuaded him to accept an exclusive arrangement to work solely for him. Carew produced a series of fine genre and mythological figures and groups for the Earl, which is still at Petworth House. On discovering at his patron's death in 1837 that he had been left nothing in the will, he brought an action against the executors, which he lost. Carew produced vigorous and baroque-inspired devotional sculpture: a high relief of the *Baptism of Christ* (1835) for St John the Baptist Catholic Church in Brighton, and another of the *Assumption of the Virgin* (1853) for the Royal Bavarian Chapel in London (now in the Chapel of the Assumption, Warwick Street). Recognition of Carew's abilities was implied by his being given the commission to execute the colossal bronze relief of *The Death of Nelson*, for the plinth of Nelson's Column in Trafalgar Square. His portrait statues include *Edmund Kean as Hamlet* (1833) at the Theatre Royal, Drury Lane, London and Henry Grattan (1857) at the Palace of Westminster. His funerary monuments include the memorial to George IV's mistress, Mrs Fitzherbert, in Brighton, and the memorial to William Huskisson (1832), in Chichester Cathedral.

Sources: Strickland, W.G., *A Dictionary of Irish Artists*, Dublin and London, 1913; Gunnis (1968); Ward-Jackson (2003).

Michael Clark (1918–1990)
Sculptor. Born Cheltenham, son and pupil of Philip Lindsey Clark. Studied at Chelsea School of Art 1935–37 and CGLAS 1947–50. Largely producing religious works, in stone, wood, bronze and glass fibre, he is represented in over 100 churches, schools and public buildings in Britain. Major works include: relief of *Christ, St Edward and St Peter*, awarded the RBS 'Best work of the year' medal; *Glorious Assumption*, carving in wood, The Friars, Aylesbury (awarded the Otto Beit medal in 1960); *Risen Christ*, Church of Our Lady, St John's Wood, London. He exhibited at the RA from 1949 onwards. ARBS 1949; FRBS 1960; PRBS 1971–6.

Source: Noszlopy, G., *Public Sculpture of Birmingham*, Liverpool, 1998.

Philip Lindsey Clark (1889–1977)
Sculptor. Born London, son of the sculptor

Robert Lindsey Clark. Studied with his father, at Cheltenham School of Art (1905–10), CGLAS (1910–14), RA Schools 1919–21. Exhibited at the RA 1920–52 and showed work at the Paris Salon from 1921. Clark produced a number of War Memorials, including one for Southwark (1923–24), and one commemorating the Cameronians for Kelvingrove Park, Glasgow. From 1926 to 1928 he provided architectural sculpture for buildings in London by the architect G. Val Myer. From 1930 all his RA exhibits were of religious and often specifically Catholic subjects, and from this time he worked largely on church commissions. He became a Carmelite Tertiary, and eventually retired from London to live in the West Country. Among many religious works from his later years are the Hanging Rood (1950) for St Mary's Church, Crewe, and the reliefs of St Augustine and the Virgin and Child (1962) on the west front of St Augustine's Church, Hoddesdon, Herts.

Source: Buckman (2006).

Geoffrey Clarke (b. 1924)

Sculptor, etcher, and designer in stained glass and mosaic. Born Darley Dale, Derbyshire. Studied at Preston School of Art, 1940–41, Manchester School of Art, 1941–42, Lancaster and Morecambe School of Arts and Crafts and the RCA 1948–52. He later taught at the RCA in the Light Transmission and Projection Department, 1968–73. Clarke won the Silver Medal at the Milan Triennale, 1951, and appeared at the Venice Biennales of 1952 and 1960. He is best known for his large-scale abstract works. His commissions include an iron sculpture for the Time-Life Building, Bond Street, London (1952); the High Altar Cross and candlesticks, Flying Cross and Crown of Thorns for Coventry Cathedral (1953–62); *The Spirit of Electricity*, for Thorn House in London (1958); cast aluminium relief for Nottingham Playhouse (c. 1964); *Bubble Chamber Tracks* relief for the University of Liverpool (1966–68); and ceremonial entrance portals for the civic centre at Newcastle upon Tyne (1969). Examples of his work are in the collections of the Arts Council, Tate Gallery, V&A and Leeds Sculpture Collections. ARA 1970; RA 1976.

Sources: Buckman (2006); *Who's Who* 1999; Cavanagh, T., *Public Sculpture of Liverpool*, Liverpool, 1997.

Pete Codling (b. 1969)

Sculptor. Born Zambia, raised in Cornwall and Scotland. Studied at Portsmouth College of Art, East London Polytechnic, Wimbledon School of Art and University of Portsmouth. Lives and works in Portsmouth. Codling views his work as contributing to the built environment and helping communities build a sense of place. He works across the disciplines of landscape, furniture, architecture and sculpture and is known for the variety of materials he uses. His work has attracted national awards and recognition from CABE, The Arts Council of England and the private sector. Public commissions include: *Meeting of Minds* (2007–08) for the Humanities garden at Everest Community College, Basingstoke; *Sun Sculpture* (2007–08) in Bognor Regis and *Mamgu* (2008–10), a 40-ft high sculpture in Glan Y Nant, South Wales. Member of Hampshire Sculpture Trust, and The International Sculpture Centre.

Source: artist's website.

Henry Collins (1910–1994)

Sculptor, painter and designer. Studied at Colchester School of Art and Central School of Arts and Crafts. With his wife, Joyce Pallot, he designed murals, including those at the Shell Centre, the General Post Office Tower and for British Home Stores. The couple also worked on a number of important projects, including the 1951 Festival of Britain and Expo 70 in Japan. Collins taught graphic design at St Martin's School of Art and Colchester School of Art.

Sources: Buckman (2006); Wyke, T., *Public Sculpture of Greater Manchester*, Liverpool, 2004.

Joyce Collins (née Pallot, 1912–2004)

Muralist and painter. Born Brightlingsea, Essex. Studied industrial design at Colchester and Southend Schools of Art. In 1938 she married Henry Collins and is best known for the concrete mural reliefs, created with her husband, which adorn a number of Colchester's pedestrian subways. Pallot was also a keen painter and a founding member of the Colchester Art Society. Member of the Society of Industrial Artists and Designers, the Colchester Art Society and the Society of Chartered Designers. She exhibited at the Trafford Gallery, London; York University; Cardiff; Ipswich and The Minories in Colchester.

Source: hatfieldhines.com.

Helen Collis (1938–1995)

Figurative artist. Born London. Studied at Portsmouth and Gosport School of Science and the Arts. After focusing for many years on drawing, she shifted her energies more to figurative sculpture, and created many portraits, including one of athlete Steve Ovett. Fascinated by African sculpture, she produced a BBC television documentary on the sculpture village Tengenenge with author Peter McCarthy. A founding member of the Fiveways Artists' Group in Brighton, she regularly hosted one of the Open Houses showcasing her own and others' work. She exhibited in Sussex until the end of her life. Her last work before her death from cancer is *The Juggler*, a replica of the sculpture that won her the Sussex Arts Club Award for Visual Arts. Most of her work is now in private collections in the UK and abroad.

Source: Claire Nelson (artist's daughter).

Angela Conner (b. 1935)
Sculptor and painter. Born London.
Apprenticed to Barbara Hepworth. She has
created sculptures in diverse materials,
including stainless steel, marble dust, carbon
fibre, resin, gold, silver, slate and glass and uses
natural elements such as water, sun, gravity and
wind to introduce movement into her pieces.
She has designed large-scale mobile sculptures
for public sites in Dublin, Longleat House,
Chatsworth House, Sydney, North Carolina
and Madrid. Her *Wave* for Parkwest Dublin
was the tallest water- and wind-powered
mobile sculpture in Europe. Conner's portrait
sculptures include those of General de Gaulle,
Camilla Parker-Bowles and Elisabeth Frink.
She has had solo exhibitions in London, New
York and Istanbul as well as exhibiting at the
RA, the V&A, Birmingham Museum and Art
Gallery and the Carnegie Museum of Modern
Art. Her works are in the collections of the
Arts Council of Great Britain, House of
Commons, Eton College and the National
Portrait Gallery, among others. FRBS.

Sources: Courtney, C., 'Sculpture by Angela Conner',
Architect (RIBA), vol.93; artist's website; Noszlopy,
G., *Public Sculpture of Warwickshire, Coventry and
Solihull*, Liverpool, 2003.

David Cornell
Designer, sculptor and painter. Born London.
Studied Central School of Art, Harrow School
of Art and the Academy of Fine Art, University
of Pennsylvania, USA. He worked as an
engraver in the West End of London where he
engraved personal stationery for celebrities,
titled families, Royal Regiments and Royal
Navy and Royal Air Force insignia and crests.
In 1964 he was appointed coin and medal
engraver at the Royal Mint. He was invited to
join the Bank of England to engrave the new
portrait of Queen Elizabeth II for the new bank
notes, but chose to work and study in the USA
and returned to the Royal Mint in 1970. He
then worked as Director of Sculpture at John
Pinches Ltd, Medallists and Trophy Makers,

also creating his own sculpture in his London
teaching studio. He worked in collaboration on
projects with Henry Moore, Pablo Picasso,
Salvador Dali, Manzu, Taro Okamoto, Marc
Chagall among others. He also worked on
medallic programmes with Lord Mountbatten,
Lord Montagu and Sir John Betjeman. He
designed the first official coin of Prince William
to commemorate his 21st birthday. Cornell's
work is in many private collections around the
world, including those of the British and
European Royal Families. His oil paintings
include portraits, horses, dancers and nude
studies. FRSA; FRBS; Vice-President SPS 1977;
Past President of the Society of Sculptors,
Medal and Coin Engravers.

Sources: *Who's Who in Art*; artist's website.

Mary Cox
Sculptor. Studied Chelsea School of Art under
Willi Soukop, Bernard Meadows and Elisabeth
Frink. Lives and works in Sussex, where she has
been commissioned to create works for
churches, hospitals and gardens, cast in bronze
or bronze resin. Her portrait busts include
Malcolm Muggeridge and eminent members of
the legal profession, but she specialises in
children's portraits. Her sculptures of children,
many based on her own family, are full of life
and careful observation. She also sculpts small
Limited Edition bronzes of mythological and
religious subjects. ARBS 2000.

Source: artist's website.

Sean Crampton (1918–1999)
Sculptor. Born Manchester, son of architect
Joshua Crampton. Studied silversmithing at
Vittoria School of Art, Birmingham, then
sculpture at the Central School of Art in
Birmingham. Apprenticed to Fernand Léger in
Paris. After the Second World War he became
Professor of Sculpture at the Anglo-French Art
Centre, London. His Catholic faith influenced
his art, most obviously in works such as the
Stations of the Cross, which he created for his

local church, St Edmund, Calne, Wiltshire.
Public commissions included a memorial for
the London Irish Rifles, and *The Three Judges*
(Churchill College, Cambridge, 1970). His
work was shown in group and solo exhibitions,
and he was particularly associated with the
Alwin Gallery. ARBS 1953; PRBS 1966–71.
Master of the AWG 1978.

Sources: *Who's Who*, 1999; Buckman (2006); Wyke
(2004); Obit. *The Independent*, 23 July 1999.

Joseph Cribb (1892–1967)
Sculptor, carver and letter cutter. Born
Hammersmith. His father was a graphic artist,
specialising in cartography. In 1906 he became
Eric Gill's assistant and was taught letter-
cutting and masonry skills. In 1907 he moved
with Gill to Ditchling in Sussex and entered a
formal apprenticeship (completed 1913),
assisting Gill with many of his early sculptures.
Cribb followed Gill into the Roman Catholic
Church and later the Dominican Third Order.
He worked with Gill on the Westminster
Cathedral *Stations of the Cross*. During army
service in France, 1916–19, he joined the
Directorate of Graves Registration and
Enquiries (forerunner of the Imperial War
Graves Commission, later Commonwealth War
Graves) and with Gill's brother Macdonald
(Max) designed the standard war grave
tombstone, making over 50 originals for the
many regimental badges represented. In 1920
Cribb joined Gill, Hilary Pepler and Desmond
Chute in setting up the Guild of St Joseph and
St Dominic, an association of Catholic artists
and craftworkers on Ditchling Common. He
also started taking on his own commissions,
initially for war memorials, one of the first
being a crucifix at Downside Abbey. When Gill
left the Guild and moved away from Ditchling,
Cribb took over his workshop although he
continued to assist Gill with some of his major
sculpture, for example on *Mankind* (1927–28).
He cut inscriptions much faster than most
letter-cutters and made more than 20 sets of

Stations of the Cross, including those at St Matthew's, Westminster. His sculptural style was based on the Romanesque sculptures he saw in France and in the V&A. At the time of his death he was running a successful business, employing two assistants, Noel Tabbenor and Kenneth Eager. He also inspired and trained other renowned sculptors and letter-cutters, including John Skelton, Michael Harvey and Michael Biggs.

Sources: Attwater, D., *A Cell of Good Living*. London, 1969; Collins, J., *Eric Gill: The Sculpture*, Woodstock, NY, 1998; Cribb, R. and J. (2007).

William Cure II (d. 1632)

Sculptor. Born London. His grandfather William Cure (or Cuer) was of Dutch origin, but founded a workshop in Southwark. His son Cornelius was apprenticed to a marbler and became Master Mason to the Crown in 1596. Cornelius worked closely with his own son, William Cure II, their most important work being the monument to Mary Queen of Scots in Westminster Abbey (1607–12). This was completed by William II following his father's death, when he succeeded to the post of Royal Master Mason. Inigo Jones complained about his neglect of work on the Banqueting House at Whitehall and replaced him with Nicholas Stone.

Sources: Whinney (1964); npg.org.uk.

Philip Currey (1851–1894)

Architect. Nephew of architect Henry Currey (1820–1900). Worked in the office of G.E. Street. His father Edmund was Registrar of the Archdeaconry of Lewes and largely financed his first restoration commission at the parish church at South Malling (1873). Thereafter he completed restoration work at St John sub Castro (1883–84); St Michael (1877–78) and St Thomas (1877), all in Lewes; and churches in Piddinghoe (1882) and Tarring Neville (1893). He died at Castlegate House, Lewes.

Source: sussexparishchurches.org.

George Cutts (b. 1938)

Sculptor. Born Rugby. Apprenticed as a sheet metal worker at Goole Shipyards in Yorkshire, then won a scholarships to Doncaster School of Art, training under John Skeaping. Lives and works in East Sussex. He often combines stainless steel and stone in his large-scale pieces, frequently also incorporating movement. He won the International Kinetic Art Competition in 2006. His work is in a number of private collections and has been exhibited at 'Sculpture at Goodwood' in West Sussex, Hannah Peschar Sculpture Garden, Storm King Art Center in Mountainville, New York, the RA and Chichester Cathedral and at other venues throughout Europe. He was the subject of *Walking with Sculptors: George Cutts – Reflections*, a documentary made by Jeremy Isaacs Productions for the Cass Foundation in 2009. FRBS.

Source: artist's website.

Ronald Peter Dellar (b. 1930)

Painter. Born London. A self-taught artist in watercolour and oil. He has exhibited at the Royal Society of Portrait Painters, the New Art Centre, Roche Court, Leicester Galleries, Young Contemporaries, Worthing Art Gallery and Gallery 27 in Tonbridge, Kent. He has held solo exhibitions at the Archer Gallery and exhibited several times in Germany. The Rother levels in Romney Marsh are a feature of his later pictures. He presented the Town Hall at Rye, where he formerly lived, with a painting of the town from the river Rother in 2008.

Sources: *Rye and Battle Observer*, 11 June 2008; artbiogs.co.uk.

John Leopold Denman (1882–1975)

Architect. Born Brighton, his father and grandfather were both local architects. Trained at the Central School of Arts and Crafts and articled to his father in 1898. In 1907 he became an assistant at the firm of Jones and Smithers. During the 1920s he was Head of the Architecture department at Brighton School of Art. He influenced the careers of a number of former pupils associated with the artistic community at Ditchling, including Joseph Cribb, whose carved reliefs adorn many of his buildings. Denman's first commissions in Brighton were for civic structures to commemorate the creation in 1928 of the Borough of Brighton. In 1930 he took over his father's practice and worked mostly in the Neo-Georgian style on a range of commercial, civic and religious buildings in Brighton, and pubs and hotels there and elsewhere on the south coast for Brighton's Kemp Town Brewery. He also completed much church restoration and wrote a book on ecclesiastical architecture. During the 1940s he exhibited at the RA and in 1945 was a founding member of The Regency Society, which campaigned against the planned demolition of large areas of Regency-era buildings on Brighton and Hove seafront. He continued the family practice as Denman and Son in partnership with his son John Bluet Denman. ARIBA 1909; FRIBA.

Sources: Brodie, A., *Directory of British Architects 1834–1914*, vol. 1. London 2001; Lyon and Woodham (2009); *A Guide to the Buildings of Brighton* (1987).

Chris Drury (b. 1948)

Sculptor. Born Colombo, Sri Lanka. Trained at Camberwell School of Art. Influenced by Hamish Fulton, he became interested in landscape art, using natural materials to create baskets, cairns and shelter forms. He often collaborates with scientists, doctors and technicians, making connections between different phenomena. He has completed residencies at The Nirox Foundation in The Cradle of Humankind, South Africa and at the British Antarctic Survey. Site-specific works include *Vortex* (Lewes Castle, Sussex, 1994), *Wave Chamber* (Kielder Reservoir, Northumberland, 1996), *Shimanto River Spheres* (Kochi Province, Japan, 1997), *Eden Cloud Chamber* (Eden Project, Cornwall,

2001), *Rhine Mosel Slate Whirlpool* (Koblenz, Germany, 2010), *UK Carbon Sink* (University of Wyoming, 2011) and *The Way of Earth and Trees* (Canberra, Australia, 2013). He has published *Chris Drury, Silent Spaces* (Thames and Hudson, 2004) and *Chris Drury, Mushrooms/Clouds* (Nevada Museum of Art, 2008). He received the Pollock-Krasner Award in 1995 and the Art in Health Award from University College, London in 2004.

Sources: artist's website; Wyke (2004).

Peter Fairhurst
Designer, teacher and writer. Born Lancashire, son of Joseph Fairhurst, expert in lettering and illuminated writing. Graduated in education, specialising in kinetic sculpture, from Eastbourne College of Education and Sussex University. He taught craft and technology in schools and also developed an interest in storytelling and creative writing in the classroom. He has produced pieces by commission for, among others, HRH The Prince of Wales and Cardinal Cormac Murphy O'Connor, head of the Catholic Church in England. Between 1975 and 1985, he wrote a series of eight model-making books for children and after taking early retirement, was appointed Educational Projects Manager for 'Young Engineers', a network of extracurricular clubs built on a close relationship between local companies, engineering and schools. Fairhurst is a former councillor and Mayor of Bexhill and was Chief Executive Officer of Bexhill Museum 2003–11.

Sources: childrensliteraryagency.com; bexhillmuseum.co.uk.

Henry Charles Fehr (1867–1940)
Sculptor. Trained at the RA Schools from 1885, winning several prizes including the Armitage Scholarship. Between 1889 and 1893 he was studio assistant to Thomas Brock. Fehr exhibited regularly at the RA from 1887. In 1904 he was a founding member of the RBS.

His works include *Perseus Rescuing Andromeda* (1893); portrait statues of James Watt (1898) and John Harrison (1903) for Leeds City Square; and the statue of Queen Victoria (1903) in Hull.

Source: Noszlopy, G., *Public Sculpture of Staffordshire and the Black Country*, Liverpool, 2005.

Brian Fell
Sculptor. Born Liverpool. Studied at Manchester Polytechnic, awarded an MA in 1979. Sculpture Fellow at Cheltenham College of Art (1979–80) and Henry Moore Fellow, Yorkshire Sculpture Park (1989–90). Fell works in metal, especially steel. Public commissions include the *Merchant Seafarers' War Memorial* and *Cargoes* (Cardiff Bay, 1998, 2000), *Footplate* (Flint Railway Station, 1999) and the Tern Project (Morecambe Bay, 1995–2000). *Ajax Bow* is at the Open Air Museum of Steel Sculpture, Ironbridge. Fell is based in Glossop, Derbyshire.

Sources: Groundwork Trust; Wyke (2004).

Damian Fennell
Sculptor. Studied at CGLAS 1997–2000. In 2004 he founded Art in Essence, an arts festival encompassing fine and applied arts, music, dance, film and poetry. He was on the management committee of 'Art in Action' (2004–07) and curated its new drawing section in 2006 and 2007. In 1998/99 he received the Madame Tussaud's award for outstanding figurative sculpture. Fennel has participated in several exhibitions in the UK and received public commissions, including co-designing and painting a three-storey high interior fresco cycle for Waterperry House near Oxford in 2001–05. ARBS 2002.

Source: artist's website.

Alexander Fisher
Teacher and modeller. Trained at the National Art Training School, South Kensington and also

gained a building qualification. He was Head Art Master at Brighton School of Art 1871–92. He acted as advisor for the new School of Science and Art building at Grand Parade in 1875–76, for which he provided designs for terracotta reliefs made in the nearby Ditchling pottery. He also contributed to the science curriculum with a series of lectures on mathematics.

Source: Woodham (2009).

Jane Sybilla Fordham
Painter, mosaic artist, sculptor. Studied at Middlesex and Brighton Polytechnics. In 1984 she helped set up the Red Herring Studios in Brighton. In 1995 she studied traditional Italian mosaic installation under Felix Cecconi. She has exhibited paintings, installations and theatre set design in the UK and abroad. She has received public art commissions from companies such as McAlpine, Kimberly-Clark in Dallas, Texas and local authorities in the UK, including two pieces that contributed to the civic award-winning Brighton seafront development. Her paintings have been commissioned by Anita Roddick for the Body Shop's Bergamot and Hemp ranges and by Fiachre Gibbons, arts correspondent for *The Guardian*.

Source: londonart.co.uk.

Alice Fox
Installation and performance artist. Studied at Brighton Polytechnic late 1980s and since the early 1990s has worked with people with complex learning disabilities and challenging behaviour, both in the context of arts practice and the advocacy of human rights. In 2003 she became Artistic Director of the Rocket Artists' group supporting collaborative practice for artists with and without learning disabilities. In 2008 Fox collaboratively directed and performed the *Smudged* inclusive performance with the Rocket Artists at Tate Modern and in 2010 the *Measures of Bodies* performance at the

Brussels Medical Museum. She is course leader for the MA in Inclusive Arts Practice at the University of Brighton. Fox has made several short documentary films on aspects of her inclusive arts projects and teaching and learning techniques. Her own creative practice has involved a wide variety of media. She was the singer in the Marine Girls, recording two albums and two John Peel sessions and was also a dancer in High Spin Dance Company (integrated dance company for dancers with and without learning disabilities), performing in two national tours. She also practices painting, embroidery and filmmaking.

Source: arts.brighton.ac.uk.

Neal French
Ceramicist, designer, sculptor. Studied sculpture at Mid-Essex Technical College and School of Art under T.B. Huxley-Jones (1949–53) and ceramics at the RCA under Arnold Machin (1955–58). He was a senior designer at Worcester Royal Porcelain Co. Ltd (1958–72), winning the Design Award and Duke of Edinburgh Prize in 1960. For 20 years from 1972 he taught ceramics and 3D design at Hornsey College of Art/Middlesex Polytechnic. Towards the end of this period he began his continuing connection with Rye Pottery as a freelance modeller. His work is primarily concerned with the simplification and stylisation of the human figure, using either ceramic, bronze, or resin with metal or stone finishes. Throughout his career he has also produced small-scale domestic sculpture and portrait heads, including those of Lady Thatcher and Sir Austin Bradford Hill. He has carried out several commissioned public sculptures, most recently a three-figure group in bronze, for the Grosvenor Estates, sited in Mayfair. French has published books and articles on ceramic subjects, most notably *Worcester Blue and White Porcelain 1751–1790* for Barrie and Jenkins publishers and *The Potter's Encyclopaedia of Colour, Form and Decoration* for Quarto Publications. FRBS 2002; member SPS.

Sources: artist's website; artparks.co.uk.

Christian Funnell
Sculptor and designer. Studied painting at Leeds Polytechnic 1984–87. His wide-ranging career has included commissions for the fashion industry, including for Paul Smith (1988) and Gaultier Junior (1990), part-time teaching and residencies at Hillcrest Community Centre (2002 ongoing) and Seaford Museum (2008). He has worked in the public arena, designing gates, sculptures and outdoor furniture that encourage the user to engage with the unique qualities of a space. His work combines new construction techniques with objects bought from scrap yards. His clients have included the National Trust, several property developments, churches throughout Sussex, Pride of the Valley Sculpture Park, Surrey, and hospitals in Brighton, Hastings, Salisbury and Eastleigh. He has participated in many exhibitions and has opened his house and studio, The Old Forge, near Newhaven, as part of Brighton Festival since 2005.

Source: artist's website.

Charles Godfrey Garrard (1886–1987)
Sculptor and carver. Born Ipswich. Served five-year apprenticeship at H.H. Martin & Co. Ltd, Cheltenham, then went to work for a furnishing company in London. In 1907 Garrard moved to Eastbourne, setting up his own workshop in a former stable behind Terminus Road. He specialised in ecclesiastical work and during his long career is believed to have carried out work in every church in the town. Much of this work was undertaken for the architect A.R.G. Fenning. He sculpted the bronze plaque to John Wesley Woodward on the parade opposite the bandstand at Eastbourne and the coat of arms above the town's Police Station. After the Second World War he set up a workshop at 37 Willingdon Road Eastbourne, where he had lived since 1919. Although he retired in 1951, he continued carving and sculpting until the age of 99.

Source: Muncey, F., 'Charles Godfrey Garrard, Sculptor and Carver'. *Eastbourne Local Historian*, no. 133, Autumn 2004.

Steve Geliot (b. 1962)
Sculptor. Born Chislehurst, Kent. Studied 3D Design at Brighton Polytechnic (graduated 1984) and Chelsea School of Art (MA in History and Theory of Modern Art 1991). He has held several solo exhibitions and participated in many group shows, including *The New Spirit in Craft and Design*, at the Crafts Council (1987). His first public commission was for Abbey Park in Leicester (1989); more recent work includes *Pollen* sculptures for the University of Brighton (2004); the *Compton Skyline Project*, a 300-square-metre temporary sculptural projection/installation working with his local community in Brighton (2006); Truro Health Park (2010); garden areas at St James Hospital Portsmouth (2010); *Antigravity*, an animated inflatable UFO for the *White Nights/Nuits Blanches* festival in Brighton and Amiens; *Treecycle*, using lenticular printing on the façade of the 15-metre-high recycling facility building for Southampton City Council, and a canopy commission for affordable housing in Hove (2013). He frequently runs educational projects with local schools and colleges alongside his commissions. Geliot has acted as Lead Artist, coordinating and contributing to several major development projects, including Saltmill Millennium Project (2000); Ropetackle Development, Shoreham (2005); Brighton and Sussex University Hospitals Trust (2006 continuing); Central St Leonard's Regeneration project (2009); and Combe Down Stone Mines, near Bath (2009).

Sources: Axis – Visual Arts Information Service, East Midlands Arts; Cavanagh, T., *Public Sculpture of Leicestershire and Rutland*, Liverpool 2000; artist's website.

Walter Gilbert (1872–1945)
Sculptor. Born Rugby, second cousin to Sir Alfred Gilbert, RA. After university he attended Birmingham School of Art 1898–99. In 1900 he became Master of the Art Department at Bromsgrove School of Science and Art. He also acted as agent to several craft workers, selling their products under the name of the Bromsgrove Guild of Decorative Arts which had its first major success at the Paris Exhibition of 1900, where it won nine awards. Around 1904 the flourishing business was converted into a limited company and employed several continental craftsmen. A major commission was the ornamental brass work for the Great Gates at Buckingham Palace for Sir Aston Webb (1904). Gilbert later withdrew from the Guild and set up in partnership with the Swiss modeller and brass worker, Louis Weingartner, their main commission being the sculptural details for the Great Reredos at Liverpool Cathedral in 1909–10. They had a studio in Weaman Street, Birmingham from 1923 to 1932 and, while Gilbert also worked freelance in local industries, together they produced garden sculptures as well as numerous war memorials including that for the Birmingham Conservative Club (now in the Birmingham Club, Ethel Street), and others at Crewe, Troon and Eccleston Park, Liverpool. Gilbert had a broad art-historical knowledge and wrote articles including 'Romance in metalwork', and 'The essentials of craftsmanship in metalwork'. A bronze bust of Gilbert by his son Donald was exhibited at the RA in 1931 and there is a memorial to him and Louis Weingartner, also by Donald Gilbert, at Hanbury church, Worcester.

Source: Ward-Jackson (2003).

Ernest George Gillick (1874–1951)
Sculptor and medallist. Born Bradford. Studied at Nottingham School of Art, then the RCA under Edward Lanteri. Won Italian travelling scholarship in 1902. Public commissions include figures of J.W.M. Turner and Richard Cosway on the façade of the V&A (1899–1908) and a memorial fountain to the novelist Ouida (Marie Louise de la Ramée) at Bury St Edmunds. Glasgow's principal war memorial, in George Square, was the work of architect Sir John Burnet and Gillick (1924). After the First World War he worked with J.R. Truelove on the *Memorial to The Missing*, at Vis-en-Artois, France. He executed the portrait medallion for the memorial to Sir George Frampton, a fellow member of the AWG, in St Paul's Cathedral (1928). Nottingham Museum has his bronze medallion portraits of Thomas Miller and Robert Millhouse. Gillick exhibited regularly at the RA and was elected ARA in 1935.

Sources: *Bénézit*, 1976; McKenzie, R., *Public Sculpture of Glasgow*, Liverpool, 2002.

William Glanfield (b. 1957)
Sculptor and woodworker. Graduated from Canterbury College of Art in 1979. He works mainly in green oak, making functional and non-functional pieces. His first public artwork was *Oyster Bench*, for his hometown of Whitstable, in 1989. He completed a residency in Grizedale Forest Park in 1992 and major commissions for Leeds General Infirmary in 1997 and Crawley Parks in 2001. In 2000 he created the Rouse Kent Public Art Award chair. In 2008 he commenced the living sculpture project, *Heart of Oak*, in collaboration with the Woodland Trust, supported by Arts Council England. In 2012 he began a major commission for a parkland in Bicester.

Source: artist's website.

Fleur Gray (b. 1955)
Sculptor. Born London. Studied at Jacob Kramer College of Art, Leeds and Canterbury College of Art. She was selected for the 'Young Contemporaries' exhibition at the Institute of Contemporary Arts in London. After college she became resident sculptress for Gillespie's of Farnham, modelling a wide variety of works for commercial use and specialising in sculpture enlargement for artists such as Robert Glen, Robert Clatworthy, Henry Moore and George Weil. She was also employed by Morris Singer Foundry. Her independent work included commissions for town centre sculptures, murals, graphic design, models for advertising and the BBC, portrait busts and puppet heads for Gerry Anderson's 'Terrahawks' TV series. She won the Sussex Open Art Club Prize and First Prize in the acrylic category at the Latour de France Festival and founded the Eastbourne Contemporary Arts Festival. She has exhibited at the ICA, Mall Galleries and Westminster Gallery in London and in galleries in the south of England and France. Gray currently lives in the south of France and has been President and founder member of Arts en Fenouilledes for the past 10 years.

Source: artist.

Vincent Gray (b. 1959)
Sculptor. Born Cheam, Surrey. Educated in the UK and Sweden and spent some time in Australia. Worked for WS Commercial Arts UK (1975–85). Attended life classes at Havant College, Hampshire in 1984 and went to work for Edward Lawrence Studios UK (1986–89); awarded the Edward Lawrence sculpture prize in 1988. During the early 1990s he studied Swedish language and culture at the ABF (Workers' Educational Association) and public art at KV Konst Scola in Gothenburg, Sweden. Gray worked in Philip Jackson's studio 1992–2000. He has exhibited widely in Hampshire and Sussex, contributing regularly to the Chichester Festival. His range of work includes props for museums and portrait busts of the astronomer Patrick Moore and yachtsman Chay Blyth (both 2001), actor Christopher Timothy and author Kate Mosse (both 2003). In 2006 he produced a sculpture for HMS Nelson Wardroom, Portsmouth and in 2008 was a sculptor in Tussaud's Studios London. ARBS 2000.

Source: artist's website.

Charles Hadcock (b. 1965)
Sculptor. Born Derby. Studied at
Gloucestershire College of Art and Technology
(1984–87) and the RCA (1987–89). He lives and
works near Preston, Lancashire. His works
express his interest in multiple images and the
ready-made; he has used mass-produced paving
stones to give texture and repetitive form in
some sculptures, as well as casting polystyrene
packaging in bronze and repeating it as a
multiple. His work has been enriched by his
interest in Victorian engineering, geometry and
musical rhythms. His work is largely abstract,
with the basic qualities of the factory processes
used in its creation visible in his finished pieces.
Major commissions include *Caesura IV* (1995,
Goodwood) and *Passacaglia* (1998, Brighton
beach). Hadcock received the Queen's Award
for Enterprise Promotion in 2007. FRBS 2008.

Sources: Noszlopy, G., *Public Sculpture of
Staffordshire and the Black Country*, Liverpool, 2005;
artist's website.

Benjamin Hancocks (1888–1962)
Sculptor and painter. Thought to have attended
the Mosley Road branch of Birmingham School
of Art in the early 1900s. He then won
scholarships to the Central Birmingham School
of Art and began teaching there in 1915. He
exhibited *The Studio Mirror* in the summer
show at the RA in 1916. Following a period of
military service, he returned to the art school to
work in the Department of Modelling, Stone
Carving and Letter Cutting, as an assistant to
the Head of the Department, William Bloye.
From 1921 onwards he was a sessional teacher
at the school, teaching modelling. He seems to
have continued working part-time in that post
until 1940, ill health subsequently reducing his
hours at the school. He retired to Worthing in
1953. At his death he left clay models for a
number of unfinished works in Sussex.
Source: Norton (2003).

Morris Harding (1874–1964)
Sculptor. Born Stevenage, Herts. Trained in the
studio of his uncle, Harry Bates, ARA (1850–
99) and also worked under J.M. Swan, RA
(1847–1910). He came into early prominence
with a life-size figure of G.K. Vansittart-Neale,
who died at Eton, aged 14, in 1904, in the
Church of All Saints, Bisham, Bucks. He
exhibited at the RA; the London Salon; Walker
Art Gallery, Liverpool and the Royal
Hibernian Academy (1929–53). In the 1920s he
began to establish a reputation as a sculptor of
animals. In 1925 he was invited to work with
Sir Charles Nicholson, consulting architect for
St Anne's Cathedral in Belfast. The Belfast
Cathedral commission was to become the major
work of his career; he spent some 12 years
working on seven nave columns and groups in
the portals of the West Front. He also
completed a series of portraits of dignitaries of
the Irish Church. A fellow sculptor on the
cathedral was Rosamond Praeger (1867–1954)
with whom he shared St Brigid's studios in
Holywood, Co. Down. Other commissions in
Belfast included: front and side chapel reredos
for St Peter's Church, Antrim Road; the Royal
Coat of Arms at Telephone House; lioness with
cubs over the doorway at the Masonic Hall,
Crumlin Road; the Civil Service War Memorial
in the Old Parliament Buildings. His last major
work was the tomb for the seventh Lord
Londonderry, at Mount Stewart, Co Down,
and he was also responsible for Lady
Londonderry's tomb, commissioned in advance
of her death. In 1938 Harding designed a frieze
45.7 m long, 1.2 m deep with 15 panels, for the
Northern Ireland Government's pavilion at the
Glasgow Empire Exhibition, assisted by Poppy
Mollan and John Luke. In 1951 he was one of
11 artists invited to exhibit in the
Contemporary Ulster Art exhibition held for
Festival 1951 at the Belfast Museum and Art
Gallery, and two years later at the same venue
he was represented in an exhibition of
sculpture, organised by the Council for the
Encouragement of Music and the Arts

(CEMA). ARBS 1919; member of the Society of
Animal Painters 1921; President of the Royal
Ulster Academy of Arts; member of the Royal
Hibernian Society; academician of the Ulster
Academy of Arts 1931 (President 1947–57);
Fellow of the Royal Hibernian Academy in
1933; OBE 1950.

Source: belfastcathedral.org.

Joc Hare (b. 1965)
Sculptor and arborist. Born Port of Spain,
Trinidad. Lives and works in St-Leonards-on-
Sea, East Sussex. He owned a business engaging
in a range of arboricultural and urban forestry
practices 1986–99, with clients including local
authorities, royal parks, the Houses of
Parliament and British Waterways. He designs
and builds commissions of sculpture and
furniture working with timber procured
through tree surgery works. He often creates
large site-specific public sculptures that have
furniture elements that can be reproduced for
private sale. In 2000 he was foreman for the
construction of the *Hairy Sitooterie* gazebo for
Thomas Heatherwick studio. He has completed
public arts commissions for Hastings and Rye
and held exhibitions along the south coast and
in London.

Source: against-the-dark.org.

Charles L. Hartwell (1873–1951)
Sculptor. Trained at CGLAS under W.S. Frith,
and the RA from 1896. Also studied privately
with Edward Onslow Ford and W.H.
Thornycroft. Exhibited at the RA 1900–50. His
Dawn (marble, c. 1909–14, Tate Britain,
London) is a poetic figure in the manner of
French Salon sculptors of the turn of the
century. Hartwell's humorously entitled *A Foul
in the Giants' Race* (bronze, 1908, Tate Britain,
London), a group of elephants and their riders,
was inspired by life in India. During both
World Wars, Hartwell exhibited works with
war-related subjects, such as *Blighty* (1916),

Tommy (1918) and *An Ally* (1945). In 1923, Earl Haig unveiled Hartwell's First World War Memorial for Newcastle-upon-Tyne, a dynamic equestrian group of St George and the Dragon on a tall stone plinth. A version of this group was later used for the Marylebone War Memorial, in front of St John's Wood Church in London. RA 1924; RBS silver medal for *The Goatherd's Daughter* 1929.

Sources: Christian, J. (ed.), *The Last Romantics*, London, 1990; Usherwood *et al.* (2000).

Carol Havard

Artist and facilitator. Since completing a Foundation course at Brighton Polytechnic in 1983, she has taken on a variety of roles as a facilitator for creative projects for individuals, school pupils and staff and community groups. Bespoke projects have included making of ceramics, mosaics, printing, painting, drawing, textiles, collage, wax resist, 3D, photography, video and mixed media. She is Director of Art Techniques Partnerships for Community Links and Creative Learning Projects.

Sources: art-techniques.co.uk; uk.linkedin.com.

Edward A. Heffer (1836–1916)

Architect and artist. Born London. Studied at the Government School of Design under Richard Burchett (1815–75). Worked with John Thomas (1813–62) for 4 years. Practiced in Liverpool and London, later in Norwich. He entered the competition for the Prince Albert Memorial in London and designed the memorial to the Prince Consort in Edinburgh 1872.

Sources: scottisharchitects.org.uk; Mapping (2011); Felstead, A., Franklin, J. and Pinfield, L. (eds) *Directory of British Architects 1834–1900*, London, 1993.

E.C. Henriques

Architect. Lived and worked in Mumbai, although he completed some training in the UK. He designed St Peter's Church, Bandra, 1938–39 and was president of the Indian Institute of Architects 1939–40.

Source: iia-india.org.

Lawrence Holofcener (b. 1926)

Songwriter, actor, sculptor, writer. Born Baltimore, USA. Following an early career writing music for television and stage shows and acting on Broadway, Holofcener began to build a reputation as a portrait sculptor with a first exhibition in 1979 at the Gibbes Museum in Charleston, South Carolina. His best known works include *Faces of Olivier*, Chichester Theatre (1985); *Allies* (portraits of Winston Churchill and Franklin Roosevelt unveiled in 1995 on Bond Street, London); *Queen Victoria* for the Isle of Wight Museum and Coburg, Germany; a life-size bronze of Thomas Paine at Bordentown, NJ; life-size portraits of Thomas Chatterton, William Tyndale and William Penn at Bristol, England. Holofcener has embarked on a major series celebrating the contributions made by twentieth-century icons; he also writes dictionaries, novels and poetry.

Source: artist's website.

Charlie Hooker (b. 1953)

Sculptor and installation artist. Studied at Croydon College of Art and Brighton Polytechnic 1969–74. His work crosses the boundaries between sculpture, installation, audio-works and image-making, as well as fusions of dance, music and theatre. During the 1970s and 1980s he undertook numerous site-specific performances and installations in Britain, Europe, America and Australia. Since the 1990s his pieces have featured unique sound systems, which fuse together art and science. These often concern aspects of meteorology and astronomy and combine mechanical and electrical power with natural elements such as wind, water and sunshine to generate audible and visual movement within sculptures. Recent examples include: *Stardust Collector* (2012, ongoing research into the production of a new cosmic ray audio-visual installation); *Audio Accompaniment* (2011; installation triggered by cosmic rays) and *Conductor* (symphonic audio installation controlled by sunshine recorder readings for the De La Warr Pavilion, Sussex, shown alongside the John Cage exhibition 'Every Day is a Good Day' (2011); *Antarctica* (2009) Haugar Vestfold Kunstmuseum, Tonsberg, Norway; *Rub-a-Dub/Wave-Wall III*, University of Brighton Gallery/Brighton Festival (2004). Hooker was made Professor of Sculpture at the University of Brighton in 2005 where he founded The Spring Group, an interdisciplinary research group of artists, scientists and musicians linking four universities.

Sources: arts.brighton.ac.uk ; artist's website.

Amanda Hopkins

Sculptor. Originally trained as a psychologist. Graduated in art and design from Middlesex University 1993. She occasionally exhibits in galleries but her main focus is on putting work in real social/environmental situations. Her research background emphasises process as much as product. She sees the creation of new, secular rituals as an increasingly important part of her work. She was artist consultant for Essex County Council (2001), collaborating with architects in rebuilding 13 schools. Recent public commissions include: *Ropetackle Lenses*, Shoreham (2007); *Star*, Church of Saint Peter and Saint Paul, Kent (2009); *Raw*, Shoreham and District Horticultural Cottage Gardeners Society, Kent (2010).

Sources: artist's website; csm.arts.ac.uk.

Reece James Ingram (b. 1963)

Sculptor. Trained briefly as a taxidermist at the Booth Museum of Natural History in Brighton and Snowdonia Taxidermy Studios, Llanrwst, Gwynedd before taking a BA (Hons) in Fine Art Sculpture at Brighton Polytechnic and an

MA in site-specific sculpture at Wimbledon School of Art. He carves animals and other natural forms from stone and wood and has been commissioned to make sculptures for many parks, towns, playgrounds and schools, most notably the Princess Diana Memorial Playground in London, Grizedale Forest and the Eden Project (2001). He provided seven sheep sculptures for the Horse Trials at the 2012 London Olympics, later moved to a playground in Greenwich. He has also been involved in workshops and residences, including assisting Peter Randall-Page, his tutor at Brighton, in delivering school workshops. He lives and works in Cornwall.

Source: artist's website.

Philip Jackson (b. 1944)
Sculptor. Born Inverness. Studied at Farnham School of Art and with Henry Moore. Lives and works in Midhurst, West Sussex. In 1991 Jackson won the Mozart Bicentenary Sculpture Competition to provide a statue of the composer in Belgravia, London. Other public commissions include *The Yomper* (Eastney, Hampshire, 1992), Jersey Liberation Sculpture (St Helier, 1995), Wallenberg Monument (London, 1997 and Buenos Aires, 1998), The Gurkha Monument (Horse Guards' Avenue, London, 1997), *Minerva* (Chichester, 1997), *Constantine the Great* (York Minster, 1998), *St Richard* (Chichester Cathedral, 2000), *The In-Pensioner* (Royal Hospital, Chelsea, 2000), *George VI* (Britannia Royal Naval College, 2002), the Bomber Command Memorial Sculpture, Green Park, London (2012) and *Sir Alex Ferguson* for Manchester United FC (2012). An equestrian statue of Elizabeth II, commissioned by the Crown Estate for the Golden Jubilee, stands in Windsor Great Park. Sir Otto Beit Medal 1991, 1992 and 1993; FRBS and Vice-PRBS; Commander of the Royal Victorian Order 2009.

Source: artist's website.

Sir Samuel Swinton Jacob (1841–1917)
Engineer, architect and writer. Born into a distinguished military family and joined the Bombay Artillery in 1858, qualifying five years later as a surveyor and engineer. In 1867 he was appointed Chief Engineer of the state of Jaipur, a post he retained until his retirement aged 71. He designed numerous public buildings in the Indo-Saracenic style, including the Jaipur Gate, which was transported to London for an exhibition. In 1926 it was moved to Hove, where it still stands outside the Museum and Art Gallery. He was recalled from England in 1911 to assist Edwin Lutyens and Herbert Baker in the design of New Delhi, but failing health soon forced him to withdraw. Jacob was made a Knight Commander of the Indian Empire in 1902.

Source: en.wikipedia.org.

John Johnson (c. 1850–1920)
Architect and surveyor. Born London. Key buildings include: The Clock Tower, Brighton (1888); Leyton Town Hall and Technical Institute; St Matthew's Church, Bayswater (1881–82); Clock Tower to commemorate the coronation of Edward VII in 1902, Surbiton. Member of the Architectural Association from 1863; RIBA 1881.

Sources: victorianweb.org; scottisharchitects.org.uk; Felstead *et al.* (1993).

Karin Jonzen (née Löwenadler, 1914–1998)
Sculptor. Born London of Swedish parents. Trained at the Slade 1933–36, winning painting and sculpture prizes. In 1936 awarded scholarship to CGLAS. Attended Royal Academy, Sweden in 1939 and was awarded the Prix de Rome, although the Second World War – in which she served as an ambulance driver – prevented her from going to Italy. She became convinced that modernism, which she believed 'did violence to the human form', was not the correct way forward and adopted a more classical style. In 1944 she married artist and

dealer Basil Jonzen (d. 1969) and then in 1972 the Swedish poet Ake Sucksdorff. She exhibited at the RA from 1944, had a solo exhibition at the Fieldbourne Galleries, 1974, and showed in various group and mixed exhibitions. Examples of her work are in the National Portrait Gallery; the V&A; and the Bradford, Brighton, Glasgow and Southend art galleries. Her public commissions include *The Gardener* (1971), Brewer's Hall garden, by London Wall; *Beyond Tomorrow* (1972), Guildhall Piazza; and *Bust of Samuel Pepys* (1983), Seething Lane Gardens, all in bronze and in London. Jonzen was elected a fellow of the Royal Society of British Artists in 1948.

Sources: Buckman (2006); Obits. *The Independent*, 2 February 1998; *The Times*, 31 January 1998; *Who's Who*, 1998.

Rick Kirby (b. 1952)
Sculptor. Born Gillingham, Kent. Studied Newport College of Art 1970–73. He is a figurative sculptor working mainly in metal. He has participated in numerous exhibitions, including solo shows at the Mall Gallery and RIBA sculpture court, London. He has completed residencies in Grindelwald, Switzerland, the Canadian High Commission, Gorky Park, Moscow, Wimpole Hall, Cambridgeshire and Castlemilk, Glasgow. His public commissions include sites on the South Bank, London (*Cross the Divide*, 2000), Endeavour Park, Boston, Lincolnshire (2005), The Atrium, Camberley, Surrey (2008) and Silver Street, Bedford (2008).

Source: McKenzie (2002).

Lorne McKean (b. 1939)
Sculptor. Trained Guildford School of Art and RA Schools, where she won a silver medal for sculpture combined with architecture. She was awarded Feodora Gleichen and Leverhulme scholarships. Two sculptures were accepted by the RA when she was only 20. She was commissioned to create a bust of HRH the

Duke of Edinburgh as the Queen's personal Silver Wedding present in 1972 and in 1997 a half life-size bronze of the Duke for the Guards Polo Club, Windsor Park. She was Official B.T. Artist for the London 2012 Olympic Games and completed a sculpture of Lee Pearson (paralympic winner of nine gold medals) performing dressage. McKean was married to the sculptor Edwin Russell with whom she collaborated on several projects. MSBS1969; FRBS 1972.

Sources: artist's website; artacademy.org.uk.

Kate Maddison

Public artist. Trained in architecture. She is co-founder (in 1985) and Director of Chrysalis Arts in Gargrave, North Yorkshire. The company combines the skills of artists and a range of highly skilled makers and specialist manufacturers with those of other design professionals and project managers and has extensive experience in producing work to commission for a wide range of clients, including Headingley Cricket Club (2001), East Bolton Regeneration ((2005) and Sefton council (2008). Maddison has been responsible for new guidelines for Public Art Sustainability Assessment.

Source chrysalisarts.org.uk.

Vernon March (1891–1930)

Sculptor. Born Sutton, Yorkshire. The family moved to London c. 1900. Eight of the March children became artists, three of them sculptors (Sydney, Elsie and Vernon). They lived and worked for most of their careers at the family home of Goddendene in Kent. Vernon March exhibited at the RA 1907–27. In 1926 he won the competition for the National War Memorial of Canada in Ottawa. His design was for a memorial arch surmounted by Peace and included a large group (23 figures) representing the 11 branches of the Canadian forces engaged in the First World War. Work on the memorial began in 1926 under the auspices of Canada's

Department of Public Works. However, March died of pneumonia in 1930 before completing the commission. Six of his siblings, including Elsie March, finished the large figure groups by 1932. After they had been shown in London, they were transported in 1937 to Ottawa and the memorial arch was constructed. The unveiling ceremony took place on 21 May 1939.

Source: Mapping (2011).

John Marder

Craftsman, technologist, designer, teacher. MSc in Horticulture Reading University. Professional Associate Royal Horticultural Society (RHS). Horticulture and Landscape Officer Horsham District Council. He has constructed five water-efficient demonstration gardens in SE England. He lives in West Sussex.

Source: Marder, J., *Water Efficient Gardening*, Wiltshire, 2009.

Teresa Martin (b. 1961)

Sculptor. Studied Winchester School of Art 1980–83. She has exhibited throughout the south of England and the Channel Islands. Her current work is a development of the casting process, with an innovative use of rubber moulds, using negative textures and producing original forms. In 2013 Martin exhibited *Whale Salutation* (for RHS Wisley) at Michelham Priory in Sussex and a tiger sculpture as part of the 'Saving the Sumatra Tiger' campaign at London Zoo. She won Tesco's Public Art Commission and Community venture with her concept 'Adur Portals'.

Sources: artist's website; artparks.co.uk.

Tom Merrifield (b. 1932)

Sculptor. Born Sydney, Australia. Trained as a classical dancer, becoming a soloist with the Borovonsky Ballet at 16 and later a dancer in musical theatre. Moved to Britain in 1956 where he appeared in many stage shows and in film and television. Lives and works in Hampstead.

He began drawing fellow dancers and exhibited these drawings at a West End gallery. He also experimented with sculpture, taking it up full-time when he retired from the stage. He has sculpted many of the world's most famous dancers; clients include the British Red Cross, who commissioned a bust of Diana, Princess of Wales for their London Headquarters; the Royal Festival Hall, London; the Hilton Hotel, Malta; the Victorian Arts Centre, Melbourne, Australia; Basingstoke council; the Mendel Centre for Arts, Michigan, USA; Chichester Festival Theatre; the Kinetic Centre, Borehamwood; the Playhouse Theatre, Epsom; Compton Acres Gardens, Poole. ARBS.

Source: artist's website.

Jon Mills (b. 1959)

Sculptor and designer. Born Birmingham. Mills's father and grandfathers were involved in the metalworking trades in Wolverhampton. He studied 3D Design at Wolverhampton Polytechnic (1979–82) before being awarded a grant by the Crafts Council to set up his own craft metalworking business. After moving to Brighton in 1985, he formed links with London-based galleries, the most well-known being Ron Arad's 'One-off'. His work has been featured in major Crafts Council touring exhibitions, including *The New Spirit* (1987) and *An Industry of One* (2001). He specialises in working in steel, producing architectural pieces, furniture and mechanical automata as well as sculpture. He has had solo exhibitions at Wolverhampton Art Gallery (1996), Hartlepool Art Gallery (1999) and Kings Lynn Arts Centre (1999), as well as participating in the touring group exhibition *Devious Devices* (1998).

Sources: Noszlopy (2003); artist's website.

William George Mitchell (b. 1925)

Sculptor. Born London. Trained at Southern College of Art, Portsmouth and the RCA, where he won a scholarship to the British

School in Rome. He established William Mitchell Design Consultants and produced abstract sculptures in concrete, wood, plastics, marble and brick. Public sculptures include abstract relief decoration of the porch and belfry on the Metropolitan Cathedral of Christ the King, Liverpool, *Ways of the Cross*, Cathedral Church of St Peter and Paul, Clifton and wall reliefs for watergardens at Harlow New Town, 1963. His *Corn King and Spring Queen* (Wexham Spring, South Buckinghamshire, 1964) was listed in 1998.

Source: Wyke (2004).

Edwin Roscoe Mullins (1848–1907)

Sculptor. Born London. Studied at Lambeth School of Art, the RA schools and with John Birnie Philip. Between 1866 and 1874 he studied under Professor Wagmüller in Munich, where he shared a studio with Edward Onslow Ford. Mullins was awarded a silver medal at Munich and a bronze medal at Vienna for a group entitled *Sympathy* exhibited in 1872. He suffered from poor health in the last decade or so of his life, which limited his ability to work.
Sources: Mapping (2011); victorianweb.org.

Carlo Nicoli (1843–1915)

Sculptor. Born Carrara, Italy and studied at the Accademia there, winning several awards from 1860 onwards. After graduating he moved to Florence where he worked under Giovanni Duprè. In 1868 he won the gold medal for a small piece, *The Beggar*. In 1870, he carved *L'angelo Sorvegliatore* that was heavily criticised but later gained recognition including from King Alfonso of Spain which led to Nicoli being awarded the Knight's Cross of the Order of Carlo III. The piece was carved several more times and eventually the Spanish Education Board in Madrid bought it. Nicoli moved back to Carrara and in 1875 became Honorary Professor at the Accademia. In 1876, working in a large workshop in San Francisco, he carved the statue of Cervantes for Alcalà de Henares (Cervantes' birthplace) and subsequently, in 1878, carved the sitting Cervantes. In 1885, after the death of Demetrio Carusi, Nicoli took over as the permanent sculpture teacher at the Accademia. His workshop in Carrara survives and is managed by his great-grandson.

Source: nicoli-sculptures.com.

Uli Nimptsch (1897–1977)

Sculptor. Born Charlottenburg, Berlin. Studied in Berlin at the School of Applied Art, 1915–17 and at the Academy 1919–26. He was in Rome at various times between 1931 and 1938, going to Paris for a year, and then settling in Great Britain. He had his first one-person show at the Redfern Gallery, London in 1942, and retrospective shows at Temple Newsam House, Leeds in 1944 and Liverpool in 1957. Works include a statue of Lloyd George for the lobby of the House of Commons 1961–63; *Olympia*, c. 1953–56 and *Seated Girl*, 1958 at the Tate Gallery. Exhibited at the RA from 1957. ARA 1958, RA 1967; Senior RA 1972. Master of the RA Sculpture School 1966–9.

Sources: *Uli Nimptsch RA, Sculptor*, Royal Academy, London, 1973; Nairne, S. and Serota, N. (eds.), *British Sculpture in the Twentieth Century*, Whitechapel Art Gallery, London, 1981.

Matthew Noble (1818–1876)

Sculptor. Born Hackness, near Scarborough, Yorkshire. Trained in London with John Francis (1780–1861). He exhibited over 100 works, chiefly portrait busts, at the RA from 1845 to 1876. His public statues numbered over 40, the Manchester Wellington monument establishing his reputation. His major Manchester and Salford public monuments began with Sir Robert Peel (Peel Park, Salford, 1852) and concluded with Oliver Cromwell (Manchester, 1875, removed to Wythenshawe Park). He provided statues of Peel in Tamworth (1852), Liverpool (St George's Hall, 1854) and London (Parliament Square, 1876). Statues of Prince Albert were commissioned for Manchester, Salford, Leeds and Bombay. His studio was described as 'a manufactory of busts'. His funerary monuments included Sir John Franklin (Westminster Abbey, 1847), Archbishop Musgrave (York Minster, 1860) and the Earl of Derby (Knowsley, 1872). His friend and assistant Joseph Edwards completed his unfinished works. His widow presented his models to the Corporation of Newcastle.

Sources: Gunnis (1968); Wyke (2004).

Sue Nunn (b. 1950)

Sculptor. Born Kent. Studied at Folkestone School of Art, and Gloucestershire University, graduating in 1971. Lives and works in Brighton. She has been carving in wood since the great hurricane that swept through the south of England in 1987 and continues to work with storm-felled or reclaimed timber. Her work is figurative, often involving research into local history, discussions with families, or working with community groups. She works on private commissions as well as larger pieces of public art, including *Spirit of the Village* (2000) for Chiddingly Millennium Commission, *Noah's Rest* (2003) for Robertsbridge Community Arts Partnership and *The Guildford Story Trail* (2003–04) for Queen Elizabeth Park Guildford.

Sources: artist's website; saatchionline.com.

Iain Nutting (b. 1961)

Sculptor. Studied at Canterbury College of Art and St. Martins School of Art (1981–83). His work is concerned with themes of art, nature and conservation. He was employed as a conservation technician at the Tate Gallery, and later as an assistant to Antony Gormley. During the 1990s he also worked freelance for Taylor Pearce, a sculpture restoration firm in London. He was involved in exhibitions at the RA, as well as working on the Royal Collection, restoration projects at Windsor Castle, for the V&A, the Palace of Westminster and Lincoln Cathedral, where the medieval carvings of Noah's Ark on the west front had a particular influence on him. He has regularly exhibited at the RA Summer Show, the Rebecca Hossack Gallery, London and Art London. His sculpture is sold and collected across Britain, Europe, and the USA. In 2010 he exhibited in Australia for the first time. He has completed public commissions for Leicestershire Council, Worthing Hospital, London and Quadrant Housing and Bishopsgate, London.

Source: sculpture.uk.net.

James Osborne (1940–1992)

Sculptor. Born Brighton, but was rejected by the local art college as he had left school without any academic qualifications. He undertook apprenticeships and worked on historic buildings including Brighton's Royal Pavilion. He also became a successful amateur boxer. In the 1960s he travelled widely, returning to Hove to set up a foundry where he produced other artists' work as well as his own. Osborne was commissioned in 1988 to sculpt a half-size bronze of the Queen's horse *Burmese* that was placed at Windsor. He then produced a sculpture of the famous racehorse *Eclipse* (1989) for Newmarket racecourse, *Boy on a Magic Rocking Horse* (1989–90) for Kensington Gardens and *Ballyregan Bob* (1990), the greyhound, for Coral's Stadium in Hove. Working closely with his brother Fred, Osborne raised huge amounts of money for charities including the Variety Club, Born Free and Save the Children. The number 653 bus in Brighton and Hove is named after him.

Sources: Macallister, D. 'Dufftown collector celebrates rare find by favourite sculptor of royals' *The Press and Journal*, 16 October 2010; history.buses.co.uk/history/fleethist; osg.uk.com.

David Parfitt

Visual artist. Trained at University of Wolverhampton. Based in Sussex. He worked as a research assistant at the Cass Foundation 1998–2001 and was a co-founder of Red Herring studios, Brighton. He specialises in site-specific sculpture and public art, acting as consultant, lead artist or initiator on a wide variety of projects with clients such as multinational corporations, local authorities, community groups and individuals. He has been responsible for the installation of the work of artists such as Anish Kapoor, Brian Eno, Alfredo Jarr and Bill Viola.

Source: artist's website.

Peter Parkinson (b. 1942)

Blacksmith. Studied Industrial Design at RCA. Worked as a designer with Morphy Richards, London Transport and Allied Ironfounders. Subsequently taught at West Surrey College of Art and Design until 1992. Learnt craft skills and gained work experience at Richard Quinnell's forge in Leatherhead, becoming a self-employed artist-blacksmith. Awarded Licentiateship and later became a Fellow of the Worshipful Company of Blacksmiths. He exhibits at the Fire and Iron Gallery Leatherhead and has produced public commissions for: Leatherhead town centre; City Museum and Art Gallery, Portsmouth; National Youth Theatre, London; Basingstoke; BBC South, Southampton; Middlesbrough; Hemel Hempstead; Leicester; Bradford; Crawley; Blackburn; Dorking; Guildford Cathedral; Derby Hook, Hampshire; The Oxfordshire Museum, Woodstock; and Fleetwood, Lancashire. He published *The Artist Blacksmith: Design and Techniques* in 2001.

Sources: artist's website; westdean.org.uk/CollegeChannel/Tutors.

Giles Penny (b. 1962)

Sculptor, stage designer, film animator, painter. Born Dorset. Studied at the Heatherley School of Fine Art, London, 1978–79, Bournemouth and Poole College of Art, 1980, Newport College of Art, South Wales, 1981–84. He has developed his sculptural work, which often takes a humorous approach, from a two-dimensional background having been trained in formal painting. He has exhibited throughout Britain. His public commissions include: *Two Men on a Bench* and *Man with Arms Open* for Cabot Square, Canary Wharf, London (1999); *Man and Animal* for Portishead Quays, Bristol (2004); *Signalman* at Bluebrick Development, Wolverhampton (2007); *Man in the Wind* for P&O cruise liner Ventura (2007); and *Rise and Shine* for BBC White City (2009). ARBS.

Sources: artist's website; mcvitieweston.co.uk.

William Pepper the elder (fl. 1831–1854)

Sculptor. Worked from Duke Street, then 39 Western Road, both in Brighton. Exhibited busts at the RA 1846–54. His bust of William Seymour (1850) is in Brighton Town Hall and one of F.W. Robertson, dated 1853, is in the Bodleian Library at Oxford. His signed tablets include those to the Lidbetter children (1831) and Mary Marla (1838), both at Bramber, Sussex, while in Brighton Parish Church is his large monument with a relief-bust of Joseph Allen (1851) and a miniature Gothic work to Mrs Crozier, with a small figure of a woman mourning by an urn.

Sources: Gunnis (1968); Roscoe et al. (2009).

John Birnie Philip (1824–1875)

Sculptor. Born London. Trained at the Government School of Design, Somerset House at 17. First employed as an ornamental sculptor under A.W.N. Pugin at the Houses of Parliament. His longest working relationship was with Sir G.G. Scott, much of his work being for churches the architect was either building or restoring. These included Tamworth Parish Church (1853); Ely Cathedral (1857); St George's Chapel, Windsor (1863); St Michael's, Cornhill, London (1858); and Lichfield Cathedral (1864). His best-known work for Scott is on the Albert Memorial, 1863–76, notably the marble podium friezes representing 87 great architects and sculptors

(1864–72), and the bronze figures of Geometry, Geology, Physiology and Philosophy on the canopy. Philip also ran a successful studio executing funerary monuments, including those to Queen Katherine Parr (Sudeley Castle chapel, Gloucestershire 1859), the Revd W.H. Mill (Ely Cathedral, 1860) and Lord and Lady Herbert of Lea (Wilton Church, Wiltshire, 1864). His public statues include Richard Oastler (Bradford, 1866), Lord Elgin (Calcutta, 1869), Colonel Baird (Calcutta, 1870) and Colonel Edward Akroyd (Halifax, 1875). He also carved eight statues of British monarchs for the Royal Gallery, Houses of Parliament. Exhibited at the RA 1858–75.

Sources: Gunnis (1968); Wyke (2004).

Enzo Plazzotta (1921–1981)

Sculptor. Born Mestre, near Venice. Studied at the Brera Academy, Milan, where one of his tutors was Giacomo Manzu. Active in the Partisan movement during the Second World War and commissioned to create *The Spirit of Rebellion*, showing the young David with the head of Goliath, as a tribute for the assistance to the movement given by British Special Forces. Plazzotta came to London in connection with this commission, and lived there for the rest of his life. Between 1947 and 1962 he relinquished sculpture, returning to it at first principally as a portraitist. However, his main interest was the expression of movement and vitality in human and animal bodies. Dance, and particularly ballet, is a predominant feature of his work, and some of his dance pieces possess special interest as representations of celebrity performers. Plazzotta's religious and mythological subjects are more sombre in character. He always retained contact with Italy, and in 1967 took a studio in Pietrasanta, from which he was able to supervise the casting of his many bronzes at the Tommasi foundry.

Source: Buckman (2006); Ward-Jackson (2003).

Kenneth Potts (b. 1949)

Sculptor. Studied ceramics, modelling and sculpture at Stockport College of Art, Stafford and Stoke-on-Trent College of Art and North Stafford Polytechnic (graduated 1972). He joined the Royal Worcester Porcelain Company in 1979, working as a modeller. His first major commission was a statue of Sir Edward Elgar for Worcester (1981). He also produced statues of Sir Douglas Bader for Goodwood (2001); Air Vice-Marshal Johnnie Johnson for RAF Museum Hendon (2002) and the Royal Navy Second World War memorial at Chatham (2004). Exhibitions of his work have been held in London, Tokyo and New York.

Source: Noszlopy, G., *Public Sculpture of Herefordshire, Shropshire and Worcestershire*, Liverpool, 2010.

Richard Quinnell (b. 1940)

Blacksmith. His parents founded a forge in Leatherhead in the 1930s and in 1982 he and his late wife Jinny set up the Fire and Iron Gallery on the same site, now run by his daughter Lucy. They had founded the British Artist Blacksmiths Association in 1978 and set up the Quinnell School of Blacksmithing in 1996. Quinnell was awarded an MBE in 1989 for his part in the revival of what had been, for many decades, a dying craft. He produced some of the most significant twentieth-century ironwork in the UK and overseas, including the gates to Shakespeare's Globe in London, the coat of arms for the British Embassy in Rome and the gates to the National Ornamental Metal Museum in Memphis, Tennessee. He is a Companion and Freeman of the Worshipful Company of Blacksmiths of the City of London.

Source: fireandiron.co.uk.

John Ravera (1941–2006)

Sculptor. Born Surrey. Trained Camberwell School of Art and had a studio at Bexleyheath, Kent. He worked mainly in clay or bronze. He was commissioned for public sculptures in London and the Home Counties, including *Family Group* near Battersea Bridge (1983) and versions of *Family Outing* in Solihull (1985), Haywards Heath and Bexleyheath. There are also works in Hong Kong and Tokyo. FRBS 1976; PRBS 1987–90.

Source: Cocke, R., *Public Sculpture of Norfolk and Suffolk*, Liverpool, 2013.

Michelle Reader (b. 1975)

Sculptor and stage designer. Born Cambridge. Studied at De Montfort University 1997 and Central St Martins (MA in Scenography) 2003. She has participated in many group and solo exhibitions in London, Nottingham, Leicester, Brighton and Bath. Public commissions include: *The Mugridges*, for Epsom and Ewell Borough Council (2008); Loch Ness Monster sculpture for SGA Productions (2009); penguins and camel sculptures for London Zoo (2009); Agapanthus sculpture for the Royal Horticultural Society (2010); eight awards from recycled materials for the Green Guardian Awards (2010). She occasionally collaborates with performers and theatre companies, designing sets, props and costumes.

Source: artist's website.

Penelope Reeve (b. 1945)

Painter and Sculptor. Studied in Paris in 1970, Byam Shaw School 1971–73, Heatherley School of Fine Arts 1993–95. She has painted 63 commissioned portraits, including the Countess of Leicester (1988), and produced over 29 portrait sculptures, including a limited edition of the England cricketer Peter May (1994) and the statue of Captain George Vancouver for Kings Lynn (2000).

Source: Cocke (2013).

Esther Rolinson

Installation artist. Studied Visual and Performing Arts at University of Brighton 1989–93 and since then has worked with 3D design, gallery installations, digital imaging and architectural lighting. Rolinson digitally animates found and self-generated images and her work explores the architectural applications of three-dimensional structures, animated light designs, and digital technologies. Her work includes: *Light Decks* at the Aquarium Terraces Brighton (2000); *Stream* on Hastings seafront (2003); *Air Wave* for the Lookahead Housing Trust building in Bracknell and *Drift* (2007) in New Road Brighton. She has collaborated with Freemont Landscape Architects on an urban design study for Redhill and was part of a team designing innovative housing and landscape for St Mary's Island, Chatham Kent.

Source: artist's website.

Louis Frederick Roslyn (born Roselieb, 1878–1934)

Sculptor. Born London. Studied at CGLAS before entering the RA schools where his awards included the Landseer scholarship and a travelling scholarship. Roslyn executed a large number of war memorials including examples at Darwen, Buxton, Port Talbot and Trinidad, West Indies. The Duchess of York and Duchess of Connaught were among his portrait busts. ARBS 1924.

Source: Wyke (2004).

Yvonne Hudson Rusbridge (1924–1985)

Sculptor, ceramicist, tapestry artist. Born London. Attended the Slade School of Art (in Oxford during the Second Word War). She developed an interest in sculpture, with ceramic stoneware as her favourite medium, producing life-size sculptures, smaller figures and wall plaques. She built a large kiln on the farm in Earnley, Chichester where she lived. In later life she also created tapestries, sometimes in conjunction with fellow Sussex artist Rosalie Williams. Her works, influenced to a large degree by her Christian faith, include: ceramic tile relief of Minerva in Crane Street, Chichester; a small statue of St Anne above the main door of St Anne's Church, East Wittering; a large tapestry depicting acts of five Sussex saints in Birdham Church near Chichester; two ceramic panels on each side of the chancel and an altar cloth in Earnley Church; the St Richard embroideries (with Rosalie Williams), for Chichester Cathedral; a statue of St Richard in St Mary's Church, Haverford West, in Wales. In Earnley Church there is a stained glass window by Paul Soderberg, created in Hudson's memory and using some of her designs.

Source: David Rusbridge (son).

Edwin Russell (1939–2013)

Sculptor. Trained at Brighton School of Art and the RA schools, where he won the Gold Medal and the Edward Stott Travelling Scholarship. Works include the *Suffragette Memorial*, London (1970); *St Michael*, St Paul's Cathedral; *Lion and Lamb*, Horsham, which won the Best Shopping Centre Award in 1987. Russell won the Otto Beit medal for sculpture in 1991. He worked individually and with his wife, sculptor Lorne McKean.

Source: horshamsociety.org.

Chris Rutter (see Evelyn Bennett)

Clare Sheridan (nee Frewen, 1885–1970)

Sculptor. Studied under John Tweed and Edouard Lanteri at the South Kensington Schools. In 1920 she was invited to Soviet Russia to make busts of notable revolutionaries, including Lenin and Trotsky. She also sculpted a bust of Ghandi (1931). She was a first cousin of Winston Churchill and in 1942 sculpted his bust, on display at his former home, Chartwell.

Sources: Sheridan (1945); Leslie, A. (1976).

Helen Mary Skelton

Sculptor and letter-cutter. In 1976 she completed an apprenticeship with her father John Skelton with whom she occasionally worked. Produces private commissions for memorials, plaques and sundials and runs workshops in her father's studio in Streat, near Ditchling, East Sussex.

Source: artist's website.

John Skelton (1923–1999)

Sculptor and letter-cutter. Born Norwich. Studied at Coventry School of Art 1939–40. Apprenticed to his uncle, Eric Gill, for a short period in 1940 when he learnt direct carving and lettering. After Gill's death, Skelton became an assistant to the carver Joseph Cribb, 1940–42, and after war service, joined the stone yard studios of Percival Bridgeman of Lewes. In 1950 he set up his own practice in Sussex. His works in stone, wood, bronze and *ciment fondu* are mainly figurative or figurative abstracts, sometimes using found objects. Works are in Norwich, Portsmouth, Lincoln and Hereford Cathedrals; Christ Church, Coventry (1954–58), Shakespeare Centre, Stratford-upon-Avon (1964), as well as *Aftermath of War*, Herbert Art Gallery, Coventry (1973), *Hands on Lyre*, Watergate Galleries, Washington DC, USA (1970), and *Torso*, exhibited at the RA (1975). He made two memorials to Edward James, poet and benefactor of West Dean, near Chichester (1986). Awarded RBS Silver Medal for the best work of the year 1975.

Source: Noszlopy (2003).

Allan Sly (b. 1951)

Sculptor. Born Windsor. Studied at CGLAS 1971–74 and RA Schools 1974–77. Won RA silver and bronze medals and Elizabeth T. Greenshields Memorial Foundation Award for figurative sculpture. Works include commission for new £2 coin (2003); *The Heroes of Science* (celebrating the discoverers of DNA); *Masquerade* for the Electric Theatre Guildford (2005). FRBS 1992.

Source: artist's website.

Joss Smith
Sculptor. Trained Wimbledon College of Art.
Lives and works in London. His work is mainly
studio-based and traditionally figurative, but he
has increasingly been commissioned to make
sculpture for public places, including the
Primrose Stone at Bongate weir on the river
Eden, Appleby; the Chain link sculpture for
Prince Charles Quay Cardigan Wales (c. 2009);
and the Magic Jug sculpture for Fountain Street
Belfast City Centre (2010).

Source: edenbenchmarks.org.uk.

Ray Smith (b. 1949)
Sculptor and graphic artist. Studied Cambridge
University 1968–71. As well as producing free-
standing steel sculptures, Smith has done a
substantial amount of painted, mosaic and
ceramic tile mural work for public and private
commissions. He is also a book designer and
illustrator, and has designed and edited practical
painting and drawing books. He has advised on
public art policy at Liverpool and Newcastle.
Exhibitions of his work include Ikon Gallery
(1980); Gateshead Garden Festival (*Red Army*
1990); Aspex Gallery, Portsmouth (1994); and
Sidmouth Festival (1995). Winner of the 1993
RSA 'Art for Architecture' Award.

Sources: Buckman (2006); Usherwood (2000).

Willi Soukop (1907–1995)
Sculptor. Born Vienna and worked in a factory
while attending evening classes at the arts and
crafts school there. Attended the Academy of
Fine Arts in Vienna 1928–34. In 1934 he moved
to Dartington Hall, Devon where he had a
studio and taught part-time 1935–45. In 1945 he
moved to London, teaching at Bromley (1945–
46), Guildford (1945–47) and Chelsea (1947–72)
schools of art. He was a member of the Faculty
of Sculpture at the British School in Rome,
1952–75 and Master of Sculpture at the RA
schools, 1969–82. He exhibited at the RA from
1935 onwards. His work was included in the
1949 and 1950 open-air sculpture exhibitions at

Battersea Park, and he had a solo exhibition at
the Yehudi Menuhin School, Cobham, 1979,
and a major retrospective at the Belgrave
Gallery, 1991. In 1981, following problems with
his eyesight, he involved himself in working on
sculptures for the blind. RSBA 1950; FRBS
1956; ARA 1963; RA 1969.

Sources: Buckman (2006); Obit. *The Times*, 9
February 1995; Cavanagh (2000).

Edward Bowring Stephens (1815–1882)
Sculptor. Born Exeter. Trained under E.H. Baily
in London. In 1836 he won a Silver Medal from
the Society of Arts and joined the RA, winning
the Silver Medal for his model, *Ajax Defying the
Gods*, the following year. His first commission
was for a bust of Miss Blanche Sheffield (1838).
He lived and worked in Italy 1839–41. He
returned to the RA Schools in 1842 and won
the Gold Medal for his relief, *The Battle of the
Centaurs and Lapithae*. In 1845 he executed two
reliefs for the Summer Pavilion at Buckingham
Palace and in the following year carved a
marble fireplace there. He executed statues of
Dr Priestly for the University Museum, Oxford
(1860) and Leonardo da Vinci, Christopher
Wren, and Sir Joshua Reynolds for the façade of
Burlington House, London (1873). Exhibited at
the RA, 1838–83, and at the British Institution,
1838–53. ARA 1864.

Source: Gunnis (1968); Cavanagh (1997).

Hannah Holmes Stewart
Sculptor. Following a Foundation course in
conservation and restoration, she trained at
CGLAS 1995–98, where she learnt traditional
skills of modelling and casting. She won the
Major Award from the Manchester Academy of
Fine Arts for her sculpture *Consider* in 1999
and the Alec Tiranti Prize for Young Portrait
Sculptors in 2000. Public commissions include
Iguanodon (2006) for Southwater, Sussex and
Hauling Man (2008) for the Tesco store in
Hailsham.

Source: artist's website.

Edwin Stirling (1819–1867)
Sculptor and stone carver. Born Scotland.
Apprenticed to a stone carver at Darnick, then
studied at Edinburgh School of Art. He later
settled in Liverpool, first working for, and then
in partnership with, an architectural carver
named Canavan. His work outside Liverpool
includes the statue for architect Edward A.
Heffer's Memorial to the Prince Consort at
Hastings (1863) and the statues on the south
front of Horton Hall, Cheshire (1867).

Sources: Cavanagh (1997); Gunnis (1968).

John Thomson
Sculptor and visual artist. Born Dunedin, New
Zealand. He has exhibited sculpture
internationally for over 30 years in many
countries, including Russia, Iceland and Ireland.
He was included in the survey of the RCC
Letterkenny Collection (Ireland) in 2003. His
drawings were included in *Fifty Years of British
Sculptors' Drawings* at the Musée de Beaux Arts
in Besançon. He completed a residency at
Oxford University Botanic Gardens and
Museum of Natural History in 2006.

Sources: casiad.solent.ac.uk; artist's website.

Newbury Abbot Trent (1885–1963)
Sculptor and medallist. Born Forest Gate,
Essex. Studied at the RA Schools. He married
(Phyllis) Hilda Ledward daughter of the
sculptor, Richard Ledward (1857–90) and sister
to Gilbert Ledward (1888–1960). He worked
throughout his life from a studio at 1 Beaufort
Street, London. His commissions included: a
statue to Edward VII, Brighton; the recumbent
effigy of Dean Pigou in Bristol Cathedral; and
war memorials in New Barnet, Beckenham,
Wanstead, Ilford, Tredegar and Wallsend.
ARBS 1914–25. ARA.

Source: Mapping (2011).

Anna Twinam-Cauchi
Studied Canterbury College of Art and Design,

Camberwell School of Art and Kennington Art School, before settling in Shoreham-by-Sea. Carving in wood and stone, often using salvaged materials, she has undertaken many public and private commissions. Major projects include: carved bollards for Brighton and Hove seafront (1992), a carving for Buchan Country Park (a collaboration with sculptor Bill Hackney, 2004) and a sculpture for Frederica Kommune Sculpture Park, Denmark.

Source: artist.

William Henry Tyler (active 1875–1893)
Sculptor, principally of portrait busts. Studied at RA Schools c. 1875. Exhibited at RA 1878–93, at the Grosvenor Gallery, 1879–90 and also at the New Gallery and the Royal Society of British Artists. His *Miniature Bust of Princess Mary*, in marble, is at Osborne House, Isle of Wight.

Sources: Cavanagh (2000); Mapping (2011).

Thomas Tyrwhitt (1874–1956)
Architect. Studied at the Architectural Association and became a pupil and then assistant of Sir Aston Webb. He started his own practice in London in 1901, but soon moved to Hong Kong, where he worked for Denison, Ram and Gibbs 1902–04, before going to Pretoria, South Africa. There he worked until 1907 in the Public Works Department, latterly as Superintending Architect, his work consisting largely of schools and post offices. On return to London he once more started in private practice at 3 Arundel Street, Strand, specialising in country houses (including two at Bolney, West Sussex) and cottages, although in 1919–20 he was briefly Superintending Architect, Ministry of Agriculture and Fisheries. His best-known work is the Indian Memorial Gateway outside the Royal Pavilion in Brighton, for which he won the competition. He died in the Canary Islands.

Sources: British Architectural Library *Biog file*; Obit; *RIBA Journal*, 65 (1958).

Geoffrey Fuller Webb (1879–1954)
Stained glass designer. Trained Westminster School of Art, then worked with Charles Eamer Kempe and Herbert Bryans, before setting up his own studio in East Grinstead. Examples of his work include Woolwich Town Hall (1903–06) and churches at Felbridge, East Grinstead, St George, South Africa, Cowfold, Lindfield and Oxted. He was commissioned to complete windows at Manchester Cathedral, Tewkesbury Abbey and a group of figures from *Alice in Wonderland* at the parish church at Daresbury, Cheshire, to commemorate Lewis Carroll's birth at Daresbury Parsonage in 1832. Webb also produced decorative metal work, particularly church furniture. His work can be identified by a spider's web with his initials, usually in the bottom right hand corner. He was the nephew of the architect Sir Aston Webb and brother of Christopher Webb, also a stained glass artist, articled to Sir Ninian Comper. The Webb family has continued the tradition of arts and crafts as stonemasons, ecclesiastical silversmiths and letter designers and carvers.

Sources: felbridge.org.uk; stmaryeastgrinstead.co.uk.

Peter Webster (b. 1958)
Sculptor. Born North Yorkshire. Graduated from Canterbury College of Art in 1980. He worked in a small artisan's bronze foundry casting his own and others' work. Commissioned work includes bronze portraits of actors Sir Michael Hordern, Sir Donald Sinden and Joanna Lumley, life-sized bronze statues of Olympic athlete Steve Ovett and comedian Max Miller. His work is represented in public and private collection in the UK, France, Germany, Holland, Italy, Spain the USA and Brazil.

Source: artist.

James Wedgwood (d. 1973)
Sculptor. Exhibited 18 times at RA 1927–57. He won the prize for the best work of sculpture

exhibited in London in 1943 for his stone groups *Pietà* and *Adoration*, exhibited at the United Artists' Exhibition, RA, Winter 1942–43. FRBS 1945; Member of AWG 1925–73.

Source: Mapping (2011).

Joseph Whitehead and Sons (fl. 1880s–1985)
Firm of stonemasons and carvers, based in London, with branches in Aberdeen and Carrara. Its director and best-known sculptor was Joseph Whitehead, who executed the monument to Father Damien for Molokai, Hawaii (1891). He also produced a dramatic effigy of John Rae (d. 1893) for Kirkwall Cathedral and a statue of Charles Kingsley for Bideford (1906). By 1909 Whitehead's had become the official contractor to the Metropolitan Drinking Fountain and Cattle Trough Association. After the First World War, the firm executed war memorials for London's General Post Office and for Stafford and Worthing.

Source: Ward-Jackson (2003).

Amon Henry Wilds (1784–1857)
Architect. Around 1806 he established an architectural and building partnership with his father, also named Amon Wilds (1762–1833) in Lewes. By 1820 they were firmly established in Brighton, then experiencing a period of rapid growth, and in 1822 formed a loose partnership with Charles Augustin Busby (1788–1834), an architect trained at the RA Schools. Together, they were responsible for the core of Brighton's best Regency and early Victorian architecture, including the grand schemes of Kemp Town, Brunswick Town, Regency Square, Hanover Crescent, and Montpelier Crescent. They also designed Park Crescent in Worthing. After the deaths of his father in 1833 and Busby in 1834, Amon Henry Wilds continued to build in the Regency style until well into the Victorian era.

Sources: Cooper (2007); Bianco (2005); brightonsarchitecture.com; Dale (1947).

Bruce Williams
Sculptor. Trained Winchester School of Art (1981) and Gwent College of Higher Education (1984). Lives and works in Brighton. He uses laser-cut steel to create permanent, three-dimensional photographic objects for public spaces, with special emphasis on the physical and social context of the work. Public commissions have included: *Boudica Colonnade*, Colchester (2009); *Langley Green Patterns*, Crawley (2010); *Swindon Works*, Great Western Railway Underpass, Swindon (2012); and *Waterlooville Pavilion*, Hampshire (2012). Williams' work is in collections in Belfast, Ormskirk, London, Birmingham, Cambridge and Brighton. He is a founder and former trustee of Fabrica Gallery in Brighton.

Sources: artist's website; axisweb.org.

Francis John Williamson (1833–1920)
Sculptor. Studied at RA, where he was a pupil of John Bell. Later became apprentice and then assistant to John H. Foley, with whom he worked for 20 years. He was private sculptor to Queen Victoria in the 1880s and 1890s, reputedly modelling almost all the members of the Royal Family at his studio in Esher. Portrait busts he executed for them include: Prince Alamaya of Abyssinia (1880), Prince Leopold, Duke of Albany and Prince Albert Victor, Duke of Clarence, all at Osborne House; and Arthur, Duke of Connaught (1885) at Windsor Castle. He produced a considerable number of public statues and memorials, notably a statue of Queen Victoria for the Royal College of Physicians in London, with replicas in Croydon, Australia, India, Rangoon and Ireland. His sculptures also include a series of statuettes of Princess Alice of Albany, the infant Prince Edward of York, and Lord Tennyson (1894). Williamson was particularly noted for his skilled treatment of draperies and materials, and exhibited throughout his life at the RA and leading London galleries.

Sources: Noszlopy, G., *Public Sculpture of Birmingham*, Liverpool, 1998; Spielmann (1901).

Margaret Winser (active 1904–1920s)
Sculptor and medallist. Exhibited portrait medallions at the RA in 1904, 1905 and 1912; a memorial panel and case of medals in 1913, and a medallion in 1914. She worked with the engravers G.W. De Saulles and William Midgley. She created a medallion, plaster bust and the death mask of the actress Ellen Terry (1847–1928) now in the National Trust Collections.

Sources: Mapping (2011); nationaltrustcollections. org.uk.

James Woodford (1893–1976)
Sculptor. Born Nottingham, son of a lace designer. Studied at Nottingham School of Art and the RCA, where he was awarded the Prix de Rome for Sculpture. He began to exhibit at the RA in 1926. During the 1930s he sculpted bronze doors for the Liverpool Royal School for the Blind (1931) and for Norwich City Offices (1938). For his more intimate works, he returned throughout his career to wood, most frequently oak. After the Second World War, he was commissioned to carve the War Memorial of the British Medical Association (1951–54) for its headquarters in Tavistock Square, London. This consists of four separate free-standing allegorical figures. At the same time, Woodford produced for his home town the Robin Hood Memorial (1952), an unusual arrangement of free-standing figures and reliefs in bronze, on a terrace below the outer walls of the castle. For the Queen's coronation in 1953, Woodford modelled a series of Queen's Beasts for Westminster Abbey. These were later carved in stone and are now placed in Kew Gardens. ARA 1937; RA 1945; FRBS; OBE 1953.

Source: Buckman (2006); Ward-Jackson (2003).

Cliff Wright (see **Evelyn Bennett**)

Edward William Wyon (1811–1885)
Sculptor and modeller. Son of Thomas Wyon, chief engraver of seals at the Royal Mint. Joined the RA Schools in 1829. In 1831 he began to exhibit wax portrait medallions and busts at the RA. Wyon worked for the Art Union, producing in 1842 its first sculpture offer, a reduction of John Flaxman's *St Michael and Satan*, described by the *Art Union Journal* as a 'glorious work'. Also for the Art Union he created a Tazza, 'modelled from a Greek design', which was shown at the Great Exhibition in 1851. He modelled portrait busts and reliefs of scenes from Shakespeare, for interpretation in 'statuary porcelain' by Wedgwood. Wyon's statue of *Britomart* (1856–61), for the Mansion House, marked his début as a monumental sculptor. In 1846 he produced a bronze statue of Richard Green, shipbuilder and philanthropist, for East India Dock, London, and an extensive programme of architectural sculpture for the internal courtyard of Drapers' Hall, in the City. In 1869, he produced figures of Galileo, Goethe and Laplace, for the University of London building in Burlington Gardens. Wyon executed a number of characterful reliefs for funerary monuments, including two in bronze for the monument to the Revd F. Robertson, in Brighton Cemetery (1853).

Sources: Gunnis (1968); Atterbury, P. (ed.), *The Parian Phenomenon*, Shepton Beauchamp, 1989; Ward-Jackson (2003).

Gordon Young (b. 1952)
Born Carlisle. Studied at Coventry and RCA. Lives and works in Somerset. Before becoming a full-time artist, he was curator of the Yorkshire Sculpture Park and Director of the Welsh Sculpture Trust. He focuses on producing art for the public domain, creating projects as diverse as the cursing stone in Carlisle where the 'Mother of all curses' has been inscribed into a 14-ton granite boulder, now housed at Carlisle Castle (2001); a series of 20-metre-high sculptural/climbing walls in Blackpool (2006); a forest of typographic trees in Crawley Library (2009); and a Wall of

Wishes in a Bristol school (2007). His most ambitious project to date is the *Comedy Carpet*, a 1880-square-metre granite typographical pavement made up of jokes, songs and catchphrases of comedians and writers to be permanently installed on the new promenade in front of Blackpool Tower. Among many awards, he won the Art for Architecture Award, Royal Society of Arts in 2001 and the PMSA Marsh Award for Excellence in Public Sculpture in 2012.

Source: artist's website.

'Antonio Tantardini: obituary', *The New York Times*, 29 March 1879.
'Bexhill and the late Colonel Lane', *Bexhill Observer*, 2 July 1898, p. 8.
'Bexhill's tribute to the late Col. Henry Lane, J.P.', *Bexhill Chronicle*, 1 July 1898, p. 3.
'Brighton and Hove's public artwork guide', *The Argus*, 19 September 2008.
'Calls to restore the Spirit of Rye', *Rye and Battle Observer*, 3 February 2012.
'Canopy at the Corn Exchange, Brighton', The *Architect and Building News* (Supplement), 18 January 1935, p. 282.
'Cast iron climbing frame is installed', *The Argus*, 17 March 1998.
'Dame causes a stir', *Worthing Herald*, 15 June 1990, p. 1.
'Extracts from the public journals relating to the death of Captain Pechell', *Castle Goring Archives 1547–1938*, West Sussex Records Office, Chichester.
'Feathers fly as swans "walk" to stop water wastage', *West Sussex Gazette*, 2 October 2007.
'Fund to close January 1856', *Brighton Herald*, 5 January 1856.
'Heads symbol of society', *Worthing Herald*, 22 June 1990, p. 10.
'Helen's gift', *The Argus*, 15 December 2005, p. 13.
'Indian memorial gateway: the unveiling ceremony at Brighton', *The Argus*, 26 October 1921.
'Inscriptions on the pylons', *Brighton & Hove Herald*, 17 November 1928.
'King of the chainsaw', *Worthing Herald*, 12 October 2000, p. 27.
'Landmark back in Brighton', *The Argus*, 5 November 2005.

'Memorial gateway: Indian gratitude to people of Brighton', *The Argus*, 19 October 1921.
'Memorial to Spitfire ace', *The Argus*, 10 August 2001.
'Memorial to the late Colonel Henry Lane, Bexhill', *Supplement to the Bexhill Chronicle*, 11 June 1898.
'Montague sculptures unveiling', *Worthing Herald*, 1 June 1990, p. 5.
'Obituary: Joyce Pallot', *Brightlingsea Gazette*, 29 June 2004.
'Revealed: Selsey's new £60,000 sculpture', *West Sussex Gazette*, 6 July 2007.
'Sculpture unveiled in memory of sisters', *West Sussex Gazette*, 4 June 2007.
'Seafront sculpture in bad shape', *The Argus*, 13 January 2004.
'Speculative illustrations: Eduardo Paolozzi in conversation with J. G. Ballard and Frank Whitford', *Studio International*, vol. 182, 1971, pp. 136–43.
'Statue arrives in Brighton', *Brighton Herald*, 19 February 1859, p. 2.
'Statue captures the spirit of war hero', *Hereford Times*, 16 August 2001.
'Swans on the move', *West Sussex Gazette*, 21 September 2007.
'The Opening of the Jubilee clock tower', *Brighton Gazette and Sussex Telegraph*, 30 June 1888, p. 5.
'The Pylons: gateway to greater Brighton', *Brighton & Hove Herald*, 26 May 1928.
'The scholarly murals of Henry and Joyce Collins, with a commentary by Henry Collins', *Concrete Quarterly*, vol. 104, 1975, p. 15.
'Town council accepts memorial', *Brighton Herald*, 8 January 1859.
'Tributes to two special angels', *The Argus*, 25

October 2005.
'Two teachers' training colleges: 1, Chichester', *The Architectural Review*, vol. 132, November 1962.
'Unveiled by a distinguished soldier', *Worthing Gazette*, 13 April 1921.
'Unveiling of the North Street clock tower', *Brighton Herald*, 30 June 1888, p. 4.
'War memorial for Brighton', *The Argus*, 24 September 1921.

A Pictorial and Descriptive Guide to Brighton and Hove, the South Downs, Shoreham, Bramber, Lewes, Newhaven, Seaford, etc. London, nd, c. 1937.
Adams, M., 'Churchill Square's whispering sculptures', *The Argus*, 2 September 1998.
Alexander, C., 'Faces of war', *Smithsonian Magazine*, February 2007.
Alexander, S., *Brighton Sculpture*, uncatalogued survey, Brighton History Centre, nd, early 1980s.
Aragon, L., *Paris Peasant* (trans. S. Watson Taylor), London, 1971.
Arscott, D., *Brighton and Hove: Events, People and Places over the Last 100 Years*, Stroud, 2000.
Arscott, D., *Curiosities of East Sussex: A County Guide to the Unusual*, Market Drayton, 1991.
Arscott, D., *Curiosities of West Sussex: a County Guide to the Unusual*, Market Drayton, 1993.
Arscott, D., *Dead and Buried in Sussex*, Seaford, 1997.
Ashburnham Christian Trust, *An Introduction to the History of Ashburnham Place*, Ashburnham, 2004.
Atterbury, P. (ed.), *The Parian Phenomenon*,

Shepton Beauchamp, 1989.

Attwater, D., *A Cell of Good Living*, London, 1969.

Bailey, C., 'Obituary', *The Guardian*, 3 December 1999.

Baird, R., *Goodwood: Art and Architecture, Sport and Family*, London, 2007.

Baker, M., 'Public images for private spaces? The place of sculpture in the Georgian domestic interior', *Journal of Design History*, vol. 20, no. 4, 2007.

Baker, M., *Figured in Marble: the Making and Viewing of Eighteenth-Century Sculpture*, London, 2000.

Bartley, L.J., *The Story of Bexhill*, Bexhill, 1971.

Batten, M., *Direct Carving in Stone*, London, 1966.

Bauldry, J., 'Aids memorial ideas unveiled', *The Argus*, 7 September 2007, p. 9.

Bayley, Rev. T.D.S., 'Lady Mary May's monument in mid Lavant Church', *Sussex Archaeology Collections*, vol. CVII, 1969.

Beardsley, C., *Love: The Passionate Life and Preaching of F.W. Robertson*, Cambridge, 2009.

Beevers, D. and Roles, J., *A Pictorial History of Brighton*, Derby, 1993.

Bell, Q. and Nicholson, V., *Charleston: a Bloomsbury House and Garden*, London, 1997.

Bénézit Dictionary of Artists, Oxford, 2006.

Berry, S., *Georgian Brighton*, Chichester, 2005.

Berryman, L., 'Bruce Williams: a new public sculpture', *Arts Review*, 1992, p. 229.

Bianco, D., 'Amon Henry Wilds and the last enigma of Dr Gideon Mantell', *Friends of West Norwood Cemetery Newsletter*, no. 52, January 2005.

Boyd, D., *Brightling Church Guide*, London, 1979, p. 21.

Brighton Almanack for 1898, Hove, 1898.

Brighton Remembered: a Century of Pictures from the Archives of the Argus, Derby, 2002.

Brighton Standard and Fashionable Visitors List, 13 September 1898.

British Contemporary Sculpture at Goodwood, Cass Sculpture Foundation, 2002/03.

Brodie, A., *Directory of British Architects 1834–1914*, vol. 1, London, 2001.

Brown, M., 'Artist Richard Wilson hangs out "Italian Job" bus to teeter on Bexhill Pavilion', *The Guardian*, 3 July 2012.

Buckman, D., *Artists in Britain Since 1945*, Bristol, 2006 edn.

Busco, M., *Sir Richard Westmacott Sculptor*, Cambridge, 1994.

Byford, E.C., *A Centenary Celebration of Forest Row Village Hall 1892–1992*, Forest Row, 1992.

Cannadine, D., *Lords and Landlords: the Aristocracy and the Towns 1774–1967*, Leicester, 1980.

Carder, T., *The Encyclopaedia of Brighton*, Lewes, 1990.

Castleden, R., *Ancient British Hill Figures*, Seaford, 2000.

Cavanagh, T., *Public Sculpture of Liverpool*, Liverpool, 1997.

Chapman, B., *The Village Signs of Sussex*, Lewes, 2006.

Charnot, M., Farr, D. and Butlin, M., *Modern British Paintings, Drawings and Sculpture*, London, 1964.

Christian, J. (ed.), *The Last Romantics*, London, 1990.

Christopher, A., *The Battle of Lewes Memorial*, Lewes, 1966.

Cocke, R., *Public Sculpture of Norfolk and Suffolk*, Liverpool, 2013.

Coleman, N., 'Chorus in a car park', *The Guardian*, 10 September 2007, p. 26.

Collins, J., *Dr Brighton's Indian Patients December 1914–January 1916*, Brighton, 1997.

Collins, J., *Eric Gill: the Sculpture, a Catalogue Raisonne*, London, 2006.

Collins, J., *Eric Gill: The Sculpture*, Woodstock, NY, 1998.

Collis, R., *The New Encyclopaedia of Brighton*, Brighton, 2010.

Conlay, I., 'The religious theme, such a brave experiment', *The Catholic Herald*, 15 August 1958, p. 7.

Cooper, C., 'Lest we forget', *City News*, August–September 2004, p. 10.

Cooper, J., 'A.H. Wilds rediscovered!' *Regency Review: the Newsletter of the Regency Society*, November 2007.

Countess De La Warr and Innes-Smith, R., *The Sackville Chapel*, Withyham, 1993.

Courtney, C., 'Sculpture by Angela Conner', *Architect (RIBA)*, vol. 93.

Craske, M.J., *The London Trade in Monumental Sculpture and the Development of the Imagery of the Family in Funerary Monuments of the Period 1720–1760*, unpublished PhD thesis, Queen Mary and Westfield College, London, 1992.

Crawley Arts Council, *The Crawley Heritage Trail*, 2007.

Crawley Borough Council, *Public Art Supplementary Guidance Note 11*, March 2003.

Cribb, R. and Cribb, J., *Eric Gill and Ditchling: the Workshop Tradition*, Ditchling, 2007.

Croft-Murray, E., 'An account book of John Flaxman R.A.', *Walpole Society*, vol. XXVIII, Oxford, 1940.

Crook, J., *St George's Church Brede*, Brede, revised edn 2004.

Dale, A., *Brighton Cemeteries*, Brighton, 1991.

Dale, A., *Fashionable Brighton 1820–1860*, London, 1947.

Darby, E.S., *Statues of Queen Victoria and of Prince Albert: a Study in Commemorative and Portrait Statuary 1837–1924*, unpublished PhD thesis, Courtauld Institute of Art, London, 1983.

Darke, J. (ed.), *A User's Guide to Public Sculpture*, London, 2000.

Davey, H., 'Wellington at Brighton and Rottingdean', *Notes and Queries*, London, 24 June 1916, p. 517.

Dinsmore, J., *Statues and Memorials in Hastings and St. Leonards: a Report on*

Condition and Conservation Options, Hastings, 1997.

Eastbourne Local History Society, *Eastbourne's Historic Street Furniture*, 1986.

Elisabeth Frink: 1930 1993, Sculptures, Graphic Works, Textiles, Salisbury Festival, 1997.

Elleray, R.D., *Eastbourne a Pictorial History*, Chichester, 1995.

Elliston, R.A., *Lewes at War 1939–1945*, Seaford, revised edn, 1999.

Esdaile, K.A., 'John Bushnell', *Walpole Society*, vol. XV, 1926–27; vol. XXI, 1932–33.

Eustace, K., *Michael Rysbrack Sculptor 1694–1770*, Bristol Museum and Art Gallery, 1982.

Evans, Rev. A.A, *The Selwyns of Sussex*, 1923, revised edn 2002.

Evans, Rev. A.A., *Friston Parish Church: a Short Historical Account*, revised edn 2006.

Felstead, A., Franklin, J. and Pinfield, L. (eds), *Directory of British Architects 1834–1900*, London, 1993.

Fiddler, H., *Eastbourne's 'Pathway to Health' Walk Project: The Impact of the Signs on Walking Behaviour*, University of Brighton, 2001.

Ford, H., *Steyning Conservation Area Guide*, Steyning, revised edn 2003.

Ford, J. and J., *Images of Brighton*, Richmond upon Thames, 1981.

Forvague, H.W., *1883–1933 Municipal Eastbourne: Selections from the Proceedings of the Town Council*, Eastbourne, 1933.

Foster, A., *Aspects of the Religious History of Slindon Since the Reformation*, Slindon, 2013.

Foster, P. (ed.), *A Jewel in Stone: Chichester Market Cross 1501–2001*, Otter memorial paper no. 15, Chichester, 2004.

Foster, P. (ed.), *Chichester and the Arts 1944–2004: a Celebration*, Chichester, 2004.

Gammon, A., *Historic Lewes*, Lewes, 1995.

Gardiner, S., *Frink: the Official Biography of Elisabeth Frink*, London, 1998.

Getsy, D.J. (ed.), *Sculpture and the Pursuit of the Modern Ideal in Britain c. 1880–1930*, Aldershot, 2004.

Glancey, J., 'Terminal shopping', *RIBA Journal*, vol. 95, no. 6, June 1988, pp. 26–29.

Graham, B., 'Long-term relationships: art in public', *Artists' Newsletter*, August 1993, pp. 30–31.

Graham, B., 'Long-term relationships: photography as permanent public art', *SF Camerawork Quarterly*, San Francisco, Fall, 1993.

Gray, F., *Designing the Seaside: Architecture, Society and Nature*, London, 2006.

Green, H. and Pinney, A., *Bexhill-on-Sea in Old Photographs*, Gloucester, 1989.

Greenacombe, J. (ed.), *Survey of London*, vol. 45, Knightsbridge, 2000.

Gunnis, R., *Dictionary of British Sculptors 1660–1851*, London, 1953.

Haines, P., *Hastings in Old Photographs: a Second Selection*, Sutton, 1991.

Hall, J., *The World as Sculpture: the Changing Status of Sculpture from the Renaissance to the Present Day*, London, 2000.

Hare, A., *The Story of My Life*, London, vol. 6, 1900.

Harper, C. G., 'Banished London', *Harmsworth Monthly Pictorial Magazine*, vol. 2, no. 9, April 1899, p. 215.

Harrison, L., *A Sussex Guide: 20 Sussex Gardens*, Alfriston, 2007.

Haselfoot, A.J., *The Batsford Guide to the Industrial Archaeology of South-East England: Kent, Surrey, East Sussex and West Sussex*, London, 1978.

Holloway, W., *The History and Antiquities of the Ancient Town and Port of Rye in the County of Sussex*, London, 1847.

Hutchinson, G., *Fuller of Sussex: a Georgian Squire*, Brightling, repr. 1997.

Hutchinson, G., *Fuller: the Life and Times of John Fuller of Brightling 1757–1834*, Brightling, 1988.

Hutchinson, G., *The Mary Stanford Disaster: the Story of a Lifeboat, November 15th, 1928*, Bexhill-on-Sea, 1984.

Irvine, L. and Atterbury, P., *Gilbert Bayes Sculptor 1872–1953*, Shepton Beauchamp, 1998.

James, N.P., *John Skelton: Axis Mundi*, London, 2005.

John Flaxman 1755–1826 Master of the Purest Line, Sir John Soane's Gallery, London, 2003.

John Flaxman: Line to Contour, Ikon Gallery, Birmingham, 2013.

John, M., *Bygone Brighton: Volume Two, Events*, Tunbridge Wells, 1980.

Kennedy, C., *Mayfair: a Social History*, London, 1986.

Kenworthy-Browne, J., 'The Third Earl of Egremont and neo-classical sculpture', *Apollo*, vol. CV, May 1977.

Kerney, M., 'Ammonites in architecture', *Country Life*, 27 January 1983, pp. 214–18.

Koch, A. (ed.), *Academy Architecture and Architectural Review*, vol. 20, 1901.

Kwintner, A. 'A fond farewell to Punky Rob', *The Argus*, 11 October 2005.

Le Pla, P., *The Parish Church of St. Bartholomew Rogate*, Rogate, revised edn, 2003, p. 11.

Leith, A., 'The War Memorial: a familiar face at the top of the hill', *Viva Lewes*, November 2007, p. 45.

Leslie, A., *Cousin Clare: the Tempestuous Career of Clare Sheridan*, London, 1976.

Leslie, K., *A Sense of Place: West Sussex Parish Maps*, Chichester, 2006.

Leslie, S., 'Clare Sheridan, sculptress', *New York Times*, 5 December 1920.

Lindey, C., 'The man who moulded Marx', *The Morning Star*, 4 April 2007.

Livingston, H., *Brighton and Hove Pictorial Memories*, Salisbury, 1999.

Llewellyn, N., *East Sussex Church Monuments*

1530–1830, Lewes, 2011.

Longstaff-Tyrell, P., *Front-line Sussex: Napoleon Bonaparte to the Cold War*, Stroud, 2000.

Loosemoore, J. and Burgis, J., *Chiddingly Church Guide*, Hastings, 1995.

Lord, F. (ed.), *Public Art and Artists' Commissions in West Sussex*, West Sussex Arts Partnership, Chichester, 2008.

Lower, M.A., *The Worthies of Sussex*, Lewes, 1865.

Lubbock, T., 'Patrick Caulfield: serenely secular,' *The Independent*, 14 April 2009.

Lucas, E.V., *Highways and Byways in Sussex*, London, 1984.

Lucie-Smith, E., 'Karen Jonzen: obituary', *The Independent*, 2 February 1998.

Lucie-Smith, E., *Elisabeth Frink: Recent Sculpture and Drawings*, London, Fischer Fine Art, 1989.

Lucie-Smith, E., *Elisabeth Frink: Sculpture Since 1984 and Drawings*, London, 1994.

Lydiate, H., 'Who owns Elizabeth Frink?, *Art Monthly*, no. 306, May 2007.

Lyon, P. and Woodham, J.M. (eds), *Art and Design at Brighton 1859–2009*, Brighton, 2009.

Macallister, D., 'Dufftown collector celebrates rare find by favourite sculptor of royals', *The Press and Journal*, 16 October 2010.

McEvansoneya, P., 'Lord Egremont and Flaxman's "St Michael overcoming Satan"', *Burlington Magazine*, no. 143, 2001.

McKenzie, R., *Public Sculpture of Glasgow*, Liverpool, 2002.

Malcolm, J., *Bygone Brighton: Volume Two: Events*, Tunbridge Wells, 1980.

Mapping the Practice and Profession of Sculpture in Britain and Ireland 1851–1951, University of Glasgow History of Art and HATII, online database 2011.

Marder, J., *Water Efficient Gardening*, Wiltshire, 2009.

Matthew, H.C.G. and Harrison, B. (eds), *Oxford Dictionary of National Biography*, Oxford, 2004.

Mayfield Local Historical Society, *Mayfield: Ancient Wealden Village*, Mayfield, 2005.

Mesquita, M. dos Santos, 'When art and science fuse well', *AGU Atmospheric Sciences*, vol. 1, 22 October 2007, pp. 1–3.

Middleton, J., *Encyclopaedia of Hove*, vol. 15, Hove, 2003.

Millican, J. with Fox, A. and Nunn, S., 'Art in the woods: an exploration of a community/university environmental arts project', in *Community–University Partnerships in Practice*, Leicester, 2007.

Moriarty, C., '"The sea goeth it all about": maritime themes in British public sculpture', *CRD Research Papers*, University of Brighton, 2001.

Moriarty, C., 'Remnants of patriotism: the commemorative representation of the greatcoat after the First World War', *Oxford Art Journal*, vol. 27, 2004.

Mossop, S., *Brighton Seafront Sculpture Project: Teachers' Pack*, Brighton and Hove, 1998.

Muncey, F., 'Charles Godfrey Garrard, Sculptor and Carver', *Eastbourne Local Historian*, no. 133, Autumn 2004.

Murray, J., *A Handbook for Travellers in Kent and Sussex*, London, 1858.

Musgrave, C., *The Royal Pavilion: a Study in the Romantic*, Brighton, 1951.

Nairn, I. and Pevsner, N. *The Buildings of England: Sussex*, London, 1965.

Nairne, S. and Serota, N. (eds), *British Sculpture in the Twentieth Century*, Whitechapel Art Gallery, London, 1981.

Norton, R.D.W., *Benjamin (Ben) Hancocks 1888–1962 British Artist (Sculpture/Oil/Watercolour/Drawing)*, Woodstock, 2003.

Noszlopy, G., *Public Sculpture of Birmingham*, Liverpool, 1998.

Noszlopy, G., *Public Sculpture of Herefordshire, Shropshire and Worcestershire*, Liverpool, 2010.

Noszlopy, G., *Public Sculpture of Staffordshire and the Black Country*, Liverpool, 2005.

Noszlopy, G., *Public Sculpture of Warwickshire, Coventry and Solihull*, Liverpool, 2003.

Odham, J., *Bygone Seaford*, Chichester, 1990.

Open Air Statues and Memorials: Brighton History Centre: New Pamphlet Box, nd.

Peace Celebration and War Memorial Sub-Committee Minute Book DB/B43/1, East Sussex Record Office, nd.

Pearson, F., *Goscombe John at the National Museum of Wales*, National Museum of Wales, 1979.

Pearson, L., 'Roughcast textures with cosmic overtones: a survey of British murals, 1945–80', *The Decorative Arts Society Journal*, vol. 31, 2007, pp. 116–37.

Penny, N., *The Materials of Sculpture*, New Haven and London, 1995.

Peter Randall-Page Sculpture and Drawings 1977–1992, Leeds, 1992.

Poplett, B., *Peacehaven: a Pictorial History*, Chichester, 1993.

Porter, J., *Images of England: Bexhill-on-Sea*, Stroud, 1998.

Potter, S. and Wilcox, T. (eds), *Public Art in West Sussex*, Chichester, 1995.

Powers, A., 'John Skelton: obituary', *The Independent*, 6 December 1999.

Powers, A., 'Obituary: John Brandon Jones', *The Independent*, 11 May 1999.

Prideaux, W.R.B., 'Statues and memorials in the British Isles', *Notes and Queries*, 14 January 1911.

Pugh, T., *The Church of Saint John the Baptist, Brighton 1835–1985*, Hove, 1985, pp. 11–36.

Pye, W., *Water Sculpture at Gatwick Airport*, London, 1988.

Quentin Bell a Man of Many Arts, Charleston, 1999.

Report of the Trial of the Cause, Carew Against Burrell Bart. And Another. Executors of the

Late Lord Egremont at the Spring Assizes Held at Lewes on Wednesday March 18th 1840, London, 1840.

Ridgeway, T., 'Steve Ovett statue unveiled on eve of 2012 games', *The Argus*, 24 July 2012.

Ridgway, T., 'Past and future symbol', *The Argus*, 10 October 2009, pp. 20–21.

Rieser, M., 'Brave new world', *Printmaking Today*, vol. 9, Summer 2000, p. 7.

Roberts, R. and Kynaston, D. (eds), *The Bank of England: Money, Power and Influence 1694–1994*, Oxford, 1995.

Robertson, F.W. and Brooke, S.A., *Life and Letters of Fred. W. Robertson, M.A.: Incumbent of Trinity Chapel, Brighton, 1847–53*, London, 1906.

Rogers, S., 'Angel of the knight', *St Dunstan's Review*, April 1997, pp. 8–9.

Roscoe, I., Hardy, E. and Sullivan, M.G., *A Biographical Dictionary of Sculptors in Britain 1666–1851*, New Haven and London, 2009.

Rowell, C., *Petworth House*, Swindon, 1997.

Rowland, D., *Survivors: True Stories of Airmen who Crashed – and Lived to Tell the Tale*, Peacehaven, 2004.

Royal Academy Exhibitors 1905–1970, vol. III, Yorkshire, 1978.

Sackville-West, R.W., *Historical Notices of the Parish of Withyham in the County of Sussex, with a Description of the Church and Sackville Chapel*, London, 1857.

Salt, D., *Memorials, Monuments and Modern Memorabilia of Horsham*, Horsham, 2nd edn, 2000.

Salzman, L.F. (ed.), *A History of the County of Sussex: Volume 4: The Rape of Chichester*, London, 1953.

Sankey, J., *Thomas Brock and the Critics: an Examination of Brock's Place in the New Sculpture Movement*, unpublished PhD thesis, University of Leeds, 2002.

Saunders, M., *The Churches of S.S. Teulon*, London, 1982.

School of Architecture and Interior Design,

Brighton Polytechnic, *A Guide to the Buildings of Brighton*, Macclesfield, 1987.

Seddon, J., 'From Worthing to Highgate and back: the career of Laurence Henderson Bradshaw (1899–1978)', *Sculpture Journal*, vol. 19.2, 2010, pp. 234–40.

Seddon, J., 'Landscape with statues: recording the public sculpture of Sussex' in S. Ewing *et al.* (eds), *Architecture and Field/Work*, London, 2010, pp. 65–71.

Seddon, J., 'The visual arts in Regency Brighton and Hove', *The Georgian Group Journal*, vol. XIII, 2003, pp. 273–80.

Seldon, A., *Brave New City: Brighton and Hove Past Present Future*, Lewes, 2002.

Sellars, D., 'Chantrey: the sculptor at work', in *Sir Francis Chantrey: Sculptor to an Age 1781–1841*, Sheffield, 1981.

Sellens, F., 'Amy's prize sign of the times', *The Courier*, 1 August 1991.

Sellens, F., 'Where they wanted it to be in 1920', *The Courier*, 24 January 1997.

Sellick Family, *Pashley Manor Gardens Through the Seasons*, Norwich, 2003.

Shapiro, M.S. and Hendricks, R.A., *A Dictionary of Mythologies*, St Albans, 1981.

Sheridan, C., *My Crowded Sanctuary*, London, 1945.

Skelton, T., *Lutyens and the Great War*, London 2008.

Smith, J.R., *Historical Notices of the Parish of Withyham*, London, 1857.

Smith, N., *The Royal Image and the English People*, Cornwall, 2001.

Solkin, D.H., *Painting for Money: the Visual Arts and the Public Sphere in Eighteenth-Century England*, London and New Haven, 1992.

Spielmann, M.H., *British Sculpture and Sculptors of Today*, London, 1901.

Stallwood, J., 'An interview with David Parfitt', *About Town* (Burgess Hill Council magazine), September 1996, p. 17.

Stoneham, E.T., *Martyrs of Jesus: The Story of the Sussex Martyrs of the Reformation*, Burgess Hill, 2nd edn, 1952.

Strachan, W.J., *Open Air Sculpture of Britain: A Comprehensive Guide*, London, 1984.

Strickland, W.G., *A Dictionary of Irish Artists*, Dublin and London, 1913.

Surtees, J., *Eastbourne: a History*, Chichester, 2002.

Sutton, A. (ed.), *Sussex: Environment, Landscape and Society*, University of Sussex, 1983.

Swinfen, W. and Arscott, D., *Hidden Sussex*, Brighton, 1984.

Swinfen, W. and Arscott, D., *People of Hidden Sussex*, Sussex, 1985.

The Magazine of Art, vol. 22, 1898, p. 168.

Thornton, N., *Sussex Shipwrecks*, Newbury, 1988.

Trimmingham, A., 'Those were the days', *Brighton and Hove Leader*, 23 August 2007, p. 4.

Troak, M., *Pioneer Days at Peacehaven: a Trip Down Memory Lane*, Telscombe, 2007.

Trusted, M, *The Return of the Gods: Neo-classical Sculpture in Britain*, Tate Britain, London, 2008.

Trusted, M., *The Making of Sculpture: the Materials and Techniques of European Sculpture*, London, 2007.

Uli Nimptsch RA, Sculptor, Royal Academy, London, 1973.

Usherwood, P., Beach, J. and Morris, C., *Public Sculpture of North East England*, Liverpool, 2000.

Vail, A., *The Shrines of Our Lady in England*, Leominster, 2004.

Vermeule, C., 'The ancient marbles at Petworth', *Apollo*, vol. CV, May 1997.

Wainwright, J.B., *Notes and Queries*, London, 24 June 1916, p. 517.

Wales, T., *The Archive Photographs Series: Brighton and Hove*, Trowbridge, 1997.

Ward-Jackson, P., *Public Sculpture of the City of London*, Liverpool, 2003.

Warne, H. and Brighton, T., A *Portrait of
    Bishop Otter College: Chichester 1839–1990*,
    Chichester, 1992.
Warner, M., *Monuments and Maidens: the
    Allegory of the Female Form*, London, 1985.
Watson, K., *"Ruth-Less" and Far From Home*,
    Eastbourne, 2000.
Webster, P., 'The life and afterlife of a public
    sculpture', *Public Monuments and Sculpture
    in Sussex: Memory and Manifestation*,
    symposium, University of Brighton, 24
    November 2007.
Whinney, M., *Sculpture in Britain 1530–1830*,
    London, 1964.
Wilcox, T. (ed.), *Eric Gill and the Guild of St
    Joseph and St Dominic*, Hove, 1990.
Windsor, J., 'Sculptor shapes up on the beach',
    The Independent, 20 March 1998.
Woodham, J.M. and Worden, S., *From Art
    School to Polytechnic: Serving Industry and
    the Community From Brighton 1859–1986*,
    Brighton, 1986.
Wright, M., *A Chronicle of Cuckfield*,
    Cuckfield, 1991 edn.
Wyke, T., *Public Sculpture of Greater
    Manchester*, Liverpool, 2004.

Yarrington. A., Lieberman I., Potts, A. and
    Baker, M. (eds), 'The Chantrey Ledger',
    Walpole Society , vol. LVI, 1991/92.

Index